THE DESIGN
OF
COST MANAGEMENT SYSTEMS

Text, Cases, and Readings

Robin Cooper
Harvard Business School

Robert S. Kaplan
Harvard Business School

PRENTICE HALL, Englewood Cliffs, NJ 07632

Library of Congress Cataloging-in-Publication Data

Cooper, Robin
    The design of cost management systems : text, cases, and readings
  / Robin Cooper, Robert S. Kaplan.
      p.   cm. -- (The Robert S. Kaplan series in management
  accounting)
      ISBN 0-13-204124-3   -- ISBN 0-13-204181-2 (pbk.) :
      1. Managerial accounting.   I. Kaplan, Robert S. II. Title.
  III. Series.
  HF5657.C65   1991
  658.15'11--dc20
                                              91-10186
                                                CIP

To our children
M-J, Brie, and Alex
Jennifer and Dina

Editorial/production supervision and interior design: Maureen Wilson
Cover design: Bruce Kenselaar
Prepress buyer: Trudy Pisciotti
Manufacturing buyer: Bob Anderson

THE ROBERT S. KAPLAN SERIES IN MANAGEMENT ACCOUNTING
ROBERT S. KAPLAN, *Consulting Editor*

Printed in the United States of America
10 9 8 7 6 5 4 3 2

ISBN 0-13-204124-3

CONTENTS

Foreword   *vii*

Preface   *ix*

1
INTRODUCTION TO COST SYSTEMS   *1*

Cases   Paramount Cycle Company   *6*

Bridgeton Industries Automotive and Fabrication Plant   *18*

Institutional Furniture   *23*

Stalcup Paper Company   *27*

Commonwealth Blood Transfusion Service   *30*

La Grande Alliance Restaurant Francaise   *43*

The Ingersoll Milling Machine Company   *47*

Readings   Yesterday's Accounting Undermines Production   *57*
    Robert S. Kaplan

Accounting Lag: The Obsolescence of Cost Accounting Systems   *63*
    Robert S. Kaplan

Does Your Company Need a New Cost System?   *80*
    Robin Cooper

Flexible Manufacturing Systems:
Cost Management and Cost Accounting Implications   *84*
    George Foster and Charles T. Horngren

2
THE TWO-STAGE PROCESS:
RESOURCES, COST CENTERS, AND PRODUCTS   *94*

Cases   Seligram, Inc.: Electronic Testing Operations   *99*

Digital Communications, Inc.: Encoder Device Division   *104*

Mayers Tap, Inc. (A)   *114*

Mayers Tap, Inc. (B)   *118*

Mayers Tap, Inc. (C)   *125*

Fisher Technologies   *126*

Mueller-Lehmkuhl GmbH   *136*

Readings The Two-Stage Procedure in Cost Accounting: Part One   *147*
            Robin Cooper

            When Should You Use Machine-Hour Costing?   *157*
            Robin Cooper

3
ASSIGNING THE EXPENSES OF CAPACITY RESOURCES   *165*

Cases   Polysar Limited   *172*

          Micro Devices Division   *180*

          Schulze Waxed Containers, Inc.   *188*

4
SYSTEMS FOR OPERATIONAL CONTROL
AND PERFORMANCE MEASUREMENT   *200*

Cases   Metabo GmbH & Co. KG   *206*

          Texas Eastman Company   *213*

          Analog Devices: The Half-Life System   *226*

          Texas Instruments: Cost of Quality (A)   *240*

          Texas Instruments: Cost of Quality (B)   *251*

Readings Activity-Based Information:
            A Blueprint for World-Class Management Accounting   *257*
            H. Thomas Johnson

5
ACTIVITY-BASED COST SYSTEMS FOR MANUFACTURING EXPENSES *267*

Cases   Destin Brass Products Co.   *281*

          Siemens Electric Motor Works (A) (abridged)   *287*

          John Deere Component Works (A)   *291*

          John Deere Component Works (B)   *304*

          Sentry Group   *311*

          Schrader Bellows (A)   *321*

          Schrader Bellows (B)   *328*

          Schrader Bellows (D-1)   *336*

          Schrader Bellows (E)   *337*

Readings   The Hidden Factory   *346*
             Jeffrey G. Miller and Thomas E. Vollmann

             The Rise of Activity-Based Costing—Part One:
             What Is an Activity-Based Cost System?   *355*
             Robin Cooper

             The Rise of Activity-Based Costing—Part Two:
             When Do I Need an Activity-Based Cost System?   *366*
             Robin Cooper

             The Rise of Activity Based Costing—Part Three:
             How Many Cost Drivers Do You Need, and How Do You Select
             Them?   *374*
             Robin Cooper

             Implementing an Activity-Based Cost System   *386*
             Robin Cooper

6
USING ACTIVITY-BASED COST SYSTEMS TO INFLUENCE BEHAVIOR   *396*

Cases   Tektronix: Portable Instruments Division (A)   *401*
             Tektronix: Portable Instruments Division (B)   *409*
             Hewlett-Packard: Roseville Networks Division   *414*
             Zytec Corporation (B)   *420*
             Hewlett-Packard: Queensferry Telecommunications Division   *426*

Readings   Cost Accounting and Cost Management in a JIT Environment   *433*
             George Foster and Charles T. Horngren

             The Human Element: The Real Challenge in Modernizing Cost
             Systems   *445*
             Thomas B. Lammert and Robert Ehrsam

             A Behavioral Model for Implementing Cost Management Systems   *450*
             Michael D. Shields and S. Mark Young

             Another Hidden Edge—Japanese Management Accounting   *461*
             Toshiro Hiromoto

7
ACTIVITY-BASED SYSTEMS IN SERVICE ORGANIZATIONS
AND SERVICE FUNCTIONS   *466*

Cases   Union Pacific (Introduction)   *474*
             Union Pacific (A)   *481*
             Union Pacific (B)   *494*
             Massachusetts Eye and Ear Infirmary   *503*
             American Bank   *515*

Kanthal (A)   526

Winchell Lighting, Inc. (A)   533

Winchell Lighting, Inc. (B)   546

Manufacturers Hanover Corporation: Customer Profitability Report   553

Readings   Why SG&A Doesn't Always Work   566
             Thomas S. Dudick

Customer Profitability Analysis   570
    Robin Bellis-Jones

How Weyerhaeuser Manages Corporate Overhead Costs   575
    H. Thomas Johnson and Dennis A. Loewe

FOREWORD

THE ROBERT S. KAPLAN SERIES IN MANAGEMENT ACCOUNTING

In the past ten years, management accounting has become more relevant to the needs of modern corporations. To accommodate these shifts in management accounting practice, teaching and research in the field have changed similarly. Traditional approaches, developed for the large corporations emerging in the first part of the twentieth century, have proved inadequate for today's global and technological environment. Academics have returned to field research to discover the new techniques being developed and implemented by successful organizations. The new approaches focus on improving the information provided to managers and employees about their organizations, and placing increased attention on the design of information and control systems.

The Robert S. Kaplan Series in Management Accounting represents this contemporary approach to management accounting. At the core of the series is an introductory book that presents basic management accounting topics within the philosophy of the modern management accounting approach. The introductory book, in addition to covering the core material, will expose students to the ideas and concepts that can be studied in subsequent elective courses. The remaining books in the series enable students to explore materials relating to accounting information for operations management, design of cost management systems, and management control systems. Each of the books provides the basis for an excellent course in management accounting.

For many of us, teaching and research in management accounting during the past ten years have been exciting activities. I hope that the books in the series succeed in conveying some of the enthusiasm that the authors have experienced in developing these materials. Properly taught, management accounting should be a central part of the education of accounting majors and business students. The series will encourage the development of teaching materials that can enable management accounting courses to fulfill this mission.

ROBERT S. KAPLAN
Series Editor

PREFACE

During the 1980s, the field of management accounting was reborn. Increased global competition demanded that companies make major changes in the technology and organization of their production processes and improve the effectiveness of decisions concerning pricing, product design, and product and customer mix. These demands required accurate information about production processes and about the resources consumed to produce products and to sell them to customers. Companies' cost systems, however, were unable to supply accurate, relevant information for these purposes. This book represents the findings from extensive case writing and field research that not only documented the limitations and failings of existing cost accounting systems but also identified the new cost management systems that had been developed by innovative companies around the world.

During the past five years, this new material has been introduced into the required first-year accounting course in the Harvard MBA program, become the basis of a completely transformed second-year MBA elective—"Measurement and Management of Product Costs"—and been incorporated into the general management executive programs of the school. Other business schools have also successfully introduced this material into their MBA, executive, and advanced undergraduate courses. The material represents a fundamentally new way of educating business students and executives about cost management systems. The previous academic approach emphasized cost *analysis* for isolated, well-specified decisions. That approach took the design of the cost system as given and attempted to extract relevant information from the system for specific decision purposes.

The new approach contained in this book emphasizes principles of cost systems *design.* The systems used by actual organizations are described in detail, and the managerial uses of this information for performance measurement and for strategic decisions on pricing, product mix, process technology, and product design are explored. Students learn how to identify the symptoms and causes of cost system failure in today's highly competitive and technologically advanced environment. The limitations of the information produced by existing cost systems become immediately apparent. This process is facilitated by developing the conceptual framework for cost systems design. Armed with this framework, students learn how some problems can be ameliorated by improving existing cost systems. But even the best-designed traditional cost system cannot provide all the relevant information required for management planning and process improvements. Many of the cases in this book illustrate completely new approaches and design principles for modern cost management systems.

Textual material at the beginning of each chapter presents the themes and general principles that will emerge from study of the cases in the chapter. The cases, written from actual company experiences, explore the properties of cost systems and how the design of the systems determines the type of information management receives about its products and production processes. The readings that accompany the text and cases either provide additional background about issues raised in the cases or elaborate on the conceptual framework developed in the chapter.

This book has been written primarily for classroom use. Many practitioners (including financial and operating managers) and consultants, however, may find much useful material here. The modern managerial accounting approach has developed so rapidly and recently that the text, cases, and readings in this book represent, at this time, the most available and comprehensive presentation of the emerging concepts. Practitioners who study carefully the text, cases, and readings will learn about the sources of failure in existing cost systems and the opportunities for innovative approaches in their organizations.

Chapter 1 presents introductory material and cases on cost management systems. In several of the cases, the cost system has serious design flaws. In others, the system works satisfactorily for accumulating costs for financial reporting but fails to provide information useful for managerial purposes. The cases introduce students to the various functions performed by cost management systems and some pitfalls that arise in poorly designed systems.

Chapter 2 provides the conceptual structure for traditional cost system design. The material illustrates the choice of the appropriate number of cost centers in a factory, how the expenses of support departments are traced to production cost centers, and the choice of allocation bases for assigning expenses accumulated in production cost centers to products. Each of the cases features how poorly designed systems adversely affect managerial decisions on product mix, production technology, or pricing. Two cases, Mayers Tap and Fisher Technologies, have computer modules that enable students to design, individually, a new cost system and compare the output from their system with that produced by classmates.

Chapter 3 covers a special topic on the costing of capacity resources. Many otherwise well-designed cost systems provide highly misleading information—both on production efficiencies and on product costs—because of distortions introduced by inappropriate assignment of capacity-related expenses. The text and case material illustrate these common failings and suggest preferred approaches for assigning capacity-related expenses to production departments and products.

Chapter 4, on operational control and performance measurement, introduces material on the design of new cost management systems. The chapter starts with a case on an advanced traditional cost system that provides daily financial feedback to departmental managers. Subsequent cases extend traditional financial performance systems by illustrating approaches taken by companies implementing total quality management programs. The companies introduce many operational, nonfinancial measures of quality performance and attempt to reconcile and integrate their financial and operational performance measurement systems.

Chapter 5 continues the development of new cost management systems. It shifts from the operational control and performance measurement issues covered in chapter 4 to the measurement of product cost and profitability. The cases introduce the role for activity-based cost systems in traditional manufacturing settings. Each of the cases illustrates how well-designed traditional cost accounting systems become obsolete as changes occur in a company's competitive environment, production technology, and product mix. A company's full-line product strategy becomes jeopardized because of the distorted product cost information it receives. In each case, the company develops an activity-based product costing system to provide more accurate information on the organizational resources consumed by its varied products. One case, the Schrader Bellows series, takes students through a complete cost system design cycle: diagnosis of the problem, analysis of the current production environment, design of a new system, analysis of the information produced by the new system, presentation of results to management, and implementation. This multipart series uses computer modules and videotapes as case supplements.

Chapter 6 examines the activity-based cost management approach in high-technology electronics companies that are implementing total quality management and just-in-time production processes. The activity-based approaches taken by these companies emphasize information to help improve product designs for future product generations, not just to improve decision making for existing products and processes. These systems also were designed to influence, in specific ways, the behavior of engineers, operators, and managers.

Chapter 7 extends the activity-based cost management approach to service companies in the financial, health care, and transportation industries. The chapter also contains cases that apply activity-based costing to the selling, distribution, and administrative expenses of manufacturing companies. As companies move beyond analysis of factory expenses, they discover that many organizational expenses are triggered by customer, not product, demands. Therefore, the text and case material in chapter 7 feature analysis of customer profitability, an expansion of the product cost and profitability perspective illustrated in chapters 5 and 6. This material demonstrates how activity-based costing can be applied to all organizational expenses and assets to produce a total profitability map of the company.

Much of the material in this book was developed during six years of observation and description of innovative organizations around the world. We were fortunate in receiving permission to present many of the cases in undisguised form, enabling students to appreciate that the examples represent problems and design choices faced by actual companies. We appreciate the cooperation from the managers and companies we have worked with during the past six years for allowing us to describe their experiences. Of course, this material could not have been developed without the active support and encouragement of the Division of Research of the Harvard Business School. Funding for domestic and international travel, research assistants, software development, and videotaping was essential for producing this new generation case material. The teaching environment of the school, which enabled us to teach jointly in the early stages of course development, also played a critical role in developing the conceptual framework for the book. We have also benefited from feedback from many of our academic colleagues who have taught these cases at their institutions. We especially appreciate the help of Professor Anthony Atkinson, now at Mt. Allison College in New Brunswick, and Professor William Rotch at the Darden Graduate School of Business, University of Virginia, for careful review and comments on the textual material.

In summary, the material in this book presents a state-of-the-art view of the emerging principles of cost management systems design. We have observed, after teaching this material, that our students and executives have been able to mobilize efforts to redesign the cost management systems in their organizations. Thus we feel confident that the material is actionable and practical. But the material is not a cookbook that can be followed unthinkingly. Students must master the underlying design principles for cost management systems and learn how to apply these principles sensibly, and in a cost-effective fashion, recognizing the competitive environment, product mix, process and information technology, and organizational situation in their individual companies.

ROBIN COOPER
ROBERT S. KAPLAN
Boston

1

INTRODUCTION TO COST SYSTEMS

Critical attention was focused, during the 1980s, on the limitations of cost accounting systems.[1] This book will examine the properties of both traditional and innovative cost systems. It will help the reader develop a framework for recognizing the limitations of existing cost systems and learn how the limitations may be overcome through improved designs. The cases examined in this chapter focus on relatively simple systems that exhibit common problems in existing cost systems. The analysis of the cases provides a vehicle for understanding the choices faced by cost system designers in developing systems that will provide more relevant information to operating managers. The actual design of new systems to overcome limitations in existing systems will be covered in remaining chapters.

MONTHLY PERFORMANCE MEASUREMENT

Cost systems have been used by companies to provide periodic measures of performance.[2] This is typically accomplished through the monthly reporting system. Conventional cost systems develop quantity and price standards for materials and labor, and allocate overhead to departments based on work performed. Each month, actual costs of material, labor, and overhead are compared to the standards for the quantities produced and to budgeted costs, with deviations highlighted as variances. Organizations then attempt to use the variances for feedback and cost control.

When cost centers are treated as responsibility centers, a manager is held responsible for the costs charged to the cost center. In most organizations today, variances between actual and standard or budgeted costs are determined and recorded at the cost center level, not the product level. Cost systems that only determine variances at the cost center level are called *process costing* systems. Originally applied to companies in continuous process industries, like chemicals, steel, and pulp and paper, the

---

[1]The two readings included in this section are representative of the criticisms leveled against traditional cost accounting systems; see also H. Thomas Johnson and Robert S. Kaplan, *Relevance Lost: The Rise and Fall of Management Accounting* (Boston: Harvard Business School Press, 1987).
[2]Chapter 4 of this book describes the role for both financial and nonfinancial performance measures in contemporary organizations. The text and cases in Chapter 1 feature only financial performance measures.

process-like costing systems are found now almost universally in large companies. Only companies making products that require extensive time and resources (such as building a large customer-specific machine tool) or that do only customized work would use a strict *job-order costing* system in which variances of materials and labor are charged directly to individual products. Even job-order costing systems that identify the actual materials and labor charges of specific jobs, however, assign overhead to jobs and products using standard, predetermined rates. Thus, overhead variances can still arise that are assigned to individual departments.

COST ASSIGNMENT

A second function performed by cost systems is to assign indirect production costs to products. We use the term *assignment* instead of *allocation* to denote the general procedure of tracing costs to products. The term *allocation* has become associated with arbitrariness as contrasted with an assignment of expenses that bears a direct or causal relation to the object that caused the expense to be incurred. The term *attribution* will be used when the assignment procedure causally models the consumption of resources by products, and *allocation* when a resource cost is assigned to a department or product using a measure that is unrelated to the quantity of the resource consumed by the department or product.

Much of the cost assignment process can be reduced to the following simple equation:

$$C = P \times Q$$

where *C*, representing the cost of the resource consumed, equals the unit price, *P*, of a resource multiplied by the quantity consumed, *Q*, of that resource. For example, utility expenses can be represented as the cost per kilowatt hour (the *P* measure) multiplied by the number of kilowatt hours consumed (the *Q* measure).

When the cost system *directly* attributes costs to cost centers and products, the price measure and the quantity measure relate to the resource whose costs are being attributed. Most cost systems only directly charge the cost of two resources; materials and labor.[3] The costs of all other resources are indirectly assigned to products. When costs are indirectly assigned, the systems use an aggregate burden rate, not a specific resource price, to assign the expenses of resources to cost centers and from cost centers to products. Also, instead of using the actual quantity consumed, *Q*, of that resource, a surrogate measure, often called an allocation base, is used to determine the amount of burden to be assigned to cost centers and to products.

The emphasis on direct charging for materials and labor, and indirect or surrogate charging for support and overhead resources, reflects to a large degree the economics of the early twentieth century, when cost systems were first designed and when the materials and labor were the principal cost components. Indirect and support expenses were less important expense categories and were difficult to measure and assign directly to products. Consequently, companies developed elaborate standard cost systems for control of materials and labor costs and for charging these costs directly to products. But they allocated all other expenses indirectly using allocations bases (direct labor,

---

[3]To reinforce the method of assigning these costs, these resources are typically called *direct* labor and *direct* material.

processing times, and units produced) that were already being measured for other purposes. These systems made eminent sense for the economics and the expensive information technology of early twentieth-century production. Their functionality for the operating environment of the 1990s is, however, suspect.

Direct charging, using the actual quantity consumed and actual unit price of the resource, does not introduce any distortion into the costs assigned to cost centers and products when P and Q are measured accurately. Unfortunately, systems designed primarily to support financial reporting requirements often fail to capture even the direct costs adequately. For example, an average scrap rate might be used for all material even when actual scrap rates vary significantly, or the labor standards might ignore the reality that when a line is manufacturing simple products, the supervisors lend workers to the lines producing complex products.

Direct charging is often expensive. For example, directly charging inspection costs to cost centers and products requires measuring the quantity of inspection and the actual salaries of the inspectors who work on each product. Recording such measurements might consume a sizeable fraction of the inspector's time and thus be expensive. Because of the high cost of direct charging, traditional cost systems use indirect charging for support and overhead resources so that companies do not have to measure the quantity and unit price of each overhead resource consumed by cost centers and products. This simplification greatly reduces the cost of measurement. For example, if direct labor hours are used to assign inspection costs to cost centers and products, the inspectors do not need to keep track of the time they spend in each cost center or on each product.

COST SYSTEM DISTORTIONS

The indirect assignment of costs lowers the cost of measurement of a cost system, but it can introduce considerable distortion. Distortion occurs when either the unit price or the quantity used of a resource is not attributed accurately to cost centers and products. Five factors explain the sources of distortion.[4] First, some costs are allocated to products that are unrelated to the products being produced. Examples of such unrelated but allocated costs include the research and development costs for future products, excess capacity costs, and corporate overhead costs such as the pension costs of retired workers. Life-cycle costs fall into this category. At the beginning of the life cycle of a product, engineering and support costs are typically high while production costs are small or nonexistent. Frequently, the engineering and support costs for new products are allocated to the products currently being produced rather than assigned to a project account for the new product.

Second, distortion is introduced by omitting costs that are related to the products being produced or to customers serviced. Examples of such costs that are frequently omitted include selling, general, and administrative costs; and warranty costs for existing products. Cost systems usually omit such costs because for financial reporting purposes, these costs cannot be capitalized and assigned to inventory—a perfect example of how the multiple roles for cost systems conflict.

---

[4]Most examples of cost system distortion and innovation have been documented when factory and production expenses are assigned to products. Cases and material in chapter 7 extend the analysis by showing that many organizational operating expenses are incurred to support customers, distribution channels, and geographical locations. The application of the concepts to service, as well as manufacturing, organizations is also demonstrated in chapter 7. Thus, while many expenses reasonably can be assigned to individual products, a more general view assigns many operating expenses to customers, channels, and locations.

Third, distortion can be introduced by costing only a subset of the outputs of the firm as products. For example, when the outputs of the firm include both tangible (i.e., manufactured) and intangible (i.e., service) products, cost systems may assign costs only to the tangible products. This treatment does not introduce distortion into reported costs if the costs of the intangible products are minor or expensed as period costs. However, many of the costs of the intangible products are typically allocated to the tangible products, thus causing the reported costs of those products to be too high.

Fourth, distortion can be introduced by indirectly assigning costs inaccurately to products. Inaccurate assignment can introduce two different forms of distortion. *Price distortion* is introduced when the cost system is too aggregated and average prices are used instead of specific prices. For example, some cost systems use an average price per direct labor hour despite wide differences in actual wage rates for both skilled and unskilled individuals. *Quantity distortions* are introduced when the costs are indirectly assigned to products using a basis that is not perfectly proportional to the actual consumption of resources by products. For example, labor-intensive products are frequently overcosted when direct labor hours are used to assign all overhead costs to products.

Finally, distortion is introduced by attempting to allocate common or joint costs to products. Any attempt to allocate such costs to products is doomed to be arbitrary and misleading. Joint costs emerge when the production process necessarily produces two or more products, as is the case when refining crude oil. Common costs pose similar problems to joint costs. They occur when multiple products are produced using the same indivisible resource. For example, when a machine is set up to allow a batch of products to be produced, then the cost of the setup is common to every unit in the batch.

COST SYSTEM DESIGN: BALANCING BENEFITS AND COSTS

Many of the five sources of distortion can be reduced or removed by carefully designing the firm's product costing system. For example, well-designed cost systems ensure that all major outputs are treated as products and that the costs of all of the resources consumed in their production are assigned accurately to them. Other sources of distortion may not be worth reducing because the cost of their reduction exceeds the benefits derived. The optimal product cost system for a firm, therefore, is not the most accurate one but the one where the benefits of additional accuracy are matched with the expenses of achieving the next increment in accuracy. The best system will report approximate but inaccurate product costs, with the degree of approximation determined by the organization's competitive, product, and process environment.

The design of the preferred cost system is affected by changes in three factors: the costs of the measurements required by the cost system, the level of competition faced, and the degree of product-mix diversity. Decreases in the costs of measurement and increases in the level of competition faced and the diversity of products produced all favor the development of more sophisticated cost systems that report more accurate product costs. Decreases in the costs of measurement favor more sophisticated systems because for the same costs, more measurements, with higher accuracy, can be made. Increased competition from more focused companies favors more sophisticated systems because such competitors are more likely to take advantage of any errors made when managers rely on distorted product costs to make decisions. Finally, increased product diversity favors more sophisticated systems because as diversity increases so does the level of distortion reported by a given system.[5]

In recent years, all three factors have been changing in ways that lead to more sophisticated systems being optimal for organizations. For example, increased application of information technology, such as Flexible Manufacturing Systems (FMS) and Materials Resource Planning (MRP) systems, has increased the availability and lowered the cost of measurements about the production process, while the emergence of focused foreign competitors or deregulation has increased the level of competition faced. Finally, to compete more effectively, many firms have increased the diversity of their product mixes.

Since the preferred cost system is determined by the costs of measurement, the degree of competition faced, and the diversity of the product mix produced, it is different for every firm. Firms in which the costs of measurement are low and competition is fierce should have cost systems that report relatively accurate product costs. Firms in environments where the cost of measurement is high and competition is low might be better served by inexpensive cost systems that may not measure product costs accurately.

The cost benefit tradeoff that governs the design of cost systems helps explain why cost systems do not report costs relevant only for a specific decision. One example of a decision-specific cost is the cost of making one more unit of a given product. For this decision, very few costs are relevant—possibly only material and incremental power required to run the machines for the time required to make the additional unit. In contrast, if the decision is to design and launch a major new product, or discontinue making 800 existing products, then additional costs such as direct labor, inspection, and engineering time become relevant. While it is attractive to think about generating the uniquely relevant costs for each decision being contemplated, the range of possibilities faced by managers is enormous. Just to compute, at a rate of one per second, the costs associated with all possible product mix combinations for a small firm would exceed the lifetime of the universe.[6] Consequently, it is not economical to design cost systems to report costs relevant only for particular decisions.

The product costs reported by cost systems are not designed to be used directly for decisions. They provide diagnostic information to focus managerial attention on the sources of profits and losses. This strategic objective is less demanding than reporting decision-relevant costs, but it still requires accuracy to be considered when designing cost systems. Reported product costs will only focus attention appropriately (i.e., where it can do the most good), if they capture sufficiently accurately the consumption of resources by products. If the reported costs are too distorted, they will frequently cause managers to focus their attention inappropriately. For example, managers might spend time working out how to make an apparently unprofitable product profitable when it was already profitable, or they may drop or outsource products that are actually profitable.

---

[5]Offsetting some of these forces for more sophisticated systems is the desire of some organizations to develop simpler systems that will send a clear message to influence the behavior of engineers, operators, and managers. The design of these decision-influencing systems is discussed in chapter 6.

[6]For a company that has only 100 products, it must consider 2^{100} different product-mix possibilities. Attempting to measure the costs relevant for each of these possible 2^{100} combinations is an impossible task.

CASES

Paramount Cycle Company

Paramount Cycle began operations as a small job shop in Dayton, Ohio in 1940. The firm grew rapidly during World War II by manufacturing specialty items for the military. At the end of the war, with 125 employees and $1 million in sales, the firm began searching for commercial products. Because of his interest in physical fitness, Scott Meadow, the firm's founder, decided to manufacture single-speed bicycles for adults. The firm changed its name to Paramount Cycle in 1954, when the firm became exclusively a manufacturer of bicycles. By 1969, annual unit sales were approximately 125,000 for sales of over $6 million. At that time Paramount produced four lines of children's bicycles, two single-speed adult models, and two three-speed adult models.

Paramount cycles were sold primarily through independently owned bicycle shops which carried bicycles from several manufacturers, usually Paramount and two or three foreign manufacturers. Murray and Huffy, the two largest selling U.S. bicycle lines, were sold primarily through mass merchandisers, while Schwinn was sold through an exclusive dealer network. Paramount had been able to maintain a pretax profit margin of 9% to 11% of sales, greater than those of either Huffy or Murray, but probably below that of Schwinn. Since Mr. Meadow felt that Paramount bicycles were of higher quality than either Murray or Huffy, but somewhat below that of Schwinn, he planned to continue the existing distribution system.

RAPID GROWTH

In 1968, responding to an increasing national concern for physical fitness among Americans, Mr. Meadow began developing an engineering department capable of supporting the manufacture of 10-speed bicycles. He also began contracting supply sources for 10-speed components (then located primarily in England, France, and Italy). In 1970, when Paramount produced its first 10-speed, total bicycle sales in the U.S. were 6.6 million units, approximately the same as the 1967 to 1969 annual average. Unit sales in the U.S. increased to 8.7 million units in 1971, to 13.4 million in 1972, and a record high of 15.2 million in 1973 before declining to 13.6 million in 1974.

This growth came almost entirely in the lightweight segment of the market. By maintaining high quality, Paramount was able to triple unit sales from 1969 to 1974, for a slight increase in market share. Mr. Meadow felt that Paramount had increased market share by offering higher quality components than comparably priced bicycles. Although Paramount had been unable to maintain its historic profit margins, profits had increased each year. Mr. Meadow felt that when sales leveled off the firm would regain its normal 10% pretax margin. However, when U.S. sales fell to 7.3 million units in 1975, Paramount suffered its first loss. By 1977, U.S. unit sales had increased to 9.3 million; however, Paramount's pretax margin had increased to only 5%.

ACCOUNTING

Paramount had estimated the cost per bicycle prior to the beginning of each year. Industrial engineering provided parts and component lists for material in each bicycle. By multiplying material quantity by estimated cost obtained from the purchasing manager, the finance department was able to calculate estimated material cost. The manufacturing department maintained a record of labor hours per bicycle. By multiplying hours per bicycle

This case was prepared by Assistant Professor Michael J. Sandretto.
Copyright © 1979 by the President and Fellows of Harvard College. Harvard Business School case 180-069.

times the estimated labor cost per hour (from personnel), finance was able to calculate estimated labor cost per bicycle. Using the annual budget, finance divided budgeted overhead by budgeted direct labor dollars to obtain an overhead cost per labor dollar. The total of material, labor, and overhead was used throughout the year as the cost of a bicycle for both inventory costing and for product pricing.

Although Mr. Meadow realized that these costs were only rough estimates, they had proved satisfactory until 1970. The inventory had been increased by purchases of material, labor, and overhead and reduced by unit sales multiplied by cost per bicycle. Accounting inventory at year-end had been within 5% of the priced physical inventory taken by Paramount's CPA firm. In addition, Paramount had maintained its 10% pretax margins.

In 1970, when margins had decreased, Paramount began experiencing larger differences between accounting inventory and the physical inventory at year-end. In 1974, the physical inventory had been 12% less than accounting inventory, and in 1975 and 1976 the difference had grown to 15%. Because of the inability to control costs, Mr. Meadow decided to have a standard cost system installed. In early 1977, a controller was hired and told to design a standard cost system which paralleled the manufacturing system as closely as possible.

Although Mr. Meadow desired a system which would be capable of accurately valuing inventory, he was more concerned that the system provide a means of controlling costs. In addition, he felt that the system should provide information which would permit analysis of cost by product group and by product series, if possible.

MANUFACTURING

Paramount had originally divided bicycle production into three manufacturing departments, each supervised by one or more foremen. A parts department produced components which were not purchased externally, such as seats, handlebars, fenders, and other items. A frame assembly department cut tubing to length, braized the frame, and then painted the finished frame. An assembly department assembled the bicycle using the manufactured frame and purchased and manufactured components. The assembly department also boxed bicycles for shipment.

When Paramount expanded into 10-speed bicycles, Mr. Meadow had insisted that additional departments be created. To maintain different levels of quality, he felt that it was necessary to maintain separate production lines. Paramount's bicycles were divided into three product groups, based on overall quality. Each product group was further divided into four or more series. Standard cost and selling price for different models within a series were the same since differences were minor. In the children's series, for example, slightly different seats and handlebars were provided as well as different color and trim. In the adult series, differences were limited to frame size, men's or women's frame, and, in some cases, choice of color. The current products are as follows:

PRODUCT GROUP	NO. OF SERIES	SERIES
100	4 Children's single-speed	AA–AD
	1 Children's 5-speed	AE
	2 Adult single-speed	BA–BB
	1 Adult 3-speed	CA
200	1 Adult 3-speed	CB
	4 Medium-priced 10-speed touring	DA–DD
300	2 High-priced 10-speed touring	EA–EB
	2 High-priced 10-speed racing	FA–FB

Separate production facilities are maintained for each of the product groups with the exception that parts for product groups 100 and 200 are produced on the same production line. The production lines are as shown on p. 8.

The payroll department records direct labor by department so that each foreman can be held responsible for his or her operations. Materials are issued to each line when a production order is issued. If additional material is required to complete an order, the issue is charged to the department rather than the job. Each line keeps a small supply of parts so that additional material issues will not be required each time more parts are used than had been issued. Thus, whenever a request for additional material is made, it is for enough material to cover at least two to three weeks of production.

PRODUCTION DEPARTMENTS

001	Parts department—100 and 200 series
102	Frame assembly—100 series (children's, single-speed adult, 3-speed adult)
103	Final assembly—100 series
202	Frame assembly—200 series (adult's 3-speed, medium-priced 10-speed models)
203	Final assembly—200 series
301	Parts department—300 series (high-priced 10-speed models)
302	Frame assembly—300 series
303	Final assembly—300 series

STANDARD COST SYSTEM

During 1977 and 1978, a standard cost system was developed and tested. The full system was installed in January of 1979. To verify that the system was operating properly, a special inventory was taken on June 30, 1979. That physical inventory differed from accounting inventory by less than 2%. Based on that inventory, Mr. Meadow decided that extensive use should be made of the cost information. The basic system is described next.

Engineering Standards. Engineering standards had been developed both for material quantity and labor hours for each piece part and for each operation. Dollar standards were developed for material by obtaining an estimate of material cost per unit from the purchasing department, and then reviewing any major price changes with the vice-president of manufacturing. An estimate of a plant-wide labor rate was obtained from the vice-president of industrial relations, and then reviewed with the vice-president of manufacturing. Final standards for material and labor were developed by October 31 of each year to apply to the following year.

Standard Overhead Rates. During the budgeting process, the finance department estimated total manufacturing overhead for 1979 using a form similar to schedule 5. Total budgeted overhead was then divided by budgeted direct labor dollars (standard labor cost per unit multiplied by estimated units produced) to obtain a 1979 overhead rate of $1.50 per direct labor dollar. While it would have been more accurate to calculate separate overhead rates for each department, rates were expected to be similar enough so that a single plant-wide rate was preferred because of simplicity.

Cost of Goods Sold.   Cost of goods sold shown on

the income statement (schedule 10) is the sum of cost of goods sold at standard (schedule 7) plus all manufacturing variances. Those variances are summarized in schedule 8.

Purchase Price Variance. The purchase price variance is simply the difference between the standard cost of a purchase order (units × standard price) and the amount shown on an invoice. Since there is considerable overlap between series within a product group, but very little overlap between product groups, the purchase price variance report is summarized by product groups. A portion of the monthly report is shown in schedule 1.

Material Usage Variance (Material Scrapped). A primary feature of the cost system is that it is designed to utilize paperwork used by the manufacturing department. When a production order is scheduled on one of the manufacturing lines, a pick list is prepared for that order. The pick list is a schedule of raw material and parts required to produce an order. As an example, a pick list for seats would list a standard quantity of rivets, nuts, and bolts and a standard amount of bar steel, steel wire, and leather. If an order were placed for 100 seats to be produced on line 301, the raw material and parts inventory clerk would issue enough material to the line 301 foreman to manufacture 100 seats.

At any one time between 50 and 100 orders are in process on lines 001 and 301, while between 5 and 25 orders are in process on most other lines. To minimize paperwork, a foreman can produce either fewer or more parts than an order called for. In addition, foremen are permitted to request additional material without reference to a specific production order. This permits lines to carry a small supply of parts so that manufacturing operations are not disrupted by shortages. It is also common for foremen to split orders so that the final part of an order might be turned in several weeks after the initial turn in of finished parts, frames, or bicycles. Because of these and other complications, the controller decided to produce one material usage variance for each line, rather than a variance by product or by production order. The basic technique is that beginning inventory on a line plus material issued to that line is the material available. Of the total available, some is transferred to stock, some is lost, and some remains on the line as ending inventory. Because of the large number of parts in process at any one time and because of the complexity of the operation, it was not considered feasible to count in-process inventory on a line without stopping operations. As a reasonable approximation, all orders in process are valued at 100% of standard material. While some material issued will have been lost through scrap, a small supply of additional material is kept on each line to avoid disrupting manufacturing operations. These offsetting factors tend to make the 100% valuation of material on a line a reasonable estimate.

The material usage variance is calculated as the balance after subtracting ending inventory and material to stock from the material available. Schedule 2 shows production orders open as of June 30 (beginning inventory) and as of July 31 (ending inventory) for line 303. Those are summarized by product at the bottom of the schedule, as are total units to stock. Schedule 3 calculates the value of material in beginning and ending inventory and in goods to stock. Schedule 4, panel A, shows the calculation of the material usage variance, by production line, based on data from schedule 3 and from total material issued to each production line.

Scrapped Labor Variance. Since some of the material scrapped also includes labor from previous operations (previous hours), labor is also scrapped. That calculation is identical to the material usage variance except that previous hours are used rather than material. Labor hours scrapped are removed from standard inventory at the standard labor rate of $6.50 per hour (schedule 4, panel B). Since overhead is in inventory as a fixed percent of labor dollars (150%), overhead is also scrapped.

Labor Rate Variance. Direct payroll is maintained by production line. Since a plant-wide standard labor

rate of $6.50 per hour is used, calculating a labor rate variance by line is straightforward. As shown in panel C of schedule 4, labor hours paid to a line are multiplied by $6.50 to obtain standard labor dollars. Actual wages paid are subtracted from standard to obtain a labor rate variance.

Labor Efficiency Variance. Although each direct labor employee fills out a time card listing hours worked by production order, the controller questioned the validity of those time reports. Since employees were not on a bonus system, he felt that the time cards were probably not that accurate. He was also concerned because in many cases items could be produced on one of several machines. Newer machines were generally more efficient, so that depending on the current machine loading, an order might take more or less labor than standard simply because of availability of a machine. Rather than look at variances by either operator or production order, he decided to accumulate labor efficiency variances by line, as was done for material usage.

The calculation was similar to the process used to calculate material usage variance, except rather than valuing units in process at 100% of standard, units were valued at 50% of standard labor required to complete a unit on a line. The 50% figure was

Exhibit 1

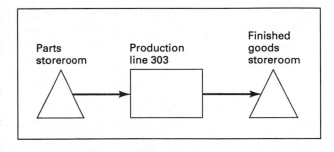

Material for a production order	100%	100%
Average	100%	
Labor for a production order	0%	100%
Average	50%	

based on a sample inventory of three lines which showed that, on average, 50% of total standard labor had been expended on parts and units in process (on average, units were half completed). See Exhibit 1.

Using units in inventory and to stock from schedule 2, labor hours are calculated for line 303 inventory and for goods to stock on schedule 3. Both beginning and ending inventory of total standard hours on line 303 are multiplied by 50%. Those hours are then used in panel D of schedule 4 to calculate a labor efficiency variance. Since the hours are lost (removed) from inventory at a standard cost of $6.50

per labor hour, overhead must also be removed at $1.50 per labor dollar.

Inventory.   Inventory is maintained at standard cost. Schedule 9 lists journal entries which affected the inventory account during July. Purchases of material, labor, and overhead are initially recorded in purchases accounts (material purchases, direct labor, and manufacturing overhead), and then transferred to inventory at standard cost. Any manufacturing variances are recorded to maintain the inventory at standard cost. Finally, all shipments are removed from inventory as cost of goods sold at standard.

SCHEDULE 1

Purchase Price Variance Report

July 1979

PRODUCT GROUP 300

PART NO.	DESCRIPTION	VOUCHER NO.	QUANTITY	STANDARD COST PER UNIT	STANDARD COST TOTAL	INVOICE AMOUNT	VARIANCE
A021-22	Tires	36058	100	$ 2.52	$ 252.00	$ 304.84	$ 52.84
A021-23	Tires	36035	100	2.61	261.00	321.39	60.39
A021-24	Tires	36104	100	2.80	280.00	336.84	56.84
A022-21	Chains	36072	50	4.12	206.00	281.14	75.14
A022-23	Chains	36023	50	4.83	241.50	306.94	65.44
A023-20	Brakes	36127	60	8.14	488.40	522.84	34.44
A023-23	Brakes	36041	40	9.52	380.80	415.61	34.81
A024-19	Crankset	36084	25	8.63	215.75	284.14	68.39
A024-21	Crankset	36014	40	9.12	364.80	486.12	121.32
A024-22	Crankset	36117	60	10.14	608.40	709.31	100.91
A025-21	Derailleur	36091	50	18.29	914.50	1421.16	506.66
A025-23	Derailleur	36042	60	21.17	1270.20	1846.31	576.11
A026-19	Hubs	36063	100	2.56	256.00	316.21	60.21
A026-22	Hubs	36029	120	3.19	382.80	489.14	106.34
	Total, Group 300				$141316.35	$160336.48	$19020.13
	Total				$682419.48	$701941.48	$19522.00

Variance by product group

100		$ 283
200		219
300		19020
Total		$19522

SCHEDULE 2

Manufacturing Work in Process (WIP) Summary Report
July 1979

DEPT. 303—FINAL ASSEMBLY
    RACING/TOURING

PRODUCTION ORDER #	SERIES	MODEL	UNITS STARTED	UNITS IN PROCESS JUNE 30	UNITS IN PROCESS JULY 31	UNITS TO STOCK JULY	
6-18	FA	2209	100	100	0	100	
6-33	EA	1012	200	150	0	150	
6-42	EB	1209	150	100	0	100	
6-47	EB	1205	100	60	0	60	
6-61	FB	2214	150	150	0	150	
6-66	EA	1018	150	150	0	150	
6-70	FA	2216	100	100	0	100	
7-4	EB	1205	150	0	0	150	
7-11	EA	1013	200	0	0	200	
7-19	FA	2216	100	0	0	100	
7-32	EA	1013	200	0	0	200	
7-43	EB	1209	100	0	0	100	
7-47	EA	1012	150	0	50	100	
7-52	FB	2214	100	0	70	30	
7-58	FA	2209	100	0	40	60	
7-60	EB	1209	200	0	120	80	
7-63	EA	1018	100	0	0	100	
7-72	EA	1012	150	0	150	0	
7-78	FA	2209	100	0	100	0	
7-85	FB	2214	100	0	100	0	
7-88	FA	2209	200	0	200	0	
Totals	EA			300	200	900	To
	EB			160	120	490	schedule 3
	FA			200	340	360	
	FB			150	170	180	

SCHEDULE 3

Extension of Work in Process Report

July 1979

DEPT. 303 — FINAL ASSEMBLY
RACING/TOURING

	UNITS	STANDARD COST PER UNIT			TOTAL STANDARD COST		
		MATERIAL	PREVIOUS LABOR HOURS	LABOR HOURS LINE 303	MATERIAL	HOURS FROM PREVIOUS DEPARTMENTS	HOURS LINE 303
Beginning Inventory							
EA	300	$57.57	5.12	2.14	$17271	1536	642
EB	160	69.43	6.27	2.68	11109	1003	429
FA	200	63.86	5.45	2.41	12772	1090	482
FB	150	73.64	6.64	2.67	11046	996	400
					$52198	4625	1953
				× 50%			976
Ending Inventory							
EA	200	$57.57	5.12	2.14	$11514	1024	428
EB	120	69.43	6.27	2.68	8332	752	322
FA	340	63.86	5.45	2.41	21712	1853	819
FB	170	73.64	6.64	2.67	12519	1129	454
					$54077	4758	2023
				× 50%			1012
To Stock							
EA	900	$57.57	5.12	2.14	$51813	4608	1926
EB	490	69.43	6.27	2.68	34021	3072	1313
FA	360	63.86	5.45	2.41	22990	1962	868
FB	180	73.64	6.64	2.67	13255	1195	481
					$122079	10837	4588

Totals to schedule 4

SCHEDULE 4

Calculation of Manufacturing Variances—Work in Process

July 1979

	Department	001	102	103	202	203	301	302	303	Total
A	Beginning inv., matl.	$ 41216	$23684	$120364	$24618	$ 132816	$18362	$ 23425	$ 52198	$ 436686
	+ Material issues*	86219	49302	263879	42619	271319	39814	47286	127042	927480
	Goods available	127435	72989	384243	67237	404135	58176	70711	179240	1364166
	− Goods to stock	85326	51206	251312	42106	267108	31612	32725	122079	883474
	− Ending Inventory	42778	20833	131618	25218	134318	17017	21812	54007	447601
	Material usage var.	$ 669	$ −950	$ −1313	$ 87	$ −2709	$ −9547	$ −16174	$ −3154	$ −33091 (u)
B	Beg. inv., previous hrs.		623	13104	718	12378		856	4625	32304
	+ Hours in matl. issued*		1314	26518	1268	25318		1932	11363	67713
	Hours available		1937	39622	1986	37696		2788	15988	100017
	− Previous hours to stock		1361	25733	1210	25023		1760	10837	65924
	− Ending inv., previous hours		542	13612	780	12604		741	4758	33037
	Labor hours scrapped		− 34	−277	4	− 69		−287	−393	− 1056
	Labor $ scrapped (× $6.50)									$ − 6864 (u)
	Overhead scrapped (× $1.50)									$ −10296 (u)
C	Labor hours worked (paid)**	23625	11628	10794	12418	13206	4210	7486	4612	87979
	× $6.50 standard	$153562	$75582	$70161	$80717	$85839	$27365	$48659	$29978	$571863
	− Wages paid**	152807	76347	71231	80653	86107	27518	48587	30315	573565
	Labor rate var. ($)	$ 755	$ −765	$ −1070	$ 64	$ −268	$ −153	$ 72	$ −337	$ −1702 (u)
D	Beginning inv., in process hours (50% of std.)	6806	3107	2823	2916	4384	1481	1618	976	24111
	+ Labor hours paid**	23625	11628	10794	12418	13206	4210	7486	4612	87979
	Hours available	30431	14735	13617	15334	17590	5691	9104	5588	112090
	− Hrs., to stock (100%)	23216	11014	10874	12273	13407	3912	6314	4588	85598
	− Ending inv., in process Hours (50% of std.)	6683	3612	2796	3023	4326	1217	1527	1012	24196
	Labor eff. var. hours	− 532	− 109	53	− 38	143	− 562	−1263	12	−2296
	Labor efficiency var. (× $6.50)									$ −14924 (u)
	Excess overhead (× $1.50)									$ −22386 (u)

* From computerized listing of material issued by department.

** From computerized payroll by department.

(u) Unfavorable

13

SCHEDULE 5

Manufacturing Overhead Budget Comparison

ACCOUNT NO.	DIRECT LABOR $	1979 BUDGET		JULY			YEAR TO DATE		
		BUDGET PER DIRECT LABOR $	FIXED BUDGET	FLEXIBLE BUDGET	ACTUAL EXPENSE	SPENDING VARIANCE	FLEXIBLE BUDGET	ACTUAL EXPENSE	SPENDING VARIANCE
	DIRECT LABOR $			$ 571863			$3659344		
014	Foremen's salaries		$ 35200	35200	$ 36430	$ − 1230	246400	$ 253210	$ − 6810
015	Indirect labor	$ .5643		322702	327324	− 4622	2064968	2097326	− 32358
017	Mfg. engineers		17200	17200	16832	368	120400	114279	− 6121
020	Clerical		7850	7850	8727	− 877	54950	59324	− 4374
101	Payroll tax	.1051		60103	61394	− 1291	384597	391622	− 7025
102	Overtime & shift premium	.1122		64163	74362	− 10199	410578	443117	− 32539
103	Holiday & vacation	.1444		82577	85118	− 2541	528409	539723	− 11314
104	Employee benefits		85600	85600	86321	− 721	599200	602831	− 3631
105	Workmen's comp. ins.	.0161		9207	9731	− 524	58915	57986	929
202	General insurance		5600	5600	5520	80	39200	38230	970
204	Outside services		5000	5000	4650	350	35000	34650	350
201	Office supplies		1800	1800	1603	197	12600	13619	− 1019
304	Factory supplies	.0232		13267	14003	− 736	84897	93910	− 9013
305	Repair & maint.—bld.		25000	25000	23285	1715	175000	193214	− 18214
306	Repair & maint.—equip.	.0301		17213	16683	530	110146	114369	− 4223
308	Depreciation		33150	33150	32120	1030	232050	238628	− 6578
311	Heat, light, & power	.0231		13210	12380	830	84531	92612	− 8081
312	Tax—sales & use	.0251		14354	12394	1960	91850	103229	− 11379
401	Shipping supplies	.0273		15612	16318	− 706	99900	105392	− 5492
	Total	$1.0709	$216400	$828808	$845195	$ − 16387	$5433591	$5587271	$ − 153680

SCHEDULE 6

Calculation of Overhead Volume Variance
July 1979

Labor hours worked (sch. 4)	87979 hrs.	
× std. labor rate ($6.50)		
Standard labor to inventory	$571863	
× std. overhead rate ($1.50)		
Standard overhead absorbed in inventory		$857795
Less: budgeted overhead (from sch. 5)		828808
Variance due to volume:		$ 28987

JOURNAL ENTRY

Inventory	857795	
Spending variance	16387	
Volume variance		28987
Manufacturing overhead		845195

SCHEDULE 7

Cost of Goods Sold at Standard
July 1979

PRODUCT GROUP	SERIES	UNITS SOLD	STANDARD COST PER UNIT MATERIAL $	STANDARD COST PER UNIT LABOR HOURS	TOTAL STANDARD COST MATERIAL $	TOTAL STANDARD COST LABOR ($6.50/HR)
100	AA	2040	$ 13.60	1.59	$ 27744.00	$ 21083.40
	AB	2480	15.92	1.88	39481.60	30305.60
	AC	3010	16.01	1.84	48190.10	35999.60
	AD	2580	18.23	2.16	47033.40	36223.20
	AE	2040	21.47	2.43	43798.80	32221.80
	CA	1840	27.14	3.03	49937.60	36238.80
	Total 100				256185.50	192072.40
200	CB	1950	30.14	2.58	58773.00	32701.50
	DA	1010	32.07	3.89	32390.70	25537.85
	DB	1600	37.16	4.63	59456.00	48152.00
	DC	1620	42.94	5.14	69562.80	54124.20
	DD	1230	47.07	5.83	57896.10	46610.85
	Total 200				278078.60	207126.40
300	EA	820	57.57	7.26	47207.40	38695.80
	EB	420	69.43	8.95	29160.60	24433.50
	FA	430	63.86	7.86	27459.80	21968.70
	FB	210	73.64	9.31	15464.40	12708.15
	Total 300				119292.20	97806.15
	Totals				$653556.30	$ 497004.95
	Overhead ($1.50 × labor $)					$ 745507.42
	Total COGS at standard					$1896068.67

SCHEDULE 8

Cost of Goods Sold Summary
July 1979

	FROM SCHEDULE		
Material			
COGS—standard	7	$653556.30	
Purchase price var.	1	19522.00	
Material usage var.	4	33091.00	
			$ 706,169.30
Labor			
COGS—standard	7	$497004.95	
Scrapped labor	4	6864.00	
Labor rate var.	4	1702.00	
Labor efficiency var.	4	14924.00	
			$ 520,494.95
Overhead			
COGS—standard	7	$745507.42	
Scrapped overhead	4	10296.00	
Overhead on excess labor	4	22386.00	
Spending var.	5	16387.00	
Volume var.	6	(28987.00)	
			$ 765,589.42
Total COGS			$1,992,253.67

SCHEDULE 9

Inventory Journal Entries
July 1979

1. Inventory at standard	$ 682419.48		
Purchase price variance	19522.00		
Material purchases			701941.48
Inventory at standard	571863.00		
Labor rate variance	1702.00		
Direct labor			573565.00
Inventory at standard	857795.00		
Spending variance	16387.00		
Volume variance			28987.00
Manufacturing overhead			845195.00

To transfer material, labor, and overhead to inventory at standard cost

Material usage variance	33091.00	
Scrapped labor	6864.00	
Scrapped overhead	10296.00	
Inventory at standard		50251.00

To record material usage variance

3. Labor efficiency variance	14924.00	
Overhead on excess labor	22386.00	
Inventory at standard		37310.00

To record labor efficiency variance

4. Cost of goods sold at standard	1896068.67	
Inventory at standard		1896068.67

To record COGS at standard

SCHEDULE 10

Income Statement
July 1979

Sales	$2689103
Cost of goods sold	1992254
Gross margin	$ 696849
Manufacturing	122841
Engineering	121495
Marketing	105217
Sales	83418
Finance	67502
Administration	79283
Total	579756
Net income before tax	$ 117093
Income tax	58000
Net income	$ 59093

Bridgeton Industries
Automotive Component and Fabrication Plant

The union has worked with us and has even led in cost reduction programs. Now corporate is talking about outsourcing additional products. What more can we do to keep the business?

MIKE LEWIS, PLANT MANAGER

The Automotive Component and Fabrication Plant (ACF) was the original plant site for Bridgeton Industries, a major supplier of components for the domestic automotive industry. The history of the plant dated back to the 1840s when the adjoining river attracted mills that processed the rich lumber resources in the area. The site progressed through several industrial uses, including an early wagon works, until it was finally purchased by the founder of Bridgeton. He opened his first office there in the early 1900s.

All of ACF's production was sold to the Big Three domestic manufacturers. Competition was primarily from local suppliers and other Bridgeton plants. As long as the market was growing and dominated by U.S. manufacturers, this strategy worked. It became less effective when foreign competition and scarce, expensive gasoline caused domestic loss of market share. Suppliers found themselves competing for a shrinking pool of production contracts. Throughout the 1980s, ACF experienced serious cutbacks due to this competitive pressure. However, as the 1989/90 model year budget approached, ACF was still considered a critical plant. Model years ran from September 1 to August 31 and were the basis for budgeting. Production contracts were usually awarded for a model year.

THE ENGINE PLANT SHUTDOWN

ACF first felt the effects of domestic loss of market share in 1985. After the first oil crunch in the mid-1970s, Bridgeton had built two plants for manufacture of fuel-efficient diesel engines in anticipation of a continued growth in the market. One of these plants was at the ACF facility. When the growth in diesel-powered cars was not sustained, one of the operations had to be shut down.

Special studies were made of the relative costs of the two plants, and ACF's facility was the one chosen to be closed. When the production workers at ACF were told they were not cost competitive, they took actions to reduce unit product cost, bringing it down to within a few cents of the competing quote. Despite these efforts, ACF's facility was closed. "Management told us we were not cost competitive. We worked ourselves into the ground and lowered the unit cost, and still lost the business," recalls Ronald Peters, a long-time production worker in the old engine facility.

When the engine plant closed at the end of 1985/6 model year, all of the related production jobs were eliminated. The skilled trades positions were eliminated where possible. However, tradespeople who had unique skills that were needed in other areas of the plant were retained. The physical machinery, equipment, and building were written down and taken off the plant books.

STRATEGIC ANALYSIS

During the 1986/7 model year, the corporation hired a strategic consulting firm to examine all of Bridgeton's products and classify them in terms of world-class competitive position and potential. Four criteria were considered: (a) quality, (b) customer

service, (c) technical capability (engineering and sophistication of plant processes), and (d) competitive cost position.

The data used to evaluate quality included warranty failure rates, product rejects per million, percent scheduled maintenance versus breakdown maintenance, customer complaints per million, and published user rating service scales.

To evaluate customer service, in addition to interviews, the study examined percent on-schedule production and shipments, percent variation in these schedules, time to respond to requests for information, time to respond to customer complaints, lead-time from design of concept to production of product, and degree of manufacturing flexibility.

Technical capability was largely estimated by interviewing customers. Internal data were gathered about product feature innovations, degree of technological proprietary, and depth of engineering expertise.

Competitive cost position was evaluated by interviewing financial, purchasing, and engineering personnel and undertaking a cost analysis which examined the cost of production by breaking each product cost into three elements: materials, direct labor and benefits, and overhead. The product costs used for the study were total full-factory costs based on examination of the manufacturing cost reports generated by the facility's cost system. The details were provided by the plant financial personnel. Comparative competitive costs were obtained through plant tours and interviews with engineering and purchasing people at other Bridgeton plants (internal competitors), information from competing component suppliers (external competitors), and discussions with financial personnel.

The budgeted unit costs provided by the plant for the 1986/7 model year study included overhead (burden) applied to products as a percent of direct labor dollars. The overhead percentage was calculated at budget time and used throughout the model year to allocate overhead to products using a single overhead pool. The overhead rate used in the study was 435% of direct labor dollars.

Product costs were analyzed by the consultants to classify products by degree of cost competitiveness. Product classification was finished and reviewed at the corporate level with little plant adjustment or involvement after initial data collection. Products classified as world class (having costs equal to or lower than competitors' manufacturing costs) were considered Class I. Products which had the potential of becoming world class (having costs 5% to 15% higher than competitors' costs) were classified as Class II. Products which had no hope of becoming world class (having costs more than 15% higher than the major competitor) were classified as Class III.

The other criteria (quality, customer service, and technical capability) were weighted into a factor that determined the final classification of the products. The consultants recommended that Class I products should remain at their present locations. Class II products were to be watched closely for improvement or deterioration. Class III were designated to be outsourced (i.e., the business was awarded to another Bridgeton location, or purchased from an outside competitor) or eliminated.

The consultants advised ACF's management that their products fell into the following classifications (for a description of these products see Exhibit 1): (a) Class I: Fuel tanks; (b) Class II: Manifolds, front and rear doors; and (c) Class III: Muffler-exhaust systems, and oil pans.

PRODUCT OUTSOURCING

At the end of the 1987/8 model year, oil pans and muffler-exhaust systems were outsourced from ACF. This outsourcing resulted in a loss of 60 direct labor (production) jobs and 30 indirect (skilled) jobs. These 90 people were transferred to a retraining job pool, which was administered and paid by the union. The job pool cost was not part of plant burden costs.

With this second major cutback, plant management and labor moved toward more cooperation and openness in efforts to retain the remaining business. Several programs were introduced to improve product quality and increase productivity. These programs stretched the traditional union/management boundaries as both sides worked toward creative solutions to meet these challenges.

One of these efforts, led by Fred Simmonds, an experienced die maker, involved union formation of teams to lower the time required to change dies, a major constraint in the production process. By combining union labor classes and skill levels on press line die change teams, ACF lowered the required time to change dies from 12 hours to 90 minutes. This was the best in Bridgeton. Other locations averaged between four and five hours. The world-class times of Japanese assembly lines, approximately 10 minutes, required special plant layouts.

Another productivity improvement program created by Simmonds and Peters used "hourly to time hourly." In this program, hourly workers kept track of the causes of downtime and categorized them as being related to personal time, tools and equipment, or startup. People from the retraining job pool formed by the union at the time of the prior layoffs were asked to time the lines. Production personnel's knowledge of the process and experience on the line resulted in highly accurate activity times for the operations they observed. Their reporting emphasized the positive side of the information using uptime reports to show progress toward the world-class goal of 80% uptime set by the Japanese. Through identifying problem areas and working with industrial engineers, they increased their uptime from an average of 30% to 65%, the best in Bridgeton.

In spite of these improvements in the production process, manifolds, designated Class II in the initial study, were downgraded to Class III in the 1989/90 model year budget and identified as candidates for outsourcing (for the 1986/7 through 1989/90 model year budgets, see Exhibits 2 and 3). Any decision to outsource manifolds was complicated by the possibility that increased emission standards would require new vehicles be fitted with lighter weight, more efficient manifolds. If this occurred, the demand for stainless steel manifolds could increase dramatically and so, probably, would its selling price.

Reacting to the change in status of the manifolds, Lewis called together his plant superintendents and union representatives. "This doesn't make sense. I know we are more competitive. We have made all kinds of improvements, but our costs keep going up and we're still losing business. What more can we do?"

EXHIBIT 1

BRIDGETON INDUSTRIES

Product Lines in 1990 Budget

Fuel tanks: These are produced on six stamping lines from coated sheet metal, which is stamped in halves and then placed together and automatically seam welded.

Manifolds: Stainless steel exhaust manifolds are produced in a highly automated production process. The parts are loaded on fixture and robotically welded. These manifolds are superior to the older technology cast iron manifolds in pollution control. The disadvantage of using stainless steel is its high relative cost.

Front and rear doors: These are the front doors and rear cargo doors for vans. They are produced on four press lines with up to six presses per line.

Muffler-exhaust systems: These are formed from sheet metal that is bent to shape and robotically welded.

Oil pans: These are small steel stampings. They are produced on two lines containing one press each.

EXHIBIT 2

BRIDGETON INDUSTRIES

1986/7 through 1989/90 Model Year Budgets

$(000)

| | MODEL YEAR | | | |
	1986/87	1987/88	1988/89	1989/90
Sales				
Fuel tanks	70,278	75,196	79,816	83,535
Manifolds	79,459	84,776	89,323	93,120
Doors	41,845	45,174	47,199	49,887
Muffler/exhausts	62,986	66,266	0	0
Oil pans	75,586	79,658	0	0
Total	330,154	351,071	216,338	226,542
Direct material				
Fuel tanks	15,125	15,756	16,312	16,996
Manifolds	31,696	33,016	34,392	35,725
Doors	14,886	15,506	16,252	16,825
Muffler/exhausts	28,440	29,525	0	0
Oil pans	32,218	33,560	0	0
Total	122,365	127,363	66,956	69,546
Direct labor				
Fuel tanks	4,169	4,238	4,415	4,599
Manifolds	5,886	6,027	6,278	6,540
Doors	2,621	2,731	2,884	2,963
Muffler/exhausts	5,635	5,766	0	0
Oil pans	6,371	6,532	0	0
Total	24,682	25,294	13,537	14,102

(continued)

EXHIBIT 2 *(cont.)*

Overhead by account number

1000	7,713	7,806	5,572	5,679
1500	6,743	6,824	5,883	5,928
2000	3,642	3,794	2,031	2,115
3000	2,428	2,529	1,354	1,410
4000	8,817	8,888	7,360	7,433
5000	24,181	24,460	20,063	20,274
8000	5,964	5,946	3,744	3,744
9000	6,708	6,771	5,948	5,987
11000	5,089	5,011	3,150	3,030
12000	26,954	28,077	15,027	15,683
14000	9,733	9,784	8,025	8,110
Total	107,954	109,890	78,157	79,393
Factory profit	75,153	88,524	57,688	63,501

EXHIBIT 3

BRIDGETON INDUSTRIES
Description of Chart of Accounts

ACCOUNT NUMBER	DESCRIPTION
1000	Wages and benefits for nonskilled hourly personnel such as janitors and truck drivers
1500	All plant salaried personnel expense, including benefits, except industrial engineers (included in account number 11000)
2000	Production supplies such as gloves, safety goggles, and packing material
3000	Small wearing tools such as grinding wheels, hammers, and screwdrivers
4000	All purchased utilities including coal and compressed gas
5000	Wages for nonproduction employees with specialized skilled classifications used for plant maintenance and rearrangement; the benefits associated with these wages are in class 14000
8000	Depreciation, on a straight-line basis, and property taxes
9000	Various relatively constant personnel-related expenses including items such as training, travel, and union representation
11000	Project expense for one-time setup and some rearrangement of new equipment and machinery
12000	Benefits and overtime premium for production hourly workers including COLA (Cost of Living Adjustment), state unemployment, and pension (Wages are in direct labor.)
14000	Benefits for skilled hourly workers similar to those for production workers (Wages are in account 5000.)

Institutional Furniture

Edwin Nixon founded Institutional Furniture 15 years ago after a successful career in secondary education where he had responsibility for selecting school equipment. The first few years were difficult, but the company gained experience and finally won three large contracts.

For the 10 years until 19X2, the company maintained a steady growth rate. Then in the spring of 19X2 the company began experiencing a profit decline. One of the first actions management took was to install a standard cost system, which was fully operational by the end of 19X3. The standard cost system, including the updating of the standard cost cards, was manually operated until June 19X4 when the company began using a computer service bureau. The major reason for turning to a computerized system was the ability to update standard cost cards on the 276 product-line items on a day-to-day basis.

The standard cost system adopted was an actual-in, standard-out system. Standards are applied to production costs only; the marketing, administrative, and product development costs are accounted for on an actual cost basis. The philosophy of setting the standards can best be described as "expected actual." That is, if all went as planned, the actual costs and standard costs would be identical and all variances would be zero.

During the first two years the standard cost system appeared to operate smoothly. The problem of declining profits seemed under control when the earnings per share increased. The variance balances were becoming progressively larger each period, but the variances were matched against revenue without managerial comment.

When Mr. Nixon received the financial statements for the 12 months ended December 31, 19X4, he was completely shocked. The income statement, shown in Exhibit 1, showed a total unfavorable variance of $164,011. Mr. Nixon was at a loss to understand the problem but because the final net profit figure was satisfactory he took no action

Exhibit 1. Institutional Furniture
Unaudited Income Statements
For the 12 Months Ended December 31

	19X4	19X5
Net Sales	$5,370,786	$5,786,581
Standard cost of sales	4,340,552	4,640,218
Standard gross profit	$1,030,234	$1,146,363
Over/Under* Absorbed overhead	255,510	9,133
Gain/Loss* variances	164,011*	226,231*
Gross profit	$1,121,733	$ 929,265
Marketing expense	$ 390,523	$ 435,562
Administrative expense	269,989	342,027
Product development and field installation expenses	152,661	156,416
Total expenses	813,173	934,005
Net operating profit	$ 308,560	$ 4,740*
Other income	31,363	24,662
Net profit before taxes and bonuses	$ 339,923	$ 19,922
Provisions for bonuses	39,355	5,533
Net profit before taxes	$ 300,568	$ 14,589
Federal income tax	144,165	3,209
Net profit after taxes	$ 156,403	$ 11,380

*Indicates loss or unfavorable variance

This case was prepared by Professor Don T. DeCoster of Seattle University. It appeared in Don T. DeCoster, Eldon L. Schaffer, and Mary T. Ziebell, *Management Accounting: A Decision Emphasis*, 4th edition (New York: Wiley, 1988). Reproduced with permission.

except to ask for monthly reports. (See Exhibit 2 for the December 19X5 monthly report.)

After December 31, 19X5, the auditors informed Mr. Nixon that in order to certify the financial statements it would be necessary to reduce the book inventories by $266,669 (see Exhibit 3 for the auditor's schedule). This reduced after-tax profits for the calendar year even further below the $11,380 reported on the unaudited statement (see

Exhibit 1). This inventory write-down, coupled with the low net income, resulted in the rejection of a substantial bank loan requested for capital equipment procurement. Mr. Nixon was crestfallen and totally unable to determine the reasons for the loss or its magnitude. As a first step he called for monthly inventories in the future; he also called upon a management consulting firm to (1) identify what had caused the loss and (2) recommend chang-

Exhibit 2. Institutional Furniture
Statement of Gain or Loss*
Caused by Variances
For Period Ended Dec. 31, 19X5

	CURRENT MONTH THIS YEAR	YEAR TO DATE THIS YEAR
Purchase variance		
Veneer	$ 60	$ 3,137
Plastic	434	2,465
Hardware	1,079	734*
Miscellaneous	1,019	12,477
Lumber	355	10,693
Core stock and hi gard overlay	51*	8,076
Colorlith	—	—
Subcontract	157*	15,424*
Total gain/loss*	$ 2,739	$ 20,690
Average labor		
Rate variance		
Cutting	$ 23	$ 2,445*
Veneer	231*	2,885*
Plastic	67	280
Machine and sand	549	1,449
Assembly	211*	5,123*
Finishing	317*	7,329*
Packing	139*	3,208*
Modification	670	5,481
Hi gard	—	2,015*
Total gain/loss*	411	15,795*
All other variances		
Veneer	$ 21,311*	$ 23,807*
Plastic	8,091*	4,181*
Hardware	2,678	58,871
Miscellaneous	18,814*	8,931
Lumber	36,163*	51,963*
Core stock and hi gard overlay	49,072*	25,365*
Process labor	62,052*	102,921*
Process overhead	95,542*	189,228*
Finished goods other	13,995	32,101*
Finished goods—burden rate change	8,513	128,060
Colorlith	2,578	2,578
Total gain/loss*	263,281*	231,126*
Total gain or loss* due to variance	$260,131*	$226,231*

*Indicates loss variance

Exhibit 3. **Smith and Smith, CPAs**
Schedule of Inventory Reduction
for Institutional Furniture
Dec. 31, 19X5

	PHYSICAL INVENTORY 12-31-X5	AUDITOR'S BOOK INVENTORY 12-31-X5	ADJUSTMENT TO BOOKS 12-31-X5
Veneer	$ 90,199.99	$ 111,293.20	$ (21,093.21)
Plastic	20,903.01	29,356.15	(8,453.14)
Hardware	134,992.77	137,226.95	(2,234.16)
Glue	3,561.78	9,696.86	(6,135.08)
Finish	6,991.88	13,020.64	(6,028.76)
Packing	23,120.68	33,113.23	(9,992.55)
Lumber	81,598.43	116,252.59	(34,654.16)
Core	192,620.14	244,502.96	(51,882.82)
Labor	90,662.18	148,109.82	(57,447.64)
Overhead	139,619.74	228,110.77	(88,491.03)
Finished goods	816,092.61	798,926.74	17,165.87
Colorlith	50,797.51	48,219.69	2,577.82
	$1,651,160.74	$1,917,829.60	$266,668.86

es in the plant operations and accounting system that would correct the problem.

The factory is divided into two production areas. In the first area lumber and core are prepared, covered with plastic or birch veneer, and cut to form the parts necessary for assembly. These parts are stored in a large area under the supervision of the wood parts controller, who keeps a cardex quantity record and locator file of all parts in his area. As necessary, parts are withdrawn and taken to the second area where they are assembled, finished, and packed for shipment. All work in the factory is cycled every two weeks, and no work is begun without written orders from production control. For products within the 276-standard product line the production control personnel add a small percentage to the quantity needed for production to ensure an adequate quantity. If spoilage is not as large as the percentage allowed, the overage is stored in the wood parts controller's area.

All raw materials are issued to the Work-in-Process Inventory when purchased; that is, there are no Raw Material Inventory accounts. To facilitate accounting control there are eight raw material subclassifications in the Work-in-Process Inventory. All raw materials are costed in the Work-in-Process Inventory at standard cost. Purchases are recorded with the following entry:

Work-in-Process (e.g., lumber)	$AQ \times SP$
Purchase Variance	$(SP - AP)AQ$
Accounts Payable	$AQ \times AP$

(AQ is the actual quantity purchased, AP the actual price paid per unit of raw material, and SP the predetermined standard price per unit.)

The purchasing agent, whenever cognizant of a price change, notifies the production control manager, the accounting department, and the industrial design department of the impending price change. The standard costs are then changed in the next available computer run to reflect the new prices.

Lumber, a basic material, is purchased in large quantities from three principal suppliers. Only one supplier provides certified lumber. Daily reports are prepared by the lead cutter showing the board feet of lumber bundles opened and board feet of usable lumber obtained. In past years the yield of "clear or better" lumber has run about 57%. Beginning in 19X5, the company instituted a policy of purchasing "Grade 1 or better" instead of "clear or better" (about $161 per 1,000 bd ft). After the shift the yield dropped to 55–56%.

The yield is the direct responsibility of the lead cutting man. As the boards pass his area all unacceptable parts are cut out and thrown onto a conveyor belt that leads to the "hog"—a machine that grinds the materials into sawdust. The sawdust is sold at current market prices; the proceeds are not significant. The lumber, after cutting, is then bonded into suitable panel sizes for veneering.

The veneer is held by the company on consignment. The company has entered into an agreement with a broker to store veneer for both themselves and the broker. The veneer is sent directly to Institutional Furniture by the broker's suppliers. When veneer shipments are received the veneer supervisor checks the marked bundles against the master packing list. Whenever a bundle is used by Institutional Furniture, the supervisor indicates the specific bundle on the master packing list. Monthly, these master packing lists and a list of usage are sent to the broker, who then bills the company. When one of the broker's other customers needs veneer, the broker comes to the factory and makes a withdrawal. No formal records of these external withdrawals are made because all accounting and responsibility lie with the broker. All parties think this is an excellent arrangement because the company has a constant supply of veneer available in a tight market, because there is no working capital invested in veneer inventory, and because the supervisor can choose the best bundles for company use. At the same time the broker has free storage space.

The core materials are used in places where the bonded lumber panels are inappropriate: doors, drawer bottoms, under plastic on table tops, and unexposed backing. The core, purchased from four suppliers, is received directly by the department where physical counts are made and recorded on the incoming packing slips. The core is stored in the factory and used as needed. The price of core has been dropping consistently from $128 to $112, and finally to $103 per 1,000 bd ft on the last invoice.

Hardware and plastic are purchased on an annual purchase order based on last year's usage. Shipments against the annual purchase order are requested whenever the storeroom reports a shortage. All receipts come directly to the storeroom where a cardex file is maintained on a periodic inventory basis. Hardware is issued to the factory without paperwork upon request of a supervisor; furthermore, there are no records of the hardware at the workbenches. Once a year all hardware throughout the plant is collected, returned to the

storeroom, counted, and reentered on the cardex records. Plastic is issued in full-roll quantities upon supervisor requests.

There are nine departments for labor cost accumulation. Each department is charged monthly for its labor costs by the following entry:

Work-in-Process (department) $AH \times SP$
Labor Price Variance $(SP - AP) AH$
   Payroll Payable $AH \times AP$

(AH is the actual hours worked; AP the actual hourly wage paid the workers; and SP the average standard hourly wage of the specific department.)

Overhead is applied to the Work-in-Process Inventory on the basis of a predetermined rate. Currently the application rate is 154% of labor cost.

When the goods have been manufactured and packed into cartons the production control forms are completed. These forms notify production control of the completion of the jobs and also serve as an accounting document. The slips are accumulated by product on a spread sheet in the accounting department. Each product total is then multiplied by the standard cost of the item. The sum of the standard costs for the items packed is then debited to Finished Goods and credited to Work-in-Process. When the items are billed to the customers, they are charged to Cost of Goods Sold, and the Finished Goods Inventory is credited for the standard cost of the items billed.

There are at least three types of unusual transactions that do not follow the same accounting procedures.

1. *Modifications.* Last year the company made about $556,000 in sales of modified units. The modification could be major (replacement of doors with drawers) or minor (changing a color). Since these items are not in the normal product line, there are no standard costs. All actual costs are charged to Work-in-Process. To relieve the Work-in-Process Inventory and charge the Finished Goods Inventory, the company uses a predetermined formula. This formula is (AQ packed × Selling price quoted by sales personnel) × 78%. The relief of the inventory subaccounts for raw materials is also done by formula: 10% veneer, 15% hardware, etc.

2. *Sales on a bid basis.* Some jobs are accepted on a bid basis. There is no standard cost card for these products. Work-in-Process is charged for the actual costs incurred. The relief to the inventory is for the original

bid cost prepared by the sales force. At least one extra unit of each type is manufactured. Any production overruns on the bid items are shipped to the purchaser without inventory relief because they are not counted on the packing slips.

3. *Spoilage and rework.* The company has a particular problem with "falldown"—products that do not pass an inspection point. When feasible the company reworks these items to obtain a usable product. The product is returned to the responsible department and left for rework. This rework is not rescheduled by the production control area. The department is expected to find a way to integrate this extra effort into its normal workday. If the existing part cannot be repaired, a replacement is drawn from the wood parts controller. The defective part goes directly to the hog. If the piece cannot be reworked, it is isolated into a separate area for a warehouse sale of "seconds" once per year. No records have been kept on the rework quantities.

Stalcup Paper Company

In March 1985, the president of the Stalcup Paper Company, while examining a group of charts regarding unit costs submitted to him by the cost department, noted that the unit costs of sorting rags had been rising for approximately two years. To determine the reason for this increase, he invited the manager of the rag sorting department and the head of the cost department to his office to discuss the matter. The head of the cost department submitted the information shown in Exhibits 1, 2, and 3, giving the details of the upward trend in costs shown in the charts. The manager of the rag sorting department said that his costs were lower rather than higher than they had been in past years, and that the basis of the cost department's estimates was unsound. He submitted Exhibit 4 in support of this contention.

The Stalcup Paper Company used old rags, new rags, and pulp in manufacturing its papers. The proportions in which these materials were mixed were varied in accordance with the requirements for different grades and types of paper. The new rags, which were purchased from textile converters, cost substantially more than old rags, which were purchased through junk dealers. The old rags were usually received in the form of garments, from which it was necessary to remove carefully all foreign materials such as buttons, rubber, and metal. New rags were largely remnants containing only a small percentage of foreign matter requiring removal and as a result could be sorted much more rapidly than old rags.

The sorters sat at benches. Their task was to remove all foreign matter from the material placed before them and to distribute the usable cloth, according to quality, into containers placed beside them. The sorters inspected and graded, on the average, 55 pounds of old rags or 575 pounds of new rags per hour. They were paid on a day-rate basis, because management discovered that payment on a piece-rate basis resulted in picking over rags less carefully.

Between 1982 and 1984, the composition of rags purchased by the Stalcup Paper Company changed considerably, as shown in Exhibit 1. The percentage of old rags to the total dropped from approximately 80% to approximately 50%. During the same interval, the amount of rags handled increased nearly 25%. In spite of the large increase in total volume, labor costs declined over the period because of the smaller amount of old rags handled.

Costs charged to the rag sorting department were of three types: first, those incurred for direct labor in the department; second, overhead burden charged directly to the department; and third, general factory overhead. It was the practice of the cost department to charge all burdens incurred directly by each department to all products processed within it as a uniform percentage of direct labor. This percentage was obtained by dividing the total department burden by total department direct labor. The amount of general overhead charged to a department was obtained by multiplying the direct

This case was written by A. Grimshaw and updated by Robin Cooper.

labor in the department by the ratio of total general overhead to total direct labor in the plant.

The items included in rag sorting department burden were as shown in Exhibit 2. The most important of these were indirect labor, including the salary of the manager and wages of employees engaged in taking material to and from the sorters; and investment, which included the charge against the department for taxes, depreciation, and insurance on the premises and equipment it used. General overhead included factory-wide waste collection, miscellaneous labor, building repair labor and materials, manufacturing executive salaries, and expenses of functional departments, such as planning, costing, and research.

The head of the cost department pointed out to the president that between 1982 and 1984 the rag sorting department burden charge had increased from 122% of direct labor to 153% and that the difference in cost of sorting in the two years was, as shown in Exhibit 3, almost entirely attributable to this increase.

The manager differed with the cost department's estimated unit costs and pointed out that it was hard to conceive of unit costs increasing while total costs were diminishing and volume of output was rising. He stated that the cost department was not charging the proper proportion of overhead charges to the new rags and that, therefore, old rags were taking more than their share of total department burden. He said that, in his opinion, a much sounder method of allocating burden charges would be on a per-pound basis rather than on the percentage-of-direct-labor basis previously used, and he recommended that costs in the rag department in the future should be calculated on the basis shown in Exhibit 4.

The unit cost for old and new rag sorting, as calculated by the cost department, was used in setting up standard costs. These standard costs, however, were only rarely used in setting prices of finished paper since most of the company's paper was sold in a competitive market at prices established by competition. The company used the standard costs mostly as a check on the profit and loss incurred on the various lines of paper manufactured to determine which were relatively more profitable. When the plant was being operated at capacity and orders were being refused, the relative profitability of lines was a factor in determining what lines should be discontinued. In 1985, the Stalcup Paper Company was operating at about 55% of capacity.

EXHIBIT 1

STALCUP PAPER COMPANY

Output of Rag Sorting Department in Pounds

	1982	1984	CHANGE
Old rags	3,220,000	2,460,000	− 23.6%
New rags	810,000	2,520,000	+211.1%
	4,030,000	4,980,000	+ 23.6%
Percent of old rags	79.9%	49.4%	
Percent of new rags	20.1%	50.6%	

EXHIBIT 2

STALCUP PAPER COMPANY

Expenses of Rag Sorting Department

	1982			1984	
		PERCENT OF DIRECT LABOR			PERCENT OF DIRECT LABOR
Direct labor		$314,475			$257,775
Rag sorting dept. burden					
Indirect labor	$ 127,995			$ 143,100	
Repair labor	9,150			7,620	
Repair materials	1,845			4,065	
Supplies	2,340			2,400	
Power	9,180			8,295	
Investment	233,235			228,060	
		383,745	122%	393,540	153%
General overhead		286,920	91%	227,790	88%
		$985,140		$879,105	

EXHIBIT 3

STALCUP PAPER COMPANY

Rag Sorting Department

Costs of Sorting Old and New Rags

(as shown in cost records)

	1982		1984	
	DOLLARS	CENTS PER POUND	DOLLARS	CENTS PER POUND
Old rags				
Wages	307,188	9.54	234,684	9.54
Department overhead	374,808*	11.64	359,160**	14.60
General overhead	280,140	8.70	207,378	8.43
	962,136	29.88	801,222	32.57
Increase				2.69
New rags				
Wages	7,371	0.91	23,184	0.92
Department overhead	8,991	1.11	35,532**	1.41
General overhead	6,723	0.83	20,412	0.81
	23,085	2.85	79,128	3.13
Increase				0.28

* 122% of wages
**153% of wages

EXHIBIT 4

STALCUP PAPER COMPANY

Rag Sorting Department

Costs of Sorting Old and New Rags

(as estimated by manager)

	1982		1984	
	DOLLARS	CENTS PER POUND	DOLLARS	CENTS PER POUND
Old rags				
Wages	307,188	9.54	234,684	9.54
Department overhead	306,544	9.52	194,340	7.90
General overhead	229,264	7.12	112,442	4.57
	842,996	26.18	541,466	22.01
Decrease				4.17
New rags				
Wages	7,371	0.91	23,184	0.91
Department overhead	77,112	9.52	199,080	7.90
General overhead	57,672	7.12	115,164	4.57
	142,155	17.55	337,428	13.38
Decrease				4.18

Commonwealth Blood Transfusion Service

Until a few years ago product cost information was never produced here. Since then we've moved some way towards the identification of our products' cost, partly to help us manage more effectively and partly to meet new reporting requirements which will necessitate regular conventional inventory valuations for the first time.

Blood product costing is a very sensitive issue at the moment. There are several vested interests for whom information of this type assumes a great significance. The government, staff, health associations and donors are all interested and affected by it.

There's also the horrendous technical accounting problem of joint costs which we face.

J. INNES, CHIEF ACCOUNTANT, COMMONWEALTH BLOOD TRANSFUSION SERVICE

INTRODUCTION

The Commonwealth Blood Transfusion Service (CBTS), formed in 1950, served a population of 9 million by gathering blood donations from a panel of approximately half a million donors. The program sustained a national self-sufficiency in blood

and most blood products. A steady growth in attendance was planned into the mid-1990s in response to anticipated increases in clinical demand. All blood donations were given voluntarily. Hospitals were statutorily debarred from purchasing blood on the commercial market. Consequently the

This case was prepared by Falconer Mitchell, Senior Lecturer in Accounting, University of Edinburgh, and Professor Robin Cooper.

recruitment of suitable numbers of donors and the maintenance of their goodwill was crucial to the continuing self-sufficiency of the service.

The CBTS was a government-funded body. It comprised three Regional Centers (RC) and a Plasma Fractionation Plant (PFP). The senior management of CBTS consisted of the directors of the three RCs, the director of the PFP, a general manager, and a medical director (John Black). A small central team led by John Innes provided accounting services to the operational units.

Each RC was responsible for donor contact, blood collection, testing, and grouping. The outputs of the RC were used directly for clinical purposes and also as the source of supply for the PFP. Most of the blood plasma obtained by the RCs was sent to the PFP for further processing. The PFP was a sophisticated manufacturing facility that produced a wide variety of biological products from plasma.

BLOOD PRODUCTS

Typically, less than 10% of blood donations were used in their whole blood form. The other 90% were fractionated to produce a wide range of blood products. Some basic fractionation was performed at the RCs to meet local clinical demand and to separate blood into red cell concentrate and plasma. The majority of the plasma from 440,000 donations, weighing 110,000 kg, was forwarded to the PFP for further, more sophisticated processing into approximately 15 distinct blood products (see Exhibit 1).

The production process at the PFP, or the "factory" as it was known to the staff, consisted of a series of distinct steps. The incoming plasma was pooled into batches, prepared, and then centrifuged. Centrifuging precipitated out the solids, or cryoprecipitate, leaving behind a liquid residue, or supernatant. The cryoprecipitate was further processed to give Factor VIII, a blood coagulant used for treating hemophiliacs. The supernatant was filtered to separate out Factor IX, another coagulant, or centrifuged to produce intravenous and intramuscular immunoglobulin and human albumin. The residual from this final step was used to produce plasma protein solutions, which were manufactured in two dosages and used in the treatment of shock, major blood loss, and burns.

Immunoglobulins were used in the prevention and treatment of viral and bacterial diseases. There were several forms of both types of immunoglobulin. For example, included among the intravenous products were vaccinations against several diseases such as tetanus, rabies, and measles, and among the intramuscular products were vaccinations against measles and tetanus. In addition, several of the intramuscular products were produced in different concentrations, which were required to provide the different dose strengths that were necessary, for example, to treat pediatric and adult patients. A simplified processing schematic for both fresh and outdated frozen plasma is shown in Exhibit 2.

The PFP maintained four types of inventory, and during the year had pursued a policy of increasing all inventory levels substantially (see Exhibit 3). Raw material inventory consisted of unprocessed plasma. Since the production process was predominantly batch-oriented, frozen plasma was inventoried until a full batch was available and then processed. Intermediate products consisted of blood fractions that were stored until required. For example, supernatant was stored to provide the flexibility to produce immunoglobulin within a shorter time scale. Work-in-process consisting of products currently being processed could be quite high because some of the fractionation steps were lengthy. Finished goods inventory consisted of completed products. Substantial quantities of intermediate and finished product inventories were maintained to ensure availability of products at all times. Large buffer inventories were necessary because clinical demand for products could vary quite dramatically (for example, in response to disasters such as air or rail crashes and major fires). The costing of these large inventories significantly affected the reported annual performance of CBTS.

The products of the PFP came in a variety of forms, including powders, liquids, and solids. Their measurement fell under three classifications:

1. *International Units (IU).* When the clinical efficacy of a product varied, an internationally agreed measure of dose strength was used to measure output. Depending on the quality of raw material input and the efficacy of processing activity, a dose of, say, 10 IUs of Factor VIII may be represented by considerably different weights or volumes of actual output.

2. *Weight.* Weight, such as milligrams (mg) of normal

immunoglobin, was used for any solid product whose clinical efficacy did not vary.

3. *Liquid Volume.* Volume, such as milliliters (ml) of plasma solution, was used for any liquid product whose clinical efficacy did not vary.

Detailed records of inputs, yields, and outputs were maintained by the PFP and a clear trail was kept between original blood donations and batches of final products so that batch or product recall was possible should a contaminated donation be discovered (as was the case in the early 1980s with the AIDS virus).

The PFP products were supplied free of charge to hospitals, although clinicians did have the option of purchasing competing commercial products if there was a shortage or if they were not satisfied with the quality of PFP products. A thriving international market existed for these products (see Exhibit 4 for some recent prices). Prices were extremely volatile for these products; for example, the commercial price of human albumin products had varied by amounts of 100% or more within periods of a few days.

THE PRESENT COSTING SYSTEM AND CURRENT DEVELOPMENTS

The basic costing system at the CBTS was designed to assist staff in controlling cost in accordance with budgeted levels which were negotiated annually with government officials. The budget was analyzed by type of expenditure, and a report, known as a management statement, comparing budgeted and actual spending was prepared monthly.

In recent years, product cost information had started to be prepared within the CBTS. The motivations for cost information included:

- CBTS management hoped that product cost information within the RCs would provide intra-organization comparison and stimulate operational changes in the higher cost RCs.
- The increasing provision of blood and blood products to the private hospital sector required cost recovery charges to be made.
- Management considered that product cost information would be relevant to make or buy decisions where commercial alternatives were available.
- The government was considering charging all hospitals for blood products.

Product cost information was first generated for the RCs. These costs were prepared in a set of comprehensive, one-off studies. These studies determined the build-up of costs for the various activities of the RC. The average cost of collecting a blood donation at the three RCs was determined to be $30, the cost of grouping, testing, and banking a donation of whole blood $15, and separating it into red cell concentrate and fresh plasma for clinical use for further processing at the PFP $5 per donation.

Once these activity costs were determined, individual product costs could be calculated. Unfortunately, several of the products were joint products and individual product costs required some arbitrary allocation of costs to products. For example, plasma and red cell concentrate were joint products, since it was not possible to produce one without the other. The joint cost problem was resolved at the RCs by assigning the costs of processing to the products based upon the number of donations consumed. For example, of every 100 donations kept as whole blood for clinical use, on average only 60 would be used in transfusions. The other 40 became outdated before they were used and were then converted to plasma for separation at the PFP. The $200 costs of banking these 100 donations were split between the 60% used for transfusions ($120), and the 40% used for outdated plasma production ($80). Exhibit 5 illustrates the procedures used for product costing at the RCs. The cost of plasma supplied to the PFP was calculated at $25 per plasma content of each donation.

By mid-1990, the focus shifted to costing the PFP products. Management decided to first determine product costs that related solely to the PFP with plasma treated as a free good. Further cost information relating to processing activity is contained in Exhibit 6. Again the joint cost problem was encountered. The problem faced by Innes was to select an admittedly arbitrary way of allocating the joint costs that was acceptable to the various constituencies interested in how CBTS recovered its costs.

THE CONSTITUENTS

The CBTS was a public body, wholly funded by taxpayers' money. As such, it was affected by and must take account of the views and requirements of a variety of interested parties. The issue of blood and blood product costing was of considerable significance to each of these parties.

The government

Throughout the 1980s the government had pursued a policy of stringently limiting public expenditure and ensuring, where possible, that resources were managed by private enterprise. This policy had been implemented by privatizing such services as telephones, gas, and water.

In the Commonwealth Health Service (CHS), while public ownership had been retained, efforts had been made to improve efficiency. For example, more comprehensive budgetary control systems had been introduced to encompass many areas of medical treatment, and the costing of medical services and procedures had been encouraged to aid efficiency monitoring and to permit notional cost-based charges to be levied. These proposed charges for blood products had been met with extremely negative public reactions (see Exhibit 7).

Health associations

Health associations existed for each health region and acted as consumers' watchdogs over the operation of the Health Service in that area. The issue of blood and blood product costing was taken up by a member of the largest Health Association (see Exhibit 8). His views were stimulated by the growth in private sector hospitals and the increasing provisions of CBTS blood and blood products to them. The notion that the CHS might be subsidizing the private hospital sector by the free (or below cost) provision of these products was one which had considerable political sensitivity (see Exhibit 9).

Blood donors

The motives of blood donors were altruistic rather than pecuniary as all donations were given voluntarily and without remuneration. Perhaps because of this, the supply of blood was extremely sensitive to many factors.

Typically donors were very concerned about what happened to their blood donations. For example, the issue of supplies to the private sector was given considerable publicity early in 1989 when a proposal for a new private hospital in an area serviced by one of the RCs was announced. A significant drop in donations at the RC was attributed to this announcement. The issue of blood costing was also highly pertinent. As one RC director suggested:

> Donors care about what we do with their donations. Some are not happy to see blood going to the private sector at all, others would be happy only if a full cost recovery charge were to be made. This problem is even greater where the private sector treats foreign nationals who pay no local taxes. Donors are also extremely sensitive to the idea that a profit might be made out of their donation; after all they have given it freely. So if private hospitals charge on a cost plus basis to their patients or if we charged more than cost for our supplies they might well stop giving. We need credible costs if we are to ensure that only a strict cost recovery charge is made.

CBTS staff

The final constituents that had to be considered were the staff of the PFP. David Hatherly, the PFP's General Manager, expressed the following view:

> We are producing life-saving products which are critical for many patients. Our primary concern is therefore to produce enough of these products to meet clinical needs as they arise and to make sure that our products meet the quality criteria necessary to ensure their effectiveness. We try to do this and keep within our budget but cost has to come after patient need in our priorities.

The emphasis on cost and the moves toward generating product cost information had the potential to pressure staff into compromising their other objectives. Moreover, staff believed that costing blood products and attaching even cost-based transfer prices to them could have significant adverse effects on the volume of voluntary blood donations (see Exhibit 10).

In September of 1990, Innes began to explore solutions to the product costing problem at the PFP. While well aware that there was no theoretical solution to the joint cost problem, he felt that he had to be able to make some recommendations to management. He wanted to pick the allocation procedure that would best satisfy the various constituents. Although arbitrary, the procedures selected to allocate the joint costs would not be irrelevant. The product costs reported by the RCs had already produced some benefits. As he had commented at a recent staff meeting:

> Our costing system is still developing, we haven't yet derived the full cost of final outputs from the PFP and we accept that our approaches to the joint cost problem are arbitrary. But the product cost information we have produced so far has had an impact already. Our Regional Center directors are already making changes to bring their own operations into line with lower cost producers. That's what management accounting's all about!

EXHIBIT 1

COMMONWEALTH BLOOD TRANSFUSION SERVICE

Blood Product Outputs: Plasma Fractionation Plant 1989/90

PRODUCT	UNIT SIZE	NUMBER PRODUCED (UNITS)	NUMBER DONATIONS	HOURS
Coagulation Factors:				
Factor VIII IU	200	50,000	326,000	6,730
Factor IX IU	200	8,000	68,500	7,930
Immunoglobulins— Intramuscular:				
Normal mg	750	5,000	28,000	8,510
Normal mg	250	15,000	26,000	8,490
Rh (D) IU	500	6,000	25,500	8,250
Rh (D) IU	250	4,000	16,500	7,960
Tetanus IU	250	3,000	15,000	8,130
Hepatitis IU	1,000	1,500	42,000	8,480
Varicella-Zoster mg	500	1,000	13,000	7,770
Rubella IU	25,000	200	7,000	7,890
Immunoglobulins— Intravenous:				
Normal gms	3	10,000	48,000	9,600
Tetanus IU	3,000	250	60,000	8,560
CMV gms	3	1,000	37,000	7,820
Albumin Products:				
Human albumin gms	20	4,000	43,500	8,050
Human albumin gms	1	700	8,500	7,630
Plasma solution mls	400	80,000	168,000	10,150
Plasma solution mls	100	1,000	1,000	6,700

Source: CBTS Annual Report 1988-89.

EXHIBIT 2

COMMONWEALTH BLOOD TRANSFUSION SERVICE

An Overview of Plasma Fractionation Plant Processing

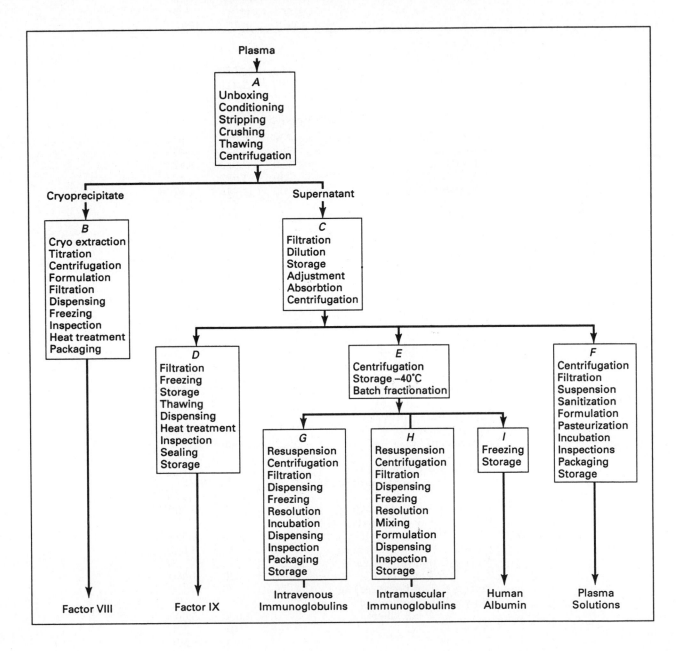

EXHIBIT 3

COMMONWEALTH BLOOD TRANSFUSION SERVICE
Inventory Levels at the Plasma Fractionation Plant in 1990

	UNIT SIZE	START OF YEAR (# OF UNITS)	END OF YEAR (# OF UNITS)
I. Finished Products			
Coagulation Factors			
Factor VIII IU	200	20,800	44,962
Factor IX IU	200	2,410	6,204
Immunoglobulins—Intramuscular:			
Normal mg	750	1,987	4,322
Normal mg	250	6,040	15,019
Rh (D) IU	500	2,834	6,050
Rh (D) IU	250	2,060	3,824
Tetanus IU	250	1,582	3,075
Hepatitis (HBV) IU	1,000	1,046	1,629
Varicella-Zoster mg	500	422	1,002
Rubella IU	25,000	100	150
Immunoglobulins—Intravenous:			
Normal gms	3	5,106	10,194
Tetanus IU	3,000	43	204
CMV gms	3	261	810
Albumin Products:			
Human albumin gms	20	2,311	4,197
Human albumin gms	1	302	574
Plasma solution ml	400	30,690	69,238
Plasma solution ml	100	619	1,146
II. Unprocessed Plasma kg		890	1,265
III. Blood Plasma Fractions			
Cryoprecipitate kg		8,000	15,000
Supernatant kg		12,000	20,000
IV. Work In Process (which is assumed to be half-processed)			
Process A (half-processed) kg		4,000	6,000
Process B (half-processed Factor VIII) IU	200	5,694	9,423
Process C (half-processed) kg		2,351	4,602
Process D (half-processed Factor IX) IU	200	620	1,040
Process E (half-processed) kg		140	190
Process F (half-processed P.P.S.) liters		2,000	5,000
Process G		NIL	NIL
Process H		NIL	NIL
Process I (half-processed Human albumin) gms		9,462	14,387

EXHIBIT 4

COMMONWEALTH BLOOD TRANSFUSION SERVICE
Commercial Prices For the Plasma Fractionation Plant
September 1990

PRODUCT	UNIT SIZE	UNIT PRICES ($)
Coagulation Factors:		
Factor VIII	200IU	300
Factor IX	200IU	600
Immunoglobulins— Intramuscular:		
Normal	750mg	45
Normal	250mg	15
Rh (D)	500IU	120
Rh (D)	250IU	60
Tetanus	250IU	75
Hepatitis	1,000IU	1,050
Varicella-Zoster	500mg	750
Rubella	25,000IU	600
Immunoglobulins— Intravenous:		
Normal	3g	300
Tetanus	3,000IU	1,800
CMV	3g	1,800
Albumin Products:		
Human albumin	20g	225
Human albumin	1g	15
Plasma solution	400mls	180
Plasma solution	100mls	60

EXHIBIT 5

COMMONWEALTH BLOOD TRANSFUSION SERVICE
The Basis of Allocating Joint Costs
at the Regional Centers

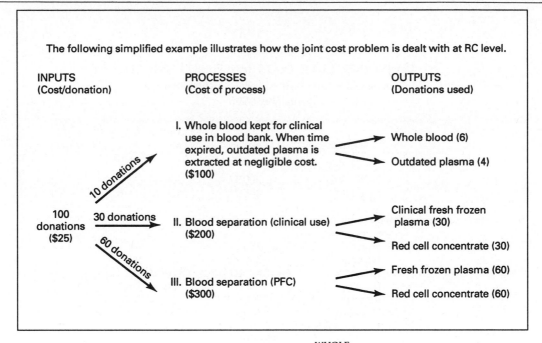

The following simplified example illustrates how the joint cost problem is dealt with at RC level.

PROCESS	PRODUCTS	DONATIONS USED	WHOLE BLOOD COST (PRO RATA)*	JOINT PROCESSING COST*	FULL PRODUCT COST
I	Whole Blood	6	150	60	210
	Outdated Plasma	4	100	40	140
II	Clinical Fresh Frozen Plasma	30	375	100	475
	Red Cell Concentrate		375	100	475
III	Fresh Frozen Plasma	60	750	150	900
	Red Cell Concentrate		750	150	900
		100	2,500	600	3,100

*Rationale: Joint product costs are split equally between the product outputs as each final product creates an equal volume demand for the whole blood.

EXHIBIT 6

COMMONWEALTH BLOOD TRANSFUSION SERVICE

Plasma Fractionation Plant Operating Costs*
and Processing Hours: 1989/90

PROCESS (AS LABELLED IN EXHIBIT 2)	COST $ MILLION	PROCESSING HOURS
A	2.1	1820
B	4.7	4910
C	1.9	4860
D	2.6	1250
E	1.4	890
F	5.3	3490
G	6.8	3270
H	6.3	4920
I	1.1	540
	32.2	

*Excludes blood plasma cost.

Plasma Fractionation Plant Processing Hours
Detailed Breakdown By Product: 1989/90

PRODUCT	UNIT SIZE		
Albumin Products:			*Process F*
Plasma solution	400mls		3,470
Plasma solution	100mls		20
		Total:	3,490
Immunoglobulins—			
Intravenous:			*Process G*
Normal	3g		2,030
Tetanus	3,000IU		990
CMV	3g		250
		Total:	3,270
Immunoglobulins—			
Intramuscular:			*Process H*
Normal	750mg		940
Normal	250mg		920
Rh (D)	500IU		680
Rh (D)	250IU		390
Tetanus	250IU		560
Hepatitis	1,000IU		910
Varicella-Zoster	500mg		200
Rubella	25,000IU		320
		Total:	4,920
Albumin Products:			*Process I*
Human albumin	20g		480
Human albumin	1g		60
		Total:	540

EXHIBIT 7

COMMONWEALTH BLOOD TRANSFUSION SERVICE
Reaction to Government Proposals to Charge for Blood Products

BLOOD SUCKER

"COUNT DRACULA" REITH MAKES US PAY FOR OUR OWN BLOOD

Confidential proposals drafted by the Government will ensure that our hospitals will have to pay for every drop of blood they use. This could curtail the use of blood in hospitals and involve serious cutbacks in surgery. Worse still, it could lead to massive reductions in blood donations.

The sinister figure of Health Minister John "Count Dracula" Reith is behind the plan which is due to come into operation in just under one year's time.

The full repercussions could be enormous:

- The Blood Transfusion Service will have to operate only on the funds it can raise from "selling" blood.
- The Service is likely to go into the red so cutbacks in jobs, research and training will quickly be implemented.
- Donors will disappear in droves when they realize their free donations are being "sold."

Strong criticism of the government plan has been made by Medical Staff Association national coordinator David Rathbone.

"Our national health service has been decimated already by financial cutbacks. The need to budget for blood is one of the last nails in the coffin. We're being forced to act like commercial undertakings, hospitals competing with each other on the prices of services on offer. The quality of service is bound to fall. The end loser will be the patient."

This new blood charge may be another step towards the privatization of parts of the health service. If blood is priced then the whole blood transfusion service including the blood products centers has financially measurable, self-generated revenues for the first time. It can produce a profit and loss account and it can be made financially attractive to private investors. After all there are few commodities as essential as blood.

If it does enter the commercial domain all sorts of problems can arise. Will those hospitals prepared to pay premium prices get preferential treatment? Will private sector hospitals outbid health sevice hospitals? Will donors be bled more often than is advisable? Attempts to balance the books are fraught with danger.

"If blood became a marketable commodity, waiting lists will become longer as budget overspends preclude treatment and private hospitals fix their supplies on a contracted basis. The whole question of supply is also problematic. Donors give their blood free. How will they feel when they find their local hospital can't afford their free gift? It was the same with organ transplant donations. Any suggestion of payment and supply stops," said Dr. Rathbone.

A spokesman for the Ministry of Health told the *National Standard* that the planned system of charges would represent a more equitable way of paying for the resources of blood transfusion. There was no profit making aim, just a long-term objective of ensuring scarce resources were used in the best possible way.

However the whole scheme must add to cost. Bureaucracy and administration will increase. More people will be paid for shuffling more paper amongst themselves. Medical decisions will no longer represent the best clinical interests of patients. Patients are bound to suffer. As Dr. Rathbone put it:

"Fairness and equality of treatment may well determine the quality of treatment. We must try and ensure that we have all our major disasters near the hospitals which are in the best financial position."

National Standard, July 1990.

EXHIBIT 8

COMMONWEALTH BLOOD TRANSFUSION SERVICE
Reaction to CBTS Supplying Private Hospitals

PUBLIC SERVICE SUPPLIES THE PRIVATE SECTOR

Sir,

It is now only a matter of time before the growth in private hospitals creates a demand for blood and blood products which will result in severe shortages being experienced in the public health sector. Profit making hospitals are now supplied with more than 25,000 units of blood and blood products each year. Up until 1985 no charge was made for these supplies. This free subsidy by the taxpayer and the blood donor of private health organizations must run to well over $1 million.

The Northern Health Association initiated the campaign which led to charges being made for these supplies. But we feel the charges are a mere token, covering less than a quarter of full cost. The charges have also remained fixed for the last three years. We are told their revision awaits . . . accountant's report.

Donors don't realize so much of their blood goes to the private sector and at a discount price. We demand that public sector demand should be met as the priority. Only then should the private sector be supplied and only at a price which fully recovers all public cost.

Jock Cranston
Chairman
Northern Health Association

Daily Chronicle, 17 October 1990.

EXHIBIT 9

COMMONWEALTH BLOOD TRANSFUSION SERVICE
Defense of Current Practice

THE BLOOD BANK HAS A BALANCE

Sir,

Mr. Cranston's observations (Letters, October 17th) in respect of blood supplies to private sector health care organizations are completely in error. A response to them is necessary in order to correct his mistakes and to avoid any damage which they may do to the Commonwealth Blood Transfusion Service's good relations with its donors.

In supplying private sector hospitals we attempt to preserve the altruistic motives of donors who provide us with their blood as a free gift. This we do by charging a fee which will make neither a profit nor loss for the service. Our processing and distribution costs are covered and no more. The current charge, far from covering only a quarter of these costs, as Mr. Cranston suggests, does in fact achieve its objective.

Consequently we are not subsidizing the private sector through our supplies of blood and blood products to them. Furthermore priority is always given to the public sector where supply shortages occur.

The false claims of Mr. Cranston can lead to a fall in blood donor support if they are widely publicized and believed. He should rescind his accusations and in future act in a more responsible manner.

Yours sincerely
Dr. J. Black
Medical Director
Commonwealth Blood
Transfusion Service

Daily Chronicle, 24 October 1990.

EXHIBIT 10

COMMONWEALTH BLOOD TRANSFUSION SERVICE
The Dangers of an International Blood Market

DONORS' DISASTER IF BLOOD MARKET GOES AHEAD

In a Medical Society speech last night, Dr. Black, Medical Director of the Commonwealth Blood Transfusion Service, condemned a government proposal to institute a wider inter-country market in the buying and selling of blood and blood products. He stated afterwards,

> If the public think their donations will be resold elsewhere, perhaps for a profit, then few will give voluntary donations. There is also a strong feeling among donors that they are benefitting their own kinsmen when they make a donation. If these twin

Dr. Black argued during his speech that certain items were beyond price and were unsuitable for buying and selling. Blood associated products and organs for transplantation were of this type. He suggested that countries should follow the World Health Organization recommendation encouraging each individual nation to become self-sufficient in blood from unpaid donors.

The Financial Press, January 1990.

La Grande Alliance Restaurant Francaise

In April 1976, one week before La Grande Alliance was opened to the public, M. Pierre Jacquard, maitre d'hotel and manager of the new restaurant, faced the problem of determining final prices for the menu. M. Jacquard did not believe he could relinquish the task of setting prices to a subordinate or an accountant, for it required the delicate balancing of factors of profitability, volume, and restaurant image. Because the prices were printed on a large, artistic menu which was both difficult and expensive to reprint, the prices M. Jacquard determined in April would have to stand, except for extremely minor alterations, for at least six months. The initial six months of a restaurant's operation were known to be crucial in determining its reputation and the size of its clientele for months and years to come.

La Grande Alliance was the major showpiece restaurant of the Hotel Lafayette, a brand-new luxury hotel in downtown Boston, which opened its doors in April 1976. The Lafayette was owned by a consortium of European investors, mainly French, and was managed by L'Union des Grands Hotels (UGH), a highly respected French hotel chain which had a substantial equity investment in the enterprise.

M. Pierre Jacquard, 33, was a long-time employee of UGH with 10 years of experience in European restaurants of the first rank. He was generally recognized as having a bright future in restaurant and hotel management with a flair for atmosphere and presentation as well as the ability to work within a budget and make profits.

To facilitate the pricing of individual items on the menu, M. Jacquard prepared (with the cooperation of M. Florentine Lestrade, the chef, as well as Gilles and Roger, the sous-chefs) the menu fact sheet shown in Exhibit 1. The fact sheet held for each dish on the menu an estimate of (1) cost of raw materials, (2) preparation time (time for a moderately experienced chef to prepare a batch of the dish in question), (3) minimum number of servings per preparation (the nature of some dishes made it impossible to prepare a single serving although there was usually no problem in stretching the number of servings per batch), and (4) difficulty—rated from least difficult to most difficult on a scale from 1 to 5.

In conversation with M. Jacquard on the subject of the fact sheet, chef Lestrade emphasized two points. First, the cost of raw materials shown was a *normalized estimate* of the *target cost* of an individual dish, as of April 1976. In general, the cost of food varies greatly from week to week and month to month. Some fluctuations are seasonally determined and predictable, others are random: Lestrade's estimates took into account foreseeable fluctuations from April to November (i.e., they were *normalized* over the six months starting April 1976). Lestrade's normalized estimates were further idealized in that they reflected the theoretical cost of the food content of an individual serving. In practice, raw food usage, and therefore cost, would be increased by waste in preparation, imperfections in measurement, fix-ups (usually necessitating the addition of butter or cream to a recipe), and simple mistakes. Even after adjustment for such considerations, the total cost of food served would understate the restaurant's total expenditure on food, since provision would have to be made for feeding the kitchen and dining staffs, spoilage, and pilfering. Chef Lestrade had indicated with extreme vehemence that management of food, including forecasts, purchasing, utilization of leftovers, and food control, was a major responsibility of the chef and an extremely important dimension of his skill.

Chef Lestrade's second point with regard to the fact sheet was that preparation time as shown represented time spent on an individual dish and did not take into account time spent on prior preparations. In any well-managed restaurant, to minimize final preparation time, the kitchen keeps on hand many intermediate preparations—stocks, sauces, dough, etc. These preparations are made in

This case was prepared by Research Assistant Carliss Y. Baldwin (under the direction of Assistant Professor Claudine B. Malone).

43

large quantities at times when the kitchen is relatively free and are used in numerous dishes. Chef Lestrade felt it almost impossible to include time spent on prior preparations in the estimates of preparation time for individual dishes. When pressed by M. Jacquard, the chef indicated that as much as 30% of his staff's time would be spent on prior preparations.

La Grande Alliance could seat 100 people at one time in the Salle Franklin and Salle Vergennes dining rooms combined. Given its location near the center of the shopping and financial districts of downtown Boston, M. Jacquard and executives of the Hotel Lafayette felt they could expect to serve 1½ seatings (150 people) at lunch on every working day. For dinner (including Sunday dinner at noon), they expected to accommodate, on average, 700 people per week; but they expected that the pattern of weekly usage would on average be as follows:

DAY	NUMBER OF MEALS SERVED
Sunday (noon)	60
Monday	85
Tuesday	85
Wednesday	85
Thursday	85
Friday	150
Saturday	150
	700

Thus, plans and budgets for La Grande Alliance were based on volume projections of 750 lunches and 700 dinners served per week, 4.3 weeks per month. A rough rule of thumb which M. Jacquard felt could be applied in Boston held that in the customers' eyes, lunch is half of dinner; in other words, that people generally spend one half as much on lunch as they would in the same restaurant on a full-course dinner. M. Jacquard was of the opinion that, as a fine restaurant in a sophisticated urban setting, La Grande Alliance could aim for an average check of $15.00 for dinner and $7.50 for lunch (not including liquor). (Lunch and dinner menus were separate and substantially different at La Grande Alliance; the dinner menu alone is the subject of this case.)

When making the menu price decision in April 1976, M. Jacquard had already received from the hotel's accounting department the restaurant's projected expense budget for May 1976 (Exhibit 2). The budget which had been drawn up by the accounting department in consultation with M. Jacquard reflected the restaurant's present staffing (as of the day it opened) and projected raw foods costs based on forecast number of meals served. The budget also included charges for breakage and supply replacement, depreciation of kitchen equipment (brand-new), and an assessment for advertising and for general overhead. As part of a large hotel establishment, La Grande Alliance did not pay directly for a number of services shared with other hotel areas (e.g., laundry, cleaning); thus the overhead assessment was naturally quite large.

The budget did not provide for the cost of sommeliers (wine waiters) nor for the cost of wine and liquor served in the restaurant. It was standard UGH practice for the wine cellar to be managed by the beverage department, which also managed all liquor inventories and the hotel bars. Although La Grande Alliance would receive a partial credit for wine and whiskey sold through the restaurant, it was not within M. Jacquard's power (except as a consultant) to determine either the wine list or wine prices. It was Jacquard's goal, therefore, that La Grande Alliance be sustained (financially, that is) by food alone—that the restaurant would not use food as a loss leader in the purveyance of liquor.

Although La Grande Alliance was a new restaurant in a new hotel, the internal accounting staff of UGH had considerable experience in budgeting for restaurants within hotels. M. Jacquard had been consulted in detail on the preparation of the budget and believed it to be fair. Jacquard was willing that the profitability of La Grande Alliance as well as his own success as maitre d'hotel and manager of the restaurant be measured according to the budgeted format.

In reviewing his pricing strategy, M. Jacquard was aware of two not mutually exclusive goals. First, he was ambitious to run a profitable center within the UGH establishment. Second, he was eager that La Grande Alliance be known as the finest restaurant in Boston.

EXHIBIT 1

LA GRANDE ALLIANCE RESTAURANT FRANCAISE

Selected Menu Costs—Dinner

	COST OF RAW MATERIALS (ONE SERVING)	RECIPE PREPARA- TION TIME (MINUTES)	RECIPE NO. SERVINGS PER PREPARATION	DIFFICULTY (1−5)
Appetizers				
Artichoke Hearts Biarritz	$1.35	30	10	3
**Quiche Lorraine	.75	20	10	2
Escargots à la Bourguignonne (6)	1.75	5	1	1
Oyster Cocktail (6)	1.50	10	1	2
**Paté de Foie en Brioche	1.25	45	15	4
Soups				
Consommé à la Royale (hot)	$ .25	10	20*	2
Soupe à l'Oignon, Gratinée (hot)	.25	35	20*	3
Créme Vichyssoise Glacée (cold)	.30	30	20*	2
Entrees				
Filet of Sole Dugléré	$2.00	40	6	2
**Crab Créole en Casserole	2.55	20	1*	2
**Coquilles St. Jacques Florentine	2.35	30	1*	2
Poulet Poché a l'Estragon	1.65	40	10	4
**Duckling, Sauce Bigarde	2.05	40	2*	4
Escalope de Veau Parisien	2.80	10	1*	3
**Lamb Ragout Printanière	2.55	60	10*	4
Tournedos Rossini	3.50	10	1*	2
**Roast Filet de Boeuf, Béarnaise	3.15	20	10*	2
All entrees include:				
Salad	$ .20	15	10*	1
Potato	.20	15	10*	3
Vegetable	.25	10	10*	2
Desserts				
Strawberries Parisienne	$ .75 ⎫			
Crème Bavaroise	.65 ⎬ Purchased from outside supplier			
Pastry assortment	.80 ⎭			
Bananes Flambées	.60	5	2	1

*Up to three or four mutiple recipes of these items may be prepared with no additional preparation time.
**These items require prior preparation.

EXHIBIT 2

LA GRANDE ALLIANCE RESTAURANT FRANCAISE
Monthly Expense Budget

Sales		
700 dinners[1]	$45,150	
750 lunches[2]	24,187	$69,337
Cost of Food		
700 dinners[3]	$13,545	
750 lunches[4]	7,256	$20,801
Salaries		
1 chef $2,500	$ 2,500	
2 sous-chefs $1,500	3,000	
2 apprentice chefs $833	1,666	
1 maitre d'hotel $2,333	2,333	
2 captains $1,250	2,500	
8 waiters $667[4]	5,336	
2.5 busboys $582[5]	1,455	
2 dishwashers $500	1,000	19,790
Material, breakage, and supplies		$ 1,500
Depreciation of kitchen equipment		1,000
Advertising and promotion (first six months)		5,000
Allocation for general overhead:		
Includes charges for laundry, cleaning, heat, electricity, maintenance, depreciation (on building), and general administration		$10,571
Total expenses		$58,625
Profit before taxes		$10,712
Net investment in restaurant		$500,000

[1]Assumes 4.3 weeks per month, average dinner check $15.00.
[2]Assumes 4.3 weeks per month, average lunch check $7.50.
[3]Assumes raw food cost to average 30% of sales.
[4]Fine restaurants average one waiter to every 10 or 15 customers.
[5]Busboys are hired on a part-time basis. Their schedules may be made to coincide with the restaurant's busiest hours.
[6]For the first six months of its operation, The Lafayette Hotel was committed to a nationwide advertising and promotion campaign, a portion of which expense was allocated to La Grande Alliance. The restaurant had also been given discretionary funds for local advertising. As the hotel became well established, both national and local advertising would decrease (M. Jacquard believed) to an average $2,000 per month.

The Ingersoll Milling Machine Company

The challenge is not to remove all the people from the production floor. Our goal is to give skilled machinists the equipment and support they require to make them as productive as possible. The flexible machining system has allowed us to expand throughput dramatically. If we were still using isolated manual machines we would require 40 machines and 120 skilled machinists. The flexible machining system provides the same output using nine machines and 39 personnel. We could not have hired enough skilled machinists to operate conventional technology machines for the higher demand we are now experiencing.

GEORGE E. FRAWLEY, MANAGER, FLEXIBLE MACHINING SYSTEMS

INTRODUCTION

The Ingersoll Milling Machine Company (IMM) manufactured about 30 large-scale custom-made metal cutting machines and machining systems for special applications per year. While the firm would build any special machine requested by a customer, its output tended to consist of four distinct types of machines or machining systems:

- *Portal-type milling machines* are large machines, typically numerically controlled (NC), that mill large parts (milling is a metal cutting operation that produces a machined surface). Until the late 1970s, milling machines formed the backbone of the firm's sales. Recently, however, other product lines have become equally significant.
- *Transfer lines* are groups of metal cutting machines, each designed for a limited range of operations, that are connected by an automated material handling system and controlled by a central control system. Transfer lines are designed to produce a given machined part (e.g., automobile engine cylinder blocks) at very high volumes. Increasingly, computer control and flexible work stations are being incorporated.
- *Composite manufacturing machines* are numerically controlled (NC) machines designed to manufacture continuous length structural shapes (e.g., airframes) out of composite materials such as carbon graphite tape.
- *Flexible machining systems (FMS)* are collections of numerically controlled machines, each designed for a broad range of functions, that are connected by a material handling system and controlled by a central computer system. Unlike transfer lines, FMSs can machine a wide variety of small volume parts.

The last two product lines had only been recently introduced, the composite tape layer in 1978 and the FMS in 1982. Both represented the latest in manufacturing technology and demonstrated the firm's commitment to remaining at the forefront of production technology.

The 1986 budget for IMM was approximately $100 million (Exhibit 1) with direct labor accounting for about 25% (Exhibit 2). This excluded the cost of materials purchased directly against a job.

IMM was a subsidiary of Ingersoll International, Inc., a privately owned holding company. In addition to IMM, Ingersoll International contained three other companies: Ingersoll Cutting Tool Company, a manufacturer of specialized cutting tools; Ingersoll Engineers Incorporated, the firm's consulting arm; and Ingersoll Machines and Werkzeuge, its German operation. Ingersoll in Germany also operated Waldrich Siegen, Bohle, and Waldrich Coburg.

THE FLEXIBLE MACHINING SYSTEM

When IMM decided to enter the FMS market, it chose a spectacular approach (see Press Release in Exhibit 3). It built its own FMS to manufacture a majority of the small parts (within a 40" cube) required for the business. Construction of this FMS, which was expected to cost about $20 million, began in 1982, and by late 1984 the FMS was operational. Installation of all equipment was expected to be completed sometime in 1987.

The decision to become an FMS supplier was driven by several forces. First, the firm's leading edge strategy prompted them to master the technology of the factory of the future. Second, the industry as a whole was slowly turning toward FMS technology, and customers were beginning to request machines with FMS capability.

IMM decided to build an in-house FMS for several reinforcing reasons. First, management believed FMSs were cost-justified. Second, they believed that IMM needed to demonstrate to potential customers the practicality and value of an FMS production process. Finally, they felt the best way for the firm to learn about the technology was firsthand.

A formal economic analysis to justify the IMM FMS was never undertaken. Management was convinced the firm had no choice. If it wanted to maintain a technological competitive edge, it had to become a leading supplier of FMSs. Despite this statement of faith and commitment, management believed the increased capacity, improved quality, reduced inventory, and savings in labor more than offset the high initial cost of the new productive facility.

The FMS, which was part of the light machining shop, produced about 25,000 different parts annually. The average batch size was under two, with 70% of the parts produced in batches of one. Because of the customized nature of each product, 50% of all parts manufactured will never be manufactured again. In 1985, the FMS was about 75% complete with five Bohle W2 horizontal and four Le Blond MC40 machining centers in place. The completed FMS was expected to contain 12 machines, six of each type and an automated materials handling system that would manage the part from cut-off to work in process. When fully operational, IMM planned to air condition the building. This would allow them to meet the extreme part accuracies required.

THE COMPETITIVE ENVIRONMENT

In an industry known for being fragmented and undercapitalized, IMM was unique. Its stated objective was to remain at the cutting edge of production technology; every year, nearly all of its profits were reinvested in new equipment. While one third of a typical competitor's machines were over 20 years old, 80% of IMM's machinery had been purchased in the last five years. This practice was a consistent part of the firm's long-term strategy, and manage-

ment believed this strategy provided a substantial competitive edge.

IMM perceived itself as being in two distinct markets: the production machine market, which included transfer lines, and the special machine market, which included heavy NC machining centers, composite tape layers, and FMSs.

The company recognized six major competitors. Three, F. Joseph Lamb, the Cross unit of Cross and Trecker, and the Comau subsidiary of Fiat, produced production machines. The other competitors, Toshiba, SNK, and Cincinnati Milicron, produced special machines. No single company competed with IMM in both markets.

The IMM salesforce worked with corporate customers to develop solutions to their machining problem. A customer proposal contained a description of the solution, the quoted price, and an approximate delivery date. Preparing a proposal was a major undertaking. The engineering department scoped the job and estimated the cost to complete. The cost estimated was prepared using the firm's historical cost data base. While nearly every machine designed for a customer was unique, each contained a large number of common subassemblies. The actual cost of subassemblies manufactured for previous contracts was known fairly accurately, and a skilled estimator could use these historic costs to develop an acceptable cost estimate for the cost of designing, building, and assembling most machines produced by the firm.

MANUFACTURING PROCESS

When a proposal was accepted and the contract signed, the final delivery date was confirmed. As soon as possible after the contract was signed, the marketing department prepared a specification document describing the job, the intricacies involved, and major unresolved items. After this document was completed, a transmittal meeting was held to discuss the specification document with representatives of the other functional areas.

The master scheduler determined two additional dates: the engineering date, when the design engineering was expected to be completed; and the machine work date, when manufacturing was expected to be finished. These two dates, along with the shipment date, defined the major milestones of the project. For a typical project, engineering was finished in six months, machine work completed by the thirteenth month, and the product shipped at the end of 18 months.

Engineering's first task was to design the machine. This task typically took three to four months. The first few weeks of the design process were considered the most critical; during that period the general design philosophy of the machine was identified and the overall level of profitability determined. Once the specifications were clear, the cost of the machine was reestimated. This estimate, called the planned cost, was used to measure the performance of the project.

The completed machine design was transmitted to the purchasing department to initiate the procurement process. Procurement took about two months to complete. The lead times of the required parts were fed into the scheduling system to help plan the manufacturing sequences. Once finalized, the design drawings (completed on the firm's computer-aided design [CAD] system) and associated bill of materials were released to manufacturing.

Since all of the firm's major in-house production machines were numerically controlled, the routing sheets prepared by manufacturing engineering had to be converted into NC programs. The routing sheets defined the fixtures required, the orientation of the part in the fixtures, and the operations to be undertaken. The NC programs were detailed machine instructions that enabled the firm's NC machines to machine the required parts. Programming typically took about two months. In 1985 the firm employed 60 numerical program programmers, of whom 27 were dedicated to programming for the FMS.

Production occurred in three major areas of the plant: In fabrication, steel plates were welded together to form weldments; in light machining, the smaller weldments and bar stock were machined; and in heavy machining, the larger weldments were machined. Total manufacturing time was typically seven months, split about evenly between fabrication and manufacturing (machining).

The final step, assembly, required about six months and was the most uncertain of the entire production process. An average machine contained several thousand machined parts and about four times as many purchased parts. Each of these parts had to be fitted together to produce a working machine. The assemblers were highly skilled workers. They often hand-worked machined or purchased parts to make them fit together. If the parts were too far out of tolerance, they were returned to the machining areas as rework.

On occasion, design problems did not become apparent until the assembly process. Engineers were then brought back into the process to redesign parts, culminating in an Engineering Notice of Correction (ENOC), which provided new specification for a part or parts. Thus, a significant part of the workload in machining centers arose from the ENOCs, errors, and defective work which was not detected until the assembly process.

Rework was typically a rush job and had to be expedited. Management estimated that about 25% of the machining area's time was spent on such high-priority rework and ENOCs.

FMS PRODUCTION

To avoid work-in-process buildup, production in the FMS was not started until (1) NC programming was complete, (2) the bar stock was cut to size or the weldment manufactured, and (3) the appropriate tooling and fixtures became available.

Six tool setters (two on each shift) collected the tools identified by the NC program from inventory bins. After offsetting and gauging, the setters put the tools onto a special trolley. This trolley kept together all the tools required to machine a given part. This allowed the tools to be easily moved around the department while guaranteeing that they were available when the part was being machined.

Parts released for production were moved to the setup area, where setup personnel placed the parts into fixtures. The fixtures were universal in design (i.e., not specially designed for the part), consisting of a part holder, such as a vise, and a pallet. To achieve the very high tolerances possible in the FMS (machining to accuracies of .00015 of an inch), the parts had to be held firmly in place. This required heavy part holders and pallets; for example, the pallets were steel and cast iron plates several inches thick.

An automatic guided vehicle (AGV) transported each part and its pallet between stations. When the central computer determined that an appropriate machine was available (i.e., that its input station would soon be empty), the AGV was sent to the setup area to pick up the part, move it to the available machine, and deposit it on the machine's input station.

The machine, when ready, moved the part from the input station onto the work station. A set of machining tasks that can be completed without repositioning the part was called an operation. A typical operation contains several transformation activities; for example, a part might be milled on two surfaces, have five holes drilled and three tapped. The ability to perform multiple operations for a given part on the same machine was one of the greatest benefits from using the FMS. With conventional technology, each operation (rough milling, drilling, smooth milling, boring) would be done on a different machine, requiring transport time, scheduling, and startup time for each processing stage. A preliminary study indicated that about 20% of machining time could be saved when parts were processed on the FMS rather than on conventional machines. When the operation was complete, the machine moved the part to the output stage. The AGV collected the part from the output stage and returned it to the setup area, where it was removed from its fixture and, if finished, sent to assembly. Otherwise, the part was prepared for the next operation.

In September 1985, 27 operators were working in the FMS, one per machine per shift. While they did not perform the actual machining, the operators had specific tasks to complete. The operators were, in order of importance, expected to do the following:

- Detect programming errors. If the program was incorrect, the operator was expected to intervene and stop the machine before any damage occurred. Damage can take several forms, as follows:

  If the cutting tool collided with the part at high speed, then probably the tool would be destroyed, the part might be ruined, and the machine could be put out of alignment. There was no way to guarantee that collisions would not occur, so machines were designed to "give" if a major collision occurs. Even with this designed-in "give," it still took several days to realign the machine if a collision occurred. In 1985, the firm estimated that without operator assistance, the FMS would average nine collisions per week.

  However, there was a process of scheduled unmanned operations in which the parts and proven programs ran unattended. This approach has been successfully tested and was expected to become a normal part of the process. The operators participated in deciding which machines should run unmanned, and the excess labor was redirected to setup, training, programming, or planned absence.

  If a cutting operation began in the wrong place, the part was ruined. The operator was expected to watch the first cut to ensure that it started at the reference point. The reference point is that point in space from which the NC program is oriented. Thus, each cut is defined as moving from a position (x,y,z) to (x',y',z') relative to a $(0,0,0)$ reference point. In 1985, the FMS machines did not have adequate sensors to detect the reference point. If the part was not in the expected position or if the program misspecified the reference point, then the part would be machined incorrectly.

  If the operations are to be performed on faces 2 and 3 and the part was oriented so that faces 4 and 5 were machined, the part was ruined and the risk of collision increased. The operator was expected to ensure that its faces were correctly oriented. The company was currently exploring the use of automatic probing to ensure that the part was correctly positioned.

- Manually alter the programmed speed if the part was being machined at an improper cutting speed. The firm had completed an analysis of operator interventions and determined that nearly all of the interventions were to reduce, not increase, the cutting speed. Management believed this occurred because the new machines cut at higher speed than the old NC machines and the operators had yet to become comfortable with these higher cutting speeds. Another problem was that some operators failed to allow the FMS to work without intervening. Prior to the FMS, the operators were rewarded for their skill in adjusting the cutting conditions to improve productivity. Some of the operators were finding it impossible not to try and "tweak" the system. In effect, they were not making the transition from machine operators to machine supervisors.

- Suggest improvement in the programming so that a library of efficient programs could be developed.

- Provide helpful suggestions about how to reduce the need for operator involvement or to improve the efficiency of the FMS. Examples of the types of suggestions received include (1) using three coolant streams aimed at different distances from the machine to guarantee that all tools, irrespective of length, received sufficient coolant automatically; and (2) pointing out where common tools, rather than special tools, could be used to machine a part, thus reducing the cost and quantity of tools required.

- Undertake in-process gauging and adjust the cut to compensate for any tool wear.
- Insure that, when a large-diameter long drill emerged from the other side of the part, the coolant, which was pumped through the tool to keep it cool, did not squirt on the floor. This had happened recently, and the coolant landed in the path of the AGV. The coolant was very slippery and caused the AGV to leave its path and crash into a wall.
- Deburr the machined parts while they were on the output stage waiting for the AGV to arrive. They were also expected to remove any metal tangled around the cutting tools. In the next 12 months, the company expected to automate about 95% of all part and tool deburring.

The operators' responsibilities in the FMS were very different from what they were in the rest of the light machining shop. In particular, the FMS operators spent more time watching and less time machining. The company was attempting to increase the operators' job content. The most significant change currently planned was to have them set up jobs at the setup station during the operating cycle of the machine. Thus, while one part was being machined, the operator would be setting up the next part.

Because of the limited number of pallets available, parts were machined in lots of one even when more than one was required. The number of pallets was purposely kept low to avoid a gridlock condition in which the AGV would try to deliver a part to an input station when all input stations were occupied or to the setup area when all setup stations were occupied. The designers of the FMS were concerned that the current software could not detect a gridlock situation and had decided to restrict the number of pallets that could be in use at one time to 15 (one per available station). Given the limited number of pallets, it was often impossible to set up a second part until the first was completed. For this reason, the majority of multiple product lots were actually machined as single lots. For the same reason, it was not usual to complete only one operation per day on a part. As most parts require two or three operations, the parts tended to stay in the FMS for several days.

COST ACCOUNTING SYSTEM

The cost accounting system at IMM captured the total cost of each finished product, including engineering, NC programming, machining, inspection, and assembly. The cost system was part of a company-wide central data base. The cost of each of thousands of machined parts within a finished product was collected. Management considered individual part costs to be valuable but overwhelming. Therefore, it was more useful to capture costs at a higher aggregate level than individual parts, such as by subassembly or by subshop order, depending on the needs.

Indirect costs in the engineering department were allocated to projects based on engineering direct labor dollars using an overhead rate of 175%. Roger Dougherty, IMM's controller, explained the rational for this procedure:

> Engineers cannot realistically assign their time to individual parts. They work on designing subassemblies and may be working on several parts at once. When they change the dimensions of one part it often affects several others. They cannot design each part on its own. For example, an engineer may use CAD libraries to create the subassembly on the screen and then make only slight adjustments in individual parts. He charges his time against the subassembly, not against each part.

NC programming charges were also accumulated at the sub-shop-order or subassembly level.

Machining costs, however, were traced to individual parts. In addition, manufacturing overhead was allocated to the manufactured parts based on direct labor dollars. Dougherty explained the rationale behind the more detailed part costing in manufacturing in contrast with the philosophy for costing engineering and NC programming.

> Part numbers are established to direct part movement through the shop. Because it is available, it is easy for an operator to measure the time spent working on individual parts. Therefore, we collect manufacturing time spent at the part level. This is quite different from Engineering, where it is unrealistic to capture part time.

Manufacturing costs were aggregated in several ways. First, for cost control purposes they were combined to give the cost of each subshop order. These costs were measured against earlier estimates.

In addition, estimators could use this information to develop bids for future machines.

The procedures used to collect direct labor and to allocate overhead costs were basically the same for all manufacturing cost centers. The setup person and machine operators entered the start and end times for each operation on their daily time cards, and these times were used to assign labor costs to parts.

Overhead costs were allocated to parts based on the direct labor dollars charged to the part. There were 14 overhead pools representing the major manufacturing processes required to manufacture a machine, and an overhead rate had been calculated for each pool (Exhibit 4). The FMS was part of the machining centers. The centers' overhead rate had dropped when the FMS was installed because the FMS had a much higher capacity rate than the older machines (Exhibit 5). This rate continued to drop as the firm gained experience and more parts were manufactured using the FMS. In 1986 it was expected to be even lower.

Prior to 1978, the manufacturing division used a single burden rate for the entire plant. The 250% rate was fixed for many years. Engineering (100%) and the service departments (65%) used different overhead burden rates for absorbing costs.

In 1978 and 1979, a massive renovation started in the plant. Nearly $50 million of capital was invested during the next five years. This investment was directed disproportionately within the plant and within machining departments, and the use of a single plant-wide rate was no longer considered adequate. Initially, up to 40 different overhead rates were calculated, almost a separate rate for each cost center.

But the use of so many different overhead rates created new problems for cost estimators. In advance, the estimators did not know whether a particular subassembly would be machined on a manual or an NC machine. The actual job cost, however, was dependent on machine choice because of the different hourly rates between the two types of machines. Therefore, the cost system was changed to group machines into the same overhead pool if they performed essentially the same function, even if the machines were geographically dispersed about the factory. Roger Dougherty commented on this experience.

We learned an important lesson. First, it was difficult for estimating departments to cope with overhead rates that try to cover every manufacturing situation. Estimating cannot predict which machines will be used to manufacture a given task. Secondly, manufacturing management learned quickly that manual machines with lower overhead rates resulted in less costs while new technology with higher rates resulted in apparently higher cost. We did not want to offer incentives to use manual machines, so we grouped similar manual and advanced machines together into a single pool.

By reducing the number of cost pools from 40 to 11, we maintained adequate accuracy for product costing while still not overloading the estimators.

This logic was applied when developing the overhead rate for the FMS. Instead of treating *it* as a separate cost pool, we group the new FMS with two older stand-alone machining centers.

In the next seven years two more cost pools, materials handling and quality control, were added. Dougherty noted the following:

Initially, we grouped all material overhead costs—inbound freight, purchasing, receiving, inventory control, and inventory adjustments—into one overhead category and allocated these costs to purchased materials using a single overhead rate of 6%. Recently, we decided to use separate rates for steel and for other purchased parts. Basically, the cost of freight and handling for steel was much higher than for all other purchased materials, and we wanted to trace these higher costs more accurately. Currently, the overhead rate is 10% for steel purchases and 5% on the price of all other purchased parts.

I suppose we could have added the freight cost to the purchase price of everything we order, but we prefer to keep freight cost in a separate category so that it becomes more visible and, we hope, more controllable.

Breaking out quality control costs was driven by another factor. We used to trace the direct labor cost of inspectors to individual parts, but we didn't bother with adding on any overhead costs to inspection labor since the amounts involved were trivial. Then we acquired our first Mauser, a machine which can measure with extreme accuracy the dimensions of an entire subassembly. It is a superb but expensive machine, and without any charge for its use, we soon found that engineers were directing that the more complex parts of products be built directly on the Mauser. While this permitted these parts to be assembled with fine accuracy, during the three months or so that the subassembly was being built, no one was able to inspect or test any other parts on the machine. Consequently, we introduced an overhead charge for Mauser machine time, and now it is used only as originally intended, for inspection of finished subassemblies.

Support department costs were allocated to the manufacturing cost centers on a number of different bases, though direct labor hours was the predominant basis (Exhibit 6).

On the whole, management was satisfied with the cost accounting system and felt that it provided accurate cost data. There was a growing concern, however, about how well the system was reporting manufacturing costs for the FMS. This concern was reinforced by their belief that the amount of FMS manufacturing would increase across time until it amounted to about 50% of all light machining. Dougherty commented as follows:

> We are rapidly reducing the amount of manufacturing direct labor in our product. FMS technology is part of a natural progression to substantially increase our productivity. As we develop FMS technology further, we will continue to make progress. At some point we will be forced to move to some kind of machine hour or elapsed time system.

Other IMM personnel also expressed their belief that the FMS environment was sufficiently different from the other machining centers that new accounting measures would eventually be called for. For example, one of the project managers felt that direct labor hours were inappropriate for costing time in the FMS. He believed that a machine hour rate based on the actual time a part is on the machine makes more sense. He hedged his recommendation, however, with his concern about the impact of any new system on the pricing and bidding for new businesses. Bidding, pricing, and estimating were such important functions for the success of the business that any change in the existing system introduced "an element of risk that needed to be addressed."

Tom Linden, vice-president for technology and one of the prime movers for promoting the FMS environment throughout IMM, believed that cost accounting could greatly expand its influence by capturing more of the data after the NC program for a part was written; it would be possible to obtain an estimate for the amount of time implied by the program to drill a hole, mill a surface, grind an edge, etc. These estimates could serve as a standard against which actual machine operations could be compared.

EXHIBIT 1

THE INGERSOLL MILLING MACHINE COMPANY
1986 Budget
($ thousands)

Direct labor	$ 25,300
Indirect labor (including supervision)	30,000
Fringe benefits/premium pay	20,500
Operating supplies	2,500
Tools, jigs, and fixtures	2,600
Purchasing services (including legal, consulting, and auditing)	4,500
Travel	2,100
Communication	700
Miscellaneous expenses, net (warranty, freight, service)	2,700
Transfers (charges to affiliates)	(2,100)
Utilities	2,800
Depreciation, insurance, taxes	7,200
Maintenance	2,700
Total	$ 101,500

EXHIBIT 2

THE INGERSOLL MILLING MACHINE COMPANY
1986 Budget
Analysis of Direct Labor Expenses by Function
($ thousands)

Engineering	6,700
NC programming	1,200
Fabrication	1,200
Light shop (including FMS)	4,000
Heavy shop	1,900
Assembly	8,000
Services (e.g., installation)	1,500
Paint shop	500
Sheet metal	300
	$ 25,300

EXHIBIT 3

THE INGERSOLL MILLING MACHINE COMPANY
Press Release
Description of FMS

Twelve machining centers in a computer-integrated flexible manufacturing line will replace 40 standalone machines at The Ingersoll Milling Machine Company Main plant in Rockford, Illinois.

With the third shift running unattended, there will be approximately 75% fewer operators than now required. However, this saving is incidental to the reduction in overhead costs that will be realized. Primary objective of the installation are uninterrupted workflow, reduced inventories of work in progress, release of needed floor space, and less manufacturing-support manhours. The investment is the latest step in what has been a long-continuing management program to stay cost-competitive internationally.

As part of Ingersoll's light machine shop, the automated system will process workpieces of 40-inch cube and less in the small lots peculiar to the company's special machinery business. History indicates that of 25,000 different parts to be produced annually, 70% will be in lots of one, and half will never be made again. The new FMS thus has been planned to provide unique flexibility and efficiency.

SYSTEM FEATURES

Centralized parts storage and setup will serve the workhandling system, with modular fixtures automatically drawn from high-rise storage. Automatic guided vehicles will transport palletized work to and from automatic pallet changers at each machine. Scheduling and monitoring of workflow will be computer managed. Tool management will include monitoring according to normal life cycles and current condition, with automated replacement of worn and broken tools. Other features include an automated parts cleaning area and inspection of finished work by computer-directed coordinate measuring machines.

Because of the close tolerances specified for critical Ingersoll machine tool components, the production area will be temperature controlled. This will help assure uniformity of work quality attainable with nine Ingersoll/Bohle machining centers included in the system. These machines have inherent ability to perform full-horsepower milling and rough boring followed by finishing to jig-borer accuracy.

The new FMS is an integral part of Ingersoll's corporate-wide computer-integrated manufacturing (CIM) system. The DEC/VAX system manager computer is in constant two-way communications with the corporate host computer, receiving new work assignments from the corporate planning and scheduling data base and feeding back lot-completion notices as parts exit the FMS headed for the assembly floor. The concept is a natural evolution of Ingersoll's award-wining CIM system into the CIFM (computer-integrated flexible manufacturing) system of the future.

MACHINING CENTER CAPABILITIES

Ingersoll/Bohle machining centers selected for the line are 40-horsepower horizontal spindle models. Their design is particularly suitable for automatic around-the-clock operation with provision for periods of unmanned operation. Capabilities include the following:

- Fail-safe seating accuracy of pallets through sensing of foreign matter on pallet changer rest pads.
- Automatic release of spindle drive in event of overload.
- Automatic release of axis drives in event of a collision.
- Automatic changing of a servodriven boring/backing head with slide feed for taper turning, profiling, and other complex operations.
- Air-jet cleaning of spindle and tool tapers during tool-change cycle.
- Diagnostic and maintenance alerts with pinpointing of problem locations.
- Hard-copy data reporting to management of work interruptions and operator-initiated adjustments.

Direction of system planning has been the responsibility of manufacturing management with assistance from Ingersoll Engineers Incorporated, the company's independent consulting organization.

EXHIBIT 4

THE INGERSOLL MILLING MACHINE COMPANY
Cost Pool Overhead Rates[a]

NC programming	350	Roll grinder	350
Paint shop	250	Small mills	250
Fabrication and sheet metal	300	Heavy machine shop	500
Heat treat	550	Assembly	200
Gear cutting and grinding	300	Quality control	300
Machining (includes FMS)	500		
Small drilling and boring	350	Material (10% steel, 5% purchased parts)	7
Lathe and cutoff	400		

[a]Allocated on direct labor dollars with the exception of materials, which is allocated on the basis of material cost.

EXHIBIT 5

THE INGERSOLL MILLING MACHINE COMPANY
Machining Cost Pool: 1981–1986[a]

	ACTUAL					PLAN
	1981	1982	1983	1984	1985	1986
Direct Costs						
Direct labor	$112.5	$ 97.5	$112.5	$199.5	$681.0	$789.0
Helper labor	75.0	75.0	46.5	69.0	165.0	192.0
Helper overhead	112.5	112.5	69.0	103.5	249.0	286.5
Total direct	300.0	285.0	228.0	372.0	1095.0	1267.0
Variable Overhead						
Indirect salaried	84.0	85.5	103.5	165.0	361.5	438.0
Overtime premium	12.0	10.5	6.0	30.0	118.5	102.0
Shift premium	43.5	49.5	45.0	66.0	177.0	183.0
Fringe benefits	79.5	87.0	85.5	144.0	385.5	450.0
Supplies	4.5	7.5	1.5	4.5	19.5	79.5
Tools, jigs, and fixtures	67.5	51.0	34.5	106.5	481.5	150.0
Maintenance	85.5	187.5	157.5	180.0	400.5	369.0
Other	4.5	7.5	6.0	19.5	84.0	81.0
Total variable	381.0	486.0	439.5	715.5	2028.0	1852.5
Fixed Overhead						
Supervision	42.0	48.0	51.0	54.0	0.0	0.0
Utilities	7.5	7.5	6.0	15.0	36.0	39.0
Depreciation	292.5	141.0	115.5	283.5	499.5	792.0
Insurance	4.5	6.0	6.0	7.5	24.0	69.0
Total fixed	346.5	202.5	178.5	360.0	559.5	900.0
Support departments	225.0	238.5	415.5	354.0	1027.5	1192.5
Helper overhead	(112.5)	(112.5)	(69.0)	(103.5)	(249.0)	(286.5)
Total overhead	840.0	814.5	964.5	1326.0	3366.0	3658.5
Full absorption rate (%)	747	835	857	665	494	464
Applied rate	750	750	750	750	600	500

[a]This cost pool contains the costs associated with the FMS and two other standalone Bohle machining centers.

EXHIBIT 6

THE INGERSOLL MILLING MACHINE COMPANY
Allocation Bases for Support Department Costs

Direct Labor Hours
  Manufacturing administration (all departments)
  Heavy shop administration (heavy machining, fabrica-
    tion, and paint departments)
  Customer service materials (all departments)
  Customer service operations (all departments)
  Facilities/advanced manufacturing engineering (all de-
    partments)
  Product manufacturing engineering (all departments)
  Process planning (heavy machining, light machining,
    fabrication)
  Manufacturing engineering/administration (50% NC,
    50% in-process planning)
  Shipping (all departments)
  Plant facilities, garage, and grounds (all departments
    excluding NC programming)

Direct to Department
  Light shop administration
  Machine shop production control (2/3 light machining
    shop, 1/3 heavy machining shop)
  Assembly storeroom (assembly)
  Assembly production control (assembly)
  Machining maintenance (10% paint, 4% fabrication,
    50% light machining, 45% heavy machining)
  Burr bench (50% light machining, 50% assembly)
  Assembly administration (assembly)

Direct Labor Hours and Direct to Department
  Advanced manufacturing engineering (assembly 10%,
    rest to heavy machining, light machining, and fabri-
    cation using direct labor hours)

Material
  Manufacturing operations—material
  Receiving
  Steel receiving
  Purchasing
  Inventory control

READINGS

Yesterday's Accounting Undermines Production

Robert S. Kaplan

The present era of intense global competition is leading U.S. companies toward a renewed commitment to excellence in manufacturing. Attention to the quality of products and processes, the level of inventories, and the improvement of work-force policies has made manufacturing once again a key element in the strategies of companies intending to be world-class competitors. There remains, however, a major—and largely unnoticed—obstacle to the lasting success of this revolution in the organization and technology of manufacturing operations. Most companies still use the same cost accounting and management control systems that were developed decades ago for a competitive environment drastically different from that of today. Consider, for example, the following cases drawn from actual company experiences.

During Richard Thompson's two years as manager of the Industrial Products Division of the Acme Corporation, the division enjoyed such greatly improved profitability that he was promoted to more senior corporate responsibility. Thompson's replacement, however, found the division's manufacturing capability greatly eroded and a plunge in profitability inevitable.

Careful analysis of operations during Thompson's tenure revealed that:

- Increased profitability had been largely caused by an unexpected jump in demand that permitted the division's facilities to operate near capacity.
- Despite this expansion, the division's market share had decreased.
- Costs had been reduced by not maintaining equipment, by operating it beyond rated capacity, by not investing in new equipment or product development,

and by imposing stress on workers to the point of alienating them.
- Many costs had been absorbed into a bloated inventory position.
- Unit productivity had actually fallen.

By this time, however, Thompson was secure in his senior position and was still receiving credit for the high profits Industrial Products had earned under his direction.

The Carmel Corporation had made significant investments in labor-saving equipment. Yet with total costs, particularly overhead, still increasing, it was hard pressed to maintain market share with prices that fully recovered all of its costs. Carmel used a standard cost accounting system that allocated all nondirect costs on the basis of direct labor hours. The company had installed this procedure many years ago when direct labor accounted for more than 60% of total costs and machinery was both simple and inexpensive. Over the years, however, investment in sophisticated new machinery had greatly reduced the direct labor content of the company's products.

Staff costs rose as Carmel expanded its design and engineering staffs to develop specialized high-margin products. Because these new products required advanced materials, Carmel also expanded its purchase of semifinished components from suppliers. With direct labor (at an average wage of $12 per hour) plunging as a fraction of total costs, the accounting system was allocating the growing capital and overhead costs to a shrinking pool of direct labor hours.

The predictable result: a total cost per direct labor hour in excess of $60—and projections that it would soon rise to $80. Worse, efforts to offset these higher hourly rates by substituting capital and purchased materials for in-house production only compounded the problem. The accounting system was distracting management attention from the expansion of indirect costs.

Both these examples offer a pointed reminder that poorly designed or outdated accounting and control systems can distort the realities of manufacturing performance. Equally important, such systems can place out of reach most of the promised benefits from new CIM (computer-integrated manufacturing) processes. As information workers like design engineers and systems analysts replace traditional blue-collar workers in factories, accounting conventions that allocate overhead to direct labor hours will be at best irrelevant and more likely counterproductive to a company's manufacturing operations. And with the new manufacturing technology now available, variable costs will disappear except for purchases of materials and the energy required to operate equipment.

Not only will labor costs be mostly fixed, many of them will become sunk costs. The investment in software to operate and maintain computer-based manufacturing equipment must take place before any production starts, and of course that investment will be independent of the number of items produced using the software program. With the decreasing importance of variable labor costs, companies that allocate the fixed, sunk costs of equipment and information systems according to anticipated production volumes will distort the underlying economics of the new manufacturing environment.

In this environment, companies will need to concentrate on obtaining maximum effectiveness from their equipment and from their increasing investment in information workers and in what they produce. Controlling variable labor costs will become a lower priority. This major change in emphasis requires that managers learn new ways to think about and measure both product costs and product profitability.

NONFINANCIAL ASPECTS OF MANUFACTURING PERFORMANCE

It is unlikely, however, that any cost accounting system can adequately summarize a company's manufacturing operations. Today's accounting systems evolved from the scientific management movement in the early part of the twentieth century. They were instrumental in promoting the efficiency of mass production enterprises, particularly those producing relatively few standard products with a high direct labor content. Reliance on these systems in today's competitive environment, which is characterized by products with much lower direct labor content, will provide an inadequate picture of manufacturing efficiency and effectiveness.

Measurement systems for today's manufacturing operations must consider:

Quality.   To excel as a world-class manufacturer, a company must be totally committed to quality—that is, each component, subassembly, and finished good should be produced in conformity to specifications. Such a commitment to quality entails major changes in the way companies design products, work with suppliers, train employees, and operate and maintain equipment. But this commitment must also extend to a company's measurement systems. Data on the percentage of defects, frequency of breakdowns, percentage of finished goods completed without any rework required, and on the incidence and frequency of defects discovered by customers should be a vital part of any company's quality-enhancement program. Otherwise, the impact of variations in quality will show up in cost and market share data too late and at too aggregate a level to be of help to management. Direct quality indicators should be reported frequently at all levels of a manufacturing organization.

Inventory.   A second nonfinancial indicator of manufacturing performance is inventory. American managers are well versed in optimizing inventory levels according to the economic order quantity (EOQ) model, which balances the cost of additional setup time with the cost of carrying inventory. They are less familiar with the effort, common among Japanese producers, to eliminate setup times and to implement just-in-time inventory control systems, which together reduce drastically overall levels of work-in-process (WIP) inventory.[1]

---

[1]See, for example, Jinichiro Nakane and Robert W. Hall, "Management Specs for Stockless Production," HBR May-June 1983, p. 84; Larry P. Ritzman, Barry E. King, and Lee J. Krajewski, "Manufacturing Performance—Pulling the Right Levers," HBR March-April 1984, p. 143; and Hal F. Mather, "The Case for Skimpy Inventories," HBR January-February 1984, p. 40.

Many of the savings in reduced working capital, factory storage, and materials handling from cutting WIP will eventually be reflected in lower total manufacturing costs. But many of the savings that arise from transactions *not* taken—less borrowing to finance inventory, for example, or less need to expand factory floor space—will not be reflected in these costs. Therefore, such direct measures as average batch sizes, WIP, and inventory of purchased items will provide much more accurate and timely information on a company's manufacturing performance than will the behavior of average manufacturing costs.

Productivity. Direct measures of productivity are a third important set of nonfinancial indicators. Even in companies publicly committed to productivity improvements, accurate measurement of productivity is often impossible because accounting systems are designed to capture dollar-based transactions only. Without precise data on units produced, labor hours used, materials processed, energy consumed, and capital employed, administrators must deflate dollar amounts by aggregate price indices to obtain approximate physical measures of productivity. But errors in approximation often arise that can easily mask any period-to-period changes in real productivity.

Alternatively, managers rely on partial productivity measures, such as value added per employee or output per direct labor hour, which attribute all productivity changes to labor. These measures tend to overlook gains from the more efficient use of capital, energy, and managerial effort and so encourage the substitution of capital, indirect labor, energy, and processed materials for direct labor. But as direct labor costs decline relative to total manufacturing costs, it becomes more—not less—important to focus on total factor productivity.

Nor can managers finesse these measurement problems by looking only at aggregate data on profitability. In the short run, product profitability may be caused more by relative price changes and holding gains not recognized by historical cost-based systems than by structural improvements in the production process. A temporary expansion of demand can, for example, enable a company to boost its prices faster than its growth in costs. In the long run, however, the higher wages paid by U.S. companies will lead to competitive difficulties—

unless offset by higher productivity. During the 1960s and 1970s, many U.S. companies earned a comfortable profit and did not notice that their productivity had begun to stagnate or even decline. They are noticing now.

Innovation. Some companies choose to compete not by efficiently producing mature products that have general customer acceptance and stable designs but by introducing a constant stream of new products. Customers buy the products of these innovative companies because of the value of their unique characteristics, not because the products are cheaper than those of competitors. For innovating companies, the key to success is high performance products, timely delivery, and product customization. Attempts to impose cost minimization and efficiency criteria—especially early in the product development process—will be counterproductive.

Cost accounting systems, however, rarely distinguish between products that compete on the basis of cost and those that compete on the basis of unique characteristics valued by purchasers. Thus, it is difficult to manufacture new products in facilities that also manufacture mature products since plant managers, evaluated by an accounting system that stresses efficiency and productivity, find it disruptive to make products for which both the designs and the process technology are still evolving. Companies that cannot afford the luxury of a separate facility for new product manufacturing must learn to de-emphasize traditional cost measurements during the start-up phase of new products and to monitor directly their performance, quality, and timely delivery.

Work force. Another limitation of traditional cost accounting systems is their inability to measure the skills, training, and morale of the work force. As much recent experience attests, if employees do not share a company's goals, the company cannot survive as a first-rate competitor. Hence, the morale, attitudes, skill, and education of employees can be as valuable to a company as its tangible assets.

Some companies, noting the importance of their human resources, conduct periodic surveys of employee attitudes and morale. They also monitor educational and skill levels, promotion and training, and the absenteeism and turnover of people under each manager's supervision. These people-based measures are weighted heavily when managers' performance is evaluated. Meeting profit or cost budgets does not lead to a positive job rating if it is accompanied by any deterioration in these people-based measures.

In summary, the financial measures generated by traditional cost accounting systems provide an inadequate summary of a company's manufacturing operations. Today's global competition requires that nonfinancial measures—on quality, inventory levels, productivity, flexibility, deliverability, and employees—also be used in the evaluation of a company's manufacturing performance. Companies that achieve satisfactory financial performance but show stagnant or deteriorating performance on nonfinancial indicators are unlikely to become—or long remain—world-class competitors.

IMPROVING CONTROL SYSTEMS

Improving manufacturing performance requires more of accounting systems than the timely provision of relevant financial and nonfinancial data. Fundamental changes in management control systems are also needed. In particular, there is a need to rethink the way companies use summary financial measures like ROI to coordinate, motivate, and evaluate their decentralized operating units.

The ROI measure was developed earlier in this century to help in the management of the new multi-activity corporations that were then forming. ROI was used as an indicator of the efficiency of diverse operating departments, as a means for evaluating requests for new capital investment, and as an overall measure of the financial performance of the entire company.

Through the use of ROI control, early twentieth century corporations achieved a specialization of managerial talent. Managers of functional departments (manufacturing, sales, finance, and purchasing) could become specialists and pursue strategies for their departments that increased the ROI of the entire company. Senior managers, freed from day-to-day operating responsibility, could focus on coordinating the company's diverse activities and developing its long-term strategies.

In practice, decentralization via ROI control permitted senior executives to be physically and organizationally separated from their manufacturing operations. For many years, this separation was a valuable and necessary feature that enabled corporations to expand into many diverse lines of business. Recently, however, problems with running corporations "by the numbers"—that is, with excessive reliance on ROI measures but without detailed knowledge of divisions' operations and technology—have become uncomfortably apparent.

Inflation & ROI

The financial executives who pioneered in the application of ROI measures were not concerned with the distortions introduced by inflation. After World War II, however, as ROI-based control systems came into widespread use, continuous price increases gave a steady upward bias to ROI.

When fixed assets and inventory are not restated for price level changes after acquisition, net income is overstated and investment is understated. Thus managers who retain older, mostly depreciated assets report much higher ROIs than managers who invest in new assets. Such apparent differences in profitability, of course, have nothing to do with actual differences in the rates of return of the two classes of assets.

Financial accounting mentality

Such distortions of economic performance are but one manifestation of a broader problem: the use in a company's internal reporting and evaluation systems of accounting practices and conventions developed for external reporting. This is, for the most part, a recent phenomenon and is more common in the United States than in other parts of the world.

In Europe, many companies have one department to collect and analyze data for internal operations and another to prepare external reports. Some companies, like Philips in the Netherlands, even report to stockholders on the basis used to evaluate internal operations. By contrast, contemporary practice in the United States is to use for internal purposes conventions either developed for external reporting or mandated by such external reporting authorities as the Financial Accounting Standards Board and the SEC.

Interest expense.   For example, many American corporations regularly allocate corporate expenses —say, interest costs—to divisions and profit centers according to some arbitrary measure of a unit's assets or working capital. Now, it is sensible to charge divisions for capital employed. It is not sensible, however, to use a pro rata share of the interest expense reported on external financial statements as the appropriate internal cost of capital. Such a procedure implies that a company financed entirely through equity would allocate no capital charges to divisions since it has no recorded interest expense.

Consider, at the other extreme, an autonomous division engaged in real estate whose assets are mostly debt financed. The financial accounting mentality would have this division bear a higher interest charge against earnings than would divisions financed more heavily by equity. But does anyone believe that the cost of debt capital is higher than that of equity capital?

Divisions should be charged for their investment in net controllable assets through a divisional cost of capital, perhaps adjusted to allow lower charges for working capital than for higher-risk fixed assets. Few companies use such a method today, perhaps because the divisional capital charges will "over-absorb" a company's actual interest expense. But considering actual interest expense as a company's only cost of invested capital is more a limitation of contemporary financial reporting than it is a criticism of charging divisions for the full cost of their investments.

Pension costs. Financial accounting practices can also lead to bad cost accounting in the allocation of pension costs. For example, prior service costs are sunk costs. They represent an obligation of a company for the past service of its employees. No current or future action of the company can affect this obligation. The amortization of prior service costs must, however, be recognized as a current expense in the company's financial statements. Therefore, many companies allocate prior service costs to divisions.

One company allocated these costs in proportion to pension benefits accrued. A plant with an older work force received almost all of its division's prior service costs, but several newer plants with much younger workers bore almost none. This arbitrary allocation produced a $4 per labor hour cost penalty on the older plant. As a result, the company was shifting work from the older plant to the newer ones. In addition, the older plant was losing market share as it raised prices in an attempt to earn a satisfactory margin over its high labor costs. Put simply, the company became a victim of its financial accounting mentality: first it allocated a noncontrollable, sunk cost to its plants and then it relied on this arbitrarily allocated cost for pricing and product sourcing decisions.

Other distortions. Distortions created by the financial accounting mentality intrude on many other internal measurements. How often, for instance, do executives, when measuring a division's investment base for an ROI calculation, include leased assets only when, according to FASB regulations, they must be capitalized on the external financial statements? Are development and start-up expenses, including software development, considered part of the investment in a computer-integrated manufacturing process, or are these investments in intangibles expensed as incurred because, according to SFAS 2, this treatment is mandated for external reporting? Do companies translate operations in foreign countries according to their economic exposure overseas, or do they use whatever translation method the FASB happens to be mandating at the time?

The point, of course, is that companies seeking to compete effectively must devise cost accounting systems that reflect their investment decisions and cost structures. Internal accounting practices should be driven by corporate strategy, not by FASB and SEC requirements for external reporting. Surely, the cost of record keeping in an electronic age is sufficiently low that aggregating transaction data differently for external and internal purposes cannot be a burdensome task.

Financial entrepreneurship

Another set of difficulties with ROI-based measurements stems from the ability of executives to generate greater profits from financial activities than from managing their assets better. Sixty years ago managers knew that higher profits and ROI came from efficient production, aggressive marketing, and a continual flow of product and process improvements. During the past 20 years, however, as it has become more difficult to increase profits through selling, production, and R&D, some companies have looked to accounting and financial activities to generate earnings.

At first, these activities—switching from accelerated to straight-line depreciation, for example—did little harm. Occasionally they proved costly, as when companies opted to pay unnecessary taxes by delaying or refusing a switch to LIFO because of its adverse impact on reported profits. Today, however, the romance with these devices is in full swing: mergers and acquisitions, divestitures and spinoffs, debt swaps and discounted debt repurchases, debt defeasance, sale-leaseback arrangements, and leveraged buyouts.

Some of these activities may create value for shareholders (current research is still attempting to sort out the net effect of these financial activities). Still, it is hard to imagine that a focus on creating wealth through the rearrangement of ownership claims rather than on managing tangible and intangible assets more effectively will help companies survive as world-class competitors. Ultimately, wealth must be created by the imaginative and intelligent management of assets, not by devising novel financing and ownership arrangements for those assets.

Intangible assets

The final and most damaging problem with ROI-based measures is the incentive they give managers to reduce expenditures on discretionary and intangible investments. When sluggish sales or growing costs make profit targets hard to achieve, managers often try to prop up short-term earnings by cutting expenditures on R&D, promotion, distribution, quality improvement, applications engineering, human resources, and customer relations—all of which are, of course, vital to a company's long-term performance. The immediate effect of such reductions is to boost reported profitability—but at the risk of sacrificing the company's competitive position.

The opportunity for a company to increase reported income by forgoing intangible investments illustrates a fundamental flaw in the financial accounting model. This flaw compromises the role of short-term profits as a valid and reliable indicator of a company's economic health. A company's eco-nomic value is not merely the sum of the values of its tangible assets, whether measured at historic cost, replacement cost, or current market prices. It also includes the value of intangible assets: its stock of products and processes, employee talent and morale, customer loyalty, reliable suppliers, efficient distribution network, and the like.

Suppose this stock of intangible assets could be valued each period. Then, when the company decreased its expenditures on these assets, their subsequent decline in value would lower the company's reported income. We do not, however, have methods to value objectively intangible assets. Therefore, reported earnings cannot show a company's decline in value when it depletes its stock of intangible assets. It is this defect in the financial accounting model that makes the quarterly or annual income number an inadequate summary of the change in value of the company during the period.

THE TASK AT HAND

Present cost accounting and management control systems rest on concepts developed almost a century ago when the nature of competition and the demands for internal information were very different from what they are today. When companies now make arbitrary allocations of corporate expenses to divisions and products, accounting systems may provide even less valid cost data than did the cost accumulation systems in use 50 years ago. In general, though, an accounting model derived for the efficient production of a few standardized products with high direct labor content will not be appropriate for an automated production environment where the factors critical to success are quality, flexibility, and the efficient use of expensive information workers and capital.

General managers must be alert to the inadequacies of their present measurement systems. It is doubtful whether any company can be successfully run by the numbers, but certainly the numbers being generated by today's systems provide little basis for managerial decisions and control. Managers require both improved financial numbers and nonfinancial indicators of manufacturing performance. Because no measurement system, however well designed, can capture all the relevant information, any operational system must be supplemented by direct observation in the field. The separation of senior management from operations that the ROI formula made possible 80 years ago will have to be partially repealed. Successful senior managers must be knowledgeable about the current organization and technology of their operations.

For their part, accounting and financial executives must redirect their energies—and their thinking—from external reporting to the more effective management of their companies' tangible and intangible assets. Internal management accounting systems need renovation. Yesterday's internal costing and control practices cannot be allowed to exist in isolation from a company's manufacturing environment—not, that is, if the company wishes to flourish as a world-class competitor.

Accounting Lag:
The Obsolescence of Cost Accounting Systems

Robert S. Kaplan

Existing cost accounting and management control practices are unlikely to provide useful indicators for managing contemporary firms' manufacturing operations.[1] Traditional cost measurement systems will imperfectly reflect, and with considerable lags at best, the dramatic increase in manufacturing efficiency and effectiveness that occurs when firms achieve total quality control, Just-In-Time (JIT) inventory systems, and computer-integrated manufacturing processes. Financially oriented measurement systems will not capture the benefits from decreased new product launch times, from the flexibility afforded from computer-controlled production systems, and from the large decrease in throughput and lead times which modern manufacturing organization and technology make possible. Further, short-term profitability indicators will not signal the decrease in firms' value when they reduce discretionary expenditures for developing new products, for improving production processes, for maintaining the skill, loyalty, and morale of the work force, for expanding distribution networks and customer awareness, for developing improved software for production and information systems, and for maintaining and improving their physical capital

resources. Quite the contrary, the existing financial accounting systems signal short-term increases in accounting profits when firms decrease their economic wealth by foregoing investments in their long-term information and productive capital.

Effective managerial accounting systems must reflect the value-creating activities of companies: in operations, in marketing and sales, and in product and process development. In particular, they cannot be developed and maintained in isolation from the organization and technology of a company's manufacturing processes. If substantial changes are taking place in manufacturing processes, the management accounting systems must also change if they are to provide relevant information for managerial decisions and control.

In an attempt to learn how firms are modifying their accounting and control systems to help them manage in the new manufacturing environment, I visited a select set of innovative firms. These firms were not chosen at random. They were selected to be representative of those U.S. industrial corporations that seemed determined to survive and prosper in the new industrial competition. Thus, they were either leaders in high-technology growth industries or firms in mature industries which were actively promoting productivity and new manufacturing technologies in order to be globally competitive. The goal of the study was to learn from innovative firms what changes were being made in their accounting, measurement, and control systems to support the current emphasis on new product and manufacturing technologies.

The study was not approached with a formal research design nor with a set of specific hypotheses to be tested. Our current paucity of knowledge of the accounting and control systems used by innovative firms precludes such a well-structured mode of inquiry. The broad agenda for this initial investigation—encompassing modifications in traditional cost accounting systems, nonfinancial measures of manufacturing performances, and an expanded set of short-term performance indicators for decentralized cost and profit centers—suggested a wide-ranging look at contemporary practices.

To anticipate the findings and conclusion of this preliminary investigation, I found there were many unexploited opportunities to improve the links between firms' measurement systems and their innovations in product technology and manufacturing processes. While it was obvious that each of the firms visited was making significant changes in its manufacturing operations, it seemed equally clear that comparable changes were not being made in its accounting and control systems. Some may argue that existing accounting and control procedures, developed 75 years ago, are robust enough to still be useful in today's radically changed manufacturing environment. Therefore, a discovery of little innovation in contemporary accounting and control systems would be consistent with firms having made appropriate choices for their information systems. Based on my observations and discussions with senior financial and operating executives, I do not share such a complacent or sanguine view of the current state of managerial accounting systems in U.S. industrial firms. I will attempt to convey to the reader the basis for my conclusions by describing the situations in the firms I visited. In order to offer candid observations and appraisals of the accounting systems of organizations that I (and many other observers) consider to be among the best managed and most successful U.S. corporations, anonymity has been preserved by referring to companies by coded initials.

COMPANY EXPERIENCES

Company V

Company V is a broadly based manufacturer of electrical products and equipment. The corporate-wide commitment to improve productivity and product quality was underscored in the 1982 Annual Report by the Chairman's Stockholder Letter and 10 subsequent pages of pictures and text. I examined a division that had recently (in Autumn 1982) implemented a major change in its organization of manufacturing operations. The division builds electrical propulsion units for mass-transit vehicles. A given propulsion unit could contain between 5,000 and 10,000 different parts. The division has a high percentage of white-collar employees, especially engineers who custom-design the units and who are responsible for installation and service of finished units. The production process is predominantly assembly operations and increasingly is using automated equipment.

Under the old production procedures, raw material and work-in-process inventories were stacked on the floor near each work station. Workers were kept busy on a production run until they ran out of operative parts or subassemblies. Partially assembled units, whose production was interrupted because of a faulty or missing part, were stored around the work station until a new part could be delivered and the worker able to start working again on that unit. A local operating rule was to attempt to keep all workers busy at their work stations even if this led to sub-assemblies being produced well before they could be processed or assembled at the subsequent stages.

Costs were accumulated on a total project basis, where a typical project produced between 30 and 50 identical units. Factory costs were allocated based on Net Allowed Hours, a projection of the total direct labor hours to be worked in the factory during the year. In 1982, this produced a shop labor rate of about $36 per hour of which only 25 percent represented actual direct labor costs. In 1983, the shop labor rate had escalated to more than $50 per direct labor hour; less than 20 percent of this amount represented direct labor costs. The increase in the shop labor rate was caused by a significant reduction in estimated Net Allowed Hours because of increased efficiencies from the new organization of manufacturing (to be described shortly), increased usage of automated equipment, and the higher overhead costs to accumulate and distribute information that enhanced manufacturing efficiencies. Engineering charges were accumulated and allocated to contracts separately. These charges were actually billed at lower rates than the current shop labor rate because of the cost allocation procedure that levied all factory overhead costs onto direct labor.

The division moved to a new organization of manufacturing because it had been steadily losing money for the prior decade. When bidding on jobs, all labor and overhead costs were forecast for the proposed job, and reduced to a cost per estimated labor hour figure.[2] The full cost per-hour figure was then multiplied by the total labor hours for the project, escalated for anticipated inflation, and marked-up for a planned profit percentage. This procedure of marking up and escalating estimated full costs per hour, at a time when business was contracting, led to high, noncompetitive bids that won few orders. Eventually, the division had slashed cost markups to win new business so that it could maintain an experienced, skilled work force. The division hoped to cut costs below its estimates while working on contracts.

The new concept of manufacturing was explicitly designed to make this division more competitive. A commitment of several million dollars for the computer-controlled equipment was made (without formal benefit-cost analysis such as discounted cash flow). An additional major investment was to reeducate and retrain workers, supervisors, managers, and engineers in a new way of conducting business.

The goal of the new system was to have work flow through the assembly process in a smooth, predictable fashion. The new flow process started with 100 percent inspection of purchased items with batches returned to the vendor if any defects were found. The formerly omnipresent (mostly underfoot) raw materials and work-in-process inventories were replaced by limited access, computer-controlled inventory storage locations. Sub-assemblies were scheduled for production only when they would be needed by a subsequent stage of assembly. Also, work on a subassembly or assembly was not initiated until availability of 100 percent good material was assured. Thus, items were built only as needed, not to keep production workers busy. Inventory was kept in the lowest value state as long as possible. Temporarily idle workers were assigned to other tasks.

A further innovation was a commitment to a model shop where 3 to 5 complete prototype units were to be built, tested, and approved before drawings would be released for shop floor production. In this way, design and manufacturing problems would surface early, and efficient manufacturing procedures implemented even for the early production runs. Previously, problems and procedures were worked out on the shop floor based on experience in actual assembly and test of finished items. While this trial-and-error approach produced a lovely learning curve over the life of a contract, it led to highly inefficient production for the first batches of units. By developing efficient manufacturing procedures in a model shop and videotaping actual assembly techniques to train factory workers, the efficiencies previously learned towards the end of a production run could now be realized much earlier.

This situation seemed to provide an ideal setting to study the benefits from changing the organization of manufacturing operations. The division had recently won a follow-up order from a customer so that it would be producing a batch of propulsion units in the "new" factory that were identical to a batch produced under the old, traditional manufacturing procedures. A certain degree of care would need to be exercised to control for experience curve effects during production of the first batch of units, differences in quantity discounts from suppliers between the two orders, and changes in price levels since the first batch of units were built. But in principle, these complications could be overcome and it was hoped that increases in productivity, reductions in WIP, production defects, rework, and scrap, and shortened throughput times would occur and could be documented. Such evidence would provide quantitative measures of the benefits from the new organization of manufacturing, and the returns from the company's investment in the new technology and in training and reeducation costs.

Unfortunately, it proved impossible to perform such a study. The accounting system had been designed to accumulate total project costs, not to measure production efficiencies. The system accumulated detailed product costs, using many subclassifications, on a monthly and contract-to-date basis. But with the exception of direct labor hours, no physical amounts were recorded. Thus, there was no record of the quantity of materials consumed during each month nor the amount of indirect and supervisory labor, and most devastating of all (for the proposed study), no figures on the amount of actual production during the month. Thus, there was no obvious way to relate inventory levels or quantities of labor and materials consumed to quantities of items produced each period. Discussions were held with program managers and production control supervisors to see whether production quantities could be obtained from a production information system, but they did not have this information either.

During the course of these discussions, it became clear to me that not only would it be impossible to reconstruct the unit cost of items produced in the past, but also there would be no way to compute productivity measures or unit costs for items currently being produced using the new manufacturing philosophy. The computer-based cost accounting system was well designed to capture all costs on a total project basis, but was too inflexible to be modified to produce unit cost and productivity measurements in the new manufacturing environment.[3] The system also produced monthly financial statements to be sent to corporate headquarters for review and for consolidation, but there was little correlation between these monthly financial statements and the actual value-creating activities in the factory.

The senior managers of the division were convinced that significant benefits would be produced from the new organization of manufacturing. Some of these were obvious by inspection. For example, floor space savings up to 50 percent were achieved by eliminating the storage of raw material and work-in-process on the factory floor and at each work station. The division was planning to move the production facilities of a nearby factory into the large space freed up in the redesigned factory. This space became available even after reserving room for the new model shop. But until the division installed a new cost accumulation system, it would not be possible to quantify the benefits from lower defect production, reductions in inventory, and a more orderly flow of production through the assembly process. We see here a theme that will unfortunately be repeated in most of our sites. Firms are implementing imaginative and innovative changes in their manufacturing operations, but continuing to measure and evaluate the performance of these operations using accounting systems from earlier eras.

Company N

Company N is a leading producer of specialized products for the lumber industry and a manufacturer of diverse products for outdoorsmen and "do-it-yourself" enthusiasts. The company's products are mature and competition takes place along quality, performance, and price dimensions. The company has a long history of emphasizing productivity and performance, but a real impetus for change occurred when a senior operating officer made a trip to Japan several years ago. The executive, who had extensive experience in manufacturing operations, reported:

In October of 1981, I joined 12 other American executives on a trip to Japan. Our mission was to study the reasons for Japan's remarkable achievements. We visited 12 large Japanese manufacturing plants and spent a full day in each. We discussed management philosophy with the Japanese managers and toured the plants to see their methods of operation. As a result of what I saw on that trip, I very quickly lowered my assessment of our own company's performance in the area of human resource management. I quite suddenly lost my complacency about our invincibility as a manufacturer. Quite frankly, I received a shock when I saw how advanced the Japanese were at managing their people and in their manufacturing methods.

Company N promptly organized a team to study in-depth what would be required to implement Japanese manufacturing concepts in a U.S. environment. By mid-1982, senior executives had articulated a new Statement of Philosophy for the company that built upon the strong value system already in existence, expanded the company's commitment to people involvement and quality, and articulated a major new thrust to achieve a Just-in-Time Inventory System (JIT). A company-wide education and planning program to implement JIT occurred in Autumn 1982, and by May 1983, a week-long conference involving worldwide production personnel, and divisional and corporate management, could be held to evaluate progress.

Obviously, with less than half a year of effort, the progress reported at the conference represented only a fraction of what ultimately will be realized, but the results were still strikingly impressive. The vice president and controller, who organized the conference, reported:

> In our——Project, inventory is down 92 percent, scrap and rework down 20 percent. In the manufacture of——kits, lead times were cut from two weeks to one day. In changing the presses for manufacturing——, die change time was cut from two and one-half hours to two and one-half minutes. In the manufacture of——products, lot sizes were cut from 500 to 30, inventory was reduced by 50 percent and lead times were shortened from six weeks to two days, making possible a make-to-order business.
>
> The award-winning plant had a small but beautiful project. By Value Analysis, they cut the number of models of handles from 11 to 2. Lead time was cut from 30 days to a few minutes and they now make to order. Work-in-process was reduced from a 40-piece average to one. An amazing feature was that travel distance was cut from 2,000 feet to 18 inches.

Summary data from the conference showed that in five months, inventory was reduced 31 percent, from 194 to 134 days of sales (four months later, on September 30, 1983, inventory had been reduced further to 116 days of sales). Table 1 shows the reduction in setup time to exchange dies for various products or locations.

The goal was to achieve Single-Minute Exchange of Dies (that is, less than 10 minutes) throughout the organization, a goal that had been realized already by many of the locations noted in Table 1.

A tour of a metal fabrication and machining division provided a graphic picture of the improvements that were accomplished within one year of adopting the JIT manufacturing goals. In one welding operation, the substitution of a microprocessor-controlled, general-purpose welding machine for a manually operated one had reduced setup times

Table 1.

LOCATION/PRODUCT TYPE	EXCHANGE TIME (12/31/82)	EXCHANGE TIME (5/31/83)
1	83 minutes	53 minutes
2	378	162
3	20	.02
4	150	2.5
5	165	.5
6	360	1.7
7	43	17
8	8	2
9	240	10
10	60	20

from 30 hours to several minutes. This permitted a reduction in lot size from 10,000 to 250 units. With smaller batch sizes throughout the plant, items were moving continually from one stage to the next rather than lying around for a week or more waiting for a large block of time to be freed up on the next machine.

The continual flow of small batches through the factory not only greatly reduced inventory and space requirements, but also permitted a large increase in quality. Previously, if a machine or the material being fed to the machine was not in conformance with specifications, an entire batch of 10,000 items could be defective. These defects would be detected at subsequent stages of processing, frequently a week or more later. Engineers would then have to be assigned to salvage the large batch of defective items, either devising some new product that could use these items or conceiving of a rework program to bring the defective items back into specifications. When production shifted to continuous processing of small batches, nonconforming items were detected much sooner and the problem remedied immediately. Engineers, no longer having to devise schemes to salvage tens of thousands of defective items, could devote all their time to process improvements, thereby producing even greater savings in the near future.

Space savings were enormous. By rearranging machines, moving to Just-in-Time production within the factory, and working with suppliers to deliver in smaller lots, more frequently, and directly to the factory floor, savings in floor space up to 50 percent had been achieved. Formerly, this division anticipated building a new plant in the near future. With the space savings already achieved and anticipated for the future, the division management was confident that a new plant would not be needed before 1988. Travel distance of an item going in and out of inventory, and from one process to the next, had been reduced from 3 miles to about 100 yards.

The labor savings from these production improvements had also been significant. The company was operating with a no-layoff policy in order to encourage an active flow of suggestions from the factory workers. In the short run, labor savings were captured by eliminating all temporary jobs, plus the normal attrition of 1½ percent per month. With the extra space, machine time, and permanent labor time now available from the early success of the JIT program, pressures were building on the R&D program to develop new products that could be produced with the new capacity the division had created through its manufacturing efficiencies.

One more sign of the benefits from the JIT program was the reduction in order lead times from 6 weeks to less than 1 week even during a period of increasing sales. Throughput time for some products, measured from the time a batch of units was started into production until the units were ready for shipment, had been reduced from 4 weeks to 1 shift (8 hours). This increase in order responsiveness was viewed by management as developing a significant marketing advantage for the division.

Accounting System for Company N. At the time of my visit, the accounting and measurement system had yet to be modified to reflect the new organization and technology of manufacturing. At the large division whose production operations I just described, a traditional standard process costing system was still being used. Production variances were computed at an aggregate plant level so that the significant cost savings achieved by particular products in the plant could not be highlighted. The system itself seemed inconsistent with the major changes occurring in the factory. For one process I examined (chosen at random), detailed standards were being maintained for each of a sequence of labor procedures. None of these separate procedures existed any longer. They had been combined into a single process that was now being performed by a machine. Thus, in many ways, the highly detailed and complex standard cost system was no longer representative of the simplified production

process one could easily observe by walking through the factory. As another indication of problems with the cost system, standard labor times for each process step were calculated to 5 significant digits even though factories would be considered operating well within control if labor times were within one percent of standard. The ability of industrial engineers to estimate labor standards accurately to within .001 of one percent is probably one of the arcane secrets of the profession. Finally, no measures of quality improvements had been developed for reporting systematically to higher levels of management.

The good news side of the accounting story in Company N was the general awareness of the value of supplementing the firm's accounting and control system. Efforts were underway to compute partial productivity indicators such as units produced and value added per labor hour, days sales in inventory, and throughput time per product. In order to motivate the efficient use of physical resources, cost centers were allowed to "sell" space and equipment that was no longer needed back to the corporation. These departments were credited for such savings even if they had not yet been realized by the corporation. Manufacturing managers were developing new evaluation criteria based on the percentage of on-time deliveries each month and reductions in lead time rather than the traditional measures of production rates and machine utilization. Cost analysts were attempting to measure actual product costs and provide this information frequently to manufacturing managers so that the benefits from improved production processes could be seen rapidly. This effort, which was still at an experimental stage, revealed that the production cost of one standard metal part (including materials) had been reduced by 40 percent in one year.

There was a general awareness that the JIT production system should eventually permit an enormous simplification and reduction in the cost of operating the firm's accounting system. At present, much of the effort in maintaining an "accurate" cost system was devoted to the detailed recordkeeping and reporting of in-plant inventories. As the company succeeds in reducing all inventories at the plant level to bare minimum levels (including immediate shipment or assignment of finished goods inventory to marketing departments) and reducing product throughput times from several weeks to several hours, the inventory accounting system can be scrapped. For periodic income measurement, it becomes much simpler and cheaper to do a physical count of the few items around the factory at the end of each period. It seems simpler, however, to eliminate inventory from actual production operations than to modify the recordkeeping for inventory in the firm's accounting system.

Company H

Company H is a broad-based manufacturer of computer systems. Division S of Company H designs and produces various models of a major peripheral storage device for the company's computer systems using highly automated and capital-intensive production processes. The division has large numbers of "knowledge workers": engineers for product and process design, industrial and manufacturing engineers for process development and improvements, cost accountants and cost engineers, quality engineering and assurance personnel, information systems specialists, test engineers, and materials planners, schedulers, purchasers, and distributors. Given the capital- and knowledge-intensive production process, direct labor represents less than 10 percent of total costs.

Company H had recently adopted goals of total quality control and just-in-time production in order to become among the most efficient global producers of computer systems and equipment. Division S had already realized a 50 percent increase in its inventory turnover ratio and anticipated another 50 percent increase during the next 3 to 5 years.

As with the other innovative companies we examined, however, the pace of change in Division S's accounting system was much more leisurely than the changes in the organization and technology of the division's production processes. The cost accounting system was traditional, accumulating all overhead expenses into large cost pools. The over-head and indirect expenses included manufacturing engineering and information systems, test engineering, quality engineering, capitalized engineering expenses, depreciation on machinery and facilities, general employee benefits, manufacturing support services, site services, and financial services. These overhead expenses were added together into large aggregate cost pools and allocated to production departments on some objective but arbitrary basis, and subsequently to products on a direct labor hour basis. With direct labor representing a small fraction of total costs, this procedure produced a total burden rate of $90/DLH in 1983 and was forecasted to rise to more than $140/DLH by 1986.

A graphic illustration of the impact of the division's cost accounting procedures is shown in Table 2, which traces the productivity gains and total manufacturing costs for one of the division's fastest growing products (numbers have been disguised to maintain confidentiality, but rates of change over time have been preserved).

We see from Table 2 that the division achieved substantial efficiencies in its manufacturing process. From 1981 (the second year of production) to 1983, the yield of good items doubled and direct labor hours per unit were cut in half. Despite these dramatic improvements in direct labor and material efficiency, total manufacturing costs remained about constant over this three-year period. Since the product was experiencing large increases in sales, one would have expected the per-unit allocation of fixed expenses to have decreased. Therefore, the total manufacturing costs should also have decreased, given the increased productivity of labor and materials and the expansion in production volumes. But manufacturing costs remained constant, clearly showing that the indirect and overhead expenses allocated to the product were increasing at least as fast as the increases in production volumes. How much of this indirect and overhead cost increase represented actual increases in the division's ex-

Table 2. Yields, Hours, and Production Costs per Unit

	1980	1981	1982	1983
Quantity Produced (1983 = 100)	3	11	58	100
Labor Hours/Unit	4.0	2.4	1.6	1.2
Yield (%)	32	38	67	75
Total Manufacturing Cost/Unit (1983 = 100)	152	102	95	100

penses in these categories and how much represented reallocation of already existing costs away from other products could not be determined from the available product cost data. It is obvious, however, that despite the direct labor focus of the cost accounting system, the cost components that need to be managed and controlled were in the overhead and knowledge worker categories.

Applying overhead and indirect costs on direct labor hours caused managers to focus a large share of their attention to controlling and improving direct labor utilization, even though direct labor was a small percentage (<10 percent) of total manufacturing costs.[4] The following behavioral responses to the cost allocation system were described to us:

- Product managers in several cost centers were recommending a shift from internal production to external vendor supply. Internal production of technically unsophisticated parts at labor rates approaching $90/DLH was hardly competitive with external suppliers. Purchasing externally saves direct labor but increases the personnel required in departments for materials specification and purchasing materials planning and scheduling, materials production and control, and materials distribution (these were actual departments in Division S). The costs of these personnel, however, are aggregated into a common overhead pool and allocated out on an average basis to the remaining direct labor hours. Therefore, the "buy rather than make" decision will lower the costs assigned to the cost center even though total costs to the division may have increased.

- Enormous attention was directed at the measurement of direct labor hours. Cost center managers were held responsible mainly for on-time delivery and direct labor hours used. Many hours at meetings were spent discussing increases or decreases of .01 hours (or smaller) of direct labor per unit. Thousands of dollars of industrial and manufacturing engineering time were spent for process improvements to reduce direct labor content by 0.1 hours. Also, managers attempted to have manufacturing engineers reclassified from a direct, traceable category into the common pool where their costs would be shared by other products.

- Labor-intensive processes seemed much more expensive than capital-intensive ones. Traceable equipment costs were not allocated to processes that used the equipment. Rather, the equipment costs were aggregated into a large overhead pool and allocated back to processes and products on a direct labor hour basis. This encouraged further capital-labor substitution and buy-vs.-make decisions for assembly and other labor-intensive processes.

- There was no incentive for product managers to

influence or control the rapid growth of support personnel. First, they never saw the actual costs of the personnel since such costs were aggregated into large overhead pools. Second, they would receive only a fraction of the benefits from reducing or containing the numbers of these personnel, since the savings would be averaged across all product groups in the division.

- Expensive clean room space was used inefficiently. Clean room space cost twice as much as nonclean room space because of more costly utilities (to operate air-cleaning equipment), raised floor construction, and higher capital, installation, and maintenance expenses. But all space expenses, clean and nonclean rooms, were added together and allocated to products on a dollar-per-occupied-square-foot basis. Thus, charges for clean room space were the same as for nonclean rooms. Predictably, clean rooms ended up being used (and built) to perform routine operations and to store items that did not really need a clean room environment.

- Direct labor time was measured in exquisite detail since the fully allocated labor rate was charged only for hours actually worked. Worker time during idle periods, changeovers, and breakdowns and repairs was charged to overhead categories. One senior financial analyst at the division estimated that 65–70 percent of the computer code for the general ledger was devoted to keeping track of direct labor costs that were less than 10 percent of total manufacturing costs. Also, while (or because) direct labor occupied so much attention in the accounting system, physical measures of materials consumed or capital employed in the production process were not available so that productivity measures could not be easily computed.

Fortunately, there is also a "good news" counterpart to the above litany: In early 1983, the product manager for one of the four major components in the storage device established a task force to study and make recommendations to improve production costing and organizational procedures. The task force's recommendation, to create "a focused factory" within the larger plant organization, was adopted and implemented as of January 1984. The focused factory was somewhat fictitious but it connoted a specific identification of all overhead, support, and indirect personnel and costs necessary to produce the component. (Perhaps coincidentally, another division of Company H at a completely different site had implemented the identical concept, calling it the "plant within the plant.") With this scheme, the product manager is charged directly for almost all the overhead personnel and costs being allocated to the component, and he contracts with the various support functions for an appropriate level of service.

Many expenditures that previously were lumped together and allocated on a common basis would now be collected and allocated on a disaggregate basis. For example, separate occupancy rates would be developed for clean and nonclean room space. The single gas or electric meter for the entire site would be replaced by local meters for energy consumption at each cost center. The single rate previously used to allocate all manufacturing engineering costs would be replaced by five separate rates that will reflect better the different tasks performed by various categories of support engineers. Only a few service functions, considered inherently nontraceable, such as payroll, accounting, and personnel, will remain in a common overhead pool to be allocated on a basis such as head count.

All these overhead costs for the component will be allocated to finished products based on expected production volumes; that is, overhead cost will be reduced to a cost per unit produced, rather than a cost per direct labor hour. The allocation on a unit basis is possible because there was little product variety in the cost center; whatever variety did exist could be handled by developing relative complexity factors for the different products and using these to compute a weighted average of equivalent production volume each period.

In summary, the focused factory proposal at Division S will make overhead costs visible to the product manager at a much more disaggregate and controllable level of detail. The manager can then negotiate to reduce support services that he feels are redundant or too expensive. The proposal is being implemented for the simplest component in the storage device produced by the division. Costs for the other components will continue to be collected and allocated on the old basis during the experimental period. While it is too early to determine the impact of the focused factory accounting approach, some reductions in the controller's and Industrial Engineering staff were already appearing. Significant personnel reductions in other engineering and overhead functions are expected to occur during the initial year as the product manager attempts to eliminate superfluous tasks and makes the continual tradeoffs between costs and work performed that are necessary for efficient operations.

Company M

Company M is a worldwide semiconductor manufacturer. The company's senior management consists of the engineers and scientists who founded the company. The influence of these technically sophisticated leaders pervades the operations and reporting systems of the organization. To a degree not closely approached by any other organization I visited, the executives of Company M rely on raw operating statistics, rather than financial data, to understand and manage their business.

This operating philosophy probably has several origins. First, with their technical backgrounds, the top managers have more faith in measures of physical quantities than in summary financial measures. As one senior executive said, "I have a need to see 'inside' the process, to be assured everything is running smoothly and operating properly." Second, there exists one physical variable that has more to do with the success of the company than any set of financial variables. Production costs arise from fabrication of silicon wafers into usable chips. If the yield of chips increases by 50 percent, then production costs per chip can drop by one-third. Therefore, the single most important factor affecting unit production costs is the percentage yield of good chips. Third, the company has been in existence for only slightly more than a decade. It does not have professional managers who would tend to run the company via financial numbers because they do not understand or are not interested in learning about the manufacturing technology. Thus, the use of summary financial statistics to shield the senior managers from the details of week-to-week operations has not occurred and will not occur in the foreseeable future, given the strong technology culture in the corporation.

Charts are used everywhere in the organization. As one walks in the corridors surrounding every production facility, one sees charts of yields, quality, activity levels, and deliveries. Production supervisors are provided with more than one hundred indicators on a frequent and regular basis. Senior managers, up through the vice presidents and the president of the company, receive about 100 charts of key indicators every week. Table 3 summarizes the nature of the charts seen by these executives.

Table 3.   Charts of Manufacturing Performance

FABRICATION	ASSEMBLY	TEST
Yield	Number Units Shipped	Number Units Shipped
Wafers Out/Wafers In	to Test	Number Units Processed
Rework Percentage	Number Units Assembled	Average Test Time
Production	(by package type)	Throughput Time
Activities Performed	Number Leads/Package	Test Yields
Wafers Produced	Yields by Package Type	Tests per Operator House
Chips Produced	Leads Completed per	% Lots Rejected
Equivalent Chips Produced	Operator Hour	Equipment Uptime
% Delivery Commit-	Shipment per Indirect Labor Head Count	Personnel Turnover
ments Met	Cost per Unit Shipped	Test of Ongoing Quality
Throughput Time	% Units Shipped on Schedule	Costs per Unit
Productivity		% Units Tested on Schedule
Activities/Operator		
Hours		
Activities/Payroll $		
Chips/Payroll $		
Equipment Maintenance		
Equipment Utilization		
% Hours with no		
Unscheduled		
Downtime		
Engineering		
Equivalent Chips		
Produced/Good		
Wafers		
Financial		
Total Expenses		
Average Cost/Chip		
Revenue/Chip		
Margin/Chip		
Summary Measures		
WIP Measures		
WIP Turnover		
Personnel Turnover		
Absenteeism		

The items in Table 3 illustrate the diversity of indicators seen by Company M's management. They include measures of output, productivity, resource utilization, and unit costs. While costs are certainly among the set of data monitored by managers, costs are never among the first measures (or even in the top half of measures) to be reported. The managers seem satisfied with the indicator system. The only complaint that emerged during my discussions was not on the quantity of measures produced, but that the indicators have not changed as rapidly as the business; that the system was getting too ponderous and was not responsive to changing conditions. I will return to the issue after a brief description of the cost accounting system used by Company M.

The company uses a relatively simple process cost system. Actual costs are accumulated into 10 major cost pools: Raw Materials, Masking Plates, Direct Labor, Indirect Material, Equipment Maintenance, Depreciation, Facilities, Process Overhead, Plant Overhead, and General Overhead. Each cost pool is allocated to processing activities based on the relative difficulty or complexity of that activity. Thus, detailed costs are not collected for each activity. But rather than allocating costs to activities on a simplistic basis (such as direct labor hours), costs are allocated after a study of the degree of difficulty of each process. Also, as in any process cost system, the accumulated cost of scrapped wafers is spread over the remaining good wafers. Yields, therefore, have a dramatic impact on the unit cost of completed wafers.

It was interesting to learn that up to three years ago, costs were allocated on a direct labor hour basis. It was even more interesting to have a vice president state that only in the last three years have cost numbers begun to be developed seriously. My interpretation of these seemingly contradictory statements is that managers did not use product cost numbers derived by allocating overhead costs based on direct labor hours. In summary, the cost system struck me as reasonable and functional. It did not seem expensive to operate and probably did a sensible job in tracing and allocating costs to products. As mentioned already, the main influences on unit costs are wafer and chip yields. Beyond this, and once the obviously traceable costs are allocated to specific products, it would not matter greatly how costs are allocated among the different types of wafers produced.

Even the extensive set of indicators used by Company M, though, were not adequate to reflect changes in the product and process technologies and in the market conditions for the firm's products. We can see in Table 3 that many of the indicators are either simple counts of output (Number of Wafers produced, Number of Chips produced, Number Units Shipped, Number Units Assembled and Tested) or ratios involving simple counts of output (Wafers Out/Wafers In, Rework Percentage, Chips Produced/Good Wafers, Number Leads/Package, Tests per Operator Hour). These measures were developed when the company had only a few principal products, all using a similar production technology. Over time, the product line has diversified into many component types so that current production includes static Random Access Memories (RAMs), dynamic RAMs, microprocessors, and microcontrollers, among others. In addition, much higher densities of patterns can now be engraved on the silicon wafer by exploiting new technology developments. The company is simultaneously producing chips using three fundamentally different technologies, each having differing processing characteristics and yields. Thus, summary measures of numbers of wafers and chips produced or units

assembled and tested no longer reflect the varying diversity and complexity of the output. This tends to distort output and productivity measures.

This output measurement problem has been recognized by management but a solution is still in the experimental stage. A complex normalized measure of output, called an equivalent functional chip, has been developed that controls both for the shrinking size of each chip (when using the more advanced technology) and for the density of the patterns given the chip size (to control for the alternative functions a chip could perform). Manufacturing managers consider this normalized measure more representative of actual output but other managers are reluctant to reduce their reliance on the simpler and more familiar measures that sum up the actual wafers, chips, and finished units produced, regardless of the technology or function of the units. The episode is an example where a company has made great advances in its product and manufacturing technology, but has been slower to update its measurement and control system to be consistent with the new product and process environment.

The use of a simple sum of diverse and noncomparable items had also created a problem in measuring production activity. Initially, wafer output was used as an indicator of production activity. As the diversity and complexity of wafers increased, simple counts of wafer capacity or wafers produced were no longer meaningful. Some wafers can be produced rapidly and in great quantities while the more complex and dense wafers require both many more processing stages and increased time at each stage. Therefore, six years ago, the company changed its production measure from counting wafers to counting the number of activities required to produce each type of wafer. The basic unit of production was defined to be one wafer processed through one machine stage. Complex wafers have many machine processing stages; simple wafers have only a few. Thus processing complex wafers to completion requires more "activities" than to complete simple wafers. Manufacturing output each month is measured by a simple (unweighted) sum of the number of activities accomplished (total number of wafers processed through each major machine process).

Unfortunately, problems with this measure

arise because of the enormous variation in the complexity of activities. An easy step in wafer production has a throughput of 300 wafers in an hour (an output rate of 300 activities/hour) whereas a complex printing process requires 8 hours to finish one wafer (a rate of only .125 activities/hour). When the time to accomplish a unit of activity varies by more than three orders of magnitude, it is unlikely that an unweighted sum of all activities accomplished can be a useful measure of the production output from different facilities.

Again, some normalized measure of production activity, to reflect the great variation in time and complexity of different stages in the wafer production process, would seem to provide a better summary both of production capacity in a facility and of the actual production accomplished in a period. As an extreme case, perhaps only one or two stages of a 40-stage fabrication process may be limiting the output of finished wafers: that is, these one or two stages represent bottleneck resources. At a time when potential sales are considerably in excess of production capacity (the situation from mid-1983 up through the present time in March 1984), these bottleneck resources should become the focus of all managers' attention. Unlike the previous situation, however, where a new summary product measure was being developed, the managers of Company M were still using the old summary measure of total activities accomplished each period to monitor and evaluate production performance. It is another example where a measurement system developed for one environment was not modified when production technology and market conditions changed.

A third measurement issue also became obvious for the first time during 1983 when sales began to exceed production capacity. Product yield had historically been used as the key measure of manufacturing effectiveness and becomes even more critical when demand exceeds current capacity. But other factors that increase production rates should also be highlighted for managerial attention. Improved use of bottleneck resources is one such factor, as discussed in the preceding paragraphs. Another factor is to obtain maximum use of equipment by avoiding unscheduled downtime. Indicators of unscheduled downtime and percentage of working hours without unscheduled equipment downtime had only been recently formulated and

had not yet become a permanent part of the reporting system. Thus the measurement system was slow to provide information on machine availability, a key target now for management attention and control.

These examples illustrate an underlying theme that has emerged throughout this article. Managerial accounting systems which have been maintained in isolation from changes in the organization and technology of a firm's manufacturing processes become obsolete. They no longer can provide relevant information for management decisions and control.

DISCUSSION

Let us summarize the incidents we found in the four companies. The electrical propulsion division of Company V had completely reorganized its manufacturing operations. The benefits from this reorganization were impossible to quantify, however, since the accounting system accumulated only total project costs. Thus, per-unit reductions in labor hours and average inventory levels could not be determined. Nor could we learn whether the introduction of a model shop, to build a few prototypes and debug product designs and manufacturing techniques, succeeded in flattening out the learning curve.

Company N had made great progress within a short time period to achieve its goal of a Just-in-Time Inventory System. Set-up times, batch sizes, material travel distances, WIP and raw material inventory, product throughput times, and space requirements had been greatly reduced, some by remarkable percentages. Yet the company was still using a standard cost system based on highly detailed and frequently obsolete labor assignments. Actual product costs had to be calculated by a separate process that was still under development. A systematic reporting system had yet to be established to monitor progress on reducing inventory levels or in the cost reductions that were the consequence of inventory reduction activities.

The cost accounting system in Division S (of Company H) allocated all costs to departments and products through a burden rate on direct labor hours, even though direct labor represented less than 10 percent of total manufacturing costs. The focus on direct labor hours was accompanied with excessive growth and inefficient use of nondirect personnel. Some evidence of distortions in make-vs.-buy decisions, in the use of scarce capital (such as clean room space), and in the resources used to record and process direct labor time also were associated with the cost allocation procedure.

Company M relied much less on financial measures to monitor its manufacturing performance. But even with its extensive use of direct physical measurements, the periodic management reporting system was not revised responsively when major changes in product characteristics, process technology, and the market environment made the critical measures in the system unrepresentative of current conditions.

These examples were not isolated instances designed to provide support for a prior hypothesis of an accounting lag phenomenon. These companies and divisions were chosen because we knew they were innovative manufacturers and therefore offered the best hope for finding either new management accounting procedures or new procedures to integrate management accounting personnel closer to the production environment. In fact, three of the companies were in the process of making experimental changes in their accounting and control systems, but these changes were lagging their innovations in the organization and technology of manufacturing operations.

I have also talked with senior partners active in the manufacturing consulting practice of four of the "Big 8" public accounting firms. They confirmed the view that corporations have been slow to modernize their cost accounting systems. Other companies that I am talking to or working with also fail to provide instances of innovative or responsive management accounting systems. A division controller in one company indicated that not only were the cost accounting systems of the 13 plants in his division incompatible with each other, but that he would classify 9 of them as below a minimal level of adequacy.[5] In another company I visited, a company with a deserved reputation for product excellence and customer service, the major financial controversy was on the allocation of company profits to manufacturing plants, even though the plants were totally managed as cost centers. An effort was just underway to develop improved measures of manufacturing performance, such as timeliness, quality,

and inventory management, but this effort had been sidetracked until the role of manufacturing plant "profitability" could be settled.

Therefore, a primary goal of this exploratory investigation was not realized. I had hoped to be able to document the incidence and value of innovative accounting and control systems for the new industrial competition; to learn how firms making major changes in their manufacturing operations were developing and using measures of quality, inventory reductions, manufacturing flexibility, employee morale and abilities, productivity, and new product effectiveness. Instead I found that changes in accounting procedures lag far behind changes in the real production phenomena they are supposed to represent. Indeed, the cost accounting systems seemed inadequate even for traditional operations, much less for the new production processes being introduced by innovating companies.

The demand for changes in management accounting systems can only accelerate in the years ahead. Seventy-five years ago, the emphasis was on using direct labor and materials efficiently. The cost accounting systems developed at that time, and which have persisted until today, reflected this goal by keeping detailed records of direct labor and inventory. With the new organization and technology of manufacturing operations, variable direct labor and inventory are vanishing from the factory. Cost accounting systems should reflect this phenomenon and start to provide meaningful, detailed costs on the capital and knowledge worker inputs that are much more critical to manufacturing success than being able to keep track of and allocate all costs to direct labor.

Existing cost accounting systems will become even more obsolete as companies invest further in computer-integrated manufacturing processes. With this technology, almost all relevant manufacturing costs become fixed costs; in fact, they are not only fixed, they are largely sunk costs because the expenditures on the equipment and on the extensive software required to operate this equipment must be incurred before production can ever begin. Attempting to manage virtually unmanned production processes with a cost accounting system designed to control direct labor costs will certainly provide an interesting new challenge to U.S. executives. Surely, however, there will be enough new challenges in the coming decades that we do not have to create unnecessary ones.

SUMMARY OBSERVATIONS

Companies are making fundamental changes in the organization and technology of their manufacturing processes. The four companies described in this article provide good examples of the new procedures and equipment for contemporary manufacturing operations. Set-up and lead times have been reduced by one and two orders of magnitude; microprocessor and other computer-controlled equipment acquired, installed, and made operational; personnel retrained to produce with greatly reduced defects and buffer inventory levels; much WIP inventory removed entirely; suppliers trained to deliver items 100 percent in conformance with specifications and just when needed; and large machinery modified and moved around to facilitate the smooth flow of products through the factory. Amidst all these changes, the one constant is the firm's management accounting system.

Relative to the real changes occurring in the firm's manufacturing operations, it would seem simple for accountants to change the way they move numbers around on their ledgers or in their computers. Transforming symbols should be easier than transforming real objects or motivating, educating, and training real people. Yet when manufacturing operations change, the last and most difficult component to change is the accounting system. Ironically, if the accounting system is not representative of actual operations, and not useful in understanding or controlling these operations, it has little other justification for existence. Why then do accounting systems lag so far behind the pace of change in the phenomena they purport to represent?

One reason for accounting lag may be the lack of adequate role models. Much of the impetus for the dramatic changes in the organization and technology of manufacturing operations came from observation of Japanese manufacturers. The experience of the CEO of Company N was typical of the reaction of many U.S. executives when they learned what leading Japanese firms could accomplish with a commitment to total quality control and zero inventory production systems. As this realization

sank in (either by direct observation of Japanese production techniques or from the competition of high-quality, low-priced Japanese products), alert U.S. manufacturers started to adapt innovative quality and inventory-reducing practices to their own operations. It seems, however, much more difficult to observe the details of Japanese accounting and control systems. Therefore, comparable examples of innovative accounting systems are not available to U.S. firms.

Other sources of innovation for U.S. manufacturers are the suppliers of computer-integrated manufacturing equipment such as robots, CAD CAM, flexible manufacturing systems, and cellular technologies. The analogous suppliers of accounting systems, such as the major public accounting firms, have not been quite as imaginative in devising new accounting systems for the contemporary manufacturing environment. Also, textbooks and articles on managerial accounting mostly employ the simple, static, single-product, single-stage, high direct labor model of manufacturing processes as articulated 75 years ago by the scientific management engineers. Therefore, even firms that recognize inadequacies in their existing management accounting systems do not have alternatives readily available to use in their place. Each firm has to innovate on its own rather than being able to share in the experiences of successfully innovating firms.

A *second* possible explanation for accounting lag is the prevalence of computer-based accounting systems. In theory, having an accounting system stored in a programmable computer should permit considerable flexibility for implementing changes. In practice, however, it seems difficult to modify accounting programs without risking damage to the entire transactions-based accounting system that provides the entries for the firm's financial and tax statements. Thus, complex and not easily modified computerized accounting systems provide a barrier to innovative and adaptive changes in the firm's managerial accounting system. Computerized systems supply efficient processing of transactions data but the potential flexibility from modifying instructions in stored programs is rarely achieved in practice.

One is also struck by the aggregation and simplifications built into existing computerized cost accounting systems. Many overhead cost categories (supervision, utilities, space charges, equipment and building depreciation, maintenance, data processing, production control, and setup costs, among others) are added together into a large overhead pool and allocated to products via a direct labor burden rate. Given the great and inexpensive calculating capabilities of computers, one must wonder why each major overhead cost category could not be allocated separately to products based on the demands each product places on each overhead resource and using an allocation basis appropriate for each overhead category.

I can only speculate on why simplistic assumptions were built into computerized cost systems. Computers were applied to cost accounting systems during the early to mid-1960s, shortly after achieving considerable success in automating financial transactions systems (payroll, accounts receivable, and accounts payable). By the 1960s, companies' products and processes were already extensive and complex. In order to allocate costs manually, to the myriad cost centers and products in the factory, plant accountants undoubtedly had to adopt simplifying practices such as large, aggregate and heterogeneous overhead pools and summary measures of production activity (direct labor hours or dollars). Thus, by the time MIS and programming specialists (trained in neither cost accounting nor manufacturing operations) showed up in the factory to develop a computerized cost accounting system, they encountered a system simplified to permit accounting clerks to manually allocate overhead costs to products. With cost accountants not realizing the enormous increase in calculating abilities of computers (or, also likely, not understanding the consequences of their simplifying cost allocation assumptions), and with MIS programmers not understanding the managerial relevance of product and process cost allocations, neither party was in a position to redesign the existing system; to keep overhead costs in disaggregate, homogeneous pools; and to allocate each overhead pool using an appropriate activity measure for that pool. Thus, we basically automated a manual cost accounting system and never got a chance to design a system that better reflected the causes and incidence of overhead costs.

Fortunately, some relief from the inflexibility and irrelevance of large, centralized cost accounting systems is now possible. The growing availability of inexpensive yet powerful personal computers (PCs) will permit much latitude for local initiatives to develop more relevant and responsive managerial accounting systems. Plant controllers can customize their internal reporting systems to aid the accounting, planning, and control requirements of manufacturing and plant managers. Ideally, much of the transactions data for the local accounting system can be obtained from the same system used to collect and report information for the companywide accounting system. Even if local PCs cannot access the centralized data base, however, the relevant data may still be entered manually and the processing and graphics capabilities of the PC used to prepare regular reports for shift supervisors and manufacturing and plant-level managers. One can be quite optimistic that the increased supply of inexpensive personal computers, excellent financial software packages, and computer-literate accounting personnel will permit much more innovation in local managerial accounting practices than was previously possible.

The role for divisional management will be to encourage such innovation and not put imaginative accounting personnel in a straitjacket by insisting that all internal financial reports be prepared in accordance with centralized accounting practices. It should be obvious that the traditional ways of measuring and motivating manufacturing performance are not adequate for the contemporary organization and technology of manufacturing operations. The alternatives to the traditional and accounting system, however, are not so obvious. A period of experimentation is needed to adapt managerial accounting practices to each company's and each factory's particular needs.[6] It is fortunate that low-cost, high-capacity local computing capacity is now available to permit such experimentation without compromising or jeopardizing the integrity of the transaction-based centralized system.

A *third* explanation for the lack of responsiveness of current accounting systems arises from the emphasis on financial accounting even among managerial accountants. Recall that most of today's cost accounting practices can be traced to the scientific management movement. The innovators of the scientific management movement were engineers, intimately involved in their company's manufacturing operations. In the past 70 years, however, the operation of the firm's accounting system has been delegated to professional accountants frequently separated from plant operations. During this time, there has been a great growth in the importance of the financial reporting system for external constituencies (stockholders, investors, lenders, public regulatory and tax authorities). The firm's accountants became more concerned with recording transactions and allocating costs in a consistent and objective manner for these external constituencies. They became removed from concerns as to whether the numbers they were objectively and consistently recording held any relevance for describing, motivating, and controlling the firm's manufacturing performance.

The emphasis on external reporting and the de-emphasis on internal relevance was also reflected in the academic training of accounting professionals. Educational programs, strongly influenced by the training demands of the public accounting profession, concentrate on financial accounting courses (introductory, intermediate, and advanced financial accounting, auditing, tax, financial accounting theory). These financial accounting, auditing, and tax courses have undergone major changes over the years in response to changes in the regulatory and legal environment. In contrast, cost accounting courses remain focused on the simple production model of the turn-of-the-century firm. Embellishments have been added to emphasize the importance of distinguishing fixed from variable costs, and the decision relevance of incremental and opportunity costs. But the greater complexity of manufacturing processes in the past 70 years has not changed the production model used to illustrate cost accounting practices. Certainly, the major innovations now underway in the organization and technology of manufacturing operations are hardly anywhere reflected in contemporary cost accounting courses and materials. Also, it would be unusual for an accounting major to take a course in production, manufacturing processes, or technology.

Thus, accounting students receive extensive training in external reporting requirements and innovations but virtually no training in contemporary manufacturing operations. Industrial companies aggravate this imbalance by frequently hiring their key financial people from public accounting firms. An alternative, but rarely followed, practice

would have firms promoting their manufacturing engineers and production supervisors into managerial accounting positions. Personnel with good technical backgrounds should not find it difficult to master the relevant features of the standard cost model, overhead allocations, variance analysis, and cost-volume-profit analysis. Promoting manufacturing engineers into responsible financial positions would generate a supply of personnel for operating the firm's internal measurement and control system who would be more comfortable with the underlying manufacturing operations. We could even hope that such personnel, knowledgeable about the technology and organization of manufacturing, could devise appropriate performance measures; in effect, to recreate the innovative environment that occurred earlier in this century when engineers were intimately involved both in redesigning the factory and in developing representative measurement systems. Also possible is for companies to increase the production expertise of their financial personnel by having them spend several years in operating positions.

One company we spoke with has instituted an imaginative program with a nearby university to train a new generation of management accountants. It has encouraged, and helped to finance, a joint undergraduate degree program between the industrial engineering and accounting departments. Students in this program will receive training both in contemporary manufacturing processes and in accounting, particularly management accounting. It is interesting to note that the large state university near the company, with one of the largest and finest accounting departments in the nation but with close ties to its public accounting firm constituency, was not receptive to instituting such a joint program on its campus.

The *fourth* and most important explanation for accounting lag, however, is that senior company management have not emphasized the need to improve the relevance and responsiveness of their management accounting systems. Top executives must recognize that they have complete control over choosing their measurement and control systems. The internal accounting procedures can and should be different from those used to prepare financial and tax statements. Also, the accounting system should be continually scrutinized so that it remains consistent with and relevant to current manufacturing technology and operations.

A strong recommendation from the case studies described in this article is that accounting personnel should be working much more closely with manufacturing managers and product and process engineers. When significant changes are made in manufacturing operations, the former accounting system will become obsolete. Rather than wait for confusing and misleading information to be produced from the old accounting system, it would be preferable for a new set of measures, aggregations, and allocations to be available simultaneously with the introduction of the new production procedures. This will require accounting and control personnel to be part of any task forces responsible for developing and implementing manufacturing process changes so that measurement systems can be developed that will be functional for the new manufacturing environment. In this way, firms will avoid the current practice where accounting measures and reports continue to be produced long after major changes have occurred in the environment for which they had been designed.

Accounting systems must serve the objectives of the firm. We do not have a universal accounting model that works well in all circumstances. While the choice of appropriate measures, aggregations, and allocations is an art, it is an art that must be practiced in conjunction with the strategic goals of the firm and in close communication with the rapid changes occurring in firms' manufacturing processes. This requires that the choice of an internal accounting system be made explicitly and simultaneously with the choice of a firm's corporate and manufacturing strategy.

REFERENCES

1 Robert S. Kaplan, "Measuring Manufacturing Performance: A New Challenge for Management Accounting Research," *The Accounting Review* (October 1983), pp.

686–705; Robert S. Kaplan, "The Evolution of Management Accounting," *The Accounting Review* (July 1984), pp. 690–718; Robert S. Kaplan, "Yesterday's Accounting Undermines Production," *Harvard Business Review* (July/August 1984), pp. 95–101.

2 Interestingly, the fully loaded shop labor rate was approximately $50 per hour, well in excess of the $30 per hour figure used to cost out engineering design time. It is a curious consequence of direct-labor burden cost systems to have an engineer's time priced below that of semi-skilled workers.

3 In principle, one could compare the total costs of two orders for the same propulsion units performed before and after the reorganization of the factory. In practice, one would be unable to disentangle the experience curve effects during each order, different material price discounts, and changes in the price level for material and labor. Also, working with only a single estimate of unit costs (computed as total project costs divided by number of units produced) gives the analyst no degrees of freedom to compensate for random, noncontrollable influences on costs. Also, lacking data on monthly production, one cannot determine the division's success in reducing average inventory levels.

4 Ridgway pointed out, three decades ago, the problems which arise from excessive focus on an inappropriate performance measure. V. F. Ridgway, "Dysfunctional Consequences of Performance Measurement," *Administrative Science Quarterly* (September 1956), pp. 240–247.

5 The incompatibility of cost accounting and management control systems of similar plants in the same division points out a hidden cost of growth through acquisition. As we understand better the rigidity of existing accounting systems, we can expect that growing by acquisition will likely lead to a division, or company, having multiple, noncomparable measurement systems in various plants. In contrast, internally generated growth gives companies the opportunity to install its preferred measurement system in newly established plants.

6 See, for example, the innovative practice of shifting direct labor to an overhead cost category for a production process where direct labor is less than 5 percent of total manufacturing costs. Rick Hunt, Linda Garrett, and C. Mike Merz, "Direct Labor Cost Not Always Relevant at H-P," *Management Accounting* (February 1985), pp. 58–62.

Does Your Company Need a New Cost System?

Robin Cooper

Almost a quarter of a century ago, Peter F. Drucker wrote "Managing for Business Effectiveness" for the Harvard Business Review.[1] *I don't know how much effect that article had then, but it has little or none today—and, in my opinion, that is a tragedy.*

Drucker argued that management's primary responsibility is "to strive for the best possible economic results from the resources currently employed or available." Then he exposed how ineffective cost accounting can obfuscate the route management should take to satisfy this responsibility. Drucker concluded his article with the following advice:

> "And while the job to be done may look different in every individual company, one basic truth will always be present: every product, every operation, and every activity in a business should, therefore, be put on trial for its life every two or three years. Each should be considered the way we consider a proposal to go into a new product, a new operation or activity."

The underlying message is clear. Every product should be reviewed to ensure that the company benefits from its production and distribution. Even if a firm is making an acceptable profit, management should still ensure that every product is making a profit or that there is a strategic reason for selling it at a loss (e.g., razor with blades).

In the past two decades, cost accounting has undergone few innovations. Practitioners have developed an "if it ain't broke, don't fix it" mentality, and academics have paid little attention to cost accounting.[2] The major changes that have occurred —the increased use of machine-hour and material-dollar costing—unfortunately do little to overcome the most serious problems in existing cost system designs.

In most companies, a product profitability analysis offers valuable insights into the sources of profits and losses. Such an analysis requires accurate measurement of each product's production and marketing costs. In most firms, the cost accounting system is expected to perform this task. Unfortunately, considerable evidence suggests that these systems fail to accurately report product costs, for two reasons. First, they were never designed to report accurate product costs; their primary objective was to report inventory values.[3] Second, they have not been modified as production processes have changed. These systems no longer adequately measure the flow of a firm's costs.[4] In effect, they are obsolete.

THE SYMPTOMS

To determine whether a firm's cost system is reporting accurate product costs and to guard against its obsolescence, management should periodically evaluate it. Managers should ask themselves, "Do I really know what my products cost?" Answering this question requires a detailed analysis of the firm's cost system—an expensive and time-consuming process. Fortunately, management can significantly reduce the risk of undertaking such an analysis unnecessarily by looking for symptoms that usually accompany a poorly designed or obsolete cost system. These are discussed in the following sections.

Products that are very difficult to produce are reported to be very profitable even though they are not premium priced. Not all products are easy to manufacture: some are new, and the work force is still learning how to make them; others are just inherently difficult to make. The second type provides a good test of how well a cost accounting system is operating. If the system is capturing the additional manufacturing costs, these difficult-to-manufacture products should either be selling at a premium or have low margins.

Reprinted from *Journal of Cost Management* (Spring 1987), pp. 45-49, with permission.

All too often, however, these complex products appear to be highly profitable. They may be sold at a small premium, reflecting the market's willingness to pay more for the product, but their reported product costs do not reflect the difficulty of manufacturing them. In this case, the cost system fails to capture actual costs and instead reports costs that reflect average levels of manufacturing difficulty.

Profit margins cannot be easily explained. Management should usually be able to identify why some products are more profitable than others. Factors that influence profitability include market share, quality differential, production process differences, and economies of scale. If the cost system is accurately reporting product costs, management should be able to explain the overall patterns of product profitability. If management cannot explain the pattern, yet believes it understands the market, the cost accounting system is probably to blame.

Some products that are not sold by competitors have high reported margins. If there is no simple explanation for this situation, the cost system may be at fault. It may be reporting phantom profits; the competitors' systems did not. Obviously, this explanation is invalid if the firm has such competitive advantages as patent protection, high brand recognition, or proprietary production processes.

If the competition purchases the firm's products, repackages them, and then resells them at a higher price, or as part of a larger order at the same price, these products are probably improperly costed and priced. Alternatively, if the competition goes out of its way to identify the firm as the sole source for these products, the competition believes that selling these products at the listed price is detrimental.

The results of bids are difficult to explain. Firms that commonly bid for business can sometimes use the outcomes of their bids to determine how well their cost accounting system is working. If management is unable to accurately predict which bids they are going to win, the cost system may be reporting inaccurate product costs. Management should look for bids that were either priced low to win or priced high and were expected to lose. If the aggressively priced bids are frequently lost and the high-priced bids win, the cost system should be examined.

The competition's high-volume products are priced at apparently unrealistically low levels. When smaller competitors with no apparent economic advantage are pricing high-production-volume products at very low levels and are simultaneously making good returns, the cost system is the prime suspect. Cost systems tend to report averaged costs. High-volume products are inherently less expensive to produce than low-volume products, and most cost systems fail to accurately account for this difference. In fact, high-volume products are usually overcosted and low-volume products are undercosted. Smaller companies that manufacture fewer products, however, often suffer less distortion and therefore have a better understanding of their product costs.

Even if cost-plus pricing is not used, this volume-based distortion of reported product costs can be a very serious problem. Because the low-volume products appear more profitable, the full-line producer is tempted to concentrate on them and leave the high-volume products to the focused competitors. If the cost system is distorting the source of profits, the firm could be chasing imaginary profits and the profitability may be slowly deteriorating. This deterioration may be difficult to explain because no clear competitive disadvantage exists and no changes in the fundamental market structure have been made.

Vendor bids for parts are considerably lower than expected. Parts are often put out to bid because they appear to be too expensive to manufacture in-house. If vendors' bids on these parts are much lower than expected given the estimated production economies involved, the cost system may be at fault.

Cost information plays an important role in make-or-buy decisions. Unfortunately, conventional cost systems cannot provide the appropriate cost data. In particular, these systems fail to accurately specify the amount of overhead that is actually avoided by buying. They overestimate the savings, thus favoring the buy decision. When this bias is coupled with the overestimation of production costs, the buy decision might be adopted too frequently.

Customers ignore price increases, even when there is no corresponding increase in cost. When prices increase, customers usually react negatively. If there is little or no reaction, the cost system may be underestimating product costs. This concern is increased if the competition's prices also increase and the firm is not the price leader.

If customers don't complain, they were probably paying less for the product than its perceived value. If competitors also raise their prices, they may have been aware that the product was underpriced but wanted another firm to take the risk of increasing prices. For cost-plus pricers, the apparent excess profitability is the final clincher. By supplying costs that were too low, the system caused management to underprice the product in the first place. These symptoms can be detected only if the cost system is reporting product costs that are significantly incorrect. This occurs only if the design of the cost system is badly flawed.

THE DESIGN FLAWS

Cost accounting systems can be flawed in several ways. The flaws discussed in this section are very common and can result in a significant distortion in reported product costs.

Only direct labor hours (or dollars) are used to allocate overhead from cost pools (cost centers) to the products. The dependence on direct labor can be traced to the very origins of cost accounting. At the end of the last century, managers installed elaborate direct labor measurement systems to keep the direct labor force productive. The designers of early cost accounting systems took advantage of these systems and adopted direct labor hours for all allocation purposes, even when other bases would have been just as effective. At that time, this simplification was acceptable because manufacturing processes were highly labor-intensive, overhead was a smaller percentage of total cost, and product diversity (i.e., the range of different product cost structures) was lower. Under such conditions, the quantity of direct labor in a product was generally a reliable measure of the total value added.

Today, direct labor costs are usually less than 10 percent of the total production cost of the product, whereas overhead is more than 30 percent of total cost. No longer are direct labor hours necessarily a good predictor of the value added to a product. Nevertheless, most cost systems still rely heavily on direct labor hours to allocate costs to the products.

Only volume-related allocation bases (e.g., labor hours, machine hours, and material dollars) are used to allocate overhead from cost pools to products. These bases assume that the cost of producing a production lot is directly proportional to the number of items in that lot. This assumption is correct for volume-related activities (e.g., direct labor, production supplies, and parts) but not for such non-volume-related costs as inspection, setup, or scheduling. These costs vary with the number of inspections performed, the number of setups, and the quantity of scheduling, respectively.

Allocating a non-volume-related cost requires the selection of an allocation base that is itself non-volume-related. In manufacturing processes whose percentage of non-volume-related costs is high, cost systems using only volume-related bases produce inaccurate product costs. The error in reported product costs increases significantly if products are manufactured in highly varied lot sizes. Many non-volume-related costs depend on the number of lots being manufactured. Traditional cost systems usually undercost the small-volume production lot products and overcost the high-volume production lot products.

The early designers could ignore this problem for two reasons. First, the percentage of non-volume-related costs was much smaller. Consequently, the error in reported product costs from using only volume-related allocation bases was much lower. Second, a single facility typically manufactured a smaller range of products in less diverse lot sizes. Today, the percentage of non-volume-related costs is high and often accounts for about 25% of total production costs. Therefore, low-production-volume products may be significantly undercosted, whereas high-volume products are slightly overcosted. This distortion in the reported product costs also distorts the strategy selected by the firm. Low-volume products appear to be more profitable than they really are, tempting management to focus incorrectly on low-volume, specialty business.

Cost pools are too large and contain machines that have very different overhead cost structures. This problem is caused by simplifications made by the early designers. First, the production processes that they dealt with were much simpler than today's; although different machines might have been used in the process, within each major step the machines tended to have similar overhead cost structures. This allowed each step to be treated as a cost center without a major distortion in reported product costs. Second, to minimize the number of calculations required to cost products, early designers kept the number of cost centers as low as possible. This constraint reflected the high cost of performing calculations in a precomputer society.

Because of extensive automation, cost centers now contain a mixture of conventional and automated machines. This guarantees the reporting of distorted product costs. Although automated machines generally have higher overhead costs than their conventional counterparts, they require less labor. The cost system charges each product an average overhead charge that is too high for conventional machines and too low for automated machines. Products manufactured on labor-intensive conventional machines are allocated a higher proportion of the overhead costs than they warrant.

The cost of marketing and delivering the product varies dramatically by distribution channel, and yet the cost accounting system effectively ignores marketing costs. Cost accounting principles are applied only to production costs; other costs (e.g., marketing) are ignored and treated as single line items. This omission reflects the domination of the inventory valuation objective in cost accounting. Although production costs can be inventoried under generally accepted accounting principles, marketing costs must be treated as a period cost and written off. Therefore, marketing and distribution costs are not allocated to products by conventional accounting systems.

Many firms currently sell their products through a multitude of distribution channels, and the costs associated with these channels can be as high as 25 percent of total cost. For example, one channel might require a specially trained sales force that frequently calls the customer before the sale is made, whereas in another channel the customer can simply call and place an order. Obviously, the cost of doing business in the two channels is very different, but if the firm is trying to maximize gross margin, this difference is ignored. Cost accounting systems similarly ignore a wide range of selling and administrative expenses because they are period costs. If these costs differ systematically by product or product line, using gross margin to rank products is a dangerous technique.

CONCLUSION

Distorted knowledge of product costs makes it difficult for management to know how to best employ the resources available and, in Drucker's terms, satisfy its primary responsibility. Unfortunately, although it is relatively easy to prove that a cost system is reporting inaccurate product costs, it is extremely difficult to prove that the firm is suffering because of it. No business decision depends solely on product costs; product cost information is commonly used in decisions that rely on a wide range of information.

The symptoms of reliance on distorted costs can be used to determine whether the cost system needs redesigning. This approach is advantageous because it is relatively fast and inexpensive. It is not, however, a perfect test. First, the symptoms are not always easy to detect, and the inability to detect them does not guarantee that the firm is not suffering. Second, there are several competing explanations for each symptom, and it is not always possible to rule them out. The risk of unfairly blaming the cost system can be reduced by determining whether it suffers from one of the more common design flaws.

It is not sufficient just to check for the design flaws. There is no easy way of telling that the distortion in reported product costs is sufficient to cause problems. The level of distortion depends on the production process, the range of products produced, and the distribution channels used. It is the joint occurrence of the symptoms with the flaws that heralds the need for a new cost system.

NOTES

1 P.F. Drucker. "Managing for Business Effectiveness." *Harvard Business Review* (May-June 1963): 33–60 (Reprint No 63303).

2 R.S. Kaplan. "The Evolution of Management Accounting." *Accounting Review* (July 1984): 390–418.

3 H.T. Johnson and R.S. Kaplan. *Relevance Lost: The Evolution of Management Accounting* (Boston: Harvard Business School Press, 1987); R. Cooper and R.S. Kaplan. "How Cost Accounting Systematically Distorts Product Costs." *Harvard Business School Working Paper.* (1986).

4 R.S. Kaplan. "Yesterday's Accounting Undermines Production." *Harvard Business Review* (July-August 1984): 95–101 (Reprint No 84406).

RECOMMENDED READING

R.G. EILER, W.K. GOLETZ, and D.P. KEEGAN. "Is Your Cost Accounting System Up to Date?" *Harvard Business Review* (July-August 1982): 133–139 (Reprint No 82403).

M.J. SANDRETTO. "What Kind of Cost System Do You Need?" *Harvard Business Review* (January-February 1986): 110–118 (Reprint No 85113).

Flexible Manufacturing Systems:
Cost Management and Cost Accounting Implications

George Foster and Charles T. Horngren

Firms are increasingly adopting flexible manufacturing systems (FMSs) as one approach to gaining a competitive advantage. Industrial marketing consultants are forecasting an expansion in the use of FMSs in a diverse set of industries over the next decade. This article examines the cost management and cost accounting implications of adopting an FMS. The research underlying the analysis includes plant tours and interviews with the managements of firms implementing FMSs, and also with vendors of FMS equipment. Twenty-five firms in the United States and the United Kingdom were interviewed over a six-month period.

An FMS is an integrated system for the automatic random processing of work units through various work stations in the system. Key elements in a FMS include the following:

- Automated material handling;
- Semi-independent work stations; and
- A network of supervisory computers.

Setup times are minimal in many FMSs; in the extreme, a batch size of one is possible.[1]

General Dynamics, in Forth Worth, Tex., is an example of an FMS. This facility, which machines over 80 different parts for the F-16 aircraft, consists of the following:

- Six, five-axis machining centers. Each machine is equipped with a 114-tool magazine.
- Two coordinate measuring machines.
- Automated stores, transport, billet preparation, and work-piece handling.

This plant can be (and sometimes is) run totally unstaffed. When raw material is delivered to the start of the process, the material can be machined and inspected without any human intervention. The entire manufacturing system is integrated through a single common data base. There is an automated interface that "links engineering and manufacturing, including automated process planning, automated numerical control, manufacturing resource planning, and an advanced, paperless shop floor control system."[2]

Terminology.   "Flexible manufacturing system" is an umbrella term that covers a broad variety of specific applications. These include the following:

- Flexible assembly systems;
- Flexible fabrication systems;
- Flexible machining systems; and
- Flexible welding systems.

Reprinted from *Journal of Cost Management* (Fall 1988), pp. 16-24, with permission.

Key characteristics of many of these applications include the ability to process many variations within a single-product family and the ability to make rapid extensions of an existing product line.[3]

Organizations differ in the use of the terms flexible manufacturing *cell* (FMC) and flexible manufacturing *system* to describe their facilities. Generally, a *cell* is a smaller site than a *system*. However, the criteria used to make this distinction differ. One criterion is based on the absolute scale of activity. Using this criterion, the dividing line between an FMC and an FMS might be, for example, whether the cost exceeds $5 million or not. Alternatively, the cutoff could simply be the number of machines (e.g., four or more for an FMS and less than four for an FMC). A second criterion is based on the relative importance of the flexible manufacturing activities at the plant relative to total activities at the plant. Thus, the flexible manufacturing center at one aerospace company's plant is called an FMC because it takes up less than 10 percent of the total floor space of the plant. Nonetheless, several other companies with standalone flexible machine centers that were actually smaller than the one at the aerospace company called their centers FMSs.

Industry Adoption of FMS.   Exhibit 1 presents European statistics on FMS adoption. The most widespread adoption is in Germany, the United Kingdom, France, and Italy. Light automotive and heavy automotive are the most frequent industry adopters. Adoptions in these industries typically are either in machining of parts or assembly of engines or bodies.

Exhibit 1.   FMS adoptions in Europe

A. GEOGRAPHIC DISTRIBUTION

COUNTRY	NUMBER OF SYSTEMS
Germany	35
United Kingdom	33
France	20–30
Italy	25
Holland	2
Belgium	2

B. INDUSTRY BREAKDOWN INDUSTRY	PERCENT BY NUMBER OF FMSS
Light automotive (Cars, motorcycles)	20%
Heavy automotive (Tractor, truck, bus)	14
Auto Parts	9
Aerospace	9
Machine tools	9
Other mechanical equipment	8
Other mechanical engineering	7
Other	24
	100%

SOURCE: *Flexible Manufacturing and Machining Systems Markets in Europe* (London, UK: Frost & Sullivan, 1984).

Evidence regarding FMS adoptions in the United States is in Exhibit 2. Machinery, transportation equipment, and electrical/electronics are the three industries with widespread FMS adoption.[4]

A Japanese survey on FMS adoption ranked the following industries in terms of level of introduction:

1. Transport equipment;
2. Electrical equipment;

Exhibit 2.   FMS adoptions in United States

INDUSTRY	USING FLEXIBLE MANUFACTURING CELL	USING FLEXIBLE ASSEMBLY SYSTEM	USING FLEXIBLE MANUFACTURING SYSTEM	TOTAL
Fabricated metal parts	2	—	2	4
Machinery	8	3	22	33
Electrical/ electronics	1	7	2	10
Transportation equipment	9	15	20	44
Total	20	25	46	91

SOURCE: *Flexible Manufacturing Systems (FMS) Markets in the U.S.* (New York: Frost & Sullivan, 1985).

3. Shipbuilding;
4. Precision instruments;
5. Iron and steel; and
6. Fabrics and apparel.[5]

Dramatic differences between U.S. and Japanese FMS machining centers have been reported:[6]

	U.S.	JAPAN
Number of machines per system	7	6
Number of parts produced per system	10	93
Number of new parts introduced per year	1	22

An earlier survey of 26 U.K. machining centers reported that U.K. sites were more similar to U.S. sites (e.g., the mean number of parts produced per system was ten).[7]

MOTIVATIONS FOR ADOPTING FMS

Firms are adopting FMS for diverse sets of reasons. These reasons can be grouped into five general categories: cost, time, marketing, quality, and technology.

Cost Reasons. The sources of cost reduction include the following:
Lower inventory levels. This reduction occurs primarily via a reduction in work in process (because of reduced cycle or throughput time).
Reduced labor costs. Reductions both in direct labor (e.g., machine operators) and in indirect labor (e.g., materials handlers) have been reported. These labor categories are sometimes called "touch labor."
Reduced scrap and rework. Increased automation at some FMSs has been associated with increased first-time yield.
Reduced floor-space requirements. Reductions in required floor space of between 30 percent and 70 percent have frequently been reported at FMS installations.
Reduced information-tracking costs. The typical FMS installation has on-line computer collection and monitoring of information. This on-line capability can substantially increase the accuracy of information collected and reduce the number of people associated with information gathering.

Time Reasons. FMSs can reduce time in key areas of the cycle that starts with product design, then moves to product development, to manufacture, and then ends with delivery to the customer. These reductions can support a corporate strategy that emphasizes shorter times in all aspects of operations.

The time between product-design change and manufacture of the new design is relatively short in many FMSs. For example, flexible assembly lines for printed circuit (PC) boards can accommodate changes in the number of components in each board, in the length or width of each board, and in the percent of components automatically inserted. This ability to move rapidly from design change to manufacture reduces the time between a customer request for a new PC board and its delivery.

Sizable reductions in production-cycle times have also been reported at some FMS facilities. Consider flexible machining centers. Cycle-time reduction sources include the following:

1. The ability to route around bottlenecks and machine breakdowns;
2. Lower set up times,
3. Reduction in fixture and tooling errors; and
4. Reduced human intervention in all phases of manufacturing.

A company reported that the reduction of their production-cycle time from forty-five days to five days was accompanied by a large reduction in change-orders from their customers.

Marketing Reasons. Marketing reasons for investing in FMSs relate to either the products made on the FMS or the FMS products themselves. The marketing advantages of producing products on FMSs include:

• Shorter delivery times (see time-based reasons);
• The ability to maintain the production of low-volume products;
• The ability to make rapid changes in product mix and volume to accommodate market shifts; and
• Quicker introduction of new and modified products.

An example is the FMS installation by Remington

Arms Company, manufacturer of firearms equipment:

> "Capable of changing product mix in four hours instead of six days, the FMS makes it possible for the company to introduce new products in six months rather than the eighteen months previously required. This will enable the company to capture niche markets by producing small numbers of collector's items, and of recreating some of the company's classic discontinued lines, which could not be reproduced cost effectively on traditional manufacturing equipment."

The vendors of FMS equipment sometimes themselves use FMSs in their own manufacturing facilities. One rationale is to demonstrate to potential clients the applicability of this approach to manufacturing. A second rationale is to develop in-house consulting skills about FMS implementation problems and their solutions.

Quality Reasons. Many FMS facilities, once operational, can operate at very high first-time-through quality levels and can maintain high consistency levels with which parts are processed.

Technology Reasons. The use of advanced technology often creates or maintains a competitive advantage. Related reasons for adopting FMS include the desire to experiment with new technologies and the desire to be on the technology frontier.

POSITIVE CONSEQUENCES OF ADOPTING FMS

Evidence on the consequences of adopting FMS comes from several diverse sources. Twenty U.S. firms were surveyed, and they reported the following.[8]

- Reductions in direct labor ranging from 50 percent to 88 percent;
- Increases in machinery efficiency ranging from 15 percent to 90 percent;
- Reductions in production-cycle time ranging from 30 percent to 90 percent; and
- Reductions in floor space ranging from 30 percent to 80 percent

A survey of thirty U.K. engineering companies reported the following:[9]

- Mean reduction in production-cycle times of 74 percent;

- Mean reduction in work in process of 68 percent; and
- Mean increase in machine use from 40–50 percent with conventional machine tools to over 90 percent with FMS.

Many of the companies visited for the research underlying this paper reported similar dramatic gains associated with the adoption of FMS.

NEGATIVE CONSEQUENCES OF ADOPTING FMS

Four main classes of negative experiences have been reported:

1. *Cost related.* This class includes dramatic underestimation of the cost of installing the FMS, not being able to eliminate the labor time predicted in the proposal, and not achieving the planned machine use.
2. *Time related.* Long delays in making the FMS operational have been reported by several firms.
3. *Technology related.* This class includes breakdowns in hardware (e.g., automated guided vehicles (AGVs), machines, and tools) or software (e.g., tool record programs and system supervisory programs).
4. *Labor related.* Problems with labor unions were encountered at several firms visited. Firm X previously had a piece-rate labor incentive scheme based on individual worker productivity. Considerable delays in implementing the FMS occurred at firm X. Management attributed these delays to protracted negotiations over the form of the group based labor incentive scheme to be adopted at the FMS plant. At firm Y there was a six-month delay in implementing an FMS. This delay was attributed by management to problems in negotiating premium wage rates for the third shift per day that was not possible at the FMS plant.

FMS PLANNING AND COST INFORMATION

This section focuses on the reported role of cost information in (1) deciding how to install an FMS, and (2) deciding which products to process on an FMS facility.

Mix Between Internal Development and External Vendor. A key decision in planning an FMS is the mix between internal development and external vendors.[10] There can be minimal internal development. External vendors can provide "turnkey systems" in which all aspects of AGVs, machines, hardware, software, and personnel training are provided by external parties. Technical expertise of the vendors, past experience, and cost comparisons are key factors in deciding on the mix between internal development and external vendor.

Another factor reported as important by four companies was the accounting policy (capitalize versus expense) with respect to internal systems development costs. These four companies immediately expense such costs. This policy created a bias toward the use of external vendors over internal development; external vendor costs were all capitalized, resulting in lower current expenses.

Choice of Products to Process on FMS.

In many installations, decisions are made about which products to process on FMS facilities. Several companies reported that cost accounting issues influenced these decisions.

Example 1:   Company *XYZ* has over 1,000 products being processed at a facility. This facility has two production areas—a dedicated area and an FMS area. The dedicated area consists of many stand-alone machines that individually process a small range of products. The FMS occupies less than 20 percent of the total facility area but can process over 600 different products. *XYZ* produces many products on a cost-plus reimbursement contract basis. The contracts provided that burden costs were a stipulated dollar-rate per machine hour. At the dedicated facilities, both set up and metal cutting were done at the machines and were included in machine-time computation. In contrast, set up was done off line at the FMS and thus was excluded from the computation of machine time. In addition, the FMS machines had faster metal-cutting time. The consequence was a bias against switching products on a cost-plus base from the dedicated facility to the FMS facility. (An option here would have been to revise the cost-plus reimbursement contract. *XYZ* reported that the other parties to the contracts were not willing to revise one clause without renegotiating other clauses that *XYZ* viewed as favorable.)

Example 2:   Company *PQR* produced PC boards on a flexible assembly line using direct-insert technology. A second flexible assembly line using surface-mount technology was then added. *PQR* used separate overhead cost pools for each assembly line. All PC boards were produced for internal customers. These internal customers specified the PC board assembly mode. A factor affecting this decision was

the quoted cost, which was a function of direct material cost plus a budgeted overhead rate based on the number of components on each PC board. The direct-insert assembly line ran at over 90 percent capacity, whereas the surface-mount line rate ran at less than 20 percent capacity. The consequence was much higher overhead rates on the surface-mount line. These higher overhead rates created a bias against internal customers using the surface-mount line. *PQR* decided to exclude overhead costs on the quoted cost for surface-mount PC boards to encourage use of this assembly line. The result was that a sizable number of customers switched from direct-insert to surface-mount PC boards.

The previous two examples are *not* unique to FMS. They illustrate, however, that when new technologies are introduced, the existing cost accounting system can influence decisions made about their mode of implementation and their use.

FMS OPERATIONS MANAGEMENT AND COST INFORMATION

This section examines the role cost information plays in day-to-day operating decisions (e.g., the routing of individual jobs to machines and the size of production runs of each job).[11]

The allocation of jobs on an FMS is typically guided by a computer scheduling algorithm. Possible criteria for constructing these algorithms include the following:

- Time based (e.g., minimize throughput time);
- Machine based (e.g., maximize machine use); and
- Cost based (e.g., minimize short-run operating costs).

No firm interviewed reported that cost plays an explicit role in the algorithms used. The following algorithm at Vought Aero Products in its flexible machining site at Dallas illustrates the nonexplicit role of cost information:

> "The computer system selects enough work orders for a twenty-four-hour production run. The scheduler optimizes the twenty-four-hour period
> —to meet production schedule;
> —minimize cutter tool changes;
> —maximize machine use; and
> —to reserve a selection of parts with high machining times for fabrication on the unstaffed third shift."[12]

Simulation is often used to anticipate potential bottleneck situations in scheduling.

Our surveyed firms provided various reasons for the explicit exclusion of cost information in the scheduling algorithms, including:

- Nonfinancial variables were paramount in scheduling decisions. For example, time is critical for some jobs at a machining shop of an aerospace company—AOG (aircraft on ground) jobs are given highest priority
- Nonfinancial variables included in the scheduling algorithms were perceived to be good proxies for cost-related factors. Several manufacturing managers reported that maximizing machine use and minimizing tool changeovers were operational ways to minimize operating costs. They were, to use the current jargon, the operating cost drivers at an FMS.
- Belief that operating costs are relatively insensitive to changes in the scheduling algorithms. For instance, at several flexible assembly lines all units make similar usage of different assembly-line parts. If setup costs of each production run are minimal, operating costs will be little affected by variations in the production schedule.
- Belief that the existing cost accounting system measures operating costs imperfectly. Comments made here focused on existing depreciation costs as an imperfect measure of machine cost use.

There are numerous individual algorithms that can be used to schedule jobs on FMSs. An important unresolved issue is how to evaluate the chosen algorithm. Interviews disclosed no cases of firms doing systematic analysis of the cost implications of their chosen scheduling algorithm vis-à-vis alternative algorithms.

The computer database underlying many FMSs helps detailed cost planning. An example is the cost of cutting tools. With bar-coding of each cutting tool, a record can be kept of how long and on how many different jobs each cutting tool has been used. This information enables operating managers to resharpen or scrap tools prior to their breaking during machining. Anticipating breakdowns means that production time is not lost and rework on jobs damaged by tooling breakages is reduced.

An area in which the production literature suggests a role for cost information in operating management is determining the optimal batch size (OBS) for each production run of separate products. The assumption underlying OBS formulae is significant setup costs for each product run. A key aim of many FMS facilities is to eliminate setup costs so that a batch size of one is the unit of analysis. Not one manufacturing manager interviewed responded yes to the question of whether OBS computations are made. Indeed, several were adamant that the FMS approach to manufacturing was adopted to make OBS computations "a thing of the past."

FMS PERFORMANCE MEASURES AND COST INFORMATION

Many performance measures found in FMS sites are similar to those used in other highly capital intensive manufacturing environments. In addition, some sites have specific measures that capture a flexibility-related aspect of performance.

Cost Measures.   Materials costs are major operating cost components in many FMS sites. Material usage variances are a frequently encountered performance measure. One Japanese company with plants in Japan, the United Kingdom, and the United States uses the actual material usage at its most efficient plant in Japan as a materials performance benchmark at its non-Japanese plants. Inventory turnover ratios are also widely used—their use is consistent with inventory reduction being a major reason for FMS adoption by firms.

Many firms (but by no means all) report placing less emphasis on labor-based performance measures. A reason is the reduction in the relative percentage of labor costs to total costs at most plants. Indeed, in some cases the FMS can operate in a completely unstaffed mode. The following productivity measure, used at one plant visited, was reported as causing problems:

$$\frac{\text{Good units produced for finished goods}}{\text{Actual direct labor dollars}} \times \frac{\text{Standard direct}}{\text{labor dollars per unit}}$$

The criticisms made by existing management of this measure included: (1) It focuses only on direct labor costs and not total manufacturing costs; and (2) the use of good units produced rather than good units sold means that management can improve the measure by producing for inventory.

Time Measures.   As noted previously, time criteria are included in many scheduling algorithms. Time-related variables are included in the performance measures used in some FMS sites (e.g., schedule attainment and throughput time). Some time-related performance measures are tied to key goals of FMS facilities. For instance, in several aerospace machining shops, measures of responsiveness time for AOG time are monitored.

Quality Measures. Two key quality performance measures in some FMS sites are (1) first-time-through quality percentage and (2) rework and scrap percentage and dollar trends. Within several sites, there is increased focus on quality performance measurement of subcomponents and at interim stages of the production line. A benefit of this focus is that the dollar amount of work in process tied up in quality testing is reduced: There is no waiting until the final production step before quality testing.

Operating Performance Measures. The definition of an FMS previously given noted that a key element is a "network of supervisory computers." Many aspects of the production process are monitored by this network of supervisory computers. Explicit performance measures related to the production process found in practice include:

Systems downtime percentage. These percentage figures frequently are reported for each subarea (e.g., AGVs, tooling, setup, and machining) along with explanations for the downtime.

Systems usage percentages. The utilization rates for individual areas are frequently monitored, in part to anticipate bottleneck problems.

Flexibility Measures. Performance measures used at three plants that relate to flexibility are product switch-over-times at machines and number of different products manufactured. At some U.S. FMS plants, there was little or no emphasis on producing a large number of different products. Indeed, two companies reported using their FMS is the initial year to manufacture their highest volume products. Their rationale was that these were the products they had the most "experience" in manufacturing. (This is consistent with Jaikumar's finding that U.S. FMS plants average ten products per system compared to ninety-three products per system for Japanese plants.[13])

A major concern of managers at two companies was the failure of their existing performance measures to reinforce the original motivations underlying adoption of the FMS. Of particular concern was the lack of explicit emphasis on time and flexibility measures when in the initial FMS approval these factors were given much emphasis.

PRODUCT COSTING IN FMS SETTINGS

Reported changes fall into one or more of the following categories:

- Changes in components of direct costs;
- Changes in the allocation of indirect costs; or
- Changes in the costs treated as period costs.

Subsequent subsections illustrate responses in each of these three categories.[14]

Changes in Components of Direct Costs. Respondents indicated two movements in the components of direct costs: (1) a movement of a cost item from the indirect to the direct category, and (2) a movement of a cost item from the direct to the indirect category.

The network of computers that are an integral part of many FMSs aids the tracing of costs to individual products. In some traditional machining shops, cutting tools have been classified as indirect costs and allocated to individual products via a single overhead rate. When an FMS was adopted, however, the costs of cutting tools used only for machining an individual product could be easily traced to that product. Two machining shops reported switching the classification of these cutting tools costs from the indirect to the direct cost category.

The labor component of total operating costs is often reduced when firms switch from dedicated facilities to an FMS. Indeed, several facilities we visited can operate their facilities in a completely unstaffed mode. Changes observed in direct labor reporting were all in the direction of simplification or elimination. Simplification was achieved by either:

- Reducing the number of labor categories; or
- "Passive vouchering" as opposed to "active vouchering." ("Active vouchering" is when each hour of direct labor is recorded in the internal accounting system. "Passive vouchering" is when there is only recording of hourly labor times in the internal accounting system when direct labor is not engaged in its primary activity.)

Those facilities eliminating the direct labor category either included labor costs as a part of manufacturing overhead or expensed labor costs to the current period.

The elimination (or at least reduction) of piece-rate labor incentive schemes at the time FMSs are implemented explains the reduction in labor categories at some plants. At one plant, for example, a change from individual piece rates to group-based labor incentive rates was associated with a reduction of labor rate categories from twenty-eight to five. This reduction considerably reduced the costs of maintaining labor records in the internal accounting system.

Changes in Allocation of Indirect Costs. There is considerable diversity across FMS facilities in the bases used to allocate indirect costs to products. Flexible machining facilities typically use direct labor hours (dollars) or machine hours as the allocation base. The rationales most frequently offered for direct labor hours as an allocation base were "tradition" and "the desire of the company to have a single product costing system." No firms making changes in the allocation base(s) changed from a non-labor-based to a labor-based base. The most common change made (or being considered) was a switch to machining hours as the allocation base. The main concern with the machine-hour allocation base was operationally defining a machine hour. Individual machines can differ in their cost and cutting speed. Although no firms interviewed had created separate overhead pools for each different class of cutting machine, several were conducting special studies to measure the effect on reported product costs of a move in this direction.

Direct labor hours (dollars) is the most frequently used base for allocating indirect manufacturing costs in the flexible assembly facilities we visited. Movement away from this basis was reported by several flexible assembly shops for PC boards. In one case, the assembly line was divided into eleven separate overhead cost pools, and separate bases were used for each of the cost pools. For example:

OVERHEAD COST POOL	ALLOCATION BASE
Automatic insertion of integrated circuits	Number of inserts per board
Wave soldering	Number of boards

Two motivations were given for making these changes: (1) To signal to PC board product designers the relative cost of the design options available, and (2) to set prices that "better reflect" the different costs of assembling different PC boards for both external and internal customers.

Changes in the Costs Treated as Period Costs.
Two flexible assembly facilities visited traced only direct materials to each product. In both cases, the facility was relatively new and the product costing system implemented represented a change from that used at other facilities of these two companies.

Example 1: Company R operates an assembly line for electrical equipment. There are approximately 700 different product variations assembled (although there are only two different product facilities). The production run time for each unit is less than one hour. The following reasons were given for expensing to the period all costs except direct materials:

- Cost plays no role in pricing. They accept the world market prices as a given.
- Individual products vary little in their use of the manufacturing overhead; detailed tracing of overhead costs to different products was believed to yield no new insights.
- Company R holds no inventory. It uses just-in-time purchasing so that materials are delivered each day. It produces to demand. As goods are completed, they are immediately shipped to distributors.

Company R has excess capacity at the plant and has not yet faced decisions about allocating scarce production facilities to individual products.

Example 2: Company S manufactures large-scale machines for metal cutting. There are five main types of machines assembled; the production-cycle time averages twenty-one days. Materials costs are the only costs traced to each individual machine being assembled. All other manufacturing costs are directly expensed to the period. Materials costs were said to be a "small" percentage of total manufacturing costs. Company S puts high emphasis on managing capacity so that they do not face the problem of rationing among potential consumer demand. Management strongly believed that manufacturing costs were not a key factor in setting prices. They face a highly competitive market where the ratio of variable operating costs to selling price was "relatively low." Given this situation, they reportedly did not look at their cost structure when deciding whether to drop, for example, the price of a machine 5 percent to match a competitor's price.

Reasons for not making changes in product costing systems. Respondents not making changes in their product costing systems, associated with introduction of FMS, gave one or more of the following reasons:

1. The FMS site is small relative to the total manufacturing operations and the company wishes to have a single cost system that is used in all facilities.

2. External obstacles exist to making changes in the product costing system. The U.S. Department of Defense was the most frequently cited external obstacle. A similar response was reported in a survey of whether Department of Defense contractors are changing their costing systems when new manufacturing technologies are adopted.[15]

3. Cost accounting is not viewed as a high-priority investment area (e.g., one controller commented that "the most we ever do is to take the existing costing system and bend it"). One company official, in the midst of a merger, commented that "at this stage, merging two disparate cultures is higher priority than changing the cost accounting system in our two FMS plants."

4. The existing product costing system was considered satisfactory, with no indication that it was producing misleading signals. There can be two explanations for this no-feedback situation:

• The existing system provides adequate product cost information; or
• There are not effective feedback mechanisms about potentially inadequate product cost information.

A visited plant provides a possible example of the latter. The plant is a flexible machining shop for crankshafts used in outboard engines. This shop is the sole supplier to an internal engine assembly division (located 1,000 miles away). This machining shop has no external customers and no other internal customers. Hence, there are no routine market prices for judging the cost of crankshafts at either the machining shop or the assembly division. Market prices often supply helpful feedback for evaluating whether cost figures are potentially misleading.

CONCLUSION

There is considerable diversity in the types of manufacturing plants adopting FMS and in the size of the FMS site relative to the firm's other manufacturing sites. As expected, there is not a single blueprint about how cost management and cost accounting practices are affected by the adoption of FMS. This conclusion is similar to that found in our earlier research on the adoption of just-in-time purchasing or just-in-time production approaches.[16]

The reasons underlying the adoption of FMS invariably involve one or more of the following: cost, time, marketing, and quality. Many managers interviewed reported concern that there be greater consistency between the motivations underlying FMS adoption and operating management methods (including the performance measures used to evaluate activities and managers of those activities).

Firms adopting flexible machining systems had the most homogeneous responses regarding changes in cost management and cost accounting. Most changes included all or most of the following:

1. A reduction in the importance of labor variances;

2. The elimination of labor as a direct cost category; and

3. Increasing use of machine hours to allocate some or all indirect costs to products.

Firms adopting flexible assembly systems have experienced relatively heterogeneous impacts on cost management or cost accounting. The most marked changes observed were in firms' assembling of printed circuit boards. These changes involved an increase in indirect cost categories and an increased focus on the cost drivers underlying the different activities in printed circuit board assembly.

NOTES

1 An introduction to FMS is in C. Young and A. Greene, *Flexible Manufacturing Systems* (New York: American Management Association, 1986).
Individual firm case studies are frequently published in *The FMS Magazine,* published by IFS (Publications), Bedford, United Kingdom. Research oriented articles are found in *The International Journal of Flexible Manufacturing Systems* (Dordrecht, Netherlands: Kluwer Academic Publishers).

2 G. Parker, "Implementation of an Advanced FMS at General Dynamics/Fort Worth Division," *FMS '87* (Long Beach, Cal.: Society of Manufacturing Engineers, 1987).

3 Further discussion of different modes of flexibility can be found in R. Kynast, "Flexibility in High Production Manufacturing," in *Flexible High Production Machining*

Systems (Dearborn, Mich.: Society of Manufacturing Engineers, 1987).

4 Frost and Sullivan, *Flexible Manufacturing Systems (FMS) Market in the U.S.* (New York: Frost and Sullivan, 1985). In their book they provide the following definitions underlying the distinctions in Exhibit 2:

- Flexible manufacturing cell (FMC)—"based on a machining center and usually includes a robot for material handling and a programmable controller" (p.10);
- Flexible assembly system (FAS)—"provide final assembly of parts . . . are dependent upon robots to make and join parts and subassemblies" (p.10);
- Flexible manufacturing system (FMS)—"includes multimachine centers or workstations that are programmed, coordinated and monitored by computer-aided controls and supported by a material handling system that delivers workpieces in real time and in any sequence required by current manufacturing operations" (p.1)

FMCs and FMSs are oriented in part manufacture while FASs are oriented towards final assembly of parts. FMCs can be expanded into FMSs.

5 S. Inoue, "Cost Management Problems for the Varied Low or Medium-Volume Productions in Japan," forthcoming in Y. Monden (ed.) *Japanese Management Accounting* (New York: Wiley, 1988).

6 R. Jaikumar, "Postindustrial Manufacturing" *Harvard Business Review* (Nov.-Dec. 1986), pp. 69–76.

7 J. Edghill and A. Davies, "FMS—The Myth and the Reality," *International Journal of Advanced Manufacturing Technology*," (September 1985). See also G. Avlonitis and S. Parkinson, "The Adoption of Flexible Manufacturing Systems in British and German Companies," *Industrial Marketing Management* (1986).

8 Frost and Sullivan, p. 9.

9 J. Bessant and B. Hayward, "FMS in Britain—good and bad news," *The FMS Magazine* (January 1986), p. 35.

10 The sizable literature on investment decisions related to FMS is summarized in W. Wallace and G. Thuesen, "Annotated Bibliography on Investment in Flexible Automation," *The Engineering Economist* (Spring 1987), pp. 247–257.

11 Survey evidence based on "an analysis of approximately 100 documented systems worldwide, enhanced by site visits in Great Britain" is in J. Edghill and C. Cresswell, "FMS control strategy—a survey of the determining characteristics," *Proceedings of the 4th International Conference on Flexible Manufacturing Systems* (Bedford, U.K.: IFS Ltd., 1985).

12 A. Roch, "Productivity by Design—FMS Applications That Work," *Flexible Manufacturing Systems '86* (Chicago, Ill.: Society of Manufacturing Engineers, 1986).

13 R. Jaikumar, pp. 69–76.

14 See also Chapter 4 of R. Bennett, J. Hendricks, D. Keys, and E. Rudnicki, *Cost Accounting for Factory Automation* (Montvale, N.J.: National Association of Accountants, 1987).

15 R. Howell, J. Brown, S. Soucy and A. Seed, *Management Accounting in the New Manufacturing Environment* (Montvale, N.J.: National Association of Accountants and Computer Aided Manufacturing—International, 1987).

16 G. Foster and C. Horngren, "Cost Management and Cost Accounting Implications of Just-in-Time," *Journal of Cost Management* (Winter 1988).

2

THE TWO-STAGE PROCESS: RESOURCES, COST CENTERS, AND PRODUCTS

Cost systems in manufacturing companies assign indirect factory expenses to products by a two-stage procedure.[1] The first stage of this procedure assigns indirect resource expenses to cost centers, and the second stage assigns the expenses accumulated in the cost centers to products. The objective of the first stage is to assign all the factory expenses, both support- (such as quality assurance and inventory management) and production-related (such as supervision and setup), to production cost centers. Some firms do the first-stage assignment in several substages, particularly when support department expenses are reassigned among themselves as well as to production departments.

The first-stage assignment is typically used for two purposes. First, the expenses assigned to cost centers are used to evaluate the performance of the cost center manager. Second, the accumulated production cost center expenses are assigned, in the second stage of the procedure, to products to satisfy financial reporting requirements for inventory valuation. In the second-stage process, the cost system designer must choose a measure for assigning production center expenses to products. This measure is called an *allocation base* if the assignment is an allocation, and a *cost driver* if an attribution is being attempted. Dividing the total cost of the center by the total budgeted quantity of the allocation base or cost driver for the center gives the center's burden rate. Overhead expenses are assigned to products by multiplying the burden rate of each cost center by the second-stage quantity measure of each product (e.g., its direct labor hours, or machine processing time in the cost center).

Algebraically, the two-stage process can be described by modifying the fundamental cost accounting equation ($C = P \times Q$) to allow for indirect tracing of expenses to products. Let Q' equal the assignment base used to assign cost center expenses to products. The price variable, P, is replaced by a burden rate, R, that measures the rate applied to the assignment base. For example, Q' could be the total number of direct labor hours (the assignment base) and R would be the direct labor burden rate. The

---

[1]Materials and labor expenses are typically assigned directly to products.

burden rate, R, is calculated as the total costs, C, to be assigned by the burden rate, divided by the quantity of the assignment base:

$$R = \frac{C}{Q'}$$

The amount, C, to be assigned from the cost center to products is determined by the first stage of the procedure. Assigning the expenses from cost centers to products, in the second stage, is performed by multiplying the burden rate, R, by the number of units, q', of the second-stage assignment base consumed by the product.

The structure of the first-stage assignment process varies in practice from simple to complex. Simple systems assign support department expenses with one or only a few bases; for example, direct labor, floor space, headcount, and departmental expenses. Many of these assignments are allocations because they fail to capture the actual consumption of support department resources by production cost centers. More complex systems attempt to implement direct charging for the first stage by getting actual measures of production departments' consumption of support department resources. By using direct charging or attribution more extensively, these systems reduce the number of allocations required for the first-stage process.

In contrast to the diversity of practice observed in the methods for first-stage assignment, the structure of the second stage of the process, from cost centers to products, is remarkably similar in traditional cost systems. Most systems either use the same basis for second-stage assignment for all cost centers (i.e., direct labor hours or direct labor dollars) or rely on a limited number of bases. Even systems that use more than one measure frequently rely on the same three bases: *direct labor* (hours or dollars) to assign labor-paced operations, *machine hours* to assign expenses associated with highly automated manufacturing processes, and *material dollars* to assign material-related support expenses to products.

While seemingly different, all the systems that use direct labor (hours or dollars), machine hours, and material dollars for second-stage assignments are similar in one important respect: All of these bases assign costs in proportion to the number of units of a product manufactured. That is, if a product's production volume increases by 10%, it will have 10% more labor hours, 10% more machine hours, and 10% more material dollars assigned to it. Consequently, the product will have 10% more overhead assigned to it no matter which base or which combination of bases is used by the company. We refer to all such proportional overhead assignment systems as *unit-based* systems because overhead costs are assumed to be proportional to the number of units of the product produced. Field research and surveys confirm that unit-based systems are prevalent in companies today. All the companies described in the cases in this chapter use unit-based systems.

The two-stage procedure introduces distortion into reported product costs in two different ways. *Price distortions* are introduced when the cost system design leads to incorrect burden rates, and *quantity distortions* are introduced when the expenses are assigned to products using an indirect measure that is not strictly proportional to the actual consumption of indirect resources by individual products.

Price distortion arises in the first stage when resource expenses are assigned to cost centers using procedures that do not capture accurately the consumption of the support resources by the cost centers. For example, if direct labor hours are used in the first stage to assign supervision expenses to cost centers, then cost centers that consume a lot of direct labor hours will be assigned a high proportion of supervision expenses, and centers that consume only a few direct labor hours will be assigned a low proportion of supervision expenses. If supervision resources are not consumed proportionately to direct labor hours, the amount of supervision expenses assigned to cost centers will be distorted. The performance measure of the cost center manager will be distorted and the burden rates, calculated from the expenses accumulated in the cost centers, will be inaccurate and will introduce distortions into reported product costs.

Price distortion can be reduced in two ways. First, more accurate assignment mechanisms can be used in the first stage; and second, more cost centers can be created to accumulate overhead and production support expenses. The first method increases accuracy by ensuring that the dollars assigned to the cost centers are closer to the expenses of resources demanded and consumed by activities at the cost center. For example, by using supervision hours to assign supervision costs to each center, the expenses of supervisory resources are assigned more accurately to the cost centers where supervisors are spending time and effort.

The second method, increasing the number of cost centers, increases accuracy by reducing the variety of production processes within each cost center. For example, if a cost center contains both automated and manual machinery, the supervision required per direct labor hour might vary depending on the type of machinery the direct labor force is operating. In particular, more supervision may be required, per direct labor hour, for the automated machinery. Using direct labor hours as the basis for second-stage assignment will introduce distortions into reported product costs because the cost system assumes that the relationship between direct labor hours and supervision is the same for all machines and production processes within the center.

The distortion created by the heterogeneity of production processes within a cost center can be reduced by splitting the center into two cost centers, one for automated processes and the other for manual processes. The manual center will have a low burden rate per direct labor hour while the automated one will have a high burden rate. It is not unusual to see cost systems in German factories with several hundred or even several thousand cost centers to eliminate all production process diversity within a cost center. Each of the hundreds or thousands of cost centers has a separate burden rate to reflect the ratio of indirect expenses to the allocation base (direct labor or machine hours) used for second-stage assignment in that cost center.

Both ways of improving the accuracy of the first-stage assignment process, direct charging and defining more cost centers, increase the complexity of the first stage of the two-stage procedure. This increased complexity requires additional measurements. Using more direct charging of support resources to cost centers requires measuring the consumption of each resource category by each cost center. For example, supervision hours consumed in each center now must be measured whereas previously only direct labor hours were required. When adding more cost centers, more measurements per first-stage basis must be made. Continuing the example, supervision expenses for the automated and manual centers would now have to be determined separately, whereas previously supervision expenses for the combined center only were required. For the German factories, consumption of each resource category by each of the hundreds or thousands of cost centers must be measured. A well-designed system balances the complexity of the first stage with the benefits of more accurate expenses accumulated at the cost centers both for performance measurement and in computing more accurate burden rates (by reducing price distortion) for measuring product costs.

Quantity distortion arises from assigning costs to the products in the second stage using bases that are not strictly proportional to the actual quantity of resource consumed. For example, if direct labor hours are used to assign supervision costs to products, the reported costs for products that consume a lot of direct labor hours but require little supervision will be overstated, while the reported costs of products that consume little direct labor hours but require a lot of supervision will be understated. Quantity distortion can be reduced by increasing the complexity of the second stage; for example, by replacing a total reliance on direct labor hours in the second stage with a system that uses direct labor hours, machine hours, and material dollars.[2]

The amount of quantity distortion that can be reduced by improving the design of the second stage is often limited by the degree of resource aggregation in the first stage. Resources are aggregated in the first stage to reduce the number of first-stage assignments required. For example, inspection and testing might be treated as the single resource called quality assurance. When resources are aggregated, the cost system can only use a single second-stage quantity measure to assign expenses to products. Cost systems must assume that all resources aggregated together in a cost center are consumed proportionally by all products that pass through the center. If the aggregated resources are not consumed proportionately by all products, quantity distortion will be introduced. For example, if inspection and testing vary by product, aggregating the expenses of both these resources in cost centers will inevitably introduce distortion. Creating additional cost centers might reduce some of the distortion, but as long as products passing through the centers consume the aggregated resources in different proportions, distortion will occur.

RECIPROCAL SERVICE DEPARTMENT COSTS

An additional complication arises in the first-stage assignment process when support departments provide service to each other as well as to production departments.[3] The following major solutions to handle reciprocal support department interactions have emerged in practice:

1. The direct method, which ignores all of the interactions between support departments
2. The step-down method, which ignores some of the interaction between support departments
3. The reciprocal method, which captures all of the interactions

In the *direct* method, each support department assigns all of its costs to the production departments and ignores service provided to other support departments. In the *step-down* procedure, support departments are first rank-ordered. Then the cost of the highest ranked department is assigned to all of the departments, both productive and support, that it services. The cost of the second-ranked support department is assigned to all of the departments it serves with the exception of the first-ranked department. This step-down process continues until the lowest ranked department is reached. All of that department's accumulated costs, both direct and assigned, are then

---

[2]This modification can be implemented in two ways: first, by selecting the most appropriate measure for each center; second, by allowing each center to use multiple measures. In this chapter we study cost systems that use only one measure per center. Later chapters illustrate systems that use more than one assignment base per cost center.

[3]This topic is also covered in Robert S. Kaplan and Anthony A. Atkinson, *Advanced Management Accounting*, 2nd edition (Englewood Cliffs, NJ: Prentice Hall, 1989), pp. 254–62.

assigned just to production departments. In the *reciprocal* method, all interactions among support departments are captured. The reciprocal method views the interactions among departments as a matrix which is inverted to give the amount of cost in each of the production cost pools. The advantage of the direct method is its simplicity; its disadvantage is the distortions it introduces when assigning service department costs to cost centers and then to products. The reciprocal method is more accurate but difficult for managers to understand. The step-down method lies in the middle of the two methods and hence is the most commonly used of the three methods when significant interactions among service departments exist.

CASES

Seligram, Inc.: Electronic Testing Operations

We put in a piece of automated equipment a year ago that only fits the requirements of one customer. This equipment reduced the direct labor required to test his components and, because of our labor-based burden allocation system, substantially reduced his costs. But putting a $40,000 machine into the general burden pool raised the costs to our other customers. It just doesn't make sense shooting yourself in the foot at the same time you are lowering the company's cost of operations.

PAUL CARTE, MANAGER

INTRODUCTION

The Electronic Testing Center (ETO), a division of Seligram, Inc., provided centralized testing for electronic components such as integrated circuits. ETO was created as a result of a decision in 1979 to consolidate electronic testing from 11 different divisions of Seligram. ETO commenced services to these divisions in 1983. It was estimated that centralization would save Seligram in excess of $20 million in testing equipment investment over the next five years.

ETO operated as a cost center and transferred products to other divisions at full cost (direct costs plus allocated burden). Although ETO was a captive division, other divisions within Seligram were allowed to use outside testing services if ETO could not meet their cost or service requirements. ETO was permitted to devote up to 10% of its testing capacity to outside customers but chose to work mainly with other Seligram divisions due to limited marketing resources.

ETO employed approximately 60 hourly personnel and 40 administrative and technical staff members. Budgeted expenses were $7.9 million in 1988 (see Exhibit 1).

TESTING PROCEDURES

ETO expected to test between 35 and 40 million components in 1988. These components included integrated circuits (ICs), diodes, transistors, capaci-tors, resistors, transformers, relays, and crystals. Component testing was required for two reasons. First, if defective components were not caught early in the manufacturing cycle, the cost of repair could exceed the manufacturing cost of the product itself. Studies indicated that a defective resistor caught before use in the manufacturing process cost two cents. If the resistor was not caught until the end product was in the field, however, the cost of repair could run into the thousands of dollars. Second, a large proportion of Seligram's work was defense related. Military specifications frequently required extensive testing of components utilized in aerospace and naval products. By 1988, ETO had the ability to test 6,500 different components. Typically, however, the division would test about 500 different components each month and between 3,000 and 3,500 per year. Components were received from customers in lots; in 1988 ETO would receive approximately 12,000 lots of components.

ETO performed both electrical and mechanical testing. Electrical testing involved measuring the electrical characteristics of the components and comparing these measurements with the components' specifications. For example, the specifications for an amplifier may have called for a 1-volt input to be amplified into a 10-volt output. ETO would deliver a 1-volt input to the component. By measuring the amplifier's output, ETO gauged its conformance with specifications.

This case was prepared by Professor Peter B. B. Turney, Portland State University, and Christopher Ittner, doctoral student (under the supervision of Professor Robin Cooper).

Mechanical testing included solderability, component burn-in, thermal shock, lead straightening, and leak detection. Solderability involved the inspection of components to see if they held solder. Burn-in was the extended powering of components at high temperature. Thermal shock involved the cycling of components between high and low temperatures. Lead straightening was the detection and correction of bent leads on components such as axial components. Leak detection examined hermetically sealed ICs for leaks.

Components varied significantly in the number and type of electrical and mechanical testing procedures they required. This variation resulted in about 200 different standard process flows for the division. Process flows were determined by the different combinations of tests and specifications requested by the customer. Based on these combinations, ETO planners determined the routing of components between testing equipment and the type of tests to be performed at each station. ICs, for example, could follow six different flows through the facility. While some ICs only required electrical testing at room temperature, solderability, and leak detection, others also required thermal shock and burn-in.

Each type of component required separate software development, and custom tools and fixtures were often required. Software, tools, and fixtures were developed by the engineering group, which was made up of specialists in software development, equipment maintenance, calibration and repair, tooling and fixturing, and testing equipment operation. Software engineers developed programs for specific applications. The programs were then retained in a software library for future use. ETO had 6,500 different software programs on file, of which 1,300 were programs developed in the past year. ETO also had an inventory of 1,500 tools and fixtures, of which 300 had been developed in the past year. The large number of tools and fixtures allowed the testing of components with a wide variety of leads, pin combinations, and mating configurations.

The testing facility was divided into two rooms. The main testing room contained the equipment used for electrical testing. The mechanical room contained the equipment used for mechanical test-ing, plus incoming receiving and the stockroom. A total of 20 people worked in the two rooms on each of two main shifts, and 10 people worked on the night shift.

COST ACCOUNTING SYSTEM

The cost accounting system measured two components of cost: direct labor and burden. Burden was grouped into a single cost pool which included burden associated with each of the testing rooms, as well as the engineering burden costs relating to software and tooling development and the administrative costs of the division. Total burden costs were divided by the sum of testing and engineering labor dollars to arrive at a burden rate per direct labor dollar. The division costed each lot of components. Burden was calculated for each lot by multiplying the actual direct labor dollars associated with the lot by the 145% of burden rate. The resulting burden was then added to the actual direct labor costs to determine the lot's total cost. In 1988, the facility-wide burden rate was 145% of each direct labor dollar, of which more than 25% was attributable to equipment depreciation (see Exhibit 2).

SIGNS OF OBSOLESCENCE

Several trends pointed to the obsolescence of the labor-based burden allocation process. Since the founding of the division in 1983, direct labor hours per lot tested had been declining steadily. This trend was aggravated by an increased dependence on vendor certification. Vendor certification was a key component of just-in-time (JIT) delivery. With vendor certification, Seligram's suppliers did the primary testing of components. ETO then utilized statistical sampling to verify that the supplier's production process was still in control. Thus, while JIT led to an increased number of smaller lots being received by ETO, vendor certification reduced the number of tests performed. Early indications were that JIT deliveries would account for 30% of Seligram's shipments within the next five years.

In addition to declining direct labor content and fewer test lots, the obsolescence of the labor-based allocation system was intensified by a shift from simple inspection services to broader based test technology. On complex parts requiring screening, environmental conditioning, and testing, the division was consistently cheaper than outside services. Where only elementary testing was required, however, low-tech outside laboratories were often cheaper, especially on large lots. The advantage that the division brought customers over the outside labs was that the latter provided essentially no engineering support, whereas ETO with its resident engineering resources was able to support such service on a rapid and cost-effective basis. The shift to more technically sophisticated services prompted a shift in the labor mix from direct to indirect personnel. The division expected to see a crossover between engineering head count and hourly head count early in the 1990s.

Finally, the introduction of higher technology components created the need for more automatic testing, longer test cycles, and more data per part. Digital components, for example, were currently tested for up to 100 conditions (combinations of electrical input and output states). The new generation of digital components, on the other hand, would be much more complex and require verification of up to 10,000 conditions. These would require very expensive highly automated equipment. This increase in automation would, in turn, lead to a smaller base of direct labor to absorb the depreciation costs of this new equipment.

There were fears that the resulting increase in burden rates would drive some customers away. ETO had already noticed an increase in the number and frequency of complaints from customers regarding the rates they were charged for testing.

The division's accounting manager proposed a new cost accounting system to alleviate the problem. Under this new system, burden would be directly traced to two cost pools. The first pool would contain burden related to the administrative and technical functions (division management, engineering, planning, and administrative personnel). This pool would be charged on a rate per direct labor dollar. The second pool would include all other burden costs and would be charged based on machine hours. Exhibit 3 provides the proposed burden rates.

Shortly after the accounting manager submitted his proposal, a consultant hired by Seligram's corporate management prepared an assessment of ETO's cost system. He recommended the implementation of a three-burden pool system utilizing separate burden centers for each test room and a common technical and administrative pool. Burden would be directly traced to each of the three burden pools. Like the accounting manager's system, burden costs in the test rooms would then be allocated on a machine hour basis. Technical and administrative costs would continue to be charged on a rate per direct labor dollar.

To examine the impact of the two alternative systems, ETO management asked that a study be conducted on a representative sample of parts. Exhibit 4 provides a breakdown of actual direct labor and machine hour requirements per lot for the five components selected for the study.

TECHNOLOGICAL FUTURE

In 1988, the division faced major changes in the technology of testing that required important equipment acquisition decisions. The existing testing equipment was getting old and would not be able to keep pace with developments in component technology. Existing components, for example, had between 16 and 40 input/output terminations (e.g., pins or other mating configurations), and ETO's equipment could handle up to 120 terminations. Although the 120-termination limit had only been reached a couple of times in the past few years, a new generation of components with up to 256 terminations was already being developed. Similarly, the upper limit of frequency on existing components was 20 MHz (million cycles per second), whereas the frequency on the next generation of components was expected to be 50 MHz.

The equipment required to test the next generation of components would be expensive. Each machine cost approximately $2 million. Testing on this equipment would be more automated than existing equipment, with longer test cycles and the generation of more test data per part. It was also likely that lot sizes would be larger. The new equipment would not replace the existing equipment but would merely add capabilities ETO did not currently possess. Additionally, the new equipment would only be needed to service the requirements of one or two customers in the foreseeable future. Exhibit 5 provides a summary of the new equipment's economics and operating characteristics.

The impact of this new equipment would be an acceleration in the decline in direct labor hours per lot of components. At the same time, burden would increase with the additional depreciation and engineering costs associated with the new equipment. This would result in a large increase in the burden rate per direct labor dollar. As Paul Carte, Manager of ETO, saw it, the acquisition of the new equipment could have a disastrous effect on the division's

pricing structure if the labor-based allocation system remained in use:

> We plan on investing $2 million on a large electronic testing machine to test the chips of one or two customers. This machine will be very fast and will require little direct labor. Its acquisition will have a significant effect on our per direct labor dollar burden rate, which will result in an increase in charges to our other customers. It is clear that a number of customers will walk away if we try to pass this increase on. I am afraid that we will lose 25% of our customer base if we don't change our cost system.

EXHIBIT 1

SELIGRAM, INC.:
ELECTRONIC TESTING CENTER
1988 Budgeted Expenses

Direct labor	$3,260,015
Indirect labor	859,242
Salary expense	394,211
Supplies & expenses	538,029
Services[1]	245,226
Personnel allocations[2]	229,140
Service allocations[3]	2,448,134
Total budgeted expenses	$7,973,097

[1]Includes tool repair, computer expenses, maintenance stores, and service cost transfers from other divisions.
[2]Includes indirect and salaried employee fringe benefits, personnel department, security, stores/warehousing, and holidays/vacations.
[3]Includes building occupancy, telephones, depreciation, information systems, and data control.

EXHIBIT 2

SELIGRAM, INC.:
ELECTRONIC TESTING OPERATIONS
Calculation of Burden Rate
Based on 1988 Plan

BURDEN ELEMENT	
Indirect labor	$859,242
Salary expense	394,211
Supplies & expenses	538,029
Services	245,226
Personnel allocations	229,140
Service allocations	2,448,134
Total burden[1]	$4,713,982

$$\text{Burden rate} = \frac{\text{TOTAL BURDEN \$}}{\text{DIRECT LABOR \$}}$$

$$= \frac{\$4,713,982}{3,260,015}$$

$$= 144.6\%$$

Effective rate	145%

[1]*Cost Breakdown*

Variable	$1,426,317
Fixed:	
Depreciation	1,288,000
Other fixed:	1,999,665
Total burden:	$4,713,982

EXHIBIT 3

SELIGRAM, INC.:
ELECTRONIC TESTING OPERATIONS
Proposed Burden Rates
Based on 1988 Plan

MACHINE HOUR RATES

	MACHINE HRS	BURDEN $[1]
Main test room	33,201	$2,103,116
Mechanical test room	17,103	1,926,263
Total	50,304	$4,029,379

$$\text{Machine Hour Rate} = \frac{\text{Burden \$}}{\text{Machine Hrs}} = \frac{\$4,029,379}{50,304} = \$80.10$$

Effective machine hour rate = $80.00

Rate per Direct Labor Hour

Total engineering & administrative burden $ = $684,603[2]

Total direct labor dollars = $3,260,015[3]

$$\text{Burden rate} = \frac{\text{Engr \& admin \$}}{\text{Direct lbr \$}} = \frac{\$684,603}{\$3,260,015} = 21\%$$

Effective burden rate per direct labor $ = 20%

[1]*Burden $*

	Variable	Fixed Depreciation	Other	Total
Main test room	$ 887,379	$ 88,779	$1,126,958	$2,103,116
Mechanical test room	443,833	808,103	679,327	1,926,263
Total burden	$1,331,212	$896,882	$1,801,285	$4,029,379

[2]*Cost Breakdown*

Variable	$ 95,105
Fixed:	
Depreciation	391,118
Other	198,380
Total	$684,603

[3]Includes all direct labor costs, including direct labor costs incurred in both test rooms as well as engineering.

EXHIBIT 4

SELIGRAM, INC.:
ELECTRONIC TESTING OPERATIONS
Direct Labor and Machine Hour Requirements
Actuals for One Lot

	DIRECT LABOR $	MACHINE HOURS MAIN ROOM	MECH. ROOM	TOTAL
IC A	$ 917	8.5	10.0	18.5
IC B	2051	14.0	26.0	40.0
Capacitor	1094	3.0	4.5	7.5
Amplifier	525	4.0	1.0	5.0
Diode	519	7.0	5.0	12.0

EXHIBIT 5

SELIGRAM, INC.:
ELECTRONIC TESTING OPERATIONS
New Testing Equipment Economics and Operating
Characteristics

Cost	$2 million
Useful life	8 years
Depreciation method	Double declining balance (first-year depreciation costs of $500,000)
Location	Main test room
Utilization	10% first year, rising to 60% by third year and in all subsequent years, based on 4,000 hours per year availability (2 shifts × 2000-hour year)
Direct labor requirements	Approximately five minutes per hour of operation; average labor rate of $30 per hour
Engineering requirements	$75,000 in installation and programming costs in first year
Estimated overhead (nonengineering depreciation)	$250,000 ($100,000 variable, $150,000 fixed)

Digital Communications, Inc.: Encoder Device Division

INTRODUCTION

Digital Communications, Inc., a Connecticut-based company, produced a wide range of communications devices ranging from portable typewriters and hand-held walkie-talkies to complex voice and data encoding devices. Their primary customers were federal, state, and local government agencies, and 1988 sales were expected to be $100 million.

The Encoding Device Division (EDD) of Defense Communications, located in Hamden, Connecticut, specialized in classified government communication products to be used on the battlefield. There were four different basic products, each of which encoded different communication transmissions: data, video, voice ratio, and variable wire. Sales in 1988 were expected to be $30 million.

Because the four products manufactured at EDD were classified, all were produced in a factory-within-a-factory environment. That is, although the products were similar in some respects, they did not share any manufacturing facilities or staffs, for it was believed that a compartmentalized structure minimized exposure to the risk of security violations. The four production departments were Data Encoding (DE), Video Encoding (VE), Voice Ratio Encoding (VRE), and Variable Wire Encoding (VWE).

This case was prepared by Shannon Weems, doctoral student (under the supervision of Professor Robin Cooper).

There were a few exceptions to compartmentalization. The general support departments—personnel, financial, information services, and plant engineering—and the material departments—shipping and receiving, inventory control, and receiving inspection—serviced all four production departments. None of these staffs, however, had contact with classified information.

The other exceptions were the production support departments: product engineering, machine maintenance, quality control, program security, and program management and supervision. These represented hybrid departments; the people within them were completely dedicated to one of the four production areas. Nonetheless, they maintained an independent departmental structure like the other support departments.

EDD ACCOUNTING SYSTEM

EDD's cost system directly charged all material, labor, and production support department costs to the production departments incurring the costs. The material support department's costs were allocated to the four production departments based on the fraction of EDD's direct labor hours worked in each department. Each department used approximately equal quantities of direct labor to produce its annual production volume, and all direct labor earned the same hourly wage.

The general support department's costs were allocated on several factors. Prior to 1985, all costs had been allocated to production departments based on direct labor hours. Several studies indicated, however, that this did not reflect the departments' usage of these resources. Consequently, personnel costs were allocated to production based on head count; plant engineering costs were allocated on square feet of production space; and financial and information services were allocated based on a special study of the usage of their services by the production departments. Exhibit 1 details the accounting system's treatment of all 1987 costs and the resulting total annual costs of the four production departments.

THE SUBASSEMBLY CONTRACT

Customers purchased products through a lengthy, sealed bid and negotiation process. Nor-mally the final price was based on cost plus a negotiated profit. Once the contract was finalized, the manufacturer was responsible for providing internal security during all phases of manufacture. Contracts usually extended over several years and, in most cases, included any maintenance or upgrading of the product in the field that was necessary.

Occasionally, new technology would make it advantageous to upgrade a product in the middle of the contract. The upgrade to units in the field was achieved via a modification kit supplied by the manufacturer.

In 1987 a new microprocessor was developed which offered significant advantages to VRE device customers. Although the original product was otherwise acceptable, the replacement contract was subject to a sealed bid and negotiation process. The contract would entail making replacement subassemblies for the units in the field and substituting the new subassembly for the old subassembly in all future production.

EDD was particularly eager to win the contract because it was committed to making and servicing completed products. In the past it had avoided piecemeal jobs that would include subcontracting large pieces of production to other firms.

The problem for management was how to bid for the new contract. Although they had experience in constructing ground-up bids for entire programs, this was the first time they had been faced with manufacturing a single subassembly for resale.

Management was confident that they understood the total cost of each program quite well, largely because of the factory-within-a-factory environment, which yielded few shared costs. However, they felt they lacked detailed information about the costs associated with individual subassemblies.

BIDDING THE JOB

The VRE device was composed of six distinct subassemblies: three printed wire assemblies (PWAs), one of which was the mother board; two wire harnesses that connected the PWAs; and a case and cover assembly that housed the other subassemblies. Purchased materials included the case and cover, wire to make the harnesses, the bare printed wiring boards, and the components added to the PWAs during production, such as resistors and capacitors. The production process and labor and machine utilizations are detailed in Exhibit 2.

The VRE subassembly for the microprocessor upgrade (identified as board 2) was one of the PWAs, not the mother board. The replacement board would be configured differently from the compromised board but would be virtually identical in its manufacture and its components.

EDD had sufficient capacity in the PWA production process to accommodate production of the replacement PWAs in addition to those needed for future production of complete units. The volume of replacement PWAs for units in the field was approximately equal to one year's production of the PWA. Hence, EDD proposed to produce twice as many of the one PWA as required in completed units and to do so without altering its investment in equipment. The only additional costs to producing the part would be the labor and material costs, which were expected to remain virtually unchanged on a per-unit basis.

In early 1988, the top staff members of the VRE production group convened to discuss how they would develop cost estimates to bid the job. Representatives from the financial staff felt that the most expedient method of costing was to utilize detailed time reporting data to determine what fraction of departmental labor hours were used to produce board 2. The advocates of this system proposed to apply that fraction of the departmental overhead to board 2, in addition to its labor and material costs, to arrive at total cost. Exhibit 3 was submitted for review as the basis for a bid proposal.

Several production supervisors balked at this idea. In reviewing the financial department's proposal, they were shocked to learn that all three PWAs were thought to cost approximately the same. Intuition led them to believe that the PWAs should have very different costs. Although the three PWAs used similar amounts of direct labor in the whole production process, they had very different production characteristics.

"Wouldn't it be a better idea if we studied these overhead costs that we're talking about to learn how to apply them to the three boards?" asked the director of quality control. "I know my staff has almost nothing to do with direct labor. Their job is to identify quality problems, and we all know that usually means machinery problems." A number of

the other support department directors felt similarly; much of their staff actions had little to do with the direct labor content of the PWAs.

After further discussion, the VRE staff decided to undertake a study to determine how costs should be allocated to the PWAs. From the findings of this study, they decided to modify the financial department's proposal. They believed that by using two additional allocation bases, machine hours, and material dollars, they could arrive at a reasonable estimate of what it cost to produce board 2.

They agreed on the following scheme for allocating VRE support department costs to the VRE subassemblies:

Machine hours:	Product engineering Machine maintenance department Quality department Plant engineering Information services
Direct labor hours:	Product security Product management and supervision Personnel Financial
Material dollars:	Shipping and receiving Inventory control Receiving inspection

After the results of the VRE study were presented, EDD controller Don Bryant began to worry whether the costs that the support departments were charging to the production departments were sufficiently accurate.

The financial department had reviewed and updated its methods for allocating general support department costs in 1985, so a number of new allocation bases replaced the previous direct labor hour allocation base. Bryant recalled an issue that had arisen at the time of that study that was dismissed as having little impact on allocations: the reciprocal use of support departments. It was evident at the time that two of the major users of information systems support were the financial department and the personnel department. Similarly, personnel provided service to both financial and information services.

At the time of the detailed study of the service

departments, the reciprocal usage of the general support departments, as well as their usage by production, was estimated (Exhibit 4). Given the workload of the finance department at that time, it was decided to ignore these reciprocal costs and to concentrate on accurately tracing production costs to the four production departments.

The justification for ignoring reciprocal usage was that the costs associated with reciprocal services were minimal and would not significantly change the costs of any product. Consequently, these costs were allocated to production in the proportion that production used the department's services directly. For instance, all of personnel costs were allocated to production based on head count in the production departments, even though 30% of personnel services were consumed by other support departments.

In light of the new subassembly contract and the need for more accurate product costs, Bryant decided that it was worth knowing the potential impact of using more accurate allocation procedures for reciprocal costs on product costs. He hired a business school student with accounting experience for the summer and assigned her the task of evaluating different treatments of joint expenses and their impact on product costs.

The student, Rebecca Wills, consulted a number of accounting texts and learned that one common treatment of such costs was the step-down method. This allocation method was a sequence of allocations that could be ordered based on the dollars in the departments, the number of services provided by the departments, or other criteria. Once the order was determined, all dollars from the first department in the sequence were allocated to the remaining departments. Then all dollars in the second department, including dollars allocated to it by the first department, were allocated to successive departments in the sequence.

The process would continue until all support department costs reached a production department. The key to the step-down method was that it did not permit costs to be allocated to a support department that preceded it in the sequence. It effectively broke one link of the reciprocal charge so that eventually all costs were allocated to productive departments.

Wills applied the step-down method using both magnitude of dollars and number of departments serviced as her criterion for sequencing the support departments (Exhibits 5 and 6). She was surprised at the size of the difference between the two approaches. She knew that when she reported her findings to Bryant, he would ask her advice about which approach was more appropriate. The VRE assembly contract was soon to be bid, and Wills realized that her assessment was of major importance.

EXHIBIT 1

DIGITAL COMMUNICATIONS, INC.: ENCODER DEVICE DIVISION
Current Financial System's Overhead Charging Mechanism

SUPPORT DEPARTMENT	DOLLARS	CHARGE MECHANISM	% USAGE OF SUPPORT SERVICE BY PRODUCTION DEPT.			
			VWE	VRE	DE	VE
General Support						
Personnel plant	$2,190,251	Headcount	25.00%	25.00%	25.00%	25.00%
Engineering building occupancy	3,011,960	Sq ftg	25.00	37.50	12.50	25.00
Information services	2,738,860	Usage	16.60	50.00	16.70	16.70
Finance & administration	1,682,000	Usage	33.30	16.70	33.30	16.70
Production Support						
Product management & supervision	$205,009	Usage	17.10%	34.44%	18.19%	30.28%
Machine maintenance	153,756	Usage	21.03	35.25	15.23	28.49
Product engineering	205,009	Usage	19.48	32.00	24.90	23.62
Product security	410,017	Usage	25.42	29.56	20.43	24.58
Quality control	256,260	Usage	13.45	32.00	19.70	34.86
Material Support						
Shipping & receiving	$221,492	Labor hours	25.00%	25.00%	25.00%	25.00%
Inventory control	110,746	Labor hours	25.00	25.00	25.00	25.00
Receiving inspection	332,239	Labor hours	25.00	25.00	25.00	25.00

Dollars Charged From Support Departments to Productive Departments

SUPPORT DEPARTMENT	DOLLARS		VWE	VRE	DE	VE
General Support						
Personnel plant	$2,190,251		$547,563	$547,563	$547,563	$547,563
Engineering building occupancy	3,011,960		752,990	1,129,485	376,495	752,990
Information services	2,738,860		454,651	1,369,430	457,390	457,390
Finance & administration	1,682,000		560,106	280,894	560,106	280,894
Production Support						
Product management & supervision	$205,009		$35,050	$70,603	$37,288	$62,068
Machine maintenance	153,756		32,333	54,202	23,421	43,800
Product engineering	205,009		39,929	65,603	51,050	48,427
Product security	410,017		104,235	121,215	83,780	100,787
Quality control	256,260		34,463	81,993	50,471	89,333
Material Support						
Shipping & receiving	$221,492		$55,373	$55,373	$55,373	$55,373
Inventory control	110,746		27,687	27,687	27,687	27,687
Receiving inspection	332,239		83,060	83,060	83,060	83,060
Total overhead	$11,517,599	52%	$2,727,439	$3,887,107	$2,353,683	$2,549,371
Direct wages	3,543,877	16	885,969	885,969	885,969	885,969
Raw materials	7,087,753	32	1,107,461	2,214,923	1,550,446	2,214,923
Total firm costs	22,149,229					
Total program costs			4,720,869	6,987,999	4,790,098	5,650,263
% of division expenses			21.31%	31.55%	21.63%	25.51%

EXHIBIT 2

DIGITAL COMMUNICATIONS, INC.: ENCODER DEVICE DIVISION

Percentage of VRE Dollar Hours (DLHRS) and Machine Hours (MCHRS) by Component, by Process

PROCESS SEQUENCE	MCHRS OR DLHRS WORKED	BOARD 1 (MOTHER BOARD)	BOARD 2	BOARD 3	FINAL & HARNESS
Automatic insertion	Dlhrs	0.82%	2.04%	1.22%	
Kit & prep	Dlhrs	0.82	3.27	4.08	
Semi-automatic insertion	Dlhrs	4.08	1.63	2.45	
Wave solder	Dlhrs	1.39	1.35	1.35	
Touch-up I	Dlhrs	1.53	5.61	3.06	
anual insertion	Dhlrs	0.61	2.45	3.06	
Test I	Dlhrs	0.69	0.67	0.67	
Test II	Dlhrs	0.00	0.61	1.43	
Mask & boot	Dlhrs	6.12	2.04	2.04	
Conformal coat	Dlhrs	1.40	1.35	1.35	
Touch-up II	Dlhrs	1.84	1.02	1.22	
Harness build	Dlhrs				12.24%
Assembly	Dlhrs				20.41
Test III	Dlhrs				4.08
Total % dlhrs		19.30	22.04	21.93	36.73
Automatic insertion	Mchrs	7.00	17.00	10.00	
Wave solder	Mchrs	11.00	11.00	11.00	
Conformal coat	Mchrs	11.00	11.00	11.00	
Total % mchrs		29.00	39.00	32.00	0.00

EXHIBIT 3

DIGITAL COMMUNICATIONS, INC.: ENCODER DEVICE DIVISION

VRE Component Costs

COST ELEMENT	VRE $'s	BOARD 1 (MOTHER BOARD)	BOARD 2	BOARD 3	FINAL & HARNESS
VRE material $'s	$2,214,923	18.00%	45.00%	27.00%	10.00%
VRE labor wages	885,969	19.30	22.04	21.93	36.73
VRE production & general support	3,720,988	19.30	22.04	21.93	36.73
VRE material support	166,119	19.30	22.04	21.93	36.73
Total cost	6,987,999	1,319,890	2,048,701	1,644,765	1,974,643

EXHIBIT 4

DIGITAL COMMUNICATIONS, INC.: ENCODER DEVICE DIVISION

Matrix of Reciprocal Usage of Support Departments

ORIGINATING BUDGET	$	DESTINATION DEPARTMENT PERCENTAGES				
		FINANCE	INFORMATION SERVICES	PERSONNEL	PLANT ENGINEERING	PRODUCTION
Finance	$1,682,000	0%	10%	5%	20%	65%
Information services	2,738,860	50	0	20	0	30
Personnel	2,190,251	13	11	0	6	70
Plant engineering	3,011,960	10	6	4	0	80

EXHIBIT 5

DIGITAL COMMUNICATIONS, INC.: ENCODER DEVICE DIVISION

Step-Down Allocation: Ordered by Dollars in Original Budget

Matrix of Reciprocal Usage of Support Departments

ORIGINATING BUDGET	$'S FROM:	FINANCE	INFORMATION SERVICES	PERSONNEL	PLANT ENGINEERING	PRODUCTION
	$'S TO:					
$1,682,000	finance	0%	10%	5%	20%	65%
2,738,860	information services	50	0	20	0	30
2,190,251	personnel	13	11	0	6	70
3,011,960	plant engineering	10	6	4	0	80
$9,623,071						

Step-Down Matrix Based on Dollars Charged Out

ORIGINATING BUDGET	$'S FROM:	PLANT ENGINEERING	INFORMATION SERVICES	PERSONNEL	FINANCE	PRODUCTION
	$'S TO:					
$3,011,960	plant engineering	0%	6%	4%	10%	80%
2,738,860	information services	0	0	20	50	30
2,190,251	personnel	0	0	0	16	84
1,682,000	finance	0	0	0	0	100

STEP 1:

ORIGINATING BUDGET	$'S FROM:	PLANT ENGINEERING	INFORMATION SERVICES	PERSONNEL	FINANCE	PRODUCTION	DOLLARS CHARGED TO PRODUCTION DEPARTMENTS			
	$'S TO:						VWE	VRE	DE	VE
$3,011,960	plant engineering	0	$180,718	$120,478	$301,196	$2,409,568	$602,392	$903,588	$301,196	$602,392
2,738,860	information services	0	0	0	0	0	0	0	0	0
2,190,251	personnel	0	0	0	0	0	0	0	0	0
1,682,000	finance	0	0	0	0	0	0	0	0	0

EXHIBIT 5 (cont.)

DIGITAL COMMUNICATIONS, INC.: ENCODER DEVICE DIVISION
Step-Down Allocation: Ordered by Dollars in Original Budget

STEP 2:

ORIGINATING BUDGET	$'s FROM:	\$'s TO: PLANT ENGINEERING	INFORMATION SERVICES	PERSONNEL	FINANCE	PRODUCTION	DOLLARS CHARGED TO PRODUCTION DEPARTMENTS — VWE	VRE	DE	VE
$0	plant engineering	$0	$0	$120,478	$301,196	$2,409,568	$602,392	$903,588	$301,196	602,392
2,919,578	information services	0	0	583,916	1,459,789	875,873	146,271	437,936	146,271	145,395
2,190,251	personnel	0	0	0	0	0	0	0	0	0
1,682,000	finance	0	0	0	0	0	0	0	0	0

STEP 3:

ORIGINATING BUDGET	$'s FROM:	\$'s TO: PLANT ENGINEERING	INFORMATION SERVICES	PERSONNEL	FINANCE	PRODUCTION	DOLLARS CHARGED TO PRODUCTION DEPARTMENTS — VWE	VRE	DE	VE
$0	plant engineering	$0	$0	$0	$301,196	$2,409,568	$602,392	$903,588	$301,196	$602,392
0	information services	0	0	0	1,459,789	875,873	146,271	437,936	146,271	145,395
2,894,645	personnel	0	0	0	463,143	2,431,502	607,876	607,876	607,876	607,876
1,682,000	finance	0	0	0	0	0	0	0	0	0

STEP 4:

ORIGINATING BUDGET	$'s FROM:	\$'s TO: PLANT ENGINEERING	INFORMATION SERVICES	PERSONNEL	FINANCE	PRODUCTION	DOLLARS CHARGED TO PRODUCTION DEPARTMENTS — VWE	VRE	DE	VE
$0	plant engineering	$0	$0	$0	$0	$2,409,568	$602,392	$903,588	$301,169	$602,392
0	information services	0	0	0	0	875,873	146,271	437,936	146,271	145,395
0	personnel	0	0	0	0	2,431,502	607,876	607,876	607,876	607,876
3,906,128	finance	0	0	0	0	3,906,128	1,300,741	652,323	1,300,741	652,323

	PRODUCTION	VWE	VRE	DE	VE
Total allocated to productive departments from support departments	9,623,071	2,657,280	2,601,723	2,356,084	2,007,986

EXHIBIT 6

DIGITAL COMMUNICATIONS, INC.: ENCODER DEVICE DIVISION
Step-Down Allocation: Ordered First by Number Serviced, Second by Dollars

Matrix of Reciprocal Usage of Support Departments

ORIGINATING BUDGET	$'S FROM:	$'S TO: FINANCE	INFORMATION SERVICES	PERSONNEL	PLANT ENGINEERING	PRODUCTION
$1,682,000	finance	0%	10%	5%	20%	65%
2,738,860	information services	50	0	20	0	30
2,190,251	personnel	13	11	0	6	70
3,011,960	plant engineering	10	6	4	0	80
$9,623,071						

Step-Down Matrix Based Number of Departments Serviced and on Dollars Charged Out

ORIGINATING BUDGET	$'S FROM:	$'S TO: PLANT ENGINEERING	PERSONNEL	FINANCE	INFORMATION SERVICES	PRODUCTION
$3,011,960	plant engineering	0%	4%	10%	6%	80%
2,190,251	personnel	0	0	14	12	74
1,682,000	finance	0	0	0	13	87
2,738,860	information services	0	0	0	0	100

STEP 1: ORIGINATING BUDGET	$'S FROM:	$'S TO: PLANT ENGINEERING	PERSONNEL	FINANCE	INFORMATION SERVICES	PRODUCTION	DOLLARS CHARGED TO PRODUCTION DEPARTMENTS VWE	VRE	DE	VE
$3,011,960	plant engineering	$0	$120,478	$301,196	$180,718	$2,409,568	$602,392	$903,588	$301,196	602,392
2,190,251	personnel	0	0	0	0	0	0	0	0	0
1,682,000	finance	0	0	0	0	0	0	0	0	0
2,738,860	information services	0	0	0	0	0	0	0	0	0

EXHIBIT 6 (cont.)

DIGITAL COMMUNICATIONS, INC.: ENCODER DEVICE DIVISION

Step-Down Allocation: Ordered First by Number Serviced, Second by Dollars

STEP 2:

ORIGINATING BUDGET	$'s FROM: / $'S TO:	PLANT ENGINEERING	PERSONNEL	FINANCE	INFORMATION SERVICES	PRODUCTION	VWE	VRE	DE	VE
$0	plant engineering	$0	$0	$301,196	$180,718	$2,409,568	$602,392	$903,588	$301,196	$602,392
2,310,729	personnel	0	0	323,502	277,287	1,709,939	427,485	427,485	427,485	427,485
1,682,000	finance	0	0	0	0	0	0	0	0	0
2,738,860	information services	0	0	0	0	0	0	0	0	0

STEP 3:

ORIGINATING BUDGET	$'s FROM: / $'S TO:	PLANT ENGINEERING	PERSONNEL	FINANCE	INFORMATION SERVICES	PRODUCTION	VWE	VRE	DE	VE
$0	plant engineering	$0	$0	$0	$180,718	$2,409,568	$602,392	$903,588	$301,196	$602,392
0	personnel	0	0	0	277,288	1,709,940	427,485	427,485	427,485	427,485
2,306,698	finance	0	0	0	299,871	2,006,827	668,273	335,140	668,273	335,140
2,738,860	information services	0	0	0	0	0	0	0	0	0

STEP 4:

ORIGINATING BUDGET	$'s FROM: / $'S TO:	PLANT ENGINEERING	PERSONNEL	FINANCE	INFORMATION SERVICES	PRODUCTION	VWE	VRE	DE	VE
$0	plant engineering	$0	$0	$0	$0	2,409,568	602,392	903,588	301,196	602,392
0	personnel	0	0	0	0	1,709,940	427,485	427,485	427,485	427,485
0	finance	0	0	0	0	2,006,827	668,273	335,140	668,273	335,140
3,496,737	information services	0	0	0	0	3,496,737	583,955	1,748,369	583,955	580,485
	Total allocated to productive departments from support departments					9,623,072	2,282,105	3,414,581	1,980,909	1,945,475

Mayers Tap, Inc. (A)

Mayers Tap, Inc., (MTI) is a subsidiary of the Mayers Corporation, a manufacturer of machine tools and cutting tools. The parent company was founded in 1910 by Helen G. Mayers to produce drill bits and was first known as St. Louis Drill Manufacturers. The name was later changed to the Mayers Corporation in honor of the founder.

During the early 1960s, the Mayers Corporation embarked on an aggressive 10-year expansion plan to capitalize on rapid growth in the cutting-tool industry. In 1966 a tap manufacturing plant was built in Denver, Colorado, and in 1976 a second plant was built in Albany, New York. All selling and administrative activities were consolidated at the Albany facility upon its completion, and a separate subsidiary, Mayers Tap, Inc., was formed to manage the company's tap business. MTI was headed by John Mayers, the 31-year-old grandson of the company's founder. MTI was entirely family owned, and the majority ownership was held by John's father, who had run the company until his retirement in 1978. MTI was proud of its employee relations; Mayers claimed this was the major reason that MTI was one of the few nonunion firms in the industry.

In the fall of 1983 John Mayers decided to replace MTI's cost accounting system. The old system was not providing enough data to price MTI's products competitively or identify cost control problem areas effectively. For example, the company sometimes lost bids to its competitors with similar productive facilities even when MTI had quoted what it considered close to break-even prices. In other cases, the firm quoted high to avoid business because it was at capacity, and yet it was the low bidder by quite a large margin. Another major problem was the continuous discrepancy between the profits predicted by the cost accounting system and those reported by the financial accounting system. In 1983 this difference amounted to nearly $200,000, with the cost system predicting higher profitability. These and other symptoms indicated to Mayers that MTI did not know what its products cost to make.

Part of the problem was the impact of changes in the production process. Although many of the machines were typical metalworking equipment, MTI had started to invest in new automatic loading machinery that substantially changed the way taps were produced. It was clear to Mayers that the cost accounting system had to be designed with the manufacturing process in mind.

The existing cost system used a single burden rate in both the Albany and Denver plants for all labor and overhead costs. The standard cost was found by multiplying the burden rate by the total standard production hours for each product and then adding the standard raw material costs.

Three questions faced Mayers in replacing the cost system:

1. How to allocate overhead costs;
2. How many cost centers to have; and
3. Whether to drop one or more products if the new cost system showed them to be uneconomical.

MTI PRODUCTS

Mayers Tap, Inc., produced a small variety of taps and had become known for high-quality output. Taps were used to cut threads into a drilled hole. These threads allowed a bolt to be screwed into the hole without requiring a nut to hold it in place. The taps were made from hardened high-speed steel, and the production process basically involved a series of precise, specialized metal-grinding operations. The principal parts of the tap are as follows:

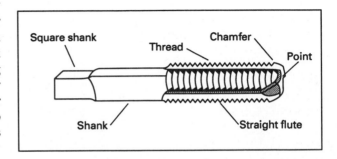

This case was prepared by Professor Robin Cooper.

Copyright © 1984 by the President and Fellows of Harvard College. Harvard Business School case 185-111.

The tap shank was squared off on one end so that it would be held securely in the tapping machine. Flutes were ground lengthwise in the tap to permit removal of the metal chips produced during tapping and to allow lubricating oil to reach the cutting surfaces. The point end of the tap was chamfered (tapered) so that the amount of thread-cutting surface gradually increased at the beginning of the tap. This increased the life of the tap by reducing the amount of heat generated during tapping.

MTI's 1984 product line consisted of 11 products. Five of the products were considered standard design taps while the remaining six taps had very specialized designs. A list of the products appears in Table A.

Table A.   MTI Product Line, 1984

PRODUCT NUMBER	TAP TYPE	DIAMETER (IN.)	FLUTES	THREADS PER INCH
1	Standard	1 1/4	4	7
2	Pilot	1 1/4	5	2
3	Pilot	1/4	4	20
4	Pipe	3/4	5	14
5	Standard	5/8	4	11
6	Reamer	1/4	4	20
7	Reamer	3/8	4	16
8	Forming	5/8	0	16
9	Standard	1/4	4	20
10	Standard	3/8	3	16
11	Standard	5/8	4	13

THE TAP INDUSTRY

Sales in the tap industry as a whole amounted to about $86 million in 1983 (see Exhibit 1). The industry was very mature. There had been relatively few new tap styles developed in the past 30 years, and except for increased automation, there were no fundamental changes in production techniques during the same period. More than 20 firms produced taps, and the largest had a 15% market share. In the last few years there had been some reduction in the conventional tap market. First, the four-cylinder engine had become more common in U.S. automobiles at the expense of the eight-cylinder engine. A four-cylinder engine requires about 50% fewer tapping operations. Second, new materials and alloys allowed for an expanded use of self-tapping screws.

MTI accounted for about 10% of the industry sales. It marketed its taps to large end users on the basis of high quality at a low price. Price competition was heated in the tap industry. Each manufacturer published list prices for its taps, but discounts of up to 50% were often given to secure a customer. Discounts were determined on a customer-by-customer basis, depending on the size of the customer and the competition.

Manufacturing operations

MTI's highly automated Denver plant was designed for high-volume production of the most common taps but could only machine taps smaller than 5/8" in diameter. The Albany plant produced taps 5/8" and larger in diameter, taps of special design, small-volume orders, and urgent orders. MTI's operations were separated in this manner because Mayers felt that two fundamentally different types of manufacturing operations were necessary for MTI's product line. He felt that this not only helped to hold down costs but made management easier, because managers in each plant could focus on one specific philosophy of manufacturing operation.

The Denver plant, which Mayers characterized as an automated production line factory, had been built using the latest machining and heat-treating equipment available. It was staffed by lower-paid machine operators, who required relatively little training to operate the equipment. Operators in Denver were trained to operate most of the machinery in the plant and therefore could be transferred among the machines as required by the production schedule. Unlike the Albany machinery, the Denver equipment could generally operate unattended. An important difference between the machines in the two plants was that the Denver equipment had autoloaders. The operator merely had to load a stack of tap blanks into a machine, and it would pick each one up and machine it automatically. The Denver equipment required longer setup times, but the machining speed of the equipment in each plant was roughly the same.

Albany was considered a specialized job shop. Most of its machinery was multipurpose metal-machining equipment such as lathes, milling machines, and grinders that averaged about 25 years old. For the most part, the production equipment was manually controlled and required skilled machinists; few machinists were trained to operate more than one type of machine. As a result, Albany's per-hour labor costs were substantially higher than Denver's.

The two plants contained 31 different types of machines and 47 machines in total (Exhibit 2 lists all 31 classes of machine). The type of labor required was dependent on the machine class in question. For example, many of the Denver machines required unskilled operators while the Albany machinery required skilled machinists.

The two-plant system allowed MTI to offer 24-hour delivery on a broad range of tools. Fast delivery was a major marketing plus for MTI. Customers were offered two levels of service, QIK and QIK-24. QIK was the normal delivery time (usually only a few working days) and provided the most competitive prices. QIK-24 orders were shipped within 24 hours for a premium price competitive with the prices of other manufacturers offering 24-hour service.

TAP PRODUCTION

Tap production, while varying from tap to tap, consisted of several distinct steps:

1. Cutoff—The bar stock was cut into proper lengths and, for large taps, the shank was square milled.
2. Heat treatment—The cut lengths were immersed in molten salt at 1,000° centigrade to harden the parts.
3. Grinding—The outer diameter of the part was ground to tolerance and the shanks of larger taps were center lapped to allow the part to fit into standard tapping equipment.
4. T-1 blanks—At this point in the process, some of the parts made in Denver were called T-1 blanks.

These could be machined into a number of different products in either of the two plants (see Table B).

5. Flute grinding—The flutes were ground into the part, one at a time.
6. Thread grinding—The fluted parts were now thread ground using diamond wheels.
7. Chamfering—The end of the tap was tapered so that cutting begins gradually.

Each of the grinding or cutting machines was lubricated by MTI's high-pressure oil system. The system pumped lubricating oil to each of the machines and sprayed the oil on the cutting surfaces to cool them and to remove steel chips. The oil was then pumped back to a filtering system that removed the steel chips.

All tap production was done in fixed volumes known as EPQs (economic production quantities). The EPQs were designed to provide the most cost-effective tradeoff between the setup costs, the inventory levels, and the production scheduling requirements. Taps were produced for inventory, and when the inventory level of a given tap dropped below a predetermined level, manufacturing would produce another EPQ batch of that tap.

Table B. Products Made from T-1 Blanks

PRODUCT NUMBER	FINAL MANUFACTURE	TAP TYPE	T-1 (IN.)
5	Albany	Standard	5/8
6	Albany	Reamer	1/4
7	Albany	Reamer	3/8
8	Albany	Forming	5/8
9	Denver	Standard	1/4
10	Denver	Standard	3/8
11	Denver	Standard	5/8

EXHIBIT 1

Tap Industry Sales

	1976	1977	1978	1979	1980	1981	1982	1983
Total sales ($000s)	$48,304	$52,171	$56,829	$61,789	$67,466	$68,043	$72,475	$86,162
Total units sold (000s)	27,761	29,146	30,553	33,015	33,565	32,871	33,942	35,168
Average price[a]	$1.74	$1.79	$1.86	$1.93	$2.01	$2.07	$2.15	$2.45

[a]As a specialty tap producer, Mayers had an average tap cost much higher than the industry.

EXHIBIT 2

Machine Descriptions

Albany

TYPE NO.	QUANTITY	TYPE OF MACHINE	YEAR PURCHASED	NATURE OF MACHINE	OPERATOR
K-40	3	Flute grinder	1979	Semiautomatic, manual loading	Specialized machinist
F-10	4	Thread grinder	1979	Automatic loading	Specialized machinist
J-22	1	Butt grinder	1970		General machinist
G-58	2	Chamfer grinder	1970		General machinist
D-34	3	OD grinder	1967		General machinist
N-68	1	Cutter grinder	1970		General machinist
C-50	2	Salt-bath furnace	1978	Manual loading	Unskilled labor
N-72	2	Cutter grinder	1960		General machinist
C-86	1	Buffing wheel	1965		Unskilled labor
N-78	1	Split-point grinder	1970		General machinist
A-39	2	Template lathe	1977	Manual operation	Specialized machinist
A-40	1	Turret lathe	1977	Manual operation	Specialized machinist
B-79	1	Milling machine	1953		Specialized machinist
C-45	2	Straightening press	1962	Hand-operated	Unskilled labor
B-86	1	Cutter grinder	1977		Specialized machinist
A-44	1	Cutoff machine	1953		Unskilled labor
A-76	1	Centering machine	1963	Specialized type of lathe	Specialized machinist
B-81	1	Milling machine	1953	Multiple head (gang)	Specialized machinist
C-59	1	Center lap	1962	Cleans and machines centers, hand-operated	Unskilled labor
F-07	2	Thread grinder	1970	Manual loading	Specialized machinist
Total	33				

Denver

TYPE NO.	QUANTITY	TYPE OF MACHINE	YEAR PURCHASED	NATURE OF MACHINE	OPERATOR
D-43	3	Flute grinder	1978	Fully automatic	
E-01	3	Thread grinder	1977	Fully automatic	
F-32	1	Chamfer grinder	1975	Fully automatic	
G-05	1	Butt grinder	1979	Fully automatic	
A-06	1	Cutoff machine	1981	Automatic operation, manual loading	
B-03	3	Salt-bath furnace	1982	Automatic loading/unloading for heat treating	Unskilled labor
C-03	1	Centerless grinder	1976	Fully automatic	
D-02	1	Square grinder	1977	Fully automatic	
A-41	1	Cutoff machine	1975	Manual loading, automatic operation	
C-31	1	Centerless grinder	1978	Fully automatic	
A-51	1	Cutoff machine	1980	Automatic loading, automatic operation	
Total	17				

Mayers Tap, Inc. (B)

John Mayers, president of Mayers Tap, Inc., (MTI) asked Lee Rhodes, controller, to conduct a major review of the company's cost accounting system [see Mayers Tap, Inc. (A) for background on the company]. Mayers was concerned that the current methods of allocating fixed and variable costs might have made unprofitable taps look profitable and vice versa.

Under the old accounting system, the company distributed overhead at only one rate. This rate was calculated by dividing the sum of the nonmaterial costs for both plants by the expected total number of direct labor hours. The resulting rate per direct labor hour, called the burden rate, was then used to allocate nonmaterial costs to the taps produced. In 1985 the direct labor burden rate was expected to be $30. Therefore, for a tap that required five hours of direct labor to produce, $150 ($30/hour × 5 hours) would be added to the raw material cost to arrive at the total cost for the tap. (Exhibit 1 shows the expected price, standard cost, and budgeted volume for MTI's 11 principal products.) Certain products were currently selling at very low prices, and Mayers thought they were close to their variable cost of production. Although the firm did not know the exact variable cost, it was thought to be about 60% of the total cost.

Mayers hoped that the new system would help MTI determine which taps were most profitable by allowing more than one burden rate. If more accurate cost information was available through the use of multiple burden rates, it would be possible to reprice the taps. Alternatively, MTI might drop some existing products and replace them with new ones. In addition, the new cost system would help MTI focus management attention on high-cost operations.

Rhodes had been asked to develop a plan to create the new cost system. He had broken it down into three major steps:

1. Determine allocation bases for each principal cost category and then allocate these costs to products, differentiating between fixed and variable costs.

2. Check whether the resulting cost data would be more accurate if each machine class was used as a cost center or whether a single rate or two plant-specific rates would be sufficient.

3. If plantwide rates were not sufficient, attempt to minimize the number of cost centers required without sacrificing the accuracy of the cost data.

Rhodes's first step was to prepare a list of the direct labor, variable overhead, and fixed overhead costs for each of the factory machines and to identify the allocation bases that should be used to allocate the costs to each machine. He started by obtaining a copy of the 1985 budget (see Exhibit 2) and a description of the contents of each of the line items in the budget (see Exhibit 3).

Obtaining an appropriate allocation base was an extremely tedious task. It required going back through MTI's accounting records to break down the costs in the necessary detail. In many instances, budget estimates had been based on only one year's data because of the amount of work required to break down the information from the existing accounting records. Often the records were not sufficiently detailed to split transactions, and Rhodes had to guess what the costs were. Although this work would allow vast improvements in the precision of MTI's cost information, the controller estimated that he would need two to three years to adequately revise and update the input data used for the system. Even then, annual adjustments would be necessary to reflect changes in factory operations and the company's product line. After several months of effort, Lee had identified 13 potential allocation bases (see Exhibit 4) and the ratios for each of the machine classes (see Exhibit 5).

Rhodes decided to develop allocations for each of the 31 machine classes. There seemed little point in differentiating among identical machines since they necessarily had very similar costs and were used interchangeably in production.

The Denver heat treatment process (machine class B-03) was used to heat-treat all products made by the firm. The Albany products were completed to a stage just prior to heat treatment, shipped to Denver, heat-treated, and returned to Albany for completion. It cost less to transport the parts than to continuously operate a second heat treatment plant in Albany. Albany had a small heat treatment facility (machine class C-50) that could be switched on and off as needed. It was used when small volumes of parts had to be completed quickly for shipment. This facility was also used to surface-treat certain products.

The cost of heat treatment at Denver was handled like any other machining operation. Consequently, the apparent budgeted expense for heat treatment in Denver was zero, since heat treatment costs were included with other line items (such as direct labor, power, and heat). The same approach was originally planned for Albany heat treatment costs, but the problems associated with allocating costs to products that only occasionally used a process were considered too difficult to overcome for a $9,000 line item. Consequently, Albany heat treatment costs were treated as an overhead item, and the operations costs were set to zero.

EXHIBIT 1

Fiscal 1985 Product Budget

PRODUCT		EXPECTED SELLING PRICE	STANDARD COST[a]	BUDGETED VOLUME (000s)
1. Standard	(1¼″– 7 4FL)[b]	$25.25	$17.17	6.0
2. Pilot	(1¼″– 2 5FL)	83.80	124.46	28.8
3. Pilot	(¼″ – 20 4FL)	35.15	24.94	8.0
4. Pipe	(⅝″ – 14 5FL)	15.00	9.04	75.0
5. Standard	(⅝″ – 11 4FL)	6.90	4.42	46.2
6. Reamer	(¼″ – 20 4FL)	4.50	3.17	24.0
7. Reamer	(⅜″ – 16 4FL)	4.75	3.40	165.0
8. Forming	(⅝″ – 16 OFL)	5.75	8.41	66.0
9. Standard	(¼″ – 20 4FL)	3.35	1.46	324.0
10. Standard	(⅜″ – 16 3FL)	1.50	1.87	255.0
11. Standard	(½″ – 13 4FL)	7.30	4.49	360.0

[a]Existing single burden rate system standard cost.
[b]FL signifies flute.

EXHIBIT 2

Fiscal 1985 Financial Budget

Budgeted sales			$9,657,070

Budgeted expenses

	ALBANY	DENVER	
Raw materials	$1,122,536	$705,846	
Direct labor[a]	1,182,012	671,172	
Nonproductive labor	110,000	68,000	
OT and night labor	82,500	51,000	
Power and heat	175,000	240,000	
Repairs and maintenance	150,000	175,000	
Grinding wheels	225,000	300,000	
Other factory supplies	50,000	80,000	
Depreciation, machines	120,000	250,000	
Depreciation, buildings	160,000	150,000	
General factory supplies	30,000	40,000	
General factory maintenance	150,000	125,000	
Factory support expenses	400,000	350,000	
General plant costs	150,000	125,000	
Oil filtration expenses	300,000	600,000	
Inspection center costs	90,000	90,000	
Heat treatment costs	9,000	0	
	$4,506,048	$4,021,018	8,527,066
Selling, general, and administrative			500,000
Net income			$ 630,004

[a]Direct labor hours budgeted: 131,778 (Albany) and 83,897 (Denver).

EXHIBIT 3

Description of Factory Costs

Raw Materials	Raw material consisted of steel bar stock purchased as needed in 25-foot lengths. The raw material cost for each tap was calculated by dividing the number of tap blanks to be cut from the bar stock by the total cost of the bar.
Direct Labor	Direct labor included wages and employee benefit costs. Labor costs varied by machine. Some machines, such as the milling machines and thread grinders, were operated by skilled machinists paid at higher rates. Other machines, such as the flute grinders, were simpler and could be controlled by operators with relatively little training who earned lower wage rates. If one machinist ran several machines at once, only a fraction of that person's hourly costs were charged to a given machine. Consequently, much of the difference in the wages of machinists versus operators was not apparent on a per-machine basis.
Nonproductive Labor	MTI hourly workers used computerized time clocks to record the amount of time they spent on each job. When a job was begun, the operator or machinist entered his or her employee number and the job number into the clock. Any paid work time (idle time, meetings, breaks, etc.) that was not directly charged to a job was considered nonproductive labor time. This usually accounted for slightly less than 10% of the total direct labor hours. The amount of nonproductive time varied by machine because of uncertainties in the availability of work for machines in the final stages of the production process.

(continued on next page)

Overtime and Night Labor	Overtime was determined much like nonproductive time. A percentage of direct labor cost for each machine was determined based on historical overtime requirements. MTI ran two eight-hour day shifts, the early shift (6 A.M.–2 P.M.) and the late shift (2 P.M.–10 P.M.). A third night shift was sometimes used for the machines that were capacity bottlenecks. Night labor hours were computed by subtracting the available daytime hours from the total required operating hours for each machine. Night labor was paid the day rate plus 10%.
Power and Heat	Electricity and gas were the only elements of power and heat. Most power was consumed by the production machinery. The factory was not heated because the heat given off by the machines and heat treatment facility was sufficient to keep the building warm. The other principal power user was the oil system. The oil was pumped at 150 psi, which required large pump motors. The administrative offices were heated by baseboard electric heat and cooled with electric air conditioners in the summer. The company received one electric bill for each building. MTI estimated that the administrative office area in Albany consumed $5,000 of electricity annually, and this was excluded from the power and heat account. The general rule for the rest of the power cost was 75% allocated to the machinery and 25% to the oil system. This was based on detailed testing of power use.
Repairs and Maintenance	Repairs and maintenance included labor and the cost of parts and supplies used in regular maintenance. No worker did repair and maintenance work exclusively. Some of the machinists that ran the production equipment regularly maintained and repaired the production equipment. MTI would subcontract particularly difficult repair work. Maintenance time was recorded by MTI workers through the computerized time clock, and parts and supplies used for repair were recorded by machine when taken from the stockroom. A machine's maintenance budget was estimated by the production manager based on historical expenses with consideration for any special maintenance that might be needed.
Grinding and Diamond Wheels	Grinding wheels and diamond wheels were one of the largest factory expenses. Grinding wheels were large abrasive stone wheels used to remove steel from the taps. The diamond wheels were small diamond-coated metal wheels that were used to reshape grinding wheels when they wore down. The amount of grinding wheel used depended on the volume of steel that had to be removed on a tap, so larger taps used much more of the grinding wheels than smaller taps. The stockroom kept track of the grinding wheels used by each machine. The budgeted expense was based on historical experience adjusted for changes in the overall estimated production volume of taps for the budgeted year.
Other Factory Supplies	Other factory supplies included all supplies used by the factory machines (other than grinding and diamond wheels), such as grease, abrasive cutoff wheels, milling cutters, and lathe bits.
Depreciation, Machines	Most of the Albany machines were over 10 years old and had been fully depreciated. The Colorado plant's newer equipment still had depreciable life remaining. All machines were depreciated on a straight-line basis over 10 years.
Depreciation, Buildings	Depreciation of the factory portion of the buildings and other equipment not directly related to the production machines was classified separately. The buildings were depreciated on a straight-line basis over 30 years.
General Factory Supplies	These consisted mostly of small general merchandise items, such as rags, nails, and glue. The budgeted amount was estimated by the production manager based on historical experience.
General Factory Maintenance	These were mostly the labor costs of the janitors who cleaned and maintained the factory area. It also included cleaning and maintenance supplies used in the factory. Three full-time janitors worked in Albany, two in Denver. The budgeted amount consisted of the janitors' salaries plus an amount for supplies estimated by the production manager.
Factory Support	Factory support was the labor costs (including benefits) of the factory's salaried workers, including the production manager, product engineers, production control supervisors, and shipping and stockroom staff.

(continued on next page)

EXHIBIT 3 *(cont.)*

General Plant Costs	General plant costs included the property taxes, rental expenses, general building maintenance, outside services such as garbage collection, the cost of employment ads, and other miscellaneous expenses. For the Albany building only, the factory share of these expenses is included. The budgeted general plant costs were estimated by the plant manager based on the historical expenses and adjusted for expected cost increases.
Oil Filtration Expenses	These were the costs incurred by the high-pressure oil system that was used to lubricate the production machines and remove the metal chips during processing. There were three major elements of cost associated with the oil system: equipment costs, oil and oil filter replacement costs, and power costs. The same oil system was used in both plants. It had been purchased in 1976 at a cost of $150,000 per plant. The oil and filter replacement costs were directly dependent on the level of production. The power cost depended on the number of hours that the system was operating and the production level. The power was consumed by the pumps used to maintain the 150 psi pressure. Some pumping was required to maintain the pressure even if no production equipment was operating, but more power was required as the number of production machines in operation at any given time increased. There was wide variation in the amount of oil required for the operation of each machine. For example, the flute grinders removed a large amount of steel relatively quickly and required much more oil than the butt grinders over an equal amount of operating time. In 1983 the power expenses of the Albany and Denver plants were $18,000 and $20,000, respectively. The oil and filter replacement costs amounted to $24,000 and $29,000.
Inspection Costs	Each plant employed one person per daytime shift to oversee the quality control of the manufacturing operations. Machine operators were responsible for checking the output of their machines. When they discovered a flaw in a tap, they would take the tap to the inspector on duty. He would record the production process, operator, and machine, and would help the operator correct the problem, if necessary. The inspector would also make periodic quality checks of the finished taps. MTI placed a great priority on its quality reputation. All of the expensive pilot taps were individually inspected. The inspection also identified machines that needed unscheduled maintenance or repair.
Heat Treatment Costs	The Colorado heat treatment equipment was a relatively new, automated, salt-bath process. It was used to harden and temper the high-speed steel used for all the taps and tap blanks produced in Colorado. The Albany equipment consisted of two old heat treatment tanks that were manually loaded and unloaded. The Albany equipment was used only for taps from Albany stock. The heat tanks in Colorado were used continuously and were maintained at the necessary temperature on a 24-hour, seven-day basis. The Albany tanks were used only when a batch of taps was produced in the Albany plant that required heat treatment. The heat tanks required almost a full day to heat up to the required temperature and would often be used for just a few hours. The biggest cost of treatment was the natural gas used to heat it. Additional salt would be added as needed, but little was consumed and the cost was minimal. To heat-treat a tap required only a few minutes in the salt bath, and little additional energy was required to maintain the tank temperature when the tank was in use.

EXHIBIT 4

Description of Overhead Allocation Bases

Budgeted Production (units)	The budgeted number of taps produced by each of the machines was easily determined.
Budgeted Raw Material Dollars	This was calculated by multiplying the unit production by the unit cost of the raw steel for each type of tap. This differed from the unit production basis because it allocated more cost to the larger taps.
Budgeted Direct Labor Hours	The number of budgeted direct labor hours was the sum of the number of operating hours (hours that the machinist was running the machine) plus the total setup time for the machine (hours that the machinist was setting up).
Budgeted Direct Labor Dollars	This basis was the budgeted direct labor hours multiplied by the respective wage rates. It allocated more cost to those machines that required highly paid labor.
Budgeted Machine Hours	This was the number of budgeted production hours. It was derived by multiplying the number of taps produced and the amount of time required to produce each tap by machine.
Nonproductive Labor	MTI hourly factory workers recorded the amount of time they spent on each job through a system of computerized time clocks. Any paid work time (idle time, meetings, breaks, etc.) that was not directly charged to a job was considered nonproductive labor time. The system recorded this by machine class.
Overtime and Night Labor	MTI ran two main factory shifts during the day. A third limited night shift was used for the machines that represented the capacity bottlenecks in the plant.
Maintenance Allocation	When the budget was prepared, MTI's production manager estimated the maintenance costs for each machine. This estimate included labor and supplies by machine and was based on both historical costs and specially scheduled maintenance.
Power Consumption	MTI machinery was powered by electric motors. To track power consumption, the company recorded the size of each machine's motor(s) as measured by wattage. This wattage multiplied by the expected run time gave the power consumption.
Oil System Usage	Due to the large costs associated with the oil system, the company identified the oil consumption of each of the machines. This was done by measuring the fluid flow rates of each of the machines when they were operating in a normal mode.
Grinding Wheel Costs	The cost of the grinding wheels used by each machine.
Floor Space	The total floor space directly associated with each of the production machines.
Machine Book Value	The net book value of the production machinery and the remaining depreciable life.

EXHIBIT 5

Overhead Allocation Ratios (%)

Albany

ALLOCATION BASES	K-40	F-10	J-22	G-58	D-34	N-68	C-50	N-72	C-86	N-78
Production (units)	13.32	14.18	15.457	14.50	4.84	1.18	0.00	1.51	0.00	7.77
Raw materials cost ($)	3.65	9.60	2.546	10.31	9.86	6.66	0.00	7.36	0.00	0.33
Direct labor hours	9.89	20.42	0.748	11.00	11.83	0.73	0.00	7.72	0.18	1.23
Direct labor cost ($)	8.69	20.71	0.808	8.81	12.31	0.76	0.00	8.05	0.20	0.99
Machine hours	9.83	20.39	0.734	10.97	11.89	0.74	0.00	7.79	0.18	1.22
Nonproductive labor	9.08	24.06	0.845	9.20	1.43	0.80	0.00	8.41	0.23	1.03
OT and night labor	12.43	26.67	0.463	12.60	0.88	0.76	0.00	8.06	0.20	1.41
Maintenance	22.00	16.50	1.100	5.50	8.80	1.10	0.00	11.50	0.10	1.80
Power	9.70	12.90	1.800	7.80	12.00	1.70	0.00	18.40	0.00	2.90
Oil system	10.40	37.50	0.400	7.20	14.00	0.40	0.00	4.10	0.00	0.60
Grinding wheel	20.50	12.90	1.800	5.60	12.60	1.80	0.00	18.60	0.00	3.00
Floor space	6.98	22.32	1.395	4.19	6.98	1.40	0.00	2.79	0.18	1.40
Machine book value	18.36	56.60	0.000	0.00	0.00	0.00	0.00	0.00	0.00	0.00

	A-39	A-40	B-79	C-45	B-86	A-44	A-76	B-81	C-59	F-07
Production (units)	4.84	1.18	1.18	0.00	1.18	3.66	3.66	3.66	4.84	3.04
Raw materials cost ($)	9.86	6.66	6.66	0.00	6.66	3.20	3.20	3.20	9.86	0.70
Direct labor hours	3.11	0.49	5.63	8.41	5.49	0.44	0.61	0.44	0.48	11.16
Direct labor cost ($)	3.37	0.54	6.20	9.09	6.04	0.47	0.66	0.48	0.52	11.32
Machine hours	3.07	0.49	5.54	8.52	5.54	0.43	0.61	0.33	0.48	11.25
Nonproductive labor	3.91	0.62	7.20	10.56	7.01	0.55	0.76	0.56	0.60	13.14
OT and night labor	3.37	0.54	3.55	9.10	3.45	0.47	0.66	0.28	0.52	14.58
Maintenance	2.30	0.40	4.20	6.20	8.20	0.20	0.50	0.30	0.30	9.00
Power	3.70	0.60	6.70	0.00	13.10	0.30	0.70	0.50	0.00	7.20
Oil system	0.60	0.10	1.10	0.00	2.90	0.35	0.10	0.10	0.00	20.15
Grinding wheel	0.90	0.10	1.60	0.00	13.20	0.00	0.20	0.10	0.00	7.10
Floor space	9.77	0.56	5.58	6.98	1.40	1.40	2.09	0.49	0.42	23.72
Machine book value	14.22	5.16	0.00	0.00	5.66	0.00	0.00	0.00	0.00	0.00

Denver

ALLOCATION BASES	D-43	E-01	F-32	G-05	A-06	B-03	C-03	D-02	A-41	C-31	A-51
Production (units)	12.00	12.001	12.00	12.00	4.45	4.45	4.45	15.85	5.37	11.40	6.03
Raw materials cost ($)	0.00	0.000	0.00	0.00	2.56	2.56	2.56	32.48	7.54	29.92	22.38
Direct labor hours	26.04	25.152	5.43	2.54	2.16	20.41	1.34	4.31	1.75	3.53	7.35
Direct labor cost ($)	26.04	25.152	5.43	2.54	2.16	20.41	1.34	4.31	1.75	3.53	7.35
Machine hours	26.25	25.339	5.41	2.55	2.10	20.66	1.26	4.30	1.69	3.41	7.03
Nonproductive labor	26.04	25.152	5.43	2.54	2.16	20.41	1.34	4.31	1.75	3.53	7.35
OT and night labor	26.04	25.152	5.43	2.54	2.16	20.41	1.34	4.31	1.75	3.53	7.35
Maintenance	51.50	18.100	2.40	3.40	1.00	13.50	0.90	2.80	0.80	2.30	3.30
Power	27.30	17.300	4.20	6.50	1.60	26.10	1.50	4.70	1.30	3.90	5.60
Oil system	30.10	50.900	3.90	1.50	0.30	0.00	1.70	5.60	0.30	4.60	1.10
Grinding wheel	60.60	17.900	3.10	6.80	0.10	0.00	1.60	5.10	0.10	4.20	0.50
Floor space	16.48	21.978	2.20	1.65	3.85	21.98	1.37	3.85	3.02	8.24	15.38
Machine book value	16.48	49.451	3.30	2.20	1.10	14.84	3.30	2.75	1.10	3.30	2.20

Note: Allocation bases total 100.

Mayers Tap, Inc. (C)

John Mayers, president of Mayers Tap, Inc. (MTI), and Lee Rhodes, company controller, were reviewing the burden rates for each of MTI's machines. MTI was revising its cost accounting system [see Mayers Tap, Inc. (A) for background on the company], and obtaining more detailed burden rates had been the first major step. Major budgeted cost items had been allocated to the machines based on a number of operating factors, and the total budgeted costs for each machine were divided by the budgeted number of direct labor hours to arrive at a direct labor hour burden rate per machine [see Mayers Tap, Inc. (B) for a description of the overhead rate calculation]. Using the most recent budget figures (see Exhibit 1), in June 1984 Mayers had prepared a final set of burden rates for each machine that MTI would use for the coming year.

Historically, the company had treated both plants as a single aggregate cost center. The new cost accounting system allowed MTI to treat each of the 31 machine classes as a separate cost center. Mayers believed that having one cost center per machine class would provide him with the most accurate data, but he was concerned that it was not worth the cost of the extra record keeping and analysis required. It would be burdensome for management to review 31 separate reports on a monthly basis, and it might be confusing for management to determine what action to take based on these reports. Mayers was convinced, however, that consolidating the machines into fewer than 31 cost centers would make an assessment of the standard costs of MTI's products less accurate. Both Mayers and Rhodes believed that industry conditions required accurate costing so that products would not be sold below variable cost.

As a first cut, Mayers and Rhodes decided to try one cost center, the old system, and then two cost centers, one per plant, to see if either of these would provide sufficient accuracy.

Rhodes pointed out that the new system allowed them to separate the variable and fixed costs. Under the old system, these were not differentiated. Mayers agreed that this was a benefit but thought that the same results could have been achieved with much less effort.

Mayers identified three products, numbers 2, 8, and 10, that would provide the acid test. These were high-volume, low-margin products. They were currently used to "fill the plant" and were priced at what the management team felt was just above variable cost. The sale price for these products varied dramatically with economic conditions. At the moment, demand was low, so prices had dropped to rock bottom. Industry competition on these items was fierce, and any attempt to raise prices would simply result in sales of the product dropping to almost zero. Fortunately, when economic conditions improved, the demand would rapidly outpace supply, the price would rise, and MTI could reenter the market. Dropping one or more of these products would not affect the sales of other products.

Although Mayers and Rhodes agreed that dropping these products without identifying substitutes was not realistic at this time, they wanted to understand the economics of maintaining the products if they were selling below variable costs.

Rhodes's first step in the analysis was to determine the three products' standard costs using 1, 2, and 31 cost centers. His goal was to determine if the resulting standard costs varied sufficiently to affect the product discontinuance decision.

For each decision scenario he decided to calculate two net income numbers. The first, standard net income, simply took the standard costs of production and multiplied them by the volume of product manufactured. The second, budgeted net income, differed from the standard net income because it kept the fixed costs at their budgeted level. It was based on a flexible budget.

This case was prepared by Professor Robin Cooper.

125

EXHBIT 1

Direct Labor Hour Overhead Burden Rates

Albany	K-40	F-10	J-22	G-58	D-34	N-68	C-50	N-72	C-86	N-78
Direct labor	7.88	9.10	9.70	7.18	9.34	9.35	0.00	9.35	9.70	7.18
Variable overhead	11.61	8.86	12.04	5.71	8.55	12.10	0.00	12.02	2.47	11.89
Fixed overhead	8.50	10.25	9.54	6.05	6.54	9.65	0.00	6.00	7.49	7.82
Total[a]	27.99	28.21	31.28	18.94	24.43	31.09	0.00	27.38	19.67	26.89

	A-39	A-40	B-79	C-45	B-86	A-44	A-76	B-81	C-59	F-07
Direct labor	9.70	9.70	9.87	9.70	9.87	9.70	9.70	9.87	9.70	9.10
Variable overhead	5.19	5.18	5.20	2.68	12.03	5.11	5.24	5.05	2.55	8.81
Fixed overhead	16.69	17.30	7.48	7.10	6.69	12.69	13.24	7.78	7.21	10.15
Total[a]	31.58	32.17	22.55	19.48	28.59	27.50	28.17	22.70	19.46	28.07

Denver	D-43	E-01	F-32	G-05	A-06	B-03	C-03	D-02	A-41	C-31	A-51
Direct labor	8.00	8.00	8.00	8.00	8.00	8.00	8.00	8.00	8.00	8.00	8.00
Variable overhead	26.08	22.86	12.69	26.31	6.62	7.41	20.34	20.38	6.88	20.44	6.80
Fixed overhead	11.17	15.93	10.35	11.92	14.58	12.91	17.92	12.04	14.74	17.63	14.97
Total[a]	45.26	46.79	31.04	46.23	29.20	28.32	46.26	40.42	29.61	46.08	29.77

[a]Column entries may not sum to total due to rounding effects.

Fisher Technologies

Automation has enhanced our ability to provide fast, reliable delivery of quality products. We can now accept an order and, within three weeks, deliver the completed parts to specification. Our competition is lucky if they can do the same in six weeks. In our industry, where you live and die by deadlines, automation has given us a real manufacturing advantage. However, it has also substantially altered the way we manufacture our products, and I am not certain that the existing cost system can cope with the changes. In particular, I question whether using direct labor hours for the allocation of costs to products is appropriate. We really need accurate cost data in this business.

PAUL FISHER

INTRODUCTION

Fisher Technologies was originally part of Harris Aerospace, a multinational conglomerate. Harris Aerospace manufactured airfoils for production and experimental jet engines. In the late 1970s, Harris decided to sell its experimental airfoil business and focus on the much larger production airfoil business. Paul Fisher bought the experimental airfoil division in late 1979 and incorporated as Fisher Technologies. By 1980, the firm achieved sales of $4 million using assets of $3 million.

Since acquiring the firm, Fisher had concentrated on modernizing the manufacturing process and was determined to develop the most modern plant in the experimental airfoil industry. The company had, by 1984, purchased 34 numerically controlled

This case was prepared by Lawrence A. Weiss and Han P. Ahmed, research assistants (under the supervision of Professor Robin Cooper).

Copyright © 1986 by the President and Fellows of Harvard College. Harvard Business School case 186-302.

(NC) machines (Exhibit 1), disposed of numerous manual machines, and doubled the production floor space.

In 1985, the experimental airfoil market was dominated by six firms. The largest three firms, Mal Tool, New England Aircraft, and TRW Danville, operated as divisions of large conglomerates and produced both experimental and production airfoils. The other firms, Fisher Technologies, Jarvis Airfoil, and Jarco Industries, were smaller independent companies and produced only experimental airfoils. Fisher Technologies ranked fourth in the industry with sales of $12 million. Exhibit 2 shows the budgeted income statement for 1985.

Airfoil firms manufacture compressor blades and vanes for jet engines. To produce the high pressures required by the engine and to survive the operating conditions inside the engine, the parts must be manufactured to very high tolerances out of high-strength, heat-resistant alloys such as Iconel and Titanium. The complex shapes, high tolerance, and hard-to-machine materials make the machining of an airfoil a very complex undertaking requiring special equipment and skilled machinists.

MANUFACTURING OF EXPERIMENTAL AIRFOILS

Fisher reflected on the relative merits of the old and current production processes with respect to technology, personnel usage, and efficiency.

When I bought the business in 1979, 65 machines with an average cost of $30,000 were acquired as part of the sale. Production of a part required many machines and each cut on a part required a machine setup. An operator was dedicated to every machine that was used during the production process. With our new production process, we have utilized technology to substantially reduce the number of machines required to produce the parts. We have also created specialized roles for the production workers. Operators now concentrate on setup and quality control and machinists focus on keeping several machines productive simultaneously. The resulting improvements produce sophisticated products quickly and accurately. The increase in revenues from $4 million to $12 million certainly attests to the efficiency of our new process.

Because the overall production approach had remained essentially constant throughout the processes, any differences in the aforementioned areas were easily discernable (Exhibit 3).

THE OLD PRODUCTION PROCESS

When the bar stock was shipped by the customer to Fisher Technologies, it was cut into pieces approximately the size of specified parts. Because the sides must be parallel and flat within .001 of an inch to allow for accurate positioning in the fixtures, the bars were sent out by Fisher to a subcontractor to be specially machined.

The first step in airfoil production was machining of the ends of the blade or vane. The smoothed parts were loaded into a universal fixture set up on a general purpose machine. A single cut was then made in each part. Loading was a lengthy and complicated manual process because parts had to be accurately positioned in the fixture. Operators typically spent about 50% of their time loading the machines. Since a three-spindle machine was used, a single cut on three parts was possible. When the first three parts were completed, they were removed and another three loaded until one cut was made to all parts in the lot. The lot was then taken to the next machine, which was set up to perform the second cut. Machining of the ends could require up to 25 machine setups, although the same machines were often used to perform several different cuts.

The parts were now ready for airfoil machining. This process required the creation of a master, either in plaster of Paris or metal. Master construction was accompanied by considerable experimentation to minimize error and obtain acceptable output. The plaster of Paris or Whaley master was handmade and about six times the size of the finished product. Since the single-spindle Whaley airfoil machine could only machine one airfoil at a time, low-volume parts were candidates for this slow process. In contrast, the metal or Cincinnati master was the same (i.e., 1:1) size as the part. Because metal masters were used on six-spindle Cincinnati machines which produced six airfoils simultaneously, this approach was used for higher volume production.

In the final major production step, the juncture between the airfoil and the ends of the part was machined to a conical or spherical form using a technique known as die sinking. This technique was slow and complex, requiring matching of the shapes of the airfoil and the ends of the part. Again, custom-built masters were used. Due to the complexity of most parts, several cuts and hence several machine loadings were required to complete the operation. Since die sinking was the last of the major production steps, the high reject rate here caused the scrap costs to be high.

When die sinking was completed, the part passed through a two-part process called gauging. Belt sanders first eliminated milling marks. The second step fit the part to a gauge with the part's specifications and sanded down excess material. The gauged part was then polished or buffed until the surface met surface specifications.

Finally, individual parts were thoroughly inspected. Inspection reports were attached to parts. Parts over tolerance (too large) were reworked. Parts under tolerance (slightly too small) were written up for acceptance or rejection by the customers. If accepted, Fisher Technologies shipped these parts along with the parts machined to tolerance.

THE NEW PRODUCTION PROCESS

The experimental airfoil business remains very competitive. Our customers are also in an increasingly competitive industry serving the airlines and the military. We risk losing important contracts if the speed and precision of our operations function below customer expectations. Given this environment, we have continually implemented new technology in our tooling and machining processes. This has radically changed and profoundly improved our performance and turnover times. It has also significantly altered our perceptions of the internal work flow from a focus on productive operator time to a concentration on optimal machine use.

Fisher's assessment highlighted the dramatic impact of new computer numerically controlled (CNC) machines on the streamlining of the production process. The use of these machines affected the speed and accuracy of setup, loading, and machining and had merged the previous five manufacturing sequences into three sequences. New technology thus had radically and irrevocably changed the company's way of manufacturing experimental airfoils.

As in the old process, the bar stock was cut to size. The CNC machines, which changed tools automatically and rotated the part on several axes, performed cuts on both ends of the airfoil in one uninterrupted machining sequence and without operator attention. All of the required cutting tools, approximately 30, were therefore loaded into the machine's tool magazine before machining began. After the part was loaded, the machine was left to complete the machining of both ends of the part. When the ends were completed, the part was removed from the machine and prepared for airfoil machining. Thus, ends machining required only one setup and a single loading per part as compared to about 25 setups and loadings under the old production approach.

Airfoil machining was being equally affected by the introduction of CNC technology. Some airfoils could be machined in the same sequence as the ends. Others, because of the configurations required by the design of new engines, were either too large or too thin for machining on a general-purpose CNC machine. They were machined on the old Whaley and Cincinnati machines. The firm had, however, just taken delivery of a custom-made CNC airfoil machine that replicated the functions of the Whaley airfoil machine but did not require a master. While Fisher had no current plans to acquire a CNC equivalent to the Cincinnati machines, the firm was committed to using CNC machines wherever possible and could not rule out the future need for such a machine.

Die sinking, which continued as a separate process, also benefited from direct machining on new twin-spindle CNC machines which eliminated custom-built masters. Parts could now be die sunk in one operation on a single machine in one uninterrupted machining sequence. The final gauging and inspection steps were unaffected by the automation of earlier steps and were likely to remain that way.

The number of fixtures required to machine a part was greatly reduced by the new manufacturing process. Under the old process, a part with 34 cuts required 102 universal fixtures (one for each of three spindles on the 34 machines). These fixtures were bolted in place on the machine before parts could be loaded into them. Substantial time was then spent positioning the parts in the fixtures to ensure that specified cuts would be produced accurately. The automated processes, however, required only 12 fixtures, or four for each of the three two-spindle CNC machines used for ends machining, airfoil cutting, and die sinking.

Because the CNC machines required this limited number of fixtures, it became economically justifiable to use shuttle technology. In this approach, parts were accurately loaded into fixtures while they were off the machine. The loaded fixture, a shuttle, was then clamped in place on the machine. A special plate, which was accurately positioned on the machine during setup, allowed the shuttle to be accurately positioned in a short period of time. The operators continued to load parts while other parts were being machined. For each CNC machine, two fixtures were in place being machined while another two fixtures were being loaded or waiting to be loaded. The machining sequence was, therefore, virtually uninterrupted except for a short pause during the removal of a completed part and the insertion of a new part. Shuttle technology was thus said to be capable of loading fixtures internal to the cycle of the machine.

Typically, the sophistication of these fixtures made them individually quite expensive, generally between $5,000 to $10,000 per order.[1] Because of the unusual shapes of specified parts, Fisher Technologies usually designed and made the fixtures itself. The higher cost of these fixtures was offset by the reduced number required. Fisher felt that overall tooling costs were the same under both approaches but pointed out that the new approach allowed considerably more cutting time and hence increased productivity.

The ramifications of automation on the tasks undertaken by the production workers were equally striking. Instead of dedicating one operator to each machine, one operator, depending on the time required to complete a cutting cycle, could run between one and four CNC machines simultaneously. More importantly, instead of operating as all-around skilled machinists, personnel became specialized. Separate personnel now handled setup and machining. Setup personnel prepared the machine for operation by loading tools, parts, and fixtures and then machined and qualified the first few parts. Qualifying ensured that parts would be machined to tolerance. It was a skilled troubleshooting process involving the resolution of cutting tool, spindle speed, shuttle, or computer program prob-

lems. When the first few parts were qualified, the machine operators took over.

The machine operators were responsible for keeping the machines busy. They loaded parts into shuttles, which were then clamped into the machines. After machining, they inspected the parts using a range of gauges. In general, the number of parts initially machined in tolerance increased from 2% to 70% (the oversize parts were reworked, and the undersize parts were written up and shipped to the customer for evaluation). Another operator function was the replacement of worn-out tools. Because the new CNC machines were more powerful and more rigid, Fisher Technologies had switched from high-speed steel to tungsten carbide cutting tools. This change not only extended the life of the cutting tools but also reduced the effect of tool wear on tolerance. Carbide cutting tools last considerably longer than their steel counterparts, and this reduced the number of out-of-tolerance parts produced due to tool wear.

The backbone of the new production system was the ability to convert CAD (computer-aided design) data sent by customers to CAM (computer-aided manufacturing) data. A DEC minicomputer converted the customer's data into CNC machine-readable data.

Initially, punched tapes transferred the program to CNC machine memory. An 800-foot reel of tape was read into CNC machine memory in 25 minutes. On average, 6,000 feet or about eight reels of tape were required to store the instructions, which could be completed in one machining sequence. On the shop floor, tapes were loaded into CNC machine memory one at a time. The machining sequences contained on one tape were completed on all parts in the lot. The next tape was then loaded and further sequences were completed. This process proved unsatisfactory since a part had to be loaded into the machine several times before it was completed. The unloading and reloading of parts several times to complete the operations also increased the number of out-of-tolerance parts.

To reduce the need for such multiple loadings, an automatic data link between the DEC and CNC machines for direct data transfer was created. Programs were loaded continuously, the machining process was virtually uninterrupted, and more in-tolerance parts were completed since the parts were

---

[1]The customer paid for all fixture expenses. The contract bid included a fixed-price estimate for fixturing and gauging.

now completed in one machining sequence. This data transfer was controlled at the shop-floor level by operators using dedicated terminals. The operators would simply call up the desired program, identify the destination machine, and then initiate the transfer by activating the CNC machine memory.

In summing up his discussion about the new production process, Paul Fisher commented as follows:

> With the CNC machines, our central objective focuses on keeping the machines busy cutting metal. At Fisher Technologies, we have increased our cutting time by moving to shuttle technology and tapeless data transfer. I anticipate that these dynamic and radical changes will be enhanced by many yet unforeseen technological improvements.
>
> However, despite all these changes, our cost accounting system has remained unchanged. The system I inherited was a good one. It has served us well, but I think it is time to consider redesigning it.

THE COST ACCOUNTING SYSTEM

When the firm had been acquired, its cost accounting system allocated all overhead costs using direct labor hours. The resulting burden rate was used to determine the cost of completed parts and to estimate costs for preparing bids. The firm continued to use this cost system for several years even though Fisher felt it was inadequate. Fisher's major concern was its reliance on a single measure, direct labor hours, to allocate all of the costs to the products. The resulting product costs were not always in keeping with Fisher's intuition, and he was convinced that the system was generating improper cost data. As the data were used to help determine appropriate bid prices, Fisher felt it was critical to have good product cost data.

In 1982, at Fisher's request, Margaret Bernier, the controller of a local firm, was asked to review the Fisher Technologies cost system and make suggestions about possible modifications. Due to work pressures, Bernier was only able to spend about a week at the plant. During that time she suggested that the single overhead rate be replaced by a two-stage allocation system using multiple cost centers. She toured the factory and discussed the production process with the production manager and

recommended that the factory be divided into about 30 cost centers. These were identified on the basis of the type of machine, the cost structure of the machines, the location in the plant, and the responsibility center in which the machines were located.

Bernier also laid out a plan to determine appropriate allocation bases for the overhead costs. This plan consisted of tracing as many overhead costs as possible to the cost centers in which they originated and, after about six months to a year, using the data collected to identify the most appropriate allocation bases for the various expense categories.

Bernier suggested that the costs be traced at the budgetary line item level (see Exhibit 4) as this would enable the cost system to be compared to the existing financial accounting system. She remarked that on her next visit she would review the appropriateness of this decision.

Unfortunately, before she could return, Bernier left the city. The rapid adoption of automated technology forced the problem of cost accounting onto the back burner. The only modifications that were made consisted of identifying new cost centers for the CNC machines and deleting old ones as machines were phased out. In 1985, only 20 cost centers remained.

As the automation process continued, Fisher again began to worry about the validity of the cost system. In particular, he was concerned about the appropriateness of using direct labor hours to allocate overhead costs from the cost centers to the products for the majority of costs. Fisher had heard that many firms, in a similar situation, were adopting or considering machine-hour-based cost systems. Unfortunately, the firm had not recorded machine hour data for any of its machines. Fisher was unwilling to initiate an expensive project to measure machine hours on an ongoing basis until he was convinced that the adoption of a machine-hour-based system was warranted.

To obtain a better grasp of the difference between direct labor hours and machine hours, Fisher requested a report on the average machine basis (the number of machines being run by a single operator simultaneously) at each cost center for the last 12 months (Exhibit 5). Reading this report caused Fisher to ask for additional reports that would shed light on the effectiveness of the firm's current cost accounting system. The first documented the percentage of costs that were traced directly to the cost centers versus those allocated for the last six months (Exhibit 6). The second report identified, for the same period, the percentage of traced costs associated with each cost center (Exhibit 7). The third report showed the resulting burden rates per direct labor hour for each of the cost centers, again for the same six-month period (Exhibit 8).

Upon reading these reports, Fisher commented as follows:

Direct labor accounts for only 12% of total costs, and it will continue to get lower. As the operators become responsible for more than one machine at a time, it is not clear to me that we can continue to use direct labor hours to allocate the majority of overhead costs from the cost centers to the products. Today, over half of our cost centers are multi-machine-based at least some of the time, and soon it will be even more of the time. I have been thinking of using machine hours, but I am not sure that it would really make any difference.

EXHIBIT 1

FISHER TECHNOLOGIES

Recent Machine Purchases

QUANTITY	DESCRIPTION
19	5,000 RPM twin spindle CNC milling machine
6	10,000 RPM twin spindle CNC milling machines
2	Mori Seki lathes
2	Japex wire electrical discharge machinery
4	Bridgeport milling machines
1	Whaley type CNC milling machine
34	

EXHIBIT 2

FISHER TECHNOLOGIES

Fiscal 1985 Financial Budget ($ thousands)

Budgeted sales		$11,550,000
Budgeted expenses		
Direct labor	1,125,000	
Indirect labor	390,000	
Overtime and night premium	280,000	
Holiday and vacation wages	115,000	
Payroll taxes	210,000	
Employee benefits—insurance	150,000	
Workmen's compensation insurance	21,000	
Repairs and maintenance—machines and equipment	120,000	
Factory supplies	535,000	
Taxes and miscellaneous	16,000	
Heat, light, and power	106,000	
Nonproductive labor	180,000	
Depreciation	542,000	
Property taxes	26,000	
Repairs and maintenance—building	32,000	
		3,848,000
Selling, general, and administrative		4,440,000
Net income		$3,262,000

EXHIBIT 3

FISHER TECHNOLOGIES

The Old and New Production Process

OLD SYSTEM	NEW SYSTEM
- Major objective was to keep operators busy.	- Major objective was to keep machines busy.
- In 1980, revenues of $4 million and assets of $3 million.	- By 1985, revenues of $12 million and assets of $10 million.
- Production equipment consisted of 68 machines, costing approximately $30,000 each.	- Production equipment consisted of 79 machines, including 34 new CNC machines costing approximately $250,000 each.
- Setup time was short due to simple fixturing and because only one tool is placed in the machine at a time.	- Setup time was long since accurate placement of the shuttle fixture was required and all tools (about 30) required for one complete machining operation are loaded at once.
- Accurate positioning during loading of fixtures was complicated since they were manually loaded.	- Loading of fixtures was simpler and faster because of new shuttle technology which guaranteed accurate placement.
- Approximately 102 cheap universal fixtures were required to accommodate the 34 machine setups in the production sequence.	- Twelve fixtures, including 6 machining and 6 loading fixtures, were required for the three machine setups in the production sequence.
- Plaster of Paris or metal masters were required for airfoil machining and die sinking.	- CNC machines eliminated mastering and performed all necessary cuts.
- Machining of the ends and the airfoils were separate manufacturing steps.	- Machining of the ends and airfoils were performed sequentially on one machine.
- Because the risk of machining out of tolerance increased with the number of machine setups, only 2% of parts were produced to tolerance.	- Seventy percent of parts were produced to tolerance.
- Because coninuous operator attention was required in all machine setups, an operator was dedicated to each machine. These operators were skilled machinists in all aspects of production.	- Because machines ran unattended, personnel became specialized. The setup personnel focused on quality control and trouble-shooting. Machine operators loaded parts, inspected parts, and replaced worn-out tools.

EXHIBIT 4

FISHER TECHNOLOGIES

Description of Overhead Budgetary Line Items

Direct Labor   Direct labor costs varied by machine. Some machines, such as the new CNC machines, were operated by skilled machinists paid at higher rates. Other machines, such as the Marvel saw, were simpler and could be controlled by operators with relatively little training who earned lower wage rates. If one machinist ran several machines at once, only a fraction of that person's hourly costs were charged to a given machine. Consequently, much of the difference in the wages of machinists versus operators was not apparent on a per-machine basis.

(continued on next page)

EXHIBIT 4 *(cont.)*

Indirect Labor	Indirect labor includes the wages of the maintenance and inspection personnel. Whenever maintenance or inspection was required, the individual was meant to enter the number of the cost center in which the work was required and the time spent on that activity. If the work was not related to a cost center, it was booked to a general account.
Overtime and Night	Overtime was determined much like nonproductive time. A percentage of direct labor cost for each machine was determined based on historical overtime requirements. FT ran two 10-hour day shifts, the early shift (6 A.M.–3:00 P.M.) and the late shift (4:30 P.M.–3:00 A.M.). Night labor hours were computed by subtracting the available daytime hours from the total required operating hours for each machine. Night labor was paid the day rate plus 10%.
Holiday and Vacation Wages	All factory personnel, direct and indirect, accrued vacation rights weekly. The amount of vacation granted increased with the individual's tenure at the factory.
Payroll Taxes	FICA and state and federal unemployment taxes for all hourly paid workers.
Employee Benefits— Insurance	Health and pension costs of hourly paid workers.
Workmen's Compensation Insurance	The cost of disability insurance for hourly paid workers. The amount of the charge per worker depended on the insurance company's estimate of the risk exposure per covered individual.
Repairs and Maintenance— Machines and Equipment	Supplies and contractor costs associated with repairing and maintaining machinery and equipment.
Factory Supplies	Includes the costs of all of the supplies associated with the factory. Also includes items such as cutters, gauges, and tools not charged to the customer, tools and tool holders, grinding and diamond wheels, and miscellaneous items such as rags and glue.
Taxes and Miscellaneous	The cost of the sales and use taxes levied by the state and minor expense categories such as prehiring physicals and employment agency fees for the hourly paid workforce.
Heat, Light, and Power	Electricity and oil were the only elements of power and heat. Most power was consumed by the production machinery. The factory was not heated because the heat given off by the machines was sufficient to keep the building warm. The administrative offices were heated by baseboard electric heat. The factory and administrative offices were cooled with electric air conditioners in the summer.
Nonproductive Labor	Hourly workers used computerized time clocks to record the amount of time they spent on each job. When a job was begun, the operator or machinist entered the job and sequence numbers into the clock. Any paid work time (idle time, meetings, breaks, etc.) that was not directly charged to a job was considered nonproductive labor time. This usually accounted for slightly less than 6% of the total direct labor hours. The amount of nonproductive time varied by machine because of uncertainties in the availability of work for machines in the final stages of the production process.
Depreciation	The depreciation charge for the machinery, equipment, and the factory. The majority of the non-CNC machines were fully depreciated, while the CNC machines were all being depreciated on a straight-line basis over 10 years.
Property Taxes	Property taxes on the factory and machinery charged by the state.
Repairs and Maintenance— Building	The cost of supplies and contractors to repair and maintain the building.

EXHIBIT 5

FISHER TECHNOLOGIES

Actual Activity for Year Ended November 30, 1985 by Cost Center

	EXPECTED MACHINE BASIS[a]	OPERATOR HOURS[b]	SETUP HOURS[c]
1 Wire EDM	2.00	2,796	417
2 Landis OD grinder	3.00	336	162
3 Mori Seki CNC lathe	3.00	2,004	619
4 New England blade potter	1.00	1,128	112
5 Marvel cutoff saw	2.00	5,088	498
6 Bridgeport milling	1.25	7,980	314
7 Bridgeport CNC milling	1.25	4,260	321
8 Circumferential dovetail	1.00	2,496	495
9 5,000 rpm CNC milling	2.00	25,284	1,089
10 K&T vertical milling	1.00	1,440	144
11 K&T horizontal milling	1.50	2,748	54
12 3-D milling	1.00	9,408	451
13 Synchotrace milling	2.00	1,404	58
14 10,00 rpm CNC milling	2.50	7,056	701
15 Whaley airfoil milling[d]	3.00	8,748	446
16 CNC Whaley airfoil milling	1.00	48	48
17 Cincinnati airfoil milling	2.00	1,788	862
18 Hand finish—belt grinding	1.00	13,008	0
19 Hand finish—polishing	1.00	22,308	0
20 Direct inspection	1.00	672	0

[a]The average number of machines being run by an operator simultaneously.

[b]The number of operator hours consumed in each cost center for the year. This excludes setup time.

[c]The number of setup hours consumed in each cost center for the year.

[d]This machine had just arrived at the end of October, and the high setup times were expected to continue for another few months before dropping to more realistic levels.

EXHIBIT 6

FISHER TECHNOLOGIES

Percentage Items Traced Directly and Allocated Using
Direct Labor Hours to Cost Centers by Budgetary Line Item
for the Six Months Ending November 30, 1985

BUDGETARY LINE ITEM	PERCENTAGE	ALLOCATION BASE
Variable overhead		
Indirect labor	20%	Indirect labor hours
	80	Direct labor hours
Overtime and night premiums	50	Overtime and night premium
	50	Direct labor hours
Holiday and vacation wages	100	Direct labor hours
Payroll taxes	100	Direct labor hours
Employee benefits—insurance	100	Direct labor hours
Workmen's compensation insurance	100	Direct labor hours
Repair and maintenance—machines and equipment	60	Repairs and maintenance
	40	Direct labor hours
Factory supplies	80	Factory supplies
	20	Direct labor hours
Taxes and miscellaneous	100	Direct labor hours
Heat, light, and power	100	Direct labor hours
Nonproductive labor	30	Nonproductive labor hours
	70	Direct labor hours
Fixed Overhead		
Depreciation	90	Depreciation
	10	Direct labor hours
Property taxes	100	Direct labor hours
Repairs and maintenance—building	100	Direct labor hours

EXHIBIT 7

FISHER TECHNOLOGIES

Percentage of Traced Costs Associated with Each Cost Center
for the Six Months Ending November 30, 1985

ALLOCATION BASES	1	2	3	4	5	6	7	8	9	10	11
Direct labor hours	2.33	0.28	1.67	0.94	4.24	6.65	3.55	2.08	21.07	1.20	2.29
Indirect labor hours	0.74	0.00	0.99	0.00	0.00	0.74	0.49	0.00	36.30	0.00	0.00
Night premium	1.81	0.00	0.84	0.60	4.70	5.54	3.13	1.08	24.94	1.08	2.65
Repairs and maintenance—equipment	0.00	0.00	3.08	0.00	2.69	12.31	5.77	0.00	32.02	0.38	0.00
Factory supplies	5.24	0.00	5.00	0.24	15.25	2.57	0.48	0.00	52.69	0.29	0.00
Nonproductive labor	12.10	0.00	51.08	0.00	0.27	0.00	0.00	0.54	16.67	0.81	0.00
Depreciation—equipment	8.16	3.74	6.80	0.00	1.70	0.00	2.72	0.00	68.03	0.00	0.00

	12	13	14	15	16	17	18	19	20	TOTAL
Direct labor hours	7.84	1.17	5.88	7.29	0.04	1.49	10.84	18.59	0.56	100.00
Indirect labor hours	5.68	0.00	10.37	43.21	0.00	1.48	0.00	0.00	0.00	100.00
Night premium	6.02	0.72	7.59	11.20	0.00	1.93	10.24	15.30	0.60	100.00
Repairs and maintenance—equipment	0.00	0.00	15.38	3.85	0.00	0.00	3.85	0.00	0.00	100.00
Factory supplies	3.43	0.33	8.38	6.29	0.00	2.10	12.43	5.96	0.00	100.00
Nonproductive labor	2.69	0.00	5.65	5.38	0.00	4.30	0.00	0.54	0.00	100.00
Depreciation—equipment	0.00	0.00	8.84	0.00	0.00	0.00	0.00	0.00	0.00	100.00

Description of Traced Costs

Budgeted Direct Labor Hours	The number of budgeted direct labor hours was the sum of the number of operating hours (hours that the machinist was running the machine) plus the total setup time for the machine (hours that the machine was being set up).
Overtime and Night Premium	The night premium charges associated with each cost center. Overtime was allocated using direct labor hours.
Repairs and Maintenance—Equipment and Machinery	The purchased supplies and contractor costs for repair and maintenance of the equipment that can be traced to the cost centers. The associated labor costs are contained in the indirect labor account. Any costs that were not traced to the cost center were allocated using direct labor hours.
Factory Supplies	The cost of the purchased factory supplies that can be traced to the cost centers. Any costs that were not traced to the cost center were allocated using direct labor hours.
Nonproductive Labor	Hourly factory workers recorded the amount of time they spent on each job through a system of computerized time clocks. Any paid work time (idle time, meetings, breaks, etc.) that was not directly charged to a job was considered nonproductive labor time. These are the charges traced to the cost center. Any costs that were not traced to the cost center were allocated using direct labor hours.
Depreciation	The depreciation charge associated with each machine. Factory depreciation was allocated using direct labor hours.

EXHIBIT 8

FISHER TECHNOLOGIES

Direct Labor Hour Overhead Burden Rates

	1	2	3	4	5	6	7	8	9	10
Direct labor	11.46	8.91	8.92	9.94	8.26	9.58	8.60	8.39	8.93	9.35
Variable overhead	21.35	11.26	36.23	12.76	23.69	14.84	14.01	11.98	22.66	13.57
Fixed overhead	15.17	55.23	17.49	0.94	2.56	0.94	4.05	0.94	14.06	0.94
Total	47.99	75.40	62.64	23.63	34.51	25.36	26.66	21.31	45.65	23.85

	11	12	13	14	15	16	17	18	19	20
Direct labor	8.90	9.11	9.23	10.54	9.07	11.16	9.00	10.62	9.28	8.25
Variable overhead	12.61	14.07	12.81	20.53	20.19	11.26	18.88	16.23	13.18	12.51
Fixed overhead	0.94	0.94	0.94	7.05	0.94	0.94	0.94	0.94	0.94	0.94
Total	22.44	24.12	22.97	38.12	30.19	23.35	28.81	27.57	23.39	21.69

Mueller-Lehmkuhl GmbH

According to Dr. Richard Welkers, president of Mueller-Lehmkuhl:

The merger with Atlas has significantly increased our ability to compete with the Japanese. As we are now the largest single manufacturer of apparel fasteners in Europe, we can reap the benefits of economies of scale. At the moment, we are cost competitive with the Japanese. While the Japanese have lower wages and overhead, we are closer to the market and have lower selling costs. Historically, the Japanese have been most successful when they were the low-cost producer.

Currently, the Japanese are pricing 20% below us. It is not enough to offset our quality advantage, but if they can match our quality or drop prices even further, we could have a problem.

COMPANY BACKGROUND

Mueller-Lehmkuhl (ML), a West German producer of apparel fasteners, was founded in 1876 as a manufacturer of shoe accessories. Soon after, other products were added, including the single-post snap fastener. Production of these items increased substantially when the company merged with a Hannover firm called Weiser. In 1929 Mueller-Weiser merged with Felix Lehmkuhl to become Mueller-Lehmkuhl. Sales growth and product diversification continued, and in 1938 the firm was acquired by the Moselhammer group.

In 1982 ML formed a joint venture with the German subsidiary of the Atlas group, an American multinational. Atlas was a conglomerate of six major businesses, one of which—Apparel Fasteners—complemented ML. At that time ML dominated a relatively small segment of the market, while Atlas Germany serviced a broader customer base. The objective of the merger was to integrate ML's technological superiority and higher margins with Atlas's access to the market. While substantially increasing its sales volume, one effect of the merger was to limit ML's potential markets to Europe and

This case was prepared by Research Associate Dagmar Bottenbruch (under the supervision of Professor Robin Cooper).

Africa: the rest of the world was serviced by other Atlas divisions. In 1986 ML had estimated revenues of $103 million[1] (see Exhibit 1).

PRODUCT DESCRIPTION

Snap fasteners are used by the garment industry to replace buttons and buttonholes. ML produced about 700 different fasteners in five major product lines: s-spring socket snap fasteners, ring socket snap fasteners, two open prong snap fasteners (brass and stainless steel), and tack buttons.

In 1985 ML introduced a new fashion line of products. These consisted of snap fasteners and tack buttons that were manufactured from a wider range of materials in a broader variety of shapes. The company's marketing manager wanted to convince the market that snap fasteners could be fashionable and could be used to replace conventional buttons in a wide array of clothing.

Each product line was designed for a specific application. The s-spring fasteners were used for medium-thick materials (1.4 mm to 2.0 mm). They could not be used for stretch materials, since they were attached centrally (through one stud) and would damage the material. The ring spring fasteners were used for thicker materials (up to 6.5 mm) and could be used on materials exposed to heavier strains. The open prong fasteners were especially well suited for use on thin (.25 mm to .75 mm) and stretchy materials, since they did not damage the materials. All fasteners could be washed, dry cleaned, and ironed. Tack buttons were used to replace conventional buttons and were usually used on blue jeans. Fasteners were customized either by applying various colors of finishes or by embossing the customer's logo on the cap.

As part of its strategy of being an integrated manufacturer, ML also manufactured attaching machines. In 1986 ML manufactured six attaching machines—three manual and three automatic. All of the machines could be modified to attach any of the company's fasteners. An operator using a manual machine placed the two parts of the fastener into the machine by hand, positioned the material, and operated the machine. In an automatic machine, one or more of the parts was positioned automatically.

The operator still had to position the material manually (for characteristics of the machines, see Exhibit 2).

Over the years, the firm had developed a policy of selling the manual machines and renting the automatic ones. Manual machines were sold because, unlike automatic machines, they did not cost much, did not require service, and were easily and inexpensively modified to allow them to attach different fasteners. Automatic machines were rented on an annual basis, though the company was willing to take them back at any time. About 10% of the 7,000 rented machines were returned in the average year. The company inventoried these machines until new orders arrived. It then modified the old machines to enable them to attach a different fastener. Modification was expensive, since it required replacing all components specific to the fastener. The company estimated that an average modification cost $2,000.

Although the rental contract did not specify free service, it was industry practice to provide preventive maintenance and emergency service at no charge. Even though most large customers had downtime insurance, ML viewed reliability and fast service response as an important sales tool. Consequently, it was not unusual for service personnel to be flown to a customer site within hours of an emergency call. In 1986, service was expected to cost about $4.5 million. To partially make up for the cost of providing this service, ML attached two conditions to the rental of a machine: (1) only ML fasteners were to be used on the machine, and (2) at least $10,000 worth of fasteners were expected to be purchased during the year. However, due to uncertain demand and overly optimistic customers, the average rented machine attached only about $7,000 worth of fasteners per year.

MARKET CONDITIONS

ML had positioned itself in the large-volume market, where automatic machines were required. Large volume referred to the quantity of a given fastener sold, not to the overall fastener consumption by a given firm. ML's preferred target market could be broken into two major segments: (1) large companies purchasing large volumes of a number of different fasteners, and (2) smaller companies need-

---

[1]In 1986, the exchange rate was $1 = DM 2.1.

ing major quantities of a single fastener. Large-volume customers accounted for 85% of fastener sales.

The European market could be characterized as a stable oligopoly consisting of four firms that together accounted for 65% of the European fastener market (Exhibit 3). An additional 13 firms (including the Japanese) accounted for the rest of the market. Most of these firms sold fasteners and attaching machines. In addition to the fastener manufacturers, there were several companies that produced only attaching machines. Their machines were usually cheaper and of inferior quality to ML's. ML's fastener sales to customers using third-party equipment were thought to be about 10%. The exact percentage was unknown because ML could not be certain on which machines its products were actually used.

The four major players, all providing equivalent services, had over the years settled into peaceful coexistence. They never initiated price wars and rarely tried to steal each other's customers. Customers had helped achieve this stability by sourcing from multiple suppliers. Customers normally identified a primary source but ordered from at least one other firm. If ML attempted to move from a secondary supplier to a primary supplier by price cutting, the adversely affected company could easily retaliate by trying to become the primary source for one of ML's customers.

There were several other factors that helped reduce the level of competition between the major players. First, the companies developed longstanding personal relationships with their customers. These relationships, coupled with high customer satisfaction, made it difficult to lure away any business. Second, the policy of renting machines, coupled with designing the fasteners so that they could be used only in the supplier's own machines, made switching an expensive undertaking. Third, there were virtually no standard prices. Each customer paid a different amount for its fasteners, making it difficult to compete on price.

Despite these limitations, the firms did compete on three dimensions:

1. The quality of the fasteners and, in particular, the tolerance to which they were manufactured (the higher the tolerance, the less likely fasteners were to cause machine downtime and the longer their life expectancy once fastened).
2. The performance of the attaching machine (in particular speed, reliability, safety, noise level, and ability to attach fasteners without scratching the surfaces).
3. The quality of service provided.

ML sold its products in approximately 20 countries. These countries differed in language, safety regulations, labor costs, taste, tariff barriers, payment terms, and currency. Even the smallest product required marketing materials, product descriptions, and labels to be in every language, adding to overhead and production costs. In some countries tariffs could add up to 100% of cost to the product, rendering a foreign producer uncompetitive with local producers. In other countries, labor costs were so low that even for large-scale production the use of manual attaching machines was still economical. In some countries, it was impossible to succeed without at least one salesperson fluent in that country's language.

To deal with these local differences, ML used agents in some countries, distributors in others, and regional sales offices in yet others to sell fasteners. Attaching machines were always purchased or rented directly from Mueller-Lehmkuhl. Agents generally represented a range of associated but noncompetitive products. They promoted ML products and were paid a 6% to 10% commission on fastener sales. Agents did not maintain inventories. Distributors differed from agents by maintaining inventory, thus reducing the uncertainty of local supply. Like agents, they enabled the local customer to deal with a fellow national. Overall, agents and distributors accounted for about 75% of sales. Product purchased through a distributor usually cost about 10% to 15% more than when purchased directly. In countries where local differences were not a major factor or ML maintained a regional sales office, large customers could purchase directly from the firm at reduced prices.

The European market was relatively mature, with overall growth expected to be 1% per annum (Exhibit 4). This low growth rate had caused ML to look for new markets, in particular Africa. The African market was more price sensitive than the European market. Low-cost producers had a significant advantage because quality was not important and no premium for a better product could be charged, making it difficult for quality-oriented producers to penetrate those markets. Since the textile industry was continuously shifting its production into less-developed countries, low-cost producers could position themselves well to service these growing markets. Unfortunately, the merger with Atlas had reduced ML's opportunities for geographic expansion, since the continuing offshore movement of the garment industry was moving ML's business into areas serviced by other Atlas divisions.

PRODUCTION PROCESS

ML's production facility was a four-story building located next to the head office in Düsseldorf, West Germany. The top floor of the building, which contained the machining and tooling departments, was primarily dedicated to the production of attaching machines. All design and prototype work for the attaching machines was completed in-house. This represented about 30% of the engineering staff's activities. Purchased parts, consisting of motors, engines, and all electrical parts, constituted about 30%[2] of the total cost of an automatic or semiautomatic attaching machine. Metal parts were cast according to ML's specifications by a local cast-iron business. After these parts were delivered to the company, they were prepared for welding, then welded, and finally the machines were assembled. Welding and final assembly required highly skilled labor, especially for the automatic and semiautomatic machines.

All product-specific parts (i.e., those that had to be changed if a machine was modified to attach a different fastener) were produced by ML. Precision was crucial to make the machine fit a customer's specifications. Therefore, testing was a major part of the production process. Frequently, up to 10,000 pieces of product had to be run through a machine before it could be delivered to the customer.

In addition to attaching machines, the company manufactured some of its own production machines. In early 1986 the company announced that it would start producing a new line of automated material-handling machines. These new machines relied heavily on the technology developed for attaching machines.

The machining department labor force was split into two groups—one producing attaching and production machines and the other refitting returned attaching machines. Management estimated that 80% of the labor force that was producing machines was dedicated to attaching machine production.

The tooling department, which was also located on the top floor, manufactured and repaired tools that were used in the production of both fasteners and machines. Tools used in the production of fasteners were very costly and were frequently reworked, whereas tools used in the production of attaching machines were relatively inexpensive and usually replaced when they showed signs of wear. No attempt had been made to determine how the tooling department's capacity was split between production and attaching machine tools.

The other three floors of the factory were dedicated to fastener production. Fastener production consisted of three major steps: stamping, assembly, and finishing. Each floor was primarily dedicated to a single step. In stamping, the material components were stamped out of large coils. If the fastener was being produced in very large quantities, then automated machines were used that could produce up to 12 components with a single stamp. These high-volume machines required expensive tooling, often costing up to $50,000. At low production volumes, less-sophisticated machines were used. The stamping department contained 47 different types of machines. In the stamping department, it was not unusual for a single operator to run several machines simultaneously.

In assembly, the stamped components were combined by machine. The tack button, for example, consisted of five components—three in the button and two in the underpart. The button was assembled from a cap (often with a logo stamped in the surface), a plastic insert that formed the locking mechanism, and a socket plate. These three parts were crimped together to form the button. The underpart consisted of two components, a stud and a cap, which were crimped together. The type of machine used to assemble the components again depended on the production volume. Altogether

---

[2]This percentage was considerably smaller in the manual machines, since they did not contain any electrical parts.

there were 112 different types of machines in assembly.

Once assembled, the parts were then washed and, if required, heat-treated before being sent to finishing. Several different finishes were produced. These included plating (the part was plated to make the surface smooth and shiny), painting or enameling (the part was spray-painted in a variety of colors), tumbling (to produce a matte surface), and polishing (to produce a smooth surface). There were 15 different types of machines in the finishing department.

Finished parts were packed ready for shipping. Only minimum work-in-process and finished goods inventories were maintained, because most fasteners were produced to order.

On the surface, fasteners seemed to be simple products requiring fairly low technology; in fact, however, they had to be machined to within a hundredth of a millimeter. This required precision stamping and high quality control. Similarly, the attaching machines were on the forefront of automated material handling technology. To maintain its technological superiority, the firm maintained a strong research and development department. The introduction of the fashion line required significant R&D resources. Management estimated that at least two-thirds of current R&D projects were related to fastener production, with the new high-fashion fasteners accounting for about 50%.

COST ACCOUNTING SYSTEM

The cost accounting system had recently been overhauled. According to the corporate controller, the old system, which consisted of about 70 cost centers, failed to differentiate appropriately between automatic and manually operated machines. The new system contained more cost centers: one per machine class.

Material, after adjustment for scrap, was charged directly to the product. The new cost system also identified a material overhead charge. This included the costs associated with purchasing, material handling, and inventory storage. Products were allocated material overhead on the basis of the material dollars they consumed.

In the stamping and assembly departments, labor costs, after dividing by the number of ma-

chines the operator was running, were charged directly to each product. Setup labor costs, after dividing by the lot size to produce a per-part setup charge, were also charged directly. Overhead was divided into two sections: machine costs and general overhead. Machine costs were those costs that could meaningfully be allocated directly to the machine: floor space, energy, maintenance, depreciation, and an interest charge for invested capital. The total cost of these items for each machine class was divided by the projected direct labor dollars (including setup) expected to be worked on that machine class to give the machine class overhead burden rate per direct labor dollar for the coming year. The resulting machine class burden rate was multiplied by the standard direct labor dollar content of each product to give the machine-related overhead portion of product cost.

General overhead consisted of factory support, factory supplies, technical administration, support department costs, machining department costs, and tooling department costs (Exhibit 5). Where possible, general overhead costs were traced directly to the fastener production departments; otherwise they were allocated to each department on the basis of direct labor dollars (including setup dollars). The general cost pool for each fastener production department was then divided by projected direct labor dollars (including setup dollars) for each department for the coming year to give the machine overtime burden rate per direct labor dollar. The resulting departmental burden rate was multiplied by the standard direct labor dollar content of each product to give the general-overhead-related portion of product cost.

Batch costing was considered the most appropriate approach for costing products in the stamping and assembly departments. In the finishing department, process costing had been adopted. Each finish process was treated as a cost center, and all of the costs associated with that center were aggregated into a single cost pool. These costs were then allocated to the products, using equivalency factors that reflected the value of resources consumed by the products.

In summary, the cost system reported standard product costs using the cost of a component in the following manner (the unit of measurement was a "mil," which was equal to 1,000 pieces):

Material	standard cost + material-overhead
Stamping and Assembly	
Labor	standard labor hours × standard pay rate/number of machines operated
Setup	standard setup labor hours × standard pay rate/lot size
Machine OH	standard labor dollars × machine burden rate
General OH	standard labor dollars × departmental burden rate
Finishing	total departmental cost × equivalency factor

While the different products appeared relatively similar to the inexperienced eye, they could actually have significantly different cost structures (see Exhibit 6 for the cost structures of five representative products).

JAPANESE COMPETITION

Hiroto Industries (HI), the major Japanese competitor in Europe, was a trading company that sold a broad range of fashion accessory products to the shoe, leather goods, and garment industries. Typical products included belts, buckles, and zippers. HI was approximately 10 times larger than ML, and the two firms competed in only 20% of HI's markets. Unlike ML, HI purchased approximately 85% of the products it sold. The 15% it produced were all high-volume, low-diversity product lines. HI's stated objective was to become number one in Japan and be a major worldwide competitor. It wanted about 25% of its business to be European based.

The existing fastener technology, which exhibited significant economies of scale, required a base market size of approximately 200 million people to support several competitors. Japan, with 120 million people, and Germany, with 60 million people, were not large enough to support domestic producers without significant international sales. The larger Japanese market provided Japanese producers with a significant economic advantage. The high price that Japanese garment manufacturers had to pay for their fasteners (120% of German prices) reflected the isolation of the Japanese market.

HI entered the European market in 1973. It faced substantial entry barriers, in particular the longstanding relationships of European companies with customers, its lack of high-quality attaching machines, and the absence of a network of distributors and service personnel. In Welkers' opinion, to help mitigate these barriers, HI had focused on the high-volume products, such as workwear, leather goods, and babywear, where the market consisted of a few customers ordering very large volumes of products.

In 1982, as part of the rationalization program between Atlas and ML, several service personnel were laid off. To strengthen its ability to deliver service in the European market, HI hired these personnel. This move enabled HI to penetrate the market even further. When ML rehired the most critical person in HI's team, this strategy failed and HI lost most of its newly acquired customers.

To compensate, HI adopted a new marketing strategy (Exhibit 7). Rather than rent the attaching machines themselves, HI identified distributors that were willing to purchase attaching machines and then rent them to its customers. These machines were purchased from the companies that manufactured only attaching machines because the firms that manufactured both attaching machines and fasteners would sell or rent their machines only to the end user.[3] HI then supplied these dealers with fasteners at about a 20% discount on the prevailing European prices. This strategy had several advantages for HI. First, HI did not own the machines and consequently did not have to provide service. Second, invested capital was kept to a minimum; and, finally, HI did not bear the risk of returned machines.

The dealers benefited because they could now compete with companies like ML. They had a significant price advantage and could "steal" those customers who were not contractually obligated to use a specific firm's fasteners.

HI's new strategy threatened two segments of ML's market. The first was the small-volume customer who used fasteners that were very popular. Several such firms were effectively equivalent to a large-volume customer. However, given that these

---

[3] If no suitable European machines were available, HI would ship its own machines and sell them to the distributor.

customers owned their own equipment, they were free to purchase fasteners from whomever they chose.

The second, a more worrisome trend, was when a large-volume customer decided to use Japanese fasteners on ML equipment. Although most fasteners were customized, some of the really high-volume fasteners, such as stainless steel spring fasteners, were standardized and could run on anybody's equipment. Certain ML customers, even though contractually obligated to purchase product from ML, were beginning to experiment with the Japanese product. ML had threatened to cancel the equipment leases if it caught any firm violating the contract. In fact, one firm had been caught, but immediately agreed to stop "experimenting" with Japanese fasteners.

HI's new strategy met with some success and by 1986 HI had achieved about a 6% overall market penetration (Exhibit 8).

ML's European sales manager voiced his opinion:

My biggest concern is keeping price levels as high as possible in the face of Japanese competition. We do not want to lose market share to them, but the problem is that their prices are so much lower than ours that matching them would be too expensive. They do not present an immediate threat because our quality is so much higher. However, even though our customers carefully analyze the situation and decide to stay with us, they are left with the feeling that they would be better off if they bought Japanese.

EXHIBIT 1

Budgeted Income, 1986 ($000)

Sales			$103,000
Cost of goods			
Materials (including material overhead)		$31,000	
Direct labor (including setup labor)		1,610	
Machine overhead		4,500	
General overhead			
Factory support	$3,020		
Factory supplies	470		
Technical administration	6,500		
Support departments	6,500		
Machining department	13,350		
Tooling department	3,050		
		$32,890	
Total			$70,000
Sales, general, and administration			
Research and development	$5,810		
Administration	2,760		
Marketing	7,930		
Shipping	3,170		
Commission	3,830		
			$23,500
Net Income			$9,500

EXHIBIT 2

Characteristics of Attaching Machines

NUMBER	M1	M2	M3	A1	A2	A3
Operation mode	Manual	Manual	Manual	Semi-automatic	Automatic	Automatic
Motive force	Hand	Foot	Pneumatic	Pneumatic	Pneumatic	Electric
Price[a]	$200	$250	$500	—	—	—
Annual rental fee[b]	—	—	—	$300	$500	$1,500
Attachment speed[c]	5/min	6/min	15/min	15/min	25/min	50/min
Application (volume)[d]	Low	Low	Low	Low/medium	Medium/high	High
Budgeted production, 1986	35	70	105	350	280	420
Budgeted rental base, 1986[e]				1,350	2,250	3,500
Life expectancy (years)	20	20	15	10	10	l0

[a]Manual machines are sold, not rented.
[b]Automatic machines are rented, not sold. Rental fee equals average paid for all outstanding models.
[c]Average number of fasteners attached per minute.
[d]Low volume is fewer than 50,000 fasteners per year. High volume is greater than 300,000 fasteners per year.
[e]Includes machines manufactured in earlier years and still on rental contracts.

EXHIBIT 3

Competitive Analysis-Predicted Sales by Fastener Product Line ($ millions)

NAME	COUNTRY OF ORIGIN	S-SPRING	RING	PRONG	TACK	TOTAL
ML	Germany	$12	$9	$60[a]	$15	$96
Piloni	Italy	44	30	16	2	92
Berghausen	Germany	63	11	11	2	87
Yost & Co.	Germany	12	21	46	4	83
Other		61	46	63	23	193
		$192	$117	$196	$46	$551

[a]$30 million prong brass + $30 million prong stainless steel.

EXHIBIT 4

Country Demographics

COUNTRY	POPULATION (000,000)	ESTIMATED MARKET ($000,000)	ML BUDGETED SALES ($000,000)	ML SHARE (%)	ESTIMATED MARKET GROWTH (%)	ML SALES THROUGH DISTRIBUTORS (%)
France	54	$84	$24	29%	+1%	100%
Germany	62	82	30	37	−1	20
U.K.	56	56	19	34	+1	0
Finland	5	12	4	33	+2	60
Netherlands	14	82	4	5	+1	50
Belgium	10	9	4	44	0	0
Spain	38	14	3	21	+1	100
Italy	57	138	2	1	+1	65
Yugoslavia	22	23	2	6	+2	60%
Other	362	51	4	8%	+1%	—
Total	680	$551	$96			

EXHIBIT 5

Description of General Overhead Accounts

Factory support included the unallocated supervision, floor space, and janitorial services that were consumed by fastener production. Production management was also contained in this account.

Factory supplies included oil, grease rags, and miscellaneous tools used in the fastener production departments.

Technical administration included attaching machine service costs and those engineering costs not included in R&D.

Support department included costs for production scheduling, fastener inventory control, the apprentice workshop, and the worker council.

Machining department included material labor, and overhead for the manufacture of production and attaching machines.[a]

Tooling department included material, labor, and overhead costs for the manufacture of tools.

[a]Under German accounting principles, given the nature of the lease agreement, the entire cost of the attaching machines was written off to general overhead in the year in which the machines were manufactured.

EXHIBIT 6

Product Cost Structures of Representative Products ($ per 1,000 units)

	S-SPRING	RING	PRONG (BRASS)	PRONG (SS)	TACK BUTTON
Average selling price	$46.75	$39.83	$15.28	$20.32	$38.40
Material					
Raw material	$ 9.70	$ 8.88	$ 6.04	$ 5.74	$11.88
Material overhead	0.54	0.50	0.34	0.32	0.67
	10.24	9.38	6.38	6.06	12.55
Stamping					
Setup	0.12	0.22	0.01	0.03	0.07
Labor	0.68	0.40	0.04	0.21	0.25
Machine overhead	1.31	1.27	0.17	1.13	1.11
General overhead	18.51	14.35	1.16	5.55	7.41
	20.62	16.24	1.38	6.92	8.84
Assembly					
Setup	0.14	0.05	—	—	0.01
Labor	0.10	0.24	—	—	0.18
Machine overhead	0.25	0.45	0.00	0.00	0.26
General overhead	2.52	3.05	0.00	0.00	1.99
	3.01	3.79	0.00	0.00	2.44
Finishing	5.66	8.28	1.88	0.56	3.84
Total	$39.53	$37.69	$ 9.64	$13.54	$27.67
Total direct labor costs[a]	$1.32	$1.32	$0.14	$0.27	$0.70

[a]Includes setup labor in all departments and the direct labor in the finishing department.

EXHIBIT 7

Comparison of Mueller-Lehmkuhl and Hiroto Industries Product Distribution Approaches

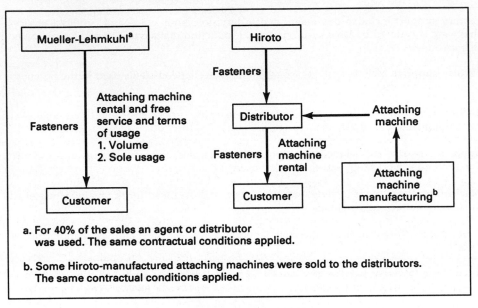

a. For 40% of the sales an agent or distributor
   was used. The same contractual conditions applied.

b. Some Hiroto-manufactured attaching machines were sold to the distributors.
   The same contractual conditions applied.

EXHIBIT 8

Estimated Japanese Market Share of European
Market in 1986

S-spring snap fastener	8%
Ring snap fastener	8
Open prong snap fastener (stainless steel)	2
Open prong snap fastener (brass)	9
Tack button	9%

READINGS

The Two-Stage Procedure in Cost Accounting: Part One

Robin Cooper

If managers are to make intelligent decisions concerning the products they market, they need to know what their products cost. In many firms, product cost information is provided solely by the cost accounting system. Understanding how cost accounting systems work helps protect managers against depending unknowingly on inaccurate product costs. Although cost accounting systems appear to be extremely complex and difficult to understand, they are actually quite simple.

This [reading] describes a simple example and four different approaches to costing products. The example demonstrates how some of these approaches report distorted product costs. In particular, they demonstrate that the more complex the approach, the more accurate reported product costs. Unfortunately, the high cost of collecting the information required by a cost system often makes it economically infeasible for management to select the approach that reports the most accurate product costs. Instead, management is forced to make a decision between doing without perfect product cost information or incurring the costs to obtain it.

One of the approaches described in this [reading], however, incorporates a procedure that reduces the amount of information required without introducing excessive distortion into the product costs. This procedure, which I call the two-stage procedure, lies at the heart of most modern cost systems.[1]

FOUR APPROACHES TO COSTING PRODUCTS

The four approaches to costing products can be illustrated with a simple example (see Exhibit 1). Approach 1, illustrated in Exhibit 2, combines the costs of supervision and direct labor and divides them by the total number of direct labor hours consumed to give a single direct labor burden rate. Costs are traced to the products by multiplying this rate by the number of direct labor hours that each product consumes.[2] This approach does not differentiate among the three machines.

Approach 2, illustrated in Exhibit 3, traces the direct labor and supervision costs to the products separately. The total cost of direct labor and supervision is divided by the total number of direct labor and supervision hours consumed respectively to give two separate burden rates for direct labor supervision. Costs are traced to the products by multiplying the number of direct labor and supervision hours each product consumes by the appropriate rate. This approach also does not differentiate among the three machines.

In the case of the example, Approach 3, illustrated in Exhibit 4, will always report accurate product costs. It traces the direct labor and supervision costs associated with each machine separately and divides them by the total number of direct labor or supervision hours consumed by the machine to give six machine-based burden rates. Costs are traced to the products by multiplying the number of direct labor and supervision hours consumed by each product at each machine by the appropriate rate.

Approach 4, illustrated in Exhibit 5, combines the direct labor and supervision costs associated with each machine. These costs are then divided by the total number of direct labor hours associated with each machine to give three machine-based burden rates. Costs are traced to the products by

Reprinted from *Journal of Cost Management* (Summer 1987), pp. 43-51, with permission.

Exhibit 1. The Example

Example Co manufactures one each of two products, A and B, per period. It consumes direct labor and supervision to produce these products. The material is supplied by the customer at no cost to the company. The two products are manufactured on three machines, M1, M2, and M3.

EXAMPLE CO
DIRECT LABOR AND SUPERVISION CONSUMPTION PATTERNS
PRODUCTS A AND B

	PRODUCT A		PRODUCT B		
MACHINE	DIRECT LABOR HOURS	SUPER-VISION HOURS	DIRECT LABOR HOURS	SUPER-VISION HOURS	TOTAL
M1	0.24	0.04	0.12	0.02	
M2	0.08	0.02	0.16	0.04	
M3	0.04	0.01	0.08	0.02	
Total Direct Labor Hours	0.36		0.36		0.72
Total Supervision Hours		0.07		0.08	0.15

	COST PER DIRECT LABOR HOUR	
M1	$5.00	$5.00
M2	$15.00	$15.00
M3	$15.00	$15.00

	COST PER SUPERVISION HOUR				
All Machines		$25.00		$25.00	
Total Cost of Resources Consumed	$3.00	$1.75	$4.20	$2.00	$10.95

The three machines consume electricity while producing the two products.

DIRECT LABOR, MACHINE HOURS AND ELECTRICITY
CONSUMPTION PATTERNS FOR PRODUCTS A AND B

	PRODUCT A			PRODUCT B		
MACHINE	DIRECT LABOR HOURS	MACHINE HOURS	KILOWATT-HOURS	DIRECT LABOR HOURS	MACHINE HOURS	KILOWATT-HOURS
M1	0.24	0.24	0.12	0.12	0.12	0.06
M2	0.08	0.16	0.24	0.16	0.16	0.24
M3	0.04	0.04	0.16	0.08	0.08	0.32
Total	0.36	0.44	0.52	0.36	0.36	0.62

	COST PER KILOWATT-HOUR	
All Machines	$5.00	$5.00
Total Cost of Resources Consumed	$2.60	$3.10

Exhibit 2. Approach 1

This approach takes all of the costs and adds them together to give a total cost of $10.95. It then divides this amount by the total number of direct labor hours, 0.72, to give an hourly rate of $15.21 per direct labor hour. The two products are now costed by multiplying the direct labor hours consumed in their production by the calculated hourly rate. This approach reports product costs of:

PRODUCT	DIRECT LABOR HOURS	RATE PER HOUR	REPORTED COST
A	0.36	$15.21	$5.47(6)
B	0.36	$15.21	$5.47(6)
Total Cost			$10.95

multiplying the number of direct labor and supervision hours consumed by each product at each machine by the appropriate burden rate. The underlying structure for each approach is illustrated in Exhibit 6.

DISTORTED PRODUCT COSTS

The reported product costs for products A and B under the four approaches are shown in Exhibit 7.

The first two approaches make inaccurate assumptions and report distorted product costs. Approach 2 assumes that all direct labor costs the same

Exhibit 3. Approach 2

This approach takes the total direct labor costs of $7.20 and divides them by 0.72, the total number of direct labor hours, to give the average hourly direct labor rate of $10.00. The equivalent calculation for supervision results in an average (and in this case actual) supervision-per-hour rate of $25.00. This approach produces product costs of:

	PRODUCT A	PRODUCT B	TOTAL
Direct Labor Hours	0.36	0.36	
Rate per Hour	$10.00	$10.00	
Total	$3.60	$3.60	$7.20
Supervision Hours	0.07	0.08	
Rate per Hour	$25.00	$25.00	
Total	$1.75	$2.00	$3.75
Total Cost	$5.35	$5.60	$10.95

Exhibit 4. Approach 3

This approach traces the consumption of direct labor and supervision separately to the products. This approach reports costs of:

PRODUCT A

MACHINE	DIRECT LABOR HOURS	RATE	TOTAL	TOTAL
M1	0.24	$5.00	$1.20	
M2	0.08	$15.00	$1.20	
M3	0.04	$15.00	$0.60	
				$3.00

SUPERVISION	HOURS	RATE	TOTAL	
M1	0.04	$25.00	$1.00	
M2	0.02	$25.00	$0.50	
M3	0.01	$25.00	$0.25	
				$1.57
Reported Cost—Product A				$4.75

PRODUCT B

MACHINE	DIRECT LABOR HOURS	RATE	TOTAL	TOTAL
M1	0.12	$5.00	$0.60	
M2	0.16	$15.00	$2.40	
M3	0.08	$15.00	$1.20	
				$4.20

SUPERVISION	HOURS	RATE	TOTAL	
M1	0.02	$25.00	$0.50	
M2	0.04	$25.00	$1.00	
M3	0.02	$25.00	$0.50	
				$2.00
Reported Cost—Product B				$6.20
Total Cost				$10.95

amount per hour. This would be an acceptable assumption if both products consumed the same mix of $5.00 and $15.00 direct labor, but they do not. The error in reported product costs reflects the difference in direct labor consumption patterns for the two products.

The cost of the supervision required to produce each product is accurately traced to the products in Approach 2, because the correct number of supervision hours consumed per product is identified, and each supervision hour costs the same amount.

Exhibit 5.   Approach 4

This approach combines direct labor and supervision by machine to produce three sets of costs. The calculations for determining the costs associated with each machine are:

| | MACHINE | | | | | | |
| | M1 | | M2 | | M3 | | |
	DIRECT LABOR HOURS	SUPER-VISION HOURS	DIRECT LABOR HOURS	KILOWATT-HOURS	DIRECT LABOR HOURS	KILOWATT-HOURS	TOTAL
Product A	0.24	0.04	0.08	0.02	0.04	0.01	
Product B	0.12	0.02	0.16	0.04	0.08	0.02	
Total	0.36	0.06	0.24	0.06	0.12	0.03	
Cost/Direct Labor Hours	$5.00		$15.00		$15.00		
Cost/Supervision Hours		$25.00		$25.00		$25.00	
Total	$1.80	$1.50	$3.60	$1.50	$1.80	$0.75	$10.95
Machine Totals	$3.30	$5.10	$2.55				

The hourly rates for these three sets of costs are then calculated by dividing the cost of direct labor and supervision per machine by the number of direct labor hours associated with each machine. This gives hourly rates of $9.17, $21.25, and $21.25 for machines M1, M2, and M3, respectively. This approach reports product costs of:

	MACHINE	DIRECT LABOR HOURS	RATE PER HOUR	REPORTED COST
Product A	M1	0.24	$9.17	$2.20
	M2	0.08	$21.25	$1.70
	M3	0.04	$21.25	$0.85
	Reported Product Cost			$4.75
Product B	M1	0.12	$9.17	$1.10
	M2	0.16	$21.25	$3.40
	M3	0.08	$21.25	$1.70
	Reported Product Cost			$6.20
	Total Cost			$10.95

Therefore, the average cost per supervision for the two products is identical to the average cost for each product, $25.00 per hour.

Approach 1 fails to trace both the cost of direct labor and supervision accurately because it assumes that both resources are consumed equally by both products. Consequently, the error in tracing direct labor costs is identical to that discussed for Approach 2. The error in tracing supervision costs is caused by the different ratio of direct labor to supervision consumed by each product. Product A consumes 0.36 direct labor hours and 0.07 supervision hours; Product B consumes 0.36 direct labor hours and 0.08 supervision hours. Only if this ratio

Exhibit 6.   The Four Approaches to Costing Products

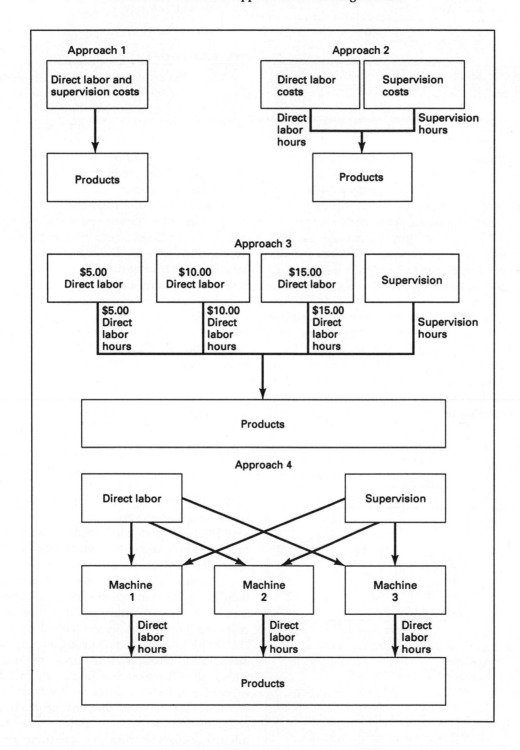

Exhibit 7. Example Co Reported Product Cost Under the Four Approaches[3]

| | APPROACH | | | |
	1	2	3	4
Product A	$5.48	$5.35	$4.75	$4.75
Product B	$5.48	$5.60	$6.20	$6.20

were constant would a direct labor–based cost system report accurate product costs.

Approaches 3 and 4 report identical and accurate product costs. Approach 4, which uses only direct labor hours to obtain the product costs, overcomes the problems encountered in Approaches 1 and 2 by tracing the direct labor costs correctly: it breaks direct labor costs into three sets, each of which contains only one type (i.e., $5.00 or $15.00) of direct labor. Splitting the costs in this way removes the distortions inherent in using an average direct labor cost.

The supervision costs are correctly traced because the creation of three sets of supervision costs removes the problem of differing ratios of supervision and direct labor consumed by each product. Exhibit 8 illustrates this phenomenon. Within each machine-based set of costs, the ratio of direct labor to supervision is the same for each product. This

Exhibit 8. Example Co Ratio of Direct Labor to Supervision Consumed by Product by Machine

| | PRODUCT A | | |
MACHINE	DIRECT LABOR HOURS	SUPERVISION HOURS	RATIO
M1	0.24	0.04	6:1
M2	0.08	0.02	4:1
M3	0.04	0.01	4:1
Total	0.36	0.07	36:7

| | PRODUCT B | | |
MACHINE	DIRECT LABOR HOURS	SUPERVISION HOURS	RATIO
M1	0.12	0.02	6:1
M2	0.16	0.04	4:1
M3	0.36	0.08	4:1
Total	0.36	0.08	9:2

equality allows accurate tracing of supervision costs using direct labor hours.

THE TRADE-OFF

Why don't managers simply implement Approach 3 cost systems, thus guaranteeing accurate product costs? The answer lies in the number of measurements and calculations required to support such a cost system. In the example, using direct labor hours to trace both direct labor and supervision costs removes the need to measure the supervision hours per product.

Instead, only the total cost of supervision per machine must be determined and direct labor hours used to trace these costs to the products. In an Approach 3 system, the supervision consumption patterns must be measured for every product. In the example, the additional number of measurements and calculations is small. For a company producing thousands of products, each consuming many resources, the additional number of measurements and calculations required by Approach 3 become prohibitively expensive.

THE TWO-STAGE PROCEDURE

The success of Approach 4 in the example explains why the procedure that underlies it is at the heart of many cost accounting systems. This procedure traces costs to the products in two distinct stages. The first stage takes such resources as direct labor and supervision and splits them up into sections, each related to a segment of the production process. These segments can be machines (as in the example), collections of machines, or even entire departments. The costs associated with each segment for each resource are then combined to form cost pools (or cost centers or burden centers). These costs are then traced, in the second stage, from the cost pool to the product using a measure of the quantity of resources consumed by the product. Although this measure is frequently called an allocation basis, I prefer the term *cost driver*, because it connotes the concept that the products drive the consumption of cost as opposed to the concept of allocating costs because they are there and must be spread to the products. The two-stage cost tracing procedure for the Example Co is illustrated in Exhibit 9.

Exhibit 9. The Two-Stage Procedure

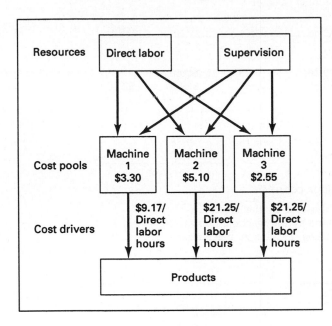

Exhibit 10. Electricity Costs Traced to Products A and B Using Direct Labors Hours, Machine Hours, and Kilowatt-Hours

	DIRECT LABOR HOURS	MACHINE HOURS	KILOWATT-HOURS
Product A	$2.20	$2.60	$2.60
Product B	$3.50	$3.10	$3.10

MULTIPLE COST-DRIVER SYSTEMS

Our example can be extended by adding a third resource, electricity, to illustrate how direct labor hours cannot always be used in the second stage to trace costs accurately to the products. The electricity costs and related direct labor and machine-hour consumption patterns are shown in Exhibit 1. The costs reported by systems that differentiate among the three machines and use direct labor, machine, and kilowatt hours to trace electricity costs to the products are shown in Exhibit 10. The calculations required to generate this table are given in Exhibit 11.

Exhibit 11. Reported Electricity Product Costs for Cost Systems Based on Direct-Labor, Machine-, and Kilowatt-Hours

	M1	M2	M3	TOTAL
Kilowatt-Hours—Product A	0.12	0.24	0.16	
Kilowatt-Hours—Product B	0.06	0.24	0.32	
Kilowatt-Hours—Total	0.18	0.48	0.48	
Total Electricity Cost @ $5.00 per Kilowatt-Hour	$0.90	$2.40	$2.40	

DIRECT LABOR COSTING

This approach divides the cost of the electricity consumed by each machine by the direct labor hours consumed on that machine to give a direct labor hourly burden rate.

	M1	M2	M3	TOTAL
Direct Labor Hours—Product A	0.24	0.08	0.04	
Direct Labor Hours—Product B	0.12	0.16	0.08	
Direct Labor Hours—Total	0.36	0.24	0.12	
Direct Labor Rate	$2.50	$10.00	$20.00	

(continued)

Exhibit 11 (cont.)

This approach reports product costs of:

	M1	M2	M3	TOTAL
Product A				
Direct Labor Hours	0.24	0.08	$0.40	
Reported Cost	$0.60	$0.80	$0.80	$2.20
Product B				
Direct Labor Hours	0.12	0.16	0.08	
Reported Cost	$0.30	$1.60	$1.60	$3.50

MACHINE-HOUR COSTING

This approach divides the cost of the electricity consumed by each machine by the machine hours consumed on that machine to give a machine hourly burden rate.

	M1	M2	M3	TOTAL
Machine Hours—Product A	0.24	0.16	0.04	
Machine Hours—Product B	0.12	0.16	0.08	
Machine Hours—Total	0.36	0.32	0.12	
Machine-Hour Rate	$2.50	$7.50	$20.00	

This approach reports product costs of:

	M1	M2	M3	TOTAL
Product A				
Machine Hours	0.24	0.16	0.04	
Reported Cost	$0.60	$1.20	$0.80	$2.60
Product B				
Machine Hours	0.12	0.16	0.08	
Reported Cost	$0.30	$1.20	$1.60	$3.10

KILOWATT-HOUR COSTING

This approach uses the $5.00 kilowatt-per-hour rate to cost products. It reports product costs of:

	M1	M2	M3	TOTAL
Product A				
Kilowatt-Hours	0.12	0.24	0.16	
Reported Cost	$0.60	$1.20	$0.80	$2.60
Product B				
Kilowatt-Hours	0.06	0.24	0.32	
Reported Cost	$0.30	$1.20	$1.60	$3.10

Using machine hours to trace electricity costs reports costs identical to those traced by kilowatt-hours. Using direct labor hours reports different and inaccurate product costs. Exhibit 12 shows the ratio of kilowatt-hours to direct labor hours and machine hours by machine. The different ratios of direct labor hours to kilowatt-hours for M2 explains the failure of the direct labor–based system to report accurate product costs.[4]

Attempting to trace direct labor and supervision costs using machine hours similarly results in distorted product costs. It is not possible to trace costs accurately in the expanded example with a single cost driver. At least two cost drivers—direct labor hours and machine hours—are required. The two-cost-driver, two-stage procedure for the Example Co is shown in Exhibit 13.

SUMMARY

The approaches described in this article differ by the number of cost pools into which the resources are traced and the number of cost drivers used to trace the costs from these pools to the products. The relationship among the four approaches is illustrated in Exhibit 14.

The four approaches report different product

Exhibit 12. The Example Co Ratio of Direct Labor and Machine Hours to Electricity Consumed by Product by Machine

| | PRODUCT A | | PRODUCT B | |
| | DIRECT LABOR HOUR/ KILOWATT-HOUR | MACHINE HOUR/ KILOWATT-HOUR | DIRECT LABOR HOUR/ KILOWATT-HOUR | MACHINE HOUR/ KILOWATT-HOUR |
MACHINE				
M1	2:1	2:1	2:1	2:1
M2	1:3	2:3	2:3	2:3
M3	1:4	1:4	1:4	1:4
Total	1:2	2:3	1:2	1:2

costs because they make the following different assumptions about the behavior of costs:

- Approach 1 reports distorted product costs in almost any realistic production environment—It assumes that the quantity of every resource consumed by all products is directly proportional to the number of direct labor hours consumed.
- Approach 2 reports distorted product costs in most production environments—It assumes that the cost per unit of any resource does not vary, depending on where in the production process the resource is consumed.
- Approach 3 always reports accurate product costs when the cost of the resources that are consumed is measurable and traceable to the products—Unfortunately, in most practical settings it is prohibitively expensive.

Exhibit 13. The Two-Stage Procedure Using Two Cost Drivers

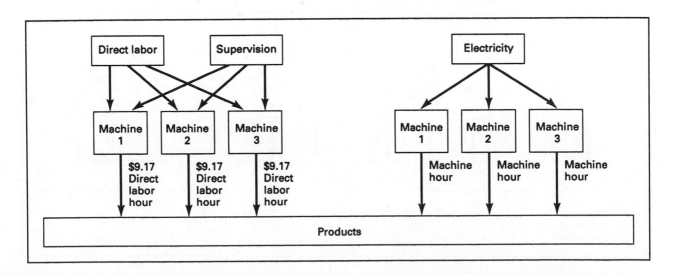

Exhibit 14. Example Co: The Four Approaches to Product Costing

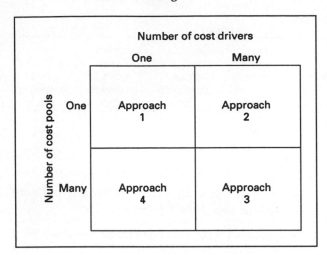

• Approach 4 frequently reports adequately accurate product costs—It assumes that for each cost pool the ratio of the quantity of resource consumed to the number of cost-driver units consumed for any resource doesn't depend on the product being produced.

The cost of collecting the information required to cost products can become extremely high, forcing management to accept inaccurate product costs. Approach 4 uses the two-stage procedure to reduce the amount of information required by the cost system without introducing excessive distortion into the reported product costs. This approach can be extended to a broad variety of production settings by using a small number of cost drivers to trace costs in the second stage. In effect, the cost system becomes a collection of Approach 4 cost systems, each tracing a different set of resources to the products using a different cost driver (Exhibit 15). In part 2 of this series, I will explore what cost drivers are required to accurately trace different types of costs to the products.

NOTES

1 Its application to manufacturing, banking, health care, and railroads has been documented in a number of Harvard Business School case studies written by my colleague Robert S. Kaplan and/or myself.

2 In the simple example the product consists of a single part. If it contains multiple parts or components, the components would be costed.

3 In a simple example with the same volume of two products being manufactured, the overcosting of one product is exactly offset by the undercosting of the other. In a more complex setting the errors still cancel, but not as obviously.

4 The total ratios for direct labor for the two products are the same. This means that a direct-labor, Approach 1 system will accurately trace electricity costs to the products. The chances of this happening when hundreds or thousands of products are involved, however, is minute.

Exhibit 15. The Two-Stage Procedure Using Multiple Cost Drivers

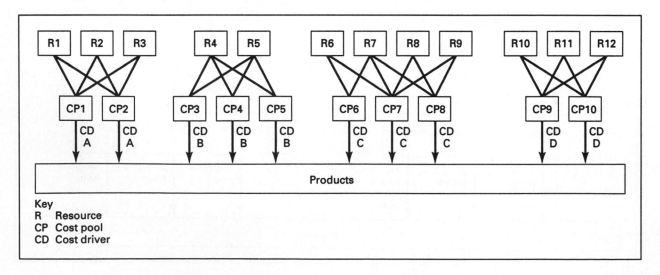

When Should You Use Machine-Hour Costing?

Robin Cooper

Machine-hour costing is not necessarily a more accurate means of reporting product cost than direct-labor-hour costing in a machine-intensive environment. This [reading] examines two sample product manufacturing scenarios in order to establish rules for when to use machine-hour costing.

A recent company memorandum illustrates some of the misunderstandings that may lead managers to believe that they need to use machine-hour costing to determine product costs. The memorandum reads, in part, as follows:

> "We have historically used direct labor hours as the base for burden absorption. . . . As the ratios of machine hours to direct labor hours and machine costs to labor costs increase, a machine-hour costing system becomes the more accurate method of costing. . . . If one operator is assigned to one machine, then direct labor hours and machine hours are equivalent; therefore, there is little justification in shifting to a machine-hour-based system. . . ."[1]

Two points must be made regarding the memorandum. First, an increase in the ratios of machine hours and machine-related costs to direct-labor hours and direct-labor-related costs does not necessarily mean that a machine-hour system is more accurate than a direct-labor-hour system. Second, assigning operators to run more than one machine does not by itself justify a shift to machine-hour costing.

This [reading] addresses the question of when to shift from direct-labor-hour to machine-hour costing. By evaluating two examples, we will demonstrate in particular that neither a high ratio of machine-hour costs to direct-labor-hour costs nor the assignment of an operator to several machines automatically requires machine-hour costing.

EXAMPLE 1

A company manufactures P1, which takes one hour of machine time to produce. The production facility consists of two cost centers. Cost Center A contains three identical machines. Cost Center B contains one machine identical to those in Cost Center A. Each cost center requires one operator. The entire facility is budgeted on an annual basis to consume $40,000 of power and 20,000 direct labor hours, 10,000 per center. The machines consume all of the power. Product P1 can be produced simultaneously on all three machines in Cost Center A or on the single machine in Cost Center B.

We need first to determine the actual cost of the power needed to manufacture product P1. We can calculate this cost as follows:

In Cost Center A, the three machines each run one hour for every direct labor hour consumed; that is, three machine hours are consumed for every direct labor hour. Therefore, Cost Center A consumes 30,000 machine hours (3 × 10,000 direct labor hours). In Cost Center B, which consists of just the one machine, the number of direct labor hours equals the number of machine hours: 10,000. Thus, in total, 40,000 machine hours are consumed. Because the entire production process consumes $40,000 of power and all machines are identical, each machine hour must consume $1.00 of power. Therefore, the manufacturing of product P1, which requires one hour of machine time to produce irrespective of the center in which it is produced, consumes $1.00 of power.[2]

In a two-stage cost-tracing procedure, the cost system for Example 1 will take on the structure illustrated in Exhibit 1.[3] In a two-stage procedure, the means of tracing costs in the first stage—from the resources to the cost center—can differ from the allocation basis used in the second stage to trace costs from the cost center to the product.[4] Thus, there are four possible direct-labor-hour or machine-hour costing systems. These include a pure

Reprinted from *Journal of Cost Management* (Spring 1988), pp. 33-39, with permission.

Exhibit 1. The Two-Stage Procedure Cost System for Example 1

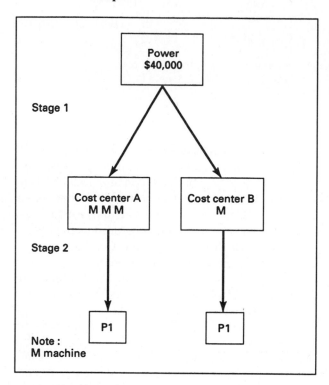

direct labor system, in which both stages rely on direct labor hours; a pure machine-hour system; and two hybrids, in which one stage uses direct labor hours and the other machine hours. (Exhibit 2 lists these four systems.) Exploring these systems helps illustrate the relationship between direct-labor-hour and machine-hour costing.[5]

The DLHR-DLHR cost system

Use of direct labor hours for the first stage results in the allocation of power costs equally to the two cost centers because each cost center consumes the same number of direct labor hours (i.e., 10,000).

Exhibit 2. The Four Cost Systems

FIRST STAGE	SECOND STAGE
DLHR	DLHR
DLHR	MHR
MHR	DLHR
MHR	MHR

Therefore, $20,000 in power costs is traced to each center.

In the second stage, this allocated $20,000 is divided by the number of direct labor hours consumed in each center—10,000—to yield direct labor consumption intensities of $2.00 per direct labor hour. In Cost Center A, each direct labor hour produces three P1 units per hour; hence, each is allocated $0.67 of power costs. By contrast, because each direct labor hour in Cost Center B produces only one P1 unit, each P1 manufactured in this center is allocated $2.00 in power costs (see Exhibit 3).[6] Consequently, the DLHR-DLHR cost system inaccurately reports product costs.

The DLHR-MHR cost system

As in the DLHR-DLHR cost system, the first stage of the DLHR-MHR cost system traces $20,000 to each cost center. In the second stage, which uses machine hours, the allocated $20,000 is divided by 30,000 machine hours in Cost Center A and by 10,000 machine hours in Cost Center B, thus yield-

Exhibit 3. The DLHR-DLHR Cost System

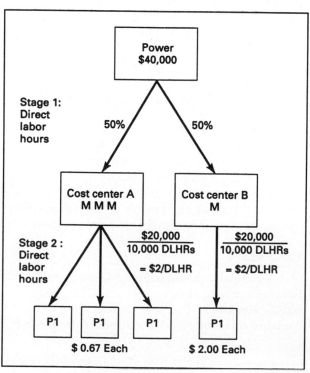

ing respective machine-hour consumption intensities of $0.67 and $2.00 per machine hour. Because each unit of P1 produced consumes one machine hour in either center, it is allocated $0.67 of power costs in A and $2.00 in B (see Exhibit 4). Consequently, the DLHR-MHR system reports product costs inaccurately in the same manner as a pure direct-labor-hour system.

The MHR-DLHR cost system

The use of machine hours for the first-stage procedure in this cost system results in the allocation of power costs according to the ratio of machine hours consumed in Cost Center A to Cost Center B, or 3:1. Thus, $30,000 is allocated to Cost Center A and $10,000 to Cost Center B.

In the second stage, the allocated $30,000 and $10,000 are divided by the number of direct labor hours consumed (10) to yield direct-labor-hour consumption intensities of $3.00 and $1.00 per hour, respectively. Because three units of P1 are produced in Cost Center A for each direct labor hour versus

Exhibit 4.   The DLHR-MHR Cost System

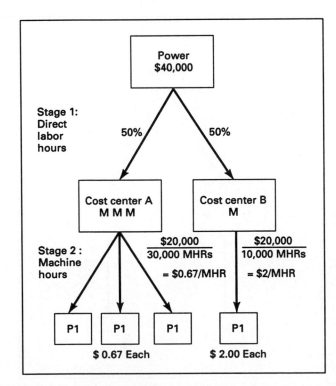

Exhibit 5.   The MHR-DLHR Cost System

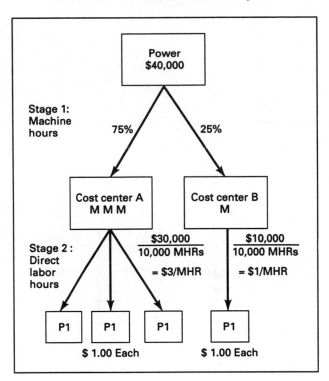

one unit in Cost Center B, P1 is allocated $1.00 of power costs in each center (see Exhibit 5). Thus, the MHR-DLHR system correctly reports product costs for P1.

The MHR-MHR cost system

As in the MHR-DLHR system, the first stage of the MHR-MHR system traces $30,000 of power costs to Cost Center A and $10,000 to Cost Center B. In the second stage, the traced costs are divided by the number of machine hours consumed in each cost center, yielding machine-hour consumption intensities of $1.00 per machine hour for both centers. Because each unit of P1 consumes one machine hour in either center, this method correctly reports product costs. (See Exhibit 6.)

RULE 1

This analysis leads to an important observation. The use of machine hours in the first stage prevents the error resulting from the direct-labor-hour system of tracing power costs equally to the two cost

Exhibit 6. The MHR-MHR Cost System

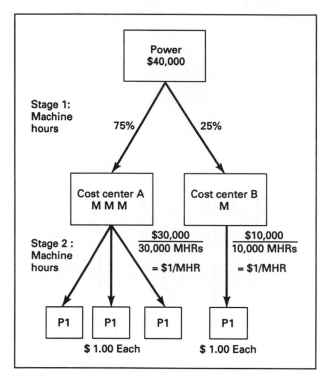

than one machine requires moving to machine-hour costing. In Cost Center A, all costs are machine related and the operator runs three machines simultaneously, yet the MHR-DLHR system reports accurate product costs.

To determine when to convert the second-stage allocation basis to machine hours, we need to expand our example.

EXAMPLE 2

The second manufacturing scenario can be summarized as follows: a company manufactures equal numbers of products P1, P2, and P3, each of which takes one hour of machine time to produce. The production facility consists of two cost centers. Cost Center A contains four identical machines, and Cost Center B contains one machine identical to those in Cost Center A. Each cost center requires one operator. The entire facility is budgeted annually to consume $40,000 of power and 20,000 direct labor hours, 10,000 per center. The machines con-

Exhibit 7. The Two-Stage Procedure Cost System for Example 2

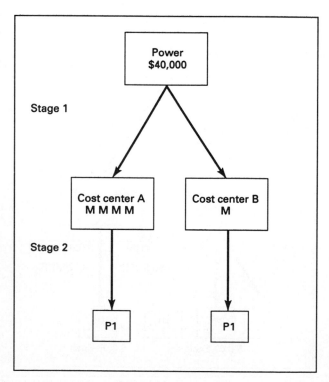

centers. Because power is consumed by the machines when running, and because Cost Center A consumes 30,000 machine hours whereas Cost Center B consumes only 10,000, Cost Center A must consume three times the power of Cost Center B. This is exactly the ratio of power costs traced by a machine-hour first stage. The failure of the DLHR-MHR cost system to trace product costs accurately demonstrates that no modification to the second-stage allocation base can compensate for an incorrect first-stage allocation.

It is now possible to state the rule for when to convert the first-stage allocation basis from direct labor hours to machine hours.

When the ratio of total machine hours to total direct labor hours varies by cost center, a machine-hour-based first stage is required to trace machine-related costs accurately. Only if this ratio is constant will a direct-labor-based first-stage system accurately trace machine-hour-related costs.

The MHR-DLHR cost system illustrates why it is simplistic to argue that a high ratio of machine-related costs or the assignment of operators to more sume all of the power. Product P1 can be made simultaneously on any three machines in Cost Center A, but not on all four. Product P2 can be produced simultaneously on all four machines, and P3 on any two. Because the operator is completely occupied in manufacturing the products, the idle machines cannot be used to make other products.

The two-stage cost procedure for Example 2 is illustrated in Exhibit 7.

Certain aspects of Example 2 are worth noting, as follows:

- The introduction of products P2 and P3 does not change the amount of power consumed by the entire facility.
- Because equal numbers of products P1, P2, and P3 are manufactured in Cost Center A and because each requires one machine hour to manufacture, the average number of machines in operation is three.
- Because 10,000 direct labor hours are consumed in Cost Center A, 30,000 machine hours are consumed —Cost Center B, with its one machine, consumes 10,000 machine hours.
- One machine hour still costs $1.00.

Exhibit 8. The MHR-DLHR Cost System for Product P2

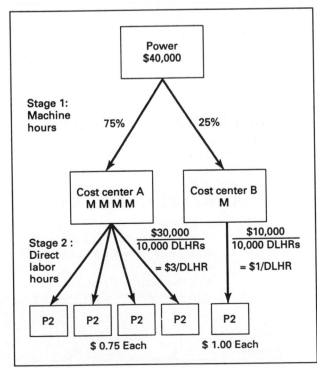

$ 0.75 Each $ 1.00 Each

Exhibit 9. The MHR-DLHR Cost System for Product P3

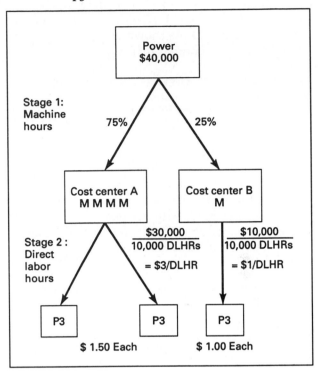

$ 1.50 Each $ 1.00 Each

- The addition of two products and an extra machine does not change the number of direct labor or machine hours consumed—In effect, for product P1 nothing has changed. The four cost systems will report exactly the same product cost for P1 as in Example 1.
- Because all three products consume one machine hour, products P1, P2, and P3 each consume $1.00 of power.

Example 1 demonstrated the inability of a direct-labor-hour first-stage system to trace machine-hour-related costs accurately to products. Example 2 illustrates the relationship between direct-labor-hour and machine-hour second-stage cost systems.

The MHR-DLHR cost system

Exhibits 8 and 9 demonstrate the product costs reported by the MHR-DLHR cost system for products P2 and P3. As shown, the MHR-DLHR cost system reports accurate product costs only in Cost Center B.

The MHR-MHR cost system

Exhibits 10 and 11 demonstrate the product costs reported by the MHR-MHR cost system for products P2 and P3. As shown, the costs for P2 and P3 are correctly reported for both cost centers.

MACHINE BASIS AND MACHINE BASIS DIVERSITY

To explain the source of the errors in the costs reported by the MHR-DLHR cost system, two concepts must be introduced: machine basis and machine basis diversity. Machine basis is the number of machines run simultaneously by a single operator, also expressed as the ratio of machines run to operators. Machine basis diversity refers to the systematic variation of machine basis by product.

Machine basis diversity occurs in at least three ways:

- The number of machines run by an operator varies systematically with the product.

Exhibit 10.   The MHR-MHR Cost System for Product P2

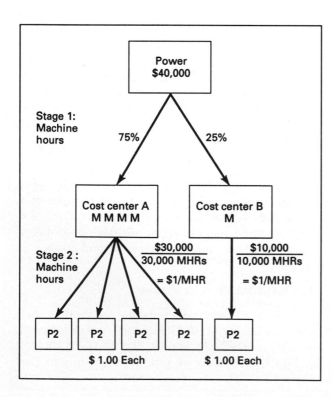

Exhibit 11.   The MHR-MHR Cost System for Product P3

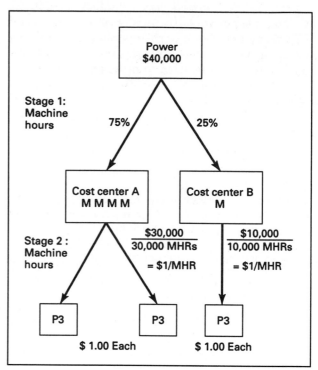

- The number of operators running a single machine varies systematically with the product.
- The operator simultaneously manufactures more than one product, and the percentage of time spent on each product varies systematically with the product.

Example 2 demonstrates the first type of machine basis diversity. The machine bases for the three products in each cost center and the average machine basis per center are shown in Exhibit 12.

Cost Center A thus demonstrates machine basis diversity, whereas Cost Center B does not.

Exhibit 12.   Machine Basis for Products P1, P2, and P3 in Cost Centers A and B

PRODUCT	MACHINE BASIS COST CENTER A	MACHINE BASIS COST CENTER B
P1	3	1
P2	4	1
P3	2	1
Average	3	1

Two important observations can now be made. First, the cost of product P1 is correctly reported by the MHR-DLHR cost system in both examples. This is because its machine basis is the same as the average machine basis for the center in which it is being manufactured (i.e., three in Cost Center A and one in Cost Center B). Second, the costs of products P2 and P3 are incorrectly reported by the MHR-DLHR cost system in Cost Center A because their machine bases—four and two, respectively—differ from the average machine basis in Cost Center A.[7] Their cost is correctly reported in Cost Center B, however, because their machine bases are identical to the average machine basis.

The role of machine basis diversity in machine-hour costing is best understood by exploring the mathematics of the second stage of the two-stage procedure. In the direct-labor-hour system, the power cost allocated to product P1 in the second stage is given by the formula:

$$\text{Power cost} = \frac{\text{Total power}}{\text{Total direct labor hours}} \times \frac{\text{Direct labor}}{\text{hours}}$$

In the machine-hour system, the power cost allocated to product P1 in Cost Center A is given by the formula:

$$\text{Power cost} = \frac{\text{Total power}}{\text{Total machine hours}} \times \text{Machine hours}$$

For product P1, the ratios of machine hours to direct labor hours are 3:1 in Cost Center A and 1:1 in Cost Center B. These are the same as the ratios in each cost center of total machine hours used to produce all products to total direct labor hours used to produce all products. That is, in Cost Center A, the machine basis is three for both product P1 and the total cost center average of all products; in Cost Center B, the machine basis is one for both product P1 and for the total cost center average. Thus, for product P1, the formulas report the same product costs in both cost centers: the machine bases for product P1 are the same as the average machine bases. For products P2 and P3, the ratios differ in Center A and are the same in Center B, so the costs reported in Center A are incorrect, but those reported in Center B are correct.

Machine basis diversity thus explains why the ratio of product-specific machine hours to product-specific direct labor hours differs from the ratio of total machine hours consumed to total direct labor hours for products P2 and P3 in Cost Center A. Only if the ratios of product-specific hours are used will the costs be correct (unless, as they were for P1, the ratios are the same).

It is now possible to state the rule for when to convert the second-stage allocation basis from direct-labor-hour to machine-hour costing.

A machine-hour-based second stage is required to accurately trace all machine-hour-related costs when machine basis diversity occurs. Machine basis diversity causes the ratio of direct labor hours to machine hours consumed to vary from product to product. Only if that ratio is a constant—if there is no machine basis diversity—will a direct-labor-hour second-stage system accurately trace machine-hour-related costs.

Adopting a machine-hour costing system will result in more accurate product costs only if at least one of the conditions noted in the two rules is true. The first stage requires converting to machine hours for machine-related costs if the ratio of the number of machine hours to direct labor hours varies by cost center. The second stage requires conversion if the number of machines an operator runs simultaneously in a cost center depends on the product being manufactured. The two rules can be applied independently, with either the first or second stages being converted to a machine-hour basis for machine-related costs.[8] A high ratio of machine-related costs and the assignment of operators to multiple machines are not, by themselves, sufficient to require machine-hour costing.

NOTES

1 To be fair, the author of the memorandum was, in fact, recommending a costing system that combines direct labor hours, machine hours, and material. A future column will demonstrate the inherent weaknesses of this approach.

2 The author of the memorandum was correct in that machine hours and direct labor hours are equivalent if one operator is assigned to each machine.

3 For a description of the two-stage cost-tracing procedure, see Robin Cooper, "The Two-Stage Procedure in Cost Accounting—Part One," *Journal of Cost Management for the Manufacturing Industry* 1 (Summer 1987), pp 43–51, and "The Two-Stage Procedure in Cost Accounting—Part Two," *Journal of Cost Management for the Manufacturing Industry* 1 (Fall 1987), pp 39–45.

4 Technically, we should use the term *cost pool* rather than *cost center*. Because we are tracing one resource only, however, the terms are synonymous.

5 These systems henceforth will be identified, in abbreviated form, as first-stage allocation basis–second-stage allocation basis systems. Thus, the pure direct-labor-hour system will be referred to as a DLHR-DLHR cost system, for example.

6 Recall that the actual power consumption is $1.00 per unit of P1 produced.

7 $(4n + 3n + 2n)/3n = 3$, where n is number manufactured.

8 An example of the impact of converting to machine-hour costing (both first and second stage) is in the Harvard Business School case "Fisher Technologies" #9, pp 186–302.

3

ASSIGNING THE EXPENSES
OF CAPACITY RESOURCES

For many organizations, expenses associated with capacity resources represent one of the largest cost components. Companies with continuous flow production processes, such as those in the chemicals, petroleum, paper, food processing, steel, and textile industries, have substantial investments in machinery and physical plant. Discrete-part manufacturing companies and service organizations (including financial institutions, hospitals, telecommunications companies, and transportation companies) have increased the capital intensity of their production processes in recent years so that the expenses associated with providing capacity for producing goods and services have become a significantly higher fraction of total operating expenses.

Capital-intensive companies face the problem of how to assign the expenses of capacity resources to the products and services that consume time on these resources. The expenses of the capacity resources typically include depreciation, maintenance, utilities expense to have the equipment ready to run (but not the incremental cost of processing units through the equipment), and the cost of the minimum crew size required to operate the assets efficiently. Some companies supplement their historical-cost financial numbers by using replacement-cost depreciation for assets plus a cost of capital or interest charge. An additional extension would attempt to approximate opportunity costs by raising the expenses assigned to machines used at or beyond rated capacity and lowering the expenses of machines currently in excess supply. Whatever choice the organization makes, it must still also decide on the denominator volume, the number that is divided into the capacity expense figure to obtain the unit cost of using the capacity resource.[1] Several choices are available for the denominator volume, and the actual choice made can have a profound impact on the way the organization calculates the cost and hence profitability of its products and services.

We can illustrate the relevant considerations with a simple numerical example. Consider the Alliant Company. Alliant's manufacturing process uses only one large piece of equipment. The annual expenses (both capital and operating) of the equipment

---

[1]The term *denominator volume*, plus descriptions of the theoretical, practical, normal, and budgeted volume bases, appears in pages 221–25 and 263–68 of Charles T. Horngren and George Foster, *Cost Accounting: A Managerial Emphasis*, 6th edition (Englewood Cliffs, NJ: Prentice Hall, 1987).

equal $120,000 per year. Alliant operates three 8-hour shifts per day, five days per week, 50 weeks per year. (The plant shuts down completely for a two-week vacation each year.) Thus, the theoretical annual capacity of the equipment is 6,000 hours of processing time. Because of scheduled, preventive maintenance and fluctuations of order arrival and scheduling, the most time the machine has ever been available for productive use, even in the busiest periods, would project to 5,000 hours per year, this figure represents the maximum practical amount of time the machine is available for processing goods. Recent adverse economic conditions in the industry and the economy, however, have reduced the time the machine is expected to be used next year to only 4,000 hours. Managers of Alliant believe that when economic conditions improve, they will have enough work to keep the machine busy for 4,800 hours.

The managers of Alliant have four choices for assigning the $120,000 of equipment-related expenses to products:

METHOD	DENOMINATOR VOLUME	MACHINE-HOUR RATE
Theoretical capacity	6,000 hours	$20/ hour
Practical capacity	5,000 hours	$24/ hour
Normal volume	4,800 hours	$25/ hour
Budgeted volume	4,000 hours	$30/ hour

Virtually no companies use theoretical capacity, since it represents a standard that can never be achieved. No matter how efficient or busy the company is, it would always have unabsorbed equipment charges. Of the three remaining methods, the budgeted volume (or actual utilization) method is the most common. It seemingly satisfies several audiences. For financial reporting, all equipment expenses are charged to products—appearing either in the cost-of-goods sold account or in an inventory account. For managerial purposes, the budgeted volume method assigns all production expenses to products so that they become an operating manager's responsibility, a goal that many senior managers impose on the product costing system. The problem is that assigning capacity costs based on budgeted volume not only leads to highly variable and distorted product costs; it also leads to incorrect, occasionally devastating decisions.[2]

If, when demand declines to only 4,000 machine hours per year, Alliant uses the $30/hour rate (based on budgeted volume) to cost products, then pressure gets exerted either to raise prices or to turn down apparently unprofitable business (business whose revenues do not exceed the total product costs when capacity costs are assigned at $30/hour). The attempt to raise prices, to cover the increased machine-hour rate, comes at exactly the wrong time; just when business for the company is slack. Several companies, however, followed exactly that route. The Alliant Company, instead of getting the expected 4,000 hours of business, ended up getting only 3,333 hours. The next year, it computed a new burden rate based on 3,333 hours of work and attempted to get business using the $36/hour rate. It got only 3,000 hours of work, and the next year Alliant raised the rate to $40/hour. Thus, companies that cost products based on expected capacity utilization run a very real danger of triggering a death spiral when demand drops below practical capacity.

A different version of the death spiral occurs when companies install a new piece of

---

[2]This situation was encountered in the Bridgeton case, presented in chapter 1 of this book.

equipment.[3] For example, a printed circuit board assembly division decided to purchase an expensive piece of equipment for surface mount insertion. (Existing technology could only do through-hole insertion on printed circuit boards.) Initially, however, because only a few newly designed boards used surface-mounted components, the equipment was used at about 10% of capacity. When the annual capital and operating expenses of the equipment were assigned based on the projected 10% utilization rate, the cost per inserted device was absurdly high, much higher than insertions on the fully utilized through-hole machines, despite the much higher efficiency of surface mounting technology. Engineers, after learning of the high unit insertion cost of surface-mounted components, avoided their use in new product designs, preferring the apparently much lower cost of older technology through-hole components. In this case, the cost system actively discouraged engineers from exploiting new technology capabilities.

We have found that practical capacity (5,000 hours for Alliant Company) provides a much better estimate than budgeted volume of the long-run cost of using capacity resources. First, the practical capacity denominator avoids death spirals and the incentives to underutilize newly acquired technology. Second, it provides a more stable basis for assessing the impacts of productivity and continuous improvement activities on product costs. Companies that have been successful in realizing productivity improvements of the order of 7% to 10% annually have found product costs holding steady or even increasing if the productivity improvements coincided with a period of decreased external demand. The reduction in capacity utilization more than swamped the steady productivity improvements. Conversely, during periods of rising demands, other organizations thought they were becoming more efficient merely because they were able to produce (and sell) more units, thereby reducing the unit cost of capacity. Only when demand stabilized or even declined did they learn that they had made no fundamental productivity improvement. Basing capacity costs on practical capacity provides a stable benchmark against which to assess the impact of ongoing process-improving activities.

After discussing an accounting issue that must be settled when using practical capacity as the denominator volume, we can understand a third reason for preferring that measure. For the Alliant Company, the projected amount of business for the year (4,000 machine hours) at the practical capacity cost rate of $24 per machine hour will assign $96,000 of expenses to products produced. Since total capacity-related expenses are $120,000, the accounting question is what to do with the $24,000 of unabsorbed expenses. If this expense is reallocated back to products at the end of the year, the result would be the same as if the budgeted volume basis had been used. We, and companies that use practical capacity, choose to label the $24,000 as excess (or idle) capacity cost and treat it as an expense of the period, not as an expense of *products*. The excess capacity cost can be budgeted at the beginning of the year, will appear as a separate line item in the income statement, and will be modified, through a production volume variance, based on actual experience (more or less production volume than anticipated) during the year. In effect, this approach treats the cost of excess capacity as the cost of products the company did not produce, rather than allocating it to the products it did produce.

A fourth advantage of the practical capacity method is that the expenses of excess

---

[3]This situation was encountered in the Seligram: ETO case, presented in chapter 2 of this book.

capacity are highlighted for management action, not buried in product costs. When allocated to existing products, the excess capacity problem appears as one of needing higher prices or greater efficiencies. With this signal, undue pressure may be exerted on the marketing and sales staff to the overall detriment of the company (by launching a death spiral). When shown as a period excess capacity cost, management gets a clear signal that the company has more capacity than it requires in its current operating environment. Management may decide to retain the capacity, looking to utilize it when demand builds or recovers; it can attempt to downsize by reducing its effective capacity, through selling off or renting time on equipment currently not needed; or it can encourage the development and launch of new products that use the currently unused capacity. Any or all of these policies may be sensible. What does not seem sensible is attempting to raise prices to cover the cost of the company's excess capacity at a time when market demand conditions are weak.

Use of the normal volume denominator (the 4,800 hours for Alliant) is a compromise between budgeted volume and practical capacity. It avoids some problems associated with measuring practical capacity while preventing a death spiral. But we believe that normal volume still distorts the economics of the company by assigning some excess capacity costs—the difference between practical capacity and normal volume—to actual production, thereby burdening these products with expenses that should be highlighted for management attention and action. Normal volume becomes a more defensible basis if the excess capacity was deliberately acquired because of the discrete quantities in which capacity can be purchased and the investment decision assumed that the normal volume (below the practical capacity) represented the expected demand.

MEASUREMENT ISSUES WITH PRACTICAL CAPACITY

We illustrated our preference for practical capacity by using a simple numerical example. In practice, many complications arise in measuring practical capacity. We have identified several questions that arise when applying this concept. We have formulated some recommended approaches, but more experience and research will be required to understand better all the relevant measurement issues and perhaps to provide more definitive and defensible solutions than those currently proposed.

What Is Practical Capacity? Practical capacity can be estimated somewhat arbitrarily or studied analytically. The arbitrary estimate is to assume that practical capacity is a specified percentage (e.g., 80% or 85%) of theoretical capacity. Donaldson Brown, the Chief Financial Officer of General Motors in the 1920s, developed the GM Pricing Formula assuming a long-run average capacity utilization of 80% of theoretical capacity.[4] The more analytic approach attempts to subtract from theoretical capacity the time required for normal maintenance, repairs, start-ups, and shutdowns. It can also incorporate an amount of time held in reserve for protective or surge capacity.

Protective or surge capacity allows the plant or piece of equipment to respond to short-term fluctuations in demand, or disruptions within the factory, without sacrificing output. Having some amount of protective capacity allows the facility to continue to

---

[4]See H. Thomas Johnson and Robert S. Kaplan, *Relevance Lost: The Rise and Fall of Management Accounting* (Boston: Harvard Business School Press, 1987), pp. 104–7; and Problem 6-3, "General Motors Corporation," in Robert S. Kaplan and Anthony A. Atkinson, *Advanced Management Accounting,* 2nd edition (Englewood Cliffs, NJ: Prentice Hall, 1989), pp. 199–205.

meet customers' demands despite short-term unexpected delays of materials receipts (either from external vendors or from prior production processes) or when short-run surges in demand occur.

Number of Shifts   The most dramatic effect on equipment costing rates can be obtained by changing the assumption about the number of shifts and days that the equipment can be operated. If Alliant operated only one shift per day, the equipment has a theoretical capacity of 2,000 hours per year, and, probably, between 1,600 and 1,700 practical hours. The one-shift assumption triples the capacity costing rate for the equipment to about $72/hour. Alternatively, if the equipment were to be used seven days per week, three shifts per day, then its practical capacity could be 40% higher, perhaps 7,000 hours per year, causing the capacity costing rate to drop below $17/hour.

Companies should be guided by their normal method of operation. If they normally operate two shifts per day, five days per week, and the plant was equipped under those conditions, then the practical capacity can be calculated as a specified percentage, say 80% or 85%, of the theoretical capacity of 80 hours/week (16 hours per day, five days per week). If the plant has always operated on one shift, only 40 hours/week, the company should use that assumption for measuring the cost of capacity. If the equipment and the plant were acquired based on an assumption of three-shift operation, but demand now and in the foreseeable future requires only a two-shift operation, the company can either show a 33% excess capacity charge each period, or, more realistically, can write off one-third of the expenses of the equipment to recognize the asset impairment of having acquired too much capacity prior to the severe downturn in demand that it experienced. In this situation, the cost of the capacity for the unused third shift reflects an event that has already occurred—the permanent decrease in demand—rather than the cost of products produced during the remaining two shifts of operation.

Machines Never   Because of the lumpiness of machine acquisition (one must acquire capacity in discrete,
Used to Capacity   not continuous, amounts), many machines may never operate at their practical capacity even when the plant as a whole is running at capacity. Such machines have permanent surplus supply; they are nonbottleneck machines. The opportunity cost approach (to be discussed later) would not assign any machine-related costs of machines with excess capacity to products that run on them. It ignores all the capital and operating expenses of supplying available time on these machines, treating them as fixed expenses that will not be affected by near-term product decisions.

The conventional capacity costing approach, described in this chapter, assigns machine expenses to products that run on the machines. In the situation where, because of bottlenecks elsewhere in the plant, a machine is permanently underutilized (and was perhaps acquired with this knowledge), the company can use a denominator volume for that machine that reflects its projected utilization when the plant is at its overall practical capacity. This procedure would eliminate any excess capacity variances from occurring when the plant runs at practical capacity. This procedure is most attractive for a newly acquired piece of equipment whose maximum utilization was projected to be at, say, 60% of capacity. If the equipment was still purchased under this projection, then a rate using the 60% expected utilization would be consistent with the machine acquisition decision. It is somewhat less attractive for a machine originally expected to be used at its practical capacity (say, 80% of theoretical) but, because of shifts in product mix, is used only at 60% of theoretical. In this situation, maintaining the original costing rate (based on 80% of theoretical) would better reflect the economics of the production decision, with the remaining expenses sent to an excess capacity account each year or written off permanently, to reflect the permanent underutilization of the asset.

Service Quality Some service businesses have customers who require different levels of service. As a simple example, consider two classes of customers. Class A requires immediate response to requests, and Class B requires responses that could be backlogged and handled in off-peak hours. Because of economies of scale in the acquisition and operation of information technology, the company provides sufficient investment to handle both types of requests in the highly responsive mode, rather than install separate systems to handle the two types of customers.

If requests from customers in Class A and Class B are costed in the same manner, some of the much higher expenses of the system installed primarily for Class A will be shifted to the Class B customers. One solution to this cost distortion would estimate the expense of providing the base service level required by Class B customers and assign this base expense to those customers. The premium over this base service level, for providing the high-quality service from the system actually installed, would then be charged only to Class A customers that require the real-time responsiveness. In this way, the higher expenses could be more appropriately attributed to Class A customers, rather than shared with the Class B customers that did not require the premium service. The value of this type of scheme depends on being able to distinguish clearly the different service levels required by different types of customers, a distinction that often can be made.

Seasonal Business Many organizations have demand patterns that are not uniform throughout the year, or even within a month, a week, or a day. The organizations are staffed and equipped to handle the peak demand, leading to excess or idle capacity in the nonpeak periods. If budgeted or normal volume is used to assign capacity expenses to products, no distinction is made between products produced in peak periods and products produced in nonpeak periods. Alternatively, if practical capacity is used, idle or excess capacity variances will be realized in nonpeak periods. The Schulze Waxed Containers case in this chapter explores various approaches for costing cyclical capacity.

OPPORTUNITY COSTS

Some would argue that it is inappropriate to assign to products the expenses of capacity resources. One version of this argument is that the machines and the buildings have already been acquired. Whether the company produces goods and services, the cash outlay has already occurred and hence will be unaffected by product-mix decisions. The accounting expenses, especially depreciation, of equipment already acquired represents a sunk cost, in this view, and hence is irrelevant for managerial decisions.

One response to this argument is to inquire whether the viewpoint would change if the facilities were rented on an annual basis, or even on a monthly or daily basis. If rental charges are considered relevant but depreciation expenses are not, the company would be permitting its method of financing to affect the way it estimates the costs of resources used in the production process. Managers get a useful signal about the long-run profitability of products and customers when all resources used in the production process—labor, materials, indirect and support employees, and capital resources—are attributed to the products and customers that benefit from and are creating the demands for the productive resources. This signal is useful whether the capital resources are purchased or rented, though the managerial actions based on the signal could differ based on the ease of disposition or acquisition of assets.

By charging for the use of capital resources, managers receive a signal about the validity of their prior investment decisions. Without such a signal, some of the discipline for accurate estimates in the capital budgeting analysis becomes mitigated. The signal provides continual information to the firm about whether current selling prices and operating expenses justify continued investment in the product line and production processes. Even though equipment may already have been purchased, active second-hand markets exist for equipment and facilities so that many capital expenses are not "sunk" at all.

Eli Goldratt and Robert Fox, in their theory of constraints, argue that operating expenses should be assigned only to bottleneck resources.[5] No costs should be assigned to machines that are not bottlenecks, and all expenses—not just equipment-related but direct and indirect labor as well—should be charged to products that consume time on the bottleneck machines. This procedure emphasizes getting maximum utilization and return from bottleneck resources and not burdening products for consuming time on non-bottleneck resources. It is an excellent procedure for short-run optimization, assuming that all resources in organization are fixed and attempting to maximize the throughput (defined by Goldratt and Fox to be selling price less materials expenses) through the facility.[6]

Signals that help to optimize short-term throughput are, however, insufficient for directing managers' attention to resource acquisition and divestment decisions, pricing and product mix decisions, product and process design decisions, and continuous improvement decisions, subjects that will be addressed in subsequent chapters of this book. For these purposes, a signal on the cost of using each of the organization's resources, not just bottleneck resources (and not just rented versus already acquired capital resources), should be useful for the organization's managers.

---

[5]Eli Goldratt and Robert Fox, *The Race* (Croton-on-Hudson, N.Y.: North River Press, 1987).
[6]Costing procedures for the short-run throughput optimizing approach are described in a four-part series by David Galloway and David Waldron, "Throughput Accounting," *Management Accounting, (U.K.)* (November 1988–February 1989).

CASES

Polysar Limited

As soon as Pierre Choquette received the September Report of Operations for NASA Rubber (Exhibits 1 and 2), he called Alf Devereux, Controller, and Ron Britton, Sales Manager, into his office to discuss the year-to-date results. Next week, he would make his presentation to the Board of Directors, and the results for his division for the first nine months of the year were not as good as expected. Pierre knew that the NASA management team had performed well. Sales volume was up and feedstock costs were down resulting in a gross margin that was better than budget. Why did the bottom line look so bad?

As the three men worked through the numbers, their discussion kept coming back to the fixed costs of the butyl rubber plant. Fixed costs were high. The plant had yet to reach capacity. The European Division had taken less output than projected.

Still, Choquette felt that these factors were outside his control. His division had performed well—it just didn't show in the profit results.

Choquette knew that Henderson, his counterpart in Europe, did not face these problems. The European rubber profits would be compared to those of NASA. How would the Board react to the numbers he had to work with? He would need to educate them in his presentation, especially concerning the volume variance. He knew that many of the Board members would not understand what that number represented or that it was due in part to the actions of Henderson's group.

Pierre Choquette, Alf Devereux, and Ron Britton decided to meet the next day to work on a strategy for the Board presentation.

POLYSAR HISTORY

In 1986, Polysar Limited was Canada's largest chemical company with $1.8 billion in annual sales.

Based in Sarnia, Ontario, Polysar was the world's largest producer of synthetic rubber and latex and a major producer of basic petrochemicals and fuel products.

Through acquisition and internal growth, Polysar had grown considerably from its original single plant. Polysar now employed 6,650 people, including 3,100 in Canada, 1,050 in the U.S., and 2,500 in Europe and elsewhere. The company operated 20 manufacturing plants in Canada, the United States, Belgium, France, The Netherlands, and West Germany.

STRUCTURE

The operations of the company were structured into three groups: basic petrochemicals, rubber, and diversified products.

The Rubber Group was headed by Charles Ambridge, 61, Group Vice-President. Polysar held 9% of the world synthetic rubber market (excluding communist bloc countries). As the largest group in the company, Rubber Group produced 46% of Polysar sales. Major competitors included Goodyear, Bayer, Exxon, and Dupont.

Rubber products, such as butyl and halobutyl, were sold primarily to manufacturers of automobile tires (six of the world's largest tire companies[1] accounted for 70% of the world butyl and halobutyl demand); other uses included belting, footwear, adhesives, hose, seals, plastics modification, and chewing gum.

The Rubber Group was split into two operating divisions that were managed as profit centers: NASA (North and South America) and EROW (Europe and rest of world). In addition to the two operating profit centers, the Rubber Group included

---

[1]Michelin, Goodyear, Bridgestone, Firestone, Pirelli, and Dunlop.

This case was prepared by Professor Robert L. Simons.
Copyright © 1987 by the President and Fellows of Harvard College. Harvard Business School case 187-098.

a Global Marketing Department and a Research Division. The costs of these departments were not charged to the two operating profit centers, but instead were charged against Group profits.

RUBBER GROUP

A key component of Polysar's strategy was to be a leader in high-margin, specialty rubbers. The leading products in this category were the butyl and halobutyl rubbers. Attributes of butyl rubber include low permeability to gas and moisture, resistance to steam and weathering, high energy absorption, and chemical resistance. Butyl rubber was traditionally used in inner tubes and general-purpose applications. Halobutyl rubber, a modified derivative, possesses the same attributes as regular butyl with additional properties that allow bonding to other materials. Thus, halobutyls were used extensively as liners and sidewalls in tubeless tires.

Butyl and halobutyl rubber were manufactured from feedstocks such as crude oil, naphtha, butane, propane, and ethane. Polysar manufactured butyl rubbers at two locations: NASA Division's Sarnia plant and EROW Division's Antwerp plant.

NASA butyl plant

The original Sarnia plant, built in 1942, manufactured regular butyl until 1972. At that time, market studies predicted rapid growth in the demand for high-quality radial tires manufactured with halobutyl. Demand for regular butyl was predicted to remain steady since poor road conditions in many countries of the world necessitated the use of tires with inner tubes. In 1972, the Sarnia plant was converted to allow production of halobutyls as well as regular butyl.

By the 1980s, demand for halobutyl had increased to the point that Polysar forecast capacity constraints. During 1983 and 1984, the company built a second plant at Sarnia, known as Sarnia 2, to produce regular butyl. The original plant, Sarnia 1, was then dedicated solely to the production of halobutyl.

Sarnia 2, with a capital cost of $550 million, began full operations late in 1984. Its annual nameplate (i.e., design) production capacity for regular

butyl was 95,000 tonnes. During 1985, the plant produced 65,000 tonnes.

EROW butyl plant

The EROW Division's butyl plant was located in Antwerp, Belgium. Built in 1964 as a regular butyl unit, the plant was modified in 1979 and 1980 to allow it to produce halobutyl as well as regular butyl.

The annual nameplate production capacity of the Antwerp plant was 90,000 tonnes. In 1985, as in previous years, the plant operated near or at its nameplate capacity. The Antwerp plant was operated to meet fully the halobutyl demand of EROW customers; the remainder of capacity was used to produce regular butyl.

In 1981, the plant's output was 75% regular butyl and 25% halobutyl; by 1985, halobutyl represented 50% of the plant's production. Since regular butyl demand outpaced the plant's remaining capacity, EROW took its regular butyl shortfall from the Sarnia 2 plant; in 1985, 21,000 tonnes of regular butyl were shipped from NASA to EROW.

Product scheduling

Although NASA served customers in North and South America and EROW serviced customers in Europe and the rest of the world, regular butyl could be shipped from either the Sarnia 2 or Antwerp plant. NASA shipped approximately one-third of its regular butyl output to EROW. Also, customers located in distant locations could receive shipments from either plant due to certain cost or logistical advantages. For example, Antwerp sometimes shipped to Brazil and Sarnia sometimes shipped to the Far East.

A Global Marketing Department worked with Regional Directors of Marketing and Regional Product Managers to coordinate product flows. Three sets of factors influenced these analyses. First, certain customers demanded products from a specific plant due to slight product differences resulting from the type of feedstock used and the plant configuration. Second, costs varied between Sarnia and Antwerp due to differences in variable costs (primarily feedstock and energy), shipping, and currency rates. Finally, inventory levels, production interruptions, and planned shutdowns were considered.

In September and October of each year, NASA and EROW divisions prepared production estimates for the upcoming year. These estimates were based on estimated sales volumes and plant loadings (i.e., capacity utilization). Since the Antwerp plant operated at capacity, the planning exercise was largely for the benefit of the managers of the Sarnia 2 plant, who needed to know how much regular butyl Antwerp would need from the Sarnia 2 plant.

Product costing and transfer prices

Butyl rubbers were costed using standard rates for variable and fixed costs.

Variable costs included feedstocks, chemicals, and energy. Standard variable cost per tonne of butyl was calculated by multiplying a standard utilization factor (i.e., the standard quantity of inputs used) by a standard price established for each unit of input. Since feedstock prices varied with worldwide market conditions and represented the largest component of costs, it was impossible to establish standard input prices that remained valid for extended periods. Therefore, the company reset feedstock standard costs each month to a price that reflected market prices. Chemical and energy standard costs were established annually.

A purchase price variance (Were input prices above or below standard prices?) and an efficiency variance (Did production require more or less inputs than standard?) were calculated for variable costs each accounting period.

Fixed costs comprised three categories of cost. Direct costs included direct labor, maintenance, chemicals required to keep the plant bubbling, and fixed utilities. Allocated cash costs included plant management, purchasing department costs, engineering, planning, and accounting. Allocated noncash costs represented primarily depreciation.

Fixed costs were allocated to production based on a plant's demonstrated capacity using the following formula:

$$\frac{\text{Standard fixed}}{\text{Cost per tonne}} = \frac{\text{Estimated annual total fixed costs}}{\text{Annual demonstrated plant capacity}}$$

To apply the formula, production estimates were established each fall for the upcoming year. Then the amount of total fixed costs applicable to this level of production was estimated. The amount of total fixed cost to be allocated to each tonne of output was calculated by dividing total fixed cost by the plant's demonstrated capacity. Exhibit 3 reproduces a section of the Controller's Guide that defines demonstrated capacity.

Each accounting period, two variances were calculated for fixed costs. The first was a spending variance calculated as the simple difference between actual total fixed costs and estimated total fixed costs. The second variance was a volume variance calculated using the following formula:

$$\text{Volume variance} = \left(\begin{array}{c}\text{Standard fixed} \\ \text{cost per tonne}\end{array}\right) \times \left(\begin{array}{cc}\text{Actual tonnes} & \text{Demonstrated} \\ \text{produced} & \text{capacity}\end{array}\right)$$

Product transfers between divisions for performance accounting purposes were made at standard full cost, representing, for each tonne, the sum of standard variable cost and standard fixed cost.

Compensation

Employees at Polysar had in the past been paid by fixed salary with little use of bonuses except at the executive level of the company. In 1984, a bonus system was instituted throughout the company to link pay with performance and strengthen the profit center orientation.

Nonmanagement employees   The bonus system varied by employee group but was developed with the intention of paying salaries that were approximately 5% less than those paid by a reference group of 25 major Canadian manufacturing companies. To augment salaries, annual bonuses were awarded, in amounts up to 12% of salary, based on corporate and divisional performance. Hourly workers could receive annual bonuses in similar proportions based on performance.

All bonuses were based on achieving or exceeding budgeted profit targets. For salaried workers, for example, meeting the 1985 corporate profit objective would result in a 5% bonus; an additional $25 million in profits would provide an additional 4% bonus. Meeting and exceeding division profit targets could provide an additional 3% bonus.

Using periodic accounting information, divisional vice-presidents met in quarterly communication meetings with salaried and wage employees to discuss divisional and corporate performance levels.

Management   For managers, the percent of remuneration received through annual bonuses was greater than 12% and increased with responsibility levels.

The bonuses of top division management in 1985 were calculated by a formula that awarded 50% of bonus potential to meeting and exceeding divisional profit targets and 50% to meeting or exceeding corporate profit targets.

INTERVIEWS WITH RUBBER GROUP VICE-PRESIDENTS

Pierre Choquette

Pierre Choquette, 43, was vice-president of the NASA Rubber Division. A professional engineer, Choquette had begun his career with Polysar in plant management. Over the years, he had assumed responsibilities for product management in the U.S., managed a small subsidiary, managed a European plant, and directed European sales.

> This business is managed on price and margin. Quality, service, and technology are also important, but it is difficult to differentiate ourselves from other competitors on these dimensions.
>
> When the price of oil took off, this affected our feedstock prices drastically, and Polysar's worldwide business suffered. Now that prices are back down, we are trying to regroup our efforts and bring the business back to long term health. Polysar will break even in 1985 and show a normal profit again in 1986. Of course, the Rubber Division will, as in the past, be the major producer of profit for the company.
>
> As you know, this is a continuous process industry. The plant is computerized so that we need the same number of people and incur most of the same overhead costs whether the plant is running fast or slow.
>
> The regular butyl plant, Sarnia 2, is running at less than capacity. Although the plant should be able to produce 95,000 tonnes, its demonstrated capacity is

85,000. Last year, we produced 65,000. This leaves us sitting with a lot of unabsorbed fixed costs, especially when you consider depreciation charges.

> Still, NASA Rubber has been growing nicely. I think that this is in part due to our strong commitment to run the divisions as profit centers. We have been pushing hard to build both volume and efficiency, and I am pleased that our programs and incentives are paying off.
>
> Our transfers to EROW are still a problem. Since the transfers are at standard cost and are not recorded as revenue, these transfers do nothing for our profit. Also, if they cut back on orders, our profit is hurt through the volume variance. Few of our senior managers truly understand the volume variance and why profit results are so different in the two regions. The accounting is not a problem, but having to explain it continuously to senior-level managers is. It always comes down to the huge asset that we carry whether the plant is at capacity or not.
>
> We run our businesses on return on net assets, which looks ridiculous for NASA. I worry that if I am not around to explain it, people will form the wrong conclusion about the health of the business. Also, you sometimes wonder if people ascribe results to factors that are outside your control.

Doug Henderson

Doug Henderson, 46, Vice-President of EROW Rubber Division, was also a professional engineer. His career included management responsibilities in plant operations, market research, venture analysis and corporate planning, running a small regional business in Canada, and being Director of European Sales.

> The Antwerp plant produces about 45,000 tonnes of halobutyl and 45,000 tonnes of regular butyl each year. In addition, we import approximately 15,000 to 20,000 tonnes of regular butyl from Sarnia each year [see Exhibit 4].
>
> We inform Sarnia each fall of our estimated regular butyl needs. These estimates are based on our predictions of butyl and halobutyl sales and how hard we can load our plant. The overall sales estimates are usually within ten percent, say, plus or minus 8,000 tonnes, unless an unexpected crisis occurs.
>
> The EROW business has been extremely successful since I arrived here in 1982. We have increased our share in the high-growth halobutyl market; the plant is running well; and we have kept the operation simple and compact.

Looking at our Statement of Net Contribution [see Exhibit 5], our margins are better than NASA's. For one thing, there is a great surplus of feedstock in Europe, and we benefit from lower prices. Also, market dynamics are substantially different.

We pay a lot of attention to plant capacity. For example, we budgeted to produce 250 tonnes per day this year and we have got it up to 275. We are also working hard to reduce our "off-spec" material as a way of pushing up our yield. If we can produce more, it's free—other than variable cost, it goes right to the bottom line.

Given these factors, Pierre loves it when I tell him jokingly that our success at EROW is attributable to superb management.

EXHIBIT 1

NASA RUBBER DIVISION
Regular Butyl Rubber Statistics and Analyses
September 1986

	NINE MONTHS ENDED SEPTEMBER 30, 1986		
	ACTUAL (000)	BUDGET (000)	DEVIATION (000)
Volume—Tonnes			
Sales	35.8	33.0	2.8
Production	47.5	55.0	−7.5
Transfers			
to EROW	12.2	19.5	−7.3
from EROW	2.1	1.0	1.1
Production costs	($000)	($000)	($000)
Fixed cost—Direct	−21,466	−21,900	434
Allocated cash	− 7,036	− 7,125	89
Allocated noncash	−15,625	−15,600	− 25
Fixed cost to production	−44,127	−44,625	498
Transfers to/from finished goods inventory	1,120	2,450	−1,330
Transfers to EROW	8,540	13,650	−5,110
Transfers from EROW	− 1,302	− 620	− 682
Fixed cost of sales	−35,769	−29,145	−6,624

Note: Financial data have been disguised and do not represent the true financial results of the company.

EXHIBIT 5
EROW RUBBER DIVISION
Regular Butyl Rubber
Condensed Statement of Net Contribution
September 1986

	NINE MONTHS ENDED SEPTEMBER 30, 1986
Sales volume—tonnes	47,850
	($000)
Sales revenue	94,504
Delivery cost	− 4,584
Net sales revenue	89,920
Variable cost	
Standard	− 28,662
Purchase price variance	203
Inventory revaluation	− 46
Efficiency variance	32
Total	− 28,473
Gross margin—$	61,447
Fixed cost to production	
Depreciation	− 4,900
Other	− 16,390
	− 21,290
Transfers to/from finished goods inventory	− 775
Transfers to/from NASA	− 7,238
	− 29,303
Gross profit—$	32,144
Period costs	− 7,560
Business contribution	24,584
Interest on working capital	− 1,923
Net contribution	22,661

Notes: 1. Fixed costs are allocated between regular butyl production (above) and halobutyl
production (reported separately).
2. Financial data have been disguised and do not represent the true financial results
of the company.

Micro Devices Division

When we built our new wafer fab facility, we thought we would have to expand within a few years. But our yields have been so high we can meet demand for our current products operating at 60% capacity. The dilemma I now face is whether I should bring more product in from the outside. With our huge fixed costs it seems to make sense. But which costs should I use to make that decision?

JERI BATINA, DIVISION MANAGER

DIVISION BACKGROUND

Micro Devices Division (MDD) was a captive supplier of integrated circuits (ICs). Located in California's Silicon Valley, the division employed approximately 3,200 hourly and salaried personnel. Its 1989 operating budget exceeded $200 million.

The IC market was extremely price sensitive. MDD had elected not to compete on a price basis with high-volume integrated circuit producers to leverage its resources and technologies. Consequently, it stayed away from the commodity chip business and concentrated on designing and manufacturing proprietary designs that gave its parent company a competitive advantage in the marketplace.

To obtain state-of-the-art semiconductor technology, MDD gave other chip suppliers a substantial share of the parent company's IC volume in return for access to the latest technical knowledge. The division then used the acquired technology to develop unique applications for its parent. In total, outside manufacturers supplied 60% of the parent's semiconductor requirements.

Each product manufactured by MDD was given a number based on criticality:

1—Proprietary
2—Can consider second supplier
3—Can buy from anyone

New business was typically won because it was proprietary. As the proprietary technology became public, the unit was frequently faced with severe competitive pressures as lower cost suppliers entered the market.

PRODUCTION PROCESS

IC manufacturing encompassed four distinct operations: raw wafer production, wafer fabrication, assembly, and test. In wafer production, purchased wafers were prepped, precleaned, and put into the production process.

In wafer fabrication, the building blocks (e.g., diodes and transistors) of an integrated circuit were made by selectively introducing impurities (dopants) into the pure silicon. This created areas (features) with dissimilar electrical characteristics. The patterns of dopant introductions were contained on a set of glass plates called masks. Since ICs were constructed in layers, several masks were required, one for each layer. A typical IC might require 10 masks, and a highly complex state-of-the-art device might have as many as 16.

In the assembly operation, the integrated circuits were packaged in their final form. Since each wafer contained from 100 to 2,000 identical ICs, the wafers were first "diced" into individual chips. Each chip was then mounted, using a die-bonding machine, onto a metal frame. Next, tiny gold wires were bonded from leads on the metal frame to aluminum pads on the silicon chip using an ultrasonic wire-bonding machine. Finally, an epoxy plastic lid was cemented or molded on top of the base leadframe to complete the integrated circuit package.

In the final test operation, the completed device was subjected to extensive electrical testing to determine its electrical characteristics. Because the number and complexity of tests was large and the required precision high, MDD utilized sophisticated computers to control the test sequence.

This case was prepared by research associate Chris Ittner (under the supervision of Professor Robin Cooper).

Several weeks were required to complete the production process, a time period typical in the semiconductor industry. MDD produced 203 different part numbers, using 82 different die. Many part numbers varied only with respect to packaging, customer, and test parameters. Products were grouped into process families, each of which contained a dozen or so devices. The only difference between devices in a family was the masks; the processing was nearly identical.

COST SYSTEM

MDD's cost system employed "yield" accounting. Direct labor, direct material, and scrap costs were traced directly to wafer lots. Overhead rates were developed for each department and subsequently allocated to wafer lots based on the actual direct labor dollars expended in producing each lot. The cost of a wafer lot was then divided by the actual number of good die in the lot to calculate individual unit costs. Packaging and test costs were developed in the same manner. The allocated cost totals were roughly evenly divided among die, package, and test costs.

MDD typically transferred products to its parent at full cost. However, the unit had some leeway in determining which costs to include in the transfer price. For example, to win a bid against an outside competitor, the division would sometimes include in the transfer price only the depreciation associated with the additional equipment acquired to provide capacity for the proposed work.

AVAILABLE CAPACITY

For the past several years, MDD had been operating far below capacity. The problem was most acute in wafer fab, where a facility designed to process 650 wafers per day was only processing 350. Several factors had contributed to this condition:

1. *Long-term yields.*   The success of the IC manufacturing process was measured by yields—the percentage of initial product started into production that, after the last step of the process, tested out as acceptable. Final yields had several components. *Line yields* referred to the ratio of good wafers to wafer starts. *Multiples* represented the number of

good dies per wafer. *Packaging yields* denoted the ratio of good packaged dies to the number of dies entered into the packaging process. As yields improved, fewer wafer starts were required to achieve the same number of good dies at the end of the manufacturing process (see Exhibit 1 for an example). As a result, yield improvements increased the amount of available capacity.

To meet increased demands, MDD had constructed a new state-of-the-art wafer fab facility. Management had originally estimated near-term capacity utilization at 80% given projected yields and demand; volume increases were expected to fill capacity by the early 1990s. Actual yields turned out to be much higher than expected, however. Within a year, the facility was meeting demand while operating at 60% capacity. Noted one engineer, "When we built the new facility we estimated yields for products we had never built before. We never knew we would be this good." Yields continued to improve as engineers identified and eliminated the sources of defects (see Exhibits 2 and 3). Because of these improvements, the number of wafer starts needed to meet demand fell far below the initial forecasts (see Exhibit 4). The reduced wafer starts created more available capacity than anticipated.

2. *Short-term yields.*   In determining the number of required wafer starts, manufacturing planners utilized average yields. Actual yields, however, could vary by as much as ± 15% from the average yields being used by the planners. Because of these statistical fluctuations, a downstream process could at times have less input than was required to produce the necessary output, while at other times it could have more than enough. Statistical fluctuations were compounded as the number of sequential operations increased.

Statistical fluctuations made it desirable to hold extra capacity. For example, MDD might need to produce 100 wafers each day for a month. Five sequential operations might be required to manufacture the wafers. Assume that on average, each operation had the capacity to produce 100 wafers per day (i.e., no excess capacity). On any production run, actual output per operation would vary between 85 and 115. The next operation would then receive either too much or too little input, even though on average the correct amount of material would be received. If too little was received, any downstream bottleneck operations would be starved for input, and output would fall below requirements. If more than 100 were received, the downstream bottleneck operation would still only have the capacity to produce 100 units on average and would be unable to make up for shortages earlier in the month. Because bottleneck operations lacked the capacity to compensate for shortfalls in earlier stages, the eventual outcome would be throughput less than the required number of wafers and a buildup in inventory. Consequently, it was useful to hold extra capacity to make up for statistical fluctuations in earlier operations.

3. *Product mix changes.*   A third source of available capacity was changes in the division's product mix. Due to technological changes and competition from outside competitors, as much as one-third of the division's volume from existing products could go away in a three-year period. This created the continual need for new products to fill capacity.

Because much of the equipment was dedicated to particular process families, however, the introduction of new products did not guarantee that existing capacity would be filled. Unless new products belonged to process families with available capacity, additional equipment had to be purchased, and equipment designed for process families with declining demand would remain underutilized. As a result, utilization of certain process family equipment was falling at the same time the division's overall volumes were rising.

4. *"Lumpy" capacity.*   MDD would sometimes purchase more capacity than was required to meet current demand. In some cases, it was more economical in the long run to provide for future needs at the time the assets were acquired. In others, the required equipment was only available in large-capacity increments. To add even a small amount of capacity, the division would need to purchase equipment capable of accommodating substantial volume increases.

Each of these factors contributed to imbalances between capacity and demand. Imbalances were found both within and between operations. For example, the wafer fabrication process consisted of numerous steps carried out in a circular flow. Individual pieces of equipment in the process flow differed with respect to the capacity they could accommodate. An equipment imbalance in this case involved differences in the capacity of one machine in contrast with the output of other machines with which it had to be synchronized. Similarly, capacity imbalances also occurred between the wafer fab, assembly, and test functions; current capacity utilization ranged from 55% in wafer fab to 75% in IC assembly.

THE IN-SOURCING DECISION

The availability of capacity prompted Jeri Batina, MDD's division manager, to explore the possibility of in-sourcing some of the ICs currently being produced by outside suppliers. In-sourcing seemed desirable for a number of reasons. First, the additional volume would allow the division's substantial fixed costs to be spread over a larger number of units. This, in turn, would reduce unit product costs. Second, wafer fabrication yields were highest when the equipment ran continuously. Wafer cleanliness, one of the primary determinants of wafer yields, was inversely related to the amount of time the wafer spent in the fabrication process. When demand fell below the capacity of the wafer fabrication equipment, the production process shifted from continuous to batch production. Consequently, until a full batch accumulated, partially completed wafers were stored in racks waiting to be processed. Additional volume would allow the equipment to run uninterrupted for longer periods of time, thus increasing yields by reducing time in the process. Finally, the credible threat of in-sourcing provided an incentive for suppliers to reduce prices.

Batina was not sure which costs to use in analyzing the feasibility of in-sourcing. The IC market was extremely price sensitive, with price swings as low as 5% determining the competitiveness of suppliers' bids. Because of the competitiveness issue, MDD struggled with which cost elements to include in the cost-estimating process. Moreover, Batina wondered whether it even made sense to consider sunk costs in her pricing decision. If new products could be produced on available equipment, no additional equipment investment would be necessary.

Strategic considerations also played an important part in the in-sourcing decision. MDD relied on outside suppliers for technology. Taking work away from them jeopardized the strategic relationships that had been developed. One engineering manager noted the following:

> A strategic issue is the key partnerships we have with some of our semiconductor suppliers. We rely on partners for technology. Because our parent is a big user, we can trade volume for technology. This allows us to keep a smaller advanced development group. We try to acquire and tweak technology for unique applications. Our strength lies in our ability to develop unique designs that give our customer strategic advantage. If we lose access to new technology because of in-sourcing, we threaten our competitive edge.

CAPACITY COSTING ALTERNATIVES

While Batina's current concern was with in-sourcing, she realized that the capacity cost allocation method also had potential implications for outsourcing of current products, future make/buy analyses, transfer pricing policy, investment decisions, and performance evaluation of the division's managers. Recognizing the importance of this decision, Batina called a meeting with representatives from engineering, manufacturing, finance, and cost estimating to discuss capacity costing options.

The initial discussion centered on the definition of capacity. Four potential alternatives emerged:

> 1. *Theoretical capacity* assumed that the facility would operate at 100% of its rated capacity. It assumed that the equipment would run continuously with no downtime for maintenance, holidays, setups, etc.
> 2. *Practical capacity* adjusted the theoretical capacity definition to account for the number of shifts worked or unavoidable delays due to holidays, vacations, time off for weekends, machine breakdown, etc. This yielded a measure of available capacity given current operating conditions.
> 3. *Normal capacity* represented the average actual utilization over a time period long enough to level out capacity highs and lows.
> 4. *Expected actual capacity* was based on the expected actual output for the next year.

The meeting participants agreed that theoretical capacity was not a viable alternative for costing decisions, but could not agree on which of the other definitions was most appropriate. (Exhibit 5 provides various capacity measures for the equipment families in wafer fabrication.)

A member of the engineering staff noted that a further distinction needed to be made between idle capacity and excess capacity. According to the engineer, idle capacity was the result of volume fluctuations; equipment idled by temporary sales declines would be restored to full use when demand increased. This was in contrast to excess capacity which resulted from greater productive capacity than the division could hope to use, or from an imbalance in equipment.

There was some resistance to allocating less than 100% of capacity costs. A representative from cost estimating argued as follows: "You have to do something with the cost of excess capacity. There's no free ride. You can't say that you have a $2 million investment but you're only going to allocate $1 million. The costs have to go somewhere."

As the meeting progressed, however, several alternatives to full cost were presented. The division's controller proposed new bidding rates based on an allocation of 80% of capacity costs. The 80% figure represented the long-term capacity utilization goal for the division; maintaining a 20% "capacity cushion" would allow the division to remain responsive to demand fluctuations by its parent.

A second proposed alternative was the allocation of capacity costs based on actual utilization within the departments. For example, a department operating at 60% capacity would only have 60% of its capacity costs allocated to products.

A third option was allocating capacity costs based on actual utilization in the bottleneck department. For example, wafer fab might be operating at 60% capacity, assembly at 75%, and test at 90%. Without additional investment in test, all of the available capacity in wafer fab and assembly could not be exploited. Consequently, under this alternative, 90% of the capacity costs in each department would be allocated to products.

Finally, the division could bid on the work at variable cost. However, Batina was not sure that the division had a good grasp of what its variable costs actually were and suspected that the only true fixed costs were building occupancy, insurance, and taxes.

As the meeting came to a close, Batina concluded that the capacity costing issue required additional study. She instructed the cost estimating group to develop a full cost estimate for a product the division was considering in-sourcing (see Exhibit 6), as well as revised estimates using each of proposed alternatives (see Exhibit 7 for details on cost structure and capacity utilization by department). When the results were ready, the meeting would reconvene and the representatives would present their recommendations. As the participants prepared to leave, Batina made the following statement:

I think we've come up with a number of good options, but I'm sure that there are others we haven't considered. We need to keep thinking about other alternatives. I'm concerned that the capacity cost allocation method we choose for our current in-sourcing decisions may not be appropriate for product costing, transfer pricing, bidding for new business, and other purposes such as forecasting and performance evaluation of departmental managers. Should the same method be used for each of these purposes? I'm not sure. When we get together again, we need to address these issues.

EXHIBIT 1

MICRO DEVICES DIVISION

Effect of Yield Changes on Number of Wafer Starts

Good output = wafer starts $\times$ line yield $\times$ multiple $\times$ package yield

	1986	1989
Line yield (% good wafers)	55%	85%
Multiple (Good dies per wafer)	200	400
Packaging yield (% good packaged dies)	85%	95%

Example—20,000 good dies required

1986

20,000 good dies = wafer starts $\times$ .55 $\times$ 200 $\times$ .85

Required wafer starts = 214

1989

20,000 good dies = wafer starts $\times$ .85 $\times$ 400 $\times$ .95

Required wafer starts = 62

Therefore, because of yield improvements, production of 20,000 good dies in 1989 required only 62 wafer starts as opposed to the 214 wafer starts required in 1986.

EXHIBIT 2

MICRO DEVICES DIVISION

Line Yield

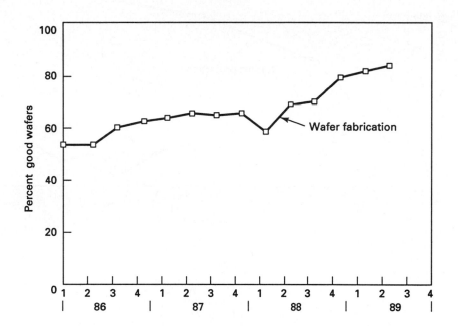

EXHIBIT 3

MICRO DEVICES DIVISION

Multiple History for a Representative Part

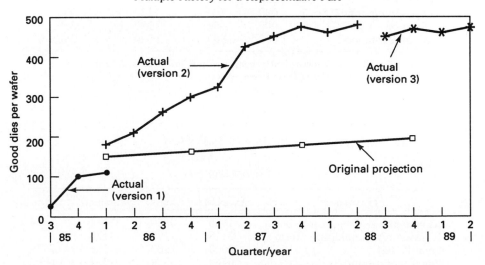

Three generations of this part were produced. Version number refers to the part generation each trend line represents.

EXHIBIT 4

MICRO DEVICES DIVISION

Shipment History for a Representative Part

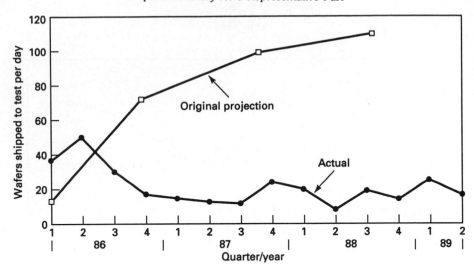

EXHIBIT 5

MICRO DEVICES DIVISION

Wafer Fabrication

Equipment Family Capacities

(Wafers per Day)

| | CAPACITY DEFINITION | | PLANNED LONG-TERM | CURRENT UTILIZATION |
EQUIPMENT FAMILY	THEORETICAL	PRACTICAL	UTILIZATION	(AVERAGE)
Oxidation	950	750	520	350
Photolithography	1,000	800	520	350
Diffusion	900	650	520	350
Ion implantation	1,000	900	520	350

Wafer fabrication had approximately 40% empty floor space that could be utilized with an additional investment of $30 million to increase practical capacity to 1,100 wafers per day.

EXHIBIT 6

MICRO DEVICES DIVISION

Fully Absorbed Cost Estimate

($ per Die)

DEPARTMENT	MATERIALS	LABOR	OVERHEAD	TOTAL
IC assembly—die and wire bond	.1830	.0820	.3314	.5964
IC assembly—mold, trim, form	.0118	.1190	.4126	.5434
Final IC test	.0000	.1483	.6506	.7989
Wafer fabrication	.6760	.0860	.9364	1.0900
Wafer test, saw, load, visual	.0000	.0153	.0947	.1100
	.2629	.4586	2.4722	3.1937

EXHIBIT 7

MICRO DEVICES DIVISION

Budgeted Departmental Cost Structures and Current Capacity Utilization

IC Assembly—Die and Wire Bond

Direct labor	$2,341,970
Overhead:	
Variable	4,023,729
Fixed	
Depreciation—equipment	698,374
Building depreciation, insurance, and taxes	120,077
Other facility costs[1]	95,381
Other fixed[2]	4,526,340

Current practical capacity utilization—75%

IC Assembly—Mold, Trim, Form

Direct labor	$4,189,427
Overhead:	
Variable	6,322,543
Fixed	
Depreciation—equipment	600,719
Building depreciation, insurance, and taxes	142,785
Other facility costs	960,042
Other fixed	6,542,842

Current Practical Capacity Utilization—75%

Final IC Test

Direct labor	$4,039,746
Overhead:	
Variable	7,150,508
Fixed	
Depreciation—equipment	2,287,558
Building depreciation, insurance, and taxes	312,382
Other facility costs	9,60,042
Other fixed	6,498,655

Current practical capacity utilization—70%

Wafer Fabrication

Direct labor	$2,348,377
Overhead:	
Variable	6,790,974
Fixed	
Depreciation—equipment	2,355,003
Building depreciation, insurance, and taxes	776,394
Other facility costs	2,866,907
Other fixed	12,779,854

Current practical capacity utilization—55%

(continued)

Exhibit 7 (cont.)

Wafer Test, Saw, Load, and Visual

Direct labor	$2,608,917
Overhead:	
Variable	6,496,947
Fixed	
Depreciation—equipment	2,515,422
Building depreciation, insurance, and taxes	360,251
Other facility costs	1,032,156
Other fixed	6,664,027
Current practical capacity utilization—60%	

[1]Other facility costs include general facility maintenance, plant security, and house-keeping.
[2]Other fixed costs include plant management and support departments.

Schulze Waxed Containers, Inc.

I told my sales force to ignore the 1987 product costs and to use the 1986 costs as the basis for their marketing decisions. Spreading fixed costs over the products causes reported costs to increase whenever production volume decreases. The 1987 product costs went up because we lost two major accounts. If we relied on 1987 costs to maintain a minimum 25% direct gross margin we, marketing, would be faced with having to increase prices, just when we needed to be more price competitive. We were clearly on a spiral that would have eventually caused us to walk away from all business.

WILLIAM WARE, VICE-PRESIDENT OF MARKETING

I was sympathetic to marketing's perspective, but in the end we need to cover all costs, not just the so-called variable ones. By taking all costs and dividing them by the number of units produced, you arrive at the average unit cost. If we priced our products in a manner that ignored the costs of idle capacity, how would we be assured that we, in the long run, will cover these costs? All that will happen is that we will drop our selling prices, increase our sales volume, and not really be any better off.

CARL BRODY, CHIEF FINANCIAL OFFICER

INTRODUCTION

Schulze Containers, Inc. (SWC), a Seattle-based manufacturer of waxed paper containers and cartons, was founded in 1941 by Fred Schulze to take advantage of the demand for waxed paper cups and containers created by World War II. After the war, the company began to face intense competition from larger, vertically integrated firms producing paper and plastic cups. In response to this challenge, the company identified its strengths and refocused its production efforts on waxed paper containers and cartons (the most common example of which is the milk carton), abandoning the paper cup product lines to the larger firms.

In 1987 sales were expected to be $23.4 million, down from $28 million the year before, a decrease due to the loss of two major customers accounting for approximately 20% of the company's business;

This case was prepared by Margaret Bernier, research associate (under the supervision of Professor Robin Cooper).

net income was expected to be $230 thousand (see Exhibit 1). In 1987 the company employed approximately 250 people.

PRODUCTS AND MARKETS

SWC manufactured waxed paper containers, ranging from small cartons (8 oz.) through half-gallon size containers (64 oz.). The smaller containers had a round cross-section and the larger ones a square cross-section. Small containers were used to package butter and for carry-out in restaurants. Large containers were used for ice cream (see Exhibit 2). The company's sales were seasonal, with 45% being sold in the four summer months (see Exhibit 3A).

The company served three major market segments, distinguished by the quantity of products produced and the extent of product customization: high-volume custom print, low-volume custom print, and stock-print items. Custom-print work comprised approximately 80% of SWC's business.

- *High-volume custom-print* products were the butter and ice cream cartons the company sold to major regional suppliers of these goods. The demand volume in this segment fluctuated somewhat throughout the year (see Exhibit 3B). The firm sold directly to five companies in 1986.
- *Low-volume custom-print* products were containers produced for customers who wanted their name to appear on the carton. These customers—primarily ice cream stands, restaurants, and bars—were highly seasonal (see Exhibit 3C). There were just under 150 accounts in this segment.
- *Stock-print* products were printed patterns that any customer could use. Since these items were primarily used for cold food, demand was high in the summer months but low in the winter (see Exhibit 3D). There were over 200 accounts in this segment.

PRODUCTION PROCESS

Manufacturing waxed paper cartons and containers was a fairly simple four-step process. The company purchased various weights of paper in bulk and stored the paper until needed. In the first step, the paper was sent to the printing machine where the customer's (or stock) design was reproduced onto the paper. The only difference between custom-print and stock-print work was the number of different inks which were required for the printing plates. Custom jobs usually required more colors than their stock counterparts.

In the second step, the paper was sent through the blanking machines, where it was cut into the precise shapes for the particular containers. In the third step, the paper blanks were assembled, coated with wax by the waxing machines, automatically counted, and inspected for quality. In the fourth and final step, the containers were packaged.

The wax coating department consisted of 60 machines which had all been developed in-house, and which ranged in age from 25 years to 8 years old. All the equipment had been modified over the years as the engineering department developed new production techniques. However, despite their efforts, the older machines still ran approximately 20% slower than the newer machines.

Each machine was dedicated to a single product. Originally, these machines had conversion kits; over the years, however, these were cannibalized for repair parts. As a result, SWC had little ability to respond quickly to changes in product demand simply by converting its machines among products.

In theory, producing for inventory in advance of actual orders was possible. Four factors made it risky to attempt to smooth production in this manner:

1. Uncertain future demand from low-volume customers in custom-print work;
2. Little or no resale value of overstock custom-print product;
3. Season-to-season demand fluctuation and difficulty in accurately predicting demanded sizes in stock-print containers;
4. Inventory carrying costs were high compared to profit margins.

Only the high-volume custom-print products had enough stability in design and customer contracts to permit some advance production. Here, too, inventory carrying costs made it uneconomic to produce more than four weeks ahead.

For these reasons, the firm had adopted a primarily seasonal production philosophy. Due to higher costs and low margins, the firm tried to avoid overtime production, which it viewed as a break-even activity. Nonetheless, in the interest of good customer relations, the firm would use overtime as necessary to meet customers' demands. For example, in 1986 SWC had exceeded capacity for the 16-oz. round containers and had gone into overtime production.

SWC had a long-standing company policy not to turn down any business on the basis of capacity constraints. If a permanent increase in demand was perceived, the company would purchase additional equipment to meet demand.

Overtime and capital expansion were the only ways available for the firm to expand capacity. Increasing capacity by increasing the operating speed of the equipment was not considered viable: The machinery tended to break down faster, and the resulting downtime and maintenance costs offset any gains made from faster operating speeds. Over the years, the company felt it had identified the optimum operating speed for each machine.

COMPETITIVE ENVIRONMENT

In the past 10 years, the paper container industry had consolidated considerably, with competition becoming more concentrated and aggressive. The major firms in the industry were roughly 10 times SWC's size and manufactured a full range of containers, including their plastic equivalents. All of SWC's customers purchased from these major firms, and SWC's position was that of a secondary supplier. SWC recognized six major national competitors and three regional ones. Since the industry's practice was not to share market information, however, SWC was uncertain of its market share and its relative position among competitors.

Distribution channels played an important role in the industry's structure. Products were sold either directly to customers or through distributors. The larger firms gained a competitive edge by establishing their own distribution networks and selling directly to customers. Smaller firms, including SWC, tended to sell through distributors, though containers with custom printing designs purchased in sufficient quantities were usually sold direct.

Smaller firms like SWC gained several advantages by using distributors. The distributors provided warehousing, local transportation and delivery to smaller accounts, carried a full line of products to supplement the smaller manufacturers' limited lines, and provided additional marketing efforts.

Distributors had a vested interest in purchasing from SWC and other smaller firms to prevent industry domination by the larger firms, who could, with their tremendous financial resources, easily bypass them and sell direct. Overall, competition was based on both price and service, with product pricing being established by the major firms. Because the industry was mature, new business was not gained by expanding the demand for products but by increasing existing market share. This was typically through competitive pricing. The current industry trend toward cut-throat pricing was a common practice among the major firms, as they sought to establish direct distribution channels to the high-volume customer. The custom-print market segment was less attractive to the larger firms because of the small-order volumes. This lack of attractiveness made this segment less competitive and hence not as price sensitive.

SWC, as a smaller player, could not compete on price for several reasons. First, it was not the lowest priced competitor. Older machinery, lack of captive supply sources, and an inability to obtain bulk purchasing discounts for other materials limited its ability to match prices. If SWC tried to cut prices to increase its market share, it would eventually lose for lack of staying power.

Without the ability to compete aggressively through pricing, customer service became a key factor in protecting market share. Maintaining an adequate stock of all products and always being willing to produce a customer's items were critical to building customer trust and loyalty. If sales of a particular item increased in the short run, SWC was willing to increase production by operating the more expensive overtime shifts to meet the customer's needs.

Another competitive tool that SWC relied on was to maintain the exclusivity of the distributor's area, thus guaranteeing each distributor a competitive advantage over other distributors in the area. Distributors' exclusivity was becoming increasingly difficult to maintain as SWC distributors were expanding their territories and thus competing with one another.

STRATEGY CHANGE

Late in 1986, unhappy with its low profitability, SWC instituted a new strategy designed to protect its dwindling profit margins. This strategy contained two major elements: (1) focus on low-volume custom-print customers, and (2) set the minimum acceptable selling price for a product as a direct gross margin of 25%.

The rationale behind the new strategy was straightforward. First, the low-volume custom-print accounts, reflecting the lower competition and willingness to pay for service, had higher gross margins than their high-volume counterparts. SWC, because it could provide the extra service required in this market and because of its willingness to work through distributors, felt it was well positioned to expand its share of this market. Historically, SWC had proven successful in negotiating higher prices in the low-volume custom-print segment (see Exhibit 4). Second, the financial planning department had analyzed the firm's financial data and determined that if a minimum direct gross margin (DGM) of 25% were achieved, overall profitability would be acceptable.

The immediate result of implementing the new strategy was a loss of competitiveness in the high-volume segment. Since profit margins were already thin on these accounts, SWC had little leeway in reducing its quoted prices to meet the competition's bids and still maintain prices within the 25% DGM guideline.

The anticipated impact of the company's new strategy came when a high-volume account began receiving low-priced bids from one of SWC's major competitors. SWC had always considered this customer to be a low-loyalty account which would leave as soon as a lower priced supplier was found. After several rounds, the price fell below the 25% DGM point, and SWC walked away from the account.

Unfortunately, the loss of this customer coincided with the loss of a high-loyalty customer handled through a regional distributor in the Midwest. SWC had a long-standing relationship with the customer, who appeared satisfied with SWC's products and service. However, SWC lost out when a recently merged large competitor, National Container, adopted a more aggressive sales strategy in the distributor's region.

National Container had threatened the distributor with going directly to the distributor's customers if the distributor did not increase National's market share by giving it a piece of SWC's and everyone else's business. The distributor refused, and National went ahead by selling directly to the distributor's customers at reduced prices, thereby gaining a significant portion of the distributor's business, including SWC's customer.

The loss of these two accounts totaled 20% of SWC's annual business: The first account represented 14% and the second 6%. While the company was satisfied with its new strategy, the losses were higher and came sooner than expected.

EXISTING COST SYSTEM

Problems with the cost accounting system surfaced when 1987 product costs were computed. The cost system treated the manufacturing plant as a single cost center and traced material and direct labor wages directly to the products. All other costs were considered either overhead costs or period costs. Overhead costs were allocated to each product based on the number of units produced.

Because the system spread all overhead costs over the existing production base, the 20% decrease in business caused the reported product costs to rise. These cost increases forced the marketing department to raise prices on some of the high-volume business. This was especially distressing since it coincided with marketing's need to be more competitive to regain the lost market share. It was at this point that William Ware, marketing vice-president, decided to ignore the 1987 product costs and use the 1986 costs for all marketing decisions. Ware stated the following:

> The 1987 product costs forced our prices to be much less competitive. At those prices, we would have never been able to match our competition or replace the lost business. It took me a while to realize what actually happened; that the lost business meant lost production volume and a decrease in the number of units to spread the total costs over. When I tried to get Michael Schulze, the president, to see this, he reminded me that it was my department's responsibility to replace the lost business and increase the volume—not to worry about how products were costed.

CFO Carl Brody, however, stated the following:

> Marketing's reaction to the 1987 product costs caused me to question the validity of the design of our cost system; in particular the way we treated the

cost of lost production volume. I asked Dick Edlund, our controller, to explore the impact on reported product costs if we shifted to a capacity-based cost system.

CAPACITY-BASED COST SYSTEM

Dick Edlund described the steps he took to determine the impact of idle capacity on the reported product costs:

> The old definition of capacity was the problem. It fluctuated year to year depending on the sales budget. I believed that the appropriate definition of capacity was the total quantity that could be produced if we kept all of the machines running all of the time.
>
> We defined capacity as the production of coated containers. The printing and blanking operations were treated as overhead and spread to the containers along with all other overhead costs on the basis of units coated.

To determine available capacity, Edlund requested from manufacturing a list of the company's 60 coating machines, indicating the size of product they made and the approximate number of units each could turn out in an hour (Exhibit 5). These machine rates were then modified by two factors: planned idle time and unplanned idle time.

Planned idle time consisted of two parts: labor related and machine related. Labor-related idle time (approximately 8% of total time) included coffee breaks and time when the workforce cleaned up the worksite at the end of the day. Machine-related idle time arose from tooling changes, paper roll changes, and machine setup time. Machine-related idle time accounted for approximately 15% of the total available production time. Unplanned idle time, caused by machine breakdown, reduced the overall capacity of the plant by an additional 10% (see Exhibit 6). While these two types of idle time varied slightly from machine to machine, the variations were not considered significant enough to require separate rates for each machine (see Exhibit 7).

Edlund commented as follows:

> I asked manufacturing to review these adjusted capacities and identify the minimum number of machines that had to be running at any one time to achieve maximum desired output. Interestingly enough, with the exception of the 16-oz. lines, there were no spare machines—all the machines had to

be in use at one point or another during the year. For the 16-oz. line, we apparently had eight machines that we could do without. However, when I asked the manufacturing manager whether the eight slowest machines from the 16-oz. lines could be removed, he said, "It's not that simple."

The efficiency with which the operator and packers could work depended on the number of machines that were running in a line. The factory consisted of 10 rows of six machines each, and the most efficient way to operate the machines was to run six in line at a time. Running six in line allowed the operator, handler, and packer to be used more efficiently. In particular, it allowed each operator to run these machines simultaneously. The eight "surplus" 16-oz. machines were often used to produce the product because of their placement in the factory even though they were slower than their newer counterparts.

Furthermore, manufacturing saw little cost savings in mothballing the equipment. Since the number of operators and packers was dependent on the number of machines in use, not the number of machines in the plant, and because both operators and maintenance workers were skilled labor which could not be utilized as floating labor, the cost of labor was relatively fixed. The only cost savings achieved by removing the machines would be some maintenance costs. If demand did increase, the machines would have to be reinstalled or new ones purchased. Edlund continued to describe the new capacity costing process:

> Once the available plant capacity was determined, the next step was to identify the fixed and variable components of cost. While I recognized that some costs might be semivariable, I decided to identify all costs as either fixed or variable on the first pass and modify the assessment in subsequent analyses if it appeared justified. [See Exhibit 8.]

Using these figures, Edlund was able to calculate the overhead cost structure of individual products under the existing cost system (see Exhibit 9). He then calculated the new capacity-based product costs using a 24-hour production rate of 7,253 thousand units and a 240-day year (see Exhibit 10) and, for comparison purposes, the product costs that would have been reported in 1987 if production volumes had been equivalent to those of 1986 (see Exhibit 11).

With the new capacity-based product costs, the effect of moving some fixed costs from product to period costs became evident. Finally, to illustrate how the accounting system would handle the cost of excess capacity, Edlund restated the projected 1987 profit and loss statements (see Exhibit 12).

Reaction to the new capacity cost was mixed, however, as evidenced by the following statements:

The new 1987 capacity-adjusted product costs allowed us to go out and really sell! At a 25% direct gross margin, we were really price competitive. I have already signed several new contracts and

expect to sign several more in the next few months. At this rate, we will soon exceed last year's volume!

WILLIAMS WARE, VICE-PRESIDENT OF MARKETING

When the cost of idle capacity was allocated to the products, it was clearly considered in the pricing decision. Now that it is a period cost, there is the risk that, on a day-to-day basis, we will ignore it. I am worried that marketing will give the firm away using these new costs. I am also concerned that we will be in trouble with the auditors. I believe GAAP does not allow fixed production costs to be expensed in the period they were incurred.

CARL BRODY, CFO

EXHIBIT 1

SCHULZE WAXED CONTAINERS, INC.

1987 Projected Profit

($000)

Sales		$23,415
Cost of goods sold		
Materials	$11,591	
Labor—direct	1,596	
Manufacturing overhead	4,843	
Total		$18,030
Gross margin		$ 5,385
Operating expenses		
Marketing and selling	$4,001	
General and administrative	1,150	
Total		$5,151
Net income (loss)		$ 234

EXHIBIT 2

SCHULZE WAXED CONTAINERS, INC.

List of Products Manufactured

CONTAINER SIZE	COMMON USES
8-oz. round	Butter, carry-out
12-oz. round	Butter, carry-out
16-oz. round	Butter, carry-out
16-oz. square	Ice cream
32-oz. square	Ice cream
64-oz. square	Ice cream

EXHIBIT 3A

SCHULZE CONTAINERS, INC.

1987 Unit Sales Forecast (000)

CONTAINER SIZE	APRIL	MAY	JUNE	JULY	AUGUST	SEPTEMBER	OCTOBER
8-oz. round	7,262	6,706	5,755	6,230	4,080	4,670	5,803
12-oz. round	8,036	6,518	7,656	10,339	3,120	3,427	3,220
16-oz. round	34,637	37,603	33,518	40,099	32,659	27,322	31,968
16-oz. square	29,339	28,934	26,052	33,604	21,437	19,848	21,502
32-oz. square	15,235	17,882	18,139	20,595	16,022	12,819	13,602
64-oz. square	2,227	3,374	3,156	3,528	3,358	1,982	1,750
Total	96,737	101,018	94,277	114,396	80,676	70,068	77,846

CONTAINER SIZE	NOVEMBER	DECEMBER	JANUARY	FEBRUARY	MARCH		TOTAL
8-oz. round	3,086	3,331	4,008	4,666	5,506		61,104
12-oz. round	2,726	2,281	5,279	4,502	4,430		61,534
16-oz. round	19,282	22,738	16,747	21,922	27,403		345,898
16-oz. square	14,522	12,604	14,635	13,108	16,627		252,212
32-oz. square	9,415	7,918	7,972	8,164	8,832		156,595
64-oz. square	988	1,603	2,306	2,340	2,820		29,435
Total	50,021	50,474	50,950	54,703	65,618		906,785

EXHIBIT 3B

SCHULZE WAX CONTAINERS, INC.

1987 Unit Sales Forecast

High-Volume Custom Print (000)

CONTAINER SIZE	APRIL	MAY	JUNE	JULY	AUGUST	SEPTEMBER	OCTOBER
8-oz. round	2,816	1,960	1,901	1,686	1,598	6	0
12-oz. round	0	0	0	0	0	1,614	2,209
16-oz. round	14,653	14,623	12,431	15,930	15,167	11,229	14,273
16-oz. square	16,799	16,436	12,570	18,696	12,751	10,528	11,694
32-oz. square	6,084	7,237	6,490	9,153	8,053	6,154	6,864
64-oz. square	0	0	0	0	0	0	0
Total	40,353	40,255	33,393	45,465	37,569	29,531	35,040

CONTAINER SIZE	NOVEMBER	DECEMBER	JANUARY	FEBRUARY	MARCH		TOTAL
8-oz. round	0	0	0	0	0		9,968
12-oz. round	1,373	1,227	1,979	1,365	1,377		11,145
16-oz. round	10,180	13,039	8,836	8,951	11,704		151,016
16-oz. square	8,617	7,604	9,367	6,585	8,687		140,335
32-oz. square	5,085	3,450	4,213	3,698	3,010		69,491
64-oz. square	0	0	0	0	0		0
Total	25,255	25,319	24,395	20,599	24,779		381,953

EXHIBIT 3C

SCHULZE WAX CONTAINERS, INC.

1987 Unit Sales Forecast

Low-Volume Custom (000)

CONTAINER SIZE	APRIL	MAY	JUNE	JULY	AUGUST	SEPTEMBER	OCTOBER
8-oz. round	1,143	980	812	680	200	0	0
12-oz. round	4,331	2,252	4,729	6,789	1,118	747	228
16-oz. round	10,340	11,810	12,794	14,781	7,448	11,612	9,307
16-oz. square	8,889	8,120	10,204	10,446	6,125	7,703	6,970
32-oz. square	7,309	8,000	9,311	8,465	5,708	5,476	5,096
64-oz. square	1,880	2,999	2,756	3,062	2,995	1,772	1,210
Total	33,893	34,162	40,606	44,224	23,594	27,310	22,811

CONTAINER SIZE	NOVEMBER	DECEMBER	JANUARY	FEBRUARY	MARCH	TOTAL
8-oz. round	232	0	0	707	338	5,092
12-oz. round	196	62	2,142	781	1,387	24,764
16-oz. round	5,079	4,861	3,748	6,748	9,197	107,725
16-oz. square	4,591	3,777	3,712	5,116	6,086	81,741
32-oz. square	3,612	3,670	2,903	3,477	5,018	68,046
64-oz. square	979	1,558	2,251	2,241	2,620	26,324
Total	14,690	13,927	14,757	19,071	24,646	313,693

EXHIBIT 3D

SCHULZE WAX CONTAINERS, INC.

1987 Unit Sales Forecast

Stock Print (000)

CONTAINER SIZE	APRIL	MAY	JUNE	JULY	AUGUST	SEPTEMBER	OCTOBER
8-oz. round	3,303	3,766	3,042	3,864	2,282	4,664	5,803
12-oz. round	3,705	4,266	2,927	3,550	2,002	1,066	783
16-oz. round	9,643	11,171	8,293	9,387	10,044	4,481	8,388
16-oz. square	3,651	4,378	3,278	4,462	2,561	1,617	2,838
32-oz. square	1,842	2,645	2,338	2,977	2,261	1,189	1,642
64-oz. square	347	375	400	466	363	210	540
Total	22,491	26,601	20,278	24,706	19,513	13,227	19,994

CONTAINER SIZE	NOVEMBER	DECEMBER	JANUARY	FEBRUARY	MARCH	TOTAL
8-oz. round	2,855	3,331	4,008	3,959	5,168	46,044
12-oz. round	1,157	992	1,158	2,356	1,666	25,627
16-oz. round	4,023	4,838	4,164	6,223	6,502	87,157
16-oz. square	1,314	1,223	1,556	1,407	1,854	30,141
32-oz. square	718	798	856	989	804	19,061
64-oz. square	9	45	55	99	200	3,109
Total	10,076	11,228	11,797	15,033	16,193	211,139

EXHIBIT 4

SCHULZE WAX CONTAINER, INC.
Average Selling Prices per Thousand Units
by Market Segment

| | CUSTOM PRINT | | |
PRODUCT	HIGH VOLUME	LOW VOLUME	STOCK
8-oz. round	$13.73	$15.94	$14.71
12-oz. round	17.60	23.03	19.65
16-oz. round	21.95	25.18	22.61
16-oz. square	22.15	22.19	20.00
32-oz. square	34.13	42.35	36.60
64-oz. square	Not sold	61.25	51.78

EXHIBIT 5

SCHULZE WAX CONTAINER, INC.
Average Hourly Output (thousands of units) by Machine

PRODUCT	NUMBER OF MACHINES	HOURLY OUTPUT PER MACHINE[*]	TOTAL OUTPUT
8-oz. round	4	6.6	26.4
12-oz. round	4	6.0	24.0
16-oz. round	22	7.5	165.0
16-oz. square	18	7.2	129.6
32-oz. square	10	7.2	72.0
64-oz. square	2	6.0	12.0
Total	60	40.5	429.0

[*]Average on all machines

EXHIBIT 6

SCHULZE WAXED CONTAINERS, INC.
Computation on Machine Capacity
8-oz. Product Line
(All 8-oz. Machines)[*]

Total labor hours available:		
3 shifts @ 40 hours/week		120.0
Planned labor idle time		
Planned relaxation or recreation per week	7.5	
Clean-up per week	2.0	
		9.5
Total effective labor hours per week		110.5
Planned machine idle time		
Machine efficiency (15%)	16.5	
Total planned machine hours per week		94.0
Unplanned machine idle time (10%)	9.4	
Total available production hours per week		84.6
Total output/hour (all 8-oz. machines)		26.4K units
Total available production per week		2,232K units
Total available production per 24-hour day		446K units

[*]All calculations rounded to one decimal place.
K = thousands

EXHIBIT 7

SCHULZE WAXED CONTAINERS, INC.

Total Available Practical Output by Product Line

PRODUCT	HOURLY TOTAL OUTPUT (000 UNITS)	TOTAL AVAILABLE PRODUCTION HOURS PER WEEK	PRODUCTION CAPACITY PER WEEK (000 UNITS)	PRODUCTION CAPACITY PER 24 HOURS (000 UNITS)
8-oz. round	26.4	84.6	2,232	446
12-oz. round	24.0	84.6	2,029	406
16 oz. round	165.0	84.6	13,948	2,790
16-oz. square	129.6	84.6	10,955	2,191
32-oz. square	72.0	84.6	6,086	1,217
64-oz. square	12.0	84.6	1,014	203
Total	429.0		36,264	7,253

EXHIBIT 8

SCHULZE WAXED CONTAINERS, INC.

1987 Projected Manufacturing Costs ($000)

Direct costs

Materials	$11,591	
Labor	1,596	
Total		$13,187

Variable overhead costs

Labor—indirect	237	
Labor—related costs	761	
Printing supplies	344	
Machinery supplies	101	
Miscellaneous	613	
Total variable overhead costs		2,056

Fixed overhead costs

Manufacturing departments	1,442	
Support departments	978	
Depreciation	368	
Total fixed overhead costs	2,788	
Total overhead costs		4,844
Total manufacturing		$18,031

EXHIBIT 9

SCHULZE WAXED CONTAINERS, INC.

1987 Product Costs per Thousand Units Reported by Existing Cost System
Based on 1987 Volumes

PRODUCTS	MATERIAL COST	LABOR COST	VARIABLE OVERHEAD COST[*]	FIXED OVERHEAD COST[*]	TOTAL COST
8-oz. round	$ 5.24	$1.90	$2.27	$3.07	$12.48
12-oz. round	7.86	2.09	2.27	3.07	15.29
16-oz. round	10.48	1.67	2.27	3.07	17.49
16-oz. square	10.48	1.74	2.27	3.07	17.56
32-oz. square	20.96	1.74	2.27	3.07	28.05
64-oz. square	41.93	2.09	2.27	3.07	49.36

[*]Based on a production volume of 906,785,000 units

EXHIBIT 10

SCHULZE WAXED CONTAINERS, INC.

1987 Product Costs per Thousand Units Reported by Capacity-Based Cost System
Based on 1987 Volumes

PRODUCTS	MATERIAL COST	LABOR COST	VARIABLE OVERHEAD COST[*]	FIXED OVERHEAD COST[*]	TOTAL COST
8-oz. round	$ 5.24	$1.90	$2.27	$1.60	$11.01
12-oz. round	7.86	2.09	2.27	1.60	13.82
16-oz. round	10.48	1.67	2.27	1.60	16.02
16-oz. square	10.48	1.74	2.27	1.60	16.09
32-oz. square	20.96	1.74	2.27	1.60	26.58
64-oz. square	41.93	2.09	2.27	1.60	47.89

[*]Computed using a volume of 1,740,720,000 units

EXHIBIT 11

SCHULZE WAXED CONTAINERS, INC.

1987 Product Costs per Thousand Units Reported by Existing Cost System
Based on 1986 Volumes

PRODUCTS	MATERIAL COST	LABOR COST	VARIABLE OVERHEAD COST	FIXED OVERHEAD COST[*]	TOTAL COST
8-oz. round	$ 5.24	$1.90	$2.27	$2.46	$12.03
12-oz. round	7.86	2.09	2.27	2.46	14.84
16-oz. round	10.48	1.67	2.27	2.46	18.04
16-oz. square	10.48	1.74	2.27	2.46	17.11
32-oz. square	20.96	1.74	2.27	2.46	27.60
64-oz. square	41.93	2.09	2.27	2.46	48.91

[*]Computed using a volume of 1,060,147,000 units

EXHIBIT 12

SCHULZE WAXED CONTAINERS, INC.
1987 Projected Profit and Loss
(Capacity-Based Costing Version)
($000)

Sales		$23,415
Cost of goods sold		
Materials	$11,591	
Labor direct	1,596	
Manufacturing overhead	3,547	
Total		16,734
Gross margin		$6,681
Operating expenses		
Marketing and selling	4,001	
General and administrative	1,150	
Excess capacity cost	1,296	
Total		6,447
Net income (loss)		$234

4

SYSTEMS FOR OPERATIONAL CONTROL AND PERFORMANCE MEASUREMENT

Cost systems have been used in companies for three primary functions: (a) inventory valuation, (b) operational and cost control, and (c) measuring product costs and profitability.

Inventory valuation is required by generally accepted accounting principles (GAAP). Companies must allocate their periodic production expenses to all items produced during the period so that these expenses—labor, materials purchased, and factory overhead—can be split between products sold (as reported in the cost of goods sold account in the income statement) and products still on hand (as reported in the inventory account in the balance sheet). Existing systems usually assign direct materials and labor reasonably accurately to products.[1] For overhead expenses, however, financial accounting principles do not require that the costs allocated to products be causally related to the demands that the individual products place on the factory's overhead resources. As we have seen in cases appearing in preceding chapters, companies have continued to use direct labor to allocate overhead to products, even though direct labor does not explain the demand for overhead resources by products and, further, has become a minor portion of total factory expenses. Also, companies may aggregate indirect expenses into a single or only a few production cost centers before allocating these expenses to products, even in a complex, highly diverse factory.

Despite using allocation bases that bear little relation to the demands by products for overhead resources and using only a small number of cost centers in factories, manufacturing companies continue to get clean opinions from their auditors. Auditors do not question companies' cost-of-sales or inventory valuation figures merely because the companies have used aggregate, simplistic methods for allocating overhead costs to products. As long as the split of costs between products sold and products still in stock is fairly accurate in aggregate and done consistently from year to year, the inventory valuation needs for financial statement purposes have been met.

---

[1]Substantial inaccuracies can arise, however, in the measurement of a product's direct labor and material expenses when companies do not measure scrap rates or rework by individual products and when they allocate labor and materials variances across all products rather than attempt to assign the variances accurately to individual products and batches.

But cost accounting systems that work well for financial reporting do not necessarily provide information relevant for managerial needs. Managers use information from cost systems for two primary purposes: for operational control—to provide feedback to production and department managers on the resources consumed during an operating period—and for measuring accurately the costs and profitability of individual products. Neither of these functions is typically performed well by the official system that allocates manufacturing expenses to products for inventory valuation. The remainder of this book illustrates the design of systems for managerial purposes. This chapter features the design of operational control and performance measurement systems. Chapters 5 through 7 introduce the design principles for activity-based cost systems that are used for strategic profitability measurement. The operational control and strategic profitability systems are sufficiently diverse that companies may prefer to develop, initially, separate customized systems for the two different managerial functions and defer for future work the integration among financial reporting, operational control, and profitability measurement systems.

OPERATIONAL CONTROL AND PERFORMANCE MEASUREMENT SYSTEMS

An effective operational control and performance measurement system should provide timely, accurate feedback on the efficiency and effectiveness of operations. The scope of the system should correspond to a manager's level of responsibility, control for known variations in cost behavior, and minimize the incidence of cost allocations. Operational control systems should also include, in addition to any financial summaries provided, a relevant variety of nonfinancial indicators. Financial summaries of departmental spending or actual batch costs provide only partial indicators of the efficiency of operations.

Timeliness is perhaps the most important criterion for a well-functioning operational control system. For companies that produce output continually, it would be most helpful to have daily or even hourly operating reports. The reports could summarize what was produced, how much was produced, the quantities and costs of variable input resources used in production (materials, labor, energy, machine time), and the quality or yield of the output. Attempting to improve production processes with present systems that provide only monthly summaries of operations is akin to training a bowler by providing feedback and information only after one month of throwing balls at pins, and then only reporting the aggregate number of pins knocked down during this period (e.g., 27,562), how this number compares to budget, and how it compares to the number knocked down during the same month a year ago. The information may be accurate (and auditable), but it does little to improve the bowler's performance.

Seventy-five years ago, it would have been prohibitively expensive to provide continual detail about operations. But today's information technology makes such measurement relatively inexpensive. For operations under computer control, the data already exist to run the process. The operational control system need only build on the production and production control system to collect, summarize, and report the relevant data. Reports do not have to be printed on paper; they can be made available to employees on video screens and their results summarized periodically for higher management review.

The financial component of an operational control system requires an understanding of which expenses are fixed, in the short run, and which expenses are expected to vary with short-term variations in production levels and mix. Fixed expenses are monitored, perhaps biweekly or monthly, by comparing actual spending to the budgeted amounts each period. Variable expenses are monitored through the use of flexible budgets that enable managers to predict the effects of changes in activity levels and mix on the consumption of labor, materials, machine time, energy, and variable support resources. Flexible budgets will be most accurate and helpful when cost system designers can capture the underlying scientific or engineering laws that govern the production process. They can design the cost control system on the production standards established by the conversion process. A production process that is stable and repetitive also helps to predict the relationship between inputs and outputs.

Operational control information will be most helpful to motivate and evaluate the continual improvement activities of employees. The old cost accounting model, derived from the scientific management movement, stressed adherence to previously determined standards. Unfavorable variances were highlighted for explanation and correction. The focus of new operational control systems has shifted from adherence to centrally determined standards to providing timely, accurate, and relevant information that will enable operators to detect problems quickly and to guide their experimentation and learning activities. This feedback should emphasize not performance against a static standard, developed by industrial engineers from study of existing internal processes, but ongoing improvement from previous levels. Meeting historically determined standards is not sufficient in a competitive world. The new model emphasizes continual improvements in operating efficiencies.

Operational control systems also need accurate measures of the quantities of resources consumed and products produced if employees and managers are to receive useful feedback on their operating performance. If, because of metering or detailed reporting, accurate measures exist for the quantity of a resource consumed by an operating department (the Q measure in our cost equation, $C = P \times Q$), the cost of that resource can be assigned to operating managers and made part of their periodic operating report. But if the actual resource quantities used by individual operating departments are not known, the aggregate cost (the C measure in the equation) should not be allocated to operating managers. The allocations found in many performance measurement systems are akin to counting all the pins knocked down in all the lanes in a bowling alley, dividing by the number of lanes, and reporting to each bowler the average for the entire bowling establishment. No useful control or performance measurement purpose is served by using allocated indirect or common costs in a short-term performance report. For example, a cost center's metered demand for kilowatt-hours of electricity or pounds of steam should be assigned to that center. But if metering is difficult, a company does not improve its cost control activities by allocating a factory-wide utility expense to cost centers. Ballpark estimates of the quantity of labor, machine time, and support resources used do not help managers improve the efficiency and productivity of their operations.

Periodic, perhaps weekly, summaries of operating expenses incurred by a department are useful, but operating reports filled with estimated and allocated costs distract responsibility managers from their primary responsibilities: to monitor and control production efficiencies and to improve productivity. If headquarters occasionally needs responsibility managers to help monitor expenses incurred at a higher level of the organization, the common expense allocation can be argued about and assigned once a year, during the budgetary process. After that annual negotiation, the allocated cost should either be held constant for each reporting period or not reported at all.

PHYSICAL AND OPERATIONAL PERFORMANCE MEASURES

Financial summaries can provide only a limited view of the efficiency and effectiveness of actual operations. Effective operational control systems will include, in addition to any financial summaries provided, a relevant set of nonfinancial indicators. Companies today are implementing total quality management (TQM) programs in which defects are measured in parts per million (PPM) and managers are expected to achieve continual reductions in their PPM defect rates. Also featured are just-in-time (JIT) procedures that attempt to keep work flowing continually without interruption. Companies able to implement TQM and JIT programs have enjoyed greatly reduced lead times for delivery of their products to customers, lowered manufacturing costs, and, in general, enhanced customer responsiveness. Yet even these successful companies have found that gains from TQM and JIT were not recognized by their organization's management accounting systems.[2] Companies attempting to improve the quality of their manufacturing process-es need continual measurements of process yields, defect rates, scrap and rework rates, and first-pass yields (the percentage of items completed without any rework required).

Companies striving to achieve JIT operations will want to monitor their performance in reducing total throughput time. The throughput time for a product (or service) can be represented as follows:

$$\underset{\text{time}}{\text{throughput}} = \underset{\text{time}}{\text{processing}} + \underset{\text{time}}{\text{inspection}} + \underset{\text{time}}{\text{movement}} + \underset{\text{time}}{\text{waiting/storage}}$$

For many operations, processing time is less than 5% of throughput time; that is, for a total throughput time of six weeks (30 working days), only one to two days of actual processing time may be required. During the remaining time, the part or product is being inspected, moved around the factory, or simply waiting—in storage, on the factory floor, or just before or after a processing operation until the next operation can be scheduled, the machine set up, and the part fixtured into place.

Manufacturing and industrial engineers sometimes call the time a product is being processed as *value-added time,* and all the remaining time as *non-value-added time.* Activities such as storing products, moving them, testing them, or setting up machines to work on them are also referred to as non-value-added activities, since none of these activities improves the product for meeting customer needs. Industrial engineers in the U.S. and many other Western countries focused their attention in the post-World War II period in making the value-added processes (such as machining and assembling products) more efficient. Only recently have they placed their attention on making improvements on the non-value-added activities: reducing setup times, improving factory layouts, and producing in smaller batches.

In an ideal JIT system, the throughput time for a part just equals its processing time (a goal that, like zero defects, may be unattainable but is still worth striving for). A key measure, the manufacturing cycle effectiveness (MCE), captures the current state of an organization's attempts to eliminate waste or non-value-added time.

$$\text{MCE} = \frac{\text{processing time}}{\text{throughput time}}$$

[2]This issue was also addressed in "Limitations of Cost Accounting in Advanced Manufacturing Environment," Chapter 1 of R. S. Kaplan (ed.), *Measures for Manufacturing Excellence* (Boston: Harvard Business School Press, 1990).

As the MCE ratio gets closer to 1, the organization knows that the amount of time wasted moving, inspecting, and storing products has been decreasing. The MCE ratio emphasizes the importance of managing time and increasing responsiveness to customers, not just the traditional cost accounting goal of managing costs. Other measures to support a JIT philosophy include average setup times, distance traveled by products in the factory, and average days production in inventory.

Vendor performance is tracked by frequency of defects and on-time delivery percentages. Performance from the customer's perspective is measured by frequency of customer complaints, returns, allowances, and warranty and field service expenses. Some companies conduct systematic surveys of their customers to compute customer satisfaction indexes. Each operating indicator provides useful information to monitor how well the company is improving its operations.

The benchmark for the quality and time-based measures should not represent engineered or historical standards. The standard for performance has become perfection: zero defects, 100% yields, zero scrap, 100% on-time delivery, and no waste in throughput times or processing. Data on current actual performance are displayed graphically so that progress toward getting closer to the ideal can be readily observed. If benchmarks short of ideal operations are desired, the goals are set based on the performance of the company's best worldwide competitor. But this can only be a short-run objective, since by the time the company achieves this performance level, its best competitor will be well beyond that performance.

In summary, operational control systems in the new competitive environment feature timely reports on actual operations, including the actual (not allocated) quantities and unit costs of resources consumed, plus a variety of nonfinancial indicators to monitor the continual improvement activities of operating managers. All the data, financial and nonfinancial, can be shown as trends, with the target for nonfinancial data being perfection or, in the short run, the performance of the company's best worldwide competitor. Each period the organization's operating performance should be improving, getting closer to the ideal.

Many financial measures, found in traditional cost accounting systems, have become actively dysfunctional by encouraging the wrong types of behavior and inhibiting the quality and JIT efforts of operating managers. Measures such as purchase price variances, direct labor and machine efficiencies, ratios of indirect to direct labor, absorption ratios, and volume variances conflict with attempts to improve quality, reduce inventories and throughput times, and increase flexibility.[3]

Some of these measures are being replaced with aggregate financial summaries of operating performance. For example, the *cost of quality* measure identifies all the expenses associated with preventing, testing for, and fixing product defects. The cost of quality measure signals to managers the large amount of operating expenses created by making and fixing nonconforming items and has been used to motivate and evaluate quality improvement programs.

To replace a narrow focus on purchase price variances by individual products and vendors, some companies have developed measures of the total *cost of ownership* of materials. This measure includes, in addition to purchase price, the cost of ordering, paying, scheduling delivery, receiving, inspecting, handling, and storing materials. It

---

[3]See Kaplan, "Limitations of Cost Accounting in Advanced Manufacturing Environment," in *Measures for Manufacturing Excellence* (Boston: Harvard Business School Press, 1990).

also includes, for each purchased material item, the cost of schedule disruptions if delivery is not made on time and the costs of scrap, rework, and obsolescence caused by the material. With this measurement, a supplier might have a higher unit price than alternative vendors but nonetheless offer a much lower cost because it can supply certifiably defect-free materials, requiring no incoming handling or inspection, in exactly the right quantities, directly to the machine, minutes before the materials are needed, with ordering, invoicing, and payment handled automatically and electronically.

Measures such as cost of quality and cost of ownership are not useful for daily or short-term operations. For those purposes, direct measurements of quality and delivery seem most suited to employee and manager needs. But the aggregate financial measures provide a useful periodic summary of how well the company has performed in lowering the expenses associated with nonconformance production and poor vendor relations. The financial summaries are informational, not control measures. They direct managers' and employees' attention and help to keep score on progress toward achieving corporate goals but are not, by themselves, the focus of near-term managerial activities.

As physical and operational measures play a much larger role in performance measurement systems, new problems arise. No longer can performance measured at a local level be easily aggregated into the financial performance measures of the plant, the division, and the company. Just how to design a hierarchical, comprehensive system of local shop-floor operating measures, departmental and plant measures, and divisional and company measures is now the subject of active research by companies, consultants, and academics. Companies are now using a full range of operating measures—of quality, throughput, cycle times, and on-time delivery—while still retaining their traditional financial measures. The task of reconciling between operational and financial measures is currently left to middle-level management, who are squeezed between the pressure to show ever-improving financial performance to their superiors while encouraging and supporting the continuous improvement activities under TQM and JIT programs among their subordinates. In good times, operational and financial performance are linked together; but frequently one set of measures is moving up while the other set is moving down. At those times, the lack of an integrated view of the organization, with a single clear focus on appropriate performance measures at all levels, leads to frustration and confusion.

CASES

Metabo GmbH & Co. KG

When our old cost system was designed and implemented, it was state of the art. But it no longer provided us with accurate numbers. The reported numbers were too aggregated to provide direct feedback on the performance of shop floor workers. Our new system, in contrast, is the best available.

MR. HÄussler, CONTROLLER, METABO

HISTORY AND PRODUCTS

Metabo, located in Nurtingen, about 15 miles outside of Stuttgart in the Swabian region of West Germany, was founded in 1924 as the Schnizler Werke company. Initially it produced hand drills and subsequently expanded its product line into hand and electric tools for craftsmen, eventually offering the world's largest do-it-yourself product line of hand-operated power tools. The company is still controlled by the three founding families (Closs, Rauch, and Schnizler), although in 1978 its legal status was changed to a limited partnership with a limited company as general partner.

Today Metabo produces a full line of power tools including saws, rotary and impact drills, screwdrivers, hammers, grinders, polishers, planers, and routers. Products are sold to do-it-yourselfers, professionals, and industrial workers. In addition to hand tools, Metabo manufactures bench- and column-mounted drilling machines, belt polishing and buffing machines, and grinding machines. Altogether, Metabo produces 500 basic and about 2,000 different final products. The company manufactures 45,000 standard parts plus customer-specified products. About 85% to 90% of turnover occurs in standard products, the remainder in special orders. All products are developed internally.

Metabo is considered the Rolls Royce of the hand-tool industry and has been able to command a price premium compared to its competition. The company's main competitors, also offering full product lines, are Bosch and AEG, two West German manufacturers, and Black & Decker. Bosch, the market leader, and AEG, the number two, offer good quality, good image, and slightly lower prices. Black & Decker competes in the lower end of the market. Recently, Japanese competitors have entered Metabo's home market. While they offer good quality and lower prices, they lack Metabo's full product line.

THE PRODUCTION PROCESS

Despite being a relatively small company, Metabo is completely vertically integrated and builds all critical components and subassemblies in-house. One of the company's founders believed, "You get quality only if you do it yourself."

Power tool production starts with raw material treatment, including components made in the aluminum foundry, by plastic injection molding, and in-steel treatment. About three metric tons of aluminum are melted daily in the foundry and cast into various small components that are subsequently cleaned, polished, and inspected. In the plastic injection molding department, granular material is fed from large storage silos into various machines to be heated and injected under pressure into molds to form plastic components (e.g., handles) for the hand tools. The molding machines come in different sizes and have different manpower requirements, ranging from one operator for one machine to one operator for six machines.

Steel treatment produces machined parts such

This case was prepared by research associate Dagmar Bottenbruch and Professor Robert S. Kaplan.

as wheels, chucks, and armature shafts. Two types of treatment occur: bar feeding, where treated bars are cut after treatment, and piece feeding, where precut parts are machined. Because of the considerable diversity of parts (about 1,500) processed through steel treatment, a large inventory of 1,000 to 1,200 metric tons of steel, worth about DM 900,000, is maintained for the area.

In the bar feeding process, the steel bars are taken by crane to the appropriate turning machine for processing. Two types of turning machines are used: six-spindle machines, which process six steel bars simultaneously, and single-spindle machines. About 1,000 different parts are produced in this department—60% on the six-spindle machines. Setup times depend on the dimensions of the components. Components with similar specifications might require only minor adjustments to the machines. If the components are completely different, setup times can range between 2 and 14 hours, even with extensive preparation work performed while the previous part is running on the machine. Twelve setup people work exclusively in the department.

Other employees in the department feed the raw material and remove the finished parts and byproducts. Because of the long setup times, production of standard parts is scheduled in large batches. For example, one part which takes 13 seconds of machining time is produced in a lot size of 20,000 pieces. The large batch would then go into inventory and be released for further processing in smaller lot sizes, depending on final demand. Some components are produced continuously; others run for between 2 to 10 shifts.

Tool preparation is another major activity in this department. A setup schedule provides information on the need for tools and machine parts. The same people do the setups and prepare the tools. Tool preparation takes an average of 2.5 hours but can, of course, be done while the machine is running. An average of 7 of the 35 machines would be in the setup stage each day. Nearly DM 6 million of inventory of fixtures and tools support the turning machines. After a part leaves a turning machine, it is hardened in a furnace, heat-treated, and inspected. Steel parts and other components are brought

together in the electrical motor production line. This department contains a fully automated line that winds wire, attaches a fan and insulators, and tests and balances the component that becomes the motor for the hand tool. This highly automated process is replicated on a smaller scale by hand for certain custom applications and for spare parts no longer in standard production.

In final assembly, purchased parts and manufactured components are manually assembled into finished products. The finished product parts list contains 80 to 100 items, all of which must be available at the right time. The finished product receives a final electrical test and is then packaged and shipped through a fully automated distribution center.

The throughput time from casting aluminum to the finished product is 6 to 8 weeks. Grinding wheels, customized special machines, and in-house tool making and production machinery are produced in separate production areas.

THE OLD COST SYSTEM

Metabo provided a complex information management environment (see Exhibit 1). The complexity was difficult to track even with extensive use of computers by the old cost system. The system's main task was to compute actual total costs. It contained the three classic cost accounting elements: accumulate costs by accounts, by cost centers, and by products. Subsystems, such as materials control and wage control, provided inputs into the product costing module. Costs were distributed from 200 different cost accounts to 250 cost centers or work orders.

Product costs were built up from material master accounts, parts lists, and work plans. Secondary (support) center costs were allocated to primary (production) cost centers, using causal relations as much as possible, such as through internal work orders. The overhead allocation was done manually twice a year (in September for budgeting purposes and to compute standard costs for the year, and at year end to eliminate errors and use actual rather than budgeted amounts). The task required three to four weeks for a highly qualified person.

Product cost components were as follows:

Materials

Materials overhead	Applied as a percentage of materials cost
Reemployed parts	The term for subassemblies

Direct Labor

Fringe benefits	Applied based on direct labor cost
Production overhead	Applied using machine-hour rates based on capacity utilization
Special costs	Such as tooling

An analytic study was conducted once per year to determine individual machine-hour rates. Costs arising at the individual cost centers were assigned to each machine in the center and divided by the machine's estimated annual volume. The rates were estimated at the beginning of each year using the actual experience from the prior year. Metabo had 1,500 such machine-hour rates. Häussler noted that many companies continued to allocate overhead to products based on direct labor. Metabo had been using machine-hour rates since the early 1970s.

Six categories of traceable costs could be directly allocated to the machines:

Depreciation	Straight line based on replacement value[1]
Imputed interest	Based on 50% of machine's replacement value[2]
Space	
Energy	Based on run time and machine horsepower
Maintenance	Estimated based on experience and industry averages (including oil and grease)
Tooling	

Costs that could not be traced directly to machines were aggregated at the cost center and allocated to individual machines as a percentage markup of the traceable costs. The rates had ranged between 200% to 300% of traceable costs, but this

procedure caused problems by heavily burdening expensive, automated machines. To avoid overburdening such newly purchased machines with large components of nontraceable costs, a compromise solution was adopted to allocate 50% of the nontraceable costs based on machine hours and 50% based on traceable costs.

PROBLEMS WITH THE OLD SYSTEM

Despite the sophistication and care taken when designing Metabo's old cost system, it no longer satisfied top management's requirements. First, the manual processing of the data at the beginning and end of year was inefficient and costly. Second, long-time lags occurred between data collection and feedback, so operators could not get timely information about what was happening in their cost centers. Thus, operators were not very cost conscious. Also, since the machine rates were only calculated once a year and not split into variable and fixed components, major errors were introduced by fluctuations in capacity utilization. After a very good year, machine burden rates would plummet, and after a bad year the rates became much more expensive. While Mr. Häussler, based on his personal experience, tried to make some adjustments to dampen extreme variations in rates, the results were not satisfactory.

No budgets were prepared, so actual results could not be compared against a standard. Even with a budget, the information would have been meaningless to cost center managers because of the inability to control for the actual level of activity in a period. The degree of aggregation at a cost center produced additional problems. For example, the aluminum foundry and injection molding department were treated as a single cost center even though several different machines with different degrees of automation and labor intensity were used in each facility. In the steel treatment area, all six-spindle machines were in the same cost center; and in the motor production area, the fully automated and the hand assembly operations were included in the same cost center.

Also producing errors was the practice of charging fringe benefits (a very high cost component in Germany) to the cost center where a worker was originally assigned, while the actual direct labor

---

[1]The calculation based on replacement costs was done for internal purposes only since historical costs were mandated for financial and tax reporting.

[2]A long-term (three- to five-year) bank lending rate was used to charge interest expense on inventory and fixed assets. Currently this rate was in the range of 5% to 6%.

charge was made to the cost center where he or she performed the work. German workers could perform a variety of skilled tasks and were rotated frequently among cost centers.

Since batch sizes varied from process to process, the job order accounting approach presented another serious problem. In the aluminum foundry, a job order could be written for 4,000 pieces of a component. If the process were running smoothly, the supervisor could decide to produce enough to release 4,500 good pieces to the next stage. Omitted from this count would be items produced in the batch but which had been set aside as scrap or rework. On the other hand, a few hundred pieces could have been added to the batch after they had been reworked from a previous batch.

With the old system, all the costs of working on the order would be accumulated and then divided by the number of good parts that left the production stage when computing a cost per unit. To get any useful information from such data, one person had to spend a month on a special study to track down the production costs associated with a single end product.

Häussler explained as follows:

> You can't expect a production supervisor or technician to explain a total product cost variance. He needs information that relates directly to the process he is controlling. Only if you show him things like excess tooling expense, indirect materials, and the actual quantity produced at that stage can he start to respond on the source of the deviation.

A final flaw in the system was the difficulty of integrating cost accounting with financial accounting. The product cost figures used internally were different from those needed for financial reporting because of differing methods of depreciation (straight-line versus accelerated, and replacement value versus historical cost), and the use of imputed interest for internal measurement of product costs that was not allowed for external reporting. The reconciliation between the two systems was tedious and painful.

IN SEARCH OF THE PERFECT SYSTEM

Mr. Häussler still gets a tortured look on his face when thinking of the old system. He was pleased when top management decided that a new cost system was needed. His background included extensive shop floor experience starting, after school, as an apprenticeship at a machine tool company. While a machining apprentice, he had to fill in for the purchasing manager who became sick. In this position he learned how little office and staff people knew of actual operations. He decided to do a second more technical apprenticeship, which occurred at Metabo. After one-and-a-half years in the technical service division of a construction machinery producer, he pursued studies in business. In 1972 he joined Metabo's control department.

Häussler, because of his technical background and his excellent relationship with the people on the shop floor, was put in charge of developing the new control system. Häussler concurred as follows:

> It is easier to familiarize an engineer or technician with some basic economic principles than the other way around. An engineer has a feeling for the production process, can relate to it. Many corporate controllers can't do that.

> While the old system was certainly better than no system at all, top management decided that they needed something better. They began their search and came across the Plaut/Kilger system and SAP software.

The Plaut/Kilger and SAP systems

Plaut—a German-based consulting firm—was a leader in developing and installing sophisticated cost systems for major industrial clients in West Germany and throughout Europe. SAP was founded in 1972 by four former IBM computer scientists to design efficient software for data processing in business and manufacturing applications. One SAP founder, Dr. Plattner, had met Plaut in 1984, and the two companies decided to combine Plaut's sophisticated cost control systems with SAP's leading-edge main frame software. Plaut would do the consulting work for the client's specific problems, and SAP would install and integrate its system with the client's operations. Mr. Häussler found that the SAP/Plaut system could satisfy the criteria top management had specified for a good system.

Implementation

The new cost management system used flexible, standard costing for cost budgeting, accounting, and control. The following functions were included:

1. Cost center accounting for manufacturing overhead cost control;
2. Production costing for product cost control;
3. Planning/simulation for strategic costing on a what-if basis.

Overhead cost control was the initial area of implementation. New cost centers had to be defined and appropriate activity bases selected for manufacturing, service, and support centers. Only similar machines with an identical relationship between incurred costs and the chosen activity base were grouped into the same cost center. Thus, highly automated machines, such as in a computer-integrated manufacturing (CIM) center, were placed in a separate cost center from operator-controlled machines. The number of cost centers had to increase from 250 to 600.

Activity bases for each cost center were chosen from operating parameters such as machine hours, labor hours, setup hours, kilograms of material, number of pieces, kilowatt-hours, and square meters of material. Occasionally, multiple activity bases, such as machining hours and setup hours, were used in the same cost center to distribute costs.

Once new cost centers and activity bases were defined, flexible budgets were prepared for each cost center. Budgeted costs were estimated, using analytic—not historical cost—methods for each manufacturing, service, and support cost center. Each cost center had about 70 different input resources identified, leading to more than 40,000 entries.

Primary costs, such as direct and indirect labor, indirect materials, energy consumption, machine costs, and outside services, were traced directly to each individual cost center. Secondary costs were allocated from service and support cost centers based on the quantities of secondary department resources used by the manufacturing (primary) cost centers. The budgeted secondary cost rates were determined by planned, not actual, volumes of consumption of secondary support resources. The budgeted cost rates were applied ex post, based on the actual volume of demands made by production cost centers, as a function of their operating activities, on the support and service cost centers. The details of this calculation are illustrated in the Appendix to this case. For the secondary cost centers where the output could not be measured easily by quantities, percentage allocations were used.

Each primary and secondary budgeted cost was split into variable (proportional) and fixed components, based on the relation between the cost element and the chosen activity base for the cost center. The final fixed and variable cost rates were used both for product costing and to authorize overhead costs at the cost center level.

Overhead cost control was accomplished with the cost center *budget performance report*. Actual costs incurred at the cost center, including both primary and secondary costs, were compared with the authorized cost for the cost center, based on the actual activity base volume at the cost center. A variety of variances—usage, price, rate, and volume—were computed and displayed.

Standard product costs could now be computed. The bill of materials and routing sheets supplied information on standard material quantities and processing times. The cost standards for material prices and manufacturing cost rates at each cost center could then be applied to obtain standard product costs for all product codes—parts, subassembly groups, and finished products—based on standard performance and standard rates. These frozen standards were used for profit planning and for inventory valuation. Updated for changes in the bills of materials, input prices, or changes in processing routes and times, they could be used for current manufacturing cost control; that is, costs would be authorized based on production work orders.

Product cost control was evaluated with the *production work order performance report*. Actual costs incurred—including direct materials use and manufacturing resource consumption—were compared with the authorized cost, which equaled the current standard product cost per unit multiplied by the actual quantity produced. Price (materials, cost rate) and performance (materials usage, manufacturing efficiency, and alternative routing) variances were separately identified. Absorption of product cost into inventory was accomplished using current standard product cost rates so that all production cost variances were expensed as period costs. In addition, management accounting cost procedures—such as straight-line depreciation based on replacement costs—which were not allowable for financial (external) accounting purposes were offset in a reconciliation routine when preparing the semiannual financial reports.

The new cost system maintained highly detailed records to measure accurately the actual activity volume at each manufacturing operation and at each of the 600 cost centers. Performance reports were produced monthly to summarize actual versus authorized performance, but the information behind these reports was continuously available, online, for immediate feedback. The detailed and accurate record keeping enabled manufacturing variances to be explained easily. For example, an unfavorable cost center variance could be traced either to events at the center itself or back to a secondary service/support center that had been reallocated to it.

Planning and simulation analysis could be performed easily because all costs, at both primary and secondary centers, could be flexed with respect to fluctuations in product volume and mix assumptions. What-if simulations could be based on changes in activity base or production quantity volumes and with respect to changes in labor rates, material prices, energy costs, tariffs, etc. Structural changes affecting the split of costs into fixed and variable components, or on resource and activity base consumption, would be entered manually before performing the simulation study.

PAYOFFS TO METABO

Häussler felt that Metabo's new cost system provided several major benefits to the company. The visibility and traceability of costs down to the lowest level in the organization enabled problems to be uncovered that had been hidden or averaged across units by the prior system. The information on marginal costs made it possible to compute accurate flexible budgets. The more accurate and detailed system gave all employees much greater confidence in the validity and reliability of the cost data. Costs could now be predicted as a function of production volume thereby eliminating a major source of uncer-

tainty in the previous system. Problems could be traced to their source and remedied immediately. Operators had to accept responsibility for costs charged to their cost centers, whereas previously they had argued that excessive costs were introduced at previous stages, were the consequence of overcharges from the secondary cost centers, or arose from errors introduced by the average, total cost system.

The ability to reconcile data between the financial accounting and the cost accounting systems was another major advantage. The two systems were now compatible, which made tax planning and audits much easier. Auditors who questioned the minutest detail could access and investigate the underlying transactions record. Thus, Metabo now enjoyed the advantages of an effective cost control system driven by the underlying production process, while still being able to produce product cost information acceptable for the financial accounting statements.

The flexibility and power of the SAP software system made complex simulations and scenario planning possible. But the system had yet to be used to make product-related decisions. Pricing, product introduction, and product elimination decisions had been unaffected by the information from the new system.

Häussler emphasized the following:

Pricing is determined in the marketplace. We cannot use product cost information to determine our pricing. Also, we must offer a full product line. Previously, our brand position was so strong that customers would purchase only Metabo products. Now, however, if we do not offer a particular product model, the consumer may purchase a competitor's product. Compromising our full product line is not a good option.

Häussler summarized his feelings about the new system as follows:

Knowing, finally, what is going on and not tapping in the dark with a pile of information that could be more damaging than beneficial has given me an incredibly good feeling.

EXHIBIT 1

METABO GMBH & CO. KG

Summary of Operations

CATEGORY	QUANTITY
Material units	45,000
Routing sheets	15,000
Parts lists	15,000
Internal work orders	2,500
Production orders	3,000
Suppliers	3,000
Orders per month	2,300
Customers	21,000
Bills per month	17,000
Average inventory moves per month	160,000
Labor inputs per month	60,000

APPENDIX

Budgeting and Charging for Secondary Center Costs

Consider the secondary (support) center 55, Inspection of Production Batches. This center inspects the output from injection molding machines in three different primary (operating) cost centers.

Step 1: Develop the annual budgeted costs for center 55.

COST ELEMENT	BUDGETED COSTS		
	FIXED	VARIABLE	TOTAL
Personnel	50,000	250,000	300,000
Supplies	300	1,200	1,500
Tools		4,000	4,000
Maintenance	1,000	3,500	4,500
Capitalized services	20,000		20,000
Occupancy	24,000		24,000
Energy		3,500	3,500
Total costs	95,300	262,200	357,500

Step 2: Distribute planned costs from center 55 to primary cost centers.

The costs planned in cost center 55 are distributed to the three molding cost centers based on expected annual operating levels of the three centers.

OPERATING COST CENTER	ANNUAL OPERATING HOURS	PERCENTAGE
22	4,350	38.3%
25	1,870	16.5
27	5,130	45.2
	11,350	100.0%

Determine the budgeted variable cost rate for center 55.

$$\frac{\text{variable}}{\text{cost rate}} = \frac{\text{budgeted variable costs (center 55)}}{\text{planned operating hours (centers 22, 25, 27)}}$$

$$= \frac{262,200}{11,350} = 23.10 \text{ per hour worked}$$

Develop the monthly budget for the three operating cost centers.

	PLANNED COSTS		
	FIXED	VARIABLE	TOTAL
22	36,500	100,500	137,000
25	15,700	43,200	58,900
27	43,100	118,500	161,600
Total planned costs	95,300	262,200	357,500

Step 3: Determine monthly actual costs in support center 55 and activity levels in the three operating cost centers.

COST ELEMENT	ACTUAL COSTS
Personnel	27,000
Supplies	200
Tools	300
Maintenance	400
Capitalized services	1,667
Occupancy	2,000
Energy	297
Total actual costs	31,864

OPERATING COST CENTER	ACTUAL HOURS WORKED
22	415
25	90
27	460
Total hours worked	965

Step 4: Analyze actual costs in support center 55.

Budgeted fixed costs equal annual budgeted costs divided by 12. Authorized variable costs equal budgeted variable cost per hour worked multiplied by the actual hours worked in the three operating cost centers in the month.

	ALLOWED COSTS			
COST ELEMENT	FIXED	VARIABLE	ACTUAL COSTS	VARIANCE
Personnel	4,167	21,258	27,000	1,575
Supplies	25	102	200	73
Tools	340	300	(40)	
Maintenance	83	298	400	19
Capitalized services	1,667		1,667	—
Occupancy	2,000		2,000	—
Energy		297	297	—
Total allowed costs	7,942	22,295	31,864	1,627

Note that the total allowed variable cost for center 55 can be computed as follows:

$$\begin{aligned}\text{allowed monthly variable cost} &= \text{actual monthly hours worked} \times 23.10 \\ &= 965 \times 23.10 \\ &= 22,295\end{aligned}$$

Under this system, all spending (or usage) variances that arise in the support center (55) remain in that center as the responsibility of the support center manager. Only budgeted fixed and authorized variable costs for the actual hours worked would be charged to the three operating cost centers. In a second step, the variances of the support center are charged to operating cost centers to get actual costs to these cost centers. But these charged variances are displayed separately in the cost center operating report.

Step 5: Distribute monthly Inspection Department costs to the three molding cost centers.

Fixed costs are distributed to the three cost centers based on planned annual usage (percentages computed in step 2). Monthly variable costs are distributed based on the annual planned variable rate (23.10 per hour) multiplied by the actual hours worked in each center.

	TARGETED COSTS		
COST CENTER	FIXED	VARIABLE	TOTAL
22	3,042	9,589	12,631
25	1,308	2,081	3,389
27	3,592	10,625	14,217
	7,942	22,295	30,237

Texas Eastman Company

Tom Wilson, Company Controller, reflected on the changing role for the Accounting Department in Texas Eastman Company's new operating environment.

Traditionally, Accounting was the recorder of history, but perhaps we were not directly relevant for the operational decisions taken every day by the departmental managers. We see the need to move accountants physically into manufacturing areas so that they can serve as financial advisors to manufacturing managers. But in order for them to function in this capacity, we need information on a real-time basis. Operators can see hundreds of observations on their processes every couple of hours, but we're issuing cost summaries only every four weeks. We need to break our frame of vision in order to develop more timely and useful information for operating employees.

COMPANY BACKGROUND

A visitor is unprepared for a first visit to the Texas Eastman (TEX) chemicals plant in Longview, Texas. No noxious smells or clouds of smoke hang over the 6,000-acre site, and one can almost imagine people fishing in the man-made ponds used as a

This case was prepared by Professor Robert S. Kaplan.
Copyright © 1989 by the President and Fellows of Harvard College. Harvard Business School case 190-039.

source of cooling water for the plant. The TEX plant is one of six companies in the Eastman Chemicals Division of the Eastman Kodak Company. (Summary data on the Division appear in Exhibit 1.)

The Longview plant, established in 1950, produces about 40 chemical and plastic products that are sold to other manufacturers for conversion into construction, industrial, and consumer products. Nearly 9 million pounds of product per day were shipped during 1988. The location in Northeast Texas gives the plant easy access to the East Texas Oil Field for the primary inputs of ethane and propane. Well served by water, rail, and pipeline transportation, the plant consumes weekly the equivalent of 700 railcars of feedstock—propane and ethane—and 50 railcars of bituminous coal. Employment in 1988 was 2,650 persons. Of these, 1,560 were production workers and 760 worked in engineering and managerial positions.

In TEX's chemical processes, feedstock is converted in a cracking plant into ethylene and propylene. These olefin products are then further processed in chemical plants to produce a variety of alcohols, aldehydes, and specialty chemicals, and in polyolefin plants to make various forms of plastics and adhesives. Computerized models are used to optimize inputs and outputs as a function of current feedstock costs and the output prices of the plant's products.

QUALITY MANAGEMENT PROGRAM

The Eastman Chemicals Division made a strong commitment to Total Quality Management in 1983. Because of the strong dollar in the early 1980s, foreign goods were increasing their U.S. market penetration and customers soon discovered that not only were Japanese and European goods lower in price, they also had higher (more consistent) quality. The automotive industry, feeling the brunt from foreign imports, began to take action by developing their own comprehensive quality programs, such as Ford's Q-1 Program. In addition to internal efforts, the manufacturers began requiring that their suppliers produce delivered goods under Statistical Process Control (SPC).

The Eastman Chemicals Division established its quality policy in 1984. The division president articu-

lated the overall quality goal, "to be the leader in quality and value of its products and services," and backed this goal with a statement of the 11 principles by which the quality goal could be achieved (see Exhibit 2). He hoped to instill an intense focus on quality throughout the organization.

The Quality Management Program was built on a Triangle Model of teamwork, performance management, and statistical process control. The teamwork leg, with its roots in the quality of work life, job enrichment, and employee participation literature, was implemented through quality management (QM) teams that permeated the organization. Every person in the plant, from the president to the lowest-skilled employee, served on at least one QM team. The teams were linked hierarchically by having members of each QM team serving on a team at a higher or a lower level of the organization so that ideas and programs developed at one level could be communicated throughout the organization.

The performance management leg was built on B. F. Skinner's behavioral school of psychology and reinforcement. It stressed the need for establishing Key Result Areas (KRA) and developing measures for each KRA. The performance management process used seven specific steps:

1. Define the *mission* in terms of the results the organization is expected to contribute.
2. Identify the *key result areas* critical to success in achieving the mission. Key result areas could be financial, safety, or environmental goals, or SPC implementation.
3. Define *measures* for each key result area that indicate how well the unit is performing its mission.
4. Decide how the measures will be *displayed* for monitoring to signal significant changes in measures.
5. Develop *control strategies* that outline a plan of action when significant changes in processes occur.
6. Develop plans to *reinforce* progress and achievements for each measure.
7. Implement *improvement projects* and *allocate resources* where they have the most impact on the key result areas.

The implementation of Statistical Process Control, the third leg of the quality management process, required an even more drastic change in TEX's operations. Prior to installing SPC procedures, operators were continually monitoring the hundreds of variables, such as temperatures, pressures, humidities, and flow rates, that governed the performance of each chemical process. As any variable moved away from its nominal mean value, operators would tweak the process, attempting to bring the variable back to its standard value. Frequently, this intervention introduced more variation into the final product than if the operators had left the process alone.

The first step along the route of complete SPC was to define upper and lower control limits for each process variable between which operator intervention should not occur. Because no computer capability existed in 1984 for manufacturing operations, the SPC charts had to be plotted by hand and analyzed manually. If an observation were outside the control limit, specific actions were defined to bring the parameter back into control. Runs tests were performed to detect consistent positive or negative biases even while each observation remained within the control limits. Taguchi methods were employed that mathematically modeled operations so that process variation—the distance between the upper and lower control limits—could be reduced even further. But TEX's quality initiatives were limited by the enormous amount of data that had to be collected, analyzed, and stored manually.

INFORMATION SYSTEMS

TEX operating personnel had, for years, been collecting extensive data on operating processes. Operators were assigned to take readings on 180 routes throughout the plant every two to four hours. The data collection process yielded between 30,000 and 40,000 observations on the plant's process parameters (such as temperatures, pressures, flow rates, and tank levels) every four hours. These data were entered on preprinted, multicolumn worksheets that the operators carried on clipboards as they toured their routes. Clerks entered output data from the worksheets into the daily production report and then sent the process sheets to a nearby warehouse where they were stored in filing cabinets.

Each day, department managers personally reviewed the data collected from operations of the day before. This next-day review, however, conflicted with TEX's current emphasis on quality. The review would frequently detect unfavorable trends in key

operating parameters much too late, enabling many pounds of product to be produced with varying product characteristics. Even though only a small fraction of off-spec material might be produced, the variations in product characteristics could create problems for customers' production processes.

When customers complained about variations in product characteristics, or when TEX people themselves detected unusual variations in products or operations, an engineer would go to the warehouse, occasionally spending many hours locating the relevant worksheets for the particular product or operating department. Once the data were located, the engineer performed an extensive analysis, attempting to learn which parameters might have been outside normal limits. The search and analysis process was tedious, requiring several days or even weeks of work, and occasionally some of the needed process sheets could not be found in the extensive and often cluttered, storage files. Attempts at process improvement were also limited by the availability of operating data only on the paper worksheets in the warehouse storage files.

The first step in providing more accessible information for real-time quality analysis was taken in 1986 with the installation of the Manufacturing and Technical (M&T) system. A stand-alone computer was acquired for manufacturing to accumulate and store operating data and perform the statistical analysis. Exhibit 3 shows the extent of the data collection in the plant by major operating division. About 15% of the observations were updated automatically, about once per minute. The remainder were updated every two to four hours. Because of the SPC analysis, fewer data points were being collected than in 1984.

By 1988, the M&T system had been significantly supplemented by a more general and flexible information system embracing both extensive Digital Equipment Corporation VAX clustered computing and advanced software packages. One package, purchased from an external vendor, monitored those departments equipped with electronic control systems to perform automatic SPC analysis, historic graphs of data, and automatic alarm processing. A second system fed data from daily production reports into the financial control system. The third, using advanced programming techniques, enabled operators to specify which SPC tests should be performed on the operating data, and if an out-of-control situation were detected, generated a recommended course of action to bring the process back into control. By early 1989, 200 such analytic models had been written. A fourth system provided statistical summaries of operations for individual departments and analysts. The reports included information on shipments and production, process improvements, control limits, historical analyses, and incidence and disposition of customer complaints.

EXISTING ACCOUNTING SYSTEM

TEX prepared fully allocated actual cost reports for its operating departments every four weeks. Direct manufacturing and delivery costs were 90% of total costs, manufacturing supervision and clerical costs were 5%, and general factory overhead and support (including computer expenses) represented the remaining 5% of costs. Almost all costs could be traced to individual plants and departments on an actual consumption basis.

An Annual Operating Plan (AOP) was prepared in October and November for the subsequent year. The AOP incorporated all budgets, standards, and plans for the next year. Sales quantities and prices were provided by Marketing. Each support group provided forecasts of prices for materials, supplies, and utilities. The Accounting Department then prepared forecasts of departmental and product costs based on this information. The departmental and product cost forecasts became the baseline against which plant performance was measured.

At the end of each four-week reporting period, Accounting received information about actual departmental costs and production quantities. It multiplied production quantities by variable standard costs and added AOP fixed-cost items to obtain a plan unit cost for each product and department. Five variances were computed and reported back to department managers.

1. *Usage variance:* The effect on unit cost of using more or less of an item than planned; measured as the change in input quantity consumed for a given level of output, evaluated at standard prices.

2. *Price variance:* The effect on unit cost of a change in the price of an input, based on actual consumption of each input. Only price variances for labor and for

materials and supplies purchased from outside vendors were included in the price variance.[1]

3. *Volume variance:* The effect on unit cost of not operating at the planned capacity utilization. The volume variance reconciled differences in unit costs due to spreading fixed costs over varying volumes.

4. *Change in standard variance:* The effect of not implementing a planned change in operations or of implementing an unplanned change. It represented the difference between the current standard and the planned standard. Any capital authorization with a justification based on cost savings or output increase was always translated into a change in future standards.

5. *Mix variance:* The effect, in a multiproduct facility, of producing with an actual product mix different from the planned mix, or of producing a nonstandard ratio of formulas for a given product class.

The sum of the five variances equaled the difference between total departmental costs and total plan cost. Exhibit 4 shows the format for a sample Departmental Cost Sheet. At the bottom of the cost sheet, the five variances were split into controllable and noncontrollable components:

CONTROLLABLE	NONCONTROLLABLE
Volume	Volume
Change in standard	Change in standard
Usage	Price
	Mix

The total volume variance was classified into both controllable and noncontrollable components. Reductions in volume due to shortages of input materials or lack of sales demand were treated as a noncontrollable variance. The manager received a *controllable unfavorable* volume variance when the department produced less than demand and demand was below capacity. The manager received a *controllable favorable* volume variance only when demand was high and he was able to operate his plant beyond rated capacity.

Controllable change in standard variances rep-

---

[1]No price variance was generated for materials and supplies produced by other TEX departments since these variances were already incorporated in those departments' cost sheets. These internal price variances, called Prior Department Variances, however, were shown on the consuming department's cost sheets so that the department manager could consider alternative suppliers or materials if the variance was significant.

resented changes in operations under the control of department managers (such as staff levels and material yield changes). In addition to the planned changes in standards resulting from capital expenditures, the standard for any cost element that had experienced a consistently favorable variance during the year would be changed by at least 50% of the annual mean favorable variance.[2] Changes in standards initiated by the Accounting Department, such as labor rates, depreciation adjustments, and changes in accounting methods, were considered department noncontrollable.

The Departmental Cost Sheets were typically issued 12 to 15 days after the close of each four-week reporting period. The Accounting Department performed analytic studies of the information before its people walked the reports over to explain the results to each Departmental Manager.

Variances for all operating departments were summarized on Division Cost Summaries for division superintendents and upper management. These summaries included the plant total cost variance as well as controllable variances for each department and division. Finally a report was issued each period for the President, Director of Administration, and Comptroller that summarized the manufacturing cost of TEX products and gave explanations for significant variances from the AOP.

Pat Kinsey, Chief Accountant, explained the rationale for the plant's elaborate hierarchy of cost reports as follows:

> The goal of our cost reporting system is to provide to managers on all levels the information they need to manage their areas of responsibility, from the production manager concerned with the efficient operation of the cost centers under his control to the senior members of management who must decide which products to produce and how to allocate company resources. Our system works fine for responsibility accounting and emphasizing controllable variances. But the information is received too late for analyzing the financial consequences from most operating decisions. Our operations personnel must rely on their daily review of key indicators (such as production, yields, and equipment availability) to learn how their operation is performing.

---

[2]The 50% factor reflected a compromise between Accounting and Operations. Departmental managers were reluctant to incorporate 100% of the gain since they did not want to risk unfavorable variances in subsequent years.

To understand more clearly the problem of delayed and aggregate financial information, you could think of the department manager as a bowler, throwing a ball at pins every minute. But we don't let the bowler see how many pins he has knocked down with each throw. At the end of the month we close the books, calculate the total number of pins knocked down during the month, compare this total with a standard, and report the total and the variance back to the bowler. If the total number is below standard, we ask the bowler for an explanation and encourage him to do better next period. We're beginning to understand that we won't turn out many world-class bowlers with this type of reporting system.

THE THREEBEE COMPANY

Steve Briley, Department Manager of Cracking Plant 3B, had recently devised a supplemental departmental financial report for his operating department.

> The diagram of the cracking process is very simple. We have two inputs of natural gas and energy, and we produce two main products, ethylene and propylene, plus several byproducts, such as hydrogen and methane gas. But inside the black box that converts feedstock into propylene and ethylene is an incredibly complex chemical process with thousands of control points, multilevel refrigerants, and recycling intermediate products.
>
> Operators had little information to help them make decisions about tradeoffs among production output, quality, and cost. For example, we could crack gas at higher temperatures and get more conversion of raw material into main and byproducts. But this is costly both in terms of achieving the higher temperatures and in wear and tear of the equipment. Also, as we push the cracking plant to maximize the rate of production, it becomes much more difficult to keep quality under control. We face constant tradeoffs among cost, production output, and quality but have virtually no information to point us in the right direction in making these tradeoffs.

Briley took an unconventional approach to solving this problem by creating a fictitious company for his employees and developing a simple financial statement for that company. The Threebee Company was formed in September 1987, and each employee in Plant 3B was issued a share of stock (see Exhibit 5). Briley then created an income statement for the Threebee Company (see Exhibit 6).

In preparing the income statement, the quantities for outputs produced and inputs consumed were readily available from the daily production report. I needed to supply prices. I estimated the prices for ethylene and propylene and several byproducts (hydrogen, methane, and steam) from nominal market values for these products. It wasn't important to get these prices precisely right, as long as I was in the right ballpark for them. I introduced one wrinkle by recognizing different prices for in-spec and off-spec material. Threebee would earn the full price for ethylene and propylene only if the product was within the upper and lower control limits (set initially at 3 sigma). If product was outside the control limits but still within rated specifications, the product price was set at half the normal price. This 50% discount was a little arbitrary, but I tried to approximate the discounts that final producers might face when selling substandard product. No revenues (zero price) would be earned for material produced outside of specifications.

The basis for the input prices for feedstock and utilities were actual costs, which turned out to be reasonably close to the plant's standard costs. But I would occasionally adjust these costs for additional emphasis. For example, I increased the price of cooling water since the company was starting a conservation drive and I wanted to encourage operators to be even more thrifty with cooling water.

For equipment costs, I computed a mortgage payment for the capital invested in the department based on a rough estimate of the replacement cost and the company's cost of capital. This figure remained constant in each report, of course, but I wanted the operators to be aware of the cost of the equipment they worked with. I also opened up a loan repayment account to repay any capital expenditures made for product or quality improvements. And I added an additional category, called Other Costs, as a target for some future cost reduction program. My goal was to start the Threebee Company off in a zero profit condition, after paying the cost of capital, so that even a zero profit would reflect a good return on investment.

Briley encountered some initial skepticism from his colleagues about whether workers would understand or respond to an income statement to evaluate their efforts. He responded as follows:

In my experience, the operators were able and willing to use a new tool, such as this profit statement, as long as they were given sufficient explanation and enough time to grow accustomed to it. Some operators had never worked with an income statement before, and it took some time to explain the concept to them. Fortunately, several of the operators had small businesses on the side, selling crops or raising livestock, and they were familiar with an income statement format. They helped to explain the concept to the others.

More than the details of the income statement, it was the whole change in culture that took some time to get used to. In the past, TEX had never shared financial information with operating people. We just gave the operators specific rules—"Do this, don't do that, watch out for this condition"—but never told them about the economics of the business they were running.

Once the daily income statement had been designed, data such as actual outputs produced, their quality, and the actual quantities of inputs consumed were obtained from the daily production record. With these data, Briley personally prepared the Threebee Company income statement each day.

The operators' first reaction to the income report was surprise about the cost of raw materials and energy consumed in the plant each day. They had no idea about the financial scale of operation of the 3B plant, or how their actions produced large effects on the costs and revenues of the plant. By varying our feedstock inputs, we can shift the ratio of ethylene to propylene production, but that change may require more inputs, decrease total production, and influence the amount of byproduct produced. On a cost basis this may look bad, but if the sales value of the production is greater, the operators can see that the company is better off even though output is down and costs are up.

As operators made suggestions for improving the format or the calculations, Briley soon found himself working 12 hours a day to keep abreast of his normal supervisory responsibilities plus producing the daily Threebee income statement.

When I was away on business, one of the first things the operators wanted me to do when I returned was calculate the profits for the days I missed. They would be disappointed if results were bad during that period because it was too late for them to correct any problems.

Briley's initial goal had been to double the current operating profit of the plant.

Even though I tried to start from a zero profit condition, our September 87 operations were yielding a period (four-week) profit of about $200K, mostly because the plant was producing more than standard. I set a goal of achieving a period profit of $400K. If we could hit that figure, I promised to install a new kitchen in the control room for the operators.

We kept charts, updated daily, of daily profits and cumulative profits for the period [see Exhibit 7]. It only took the operators four periods to achieve the $400K rate of profit, and along the way we broke five new production records for ethylene and propylene. Operators were posting quality statistics every two hours, and quality measures had improved by 50%. Operators had gotten so good at having all material within the 3-sigma limits, we agreed to set a more challenging target by reducing the upper and lower control limits to 2 sigma.

Briley felt satisfied and suspended the program when the higher outputs and quality enabled the $400K profit goal to be achieved. The operators and supervisors had their new kitchen, but they told Briley that they missed the daily calculations. They had enjoyed seeing the daily income statement and the challenge of achieving profit targets. Briley responded as follows:

One of our Threebee Company officers is a computer whiz. He decided to write software so that the daily report could be prepared automatically, using data the operators entered into the system. Now when operators come in each day at 7 A.M. to start their shift, they look first at the profit report for the previous day. When I show up, an operator immediately tells me about yesterday's profits, happy when they had had a good day and disappointed when profits had declined.

Operators and supervisors in the 3B plant were using the information from the daily income statement to make decisions that formerly they were forbidden to make or else they had taken to Briley for approval. According to Briley,

When the company started the Quality Management Program, we had told the operators not to tweak flow rates or change operating conditions without prior approval from their supervisor. They were to hold feed rates and operating conditions constant. Within several periods of operations of the Threebee Company, operators had learned how to tweak the system to *increase* profit; they're taking actions now that they formerly were not allowed to do. They have also learned to focus on a few key items and really keep an eye on those. For example, they found that if propylene quality is good, everything else was working pretty well, so propylene impurities are monitored continuously. They have also narrowed the control limits for many operating parameters to guarantee that the product is never outside the 100% price limits. In fact, they got so

good at this I had to build in a new challenge. I established a top-grade gold quality region and set a 25% price premium for product falling within the gold region. My rationale was that the higher-quality product could be sold to new outside customers at this higher price.

The operators were also more willing to take action when I wasn't around. For example, one night a hydrogen compressor failed. Normally, repair efforts would have been undertaken on a routine, nonexpedited basis. But the shift supervisor on duty had just seen the value of hydrogen gas from the income report. Knowing the value of the lost output of hydrogen gas, he made an immediate decision to authorize overtime to get the compressor repaired and back on line as soon as possible.

Briley was asked how he used the Period Departmental Cost Reports that he received from the Accounting Department:

Some data are only available from the Period Report. For example, I don't see daily maintenance records, so we're using budgeted numbers in the Daily Income Statement. The Period Report shows me actual maintenance costs and helps me to calibrate and monitor our maintenance activity. The Period Report also forces us to reconcile between meter readings we take locally and plantwide meterings. Because of metering discrepancies, we need to absorb a pro-rata allocation of deviations between local and plantwide meterings.

Gayle English, a production Division Superintendent, provided additional comments about the cost reports he received from Accounting.

The problem with the Period Report is that the information comes too late—a cost incurred near the start of a period will not be reported until six or seven weeks later—and results from all the events of that period are aggregated together. As a result, production people often pay little attention to the financial reports since they already know about any chronic problems.

TEX, historically, had shared cost information with departmental managers but was reluctant to disclose information on product profitability. Virtually no financial data had been provided to the operators. With the new report, operators were really surprised about the costs of materials being consumed in the cracking process. Even the costs of small items like filters or half-filled bags of material that they might have been throwing away or discarding surprised them. They never appreciated the cost consequences of things they were doing.

Jerry Matthews, an Assistant Department Superintendent, offered his observations on how the Daily Income Statement changed the roles of the operators.

> Initially the work teams were not used to selecting and working on projects. They had to be fed ideas from department managers. But as they got more comfortable with the reports and with the freedom they had, they started to take more initiatives. Without having good measures, it would have been difficult to get them interested and involved and to take the ownership for the processes they were controlling. The financial data, on costs and profits, turned out to be a lot more meaningful to them than just trying to control quantities of steam. It helped them set priorities among different projects. Before, they may have been concentrating on controlling one part of the process which cost only $200 per day. Now they can set priorities to focus where their efforts can have the greatest impact.
>
> For example, before we established different prices for in-spec and out-of-spec material, it was hard to mobilize enthusiasm about quality. Occasionally, the cracking department might ship off-spec material to downstream processing plants. Those plants accepted the material but eventually paid a higher price for doing so. They had to perform more purges to get rid of impurities from their chemicals, they might have more rework, and their catalysts would get fouled up sooner. This really ran up the costs of the processing department, but the costs were attributed to that department, not to the supplying department that created the problem. Now, by putting a lower price on off-spec material from the cracking plant, we have everyone's attention.
>
> The daily financial reports have also become a tool for my decision making. I need to decide whether to shut down the plant for maintenance for six days or for eight days. The Daily Income Statement helps me decide whether the additional improvements are worth two more days of shutdown. I can trade off overtime and higher rates of spending during the maintenance period in return for getting the plant back on line one or two days earlier. When demand falls, I can ask whether it is better to run at a reduced rate or to keep producing at capacity and then shut down for a few days.

Matthews reflected on the changes brought about by the new systems at TEX.

> There's so much information out there, and we're still learning how to use it effectively. An operator always has more demands for his time than he can

deliver. Which problems should he solve to have the greatest impact? Operators can now see the relative priority of raw material costs versus maintenance costs versus other categories. With the Daily Income Statement, we've empowered the operators, making our mission statements about teamwork and ownership real. Doors are opening up; it's mind boggling. It's like giving someone a car who formerly only had a horse. There are new directions and distances we can now consider traveling.

ACCOUNTING DEPARTMENT REACTIONS

Jess Greer, a cost analyst in the Accounting Department, wondered about the changing role for the finance function in the new operating environment of the TEX plant.

> There's certainly been a lot of interest in Threebee's Daily Income Statement, and the people seem very enthusiastic about it. In finance, we have been trying to be responsive. Financial information is being used for more and more things. We introduced statistical control limits on some of the variance analysis reports and adjusted standards rapidly to current operating conditions. We're also doing a lot more analytic work on the numbers to explain deviations between actual and standard. The finance people are working much more closely with operations, giving them information which seems to be helping them to manage. But we can clearly do more to improve the delivery of the existing cost system, to make it more timely and to switch from paper to electronic presentation.

Tom Wilson, Company Controller, concurred with the need for the finance function to go beyond its traditional role.

> Continuous improvement requires very rapid, accurate timely feedback. I don't see how we can maintain our continuous improvement efforts without some kind of daily operating report. Our focus of attention has to be to get cost information to the first-level teams, the people on the line turning the valves that operate the plant.

The senior managers in Accounting were highly supportive of the Threebee initiative but wondered about its implications for the overall system of financial reporting at TEX. They were uncertain about the consequences if every department developed its own financial summaries. The businesspeople at the top of the organization were used to making decisions based on the Period Cost Reports, and they expected the financial reports for each department to tie into the results for the plant as a whole. They would not want individual department managers thinking they were doing a terrific job when the plant as a whole was showing poor

performance. Among the questions confronting the senior Accounting managers were the following:

Should there be two systems, the official financial one and one for departmental operations? If each department develops its own financial system, how should the local departmental reports be reconciled with the upper management reports?

EXHIBIT 1

TEXAS EASTMAN COMPANY

Eastman Chemicals Division: Summary
of Operating Results
($000,000)

	1988	1987	1986
Sales	$3,033	$2,600	$2,378
Operating earnings	628	388	227
Assets	2,875	2,514	2,266
Capital spending	475	394	314

Exhibit 2 appears on p. 222.

EXHIBIT 3

TEXAS EASTMAN COMPANY

Data Collection Statistics

DIVISION	NUMBER OF ROUTES	NUMBER OF OBSERVATONS
Olefin	27	6,800
Oxo-ethylene products	51	12,100
Polyethylene	28	3,600
Polypropylene-eastobond	30	3,700
Utilities	20	3,100
Supply and distribution	8	600
Totals	164	29,900

EXHIBIT 2
TEXAS EASTMAN COMPANY

EASTMAN CHEMICALS DIVISION

QUALITY POLICY

QUALITY GOAL

To be the leader in quality and value of products and services

QUALITY MANAGEMENT PROCESS

- Establish mission, vision, and indicators of performance.
- Understand, standardize, stabilize, and maintain processes.
- Plan, do and reinforce continual improvement and innovation.

OPERATIONAL POLICY

- Achieve process stability and reliability.
- Control every process to the desired target.
- Improve process capability.

PRINCIPLES WHICH SUPPORT AND ENABLE ACHIEVEMENT OF THE QUALITY GOAL

CUSTOMER FOCUS	Emphasize understanding, meeting, and anticipating customer needs.
CONTINUAL IMPROVEMENT	Current level of performance can be improved.
INNOVATION	Everyone searching for creative process, product, and service alternatives.
PROCESS EMPHASIS	Focus on processes as the means to prevent defects and improve results.
MANAGEMENT LEADERSHIP	Create an inspiring vision, maintain constancy of purpose, and establish a supportive environment.
EMPLOYEE INVOLVEMENT	Every employee participates in decision making and problem solving, along with teamwork among all functional areas and organizational levels.
STATISTICAL METHODS	All employees understand the concept of variation and apply appropriate statistical methods to continual improvement and innovation.
PERFORMANCE MANAGEMENT	Take pride in work through clear accountabilities, feedback, reinforcement, and removing barriers.
EDUCATION AND TRAINING	Encourage learning and personal growth for everyone throughout their career.
CUSTOMER AND SUPPLIER RELATIONS	Build long-term partnerships with customers and suppliers.
ASSESSMENT	Benchmark against world best and assess performance against the Quality Policy for improvement planning and reinforcement.

E.W. Deavenport, Jr.
President

EXHIBIT 4

TEXAS EASTMAN COMPANY

RESTRICTED INFORMATION TEX 7112-01	TEXAS EASTMAN COMPANY DEPARTMENTAL COST OF MANUFACTURE CHEMICAL ONE MFG. PLANT 1	SHEET NO. 98 THIRD PERIOD ISSUED 03/31/89

CHANGE IN STANDARD	ACTUAL	PLANNED	VARIANCE
PERIOD BASIS	$1,000*	$2,000	$3,000*
YEAR-TO-DATE BASIS	2,000*	2,000	4,000*

PRODUCTION		DEPARTMENTAL COST THIS PERIOD			DEPARTMENTAL COST THIS YEAR		
PERIOD 80,000			VARIANCE FROM STANDARD			VARIANCE FROM STANDARD	
YEAR 169,000	AMOUNT	AMOUNT	UNIT	AMOUNT	AMOUNT	UNIT	

	AMOUNT	AMOUNT	UNIT	AMOUNT	AMOUNT	UNIT
Raw materials	$35,000	$2,500	$.0313	$82,000	$8,500*	$.0503*
Recoveries						
Packing materials						
Net materials	35,000	2,500	.0313	82,000	8,500*	.0503*
Labor and benefits	10,000	2,000*	.0250*	26,000	2,700*	.0160*
Manufacturing supplies	1,200	500	.0063	1,900	3,200	.0190
Maintenance and repairs	8,800	1,200	.0150	29,000	1,000	.0060
Plant utilities	5,000	1,200*	.0150*	12,000	3,700*	.0219*
Other expenses						
Laboratory						
Planning and production records						
General plant						
Depreciation, insurance, and taxes	3,000			9,000		
Miscellaneous				700	700*	.0042*
Underground storage						
Work done for/by other						
Materials handling						
Storage and shipping						
Waste treatment						
Total conversion cost	28,000	1,500*	.0188*	78,600	2,900*	.0172*
Total departmental cost	$63,000	$1,000	$.0125	$160,600	$11,400*	$.0675*

		VARIANCES			
COST SUMMARY	DEPARTMENTAL COST	USAGE/ PRICE	VOLUME/ MIX	CHANGE IN STANDARD	AOP
Period—Amount	$63,000	$500*	$12,500	$3,000*	$72,000
Unit	.7875	.0063*	.1563	.0375*	.9000
Year—Amount	160,600	14,200*	15,345	4000*	157,745
Unit	.9503	.0841*	.0908	.0237*	.9223

Variance Analysis

	DEPARTMENT CONTROLLABLE			DEPARTMENT NONCONTROLLABLE			
	CHANGE IN STANDARD	USAGE	PRODUCT VOLUME	PRICE	CHANGE IN STANDARD	DEMAND VOLUME	PRODUCT MIX
Period	2,000*	1,000	1,335*	1,500*	1,000*	8,902*	4,933
Year	3,000*	11,400*	4,750*	2,800*	1,000*	2,228	17,867

EXHIBIT 5

TEXAS EASTMAN COMPANY

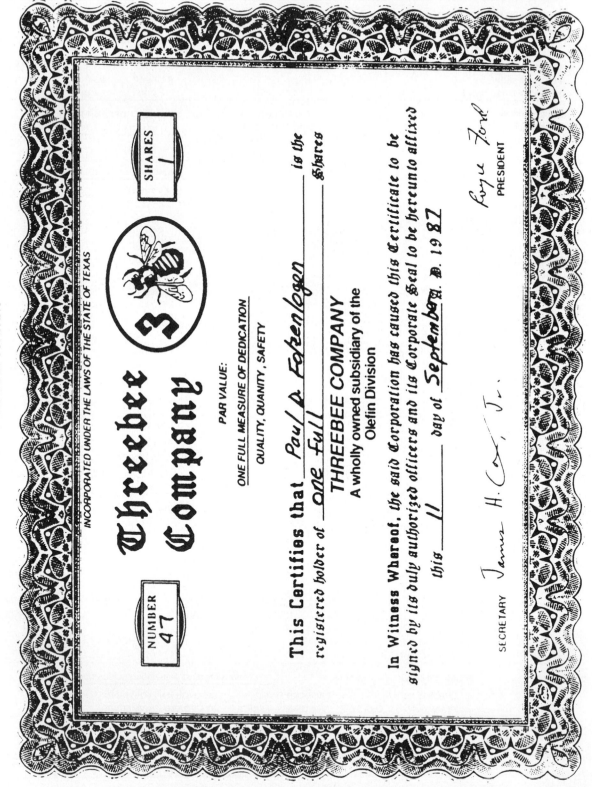

EXHIBIT 6

TEXAS EASTMAN COMPANY
Daily Profit Statement for Threebee Company 1988 April 21

				$/day	
Sales					
Steam	+ 600#	87,938	lb/hr	8,416	
	+ 160#	11,972	lb/hr	1,068	
	− pyro	24,516	lb/hr	2,368	
	− 30#	11,624	lb/hr	1,037	
	Net	63,770		$6,079	
Ethylene:	Hi grade	776,042	lb/day	124,167	
	Lo grade	0	lb/day	0	0% out
	Waste	0	lb/day	0	
	Total	776,042		$124,167	
Propylene:	Hi grade	358,280	lb/day	68,073	
	Lo grade	32,429	lb/day	3,081	8.3% out
	Waste	0	lb/day	0	
	Total	390,708		$71,154	
Hydrogen,	capacity	7	lines	$57,708	
Methane,	capacity	9	lines	5,058	
Heavies		(fixed for now)		1,732	
	Total sales			$265,898	
Costs					
Feedstock:	Ethane	227,865	lb	6,471	
	Propane	1,595,066	lb	108,305	
	Total	1,822,930	lb	$114,776	
Maintenance and repair (1987 avg.)				$4,168	
Utilities:					
Electricity		1,234	amps	8,359	
Cooling water		4.8	lines	4,109	
Natural gas		3.1	lines	3,442	
Other (typical)				607	
	Total utilities			$16,517	
Other costs				$45,714	
Total cost of goods sold				$181,175	
Loan repayment				0	
Mortgage				$54,946	
	Total costs			$236,122	
Gross profit				$29,776	
Less taxes @ 35%				$10,422	
Net profit*				$19,354/day*	

*Equivalent to $541,923/period profit.

EXHIBIT 7

TEXAS EASTMAN COMPANY

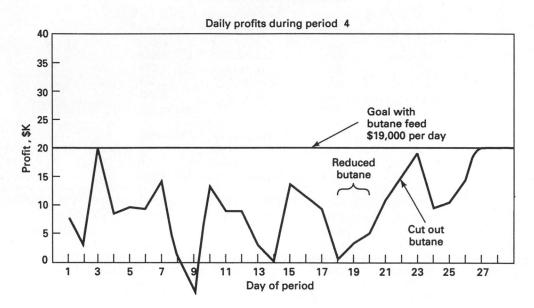

Daily profits during period 4

Analog Devices: The Half-Life System

A problem with management information systems is that they are strongly biased toward reporting financial information to stockholders and government agencies. Unless quality improvement and other more fundamental performance measures are elevated to the same level of importance as financial measures, when conflicts arise, financial considerations win out. To address this issue, we designed a division scorecard that reports only the barest of financial information and places greater emphasis on quality improvement goals.

RAY STATA, CHAIRMAN AND PRESIDENT, ANALOG DEVICES, INC.[1]

COMPANY BACKGROUND

Analog Devices, Inc. (ADI) headquartered in Norwood, Massachusetts, produces integrated circuits and systems for the high-end data acquisition market. The devices convert between physical and digital data in equipment such as high-performance computer disk drives, aircraft sensors, medical instruments, and sophisticated consumer electronics (compact disk players, digital audio tape players, and high-definition television). As a senior ADI

executive remarked, "The real world is not digital; it's analog. Someone has to measure temperatures, pressures, and velocity and convert these data into digital form."

ADI, with 5,400 employees and seven manufacturing sites worldwide, had 1988 sales divided

[1]Comments by Ray Stata throughout this case were extracted from his article, "Organizational Learning—The Key to Management Innovation," *Sloan Management Review* (Spring 1989), pp. 63–74.

This case was prepared by Professor Robert S. Kaplan.

among the U.S. (56%), Europe (28%), and Asia (16%, principally Japan and Korea). Its customers were in the military/avionics, telecommunications, computer, instrument, and industrial market segments. Summary financial data appear in Exhibit 1.

THE QUALITY IMPROVEMENT PROGRAM

Recently, the company had dedicated itself to an ongoing Quality Improvement Program. Ray Stata described the motivation for the effort.

> For more than fifteen years, Analog Devices grew consistently at a rate of about 25 percent per year. Then for the first time, between 1982 and 1987, we missed our five-year goals—and by a country mile. Like other semiconductor companies we were affected by the malaise in the U.S. electronics industry and by the strong dollar. But the external environment was only part of the problem: something was also wrong internally, and it had to be fixed.
> But what was the problem? We had the largest share of our niche market in high-performance linear integrated circuits. We had the best designers and technologists in our business. We had excellent relations with a highly motivated workforce. We were not guilty of underinvestment, nor of managing for short-term profits. The only conclusion was that there was something *about* the way we were managing the company that was not good enough.

Motivated by systems dynamics concepts articulated decades earlier by Jay Forrester at the Massachusetts Institute of Technology (MIT), Stata came to focus on organizational learning as the key management concept: "I would argue that the rate at which individuals and organizations learn may become the only sustainable competitive advantage, especially in knowledge-intensive industries."

Improved performance in customer service, product quality, yield, and cost were becoming key strategic goals for ADI. Historically, the company had played a niche strategy, focusing its attention on being the first to the market with new products whose unique performance enabled it to earn substantial margins. These applications usually required only modest production volumes. But several of the newer applications for ADI's products had developed substantial high-volume potential. For high-volume applications, customers were demanding lower prices and better delivery performance.

ADI decided to concentrate on penetrating the higher-volume markets developing in computers, communications networks, and consumer products and to use the lower-cost structure from serving these markets to maintain and increase penetration in its traditional lower-volume industrial and military markets.

Stata recalled what he believed was necessary to penetrate the high-volume markets:

> We decided to focus our attention on product quality, on-time delivery, lead time, yields, and new-product time to market. We went to seminars, read books, gave speeches, and introduced information systems to measure our performance. But three years into the mission we were not getting very far very fast.
> We knew all about error detection and correction and about doing it right the first time. But we did not have any notion of what rate of improvement was satisfactory or what we could do to accelerate the improvement process.

THE QUALITY HALF-LIFE CONCEPT

ADI believed strongly in operating with a small corporate staff, and that line managers had to take the lead in improving quality. But frustration with the slow rate of improvement led to the hiring of Art Schneiderman as Vice-President for Quality and Productivity Improvement. Schneiderman, with mechanical engineering and management degrees from MIT, had worked for many years as a consultant for Bain & Co. His consulting experience had focused on case histories of successful quality improvement programs. Schneiderman was a follower of the Juran philosophy[2] that quality goals had to be incorporated into incentive and reward systems. But to be part of the reward system, Schneiderman knew that the quality goals needed to be realistic.

> The basic flaw in current goal setting is that specific goals should be set based on knowledge of the means that will be used to achieve them. Yet the means are rarely known at the time goals are set. The usual result is that if the goal is too low, we will underachieve relative to our potential. If the goal is too high, we will underperform relative to others' expectations. What's really needed to set rational

[2]J. M. Juran, *Quality Control Handbook,* Third Edition (New York: McGraw Hill, 1979).

goals is a means of predicting what is achievable if some sort of standard means for improvement were used.[3]

Schneiderman had recently made an important discovery:

I had inadvertently made a transformation of some data provided by Yokogawa Hewlett Packard [see Exhibit 2] that suggested a simple model for the results of Quality Improvement Process (QIP) activity. Any defect level, subjected to legitimate QIP, decreases at a constant rate so that when plotted on semilog paper against time, it falls on a straight line. At the Japanese HP plant, the continuous improvement process produced a 50% reduction in the failure rate every 3.6 months over a two-year period. After reducing defects by a factor of more than 250, the process eventually slowed down probably due to inherent equipment limitations.

After this initial discovery, I gathered data on every quality improvement program reported in the literature. The reports came from a wide variety of sources including my experience, various publications, presentations from the Juran Institute and the American Society for Quality Control, and a wide variety of textbooks on quality improvement.

In analyzing this data, I used the word *defect* in its most general sense: any measurable quantity that is in need of improvement.

Among the "defects" studied by Schneiderman were errors, rework, yield loss, unnecessary reports, cycle times in manufacturing, design and administrative processes, unscheduled downtime, inventory, employee turnover, absenteeism, lateness, unrealized human potential, accidents, late deliveries, order lead time, setup time, cost of poor quality, and warranty costs. Exhibit 3 shows the graphs for five of the quality improvement programs.

In each QIP, Schneiderman measured the half-life for improvement. For each increment of time that equals this half-life, the defect level drops by 50%. For example, if the initial defect level was 10% and the defect half-life was six months, after the first six months the defect level would be down to 5%, after the next six months, 2.5%, and so on. Schneiderman proceeded to test his half-life concept at ADI.

---

[3]Comments from Schneiderman in the case were obtained both from direct interviews and from his article, "Setting Quality Goals," *Quality Progress* (April 1988), pp. 51–57.

One of the key corporate goals was to reduce the percentage of orders shipped late. We assembled a team from various organizations involved with customer service to analyze the causes of lateness. For each late shipment we determined the cause, and then we plotted their distribution. We found that a relatively small number of causes was responsible for 50% of the problems.

Next we assembled problem-solving teams to attack these major causes of lateness. When the cycle was completed, we repeated the process by prioritizing the causes for 50% of the remaining problems and then eliminating those causes. This cycle was repeated again and again; each time the most important remaining problems were identified and resources were focused on solving them.

Schneiderman commented on factors that influenced the improvement half-life.

The slope of the learning curve seems to be determined by how long it takes to identify and prioritize the causes of the problem and to eliminate those causes. The required time for each cycle of improvement is largely a function of the complexity and bureaucracy of the organization (see Exhibit 4). Ray Stata likes to rephrase this by saying that the half-life is determined by the rate of organizational learning.

IMPLEMENTING THE HALF-LIFE CONCEPT AT ADI

The ADI five-year plan for fiscal year (FY) 1987 through FY 1992 called for the following:

Sales growth	20-25% per year
Operating profits	17% of sales
Profit after tax	9.4% of sales
Return on capital	15%

The sales growth target was particularly challenging since the worldwide projected growth rate for electronic equipment was only 11% per year, and for semiconductor sales, 13% per year. ADI would have to grow profitably at a rate considerably higher than its competitors if it were to meet its objectives. Stata felt this could only be achieved if ADI was thought by its customers to be number 1 in terms of total value delivered. Rather than allow individual department and division managers to establish their own metrics and goals for customer performance, the senior executives of ADI established a top-down performance measurement system. In addition to continuing to turn out high-performance products that met customers' functional needs, specific targets were established for on-time delivery, defect levels, and lead time.

	1987	1992	HALF-LIFE (MONTHS)
On-time delivery	85%	>99.8%	9
Outgoing defect level	500 ppm	<10 ppm	9
Lead time	10 weeks	<3 weeks	9

Schneiderman knew that these ambitious goals for customer service could be met in only two ways. One way involved building and holding inventory and using lots of inspection to meet the delivery, quality, and lead-time goals. Schneiderman felt, however, that this way led to bankruptcy. The second way was to make continuing, fundamental improvement in manufacturing processes. Four measures of internal performance were established for every division and five-year goals for improvement of these measures specified:

	1987	1992	HALF-LIFE (MONTHS)
Manufacturing cycle time	15 wks.	4-5 weeks	9
Process defect level	5000 ppm	<10 ppm	6
Yield	20%	>50%	9
Time to market	36 months	6 months	24

The half-lives for improvement of both the external and internal measures had been estimated from Schneiderman's data base of 64 improvement examples. Schneiderman also pointed out that while the detailed tracking of improvement measures depended on making a quantity (such as percent of late deliveries) smaller, for motivational purposes the company executives liked to emphasize the positive aspect such as the on-time delivery percentage increasing from 60% to greater than 95%.

Stata recalled the introduction of the new performance measurement targets.

The challenge of making continuous improvements with nine-to-twelve month half lives over an extended period is awesome. The first reaction of our organization was to recoil from what looked like unrealistic objectives. But if a company really gets its quality improvement act together, there is no fundamental reason why these goals cannot be achieved. There were companies in Japan already operating at these levels on some of these measures.

Schneiderman designed a quarterly scorecard (see Exhibit 5) so that the predicted performance of each division on the external and internal metrics could be conveniently displayed.

Each year, I fill in the scorecard for the next year with benchmarks based on half-life improvement rates. Then the division managers come up with their bottom-up targets. We negotiate differences, usually ending up in the middle between our proposals.

The Corporate Scorecard [Exhibit 5] is divided into five panels. The top panel, Financial Performance, presents information of interest to stockholders. The second panel, QIP indicators, presents data on how we look to our customers and employees. The measures, such as leadtime, on-time delivery, and employee turnover, indicate what's important and what we need to improve. The third and fourth panels present measures of internal manufacturing performance. These measures are what we believe drive the external measures shown in the first two panels. The fifth panel shows how well we are doing in introducing new products and achieving the strategic goals specified in our five-year plan.

During the year, the trends on all key indicators are reported monthly and quarterly (see Exhibit 6 as a sample report for on-time delivery performance of the seven ADI divisions). Stata emphasized the importance of the reporting process.

How information is displayed makes an incredible difference. The simple summary of on-time delivery [Exhibit 6] replaces pages of information that used to be circulated to managers. With all these pages, the most crucial information—the half-life trend—was missing. For management purposes, displaying all divisions together on a single page has great motivational value. A high level of internal competition exists to generate the fastest learning curve; it is obvious and embarrassing when you are not performing.

Schneiderman reviewed the trend performance of each division quarterly.

By statistical analysis of the improvement curve, I can estimate upper and lower control limits for each observation. I circle any major variance, a red circle for an unfavorable variance, and a green circle for a favorable one. When a green variance occurs, managers are asked to share their insights, which led to a more rapid rate of improvement than had been historically achieved. For red variances, managers must explain what was controllable versus noncontrollable and give suggestions about how to make further improvements.

Over time, managers have learned that there are right answers and wrong answers for explaining unfavorable variances. The wrong answer is to claim that lots of little reasons combined to produce the bad outcome. The right answer is to identify the two or three key problems that contributed to 80% to 90% of the bad performance and to describe the program that will lead to reducing the impact of these problems in the future.

The QIP Quarterly Scorecard soon became accepted at ADI, but a new unforeseen conflict had developed. Operating managers continued to receive extensive financial summaries of their monthly performance. Frequently, the QIP Scorecard and the Financial Performance summaries pointed in opposite directions; a manager might be performing well by one scorecard and performing poorly with the other scorecard. Gene Hornsby, Director of Product Assurance, described the problem.

> We were trying to get managers to keep inventory down, improve quality, and match production to customer deliveries. But with the monthly financial reports, the operating people got stroked when volume was high and beat up when volume was low. They're not unresponsive. They soon figured out that getting stroked felt better than getting beat up. The accounting system seems to be a barrier to our attempts to implement just-in-time and short cycle times.

Active discussions and debates ensued attempting to reconcile the conflicting signals.

MONTHLY FINANCIAL SYSTEM

The ADI financial system was a traditional process-oriented system that tracked expenses to each of the major production cost centers and allocated cost center costs to products. Each production center had a direct cost center (for materials and labor) and a fixed cost center. Most of the indirect expenses were considered fixed. Material, labor, and variable overhead costs were assigned to each batch of wafers started through the fabrication process. Fixed expenses were allocated to products only when preparing external financial statements to conform to generally accepted accounting practices.

The key determinant of the cost of an individual die was the wafer yield, defined as the ratio of good dies produced on a wafer to the total number of dies that can be printed and produced on the wafer. All the wafer fabrication costs were assigned to the good dies based on estimated yield percentages. Currently yield was averaging about 35%.

Labor and overhead expenses were assigned to wafers based on estimates of machine utilization and efficiency. Russ Brennan, Semiconductor Divisional Controller at ADI, remarked as follows:

> It's been normal to have unfavorable variances equal to 20% to 25% of standard direct cost. The standards overstate the efficiency of machines and their utilization. For example, a machine may only be working for two hours per day, but the standard for the machine could be six hours of operation each day. Also, we frequently find there's a big gap between what we thought a machine's performance would be and what it is actually delivering.

> But the big issue is yield. Each quarter, planners make assumptions about yield, and these assumptions drive the production schedule. The planners' estimates of yield can be different from the existing standard and also different from recent actual experience. They are evaluated by customer service levels, not inventory levels, so that they have been reluctant to change production schedules based on short-term improvements in yield.

> For example, as some of the continuous improvement activities took effect recently, yields increased dramatically. A planner eventually noticed the large buildup of die inventory and started to slow down the number of wafer starts. The slowdown caused overhead to be underabsorbed. Yield variances were favorable, but our absorption variances were unfavorable since labor and overhead rates had been based on a higher number of wafer starts.

Weekly financial reports summarized new bookings, shipments (referred to as billings), and the key semiconductor industry ratio—"bookings to billings." A book-to-bill ratio larger than 1 signaled sales growth, while a ratio less than 1 indicated a potential industry slowdown. Also reported weekly were scrap dollars, yield percentages, yield variances from standard and plan, and detailed inventory positions by product type and production stage.

A monthly income statement (see Exhibit 7) reported bookings, backlog, sales, and several levels of profit margins. Managers focused especially on the contribution margin line, which represented gross margin less fixed manufacturing and divisional fixed expenses (marketing, engineering, and general and administrative expenses). Monthly spending summaries, by detailed account type, were prepared for each department. The monthly report also summarized absorption variances of labor and variable overhead, purchase and usage variances for materials, and efficiency and rate variances for labor and variable overhead. Brennan acknowledged the following:

> We use a pretty conventional costing system that was designed more for inventory measurement and valuation than for performance measurement. Line managers look mostly at yield, and more at percentages than the dollar variances. They also keep track of completed goods each period. As the company moves forward with its continuous improvement activities, we will need to decide when we have enough confidence in the recent operating results to incorporate them into the financial numbers and the production build plan. Historically, our product volumes have been small, and process yields can change quickly when products are not produced in a smooth learning environment.

THE IMPACT ON OPERATING MANAGERS

Goodloe Suttler, formerly a product line manager at the Wilmington facility, had recently been appointed General Manager of the Semiconductor Division. Suttler was skeptical about the value of financial information for semiconductor manufacturing.

> Two years ago, we were producing one product for a very large computer manufacturer. Every day, I was looking at the die yields from the test and probe cost center. It was the best predictor for process efficiency and for meeting the customer's delivery schedule. A handful of key results, not the accounting system, tell you what you need to know to operate in real time. With timely and accurate local indicators at critical control points, we obtain orders-of-magnitude improvements in our ability to control. You can never get the official accounting system to provide the necessary timely, relevant information.

Suttler was asked his opinion of the recently introduced half-life system.

> The half-life measurements provide the context for long-term problem solving. It made us realize that we had several chronic problems that we had learned to live with for a long time without fixing. With thousands of problems arising in our complex production environment, we can't address the most serious ones without a comprehensive measurement system. The metrics now being used will be much more useful than installing a better cost accounting system.
>
> In the past, the ADI culture was Design and Marketing; Manufacturing was a necessary evil in order to get customers to part with their money. Cost reduction programs never seemed to work; they were boring, not meaningful. They didn't address how we were adding value to customers.
>
> The QIP changes the emphasis from boring cost reduction to making improvements in measures that people can get really excited about. We are now following a three-stage program. First, identify what matters to customers. This sets the objectives for our efforts. Second, we develop metrics for these objectives, and third, we analyze the metrics to develop problem-solving activities. We try to determine what problems exist that affect our ability to improve performance along each metric and form teams to address the problems with the highest priorities.

Suttler recalled the recent incident described by Brennan, when yields had increased substantially.

> The production planners were determining wafer starts based on historic average yields and they didn't slow down starts initially. They had seen ups (and downs) in yields many times before, but this time we had really fixed some problems and yields kept increasing. A lot of extra good dies started piling up in inventory, but no real-time system was tracking it. The wafer fab manager figured out that the inventory must be building up somewhere, but he kept quiet for a while because he didn't want the unfavorable volume variances and pressure to idle workers that would result from slowing down starts. Eventually, he reported the buildup to me, but I waited another month to verify the buildup so that we produced even more inventory before finally ordering a major cutback on starts. We could have been producing the wrong mix for inventory and risking considerable obsolescence. Now we look weekly at our yields and schedule starts based on the most recent data. But until we worked off the inventory we had built, we had lower cost absorption. Wall Street analysts called us about the reductions in our short-term margins not about the long-term improvement in die yield from wafer production.

An unexpected problem from the improvement in yields was a decreased demand for workers. ADI did not want to lay off workers because of the improvement in its production processes. Suttler speculated that perhaps the future QIP improvement targets should be matched with attrition and hiring rates to avoid the pressure for layoffs. Suttler recognized, however, that a big benefit from improved yield was to increase the effective capacity of the facility and therefore to defer, perhaps indefinitely, capital additions. Suttler was asked to describe occasions when financial measurements and operating improvements conflicted.

> We always knew that manufacturing cycle time was a critical factor for improving customer service. A few years ago, however, our cycle times increased from between 22 and 24 weeks to 30 weeks. When we investigated, we learned that we were using inventories to generate rapid earnings growth. We have a cost system with only a few inventory recognition points. Any material that starts into production is treated as WIP (assumed to be about halfway finished). At the end of one quarter, we had started lots of wafers into production, and they all got valued at the midway WIP point; this really helps earnings. In a high sales growth situation, you pull third-quarter results into the first quarter. But all the wafers in WIP sat in front of new orders and had to be processed before we could get any of the new orders through the system.

Art Schneiderman described a second conflict.

> There's an obvious tradeoff between OTD [on-time delivery] and short-term financial performance. In the past, we have occasionally delayed many low-revenue shipments that were near completion at the end of a quarter and substituted high-revenue shipments that were due the next month. So the daily OTD deteriorated sharply; about a third of our late deliveries were caused by this revenue acceleration effect. And at the beginning of the next quarter, we had to go out and find all the small orders that had been delayed and reschedule them. The OTD statistics were lousy for another two weeks.

> Many companies, not just ADI, seem to go through this hockey-stick shipment phenomenon at the end of months or quarters. We have to decide whether we're going to be revenue-recognition driven or OTD-performance driven.

Lou Fiore, an operations manager in the semiconductor division, commented on his disdain of periodic financial summaries.

> Cost variances are useless to me. I don't want to ever have to look at a cost variance, monthly or weekly. Once you've decided to run a product, you don't have many choices left. Resources are already committed regardless of how the cost system computes costs among alternative processes.

Asked about what information he finds useful to look at, Fiore responded as follows:

> Daily, I look at sales dollars, bookings, and OTD—the percent of orders on time. For OTD, a late order is counted only once, on the day it was not shipped on time.

> Weekly, I look at a variety of quality reports including the outgoing QC report on items passing the final test before shipment to the customer, in-process quality, and yields. Yield is a good surrogate for cost and quality.

> Monthly, I do look at the financial reports. I want to see the bottom line P&L for the period and the actual direct margin percentages. I look closely at my fixed expenses and compare these to the budgets, especially on discretionary items like travel and maintenance. I also watch headcount. But the financial systems still don't tell me where I am wasting money. I expect that if I make operating improvements, costs should go down, but I don't worry about the linkage too much. The organizational dynamics make it difficult to link cause and effect precisely.

> The biggest challenge is OTD. We work on this continually. We meet once a week and discuss the data on missed deliveries. We develop a Pareto diagram for the reasons and decide whether there's anything important that we're not yet focusing on, or were the problems already being addressed by actions underway but not yet completed.

> The hot button we're working on now is cycle time. If we can continually reduce cycle time, the efficiency of the whole operation will increase. The previous production manager liked to run large lots because the system told him this reduced costs. My approach is exactly the opposite. We reorganized the test area from a job-shop functional layout to 30 production cells that match most of our routings. Out of the 30 groups, only three are really constraints. I focus on these cells, closely monitoring their efficiencies and making sure they don't go out of service.

> I also try to size production lots so that they can be completed in eight hours on the slowest (gating) operation in the process. This enables us to finish a lot in one shift and makes production scheduling a lot easier since we can schedule work in one-shift units. By reducing the lot size, we reduced both cycle time and the variance of cycle times. This led to dramatic decreases in WIP inventory while greatly improving our ability to spot quality problems. Production now matches customer demands more closely, and the number of expedited and late orders has decreased.

Russ Brennan, the Divisional Controller, defended the role for financial measurements. He felt that when conflicts between QIP and financial measures occurred, the financial measurements were not always at fault.

> For much of last year, overall chute yields were increasing and yield variances were favorable, so the two signals were consistent with each other.[4] Then in the last quarter, actual chute yield continued to increase, but we reported an unfavorable yield variance. This caused considerable confusion among the operating people.
>
> After investigating, we found that the mix of our business had changed in the last quarter. We were building less low-volume, high-ASP [average selling price] products and much more high-volume, low-ASP products. The standard yields on the low-ASP business are higher than on the high-ASP products, so the reported improvement in chute yield was due more to the favorable mix change than to fundamental improvements in the production processes. Actual yields did not increase as much as they should have, an effect only revealed by our financial measure, the yield variance.

CURRENT DEVELOPMENTS

The QIP program was proceeding under a three-phase program. Phase I, being worked on in 1989, concentrated on OTD performance measured relative to ADI's committed shipping date.

Phase II, to begin in 1990, would add two new measures of customer responsiveness: (1) the percentage of time ADI met customers' lead-time requests, and, when customer lead-time requests were

---

[4]Chute yield equals the ratio of good dies released from final testing to the number of total dies started into production.

not met, (2) weeks of excess lead-time, measured as the difference between the lead-time requested by the customer and the lead-time committed to by the factory. The Phase II measurements would soon be added to the division scorecards. The causes of missed OTD were also broken down by responsibility.

SOURCE	POSSIBLE CAUSE
Factory	No product available
Warehouse	Handling error
Credit	Customer on credit hold
Customer	Closed for holiday
	Requested shipment hold

In Phase III, ADI hoped to use lead-time as a strategic weapon. Schneiderman wanted to be able to offer lead-times even below those requested by customers.

ADI had recently introduced an additional incentive bonus plan to increase attention to its operating indicators. It retained a corporate-wide performance bonus tied to meeting ADI's financial goals. The plan was supplemented for divisional personnel with a bonus tied to surpassing a divisional net income benchmark while achieving an OTD percentage of 90% or better and operating with defect rates of less than 500 ppm (these target levels were to be raised each year). Annual performance reviews of professional staff highlighted setting and achieving goals that were linked to departmental or organizational objectives in support of the benchmark and five-year plan.

EXHIBIT 1

ANALOG DEVICES, INC.

Selected Financial Statistics

($000,000)

	1988	1987	1986	1985	1984	1983	1982	1981	1980	1979
Sales	$439	$370	$334	$322	$313	$214	$174	$156	$136	$100
Net income	38	19	23	30	37	18	10	5	9	7
Total assets	449	397	369	348	296	223	163	145	126	84
Capital expenditures	49	43	37	69	58	19	19	16	20	8
Sales	100%	100%	100%	100%	100%	100%	100%	100%	100%	100%
Gross margin	54%	54%	55%	53%	57%	54%	52%	48%	52%	50%
R&D	14	15	13	12	9	9	9	8	7	6
Operating income	13	9	12	14	18	15	13	11	16	15
Return on sales	9	5	7	9	12	9	6	3	7	7
Debt-to-equity	0.09	0.13	0.14	0.23	0.17	0.21	0.65	0.76	1.11	0.96

EXHIBIT 2

ANALOG DEVICES, INC.

Yokogawa Hewlett Packard: Dip Soldering Failures

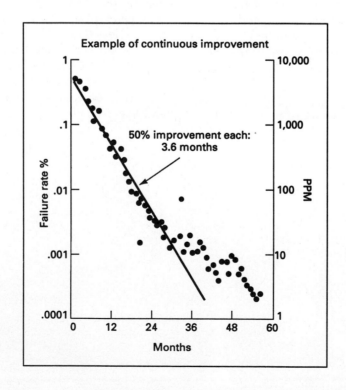

EXHIBIT 3

ANALOG DEVICES, INC.

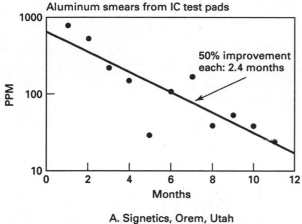

A. Signetics, Orem, Utah

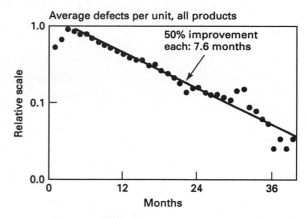

B. Eastman Kodak Copy Products Division

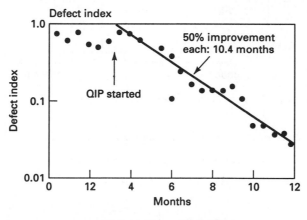

C. Rank Xerox Mitcheldean

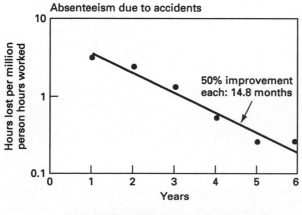

D. Japan Steel Works, Ltd., Hiroshima Plant

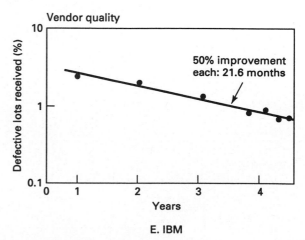

E. IBM

EXHIBIT 4

ANALOG DEVICES, INC.

Estimated Half-Lives (in months) of
Problems Amenable to Continuous Improvement

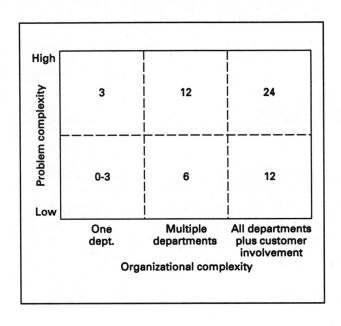

EXHIBIT 5

ANALOG DEVICES, INC.

FY 1990 CORPORATE SCORECARD

	END FY89 ACT	Q190 BHMK	Q190 ACT	Q290 BHMK	Q290 ACT	Q390 BHMK	Q390 ACT	Q490 BHMK	Q490 ACT	FY90 BHMK	FY90 ACT
FINANCIAL											
Revenue											
Revenue growth											
Profit											
Return on assets (ROA)											
QIP											
On-time delivery (to factory commit date)											
% Customer requested dates not matched											
Excess lead-time											
Labor turnover											
MANUFACTURING METRICS: IC PRODUCTS											
Outgoing ppm											
Process ppm											
Cycle time											
Yield											
MANUFACTURING METRICS: ASSEMBLED PRODUCTS											
Outgoing ppm											
Process ppm											
Cycle time											
Yield											

NEW PRODUCTS	ACTUAL	FY87 PLAN	ACTUAL	FY87 PLAN	ACTUAL	FY87 PLAN	ACTUAL	FY87 PLAN	ACTUAL	FY87 PLAN	ACTUAL
Bookings pre-86 products											
Bookings post-85 products											
Total bookings	FY89PLAN	FY87PLAN	FY90 PLAN			FY87PLAN	FY90 PLAN			FY87PLAN	FY90 PLAN
1992 ratio											
(FY90PLAN/FY87PLAN)											
Forecast 3rd year-CAGR											

EXHIBIT 6
ANALOG DEVICES, INC.
Analog Devices On-Time Customer Service Performance
Monthly Rate (August 1987–July 1988)

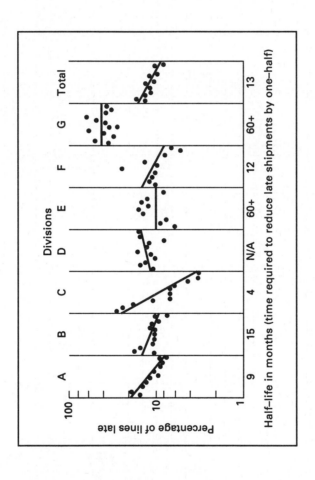

EXHIBIT 7
ANALOG DEVICES, INC.
Income Statement: June 1989 (QTD)

	FIRST QUARTER 1988	SECOND QUARTER 1988	THIRD QUARTER 1988	FOURTH QUARTER 1988	YEAR 1988	FIRST QUARTER 1989	SECOND QUARTER 1989	2 MONTHS QTD	VAR ROLL	ROLL THIRD QUARTER 1989
Bookings—trade & affiliate	103,479	115,486	114,583	111,567	438,206	113,182	117,336	70,027	(765)	115,021
Sales—total	101,207	109,608	113,284	115,107	439,206	114,145	115,003	74,800	2,542	117,420
Standard margin	80,257	87,248	89,041	91,185	374,711	91,430	92,692	59,391	1,657	93,819
% sales	79.3%	79.6%	78.6%	79.2%	79.2%	80.1%	80.6%	79.4%		79.9%
Variances	(1,007)	(1,818)	(1,629)	(1,974)	(7,220)	(1,519)	(463)	(19)	979	(1,622)
Direct margin	78,450	85,430	87,412	89,191	340,483	89,911	92,209	59,372	2,636	92,197
% sales	77.5%	77.9%	77.2%	77.5%	77.5%	78.8%	80.2%	79.4%		78.5%
Gross margin	53,134	59,617	62,906	61,007	236,843	60,497	62,677	38,597	(134)	62,937
% sales	52.5%	54.4%	55.5%	53.0%	53.9%	53.0%	54.5%	51.6%		53.6%
Division fixed	44,936	46,912	48,486	50,992	191,326	51,137	54,741	38,896	(5,368)	54,483
% sales	44.4%	42.8%	42.8%	44.3%	43.6%	44.8%	47.6%	52.0%		46.4%
Total fixed	57,507	60,613	62,646	65,381	246,227	65,405	69,117	48,246	(5,368)	69,160
% sales	56.8%	55.3%	55.3%	56.8%	56.1%	57.3%	60.1%	64.5%		58.9%
Contr margin	20,863	24,817	24,766	23,810	94,256	24,506	23,093	11,126	(2,732)	23,036
% sales	20.6%	22.6%	21.9%	20.7%	21.5%	21.5%	20.1%	14.9%		19.6%
ROA	15.3%	19.9%	20.2%	18.8%	18.6%	19.6%	17.4%	13.2%		17.2%
Deferred OH and other income	(810)	(877)	(906)	(921)	(3,514)	(913)	(920)	(598)	20	(939)
Operating prof.	21,673	25,694	25,672	24,731	97,770	25,419	24,013	11,725	(2,753)	23,976
% sales	21.4%	23.4%	22.7%	21.5%	22.3%	22.3%	20.9%	15.7%		20.4%

Texas Instruments: Cost of Quality (A)

Although you can find a technical fault with every number, the Cost of Quality system has been successful in meeting its intended objectives. But the Cost of Quality figure probably includes only half of all the costs associated with quality and may no longer provide sufficient incentives to drive further improvements. Cost of Quality numbers should be as high as possible to aid in identifying areas for improvement. During the past five years, we have reduced the biggest boulders. Now we have a conflict between comparability and the need to redefine our measurements so that the smaller rocks become visible. Today's opportunities are mostly in indirect areas, but it would take a dramatic shift in attitude to focus on measuring indirect quality costs.

WERNER SCHUELE, VICE-PRESIDENT, PEOPLE AND ASSET EFFECTIVENESS

INTRODUCTION

Texas Instrument's Materials & Controls (M&C) Group was founded in 1916 as General Plate Company, a manufacturer of clad and solid gold alloys for the jewelry industry. Following steady growth in the 1920s, General Plate merged in 1931 with Spenser Thermostat Company, a research and experimental company, to form Metals and Controls Incorporated. In 1959, serious management problems forced a merger with Texas Instruments (TI). TI added M&C's materials- and device-level strengths to its existing component and system-level capabilities and brought management leadership and sophistication that would shape the future growth of the group.

By 1987, the M&C Group was the third largest of seven major businesses within TI. Headquartered in Attleboro, Massachusetts, the group operated manufacturing facilities in four U.S. locations and nine foreign countries and had sales offices throughout the world. The M&C Group's activities centered around two primary technologies.

- *Metallurgical materials*—M&C was currently the world's leading designer and manufacturer of industrial and thermostatic clad metals. Clad metals consisted of two or more wrought metal layers that were metallurgically bonded together to offer properties not available in conventional metals. Examples of this technology included copper-clad aluminum wire, which combined the electrical conductivity of copper with lighter and lower-cost aluminum; stainless steel-clad aluminum, offering the luster of stainless and the corrosion protection of aluminum; and thermostatic metals, which enabled the controlled movement of

thermostat components through the bonding of two metals with different coefficients of expansion. M&C had pioneered the application of these layered materials in uses as diverse as cookware, coinage, cable and wire shielding, integrated circuits, and corrosion-inhibiting trim for automobiles.

- *Control products*—The Control Products business manufactured a wide range of products combining electronic and electromechanical technologies with TI's semiconductor and clad metals expertise. The business operated plants worldwide in support of a strategy based on strong, long-term customer relationships, primarily at the original equipment manager (OEM) level. Principal markets included the automotive, appliance, heating/ventilating/air conditioning, general industrial, and aerospace/defense industries. The business's products offered control, regulation, signaling, and protection functions in applications such as motor protectors, relays, automotive engine controls, pressure switches, circuit breakers, thermostats, and electronic sensors.

The last decade had brought increased competition as companies from Japan, Italy, and Brazil had improved their products while lowering costs. M&C had responded by improving quality and service so that it could compete on factors other than price alone.

ORGANIZATION

The Product Customer Center (PCC) served as the organizational building block within TI. PCCs had profit and loss responsibility for products and customers. M&C had 11 PCCs and two Fabrication Customer Centers (FCCs) located within four operating divisions (two domestic and two international).

This case was prepared by doctoral student Christopher Ittner (under the supervision of Professor Robert S. Kaplan).

Three additional PCCs were located in a Latin American division. Each PCC had its own marketing, engineering, finance, and manufacturing functions. FCCs manufactured components and subassemblies that were common to PCCs to capitalize on economies of scale and specialized expertise.

Four staff support activities existed at the group level: Research and Development, Finance, People and Asset Effectiveness (responsible for quality assurance, training, purchasing, and materials management), and Personnel/Group Services (responsible for facilities, tool making, automation, and human resources).

QUALITY AT TI

Productivity, teamwork, and problem solving had always been important at TI. During the 1950s, work-simplification programs, the forerunner of what are now called quality circles, had been established. In the 1960s and 1970s, TI's productivity programs were expanded to include asset management as well as people effectiveness. As international competition intensified in the late 1970s, TI's People and Asset Effectiveness activities began to focus more specifically on quality improvement. Despite these trends, however, TI continued to emphasize financial controls and a quality philosophy which, while never formally stated, expected a certain amount of defective product to be returned by the customer.

In 1980, the short-run economic tradeoff approach to quality was abandoned when the company decided to commit to a Total Quality Thrust. The new thrust was triggered when Hewlett-Packard, an important TI customer, publicized a study that had found the products of its best American suppliers to be inferior to those of its worst Japanese suppliers. TI management understood well the message from this study: Its long-run competitive success required a greatly expanded commitment to quality control.

The TI Total Quality Thrust was based on the following principles:

1. Quality and Reliability (Q&R) is management's responsibility.
2. Q&R is a responsibility of all organizations.
3. Managers' performance on Q&R will be a key criterion in performance evaluation.
4. Managers' commitments to Q&R will not be measured—only the outcomes.

5. The only acceptable goal for Q&R is a level that surpasses TI's best worldwide competitors at any time.

To emphasize that quality was not just a program but had to become TI's normal way of doing business, a vice-president of People and Asset Effectiveness was appointed at the corporate level. A written policy statement, signed by the CEO, was developed and communicated. It stated the following:

> For every product or service we offer, we will understand the requirements that meet the customers' needs, and we will conform to those requirements without exception. For every job each TIer performs, the performance standard is: Do it right the first time.

A massive training program for all operating personnel on the fundamentals of quality improvement was undertaken. During the first phase, 450 top managers, including 22 from M&C, were sent to quality training courses conducted by Philip Crosby, a leading quality expert. Subsequently, a series of 16 tapes on the quality improvement philosophy and techniques of Joseph Juran, another leading quality expert, was shown to all exempt employees within M&C, with classes taught by senior and operating management. Managers and operating personnel were also trained in quality tools such as control charts and statistical process control. The classes helped to instill awareness and communicate the corporate commitment to quality improvement.

A quality reporting system was implemented to supplement TI's extensive system of financial indicators. For years TI had evaluated the profit-and-loss performance of each business with a series of financial indices published each month in the Blue Book. In 1981, TI began a Quality Blue Book with indices such as product reliability, customer feedback regarding TI quality, and data on the cost of quality. The Blue Book format was deliberately chosen to communicate to TI managers that quality performance was now to be judged on the same level as financial performance.

QUALITY BLUE BOOK

Like its financial counterpart, the Quality Blue Book contained three pages of indices presenting actuals versus goals, previous period comparisons, and three-month forecasts. Unlike the highly structured Financial Blue Book, however, the Quality Blue Book performance indices were generally determined by the responsible PCC manager. This allowed managers to tailor the report to reflect the key quality indicators in each business. Performance indicators for a typical PCC unit are defined in Exhibit 1.

COST OF QUALITY

Cost of Quality (COQ) was one of the performance measures that had to be included in every business unit's Quality Blue Book. COQ represented expenditures that arose because poor quality had occurred or to prevent poor quality from occurring in the future. The COQ measure was designed to highlight the cost of poor quality, the cost of doing things wrong. J. Fred Bucy, TI's President and Chief Operating Officer, explained as follows in a statement to the company's employees:

> Some people think that quality costs money, because they see the costs of quality in terms of new testing equipment, added inspectors, and so on. But these are the costs of doing it wrong the first time. If we design a product right the first time, and build it right the first time, we save all the costs of redesign, rework, scrap, retesting, maintenance, repair, warranty work, etc.
>
> Consider how much of your time is spent in doing something over again. How much of your assets are tied up in rework, retesting, repair, and making scrap? How much material is wasted at TI? If we could eliminate these costs by doing things right the first time, we would have true People and Asset Effectiveness, and improved profitability, without having to add a dollar to billings.

The COQ system was a key component of the Total Quality Thrust. By measuring quality in financial terms, the COQ system allowed M&C management to create a major cultural change by using terms familiar to everyone—the bottom line. Tom Haggar, Controller of the Metallurgical Metals Division, observed as follows:

> COQ ties quality progress into what we're here for—to be a profitable world-class manufacturer constantly improving quality. COQ numbers shocked PCC managers. We initially showed them COQ figures of 10%: 10% of sales value, and an even greater percentage of profits, down the hole. It is now down to a less shocking 4% to 5%. Managers

are saying that they haven't found all of the costs but that the trend is right. Even today's lower percentage is not making them comfortable. A cultural change was needed from the old to the new. For example, we used to budget for 5% scrap but no longer. We now recognize that budgeting for bad quality production is ridiculous.

Implementation of the COQ system began in the fourth quarter of 1981 when the Quality Department undertook a quick top-down exercise to determine quality costs. By the following quarter, an ongoing system based on accounting data was in place. At present, Control and Finance provided PCC's Quality Department with data from the accounting system on the sixth working day following the close of the month. The Quality Department then processed this information into the Quality Blue Book.

The initial list of COQ variables included 77 items, a number that had since been reduced to 19 through the elimination of semantic overlaps between divisions and the merger of insignificant categories into other cost elements. The variables were grouped into four broad categories, as follows:

1. *Prevention costs*—Costs incurred to prevent nonconforming units from being produced.
2. *Appraisal costs*—Costs incurred to ensure that materials and products that failed to meet quality standards were identified prior to shipment.
3. *Internal failure costs*—Scrap costs and costs incurred in correcting errors caught at appraisal, before delivery of the product to the customer.
4. *External failure costs*—Costs incurred in correcting errors after delivery of the product to the customer.

The variables included in each category differed somewhat among PCCs, depending on the nature of the business. The cost elements utilized by the Motor Controls PCC are shown in Exhibit 2.

Several categories of quality costs, such as indirect costs and losses considered inherent to the manufacturing process, were not captured in the COQ system. Indirect quality costs arose from support department personnel repeating tasks because of problems with shipments (defective or incorrect parts, over- or undershipments, late deliveries, etc.) or because the tasks were not done correctly the first time. Examples included the cost of retyping orders, rebuilding tools, and rebilling customers as well as correcting paperwork errors and incorrect journal entries. Efforts were underway to determine the level of indirect quality costs through Hidden Factory reviews.

When originally implemented, the COQ system excluded costs that were considered to be a standard part of the manufacturing process. For example, a calibration process in production may have been imperfect, requiring parts to be manually checked on the line. The costs of the manual checking were not included in COQ, leading to an understatement of quality costs. Scrap costs were also underreported by a number of PCCs. The PCC managers argued that engineered scrap, such as the material left when a round part was punched out of a square piece of metal, was inherent to the process.

The COQ system had been easy to implement since it used data that already existed in the accounting system. Now, however, the desire to maintain consistency over time, so that trends would be visible, had made it difficult to add new measures such as indirect quality or engineered scrap costs. In effect, attempts to update the COQ system to make it more accurate and relevant were in conflict with the need to maintain comparability across periods.

USES OF COQ DATA

Initially, the COQ system was resented as just another number to be judged against. Carl Sheffer, General Manager of the Motor Controls PCC, recalled his concern: "I resented the system, feeling that quality was a virtue in its own right. Attempting to assign costs to quality diminished its value. Value is not in the numbers but in the areas they represent."

By 1987, however, the quality indicators and the COQ data in the Blue Book had become widely utilized management tools at M&C. Two factors had contributed to the system's widespread acceptance. First, quarterly financial forecast reviews were supplemented by quality reviews. PCC managers were now allowed to present the results of operations in a less structured format with emphasis on the areas of importance to each business.

Second, the Quality Blue Book was not used to "hammer" the PCC managers. Performance was not measured exclusively on the achievement of quality goals, nor were quality measures compared across businesses. Rather, the quality measures were used to focus on long-term trends of quality improve-

ment and to highlight potential sources of quality problems.

The Quality Blue Book was distributed to the Group President, Controller, Vice-President of People and Asset Effectiveness, and to the responsible Division and PCC managers on a monthly basis. Although not formally distributed to operating personnel, the information was widely available to them. Jim Meehan, PCC Quality Manager, noted the following:

I don't distribute Quality Blue Books to anyone below the level of the PCC manager. The PCC manager must take responsibility for getting copies to all the operating functions. Everybody probably sees them, and anyone who asks me can have a copy. Different people use different measures—the PCCs use Cost of Quality, manufacturing uses internal failures, operations is interested in on-time delivery, and marketing wants to know about external failures.

Carl Sheffer discussed his use of the data.

The reports go to all of my managers and team members. I take personal interest in Cost of Quality and ask for the numbers. At monthly meetings, the COQ numbers are discussed with the nonexempt employees. I highlight product lines that have improved and lines that have deteriorated. We primarily focus on Internal Failure and RMR [Returned Material Reports] because they are "hard" numbers. The others are more helpful for trends.

This year, the Cost of Quality numbers provided the single best indicator that problems had arisen in production, problems that had caused a bad P&L performance. The Cost of Quality showed deterioration in Internal Failure when the department claimed that scrap rates were down. The discrepancy arose from the department not realizing that it had not reduced the amount of overage (material in excess of the minimum required) issued from the stockroom. Eventually, a physical inventory check found unused material all around the shop. So, the Cost of Quality report signaled a problem that may have gone undiscovered for a while.

In addition to Quality Blue Book reports, Sheffer had developed special COQ reports for his area (see Exhibits 3 through 5). Problems reflected in the COQ reports were not always indicative of actual quality shortcomings however. Sheffer continued as follows:

A couple of years ago, we saw continually worsening trends in the Cost of Quality. After investigating, we found that the selling price had been reduced 10%. The same scrap rate led the Cost of Quality, measured as a percent of Net Sales Billed, to go way up. This is a profitability problem but not one caused by a quality problem.

COQ PROJECTS

Quality improvements were aided by management's willingness to expend funds on projects that produced intangible benefits, such as quality and service, without rigorous financial justification. Concurrent with the financial planning cycle, quality improvement teams, consisting of department managers, their staff, and representatives of support organizations such as Marketing, Engineering, Manufacturing, Production Control, Quality, Finance, and Purchasing, met to establish COQ improvement projects, using COQ system numbers as priority-setting mechanisms. Anticipated savings from the COQ improvement projects were estimated and incorporated into the product line's profit forecast. COQ savings by project were subsequently tracked by the Manufacturing Engineering department (see Exhibit 6). Bob Porter, Vice-President of Quality Assurance and Reliability, felt that the identification and implementation of COQ projects were the keys to instilling quality awareness and improving quality performance within the group.

The critical issue is the process. By that I mean getting management involved in identifying opportunities for quality improvement, establishing priorities, helping ensure that resources are available, and monitoring progress. We need to speak the right language on each of these issues, and COQ is the language of management.

Two of the organizational mechanisms that support the process are the Quality Improvement Teams (QIT) and the People and Asset Effectiveness (P&AE) reviews. The QITs, which are in place at the group, division, and department levels of the business, consist of natural work groups of managers and professionals who meet regularly to steer the quality excellence process. The quality (P&AE) reviews, which are held quarterly, are high-level management reviews in which business managers review progress against their short- and long-term quality goals.

Early in the year, the lowest-level QITs identify quality improvement opportunities. Frequently, senior management attends these department QITs where the champions of these projects discuss the opportunities. These projects are dollarized, time

phased, assigned champions, and summarized at the division level. The forecasted COQ savings are recognized in the annual plan. Key COQ projects are summarized at the group level. The COQ trend is tracked and reviewed at every group and division QIT meeting.

At the P&AE reviews, the operating departments discuss their short- and long-term goals. Much of this is focused on the progress of key COQ projects —how the QITs are using quality tools such as statistical process control to drive continuous improvement in COQ. This process is not treated as an exact science. It is not preoccupied with testing the validity of the numbers or comparison of one entity versus another. It is focused on who, what, and when, and closing the loop on results.

In summary, the operating businesses have ownership. They establish priorities and wrestle with the resource tradeoffs. The quality organization provides lots of support, but quality improvement is clearly not a program of the quality organization. Operations managers work to achieve goals they helped to establish. Progress is monitored against milestones throughout the year at the QITs and P&AE reviews.

If this process works well, the COQ numbers will take care of themselves. Without the COQ numbers, however, this process wouldn't work.

SYSTEM RESULTS

Between the formal inception of the COQ system in 1982 and the end of 1987, COQ as a percent of net sales billed had fallen from 10.7% to 7.8%. Reductions had occurred in each category of quality costs (see Exhibit 7). The system had also focused increased attention on the impact of improved quality on costs and profitability. Carl Sheffer, however, still had mixed feelings about the current COQ system.

Motivating senior management wasn't a problem. They already knew that quality was critical. COQ was most helpful for middle managers to see the consequences of poor quality on overall income. COQ gives one number that focuses several things together. If we focused just on scrap, we would get lower scrap costs but would go out of business as we passed scrap on to the customer. On the other hand, if we tried to focus on reducing external failures through inspection alone, without actually reducing manufactured defects, we would become uncompetitive cost wise. COQ forces us to think about an optimum relationship among the various factors. You have to improve the whole, not pieces at a time.

The COQ system has proven to be a good attention getter, has forced priority setting, and has stimulated quality improvement activities. It also ends up being a good scorecard. It does much less well as a diagnostic tool, partially because it uses accounting techniques. It is sometimes difficult to find out what the problem is without supplementary diagnostic tools.

Maybe the things we track well, such as Internal Failure, should be reported more often while COQ in general could be done less frequently. Indirect cost of quality tracking probably doesn't need to be continuous. We should look at each function and ask, "Why does it exist?" If the function only exists to correct errors, we can probably eliminate it. Getting rid of the function will be more appropriate than tracking secretary time, paper processing, cost of calling customers, etc. We need to focus on the big items.

THE FUTURE

As 1987 came to a close, Werner Schuele, Vice-President of People and Asset Effectiveness, was evaluating potential changes to the COQ system as part of an overall company review of its cost systems. Although the COQ system remained a valuable tool to highlight quality trends, allocate resources, and instill quality awareness, Schuele was not sure that COQ could continue to drive improvements in quality unless improvements were made. He felt strongly that the costs tracked by the system were only 50% of actual quality costs, resulting in inadequate attention being focused on major sources of quality costs. But he also knew that changes to the system might distort trends in the data, perhaps the most valuable use of the information. Schuele felt some reticence in implementing an indirect quality cost-tracking system.

I would love to track it if I knew how. We could avoid the trend distortion issue just by having two categories: direct and total [i.e., direct and indirect]. My major concern is that determining the real cost of "indirect scrap" is not precise and has no foundation in our accounting system. For example, nowhere is the cost of retyping a letter with a misspelled word tracked. My dilemma is that I'm not sure that the cost of developing the tracking system is worth it. Also, there is no organizational mandate to develop a precise indirect system.

Finally, Schuele was not convinced that monthly COQ reporting was necessary. Over the next six months, these questions would need to be addressed and recommendations presented.

EXHIBIT 1

Quality Blue Book Performance Indicators

Concurrent Indicators
Lot acceptance % | Percentage of lots accepted by Outgoing Quality Control. Tracked by product line.

Average outgoing quality level | Defective parts per million. Tracked by product line.

Lagging Indicators
RMR % quality | Returned merchandise report percentage. Percentage of shipments returned from customers due to poor quality.

RMR % total | RMR % quality + percentage of shipments returned for reasons other than poor quality. These included incorrect quantity shipped, wrong parts, and incorrect packaging.

Customer report card | Customer lot acceptance level. A sample of customers was interviewed to get feedback on M&C quality. Lack of record keeping by customers limited the availability of quantified data on this indicator.

Competitive rank | Subjective self-ranking of competitiveness. Ranking was done by marketing and field sales personnel. The fraction presented in the report represented M&C's competitive ranking relative to the number of competitors in that product line.

On-time delivery | Shipment of at least 90% of the order on or before the acknowledgement date (indicator added in 1984).[1]

Leading Indicators
First-pass calibration yields | Most products produced by this PCC were calibrated to open at a specific temperature. After processing, 100% of the units were tested either manually or automatically to determine that the units were calibrated correctly. This indicator reflected the percentage of units that passed this inspection.

Cost of quality | Calculated as the percentage of quality costs to net sales billed. Quality costs were defined as costs that were incurred due to poor quality or to prevent poor quality from occurring.

---

[1]Some debate existed as to whether on-time delivery represented a quality indicator to be put in the Blue Book. Only in the last quarter of 1987 did most divisions in the group incorporate this measure.

The on-time delivery percentage was calculated on events rather than dollars to ensure that shipments to smaller customers received equal weighting. The previous measure of delivery performance was whether a customer was ever forced to shut down, ignoring instances in which customers were forced to reschedule production due to late delivery.

In 1981, on-time delivery was less than 50%. By 1987, 97% of the 2,000 shipments per week were delivered on time.

EXHIBIT 2

Cost of Quality Variables
Motor Controls PCC

Prevention Costs
Quality engineering | Total quality engineering expense from the monthly actuals report.

Receiving inspection | Total receiving inspection expense from the monthly actuals report.

Equipment repair/maintenance | Estimated percentage of actual repair and maintenance expenses spent on preventive maintenance. An estimate of 15% of total R&M expenses was developed by PCC management in 1981. This percentage had not been revised since the original estimate was made.

Manufacturing engineering | Estimated percentage of actual manufacturing engineering expenses spent on prevention. The estimated percentage was revised every six months by the Manager of Manufacturing Engineering.

(continued)

EXHIBIT 2 (cont.)

| Design engineering | Estimated percentage of actual design engineering expenses spent on prevention. The estimated percentage was revised every six months by the Manager of Design Engineering. |
| Quality training | Actual cost of quality training from the labor reporting system. Quality training time was charged to a special labor link (charge) number. |

Appraisal Costs

TSL laboratory	Total technical services laboratory expense from the monthly actual report. The technical services laboratory was responsible for sophisticated quality-related testing.
Design analysis	Estimated percentage of actual design analysis expenses spent on appraisal. The percentage was revised every six months by the Manager of Design Analysis.
Product acceptance	Total inspection (quality control) expenses from the monthly actual report.
Manufacturing inspection	Actual cost of manufacturing inspection from the labor reporting system. Manufacturing inspection was charged to a special link (charge) number.

Internal Failure Costs

Quality scrap	Calculated as (material issued at standard) − (material scheduled for production at standard) × labor and overhead factor. The labor and overhead factor represented the amount of labor and overhead costs incurred in the assembly prior to its scrapping.[1] Obsolete parts scrapped out of inventory were not included in this measure.
Rework	Actual cost of rework from the labor reporting system. Rework was charged to a special link (charge) number.
Manufacturing/ process engineering	Estimated percentage of actual manufacturing/process engineering expenses spent on internal failure. The estimated percentage was revised every six months by the Manager of Manufacturing Engineering.

External Failure Costs

Net RMR cost	Cost of returns less good material to inventory.[2]
Marketing	Estimated percentage of actual marketing expenses spent on external failure. The estimated percentage was revised every six months by the Marketing Manager.
Manufacturing/ process engineering	Estimated percentage of actual manufacturing/process engineering expenses spent on external failure. The estimated percentage was revised every six months by the Manager of Manufacturing Engineering.
Repair	Actual cost of repair from the labor reporting system. Repair time was charged to a special link (charge) number.
Travel	Actual travel costs related to quality problems. Computed from the monthly actual report.
Liability claims	Infrequent claims. Liability claims were included when incurred or when a reserve was taken. Legal fees, which did not hit the group profit-and-loss statement, were not included.

Internal failure and net RMR costs were available at the product line level. All other elements were captured at the product (PCC) department level.

[1] In 1981, a study was conducted to determine at which point in the assembly process products were being scrapped. As a result of this study, a factor of 88% above scrapped material costs was calculated to account for labor and overhead. This factor had not been changed since the original study.

[2] If a $5 product was returned due to defects, it could either be scrapped or reworked and returned to inventory. If the item was scrapped, the net RMR cost would be $5. If, on the other hand, the item was reworked at a cost of $1, rework costs of $1 would be reported and no costs would be included in net RMR.

EXHIBIT 3

TEXAS INSTRUMENTS

Materials and Controls Group

Motor Controls PCC

Product Line Failure Costs

PRODUCT A	SEPTEMBER	OCTOBER	NOVEMBER	YEAR-TO-DATE 1987
Activity $	522,833	467,380	424,051	5,398,635
Internal failure COQ $	14,637	28,597	2,170	232,221
External failure COQ $	425	0	85	4,420
Total failure COQ $	15,062	28,597	2,255	236,641
Nonconformance COQ %	2.88	6.12	0.53	4.38
Variance prior year %	0.38	−2.86	2.73	−1.12
Variance prior year $	1,982	(13,361)	11,569	(60,645)
Cumulative $	(58,853)	(72,214)	(60,645)	

EXHIBIT 4

TEXAS INSTRUMENTS

Materials and Controls Group

Motor Controls PCC

Failure Rates By Product

	JANUARY	FEBRUARY	MARCH	APRIL	MAY	JUNE	JULY	AUGUST	SEPTEMBER	OCTOBER	NOVEMBER	DECEMBER	YEAR
Product A Overage %	7.1	8.7	10.6	11.5	8.9	1.7	7.1	−2.1	15.8	3.7	4.4	—	7.1
Internal failure	7,031	8,973	13,548	11,278	8,310	2,474	7,031	−1,595	15,341	3,995	5,914	—	82,300
External failure	2,805	3,740	1,020	0	340	0	85	8,670	0	0	0	—	16,600
COQ %	5.6	5.3	5.6	4.4	3.5	0.9	5.1	3.6	7.3	1.8	2.8	—	4.1
Product B Overage %	3.6	4.0	5.7	4.2	2.9	3.7	7.6	1.2	2.6	3.7	−8.5	—	2.3
Internal failure	932	874	1,506	1,393	1,107	1,045	1,523	600	1,255	1,543	−2,894	—	8,884
External failure	0	0	0	0	0	0	0	0	0	0	0	—	0
COQ %	2.8	4.1	4.6	3.7	2.3	3.0	14.2	1.0	2.0	4.0	−6.6	—	2.1

EXHIBIT 5

TEXAS INSTRUMENTS

Materials and Controls Group

Motor Controls PCC

Departmental Nonconformance Costs

YEAR-TO-DATE THROUGH NOVEMBER

NONCONFORMANCE SAVINGS VERSUS 1986*   YEAR-TO-DATE NONCOMFORMANCE COQ % NET SALES BILLED

Product A	$89K	Product A	1.6%
Product B	61K	Product B	2.1
Product C	52K	Product C	3.1
Product D	20K	Product D	3.3
Product E	16K	Product E	3.4
Product F	8K	Product F	3.5
		Department average	3.1%

*Represents the difference between actual 1987 quality costs and the quality costs that would have been incurred at the 1986 COQ percentage. Includes internal and external failure costs only.

EXHIBIT 6

TEXAS INSTRUMENTS

Materials and Controls Group

Motor Controls PCC

Cost of Quality Project Savings

COQ PROJECTS	1987 COST REDUCTIONS ($K)					VARIANCE FROM
	FIRST QUARTER	SECOND QUARTER	THIRD QUARTER	FOURTH QUARTER	YR87	ANNUAL PLAN
Yield improvement	26	61	55	54	196	150
Upgrade assembly	20	24	32	44	120	53
Redesign molded part	16	20	24	53	113	(55)
Nondestruct testing	10	11	14	17	52	13
Laser coding	9	10	9	10	38	30
Flash reduction	8	9	11	10	38	22
Statistical process control	93	119	128	127	467	(90)
Total	182	254	273	315	1,024	123

EXHIBIT 7

TEXAS INSTRUMENTS

Materials and Controls Group

Cost of Quality, % of Net Sales Billed

	1982	1983	1984	1985	1986	1987
Prevention	2.3	2.0	2.0	2.1	2.3	2.3
Appraisal	2.2	1.9	1.7	1.9	1.9	1.8
Internal failure	5.3	4.8	4.5	4.2	3.6	3.3
External failure	0.9	0.7	0.6	0.4	0.4	0.4
Total COQ	10.7	9.4	8.8	8.6	8.2	7.8

Texas Instruments: Cost of Quality (B)

When we implemented the Cost of Quality system in 1983, it served as the language for the cultural change. The Cost of Quality, or more appropriately the Cost of Poor Quality, acted as a philosophical driver to show how much better we could do. But Cost of Quality changes its nature as a quality culture is institutionalized. As the culture matures, the tools are bound to change. The quality tools are now statistical process control, the Taguchi method, and Ishikawa charts. We have gone eight months without formally reviewing Cost of Quality numbers. We have been focusing on other measures of quality such as cycle time and on-time delivery. But Cost of Quality is a useful measure of progress. It may be time to revisit it.

Mac McDonnell, Vice-President and General Manager of TI's Industrial Systems Division (ISD), was commenting on the division's COQ system. Over the past several years, ISD had made great strides in institutionalizing a quality culture, with COQ measurement playing a key role in the cultural transformation. Now, however, the management team questioned whether to retain the system, modify it, or drop it completely. A debate on the system's future was scheduled for the next management committee meeting.

INDUSTRIAL SYSTEMS DIVISION

The ISD manufactured programmable controllers for the industrial automation and factory control fields. A programmable controller is an industrial computer used to automate manufacturing processes in a variety of industries such as food and beverage, pharmaceuticals, petrochemicals, paper and pulp, specialty chemicals, and automobiles. Programmable controller technology had been applied to virtually all United States industries and was a foundation of industrial automation in the country. The same technology was also experiencing increased growth in the European market.

In addition to the manufacture of automation products, ISD operated a state-of-the-art facility for assembling pin-in-hole and surface mount circuit boards. Both pin-in-hole and surface mount manufacturing processes used modern automated equipment and advanced assembly techniques under statistical process control (SPC). Circuit boards were assembled under contract for other manufacturers, with end uses in products ranging from computers to talking teddy bears.

Since its founding in 1973, ISD's Johnson City, Tennessee manufacturing site had grown from a temporary plant with 500 employees to a modern, 350,000-square-foot facility employing approximately 1,500 hourly and salaried personnel organized along functional lines. A large segment of ISD's business was conducted through overseas offices that served locations throughout the world.

INSTITUTING A QUALITY CULTURE

ISD's push to institute a quality-oriented culture was an outgrowth of TI's Total Quality Thrust. Corporate managers directed divisions to implement a quality measurement system to supplement TI's extensive system of financial indicators. As part of the measurement system, divisions tracked a series of indices in a monthly report known as the Quality Blue Book. The Blue Book measured key attributes of People and Asset Effectiveness, a term which encompassed, in addition to quality, measures on productivity, material effectiveness, asset effectiveness, and automation.

One performance measure common to all Quality Blue Books was COQ. In determining COQ variables, divisions sought to incorporate cost measures for the broad sources of quality prevention, detection, and failure.

COQ SYSTEM DEVELOPMENT

In 1981, an initial attempt was made to develop a COQ system for ISD. The system was designed by

This case was prepared by Christopher Ittner, doctoral student (under the supervision of Professor Robert S. Kaplan).

a quality engineer who sent a memo instructing every cost center manager to calculate a cost of quality. The quality engineer then summarized the numbers given to him by the managers to calculate an overall quality cost figure for the division. Managers, however, interpreted the directions differently, leading to incompatible measures. Excess inventory, for example, was directed to be one component of quality costs. Some managers included the entire value of the excess inventory in their calculations, while others included only the additional carrying or financing costs arising from the excess inventory.

Monthly reviews were held to discuss each organization's COQ figures, but a negative tone soon emerged when managers were asked to explain their performance. The confrontational air of the meetings strengthened the view that quality personnel were acting as police officers. Don Schenck, Manager of Quality and Reliability, observed,

> The monthly reviews never really worked. We were comparing apples and oranges. Managers didn't believe the numbers, and monthly reviews reinforced their defensive attitude. Long-term problems couldn't be solved in 30 days. Reviewing quality costs each month produced a tactical rather than a strategic mode of behavior.

In 1983, a group of managers representing Finance, Quality, Operations, Engineering, Marketing, Sales, and Personnel began the development of a quality cost measurement system for the division. Given the disappointing results of the earlier effort, two factors were considered essential for any new system. First, the numbers needed credibility. McDonnell recalled,

> People won't get serious about the meaning of quality costs if they don't believe the numbers. We brought C&F [Control and Finance] into the task force and said, "You are the keepers of the numbers on the site. You're going to say what the Cost of Quality percentage is." The numbers don't need to include every last penny of quality costs, but they need to be consistent.

Second, the variables measured by the system needed to reflect key areas for quality improvement. Schenck noted, "In determining drivers, the question was, 'If I had to prioritize, what are the important things? Where are the hidden costs?'"

Nine variables were eventually selected for measurement: turnover costs, project management, RMR (Returned Material Report), product inspection, production planning, production rework, reliability, burn-in, and test (see Exhibit 1 for definitions of the COQ variables). The nine COQ variables served as the focus for the measurement and management of business-wide quality costs (see Exhibit 2).

Dale Geiger, Division Controller at the time the new system was implemented, summarized the development of the COQ system as follows:

> Only when you have believable numbers can trends be used. Consequently, the Cost of Quality system was developed so that a clerk could take the formulas and use the accounting reports to calculate COQ. Where judgments were required, the methodology was standardized.
>
> While some may question whether the variables we selected were actually quality related, we felt that they all related to the broad definition of quality. Take project management, for example. We were spending a lot of money on new product development, so we included project management performance as a quality variable. When a manager of a development project accepted a budget for the project, he made a commitment. We treated it as a contract. Revisions could be made if the scope of the project changed. But otherwise, the ability to meet cost and schedule was an indicator of the quality of project management.
>
> Highlighting the results of poor project management resulted ultimately in the development of enhanced MIS tools. The system has been so successful that other areas in TI have adopted it.

EVOLUTION OF COQ MEASUREMENT

Initially, COQ numbers from the new system were issued monthly to lend credibility to the information. Rather than reviewing each manager's quality costs, however, the management team took a more strategic approach by focusing on the major sources of quality costs within the entire division. Using Pareto analysis, in which the various categories of quality costs were ranked by dollar volume, management was able to identify broad categories of quality deficiencies (see Exhibit 3). Efforts were then undertaken to identify the underlying causes.

Division management sought to avoid having a multitude of independent quality cost reduction projects by designating a single key quality problem for attention. Teams were then formed to unravel the problem until the root causes were identified. Production planning quality costs, which included inventory writeoffs, carrying cost of excess inventory, air freight, and purchasing premiums for quick delivery, were soon targeted as a major area of concern. The result was a three-year program to identify and correct the sources of problems in the planning area. McDonnell recalled,

> Three or four years ago, we determined that the biggest issue in Cost of Quality had to do with the whole category of planning. The problem was flagged by a Pareto analysis that showed a large opportunity for quality improvement in the production planning area. We put together a Quality Improvement Team to discover the underlying sources. When the team got into it, all kinds of problems were discovered—forecasting, scheduling, etc. It permeated the organization. Eventually we discovered that the critical driver was cycle time. We reduced cycle time from 60 to 10 days. WIP [work in process] went down, rework fell, and we didn't build scrap.

Based on the quality improvement team's findings, extensive changes were made to reduce cycle time. These included the restructuring of the division's MRP system, improved factory planning, and implementation of just-in-time concepts and common work cells.

RECENT DEVELOPMENTS

Although management continued to measure quality costs and conduct Pareto analysis, the COQ system began receiving less formal attention as the division's management began to focus on other measures of quality such as cycle time and on-time delivery. McDonnell explained,

> We have gone a long way in institutionalizing a quality culture. As the culture has matured, the tools of quality management have also changed. We used to see only what happened last month. Now we have many production lines with statistical process controls to analyze quality on-line. Originally, Cost of Quality provided the language to change our quality culture. Today, however, the language of quality is cycle time in the factory, on-time delivery, and meeting customer demands.

For the past eight months, no COQ figures had been calculated. McDonnell did not seem concerned about the omission.

We need to look at drivers and underlying processes. You can manage costs or manage processes. If you only look at costs, you may be balloon squeezing with cost reductions in one area suddenly reappearing in another.

The deemphasis of COQ measurement made it unclear what, if any, role the system would play in the future. For McDonnell, COQ reporting was not a high priority.

> I'm much more concerned with how many lines we have under statistical process control. I don't want to depreciate Cost of Quality, but we used it as a relative measurement tool, not as a fundamental driver. Cost of Quality is just a tool, maybe just an awareness tool, and even then maybe not the most important tool.

Despite McDonnell's misgivings, other members of the management team were not ready to abandon the system. Don Schenck, the division's Quality and Reliability Manager, noted,

> I would like to reemphasize Cost of Quality. It did tell us things. Compared to six months ago, am I really doing better? Are the improvement projects really making an impact? Strategic use will only require a review every six to twelve months.
>
> Cost of Quality does tell where our most significant operations lie. Our number-one priority is now software development and testing. Obsolescense is also a big issue, which ties into supplier delivery, planning, and forecasting. Cost of Quality helps us identify areas for improvement, although it does not point to the specific actions we should take. The question is, how much attention should be paid to it? If you focus too much on dollars, it becomes a police action, a negative report card. Proper management action from a good COQ system should address underlying root causes rather than tactical police-action–type goal setting.

Sil Pena, the division's Controller, felt that merely reviving the old COQ structure would not be adequate. In his view, even greater attention to quality costs was warranted.

> You're talking to a finance guy, so my perspective may be different than Mac's or other people in operations. But I think we should be actively managing quality costs downward. Management needs to look at how to get quality dollars down. We do a good job in hindsight. But we should start looking forward. We should look at Cost of Quality on a long-term basis with a long-term plan for reducing these costs. We should also be looking at the

distribution of costs among the prevention, appraisal, and failure categories of quality costs. We should make sure that we are spending our money on prevention and appraisal activities such as training and inspection, rather than on failure costs such as warranties and returned product. While I think that indices are more useful for measuring and managing quality at lower levels, I feel that measuring quality in dollar terms provides management with better information about our overall quality performance.

These comments were just an indication of the conflicting opinions surrounding the COQ system's

role in the future. At the upcoming meeting, ISD's management team was scheduled to discuss proposed revisions to the Quality Blue Book (Exhibit 4 provides the proposed Blue Book indices). Although retention of the existing COQ structure at the divisional level was proposed, its inclusion was open to debate. Given the conflicting opinions on the value of quality cost measurement to ISD's quality management practices, the COQ system's ultimate fate was far from clear.

EXHIBIT 1

TEXAS INSTRUMENTS: COST OF QUALITY (B)

Cost of Quality Variables

Turnover costs	Productivity losses and additional hiring and training costs due to turnover. Formulas were developed by Personnel based on salary grade, length of service, and other employment and experience factors.
Project costs	Product development cost overruns. Project budgets were treated as contracts between the project manager and the division. Changes in scope were treated as changes to the contract.
RMR (Returned Material Report)	Cost of field failures and technical services used to support customer questions and problems.
Product inspection	Receiving and manufacturing inspection costs.
Production planning	Included change in reserve level for excess or obsolete inventory, carrying cost of excess inventory, air freight, and purchasing premiums for expediting deliveries.
Production rework	Scrap, rework, solder inspection, and troubleshooting costs.
Reliability	Costs associated with reliability engineers in R&D areas. (Reliability engineers were responsible for controlling the design process.)
Burn-in	Burn-in involved heating electronic components to promote premature failure of defective products. Power was applied to the components, and the temperature was raised in the testing ovens. This was continued for an extended period of time. It was assumed that any components that were likely to fail in the field would have failed the burn-in test. Costs in this category included labor associated with the burn-in test and depreciation on the burn-in equipment.
Test	All costs associated with product testing other than burn-in.

EXHIBIT 2

TEXAS INSTRUMENTS: COST OF QUALITY (B)

Cost of Quality as Percent of Net Sales Billed

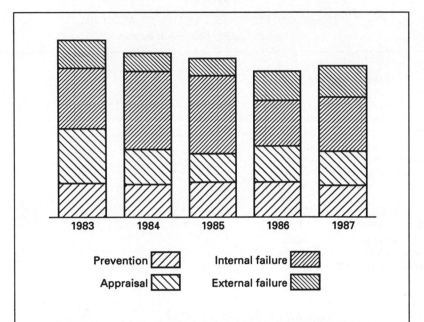

PREVENTION included most costs incurred prior to production release, including quality engineering interface with new suppliers, product development cost overruns, and new product testing and evaluation.

APPRAISAL included all costs associated with the sampling of product, including receiving inspection and manufacturing tests associated with products during the production phase.

INTERNAL FAILURE included burn-in, personnel turnover, manufacturing rework, and production planning costs associated with excess or obsolete material.

EXTERNAL FAILURE included all costs for field failures (RMR costs) as well as technical services used to support customer questions and problems.

EXHIBIT 3

TEXAS INSTRUMENTS: COST OF QUALITY (B)

Strategic Ranking Derived from COQ

	PARETO RANKING BY DOLLAR VALUE				
	1983	1984	1985	1986	1987
1.	Planning	Project costs	Planning	Rework	Planning
2.	Project costs	Planning	Rework	RMR	Turnover
3.	Rework	Reliabilty	Project costs	Reliability	RMR

EXHIBIT 4

TEXAS INSTRUMENTS: COST OF QUALITY (B)
Proposed Quality Blue Book Indices

Industrial Systems Division
Cost of Quality—% of net sales billed (NSB)
On-time delivery
Total inventory turns per year
Indirect PEI (People Effectiveness Index). Productivity index defined as revenue ÷ payroll + benefits. Index focused on indirect labor productivity due to effective tracking of direct labor by manufacturing and high indirect labor percentage (70%) within the division.
Number of products > 8 weeks lead-time
Exempt turnover (annualized %)

Control and Finance
Unresolved customer debit memos (% NSB)
Customer bad debt (% NSB)
On-time payments to suppliers (% $ due)
Automatic cash applications (% total applications)
Overdue shipments due to credit (qty/month)

Operations
Yields by product (%)
Units delivered on time (% total due)
Qty of products > 8 weeks lead-time
Factory cycle time (calendar days)
I.S.D. total inventory (turns per year)
Nonmaterial costs (% total costs)

Industrial Systems Products (Marketing and Product Development)
Field reliability by product
Factory reliability assessment by product
Software project productivity (source lines/project man-month)
Software quality (total problem reports/1,000 lines of source)
Project management schedule index
Project management cost performance index
Profit index (gross margin/total budget)

People and Asset Effectiveness
Qty stock purges (qty/1,000 lots processed)
Qty quality-related ship holds (qty/month)
Qty First Article Conformance Inspection discrepancies (qty/month). An audit was performed just prior to the release of a design to manufacturing. The checklist covered items such as correct drawings, approved suppliers, and readiness of instrumentation and test equipment.
Engineering change notice activity (qty/month)
Quality control costs (% manufacturing costs)

North American Industrial Systems (NAIS) Sales
Sales efficiency (net sales entered/field sales total headcount)
NAIS department efficiency (net sales entered/total NAIS employees)
NAIS department People Effectiveness Index (net sales entered/NAIS budget for below the line indirects)

READINGS

Activity-Based Information:
A Blueprint for World-Class Management Accounting

H. Thomas Johnson

For more than 60 years, managers have used cost information from transaction-based financial accounts to judge the impact of their decisions on company profits. Costs are used in budgets for planning and control, and they also are used to evaluate both the profitability of products and the effects on profit of resource allocation decisions. Relying on cost to evaluate the consequences of a manager's decisions succeeds if cost is the primary determinant of probability.

Today, however, we recognize that profitability no longer results exclusively from controlling costs. New management methods make quality and flexibility as important as cost in determining profitability. These new methods, pioneered in Japan and adopted since 1980 by scores of American companies, prompt a need for new sources of management accounting information.[1]

New management methods stress the need for focusing not only on cost, but also on quality and flexibility. New technologies of communication and information processing, by giving customers rapid access to the best products and services in the world, also make it imperative that businesses provide "world class" quality and cost, and be flexible enough to respond rapidly to changes in consumer demand. Profitability no longer results primarily from taking steps to control costs; it also hinges on maintaining world-class standards of customer value. To be profitable in the global economy, businesses must know if their decisions will deliver value to the customer in excess of the cost of delivering that value.

Until now, cost information was deemed suffi-cient to enable businesses to manage profitability. Now, however, profitability encompasses more than just cost. Management accounting, therefore, must look beyond transaction-based cost information to know if decisions will deliver profit. It must develop new information to achieve this objective.

A NEW APPROACH

A new approach to management accounting must be built on "activity-based information." This information is about the work (or activity) that consumes resources and delivers value in a business. People consuming resources in work ultimately cause costs and achieve the value customers pay for.

Ideally, the way to achieve profitability is to manage activities. When managers attempt to achieve profits by managing costs, as has been done for decades, they implicitly use cost to measure activities indirectly. Initially, this practice was probably a matter of convenience and economy. Until the advent of electronic information processing it was very difficult, and costly, to gather information about activities.

Cost numbers always have been easily available. Moreover, cost information can substitute for direct information about activities when businesses use relatively simple processes and produce fairly homogeneous product lines. Before the end of World War II, homogeneity and simplicity charac-terized most, though not all, American businesses. Businesses trying to compete in today's global econ-omy are neither simple nor homogeneous. In busi-

Reprinted from *Management Accounting* (June 1988), pp. 23–30, with permission.

ness today, cost and value cannot be assessed by transaction-based cost information. Achieving profitability requires activity-based information.[2]

Two types of activity-based information (see Figure 1) should form the backbone of world-class management accounting. One type is nonfinancial information about sources of competitive value (e.g., quality, flexibility, and cost) in a company's operating activities. This information indicates how effectively operating activities deliver value to the customer. The second type of activity-based information, strategic cost information, enables managers to assess the long-term profitability of a company's current mix of products and activities. Strategic cost information indicates if a company's activities are cost-effective in comparison to alternatives outside the company, and if the mix of prod-

ucts management has chosen to sell uses activities in the most profitable way.

These two uses of activity-based information resemble control and planning as defined in traditional management accounting. But activity-based information seldom comes from the transaction-based financial accounts that supply almost all information in traditional management accounting systems. It comprises any relevant information about activities across the entire chain of value—design, engineering, sourcing, production, distribution, marketing, and after-sale service. Activity-based information focuses managers' attention on underlying causes (drivers) of cost and profit unlike the distant, often distorted, financial echoes of those causes that appear in traditional cost and performance reports.

Figure 1.   Activity-Based Information for Managing Profitability

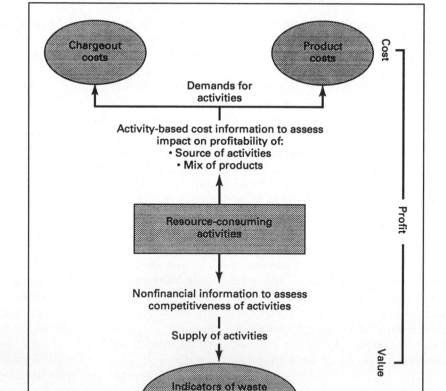

COMPETITIVE ACTIVITIES

Sources of customer value changed dramatically after 1970 causing business leaders to become concerned with value and competitiveness. Prior to the 1970s, companies competed chiefly on cost. Today's companies must compete on quality and flexibility, as well as cost.

Management accounting fails to help companies achieve world-class standards of quality, flexibility, and cost when it encourages them to manage costs. Accounting costs *per se* are not a source of competitive value. Only activities—work that consumes resources—have the power to add value. No activity adds customer value 100% of the time. Wasted effort, inevitable in human activity, detracts from the value all activities provide to customers. Thus, to achieve competitiveness, managers must monitor and remove wasted effort, i.e., nonvalue activities.[3] To do so, they must eliminate causes of delay, excess, and unevenness in all activities.

Cost accounts record results of nonvalue activity in categories such as scrap (a sign of excess), inventory (a sign of delay), and overtime for end-of-period production spurts (a sign of unevenness). But cost information about scrap, inventory, and overtime does not pinpoint activity that adds no value.

To achieve competitive operations that deliver value to customers, managers need information about sources of delay, excess, and unevenness that cause waste in operating activities. Eliminating delay, excess, and unevenness removes waste and makes activities more competitive. Let's look at a familiar example—managing setup costs.[4] This example will demonstrate the difference between managing operations with traditional cost information and managing operations with information about generators of waste.

The traditional way to manage setup cost is to produce in batch sizes that spread setup cost over as many units as possible, but not over so many units that the cost of storing output in excess of current consumption becomes prohibitive. The well-known EOQ paradigm, portrayed in Figure 2, calculates an

**Figure 2.   Managing Cost Versus Managing Activity, Part 1
Optimizing Cost with Long Setup Time**

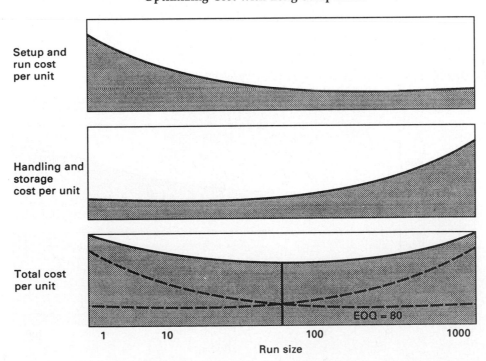

Source: Abegglen and Stalk, *Kaisha*, p. 95

"optimal" batch size that minimizes total unit cost of setup and storage. However, the paradigm takes for granted the activities (e.g., setting up and storing) whose costs we manage by optimizing batch sizes. This seems remarkable, because the resource-consuming activities that both setup cost and storage cost measure often add little value to customers. Setting-up entails delay and storing signifies excess.

As we know now, production people at Toyota over 30 years ago explored the implications of reducing waste in setup and storage activities. They began by working to reduce setup time. Reducing setup time causes EOQs to fall until, eventually, it is unnecessary ever to produce more than the amount needed for current consumption. (As shown in Figure 3, reducing setup time to a limit of zero produces an EOQ of one unit.) Producing to demand eliminates a need to store inventory, the activity that causes storage costs.

Thus, instead of managing setup cost, as we do with the EOQ paradigm, Toyota set out to curtail setup time—a source of delay that causes setup cost.

In the process, it reduced setup cost. But it did much more as well. By reducing setup time it reduced economic batch sizes and eliminated a need for inventory. Reducing batch sizes and eliminating inventory removed major causes of defective output and improved quality. Moreover, by reducing economic batch sizes, Toyota reduced turnover time and became more flexible. In short, the company improved quality, flexibility, and cost simultaneously by managing waste in activities, not by managing cost.

Improving all determinants of competitiveness simultaneously by managing setup time runs counter to what occurs when we optimize batch sizes by managing setup and storage *costs*. Indeed, the EOQ paradigm suggests a trade-off among determinants of competitiveness. To see this trade-off, consider what happens if the marketing organization asks the factory to be more flexible (i.e., change models frequently) or to improve quality, once total per unit setup and storage cost is minimized by producing at the optimal batch size. Changing models more often

**Figure 3. Managing Cost Versus Managing Activity, Part 2
Reducing Setup Time**

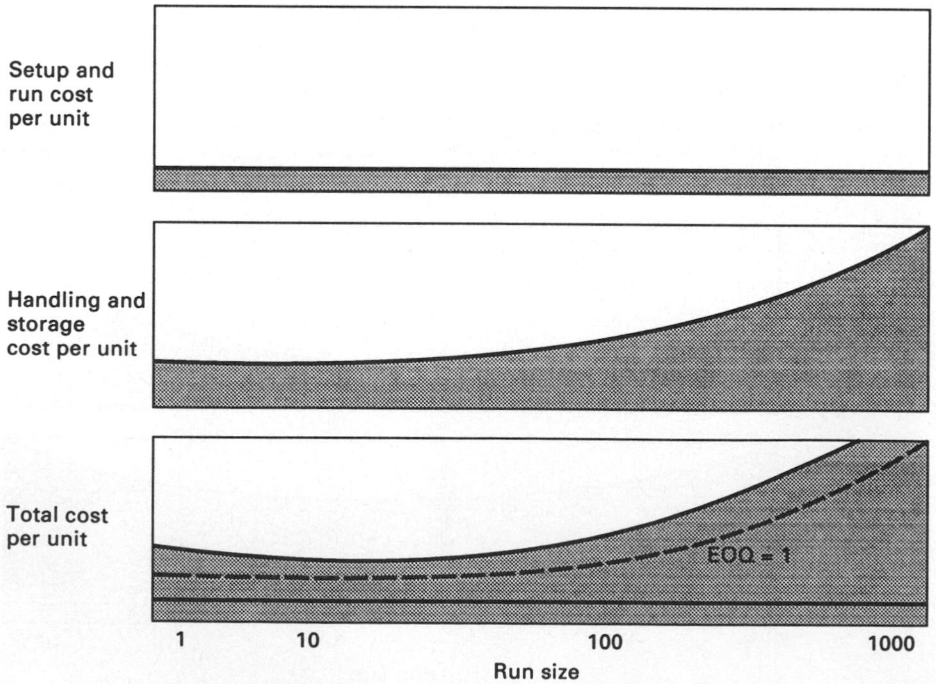

Source: Abegglen and Stalk, *Kaisha*, p. 95

means shortening run lengths, and shorter runs will raise total unit cost (see Figure 2). Thus, the factory can deliver increased flexibility only at greater cost. Likewise with quality. To improve quality when running large batches, one might stop a machine periodically and adjust its setting to eliminate out-of-tolerance pieces near the end of a run. But stopping a machine to reset it increases total unit cost. Thus, we can have higher quality, but only at greater cost.

Obviously, a company striving to achieve world-class standards of value should manage waste, not costs. The presence of nonvalue activity forces us to accept trade-offs among sources of competitiveness. By reducing waste in activities, companies can forestall the trade-offs among cost, quality, and flexibility that otherwise prevent them from becoming world-class competitors.

FOUR STEPS TO MANAGING OPERATING ACTIVITIES

There are four steps to managing waste in operating activities: chart the flow of activities throughout the organization; identify sources of customer value in every activity, and eliminate any activities that contribute no identifiable value to customers; identify causes of delay, excess, and unevenness in all activities; and track indicators of waste. The chart shows a partial list of causes for delay, excess, and unevenness in activities such as setting-up, storing, and moving. In the case of setup activity, these causes include poor training of setup personnel, conflicts in workers' assignments that interrupt setups, poorly designed machines, haphazard placement of setup tools, and more. Eliminating causes of delay, excess, and unevenness will reduce waste in activities. The presence of any nonvalue activity limits a company's ability to be as competitive as possible.

Identifying generators of delay, excess, and unevenness calls for the cooperation of everyone in an organization, from top to bottom. No activity should escape attention. Once you identify causes of waste, the entire arsenal of new management methods associated with just-in-time, total quality control, and employee involvement is required to remove them.[5]

The serious attention paid to employee suggestions in Japanese companies indicates the impor-

tance Japanese managers place on this third step. Indeed, identifying generators of delay, excess, and unevenness is a task without end, and is the pathway to that inscrutable goal of Japanese management known as continuous improvement.

Managing waste in activities involves developing measures that track a company's success at eliminating generators of delay, excess, and unevenness. Here managers need a few broad indicators of waste, such as elapsed time. The elapsed time it takes to do something—make an assembly, make a product, run a process—is an all-encompassing index of competitiveness. Less time to do something means greater flexibility; it also means higher quality and lower cost in most cases.

Other indicators of waste are distance parts move, space occupied by production activities, number of part numbers per product, and, of course, setup time. Indicators of waste help companies achieve the goal of continuous improvement by giving employees an incentive to continuously identify and remove generators of delay, excess, and unevenness. Continuously identifying and removing generators of delay, excess, and unevenness improves the indicators of a company's competitive position.

In contrast to traditional management accounting indicators of performance, the indicators of competitiveness referred to above—elapsed time, distance moved, space occupied, number of part numbers—are all *nonfinancial* measures of performance in operating activities. No financial numbers are used here to control operations. This conforms to the view of a leading authority on the new Japanese manufacturing techniques, Robert W. Hall, who says that "over time, financially oriented management should be weaned from thinking that detailed financial goals stimulate operating improvement." He argues that companies migrating toward JIT/TQC should abandon or deemphasize traditional factory measures such as budget variances, labor efficiency, and inventory turn. He goes on to say "the more confidence a management begins to have in JIT/TQC concepts, the fewer demands for this financial [information]. *It becomes obvious that any actions improving quality or reducing leadtimes will reduce operating costs* (emphasis added)."[6]

But managers should be aware that their success at eliminating nonvalue activity will not automatically reduce costs recorded in the financial accounts. Nonfinancial indicators of competitiveness such as elapsed time and space occupied can shrink without reducing book costs. The reason is clear. Expenditures do not stop automatically for resources made redundant by a campaign to reduce waste. Space or employees do not vanish just because a more competitive organization no longer needs them to get the job done. Consequently, not only must world-class operating managers develop systems to track waste reductions, they must have plans to use the excess resources productively or dispose of them.

Using nonfinancial indicators of performance to control operations does not eliminate financial cost information in businesses. Financial cost data is still compiled in budgets and other internal reports. But it is used for top-level planning, coordination, and allocation decisions—not to control operations.

World-class enterprises will not control operations by "rolling down" budgets into sub-units of an organization and then delegating to submanagers the task of achieving financial targets. Subordinate managers at the plant or department level will think in terms of nonfinancial indicators of competitiveness such as elapsed time, reject rates, and cycle time—not in terms of budgeted cost targets, net income, or return on investment. Having used budgets to plan and coordinate the allocation of resources among diverse sub-units of a complex organization, top managers may use imprest funds to control cash outlays subordinate managers are responsible for.[7]

COST-EFFECTIVE ACTIVITIES

A company may achieve world-class standards of competitiveness by removing generators of delay, excess, and unevenness from operating activities and still not be as profitable as it should. Resources consumed in an activity can supply competitive value to customers, yet do so at a cost that exceeds the value supplied. This condition may reflect a need for the company to change its mix of activities, the mix of products its activities create, or both. Two additional types of activity-based information—chargeouts and product costs—reveal how profitably a company consumes resources in its activities. Managers can use this information to assess the scale and scope of a company's operating activities.

Activity-based chargeout information

In principle, all activities in an organization supply output to meet customers' demands. The "customer" in this sense is not only the final consumer of product or service, but also the next user of an activity's output. The goal of every activity in a business, mirroring the global goal of the business itself, should be to provide value to the customer at a reasonable cost. If any activity's output costs more or provides less value than the output of an alternative activity, then the company is not as profitable as it could be. Managers need information to compare the competitiveness and cost of each activity's output with the next best alternative, whether that alternative be inside or outside the company.[8]

One type of information for this purpose is a "chargeout." Chargeouts resemble the price a company charges for output it sells to final consumers. However, a chargeout is the price an activity center charges for output it provides to its customers inside the company. A corporate accounting department, for instance, may prepare invoices for all customers the company sells to. A chargeout would be a price per invoice charged by the accounting department to any department that requests one. Chargeouts help allocate resources within a company in a manner similar to prices in competitive markets, although the comparison is not quite exact.

In one company that uses chargeouts extensively, chargeouts for each activity are expected not only to recoup costs, but also to compare favorably with alternative market prices.[9] Users of each center's services know these charges for the coming year and are free to purchase each activity from the company or, if all parties agree a superior alternative exists, buy elsewhere. Similarly, activity centers are free to sell their output outside the company if they wish. Decisions to source or sell activities outside the company must consider all facets of competitiveness —quality and flexibility, as well as cost. In the long run, this company will liquidate and reallocate resources from an activity center that fails to satisfy customers efficiently, whether they be inside or outside the company. To do otherwise would diminish the company's long-term profitability.

Chargeout information gives users of activities, not suppliers, the ultimate say in decisions about long-term allocation of resources to activities. This

Managing Operating Activities to Deliver Value

1. Chart activities over the entire chain of value

2. Identify sources of customer want-satisfaction and eliminate nonvalue activity

3. Reduce waste continuously in operating activities by eliminating generators of delay, excess and unevenness

ACTIVITY	SETTING-UP	STORING	MOVING
GENERATORS	Worker training	Setup time	Plant layout
	Work assignments	Unreliable vendor	Process design
	Machine design	Machine breakdown	
	Tool placement	LIFO policy	
	Dust, humidity		

4. Track indicators of waste

   Elapsed time, setup time, cycle time, distances moved, space occupied, and number of part numbers per product

OBJECTIVE: Achieve continuous improvement in competitiveness by reducing the indicators of waste in Step 4. Do so by continuously eliminating generators in Step 3.

gives activity managers incentive to keep their operations competitive by continuously identifying and cost-effectively eliminating generators of waste.

Chargeouts have a greater long-term impact on a company's competitiveness and profitability than do traditional methods for allocating activity center costs. Chargeouts to users, unlike cross-subsidized allocations based on company-wide denominators, do not reward intensive users of an activity and penalize light users. Compare the chargeout for invoices that a selling division pays, for instance, with a charge that is allocated over all divisions' gross revenues. In the latter case, a division selling to thousands of small-volume retail customers—the division that likely causes the consumption of most of the invoicing center's resources—is charged relatively much less for the services received than is a division with a small number of high-volume industrial customers. Chargeouts mitigate against the misuse of resources that usually is associated with such cross-subsidized allocations.

Chargeout information provides an especially powerful tool for managing corporate overhead activities, a source of the fastest growing and least controlled costs in most companies during the 1980s. Its power lies in focusing managers' attention on the resource-consuming activities that ultimately cause costs, rather than on the recorded costs themselves. Traditional flexible budget information assigns responsibility for recorded overhead costs to activity centers that supply overhead services. Chargeout information puts responsibility for the scale of overhead activities on the shoulders of users who demand activities to provide value to final consumers. Chargeout information to price activities, together with operating information about causes of waste, help companies sustain profitability while giving competitive value to customers.

Activity-based product cost information

A company may achieve world-class standards of competitiveness in its operating activities and all its activities may be as cost-effective as any in the market, yet the mix of products or services it sells may not use the company's activities as profitably as possible. This occurs when the company uses traditional product cost accounting information to evaluate the costs and profit margins of its various products or services.

Traditional accounting systems efficiently and effectively cost products for one purpose and that is to value inventories for financial reporting. Traditional cost accounts do not distort total costs, inventory costs, or "bottom-line" net income figures. However, managers who use cost accounting information to judge an individual product's costs can make serious marketing errors.[10] This happens because the overaggregated averages that cost accounting systems use to distribute indirect costs to products *systematically* distort the costs of individual products.[11] The cause of this distortion is the practice of distributing overhead costs to products according to weights that vary directly with volume of output, such as direct labor hours, material dollars or machine hours. A product containing more direct labor hours (or material dollars or machine hours, etc.) than another product is assumed to incur proportionately more indirect cost. Volume-related weights reliably distribute overhead costs to products only if overhead varies directly with volume of output.

In recent decades, however, the chief cause for growth of overhead has been increased diversity, or scope, of output, not increased volume, or scale, of output. Thus, traditional cost accounting systems tend to overcost high volume products—not the ones that cause most growth in overhead—and they undercost the low volume products that are chiefly responsible for most overhead growth. When used to guide marketing strategies, this distorted cost information encourages managers to proliferate low-volume product lines. The result in many cases is declining profit margins and perceived difficulty competing with focused (usually foreign) competitors.

A business with diverse product lines and high indirect costs cannot abide the distortions in product cost and margin data that traditional product costing systems create. Fortunately, a solution is at hand. Known as activity-based costing systems, product costing systems are beginning to appear that do not distort by distributing indirect costs with overaggregated volume-sensitive averages.[12] In fact, they turn traditional product costing on its head. Traditional product costing assumes that products cause indirect costs by consuming the driver (e.g., direct labor hours) that is used to distribute indirect costs to products.

Activity-based costing, in contrast, assumes that resource-consuming activities cause costs; products incur costs by the activities they require for design, engineering, manufacture, sale, delivery, and service. Activity-based costing traces costs to products through activities—essentially the activi-

ties that operating managers control with nonfinancial indicators of waste. By linking activities to financial costs, activity-based product cost information complements, therefore, the nonfinancial information operating managers use to achieve competitiveness in operating activities.

The importance of having activity-based cost information to assess the profit consequences of product-mix decisions is highlighted in Figure 4. This figure is based on a case study of an actual manufacturing company whose experience is typical of American businesses generally.[13] Disappointed by chronically declining profits and by difficulty competing with new Japanese competitors in the 1970s, the company concluded that its problems were caused in large part by making product mix decisions with distorted product cost information. The company always had relied on a traditional product costing system that distributed indirect costs to products with direct labor hours. In the early 1980s, it redesigned its product costing system along activity-based lines.

The two curves in Figure 4 show strikingly different views of its products' profits. Traditional cost information shows that all products make profit, some more and some less. Using this information over the years, the company's management had always pruned away products that lost money. The activity-based cost information reveals, however, that a very high percentage of the company's products actually generate losses in the long-run. Most surprising, and not evident in Figure 4, is the

Figure 4. Product Profit/Volume Profile

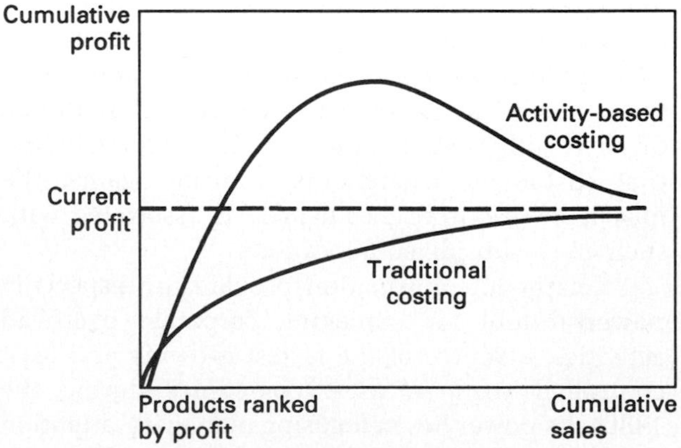

Source: Robin Cooper, *Schrader Bellows*

identity of products that generate profits and losses according to the two product costing systems. In general, those products identified as winners by the traditional product costing system were found to be losers by the activity-based system and vice versa. The company's disappointing performance in the 1970s, in the face of new Japanese competition, resulted in no small way because distorted cost information caused management to proliferate its line with unprofitable products.[14]

MANAGE ACTIVITIES, NOT COSTS

Today's global economy calls for new management accounting information. Two types of activity-based management accounting information I have described enable a business to achieve profitability by creating competitive value for its customers that exceeds the cost of creating that value.[15] To be competitive, businesses need information that will make it possible for managers to identify and to eliminate generators of nonvalue activity. To be profitable, they need additional information to manage activity costs.

Traditional management accounting systems to control operations and to cost products do not serve managers well in today's competitive environment. Companies who control operations with costs and variances reported in flexible budgets will see their competitiveness and their profits shrink. Focusing operational control on financial costs does not assure competitiveness in the global economy. Today it is also necessary to achieve high quality and flexibility. Managers can achieve low cost, high quality, and flexibility simultaneously by focusing operational control on generators of nonvalue activity. Businesses become competitive and efficient by eliminating waste in operating activities, not by managing recorded costs.

World-class competitors will not necessarily see profits rise unless they also design activity-based chargeout and product cost systems. Activity-based costs eliminate distortions and cross-subsidies caused by traditional cost allocations. Activity-based cost information provides a clear view of how the mix of a company's diverse products, services, and activities contribute in the long run to the bottom line. Combined together, nonfinancial information to control operating activities and activity-based cost information can provide the management information that businesses need in today's competitive environment. Activity-based management accounting information is the key to continuous improvement of profitability, a journey without end.

1 H. Thomas Johnson and Robert S. Kaplan, "The Rise and Fall of Management Accounting," MANAGEMENT ACCOUNTING, January 1987, pp. 22–30.

2 Activity-based information relates conceptually to the markets and hierarchies theory of Oliver Williamson and the value-chain concept of Michael Porter. Although not an influence on ideas in this paper, writings on management accounting by Gordon Shillinglaw and George Staubus also refer to "activity cost" information. Of the two, Shillinglaw in *Managerial Cost Accounting*, Richard D. Irwin, Inc., 1982, expresses ideas closer to those articulated in this article than does Staubus in *Activity Costing and Input-Output Accounting*, Richard D. Irwin, Inc., 1971.

3 R.J. Schonberger, *Japanese Manufacturing Techniques: Nine Hidden Lessons in Simplicity*. The Free Press, 1982, pp. 44–45. The origins of the nonvalue activity concept are hazy. General Electric Co. was an early advocate of the concept and contributed much to the articulation of nonvalue activity ideas in *CAM-I Cost Management Systems Conceptual Design Document, Phase I*, Computer Aided Manufacturing-International, Inc., Arlington, Tex., 1987.

4 The setup example that follows is based on Richard J. Schonberger, *Japanese Manufacturing Techniques*, pp. 18–24, and James C. Abegglen and George Stalk, Jr., *Kaisha, The Japanese Corporation*, Basic Books, Inc., New York, 1985 pp. 93–96.

5 For a concise up-to-date summary of these techniques see Ernest C. Huge (with Alan D. Anderson), *The Spirit of Manufacturing Excellence: An Executive's Guide to the New Mind Set*, Dow-Jones, Irwin/APICS, 1988.

6 Robert W. Hall, "Measuring Progress: Management Essential," *Target*, Summer 1987, pp. 1–10. An excellent discussion of nonfinancial indicators of waste that is germane to JIT operations is in Richard J. Schonberger, *World Class Manufacturing Casebook: Implementing JIT and TQC*, The Free Press, 1987, pp. xi–xxiii.

7 The budgeting procedures advocated here resemble those used by E.I. duPont de Nemours Powder Company from about 1903 to 1915. See H. Thomas Johnson and Robert S. Kaplan, *Relevance Lost: The Rise and Fall of Management Accounting*, Harvard Business School Press, 1987, ch 4.

8 H. Thomas Johnson, "Organizational Design versus Strategic Information Procedures for Managing Corporate Overhead Cost: Weyerhaeuser Company, 1972–1986," in William J. Bruns and Robert S. Kaplan, eds., *Accounting and Management: Field Study Perspectives*, Boston: Harvard Business School Press, 1987, pp. 49–72.

Also see Brandt Allen, "Make Information Services Pay Its Way," *Harvard Business Review*, January-February 1987, pp. 57–63.

9 H. Thomas Johnson and Dennis A. Loewe, "How Weyerhaeuser Manages Corporate Overhead Costs," MANAGEMENT ACCOUNTING, August 1987, pp. 20–26.

10 For more on the distinction between cost accounting and cost management information see H. Thomas Johnson. "The Decline of Cost Management: A Reinterpretation of 20th Century Cost Accounting History," *Journal of Cost Management*, Spring 1987, pp. 5–12.

11 Robin Cooper and Robert S. Kaplan, *Accounting and Management*, pp. 204–228. A condensed version of this chapter appeared in MANAGEMENT ACCOUNTING, April 1988, pp. 20–27.

12 Robin Cooper, "The Two-Stage Procedure in Cost Accounting," *Journal of Cost Management*, Part 1, Summer 1987, pp. 43–51 and Part II, Fall 1987, pp. 39–45; R. Cooper and R.S. Kaplan, "How Cost Accounting Systematically Distorts," H. Thomas Johnson and Robert S. Kaplan, "The Importance of Long-term Product Costs," *The McKinsey Quarterly*, Autumn 1987, pp. 36–48.

13 Robin Cooper, *Schrader Bellows: A Strategic Cost Analysis*, Harvard Business School, Case Series 9-186-272, 1986.

14 For additional insights, see Peter Drucker, "Managing for Business Effectiveness," *Harvard Business Review*, May-June 1963, pp. 59–62; also, Abegglen and Stalk, *Kaisha*, ch 4.

15 Michael E. Porter, *Competitive Advantage: Creating and Sustaining Superior Performance*, The Free Press, New York, 1985, p. 3.

5

ACTIVITY-BASED COST SYSTEMS FOR MANUFACTURING EXPENSES

Managers in today's competitive environment need accurate information on how decisions on product mix, product design, and process technology affect their organization's profitability. This information emerges from a strategic profitability model that links the revenues created by the sale of individual products to the expenses of resources consumed to design, produce, and sell these products. Traditionally, companies' cost systems were used to provide the linkage between revenues earned and the expenses of producing products. But these cost systems have failed to keep up with the major changes in companies' production processes and product mix. The activity-based cost systems, to be discussed in this and the subsequent two chapters, have emerged in recent years to provide managers with more accurate cost information about operations for the organization's strategic profitability model. The activity-based cost systems reflect better the underlying economics of production and thereby provide better guidance to managers for decisions on the following:

Pricing
Managing customer relationships
Product mix
Product design
Process improvement activities
Technology acquisition.

LIMITATIONS OF TRADITIONAL COST SYSTEMS

Traditional systems can measure accurately the resources that are consumed in proportion to the number of units produced of individual products. Such resources include direct labor, materials, machine time, and energy. But many organizational resources exist for activities and transactions that are unrelated to the physical volume of units produced.[1] Consequently, traditional cost systems do a poor job of attributing the

---

[1]The high percentage of manufacturing expenses required to handle transactions is described in the Miller and Vollmann article, "The Hidden Factory," presented in this chapter.

expenses of these support resources to the production and sale of individual products. The expenses are typically allocated to products using unit-based measures, such as direct labor, materials purchases, processing time, or units produced. The product costs produced by such allocations are distorted because products do not consume most support resources in proportion to their production volumes.

The distortions from unit-based product cost systems are most severe in organizations producing a diverse product mix. Products that differ in volume, complexity, and age (mature versus newly introduced products) consume support resources in significantly different amounts. As product diversity increases, the quantities of resources required for handling transactional and support activities rise, thereby increasing the distortion of reported product costs from traditional systems. This explains why companies that were early adopters of activity-based systems typically manufactured diverse products and had high overhead expenses.

The inability of unit-based systems to report accurate product costs can be illustrated using a simple example.

> Consider two hypothetical plants turning out a simple product, ballpoint pens. The factories are the same size and have the same capital equipment. Every year Plant I makes 1 million units of only one product, blue pens. Plant II, a full-line producer, also produces blue pens, but only 100,000 per year. Plant II also produces a variety of similar products: 80,000 black pens, 30,000 red pens, 5,000 green pens, 500 lavender pens, and so on. In a typical year, Plant II produces up to 1,000 product variations with volumes ranging between 100 and 100,000 units. Its aggregate annual output equals the 1 million pens of Plant I.

Despite the similarities in the products produced in the two plants and in their annual total output, a visitor walking through the two plants would notice dramatic differences. With its higher diversity and complexity of operations, Plant II requires a much larger support structure: more people to schedule machines; perform setups; inspect items; purchase, receive, and handle materials; assemble, expedite, and ship orders; rework defective items; design and implement engineering change orders; negotiate with vendors; schedule materials and parts receipts; update and program the much larger computer-based information system; and handle the large number of individual customer requests. Plant II would also operate with considerably higher levels of idle time, overtime, inventory, rework, and scrap.

Plant II's extensive factory support resources and production complexities generate product cost distortions in traditional systems. Because the number of units produced and sold by the two plants is identical, both plants have roughly the same amount of direct labor hours, machine hours, and material purchases. Therefore, the much higher operating expenses in Plant II cannot be explained by the amount of direct labor worked, the number of machine hours operated, or the amount of material purchased even though all traditional cost accounting systems use such *unit-level drivers* to allocate indirect support expenses to products.

Whether Plant II uses direct labor hours, machine hours, material purchases, or any combination of these to assign indirect expenses to products, its cost system will allocate to blue pens, which represent 10% of the plant's output, about 10% of the factory expenses. Similarly, lavender pens, which represent .05% of Plant II's output, will receive an allocation of about .05% of the factory's expenses. In fact, if the standard output per unit of direct labor hours, machine hours, and materials quantities are the same for blue pens as for lavender pens, the two types of pens will have identical reported costs—even though lavender pens, which are ordered, fabricated, packaged, and shipped in much lower volumes and require special design and handling resources, consume far more overhead per unit.

Intuitively, the reported product costs are inaccurate. It must cost more to produce one lavender pen than one blue pen given the difference in production volumes and special handling between the two products. The higher operating expenses in Plant II, caused by producing a high variety of customized low-volume products, can only be explained by introducing an activity-based cost system that expands the types of second-stage assignment bases used for assigning resource expenses to products.

THE STRUCTURE OF ACTIVITY-BASED COST SYSTEMS

Activity-based cost (ABC) systems start by assuming that support and indirect resources provide capabilities for performing activities, not that they generate costs to be allocated. The first stage of ABC systems assigns the expenses of support resources to the activities performed by these resources. ABC systems, therefore, start from the assumption that activities cause costs. For example, the expenses of performing engineering change notices might be traced to the activity Changing Product Specifications in the first stage of the two-stage procedure.

The second assumption of ABC systems is that products (and customers) create the demands for activities. Therefore, in the second stage of the two-stage ABC process, activity costs are assigned to products based on individual products' consumption or demand for each activity. For example, the expenses of the activity Changing Product Specifications might be assigned to individual products with the second-stage driver, Number of Engineering Change Notices. Products requiring more engineering changes would have more engineering expenses assigned to them than mature products that required no changes in their product or process characteristics.

Figure 5.1 shows the flow of overhead costs to products in a traditional two-stage

Figure 5.1.   Two-Stage Allocation Process: Traditional Cost System

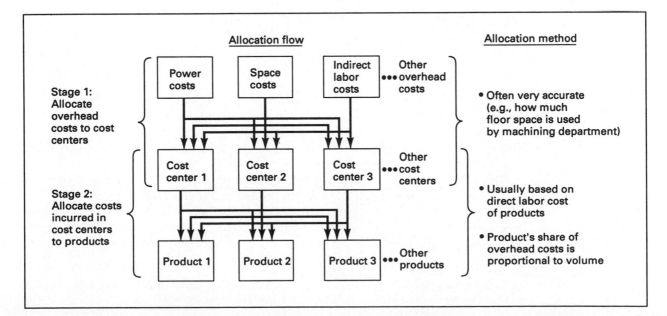

Figure 5.2.   Two-Stage Assignment Process: Activity-Based Cost System

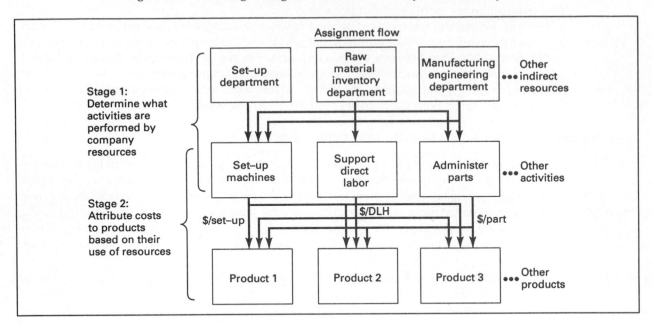

allocation system. In the first stage, overhead costs are assigned to cost centers, and then the accumulated costs in cost centers are allocated to products using unit-based drivers (such as direct labor or machine hours). Figure 5.2 shows the structure of an activity-based system in which the expenses of support departments are assigned to the activities performed (setting up machines, supporting direct labor, and administering parts). The expenses of each activity are then assigned to products based on the products' demand for the activities (e.g., number of setups, direct labor hours, and number of parts in the product). Thus, even though ABC systems use a two-stage procedure, just like traditional cost systems, both the nature of cost centers (or, more accurately, activity centers) used to accumulate operating expenses in the first stage and the method of assigning expenses from cost centers to products are quite different in activity-based cost systems.

Case writing and field research have revealed that activity-based cost systems need two new sets of activities—batch and product-sustaining—to explain the demands that individual products make on organizational resources.[2] The batch and product-sustaining activities supplement the traditional unit-level activities of consuming direct labor, materials, and machine time.

Batch-related activities, such as setting up a machine to produce a different product, are performed each time a batch of goods is processed. When a machine is changed from one product to another, setup resources are consumed. As more batches are produced, more setup resources are consumed. But the demands for the setup resources are independent of the number of units produced after completing the setup.

---

[2]See Robin Cooper, "Cost Classifications in Unit-Based and Activity-Based Manufacturing Cost Systems," *Journal of Cost Management for the Manufacturing Industry* (Fall 1990), pp. 4–14.

Processing purchase orders provides another example of a batch-driven activity. Purchasing resources are consumed each time a purchase order is prepared and issued, but the resources consumed are independent of the number of units ordered by the purchase order. Thus, the materials cost of items in the purchase order are unit-driven costs, but the cost of the purchase order itself is batch driven. Resources devoted to production scheduling, first-item inspection, and materials movement are also batch driven, varying with how many production runs are initiated in the shop but independent of how many units are produced in each run.

Product-sustaining activities are performed to enable individual products to be produced and sold. The expenses of these activities can be traced to the individual products, but the resources consumed by the activities are independent of how many units or batches of the product are produced. Examples of resources used for product-sustaining activities include the information system and engineering resources devoted to maintaining an accurate bill-of-materials and routing for each product. Other examples are the resources to prepare and implement engineering change notices (ECNs), to design process and test routines for individual products, to expedite orders, and to perform product enhancements. These activities are done more often or with greater intensity as the number of products in the plant increases. Thus, organizations with numerous products, such as Plant II, need more product-sustaining resources than do organizations that produce only a few products, like Plant I.

Activity-based systems attribute resource expenses to products based on activities triggered by the number of batches (or production runs) of products and based on the activities required to support a large and diverse product line. The activity-based approach attributes many more resources to a product for which extensive setups, ECNs, and inspections are performed. Once a richer array of drivers of resource consumption are recognized, many more of an organization's resources can be assigned directly to individual products.

The three classes of drivers can be portrayed hierarchically (see Figure 5.3). The hierarchical diagram symbolizes that expenses that vary at the batch level are fixed (or independent) with respect to how many units are made in the batch. Similarly product-sustaining expenses increase with the number of products being produced, but the expenses are independent of (i.e., do not vary with) the number of production batches or units produced of individual products.

Facility-Sustaining Expenses

One additional category of factory resources shown in Figure 5.3, *facility-sustaining expenses*, occurs in production facilities. Many facility-sustaining activities are administrative, such as managing the plant and personnel and accounting for the shop floor. Other examples include the taxes, housekeeping, landscaping, maintenance, security, and lighting for the factory building. Facility-sustaining activities are necessary to provide a factory that can produce products, but the extent of these activities is unrelated to the volume and mix of individual products. The activities are common or joint to many different products, and their costs must be considered common costs to all the products made in the facility.

The expenses of any plant-level resources caused by the volume or variety of production in the plant are assigned directly to those product-specific activities. The remaining expenses are assigned to the facility-sustaining category and not to individual products or product lines. To compute the operating profitability of the factory, we would then sum the operating margins from all product lines and subtract the facility-sustaining expenses.

Figure 5.3.   Measuring Factors Expenses: ABC Hierarchical Model

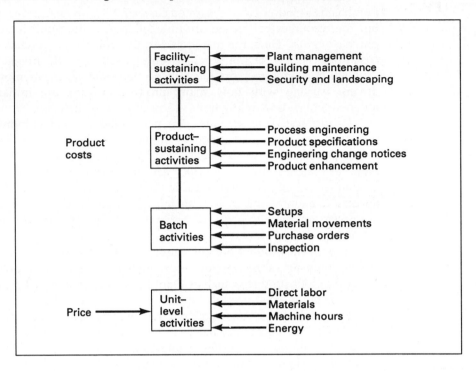

The expenses of excess capacity (not required for seasonal or peak demands) should also be assigned at the facility level so as not to allocate this expense misleadingly to the products actually being produced during the period.[3] When excess capacity becomes used as production expands in the factory, the expenses that had been assigned in the facility-sustaining category would become reassigned at the unit (or batch) level.

The four-category hierarchy of factory activities allows us to describe the process of developing activity-based cost systems for factory expenses.

1. Identify the major activities performed in the factory.
2. Classify the activities into unit, batch, product-sustaining, and facility-sustaining categories.
3. Attribute, to individual products, the expenses of the unit, batch, and product-sustaining activities using bases that reflect the underlying behavior of the products' demands for these activities.

Facility-sustaining expenses are, ideally, treated as an expense of operating the facility for the period and not allocated to products. Frequently, however, management desires to allocate all factory expenses to products. In this case, facility-sustaining expenses are allocated, in some arbitrary manner, to individual products.

---

[3]If the facility produces multiple product lines and capacity is not fungible across the different lines, excess capacity resources can be assigned more accurately to the product-line level, not the aggregate facility level.

IMPLICATIONS OF THE HIERARCHICAL ACTIVITY-BASED COST MODEL

If we return to the example of the pen factories, we can see how the hierarchy of activities can be used to differentiate between the two plants. Focused factories, like Plant I, where only blue pens are manufactured, require very few batch and product-sustaining activities. Batches are large (the production process may even be continuous) so that only a few batches may be required to produced 1 million pens. Since only a few batch activities are performed, the expenses of performing batch activities are minimal. Product-sustaining expenses are similarly small since only one product is manufactured in the plant.

In Plant II, where various products are produced, batch-level activities are more numerous. Every time a new color is produced, machines have to be set up, material moved to the machines, and first and last parts inspected. Some of the batches contain only a few units, while other batches contain large numbers of units. With these high levels of batch-size diversity, accurate product costs can only be reported by a cost system that assigns batch-level expenses to the batches and not to the units in the batches.

The product-sustaining activities also cause product cost distortions in Plant II. As the number of different products increases, so does the number of product-sustaining activities required. As product-sustaining expenses become a higher fraction of total factory expenses, only activity-based systems can attribute these expenses accurately to individual products.

The Fallacy of Unit Product Costs

Early adopters of activity-based cost systems divided the total expenses applied to a product, including its batch and product-sustaining expenses, by the product's annual production volume to arrive at a unit-product cost figure. In effect, this procedure *allocated* the batch and product-sustaining expenses to individual units. The allocation procedure can be viewed as drawing arrows downward on the vertical links shown in Figure 5.3. Such a procedure, however, to arrive at a *unit product cost,* can be misleading by implying that these expenses are in any sense causally related or directly proportional to the number of units produced. We prefer to draw arrows in the northerly direction, aggregating unit and batch-level expenses into total product expenses, where no arbitrary allocations are required.

The hierarchical activity-based analysis reveals that many expenses assigned to the product do *not* vary with how many units of the product are produced. These expenses are caused by the number of production runs, the length of setups required to produce the product, and how many materials moves were made. Other expenses are incurred just to have the ability to produce the products. These expenses will not increase in the short run if production volume increases, nor will they decrease if volume contracts. Because these expenses do not expand or contract with unit production volumes, they have traditionally been called fixed expenses. Many observers advocate ignoring these fixed expenses when making decisions about products and processes.

Experience and the example of the two pen factories, however, indicate that these expenses are not fixed at all. When analyzing whether a given expense category is fixed or variable, we recommend using the Rule of One. If only one person (or one machine) exists in a department, it can be considered a fixed expense. But when more than one unit of a resource exists in a department, it must be a variable resource. Something is creating a demand for the output from that department, and more than one unit of resource is required to satisfy that demand. Interviewing procedures are used to learn what creates demands from each department so that the expenses of the department can be linked to the factors creating those demands.

This procedure identifies a much broader set of expenses as varying with decisions made about products. But driving all these product-related expenses to the unit level, to compute a unit product cost, gives a misleading impression about the variability of the cost structure of the product. A further distortion occurs if facility-sustaining costs are also allocated to products, and divided by production volumes, to obtain fully allocated unit product costs. An alternative and more accurate perspective can be obtained by aggregating all product expenses—unit, batch, and product-sustaining—into a total product expense figure. The total product expense includes all the expenses that can be causally attributed to the individual product and does not require nor imply that all expenses are variable with the number of units produced.

The hierarchical activity-based product expense model can be used to approximate the changes in expenses as a consequence of particular decisions. If a proposed decision will reduce the number of batch-level activities required or will lower the cost of performing batch-level activities (such as by reducing setup times), the decision maker can estimate the future reduction in demands for resources formerly used to perform these activities. If a proposed decision will increase the number of products in the plant, the increased number of product-sustaining activities can be estimated and linked to subsequent demands for increased resource spending.

Not all activity-based systems rely on all four types of bases. Some only rely on two, unit level plus either batch or product sustaining. Few ABC systems separate facility-sustaining expenses into a separate category and keep these expenses segregated from product expenses. Several possible reasons may help to explain a company's omission of either the batch, product-sustaining, or facility-sustaining bases.

1. The designers may have failed to understand that all these kinds of bases existed. In at least one of the firms using only unit and batch-level bases, the costs associated with product-sustaining activities were significant.

2. In some production processes, two of the categories of activities became equivalent. For example, when products are produced in batches of size one, unit and batch-level activities are synonymous.

3. Third, the benefits associated with separately reporting one of the categories may have been small. This typically occurs when either the cost of that category of activity is relatively small or the products are homogeneous.

4. Even though cost system designers may be aware of all types of bases, they may choose, for reasons of simplicity and ease of understanding, to use only two of them.

Systems containing only two types of drivers can be viewed as partial activity-based cost systems. Cost systems can thus be viewed as a continuum starting with unit-based systems that have only one type of driver and ending with full activity-based cost systems that explicitly recognize three types of cost drivers for products, plus facility-sustaining expenses.

In summary, the ABC analysis treats spending on all factory resources as variable at some level (including the level of opening and operating the factory and maintaining excess capacity for product lines and the facility). As much as possible, factory expenses are attributed to activities required for individual products (either unit, batch, or product sustaining). But resources that are not consumed by activities performed for individual products need not be allocated to product activities. The facility-sustaining expenses provide a base level of operating capacity to permit the factory to remain open each year and to support all the production occurring within the factory walls.

SPENDING VERSUS CONSUMPTION

Activity-based systems differ from their unit-based counterparts because they model consumption, not spending. An activity-based model is not just another and more complex cost accounting system. It is, in reality, a model of organizational resource consumption. For some resources—such as materials and energy—resource consumption and spending on that resource are closely aligned. The energy to operate a production machine is consumed as the machine processes parts. As more parts are processed by the machine, more energy is consumed, and spending on energy also increases to reflect the higher energy consumption. Labor paid on a piece-work basis also has a close correspondence between resource use (labor working on a part) and resource spending (paying the worker for producing the part). The expense of purchasing materials is a third example in which using the resource (consuming stocks of raw materials) is soon followed by spending on the resource (purchasing additional materials to replenish the inventory or to allow the next items to be produced).[4] This close link between resource consumption and resource spending is why energy, piece-work labor, and direct materials are classified, both by activity-based and traditional systems, as variable costs—costs that vary with the amount of product produced.

Most traditional cost systems treat direct labor paid hourly or weekly as a variable cost. But workers paid hourly or weekly are not necessarily a variable expense if they will remain on the payroll in the short run whether or not they are producing products. Thus, the amount of time they spend working on a product does not affect the amount of money they will be paid that week or that month.

Extending beyond hourly or weekly paid workers are the expenses of indirect and support workers—people who schedule production, write purchase orders, inspect products and machines, set up machines, perform engineering change orders, move materials, or manage materials receipts, movement, and storage. Other indirect production costs include the expenses of engineers and managers who design products, manage employees, and perform a variety of support functions. The demands for these indirect, support resources arise, as with energy and materials, from decisions on production volumes and mix. But unlike energy and materials, the spending on these resources does not vary in the short run with changes in production volume and mix.

When production activity drops, indirect resources tend to remain in place for weeks or months even though less work is around for them to do. When production activity expands, the employees find ways, in the short run, to accommodate the increased demands on them by using up previously excess capacity or by working harder and longer. Alternatively, employees defer some activities viewed to be less urgent enabling increased output without short-term increases in spending. Even when the resource represents physical, not human, capital, machines can be run faster or maintenance postponed so that more output can be produced without acquiring additional physical capacity. Over time, however, people and machines become

---

[4]Inventory causes a lag between spending and consumption of raw material.

overloaded, and the quality and quantity of the service they perform drops. Continuing to postpone the deferred activities becomes difficult and expensive. For example, by reducing maintenance levels on inspection equipment, operators will have time to perform more inspections. Eventually, however, the inspection equipment will drift out of alignment and the quality of inspections will suffer.

To reduce the overload on people and equipment and to allow the deferred activities to be performed, pressure builds to acquire additional resources: people and equipment. At that time, the *spending* on the resource changes. It changes because management takes actions that allow spending to increase. For example, managers authorize more inspectors to be hired or more machines to be purchased. The higher demands for inspectors and other indirect resources were caused by the acceptance and processing of additional orders sometime in the past. But there was a lag between the increased consumption of the indirect resources and the subsequent increase in spending on the resources.

This lag between resource consumption and resource spending helps to explain a distinction already made between traditional and activity-based systems. Traditional cost systems attempt to identify expenses, like energy, materials, and perhaps direct labor, that vary in the short run with product volumes and mix. Those expenses are assigned directly to products. The remaining expenses are either allocated arbitrarily to products based on one or more direct measures (such as direct labor time, materials expense, or machine hours) or are ignored entirely for decision making about the products.

The activity-based approach is not concerned with allocating costs to products and does not attempt to measure or predict short-term spending trends. It does attempt to measure the total organizational resources required to produce a product. Activity-based systems recognize that, over periods of time measured in months or years, changes in consumption of resources are eventually followed by corresponding changes in the spending on the resources. To predict future spending trends, activity-based systems estimate the *quantities* of resources consumed by organizational activities. The resources consumed can be priced (or costed) by a variety of methods. Early adopters of activity-based systems have used prices derived from the company's historical cost accounting system. In this way, the sum of the product costs computed by their new activity-based system reconcile with the costs computed under their previous, traditional system. But to predict future spending and operating expenses, managers could also use forecasts of future prices or even resource opportunity costs to price out resource consumption. Also, activity-based systems, as models of resource consumption, assume that resources can be acquired in very small increments. In effect, the product costs reported by activity-based systems are linear approximations to what may, on closer examination, prove to be a sequence of stepped cost functions.

THE BENEFITS OF ACTIVITY-BASED COSTING

Managers implement activity-based cost systems when they believe that the costs of the additional measurements required are more than offset by the benefits provided by more accurate product costs and improved insights into the economics of production. Managers associate three major classes of benefits with activity-based costing. These benefits are improved decision making due to more informative product cost information, improved insights into managing the activities that lead to overhead, and easier access to relevant costs for a wider range of decisions. The conditions that favor activity-based cost systems are those that make it likely for significant errors to occur in traditional product costing systems and for the consequences of such errors to be high. Activity-based cost systems are likely to report significantly more accurate product costs when

> The organization uses large amounts of indirect resources in its production processes; and
>
> The organization has significant diversity in products, production processes, and customers.

The consequences from decision making with inaccurate product costs are highest when the company faces significant competition, especially from more focused competitors.

Benefit 1: Improved Decisions

Managers at many of the companies that have adopted activity-based costing believe that the more accurate product costs reported by activity-based cost systems reduce the possibility of managers making poor decisions based on available cost information. Poor decisions occur because, as field research has shown, managers frequently underestimate the level of distortion in reported unit-based costs. Managers may know before the introduction of an activity-based system that the reported costs of the low-volume products are understated, but they often do not know to what degree. Managers' failure to understand the degree of distortion can cause them to undercompensate for the distortion introduced by their unit-based systems.

More accurate product costs are particularly important for firms that face intense competitive pressures. As competition increases, a competitor will be more likely to exploit poor pricing and product-mix decisions, or to take advantage of a company using inefficient manufacturing facilities and poor product designs. Activity-based cost systems tend to emerge in firms that are suddenly facing increased competition.

Benefit 2: Continuous Improvement Activities to Reduce Overhead Costs

Many organizations today are attempting to reduce the cost of offering diverse, customized product lines, such as those manufactured in Plant II. The hierarchical activity-based model reveals the large amount of added expenses required to produce a diverse product line in a traditional manufacturing facility. Plant II has a high percentage of its operating expenses in the batch and product-sustaining categories, whereas a focused facility, like Plant I, has the bulk of its operating expenses in the unit-level category. A simplistic approach would recommend that Plant II cut overhead costs by reducing the variety of products it offers or the number of new product introductions. While such a practice might yield some short-run benefits, it entails layoffs of existing personnel to realize the operating savings and may jeopardize the company's competitive position by locking it into mature, low-growth product lines.

An alternative and frequently preferable approach could be to accept the wisdom of the customer-driven market strategy of Plant II and to accommodate this strategy by implementing operating improvements that reduce the costs of designing and producing high-variety, low-volume products. In fact, much of the emphasis in the past decade on *kaizen* or continuous improvement activities—eliminating defects and increasing first-pass yields, reducing setup times, improving factory layouts and materials flows, designing products with fewer and more common parts, and introducing advanced information technology that links design to manufacturing (computer-aided engineering [CAE] and computer-added design [CAD]) and for flexible manufacturing (flexible manufacturing systems [FMS] and computer-integrated manufacturing [CIM])—can be seen as actions to reduce or even eliminate the demands for batch-level and product-sustaining activities by individual products.

Traditional cost systems have encouraged companies to lower costs by reducing the purchase price of materials, making direct labor more efficient and running machines faster. The unit-based systems averaged the cost of batch and product-sustaining activities over many, if not all, products. Thus, engineers attempted to lower the reported cost of individual products by reducing their consumption of the unit-level drivers (materials, labor, and machine times) used to assign overhead costs to the products. The activity-based system shows that significant expense reduction can be achieved by reducing setup costs, making production scheduling and materials handling more efficient, and reducing the number of parts required to meet final customer product demands. Further, the justification to adopt continuous improvement activities and to introduce advanced information and manufacturing technologies should include the reduced expenses of performing the batch and product-sustaining activities for innovative products that meet individual customer needs.

Activity-based information supports performance-improving activities in several ways. First, it identifies the amount of expenses currently being spent on activities whose performance can be substantially improved. Many of the benefits from introducing FMS and CIM facilities become clearly identified. Second, even organizations that already are involved in quality improvement and just-in-time activities need a financial model to help set priorities so that the organization can focus on the activities that have the largest opportunities for improvement. And finally, organizations that periodically reestimate their activity-based model can learn whether operating improvements have, in fact, been translated into improved profitability through higher revenues and reduced resource spending. Improving time to market, on-time delivery, first-pass yields, and just-in-time production are laudable tactical objectives. But only a comprehensive and integrated financial system can indicate whether such operating improvements have been translated into increased profitability.

Benefit 3: Ease of Determining Relevant Costs   The product cost data from companies' cost systems are frequently analyzed in greater depth to obtain information relevant for a particular decision. The desired cost adjustments typically require an expensive special study. The degree of adjustment required for a given decision depends on the scope of that decision and the design of the firm's cost system. The scope of the decision is important because it defines the magnitude of the risk associated with relying on incorrect cost information. The design of the cost system is important because it defines the accuracy of reported product costs and their ease of modification. Activity-based systems reduce the need to perform special studies by both increasing the accuracy of reported product costs and, unlike traditional systems, by reporting separately the costs of the four different categories of activities.

If a proposed decision will reduce the number of batch-level activities required or will lower the cost of performing batch-level activities (such as by reducing setup times), the decision maker can estimate the future reduction in demands for resources formerly used to perform these activities. If a proposed decision will increase the number of products in the plant, the increased number of product-sustaining activities can be estimated and linked to subsequent demands for increased resource spending.

In one activity-based application, the company managers focused little attention on the changes in product profitability revealed by the activity-based analysis. The activity-based analysis was used to focus managers' attentions on the extremely high amounts of machine and labor time consumed by changeovers and downtime, and it helped to launch a major project to improve manufacturing efficiencies. The study also showed that significant resources had been consumed to launch new product varieties. Previously these expenses were hidden from management's attention because they were buried in direct labor and machine hour overhead burden rates applied to existing products. The activity-based analysis stimulated the company to adopt a more focused, project-oriented approach to designing and launching new products.

CHOOSING SECOND-STAGE ASSIGNMENT BASES IN ACTIVITY-BASED COST SYSTEMS

Companies installing activity-based systems use three methods for estimating the cost of performing activities. The simplest method aggregates the spending on all the resources devoted to a particular activity, such as setting up machines or writing purchase orders, and divides this total spending amount by the number of times the activity was performed (the number of setups, number of purchase orders, number of sales calls).[5] This calculation yields a unit cost for the activity (cost per setup, purchase order, or sales call) that is assigned to products or customers based on the number of times the activity was performed for them. This approach is the simplest and least expensive to implement, requiring only a measure of the number of times an activity was performed. It assumes, however, that each occurrence of the activity consumes the same amount of resources (i.e., that all setups, purchase orders, and sales calls require the same quantity of resources). Thus, it has lower accuracy than the other two methods when different products require substantially different resources for the activity.

The second method uses duration drivers, the time required to perform each occurrence of the activity, to assign indirect expenses to products. Examples of duration drivers include the length of time to perform a setup (setup hours or minutes), number of hours or days to perform an engineering change notice, length of time spent with a customer or brand, and hours of maintenance time. Duration drivers require more information about the performance of the underlying activity but will provide more accurate estimates of resource consumption when the time required to perform a given activity varies widely across products and customers. In this situation, using a simple transactions cost driver (number of setups rather than setup hours) will underestimate resource consumption for complex products that require lengthy setups and overestimate resource consumption for simple products. The benefits of more accurate consumption measures must be balanced by the higher cost of information collection.

The third and most accurate method is to measure directly the resources consumed by each occurrence of the activity. For example, we could measure all the resources used for a particular engineering change notice or for a particular maintenance job. Duration drivers assume that expenses are proportional to the length of time an activity is performed. Intensity or direct charge drivers measure the actual resources used each time an activity is performed. For example, a product that is especially difficult to manufacture may require special supervisors and quality control people to be present when machines are being set up and the first few items produced. The expenses of many product-sustaining resources—such as for product enhancement or for developing manufacturing process routines and test equipment for particular products—can be

---

[5]The volume measure for the activity (such as the number of setups) is usually referred to as the cost driver for that activity. This term has led some people to call these systems cost-driver systems, not activity-based systems.

directly assigned to the products for which the work has been performed. The direct assignment usually requires a system of work orders in which materials, computing resources, and employees' time can be measured each time the activity is performed. The information is more costly to collect but will be more accurate, especially in situations in which large quantities of resources are required for the activity, and products (or customers) differ considerably in the demands they place on that activity.

SUMMARY

Activity-based cost systems differ from traditional cost systems in two very important ways. First, they expand the range of second-stage cost assignment drivers beyond the traditional measures of labor and machine times, units produced, and material quantities to allow for drivers that measure the amount of batch-level, product-sustaining, and facility-sustaining activities performed. Second, the ABC system is a resource consumption model of the organization, not just a more complex cost accounting or cost allocation system. Early adopters of ABC systems have used unit resource and activity prices, derived from the companies' historical-cost financial system, to price out the consumption of resources by individual products. But the analysis permits other prices—future prices, or opportunity-cost prices—also to be applied to the resource consumption model. The essential message is to estimate the quantities of resources used by various activities and then to link these quantities to activities performed for individual products. The new information can help managers make better decisions about product designs, process improvements, pricing, and product mix.

CASES

Destin Brass Products Co.

Every month it becomes clearer to me that our competitors either know something that we do not know or they are crazy. I realize that pumps are a major product in a big market for all of us, but with the price cutting that is going on it is likely that no one will be able to sell pumps profitably if they keep forcing us to match their lower prices. I guess we should be grateful that competitors seem to be overlooking the opportunities for profit in flow controllers. Even with the 12½% price increase we made there, our sales representatives report no new competition.

Roland Guidry, President of Destin Brass Products, was discussing product profitability in the latest month with his controller, Peggy Alford, and his manufacturing manager, John Scott. The meeting among the three was taking place in an atmosphere tinged with apprehension because competitors had been reducing prices on pumps, Destin Brass Products' major product line. With no unique design advantage, managers at Destin had seen no alternative except to match the reduced prices while trying to maintain volumes. And, the company's profits in the latest month had slipped again to be lower than those in the prior month.

The purpose of the meeting was to try to understand the competitive trends and to develop new strategies for dealing with them if new strategies were appropriate. The three managers, along with Steve Abbott, Sales and Marketing Manager (who could not attend because he was away), were very concerned because they held significant shares of ownership in Destin Brass Products. Locally they were a success story; the company had grown to be a significant business in Destin, Florida, better known for its white sand beaches and as "The Luckiest Fishing Village in the World."

THE COMPANY

Destin Brass Products Co. was established by Abbott, Guidry, and Scott, who purchased a moribund commercial machine shop in 1984. Steve Abbott had sensed an opportunity in a conversation with the president of a large manufacturer of water purification equipment who was dissatisfied with the quality of brass valves available. John Scott was a local legend for the brass boat fittings he had always manufactured for the fishing fleet along the Florida Gulf Coast. Roland Guidry had recently retired from the United States Air Force, where he had a long record of administrative successes. The three then selected Peggy Alford, an accountant with manufacturing experience, to join them.

John Scott was quick to analyze the nature of problems other manufacturers were having with water purification valves. The tolerances needed were small, and to maintain them required great labor skill or expensive machine controls, or both. Within weeks of forming the company, Scott and his shop crew were manufacturing valves that met or exceeded the needed specifications. Abbott negotiated a contract with the purification equipment manufacturer, and revenues soon were earned.

The company had grown quickly because the demand for water purification equipment increased and Destin Brass Products became the sole supplier of valves to its customer. But Abbott and Guidry both had greater ambitions. Knowing that the same manufacturing skills used in machining valves could also be used in manufacturing brass pumps and flow controllers, they created an engineering department and designed new products for those markets. Pumps were known to be an even larger market than valves, and flow controllers were often used in the same fluid distribution systems as valves and

This case was prepared by Professor William J. Bruns, Jr.

281

pumps. By specializing in brass, the company could exploit Scott's special knowledge about working with the material.

Destin did no foundry work. Instead, components were purchased from brass foundries and then were precisely machined and assembled in the company's new modern manufacturing facility. The same equipment and labor were used for all three product lines, and runs were scheduled to match customer shipping requirements. The foundries had agreed to just-in-time deliveries, and products were packed and shipped as completed. Guidry described the factory to his friends as "a very modern job shop in specialized products made from brass."

THE PRODUCTS

Valves (24% of company revenues) were created from four brass components. Scott had designed machines which held each component in jigs while they were machined automatically. Each machinist could operate two machines and assemble the valves as machining was taking place. The expense of precise machining made the cost of Destin's valves too high to compete in the nonspecialized valve market, so all monthly production of valves took place in a single production run which was immediately shipped to their single customer on completion. Although Scott felt several competitors could match their quality in valves, none had tried to gain market share by cutting price, and gross margins had been maintained at a standard 35%.

Pumps (55% of revenues) were created by a manufacturing process which was practically the same as that for valves. Five components required machining and assembly. The pumps were then shipped to each of seven industrial product distributors on a monthly basis. To supply the distributors, whose orders were fairly stable so long as Destin would meet competitive prices, the company scheduled five production runs each month.

Pump prices to distributors had been under considerable pressure. The pump market was large, and specifications were less precise than those for valves. Recently, it seemed as if each month brought new reports of reduced prices for pumps. Steve Abbott felt Destin had no choice but to match the lower prices or give up its place as a supplier of pumps. As a result, gross margins on pump sales in the latest month had fallen to 22%, well below the company's planned gross margin of 35%. Guidry and Alford could not see how the competitors could be making profits at current prices unless pumps were being subsidized by other products.

Flow controllers (21% of revenues) were used to control the rate and direction of flow of liquids. As with pumps, the manufacturing operations required for flow controllers were similar to those for valves. More components were needed for each finished unit, and more labor was required. In recent months, Destin had manufactured 4,000 flow controllers in 10 production runs, and the finished flow controllers had been distributed in 22 shipments to distributors and other customers.

Steve Abbott was trying to understand the market for flow controllers better because it seemed to him that Destin had almost no competition in the flow controller market. He had recently raised flow controller prices by 12½% with no apparent effect on demand.

THE MEETING

After the latest month's results had been summarized and reported, Roland Guidry had called Peggy Alford and John Scott into his office to discuss what changes they could or should make in their course of actions. The meeting began with Guidry's statement, at the opening of the case. Guidry had a copy of the product profitability analysis (Exhibit 1) on his desk.

JOHN SCOTT (Manufacturing Manager):
It really is amazing to me as well that our competitors keep reducing prices on pumps. Even though our manufacturing process is better than theirs, I truly do not believe we are less efficient or cost effective. Furthermore, I can't see what their motives can be. There are many manufacturers of pumps. Even if we, or even several competitors, were to drop out of the market, there would still be so many competitors that no monopoly or oligopoly pricing could be maintained. Maybe the competitors just don't realize what their costs are. Could that be, Peggy?

PEGGY ALFORD (Controller):
That does not seem likely to me! Cost accounting is a well-developed art, and most competent managers and cost accountants have some understanding of how product costs can be measured. In manufacturing businesses like ours, material and labor costs are pretty easily related to products produced, whether in

the product design stage or after the fact. So, if anything, our competitors must be making some different assumptions about overhead costs or allocating them to products in some other way. Or, as you said, Roland, maybe they have stupidly forgotten that in the long run prices have to be high enough to provide product margins that cover corporate costs and produce return to owners.

ROLAND GUIDRY (President):

Peggy, I know you have explained to me several times already the choices we could make in allocating overhead to products. In fact, last month you almost sold me on what you called a "modern costing approach," which I rejected because of the work and cost of the changeover. I also was worried about the discontinuity it might cause in our historical data. But I feel that I might need another lesson to help me understand what is happening to us. Could you try once more to explain what we do?

PEGGY ALFORD:

I would be happy to try again. We have a very traditional cost accounting system that meets all of our needs for preparing financial reports and tax returns. It is built on measurements of direct and indirect costs and assumptions about our production and sales activity [Exhibit 2]. Each unit of product is charged for material cost and labor cost; material cost is based on the prices we pay for components, and labor cost is based on the standard times for run labor multiplied by the labor pay rate of $16 per hour. Overhead cost is assigned to products in a two-stage process. First, the overhead costs are assigned to production—in our case we have only one producing department so we know all overhead costs are assigned correctly at the first stage. Then we allocate the total overhead cost assigned to production on the basis of production-run labor cost. Every dollar of run-labor cost causes $4.39 of overhead to be allocated to the product to which the labor was applied. You can see how this works in our Standard Unit Costs sheet, which I brought with me [Exhibit 3]. This is a fairly inexpensive way to allocate overhead cost because we have to accumulate direct labor cost to prepare factory payroll, and we just use the same measurement in product costing.

ROLAND GUIDRY:

All this looks familiar to me. But remind me again what the choices we discussed earlier were.

PEGGY ALFORD:

Well, one choice advocated by some would be to forego the overhead cost allocation altogether. Overhead costs could be charged each month as period expenses. Product profitability would then be measured at the contribution margin level, or price less all variable costs, which in our situation are direct material costs. We would still have to make some adjustments at the end of any period we held inventory to satisfy reporting and tax return requirements, but the

effort to do that would be fairly trivial. The bigger danger would be that we would forget that all overhead costs have to be covered somehow, and we might allow our prices to slip.

JOHN SCOTT:

Yeah, the salesman's mentality in Steve Abbott would make that kind of direct cost accounting dangerous. He would be looking for marginal customers willing to pay marginal prices based on marginal costs. From the outset we have succeeded in part because we insisted on trying to maintain a 35% gross margin on costs *including* allocated overhead.

ROLAND GUIDRY:

John, the competitors are real and so are their prices. If we want to stay in pumps we probably have to meet them head-on. Peggy, please go on.

PEGGY ALFORD:

The last time we discussed this, Roland, I showed you these revised standard unit costs [Exhibit 4]. These are based on a more modern view of the proper way to allocate costs. I put these together in an attempt to better allocate overhead based on activities. First, I identified material-related overhead, the cost of receiving and handling material, and allocated that to each product line based on the cost of material. The justification for this change is that material handling does not have any relationship to the labor cost of machining. Second, I took setup labor cost out of the total overhead and allocated it to each product line. This is a small amount, but the cost of setups also had no relationship whatever to the total labor cost of a production run. Finally, I substituted machine hours for labor dollars as a basis for allocating the remaining factory overhead. John [Scott] has really done wonders with our machines, but our expenses for machines are probably more than double the cost of labor. Therefore, it seems to me that machine hours better reflect use of an expensive resource and should be used to allocate overhead costs.

The results of this proposal made sense to me and may contain a clue about why competitors are chasing lower prices in the pump market. The revised standard cost for pumps is more than $4 below our present standard and would show a gross margin percentage of 27% compared to our current 22%. Maybe our competitors just have more modern cost accounting!

ROLAND GUIDRY:

And you said this modern approach would not cost much more to maintain once we adopted it?

PEGGY ALFORD:

No, it wouldn't. All I really did was to divide the overhead costs into two pools, each of which is allocated on a different measure of activity.

ROLAND GUIDRY:

And we could use the same numbers for financial reports and tax returns?

PEGGY ALFORD:
Absolutely.

(John Scott had been examining the revised unit costs and suddenly spoke up.)

JOHN SCOTT:
Peggy! This new method makes valves look more costly and flow controllers even more profitable than we know they are.

PEGGY ALFORD:
. . . or thought they were! The profit for each product line will change if we change the way we allocate overhead costs to products.

JOHN SCOTT:
I realize that. But it seems to me that product costs should have more to do with the costs caused by producing and selling the product. That's usually true for material, and maybe direct labor, but it is not true for most of these overhead costs. For example, we probably spend one-half of our engineering effort on flow controllers, but whether you use direct labor dollars or machine hours to allocate engineering costs to products, flow controllers don't get much of the engineering costs.

I've been thinking about this a lot since last week when I attended an Excellence in Manufacturing conference in Tallahassee. One presentation was about cost accounting for the new manufacturing environment. I couldn't follow all of the arguments of the speaker, but the key seemed to be that activity, rather than production volume, causes costs. In our operations it is receiving and handling material, packing and shipping, and engineering orders that cause us to incur costs and not the length of any production run.

If I understood what this speaker was advocating, it was that whenever possible overhead costs that cannot be traced directly to product lines should be allocated on the basis of transactions—since transactions cause costs to be incurred. A product that required three times as many transactions to be incurred than another product would be allocated three times as much of the overhead cost related to those transactions than the other product would be allocated. Or said another way, a product which causes 3% of the total transactions for receiving components would be allocated 3% of the total cost of receiving components. At a basic level, this seems to make sense to me.

PEGGY ALFORD:
Recently I've been reading a lot in my professional magazines about this activity-based-costing (ABC) . . .

ROLAND GUIDRY:
But to cost products that way has got to be more expensive. It's more complex; also, who keeps count of transactions?

PEGGY ALFORD:
It can't be too hard. All overhead allocation is somewhat arbitrary. We could experiment with estimates to see how the product costs might be affected. The product costs for material, direct labor, and setup labor will be the same as for my revised unit costs, and to allocate other overhead costs we just need to estimate how many transactions occur in total and are caused by each product.

JOHN SCOTT:
I'd like to ask Peggy to put together an analysis for us. The managers at the conference from companies that have used these transaction-based costing systems really seemed excited about what they said they learned.

ROLAND GUIDRY:
OK. Peggy, you and John get together this afternoon to put together the activity estimates you need. Get back to me as quickly as you can. Maybe we can figure out why the competitors think they should sell pumps regardless of price.

After lunch, Peggy Alford and John Scott met in Peggy's office. They discussed transactions and effort related to each type of overhead cost. The result was the overhead cost activity analysis shown in Exhibit 5.

EXHIBIT 1

DESTIN BRASS PRODUCTS CO.
Product Profitability Analysis

	VALVES	PUMPS	FLOW CONTROLLERS
Standard unit costs	$37.56	$63.12	$56.50
Target selling price	57.78	97.10	86.96
Planned gross margin (%)	35	35	35
Last Month			
Actual selling price	$57.78	$81.26	$97.07
Actual gross margin (%)	35	22	42

EXHIBIT 2

DESTIN BRASS PRODUCTS CO.
Monthly Product and Cost Summary

PRODUCT LINES	VALVES	PUMPS	FLOW CONTROLLERS	
Monthly production	7,500 units (1 run)	12,500 units (5 runs)	4,000 units (10 runs)	
Monthly shipments	7,500 units (1 shipment)	12,500 units (7 shipments)	4,000 units (22 shipments)	

MANUFACTURING COSTS				MONTHLY TOTAL
Material	4 components 2 @ $2=$ 4 2 @ 6= 12	5 components 3 @ $2=$ 6 2 @ 7= 14	10 components 4 @ $1=$ 4 5 @ 2= 10 1 @ 8= 8	
Total material	$16	$20	$22	$458,000

Labor ($16 per hour including employee benefits)				
Setup labor	8 hours per production run	8 hours per production run	12 hours per production run	168 hours
Run labor	.25 hours per unit	.50 hours per unit	.40 hours per unit	9,725 hours
Machine usage	.50 hours per unit	.50 hours per unit	.20 hours per unit	10,800 hours

MANUFACTURING OVERHEAD

Receiving	$ 20,000	
Materials handling	200,000	
Engineering	100,000	
Packing and shipping	60,000	
Maintenance	30,000	
Total	$410,000	
Machine depreciation (units-of-production method) $25 per hour of use		$270,000

EXHIBIT 3

DESTIN BRASS PRODUCTS CO.
Standard Unit Costs

	VALVES	PUMPS	FLOW CONTROLLERS
Material	$16.00	$20.00	$22.00
Direct labor	4.00	8.00	6.40
Overhead @ 439% of direct labor $	17.56	35.12	28.10
Standard unit cost	$37.56	$63.12	$56.50

Overhead	
Machine depreciation	$270,000
Setup labor	2,688
Receiving	20,000
Materials handling	200,000
Engineering	100,000
Packing and shipping	60,000
Maintenance	30,000
	$682,688

Total run labor = 9,725 hours × $16 = $155,600

$$\text{Overhead rate} = \frac{682,688}{155,600} = 439\%$$

EXHIBIT 4

DESTIN BRASS PRODUCTS CO.
Revised Unit Costs

	VALVES	PUMPS	FLOW CONTROLLERS
Material	$16.00	$20.00	$22.00
Material overhead (48%)	7.68	9.60	10.56
Setup labor	.02	.05	.48
Direct labor	4.00	8.00	6.40
Other overhead (machine hour basis)	21.30	21.30	8.52
Revised standard cost	$49.00	$58.95	$47.96

Material-related Overhead	
Receiving	$ 20,000
Materials handling	200,000
Total	$220,000

Overhead Absorption Rate

$$\frac{\$220,000}{\$458,000} = 48\% \text{ (materials cost basis)}$$

Other Overhead	
Machine depreciation	$270,000
Engineering	100,000
Packing and shipping	60,000
Maintenance	30,000
Total	$460,000

Overhead Absorption Rate

$$\frac{\$460,000}{10,800 \text{ hours}} = \$42.59 \text{ per machine hour}$$

EXHIBIT 5

DESTIN BRASS PRODUCTS CO.
Monthly Overhead Cost Activity Analysis

	VALVES	PUMPS	FLOW CONTROLLERS
Receiving and Materials Handling:			
Receive each component once per run	4 transactions (3%)	25 transactions (19%)	100 transactions (78%)
Handle each component once per run	4 transactions (3%)	25 transactions (19%)	100 transactions (78%)
Packing and Shipping:			
One packing order per shipment	1 transaction (3%)	7 transactions (23%)	22 transactions (73%)
Engineering:			
Estimated engineering work-order percentage (subjective)	20%	30%	50%
Maintenance:			
Machine hour basis	3,750 hours (35%)	6,250 hours (58%)	800 hours (7%)

Siemens Electric Motor Works (A) (Abridged)

Ten years ago our electric motor business was in real trouble. Low labor rates allowed the Eastern Bloc countries to sell standard motors at prices we were unable to match. We had become the high-cost producer in the industry. Consequently, we decided to change our strategy and become a specialty motor producer. Once we adopted our new strategy, we discovered that while our existing cost system was adequate for costing standard motors, it gave us inaccurate information when we used it to cost specialty motors.

MR. KARL-HEINZ LOTTES, DIRECTOR OF BUSINESS OPERATIONS, EMW

SIEMENS CORPORATION

Headquartered in Munich, Siemens AG, a producer of electrical and electronic products, was one of the world's largest corporations. Revenues totaled 51 billion deutsche marks in 1987, with roughly half this amount representing sales outside the Federal Republic of Germany. The Siemens organization was split into seven major groups and five corporate divisions. The largest group, Energy and Automation, accounted for 24% of total revenues. Low-wattage alternating current (A/C) motors were produced at the Electric Motor Works (EMW), which was part of the Manufacturing Industries Division of the Energy and Automation Group. High-wattage motors were produced at another facility.

THE ELECTRIC MOTOR WORKS

Located in the small town of Bad Neustadt, the original Siemens EMW plant was built in 1937 to manufacture refrigerator motors for *Volkskuhlschraenke* (people's refrigerators). Less than a year later, Mr. Siemens halted the production of refrigerator motors and began to produce electric motors for other applications. At the end of World War II, the Bad Neustadt plant was the only Siemens factory in West Germany capable of producing electric motors. All the other Siemens production facilities had been completely destroyed or seized by Eastern Bloc countries. After an aggressive rebuilding program, Bad Neustadt emerged as the firm's primary producer of electric motors.

Through the 1970s, EMW produced about 200 different types of standard motors, at a total annual volume around 230,000 motors. Standard motors accounted for 80% of sales volumes—the remaining 20% was customized motors. The production process was characterized by relatively long runs of a single type of motor. Because identical motors were used by a wide range of customers, standard motors were inventoried and shipped as orders were received. The market for standard A/C motors was extremely competitive. The firm was under constant pressure to reduce costs so that it could price aggressively and still make a profit. Despite a major expansion and automation program begun in 1974, by the early 1980s EMW found it could not lower its costs sufficiently to offset the lower labor rates of its Eastern Bloc competitors.

CHANGE IN STRATEGY

An extensive study revealed that EMW could become a profitable producer of low-volume, customized A/C motors. To help implement this strategy, the Bad Neustadt plant was enlarged and dedicated to the manufacture of A/C motors with power ratings ranging from 0.06 to 18.5 kilowatts. These motors supported a number of applications including automation engineering, machine tools, plastic processing, and paper and printing machines.

For the new strategy to succeed, EMW needed to be able to manufacture efficiently a large variety of motors in small production runs. Between 1985 and 1988, EMW spent DM50 million a year to replace almost every machine on the shop floor and thereby create a production environment that could support its new strategy.

By 1987 the production process was highly automated with numerically controlled machines, flexible machining centers, and robotically fed production processes used throughout the factory. Large-volume common components were manufactured using dedicated automated equipment, while very low-volume components might be made in manual production processes. Where possible, flexible manufacturing was used to produce small-volume specialty components. While a normal annual production volume for common components might be 100,000 units, a single component could have up to 10,000 custom variations that might have to be produced one at a time.

To design a custom motor, modifications were made to a standard motor design. The process involved determining where standard components could not be used. These standard components were replaced by custom components that provided the functionality required by the customer.

By 1987, the EMW strategy seemed to be successful (see Exhibit 1). Of a total of 65,625 orders accepted, 90% were for custom motors; 48% for only one motor; and 74% for fewer than five motors. But EMW high-volume standard motors still accounted for almost half the total annual output of 630,000 motors.

CHANGE IN THE CALCULATION OF PRODUCT COSTS

EMW's product cost system assigned materials and labor costs directly to the products. Overhead costs were divided into three categories: materials-related, production-related, and support related. *Materials-related overhead*, containing costs associated with material acquisition, was allocated to products based on their direct materials costs. *Production-related overhead* was directly traced to the 600 production cost centers. A production cost center had been created for each type of machine. Cost centers with high labor intensity used direct labor hours to allocate costs to products. For centers with automated machines whose operation required few direct labor hours, machine hours was used as the allocation base. *Support-related overhead* was allocated to products based on manufacturing costs to date: the sum of direct materials and direct labor costs, materials overhead, and production overhead. The breakdown of each cost category as a percent of total costs is shown in the table at the top of p. 289.

Two years after the change in strategy, problems with the traditional cost system became apparent. The traditional cost system seemed unable to capture the relation between the increased support costs and the change in product mix. Management felt that most support costs related more closely to the number of orders received or the number of customized components in a motor rather than to materials expense or to the quantity of labor and machine hours required to build the motor.

An extensive study was undertaken to identify the support costs that management believed were

	PERCENT OF TOTAL COSTS	BURDEN RATE
Direct materials	29%	
Direct labor	10	
Materials overhead	2	6% of materials cost
Production overhead	33	DM/direct labor hour or DM/machine hour (600 rates)
Support-related overhead	26	35% of other manufacturing costs
Total	100%	

driven by the processing of orders and the processing of special components. The following departments' costs were most affected by the large increases in number of orders and number of special components.

Costs Related to Order Processing
   Billing
   Order Receiving
   Product Costing and Bidding
   Shipping and Handling

Costs Related to Special Components
   Inventory Handling
   Product Costing and Bidding
   Product Development
   Purchasing
   Receiving
   Scheduling and Production Control
   Technical Examination of Incoming Orders

An analysis of the order processing costs revealed that the same resources were required to process an order of one custom motor as for an order of 200 standard motors. A similar analysis indicated that the number of different types of special components in each motor design determined the workload for the departments affected by special components. The demand for work in these departments was not strongly affected by the total number of special components produced. For example, an order of five custom motors requiring 10 special components per unit generated the same amount of work as an order of one custom motor with a design requiring 10 special components. In 1987, the factory used 30,000 different special components to customize their motors. The special components were processed 325,000 different times for customized orders.

The costs in each support department associated with these two activities were removed from the support-related cost pool and assigned to two new cost pools. Exhibit 2 illustrates, for 1987, the formation of the two new cost pools. The first column presents total costs grouped by traditional costing system definitions. The new cost system removes 6.3 million from engineering support costs, and 27.0 million from administrative support costs. These expenses are then assigned to the new cost pools, 13.8 million to order processing costs, and 19.5 million to special components costs.

Exhibit 3 shows the cost buildup for five typical motor orders. The base motor cost includes direct materials and labor costs, materials and production overhead, and the portion of support overhead not assigned to the two new cost pools. To this base motor cost must be added the cost of processing the order, and the materials, labor, production overhead, and support overhead required for the special components.

EFFECT OF THE NEW COST SYSTEM

In 1987 EMW received close to DM1 billion in orders, accepted only DM450 million, and ran the factory at 115% of rated capacity. Mr. Karl-Heinz Lottes, Director of Business Operations at EMW, commented on the role of the redesigned cost system with the new strategy.

Without the new cost system, our new strategy would have failed. The information it generated helped us to identify those orders we want to accept. While some orders we lose to competitors, most we turn down because they are not profitable. Anyone who wants to understand the importance of the system can simply compare some typical orders costed with the traditional system with the costs produced by our new system.

EXHIBIT 1

SIEMENS ELECTRIC MOTOR WORKS (A)

Distribution of Orders Accepted for Production in 1987

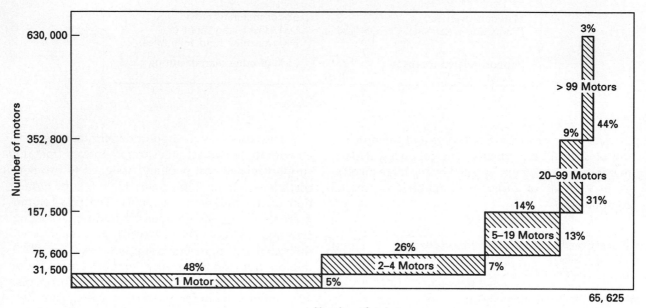

EXHIBIT 2

SIEMENS ELECTRIC MOTORS WORKS (A)

1987 Reconciliation

Transforming the Traditional Cost System

(000 DM)

	TRADITIONAL	TRANSFERRED	NEW
Materials	105,000		105,000
Materials overhead	6,000		6,000
Labor	36,000		36,000
Labor or machine overhead	120,000		120,000
Manufacturing cost	267,000 (74%)[1]		267,000 (74%)
Engineering costs	12,000	6,300	5,700
Tooling costs	22,500	0	22,500
Administrative costs	60,000	27,000	33,000
Support-related cost	94,500 (26%)[2]	33,300 (9%)	61,200 (17%)
Order-processing cost		13,800	13,800
Special components cost		19,500	19,500
Total cost	361,500	0	361,500

[1]Percent of total cost.

[2]This figure corresponds to the 26% of support-related overhead on page 289.

EXHIBIT 3

SIEMENS ELECTRIC MOTOR WORKS (A)

Manufacturing Costs for Five Motor Orders

	A	B	C	D	E
Cost of base motor (without assignment from new cost pools)	295.0	295.0	295.0	295.0	295.0
Cost of all special components[1] (without assignment from new cost pools)	29.5	59.0	88.5	147.5	295.0
Number of different types of special components per motor	1	2	3	5	10
Number of motors ordered	1	1	1	1	1

	BASE MOTOR COST	SPECIAL COMPONENTS COST
Materials	90	9.0
Materials overhead	5	0.5
Direct labor	35	3.5
Manufacturing overhead	110	11.0
	240	24.0
Support-related overhead[2]	55	5.5
Unit manufacturing costs	295	29.5

[1]For illustrative purposes, all different types of special components are assumed to cost 29.5 a piece.

[2]Support-related overhead excludes the expenses associated with processing individual customer orders and handling special components.

John Deere Component Works (A)

The phone rang in the office of Keith Williams, manager of Cost Accounting Services for Deere & Company. On the line was Bill Maxwell, accounting supervisor for the Gear and Special Products Division in Waterloo, Iowa. The division had recently bid to fabricate component parts for another Deere division. Maxwell summarized the situation:

They're about to award the contracts, and almost all of the work is going to outside suppliers. We're only getting a handful of the parts we quoted, and most

of it is low-volume stuff we really don't want. We think we should get some of the business on parts where our direct costs are lower than the outside bid, even if our full costs are not.

Williams asked, "How did your bids stack up against the competition?" Maxwell replied:

Not too well. We're way high on lots of parts. Our machinists and our equipment are as efficient as any in the business, yet our costs on standard, high-

This case was prepared by Research Associate Artemis March (under the supervision of Professor Robert S. Kaplan).

Copyright © 1987 by the President and Fellows of Harvard College. Harvard Business School case 187-107.

volume products appear to be the highest in the industry. Not only are we not competitive with outside suppliers, but our prices are also higher than two other Deere divisions that quoted on the business.

DEERE & COMPANY

The company was founded in 1837 by John Deere, a blacksmith who developed the first commercially successful steel plow. One hundred years later, Deere & Company was one of seven full-line farm equipment manufacturers in the world and, in 1963, had displaced International Harvester as the number one producer. During the 1970s, Deere spent over $1 billion on plant modernization, expansion, and tooling.

During the three-decade, post-World War II boom period, Deere expanded its product line, built new plants, ran plants at capacity, and still was unable to keep up with demand. Deere tractors and combines dotted the landscape throughout America.

During this same period, Deere had diversified into off-the-road industrial equipment for use in the construction, forestry, utility, and mining industries. In 1962 it also began building lawn and garden tractors and equipment. By the mid-1980s, Deere had the broadest lawn and garden product line in the world.

The collapse of farmland values and commodity prices in the 1980s, however, led to the worst and most sustained agricultural crisis since the Great Depression. Several factors exacerbated the crisis. The high dollar reduced U.S. exports and thus hurt both American farmers and American farm equipment producers. Farmers had been encouraged to go into heavy debt to expand and buy land, so when land values and farm prices plummeted, the number of farm foreclosures skyrocketed. Few farmers were in a position to buy new equipment, and resale of repossessed equipment further reduced the market for new equipment.

In response, Deere adjusted its level of operations downward, cut costs where possible, increased emphasis on pushing decision making downward, and restructured manufacturing processes. While outright plant closings were avoided, Deere took floor space out of production, encouraged early retirements, and did not replace most of those who

left. Employment was reduced from 61,000 at the end of 1980 to about 37,500 at the end of 1986. It implemented new manufacturing approaches such as just-in-time production and manufacturing cells that grouped a number of operations for more efficient flow-through production and placed quality control directly at the point of manufacture. To add production volume, Deere wanted its captive component divisions to supply other companies and industries.

JOHN DEERE COMPONENT WORKS

For many years, all the parts for tractors were made and assembled at the tractor works in Waterloo. To generate more production space in the 1970s, Deere successively split off parts of tractor production. Engine machining and assembly, final tractor assembly, and product engineering each were moved into new plants in the Waterloo area. By the end of the decade, the old tractor works buildings were used only for component production, ranging from small parts to large, complex components such as axles and transmissions. The old tractor works buildings in Waterloo were renamed the John Deere Component Works (JDCW).

In 1983 JDCW was organized into three divisions. The Hydraulics Division, which was soon consolidated into a nearby, refurbished warehouse, fabricated pumps, valves, and pistons. The Drive Trains Division made axles, transmissions, and drive trains. The Gear and Special Products Division made a variety of gears, shafts, and machined parts and performed heat treating, cast iron machining, and sheet metal work.

As part of a vertically integrated company, JDCW had been structured to be a captive producer of parts for Deere's equipment divisions, particularly tractors. Thus, it had to produce a great variety of parts whose volume, even in peak tractor production years, was relatively low. During the 1970s, operations and equipment had been arranged to support tractor production of approximately 150 units per day; by the mid-1980s, however, JDCW was producing parts for less than half as many tractors. The lower volume of activity had a particularly adverse effect on JDCW's machined parts and sheet metal businesses, since its machines were most efficient for high-volume production.

Internal sales and transfer pricing. Virtually all of JDCW's sales were internal. Deere equipment-producing factories were required to buy internally major components, such as advanced design transmissions and axles, that gave Deere a competitive advantage. For smaller components, corporate purchasing policy placed JDCW in a favored, but not exclusive, position for securing internal business.

Corporate policy stated that transfers between divisions would take place at full cost (direct materials + direct labor + direct overhead + period overhead). Corporate also had a make-buy policy that when excess capacity was available, buying divisions should compare component divisions' direct costs, rather than full costs, to outside bids. (Direct costs equal full costs less period overhead.) Thus, for example, if JDCW full costs were $10, its direct costs $7, and an outside bid $9, the make-buy decision rule held that the buying division should buy from JDCW. But, the transfer pricing policy required the buyer to pay $10 to the component division. Bill Maxwell described the conflict.

> The equipment divisions looked only at price and acted like profit centers rather than cost centers. They are starting to act in the interest of their factory rather than the corporation as a whole. The transfer pricing policy wasn't a problem until times got bad and capacity utilization went down. At Component Works, we said to our sister divisions, "You should look at our direct costs and buy from us." They replied, "We don't want to pay more than it would cost us from outside vendors."

In practice, equipment divisions did not always follow the corporate guidelines for internal sourcing, and JDCW lost a portion of the equipment factories' business to outside vendors.

MACHINE PRODUCTS BUSINESS

Deere's effort to push decision making down into more manageable units encouraged divisions to view their product lines as stand-alone businesses that sold to external markets. By early 1984, JDCW operations were so far below capacity that managers realized they could not wait for the agricultural market to turn around. In the Gear and Special Products Division, several people thought that complex machined parts offered a promising niche.

Turning machines transformed raw materials (primarily steel barstock) into finished components and were the most autonomous of the division's operations. As one manager put it, "We could shut down the turning machine area and not affect the rest of the plant—except that we would then have to buy machined parts from outside suppliers." Only the master schedule connected the area with the activities of the rest of the plant.

Turning machine operations were organized into three departments. These departments were distinguished by the diameter of the barstock its machines could handle and by the number of spindles on each machine. A six-spindle machine could handle six different orientations, for example, and thus make more complex parts than could a four-spindle machine.

Machine capabilities and operations. Turning machines automatically fabricated small metal parts. Raw barstock was brought to a staging area near the machines by an overhead crane, the amount depending on the lot size to be run. Barstock (in round, square, or hexagonal sections) was fed horizontally by the operator into the back of the machine. Multiple stations each performed different operations simultaneously on what would become parts; when the longest cycle time (they ranged from a few seconds to six minutes) was completed, a machine indexed to the next position. Small parts, such as pinions, collars, gears, bushings, and connectors, continually emerged from the final station. Finished parts were transported in 50-pound baskets stacked in trailers that carried up to 1,500 pounds.

Once set up, automatic turning machines were very fast, had excellent repeatability, and were particularly good at drilling, threading, grooving, and boring out large holes. New, the machines could cost as much as $500,000 each; their replacement value was estimated at about half that amount.

Operators were assigned to a battery of two or three specific machines; they did their own setups and tool changes. Setups, like runs, were timed; operators punched in and out, creating a record of how long setups actually took. Operators were also responsible for quality, machine cleanup, and housekeeping in their areas. Following first-part inspection by an inspector, operators ran the lot. Roving inspectors also checked samples from each lot or basket for conformance to quality standards.

Layout. Component Works had 120 automatic machines lined up in four long rows in an 80,000-square-foot building—almost the size of two football fields. The chip and coolant recovery system was constructed under the floor, running the entire length of the building. It was connected up to each machine, much like houses are connected to a sewer system, to carry off the tremendous amount of chips generated by the machines as well as to cool and lubricate the machines. The layout of the cooling system made it infeasible to redesign the machine layout into cellular configurations that would group attendant secondary and finishing operations together.[1] The machines could be shifted around or dedicated to certain parts, but due to the prohibitive expense of duplicating a chip coolant system, they were forced to remain in rows in S Building.

During the 1970s, secondary operations had been moved off the main floor in S Building to make room for more turning machines; this increased materials-handling distances for most parts. For example, the enormous heat treatment machines were located about one-quarter mile from the main machine area.

Process engineering. To bring a new part into production required extensive process engineering activities. Operations had to be sequenced and tooling requirements specified for each spindle. If the appropriate specialized tooling did not exist, it had to be either purchased or designed and built (usually outside). Both setups and runs had to be timed and standards established. Process engineers had to make sure that the process they had designed would in fact make the part correctly. Data bases then had to be set up for each machine.

All of these activities had to be conducted whether or not the part number ever ran. John Gordon, head of the process engineering group for automatic machining, commented, "We have to do as much work for a part we run once a year—or one we never even run—as for one we set up every month or that runs every day."

Recently, process engineering and production people had begun to make changes in how they ran machined parts. On setups, for example, they tried to "family the parts." Rather than sequencing setups so that each required a distinctly different set of tools, they started grouping similar parts (in terms of diameter, length, and shape) so they could run on the same machine, thereby reducing tool changes and setup times. They also began to reduce the number of parts being run on the turning machines. As Andy Edberg, head of process engineering for the division, noted, "The automatic machines are extremely high-volume machines so you want to dedicate them if possible." Process engineers were starting to outsource some low-volume parts or to transfer them to more labor-intensive processes. Edberg pointed to the fundamental nature of the shift.

> We always made all the components for tractors, so we ran lots of part numbers but never really looked at the costs of individual parts. What was important was the efficiency of the whole rather than the efficiency of making the parts.

Competition and strategy. By 1984, Gear and Special Products had roughed out a general strategic thrust toward marketing machined parts to the outside world, such as automobile OEMs (original equipment manufacturers). Initial efforts to gain outside business, however, soon made it obvious that competing in the external market was going to be harder than anticipated. Competition came in two forms: (1) captive producers of other vertically integrated companies (about whom Deere found it difficult to obtain information), and (2) independent machine shops. The latter had sprung up around geographical clusters of end users. On the East Coast, the independent shops fed the defense industry, particularly shipyards; on the West Coast, they supplied the aircraft industry; and in Michigan and Indiana, they sold to the automotive industry. Dick Sinclair, manufacturing superintendent, observed,

> The key to successful competition in the outside market is price. We found we have a geography problem. We are not in the midst of heavy users, and it is expensive to ship steel both in and out. We also found our range of services to be less useful than we thought they would be.

BID ON 275 MACHINED PARTS

Both excess capacity and its new thrust toward developing stand-alone business motivated Gear

---

[1]Secondary operations included heat treating, cross-drilling, plating, grinding, and milling; most parts required one or more secondary operations.

and Special Products to bid on 275 of the 635 parts Deere & Company offered for bid in October 1984. All 635 parts had high potential for manufacture on automatic turning machines. Gear and Special Products bid on a subset for which it had the capability and where the volume was large enough to exploit the efficiencies from its multiple-spindle machines. The buying group consisted of several equipment factories plus a corporate purchasing group; its aim was to consolidate turning machine purchasing by dealing with just a few good vendors and to gain improved service, quality, and price for these parts. Gear and Special Products had one month to prepare its bid. Results of the bid are summarized in Table A and represent the annual cost for the quantity quoted.

The purchasing group awarded Gear and Special Products only the 58 parts for which it was the low bidder on a full-cost basis. Most of these were low-volume parts that the division did not especially want to make. Gear and Special Products could be the source for the 103 parts on which its direct costs were below the best outside bid only if it agreed to transfer the parts at the same price as the low outside bidder. The division passed on this "opportunity."

The bidding experience generated a good deal of ferment at Gear and Special Products and confirmed the feeling of many that "we didn't even know our costs." Sinclair recalled,

Some of us were quite alarmed. We had been saying, "Let's go outside," but we couldn't even succeed inside. Deere manufacturing plants in Dubuque and Des Moines also quoted and came in with lower prices—not across the board, but for enough parts to cause concern. If we weren't even

competitive relative to other Deere divisions, how could we think we could be successful externally? And when we looked at the results, we knew we were not costing things right. It was backwards to think we could do better in low-volume than high-volume parts, but that's what the cost system said.

JDCW STANDARD COST ACCOUNTING SYSTEM

A standard cost accounting system was used throughout Component Works. The industrial engineering (IE) department played an active role in supporting the accounting function.

Industrial engineering standards. The IE department had established standard hours for direct labor run time and for setups for every operation. Hourly workers were paid on a piece-work basis; the incentive system allowed them to make up to 125% of their base pay for performing setups or runs more quickly than the standard rate. IE issued weekly efficiency reports detailing performance at different levels, including department and individual workers. It gave information concerning percentage of time on or off incentive, the level of incentive, time delays, setups, number of pieces produced, and other data. All of this information was based on labor hours and generated many percentages, often comparing actual to standard.

Materials. The quality assurance (QA) department maintained control over materials usage. No materials usage variances were computed. The QA department recorded scrap when bad material was discarded. Weekly reports were prepared that summarized dollars of scrap, high scrap parts, reasons for scrap, and an overall quality level index.

Table A. Comparison: JDCW versus Vendor ($ in thousands)

	PARTS WITH JDCW LOW TOTAL COST	PARTS WITH JDCW LOW DIRECT COST	PARTS WITH JDCW HIGH DIRECT COST	TOTAL ALL PARTS
Part numbers	58	103	114	275
JDCW direct cost	$191	$403	$1,103	$1,697
JDCW full cost	272	610	1,711	2,593
Low outside quote	$332	$491	$684	$1,507
Percent of $ value	22%	33%	45%	100%
% JDCW of low vendor				
Direct cost	58%	82%	161%	113%
Full cost	82%	124%	250%	172%

Responsibility accounting. The accounting department issued weekly and monthly reports on expenses incurred in each support department. Only costs incurred within a department appeared on these periodic reports. The reports were used primarily to see how areas were operating rather than to evaluate performance.

The weekly reports showed only actual labor overhead and materials overhead costs. On the monthly report, actual labor overhead costs were compared with budgeted rates applied to actual direct labor dollars.

PART COSTING

Standard costs were used for inventory valuation and for part costing. The standard or full cost of a part was computed by adding up the following:

```
direct labor (run time only)
direct material
overhead (direct + period) applied on
                            direct labor
overhead (direct + period) applied on
                            material dollars
overhead (direct + period) applied on
                            ACTS machine
                            hours
_____
standard or full cost
```

Establishing overhead rates. Once each year, the JDCW's accounting department reestablished overhead rates, based on two studies: the normal study and the process study. The normal study determined the standard number of direct labor and machine hours and total overhead for the following year by establishing a "normal volume." To smooth out sharp swings, normal volume was defined as the long-term "through the business cycle" volume. One of the measures for setting normal volume was the number of drive trains produced per day.

The process study broke down projected overhead at normal volume among CW's 100-plus processes, such as painting, sheet metal, grinding, machining, and heat treating. To determine the overhead rate for each process, accounting computed the rate from actual past charges and then asked, "Do we expect any changes?" (Accumulated charges were collected by charging the specific process code as production took place.) Applying judgment to past rates, next year's normal volume, and any probable changes, a new overhead rate was established for each process for the coming year.

Evolution of bases for overhead rates. For many years, direct labor run time was the sole basis for establishing overhead rates at Component Works. Thus, if $4,000,000 in overhead was generated by $800,000 of direct labor, the overhead rate was 500%. In the 1960s a separate materials overhead rate had been established. This rate included the costs of purchasing, receiving, inspecting, and storing raw material. These costs were allocated to materials as a percentage markup over materials costs. Over time, separate rates had been established for steel, castings, and purchased parts to reflect the different demands these items placed on the materials handling resources.

Both labor- and materials-based overhead were subdivided into direct and period overhead. Direct (or variable) overhead, such as the costs of setups, scrap, and materials handling, varied with the volume of production activity. Period (or fixed) overhead included accounts (such as taxes, depreciation, interest, heat, light, and salaries) that did not vary with production activity.

In 1984 Component Works introduced machine hours as well as direct labor and materials to allocate overhead. With the increased usage of automated machines, direct labor run time no longer reflected the amount of processing being performed on parts, particularly when one operator was responsible for several machines. Every process was studied and assigned a machine hour or ACTS (Actual Cycle Time Standard) rate. Labor hours were retained for processes where labor time equaled machine time; where these were different, ACTS hours were used to allocate overhead. Total overhead (other than materials overhead) was then split between direct labor overhead and ACTS overhead. As before, each overhead pool was subdivided between direct and period overhead.

LAUNCHING A COST STUDY
FOR TURNING MACHINES

Keith Williams had been aware that the existing standard cost system, although satisfactory at an aggregate level, was ineffective for costing and bidding individual parts. He was experimenting with other ways to apply overhead to products. When Maxwell called him in November 1984, Williams realized that the situation at Gear and Special Products provided an opportunity to demonstrate the weaknesses of the current system and to develop a new approach that would be more useful for decision making.

After his phone conversation with Bill Maxwell, Williams quickly put together a proposal to management at Deere & Company and to the division manager of Gear and Special Products. The study would focus on one cost center—the three turning machine departments—because turning machine ACTS hours were the biggest chunk of costs in the bid; more than 60% of total machining for the parts occurred on the turning machines. To conduct the study, Williams chose Nick Vintila, who had begun his career at Deere as a manufacturing supervisor at Component Works. During his second year, Vintila had worked in the turning machine area. Not only had he become very familiar with its operation, but he had worked with people such as John Gordon, then in methods, and Andy Edberg, then a manufacturing superintendent, who would now also be working on the cost study. Vintila had subsequently served as a liaison between systems development and manufacturing to implement a labor reporting system that tied into MRP, and he then became an accounting supervisor at the Tractor Works.

As a first step, Williams and Vintila studied a sample of 44 of the 275 bid parts. (See Exhibit 1.) This examination showed (a) an enormous range of variation among quotes for many parts; (b) a large dispersion between JDCW and vendor quotes, ranging from 50% to 60% on some parts and 200% to 300% on others; (c) that JDCW estimated standard costs exceeded vendor prices by 35% on average;

and (d) that JDCW appeared to be most cost-effective on low-volume and low-value parts. (See Exhibit 2 for summary measures of the characteristics of the 44 sample parts.) These findings raised numerous questions about the validity of the standard cost system for determining costs of individual parts and reaffirmed the need for an alternative costing method.

Vintila spent the first half of 1985 working full-time on what became known as the ABC (Activity-Based Costing) study. After detailed study of the shop process flow, he and Williams learned that use of overhead resources could be explained by seven different types of support activities: direct labor support, machine operation, setup hours, production order activity, materials handling, parts administration, and general overhead. Vintila then went through each overhead account (e.g., engineering salaries, crib attendant costs), asking others and himself, "Among the seven activities, which cause this account to occur? What creates work for this department?" He began to estimate the percentages of each overhead account that were driven by each of the seven activities. He conducted specific studies to estimate the total volume of each of the seven overhead driving activities (such as number of production orders, total machine hours). This work was circulated among people like Maxwell, Edberg, Gordon, and Sinclair, who, drawing on their experience and judgment, accepted the seven activities as the key overhead drivers and adjusted the final percentages for allocating budgeted items to each activity. (See Appendix for a description of the seven overhead drivers and how Vintila arrived at the seven overhead rates.) When the ABC method was used to allocate overhead, 41% of the overhead shifted to activity bases 3–7 (see Exhibits 3 and 4). The data needed to estimate the cost of a particular part are shown in Exhibit 5.

The detailed work to design the ABC system had now been completed. The next step for Williams and Vintila was to test and gain acceptance for their new costing approach.

EXHIBIT 1

Comparison of JDCW Bid versus Outside Vendor Bids for Sample of 44 Parts

PART NUMBER	PART DESCRIPTION	QUOTE VOLUME	JDCW EST. DIR. COST	JDCW EST. MFG. COST	COMPETING VENDOR QUOTES 1	2	3	4	5	6	7	% OF JDCW TO VENDOR 2 DIR. COST	MFG. COST	DIRECT LABOR $ EACH
Component Works Low on Full-Cost Basis:														
F382	Fitting	4,009	$2,248	$3,153	$3,940	$9,822	$13,550					23%	32%	$0.05
S209	Spacer	950	183	291	399	522	551	$1,244	$1,244			35	56	0.03
P594	Pin	692	297	430	692	796	817	1,012	1,509			37	54	0.03
T815	Stud	3,150	719	1,162	1,712	1,859	2,158	2,300	3,131	$9,356		39	62	0.03
P675	Pin	3,596	1,703	2,649	3,587	3,740	6,024	7,947				46	55	0.07
H622	Hub	4,450	3,207	4,365	5,687	6,324	6,743	7,518	8,463	12,875	$12,875	51	69	0.05
S245	Spacer	4,912	1,249	1,917	2,210	2,335	2,536	3,276	3,585	4,076		53	82	0.03
R647	Sprocket	5,167	6,792	9,196	11,907	12,142	12,400	13,124	16,116	16,674	17,516	56	76	0.10
T501	Stud	4,879	902	1,492	1,537	1,610	1,625	1,820	2,196	2,976	6,294	56	93	0.03
S071	Spacer	5,661	4,896	6,885	8,378	8,433	10,133					58	82	0.09
C784	Cap	71,200	13,101	19,537	17,088	22,072	22,606	23,332	29,832	41,253		59	89	0.04
P583	Pin	3,402	2,775	4,285	4,380	4,467	4,826	5,233	5,391	17,200		62	96	0.09
R410	Sprocket	792	878	1,226	658	1,349	2,162	2,273	2,866	2,946	3,983	65	91	0.08
	Total or average	112,860	$38,949	$56,590		$75,471						52%	75%	$0.05

Component Works Low on Direct-Cost Basis:

Part no.	Name												Unit cost
R918	Rocker	1,091	$663	$1,063	$905	$1,036	$12,655	$14,642	$18,711		64%	103%	$0.05
P220	Pin	3,204	6,685	11,754	9,048	10,413	2,306	2,985			64	113	0.45
P057	Pin	1,281	979	1,675	1,460	1,487					66	113	0.09
T566	Stud	2,452	7,925	12,037	9,563	11,843	12,628	13,461	18,568	$22,983	67	102	0.42
P736	Pin	38,955	6,837	10,475	9,181	10,167	11,492	11,492	13,323		67	103	0.03
P904	Pin	950	1,170	1,801	1,606	1,729	1,767	1,995	3,420		68	104	0.10
H355	Hub	1,155	1,947	3,090	2,552	2,872	2,979	3,026	4,775	6,846	68	108	0.13
P423	Pin	3,402	2,661	4,157	2,994	3,912	5,137	5,477	11,805		68	106	0.09
B605	Bolt	10,561	2,239	3,373	2,893	3,273	3,485	3,707	3,970	$4,718	68	103	0.03
H346	Hub	1,088	2,223	3,570	3,007	3,122	3,151	3,242	3,438	4,128	71	114	0.15
H554	Hub	1,490	1,551	2,214	1,967	1,997	2,077	2,216	2,298	2,459	78	111	0.06
P244	Pin	7,383	7,438	10,948	7,591	8,786	9,498	10,705	11,270	23,773	85	125	0.11
L209	Lever	5,351	2,480	3,827	1,578	2,745	3,692	4,334	4,486	4,826	90	139	0.05
R316	Roller	18,058	2,470	4,610	2,257	2,691	3,250	4,050	4,231	4,984	92	171	0.03
S451	Spacer	2,785	645	1,226	390	697	852	1,104	1,253	1,306	93	176	0.04
P333	Pin	4,258	6,818	12,088	6,898	7,324	9,197	11,113	12,008		93	165	0.32
P379	Pin	6,807	6,984	10,249	5,037	7,352	7,760	9,394	9,421	21,919	95	139	0.11
P682	Pin	3,402	4,037	5,880	2,824	4,208	5,035	5,817	11,533		96	140	0.11
	Total or average	113,673	$65,753	$104,038		$85,654					77%	121%	$0.08
	Cumulative	226,533	$104,703	$160,629		$161,125					65%	100%	$0.08

Component Works Not Cost-Competitive:

Part no.	Name												Unit cost
H265	Hub	4,464	$15,311	$24,341	$13,570	$15,236	$17,275	$17,454	$17,901	$20,489	100%	160%	$0.57
A152	Shaft	2,972	7,749	12,841	6,685	7,667	8,470	10,877			101	167	0.38
R717	Sprocket	4,869	6,834	10,003	6,205	6,707	7,421	7,839	7,887	$9,450	102	149	0.16
S771	Spacer	11,092	971	1,689	909	942	1,053	1,275	1,852	2,203	103	179	0.02
R428	Sprocket	3,180	4,374	6,888	3,637	4,226	4,285	4,293	4,624	5,599	103	163	0.18
R946	Roller	5,904	6,254	10,727	4,815	6,022	6,199	6,494	7,947	19,837	104	178	0.14
R157	Roller	3,181	1,651	2,934	1,082	1,565	1,645	1,749	1,890	2,004	106	188	0.08
B823	Button	18,200	3,296	5,622	2,347	3,094	3,257	3,276	3,314	6,042	107	182	0.03
T863	Stud	7,120	11,136	17,790	8,231	8,590	9,185	13,243	24,706		130	207	0.37
T237	Stop	4,258	12,719	18,713	7,877	8,516	9,112	9,623	10,228	16,606	149	220	0.35
N281	Nut	8,500	6,350	11,322	3,392	3,789	4,114	6,375	7,548	15,640	168	299	0.18
T166	Stud	5,645	8,766	16,014	3,912	5,024	5,701	13,209			174	319	0.41
T586	Stud	10,000	15,957	27,273	7,525	8,900	9,540	11,000	11,520	26,700	179	306	0.40
	Total or average	89,385	$101,367	$166,157		$80,278					126%	207%	$0.21
	Total/Avg. all parts	315,918	$206,069	$326,786		$241,403					85%	135%	$0.11

EXHIBIT 2

Characteristics of Sample of 44 Parts

CATEGORY	NUMBER	VOLUME	DIRECT LABOR $	ACTS HOURS PER 100 PARTS	ANNUAL ACTS HOURS	DL $/ MATERIAL $
Low on full-cost basis	13	4,009[a] [692; 71,200]	.05 [.03; .10]	0.4 [0.3; 1.5]	19 [2; 266]	21% [9; 51]
Low on direct-cost basis	18	3,402 [950; 38,955]	.09 [0.3; .45]	1.2 [0.3; 2.8]	31 [10; 159]	23% [9; 224]
Not cost-competitive	13	5,645 [2,972; 18,200]	.18 [0.2; .57]	1.5 [0.2; 3.4]	70 [18; 150]	57% [22; 480]
Total	44					

[a]Top number is the median value in that category. Beneath the median appears the range [minimum; maximum].

EXHIBIT 3

1985 Turning Machine Overhead Allocation Using Standard Cost System

	APPLIED BASED ON DIRECT LABOR		APPLIED BASED ON MACHINE HOURS		TOTAL $000	%
Direct Overhead						
Maintenance	$32	0.3%	$1,038	10.2%	$1,070	10.5%
Labor allowances	459	4.5	0	0.0	459	4.5
Machine setups	0	0.0	524	5.2	524	5.2
Other OH labor	130	1.3	164	1.6	294	2.9
Scrap and misc.	80	0.8	96	0.9	176	1.7
Employee benefits	1,296	12.7	556	5.5	1,852	18.2
Total direct overhead	$1,997	19.6%	$2,378	23.4%	$4,375	43.0%
Period Overhead						
Maintenance	$127	1.2%	$527	5.2%	$654	6.4%
Salaries	796	7.8	826	8.1	1,622	15.9
Depreciation	0	0.0	1,790	17.6	1,790	17.6
General and misc.	227	2.2	717	7.0	944	9.3
Employee benefits	354	3.5	432	4.2	786	7.7
Total period overhead	$1,504	14.8%	$4,292	42.2%	$5,796	57.0%
Total overhead	$3,501	34.4%	$6,670	65.6%	$10,171	100.0%
Overhead base	$1,714 DL$		242,000 ACTS hrs.			
Direct overhead rate	117%		$9.83 per hr.			
Period overhead rate	88		17.73 per hr.			
Total overhead rate	205%		$27.56 per hr.			

EXHIBIT 4

1985 Turning Machine Overhead Allocation Using ABC Method

	DIRECT LABOR SUPPORT OVERHEAD		MACHINE OPERATION OVERHEAD		MACHINE SETUP OVERHEAD		PRODUCTION ORDER OVERHEAD		MATERIALS-HANDLING OVERHEAD		PART ADMIN. OVERHEAD		GENERAL AND ADMINISTRATION OVERHEAD		TOTAL	
	$000	% TOTAL	$000	% TOTAL	$000	% TOTAL	$000	% TOTAL	$000	% TOTAL	$000	% TOTAL	$000	% TOTAL	$000	% TOTAL
Direct Overhead																
Maintenance	$0	0.0%	$899	8.8%	$45	0.4%	$62	0.6%	$63	0.6%	$0	0.0%	$0	0.0%	$1,069	10.5%
Labor allowances	329	3.2	47	0.5	61	0.6	10	0.1	12	0.1	0	0.0	0	0.0	459	4.5
Machine setups	0	0.0	146	1.4	378	3.7	0	0.0	0	0.0	0	0.0	0	0.0	524	5.2
Other OH labor	0	0.0	67	0.7	0	0.0	106	1.0	122	1.2	0	0.0	0	0.0	295	2.9
Scrap & misc.	0	0.0	141	1.4	0	0.0	30	0.3	6	0.1	0	0.0	0	0.0	177	1.7
Employee benefits	1,100	10.8	339	3.3	246	2.4	77	0.8	90	0.9	0	0.0	0	0.0	1,852	18.2
Total direct OH	$1,429	14.0%	$1,639	16.1%	$730	7.2%	$285	2.8%	$293	2.9%	$0	0.0%	$0	0.0%	$4,376	43.0%
Period Overhead																
Maintenance	$10	0.1%	$333	3.3%	$40	0.4%	$9	0.1%	$8	0.1%	$238	2.3%	$17	0.2%	$665	6.4%
Salaries	270	2.7	179	1.8	62	0.6	243	2.4	0	0.0	421	4.1	448	4.4	1,623	16.0
Depreciation	27	0.3	1,424	14.0	226	2.2	25	0.2	0	0.	43	0.4	45	0.4	1,790	17.6
Gen. & misc.	59	0.6	323	3.2	19	0.2	152	1.5	0	0.0	90	0.9	298	2.9	941	9.3
Employee benefits	103	1.0	147	1.4	34	0.3	103	1.0	2	0.0	207	2.0	190	1.9	786	7.7
Total period OH	$469	4.7%	$2,406	23.7%	$381	3.7%	$532	5.2%	$10	0.1%	$999	9.8%	$998	9.8%	$5,795	57.0%
Total overhead	$1,898	18.7%	$4,045	39.8%	$1,111	10.9%	$817	8.0%	$303	3.0%	$999	9.8%	$998	9.8%	$10,171	100.0%
Overhead base	$1,714 DL$		242,000 annual ACTS hours		32,900 annual setup hours		7,150 annual orders		15,600 annual loads		2,050 part $'s		$10,887 value added			
Direct overhead rate	83.4%		$6.77 per hr.ᵃ		$22.18 per hr.		$39.86 per ord.		$18.78 per load		—					
Period overhead rate	27.4		9.94		11.58		74.41		.64		$487 per part		9.1%			
Total overhead rate	111.0%		$16.71 per hr.		$33.76 per hr.		$114.27 per ord.		$19.42 per load		$487 per part		9.1%			

$1,714 DL$
$1,898 DL$
4,045 Mach. Oper. OH
1,111 Setup OH
817 Prod. Order OH
303 Mat.-Hand. OH
999 Part Admin. OH
$10,887 Value added

ᵃRates shown are averages across all turning machines. In practice, separate machine overhead rates were calculated for each major class of machines.

EXHIBIT 5

Elements for Costing Part A103 in 1985

Materials cost per 100 parts	$6.44
Materials Overhead Rates	
Direct	2.1%
Period	7.6%
Direct labor hours per 100 parts	.185 hr.
ACTS hours per 100 parts	.310 hr.
Labor rate for turning machine	
operation	$12.76
Machine setup time	4.2 hrs.
Part weight	0.175 lb.
Quote volume[a]	8,000
Runs per year	2
6-Spindle Machine Rates[b]	
Direct	$8.99
Period	$7.61

[a]Annual volume as specified by user.
[b]Under ABC system.

APPENDIX

ABC activities for applying overhead to turning machine parts

The ABC study used the accounting estimate of normal volume and total overhead costs as its starting point. Overhead costs were then allocated to seven rather than just two activities. A separate overhead rate was derived for each activity. (See Exhibits 3 and 4 for comparison of the two methods.) Vintila used the following approach to apportion overhead and to develop overhead rates:

1. *Direct labor support* overhead was generated by incentive employees working on parts. It included allowances for benefits, break periods, and a percentage of supervision, personnel, payroll, and industrial engineering salaries. All direct labor support overhead costs were summed ($1,898,000 in 1985) and divided by the total amount of direct labor dollars ($1,714,000) to derive an overhead rate for this activity (111%).

2. *Machine operation* overhead was generated by operating the turning machines, plus an allocation of facility and capacity charges. This activity received most of the costs of machine maintenance, small tools, jigs, and dies, as well as smaller proportions of inspection and defective work, engineering, and supervision salaries. Allocations were also made for depreciation, taxes, interest, and utilities.

The total dollars required to operate the machines ($4,045,000) were divided by the total number of machine hours (242,000) to develop the $16.70 per hour overhead rate for this activity.

Whereas the standard cost system used the same ACTS rate for all turning machines, Vintila examined the machines individually and ultimately developed separate rates for four different-size machines. He gathered data on several factors to create machine-specific estimates of the costs of running them. For example, kilowatt-hours multiplied by the load factor was used to generate utilities cost; replacement costs to estimate the share of insurance, taxes, and depreciation; square footage to calculate a proportion of facilities costs; and the "spindle factor" to allocate tooling and maintenance costs. The spindle factor took into account the number of spindles on a machine; when multiplied by its annual load (or ACTS hours), it provided a basis for allocating tooling and maintenance costs according to size and use of the machine. For all of these factors, Vintila obtained percentages by dividing the total (e.g., replacement costs of all turning machines) by that for the particular machine. To obtain an overall direct overhead rate for a machine, he divided all its direct overhead by its ACTS hours.

Once this information had been generated for each of the turning machines, similar-size machines were grouped and a single overhead rate determined for each group. In this way, machines that happened to have a lower load would not be penalized by a higher rate.

3. *Setup hours* overhead was generated by changing the job to be run. It included actual setup costs; a small share of machine and small-tool maintenance, supervision, and engineering salaries; and a share of depreciation and other facility costs. These costs ($1,111,000) were divided by the estimated number of setup hours (32,900) to arrive at an hourly overhead rate ($33.80).

The number of setup hours was estimated through an examination of production control data, which showed the average setup time to be four hours. This figure was multiplied by the average number (4) of annual runs per part number, and by the 2,050 parts in the system.

4. *Production order activity* was generated by shop activity resulting from each production order. The largest cost was materials control salaries. Percentages of crib attendant costs, inspection, defective work, and manufacturing costs were also applied. The sum was divided by the total number of annual production orders (7,150) to yield a cost of $114 per production order.

5. *Materials-handling* overhead arose from moving barstock to the machines, and then moving the parts to the next operation. The major cost elements were materials-handling labor and equipment maintenance. This activity also received a share of inspection and defective materials costs. An overhead rate ($19.42) was derived by dividing the total allocated costs ($303,000) by the number of loads (15,600).

The number of loads was estimated through a six-step process.

a. $\dfrac{\text{part weight} \times \text{annual volume}}{\text{runs/year for that part}} = \text{weight/run}$

b. $\dfrac{\text{weight/run}}{\text{pounds/load}} = \text{loads/run}$
(average of 2,000 lb. per transport container)

c. loads/run + .5, then round result to nearest full integer
(a calculation to correct for incomplete loads)

d. multiply result in (c) by no. of runs of that part/ year = no. of loads/year moved away from machines

e. loads/year × 2 (movement to and from machine) = total no. of loads/year for that part

f. repeat process for all part numbers, and add no. of loads/part (to obtain total no. of loads per year).

6. *Part administration* overhead was incurred just by having a part number in the department's repertoire. It included the cost of establishing and maintaining records and systems documentation and a share of salaries in process engineering, industrial engineering, supervision, and materials control. The sum of $999,000 in overhead, when distributed among the 2,050 parts in the system, generated a head tax of $487 per part number.

7. *General and administrative* overhead was attributed to the entire factory, not to a particular manufacturing process or activity. It included a large share of taxes, utilities, and depreciation, as well as smaller shares of salaries, such as accounting, reliability, and manufacturing engineering. The $998,000 of G&A overhead was prorated to products based on their value added: the sum of direct labor plus the other six overhead activity costs for each part. The value-added sum became the denominator for determining the G&A rate to be applied to the part.

John Deere Component Works (B)

Frank Stevenson had been appointed division manager of Gear and Special Products in September 1986 after spending 20 years in manufacturing and manufacturing engineering. He summarized his division's response to activity-based costing (ABC):

> Few things have generated more excitement. Even though it's still an allocation, it's such an improvement. Parts we suspected we were undercosting have turned out to be even more expensive than we had thought. It's proven what we suspected about the costs of material handling and transport distances, and triggered our making layout changes. When it showed us the costs added by secondary operations, we brought them back onto the main floor.

ABC COST ESTIMATING MODEL

To use ABC for costing individual parts, a model was developed that could be run using a Lotus 1-2-3 spreadsheet on an IBM personal computer (separate from the overall accounting and data processing systems). It provided considerably more information than the standard cost model, and some elements of the model were interactive. The ABC model, for example, calculated material costs on the basis of the type of steel, part length, and machine number (which affected tools used and waste). Also, materials that were delivered directly to the machines on the floor, bypassing receiving, inspection, and storage, were not charged for any materials overhead. Therefore, material costs depended on how the material was used, as well as its purchase price. (The standard cost system, by contrast, calculated an average cost for parts of a certain weight based entirely on the purchase price of the barstock.) Materials of different prices could be fed into the ABC system, and the model would make cost tradeoffs among them. The model could calculate the number of annual runs that produced the lowest manufacturing costs on an annual basis for a part number; it included inventory holding costs as a

factor in making this assessment. It could also compare setups on different machines for their differential cost effects.

Although the ABC method was developed on the basis of normal volume, the model could also calculate costs at a par (full capacity) level of utilization. Par volume was higher than current normal volume and represented what Gear and Special Products managers considered a more reasonable level of utilization than the currently existing very depressed normal volume. Par overhead rates spread period overhead across higher volumes of parts than did normal rates.

COMPLETING THE ABC STUDY

Keith Williams and Nick Vintila, the authors of activity-based costing, were able to demonstrate the change in estimated costs, from standard to ABC, for the sample of 44 parts examined earlier (see Exhibit 1).

A second study showed the impact of shifting the product mix to exploit the efficiencies from running longer jobs on the turning machines. Exhibit 2 shows the current workload on the turning machines based on the annual machine hours (ACTS) for each part. The overhead assignment (using the new ABC model) to each class of parts is shown at the bottom of the exhibit. Exhibit 3 shows a simulated overhead assignment assuming that the more than 1,000 parts with less than 100 annual ACTS hours run time were transferred from the machines, with the freed-up machine time used to produce 30 new parts that each required at least 500 annual ACTS hours. This change would reduce by 77% the number of part numbers being processed on the machines and reduce the number of setup hours and orders processed by about 60%. Williams explained the rationale for this study.

> We wanted to estimate the impact from substituting a few high-volume parts for the large number of

This case was prepared by research associate Artemis March (under the supervision of Professor Robert S. Kaplan).

low-volume parts we are now running. Overhead is reduced by $2.2 million, or about 21%. The overhead rate declines from 593% to 467% of direct labor. The key question is whether actual overhead reductions of that scale would result from such a change.

Our impression is that at least this amount of overhead reduction should occur. The reduced number of parts should directly reduce the expenses for machine setups and for material management scheduling and coordination. Process and tool and industrial engineering would be supporting only a fifth of the part numbers now being supported. Such a change should make it much easier to standardize raw material, which should reduce coordination in that area. Also, it should be much easier to implement other operational improvements such as sequencing jobs so as to minimize setups, using pick-offs or other attachments to eliminate secondary operations, or possible rearrangements to create a cell environment for the high-volume parts.

DIVISION CHANGES

Stevenson located activity-based costing in the context of a division trying to reorient itself to a new reality: "We must dramatically increase our competitive position in the worldwide market. That requires a quantum leap in manufacturing quality and in reducing our costs." To this end, the division had, during the 1985–1986 period, formally demarcated its product lines into five businesses: gears and shafts, machined parts, cast iron machining, heat treating, and sheet metal work. Wherever possible, departments were reorganized from processes to manufacturing cells and a just-in-time approach was adopted to shorten lead times, improve quality, and thus lower costs. Stevenson stated, "We want 'visual management' to replace routing; we want to stand here at the beginning of the process and see parts being completed right within our view." In addition, a marketing department had been added at the factory level.

USE OF ABC

ABC was widely embraced for decision making in the machined parts business and for implementing other changes more effectively.

Bidding. The ABC model was being used to cost machined parts and to prepare bids to both Deere and outside customers. Sinclair commented, "We

are more confident now about our quote prices. And because ABC more properly penalizes low-volume products, we now know which business we don't want." Also, the ABC model could generate costs at either normal or par volume, making it easier to prepare par-based quotes for the machining portion of the parts.

The division had also changed its transfer pricing and bidding practices. Attempting to bid and transfer at full cost had lost Gear and Special Products much internal business. It began to negotiate "market-based prices," which could be below the full costs calculated by the existing cost accounting system. After a period of experimentation, the use of market pricing became official corporate-wide policy in April 1986.

Process planning. John Gordon, head of process engineering for the machining area, was using the model to compare relative machining efficiencies for different types of steel and part numbers to decide which parts should be run on which types of machines. Because ABC revealed much higher setup and production order costs than those used in the MRP ordering formula, larger lot sizes and fewer annual runs per part number were indicated. Process engineering was using ABC to cost parts on the basis of optimal runs per year and to negotiate with customers to accept fewer runs at lower prices.

Low value-added parts. Gear and Special Products was already accelerating the movement of low-volume, short-running parts off the turning machines. About one-third (31%) of parts required over 20 hours each of direct labor, collectively these accounted for 97% of all direct labor hours and were likely to all remain on the machines. But parts with less than eight hours of labor were being outsourced or would soon go to the low value-added (LVA) jobshop that was being set up adjacent to the machining area. The fate of the remaining parts was still undetermined, but decision making was now aided by the much more accurate costing under ABC. This would eventually allow the division to determine the breakeven point; Dick Sinclair, the manufacturing superintendent, commented, "We don't yet know where the point is that says, 'Put it on the screw machine.' We've eliminated the clearly LVA parts and are working our way up."

The combination of moving LVA parts off the

turning machines and moving toward fewer runs for the remaining parts was expected to increase the average run time, reduce scheduling complexity, and eventually reduce the demands for staff support.

Cell arrangements. While physical manufacturing infrastructure constrained dramatic rearrangement from rows of machines to cells, certain machines could be clustered together and dedicated to a particular high-run part. For example, 12 adjacent machines were now dedicated to running just two parts for General Motors.

Layout. ABC was helping division managers decide how to arrange the machining departments. Sinclair noted, "We did a lot of things in the 1970s that made a lot of sense then, but now we must undo them." The high cost of secondary operations caused management to move these operations not only back into the division (they had been part of Drive Trains for years), but into a corner of the main floor in S Building where they were now being requalified. To make room for these operations, less efficient turning machines had been scrapped; relative efficiencies had been revealed by Vintila's detailed machine study. To reduce handling distances, barstock staging had been made more efficient, and packaging and shipping were being relocated closer to final operations.

These layout changes had not yet been tried out during production. They had been made during the August 1986 vacation shutdown, but the factory had been closed until January 1987 by a corporate-wide UAW strike.

One layout change implemented in April 1985, however, already had made a considerable impact. Gordon's process engineering group, formerly one-half mile from the shop floor, was now located right in the middle of the machining area. According to Andy Edberg, Division Head of Process Engineering, "The effect has been tremendous. The output of our process engineers has tripled, and communications between them and the operators have improved enormously."

FUTURE OF ABC

Useful as it was, ABC's impact was still limited. First, it was run on a personal computer and not integrated with the other division data bases; and second, it was being applied only to turning machine operations.

Extending ABC to secondary operations was Sinclair's top ABC priority: "If we are to price the whole business, we need to extend the model to secondary operations." While the model costed machine operations for parts that would eventually be assembled into major parts such as drive trains, the old standard cost system was still being used for inventory valuation and for costing major parts. Stevenson noted,

We don't want parallel systems; their development and maintenance is too costly. We would like to get rid of the standard system and have just one system —ABC.

EXHIBIT 1

Comparison of Machined Parts Overhead: Standard Costing versus Activity-Based
Costing for the 44 Sample Items—Turning Machine Operations Only

PART NUMBER	PART DESCRIPTION	QUOTE VOLUME	PART WEIGHT	ABC RUNS/ YEAR	PER	ACTS HRS. 100	ACTS HRS. ANNUAL	DIRECT LABOR
The 10 Parts Most Helped by ABC								
H265	Hub	4,464	3,703	4		3.4	150	$1,127
R946	Roller	5,904	0.600	3		2.4	139	695
R428	Sprocket	3,180	1.556	2		2.2	70	527
R717	Sprocket	4,869	1.956	2		2.0	95	713
A152	Shaft	2,972	1.252	3		1.7	51	379
P244	Pin	7,383	1.085	3		1.8	132	706
H355	Hub	1,155	3.052	1		2.3	26	130
R157	Roller	3,181	0.243	1		1.5	46	231
C784	Cap	71,200	0.166	4		0.4	266	1,994
P379	Pin	6,807	1.116	3		1.8	133	651
Total/Average		11,112	1.473	2.6		1.9	110	$7,152
The 10 Parts Most Penalized by ABC								
S771	Spacer	11,092	0.039	1		0.2	20	$100
P675	Pin	2,596	0.412	1		0.4	14	69
P220	Pin	3,204	0.743	3		0.6	19	139
T815	Stud	3,150	0.281	1		0.4	12	58
N281	Nut	8,500	0.222	3		0.2	18	135
T566	Stud	2,452	1.779	3		1.0	24	178
R918	Rocker	1,091	0.703	1		0.9	10	40
R410	Sprocket	792	2.786	1		0.7	6	42
P594	Pin	692	0.722	1		0.3	2	11
S209	Spacer	950	0.141	1		0.3	3	15
Total/Average		3,229	0.712	1.5		0.5	12	$788
Remaining Parts								
H346	Hub	1,088	3.614	2		2.8	31	$151
B823	Button	18,200	0.069	2		0.5	84	417
R316	Roller	18,058	0.042	2		0.4	80	401
T237	Stop	4,258	1.818	5		2.7	116	706
P682	Pin	3,402	1.347	2		1.8	61	325
T586	Stud	10,000	0.602	4		0.7	77	573
S071	Spacer	5,661	1.507	2		1.0	54	407
P583	Pin	3,402	1.253	2		1.5	52	258
P736	Pin	38,955	0.160	2		0.4	159	795
P423	Pin	3,402	1.354	2		1.5	52	258
P333	Pin	4,258	0.937	3		1.3	56	282
L209	Lever	5,351	0.533	2		0.8	41	204
P057	Pin	1,281	0.569	1		1.5	20	97
T863	Stud	7,120	1.110	4		1.0	74	553
T166	Stud	5,645	0.258	3		0.6	36	232
B605	Bolt	10,561	0.286	2		0.3	32	242
P904	Pin	950	2.179	1		1.8	17	86
R647	Sprocket	5,167	3.522	3		1.4	74	372
H622	Hub	4,450	1.913	2		0.6	26	130
S451	Spacer	2,785	0.120	1		0.6	17	83
H554	Hub	1,490	1.582	1		1.1	16	79
T501	Stud	4,879	0.151	1		0.3	17	85
F382	Fitting	4,009	0.711	2		0.5	20	153
S245	Spacer	4,912	0.281	1		0.4	19	94
Total/Average		7,054	1.080	2.2		1.1	51	$6,983
Total/Ave. All Parts		7,180	1,102	2.1		1.1	56	$14,924

Note: Dollar figures are annual totals for the quote quantity.

(continued)

EXHIBIT 1 (*cont.*)

JDCW OVERHEAD COST			ABC OVERHEAD COST			ABC OVERHEAD AS % JDCW		
DIRECT OH	PERIOD OH	TOTAL OH	DIRECT OH	PERIOD OH	TOTAL OH	DIRECT OH	PERIOD OH	TOTAL OH
$3,750	$4,905	$8,654	$3,347	$3,104	$6,451	89%	63%	75%
2,621	3,700	6,321	2,064	2,726	4,792	79	74	76
1,672	2,187	3,859	1,575	1,744	3,319	94	80	86
2,035	2,661	4,696	2,181	2,087	4,266	107	78	91
1,359	1,777	3,136	1,363	1,618	2,981	100	91	95
2,198	3,064	5,262	2,358	2,696	5,054	107	88	96
677	955	1,632	540	1,028	1,568	80	108	96
839	1,185	2,024	711	1,274	1,984	85	108	98
4,151	5,425	9,576	4,929	4,472	9,401	119	82	98
2,039	2,843	4,882	2,238	2,561	4,798	110	90	98
$21,341	$28,702	$50,043	$21,306	$23,310	$44,614	100%	81%	89%
$329	$466	$795	$411	$934	$1,346	125%	200%	169%
263	371	634	377	858	1,236	144	231	195
444	580	1,024	824	1,188	2,011	186	205	196
237	336	573	317	828	1,144	134	246	200
411	537	949	817	1,183	2,000	199	220	211
564	738	1,302	1,228	1,519	2,748	218	206	211
193	281	473	262	783	1,047	136	279	221
172	225	397	339	766	1,105	197	341	278
61	87	148	207	702	910	338	811	615
58	82	140	173	688	862	299	842	617
$2,732	$3,702	$6,434	$4,955	$9,449	$14,409	181%	255%	224%
$823	$1,166	$1,989	$735	$1,225	$1,960	89%	105%	99%
1,305	1,844	3,149	1,317	1,898	3,215	101	103	102
1,266	1,784	3,050	1,278	1,854	3,132	101	104	103
2,072	2,924	4,996	2,413	2,763	5,176	116	94	104
1,131	1,577	2,708	1,253	1,618	2,872	111	103	106
1,595	2,086	3,681	1,888	2,061	3,947	118	99	107
1,167	1,527	2,694	1,449	1,545	2,994	124	101	111
935	1,320	2,255	1,056	1,479	2,534	113	112	112
1,944	2,742	4,686	2,480	2,915	5,394	128	106	115
931	1,314	2,245	1,131	1,489	2,619	121	113	117
1,021	1,441	2,462	1,232	1,668	2,899	121	116	118
747	1,054	1,801	858	1,332	2,190	115	126	122
438	618	1,056	404	926	1,330	92	150	126
1,396	1,825	3,220	2,217	2,100	4,316	159	115	134
757	1,023	1,780	1,098	4,415	2,511	145	138	141
659	864	1,523	911	1,250	2,161	138	145	142
384	542	925	430	894	1,325	112	165	143
1,254	1,769	3,023	2,329	2,054	4,383	186	116	145
548	773	1,320	756	1,171	1,927	138	152	146
347	490	837	370	887	1,257	107	181	150
361	510	871	423	895	1,319	117	176	152
322	454	775	376	894	1,269	117	197	164
488	636	1,124	738	1,103	1,840	151	173	164
336	475	811	433	921	1,355	129	194	167
$22,226	$30,757	$52,982	$27,575	$36,357	$63,925	124%	118%	121%
$46,299	$63,161	$109,459	$53,836	$69,116	$122,948	116%	109%	112%

EXHIBIT 2

Assignment of Machine Overhead by Activity: Present Distribution of Parts

ACTIVITY DATA	0	1–50	50–100	100–500	500–1,000	OVER 1,000	TOTAL
						PART GROUPING BY ANNUAL ACTS HOURS	
Direct Labor ($000)	$0	$251	$207	$783	$236	$236	$1,713
% of total	0.0	14.7	12.1	45.7	13.8	13.8	100.0
Machine (ACTS) Hours	0	17,000	14,000	53,000	16,000	16,000	116,000
% of total	0.0	14.7	12.1	45.7	13.8	13.8	100.0
Number of Part Numbers							
Parts with no requirements	1,110						1,110
Parts with requirements		877	208	256	22	8	1,371
% of total		64.0	15.2	18.5	1.6	0.6	100.0
Annual Setup Hours (est.)							
Orders/part (est.)	0	4	6	8	10	12	
Hours/setup (est.)	4	4	5	5	5	3	
Total setup hours	0	14,032	6,240	10,240	1,100	288	31,900
% of total	0.0	44.0	19.6	32.1	3.4	0.9	100.0
Annual Production Orders							
Orders/part numbers (est.)	0	4	6	8	10	12	
Total production orders	0	3,508	1,248	2,048	220	96	7,120
% of total	0.0	49.3	17.5	28.8	3.1	1.3	100.0
Material-Handling Data							
Loading factor (est.)	0	0.67	0.8	1.0	1.0	0.8	
Cost weighting	0	25,373	17,500	53,000	16,000	20,000	131,873
% of total	0.0	19.2	13.3	40.2	12.1	15.2	100.0
Overhead Assignments ($000)							
Direct labor support	$0	$278	$229	$867	$262	$262	$1,898
Machine operation	0	593	488	1,848	558	558	4,045
Machine setup	0	498	211	356	37	10	1,112
Production orders	0	401	143	237	25	11	817
Material handling	0	58	40	122	37	46	303
Part administration	5	636	151	186	16	6	1,000
General administration	1	268	137	393	102	97	998
Total overhead	$6	$2,732	$1,399	$4,009	$1,037	$990	$10,173
Total overhead/DL $	na	1,088%	676%	512%	439%	419%	594%

EXHIBIT 3

Assignment of Machine Overhead by Activity: Assumed Distribution of Parts

ACTIVITY DATA	0	100–500	500–1,000	OVER 1,000	TOTAL	%	($000)
		PART GROUPING BY ANNUAL ACTS HOURS				INDICATED CHANGE IN ACTIVITY/COST	
Direct Labor ($000)	$0	$783	$465	$465	$1,713	0	
% of total	0.0	45.7	27.1	27.1	100.0		
Machine (ACTS) Hours	0	53,000	31,500	31,500	116,000	0	
% of total	0.0	45.7	27.2	27.2	100.0		
Number of Part Numbers							
Parts with no requirements	1,110				1,100	0	
Parts with requirements		256	44	16	316	−77	
% of total		81.0	13.9	5.1	100.0		
Annual Setup Hours (est.)							
Orders/part (est.)	0	8	10	12			
Hours/setup (est.)	4	5	5	3			
Total setup hours	0	10,240	2,200	576	13,016	−59	
% of total	0.0	78.7	16.9	4.4	100.0		
Annual Production Orders							
Orders/part numbers (est.)	0	8	10	12			
Total production orders	0	2,048	440	192	2,680	−62	
% of total	0.0	76.4	16.4	7.2	100.0		
Material-Handling Data							
Loading factor (est.)	0	1.0	1.0	0.8			
Cost weighing	0	53,000	31,500	39,375	123,875	−6	
% of total	0.0	42.8	25.4	31.8	100.0		
Overhead Assignments							
Direct labor support	$0	867	$515	$515	$1,897	0	$0
Machine operation	0	1,848	1,098	1,098	4,044	0	0
Machine setup	0	356	74	19	449	−60	(663)
Production orders	0	237	50	22	309	−62	(508)
Material handling	0	122	72	90	284	−6	(19)
Part administration	5	186	32	12	235	−77	(765)
General administration	1	393	200	191	785	−21	(213)
Total overhead	$6	$4,009	$2,041	1,947	$8,003	−21	$(2,170)
% Overhead/DL $	na	512%	439%	419%	467%	−21%	

Note: Assumes transfer of parts with less than 100 ACTS and replacing available ACTS hours with parts having more than 500 ACTS.

Sentry Group

The new C300 is currently budgeted to sell through the mass merchandiser chains for about $150 retail. I think this price is too high. We will only sell about 50,000 per year at that price. I think we should drop our selling price from $90 to $80, allowing the merchandisers to drop their price to just under $135. At that price we should sell at least 40% more units, and since the variable cost is about $50, our overall profits will be higher.

JIM BRUSH, SALES MANAGER

I'm not sure we really know what our products cost. I would like to really make certain that we are making a profit at $80, before I agree to drop our price, because we will not be able to change prices again in the near future.

JACK BRUSH, PRESIDENT

INTRODUCTION

Sentry Group (SG), a Rochester, New York manufacturer of fireproof home and office safes, was founded in 1931 to produce insulated metal office safes. Over the years additional metal products, including containers, files, and smaller safes, were introduced. Many of these products were aimed at the consumer as opposed to the office market. In 1984, a completely new class of products manufactured out of plastic was introduced. Due to their ease of manufacture and low cost, the plastic products made household record protection possible and practical. By 1988, these products had considerably expanded the consumer market.

In 1987, SG had total revenues of $100 million generating net income of $5 million (see Exhibit 1). In 1988, the Company was run by Jack and Dick Brush, sons of the company's founder, John D. Brush, Sr., while their younger brother, Bob, ran the distribution center on the West Coast. Jack's sons, Doug and Jim, were the marketing and sales managers, respectively.

PRODUCT DESCRIPTION

SG manufactured over 50 different models in eight product families, seven metal, and one plastic. Within a product line, the product differed only in size. Different models from the same product line could be produced in a single batch without incurring any additional costs. The only real difference was the time taken to weld and fill the insulation cavity. The eight families were as follows:

Metal products

1. Standard safes included 14 models, each approximately 2 feet tall and 1½ feet wide, with varying depths. SG used 20-gauge cold-rolled steel to make these products. The safes were certified by Underwriters Laboratory (UL) to withstand the heat from a house fire (1,500 degrees fahrenheit) for two hours. This certification was called a two-hour UL rating.

2. Design '82 was a slightly higher quality line of safes. These safes provided improved capacity and security. There were seven models in this family. These safes were 4 inches taller and 2 inches wider than the standard safes and had four active, live-bolt security locks rather than one. These safes also had a two-hour UL fire rating.

3. The large safes were the company's largest capacity safes. They were almost 3 feet high and 2 feet wide. They were purchased mainly by businesses and carried a two-hour UL fire rating. There were four models in this line.

4. Small safes were smaller and lighter versions of the safe line. These products used a 24-gauge steel and only carried a one-hour UL fire rating. There were two 11 × 13 models. These were about 5 inches shorter and 3 inches narrower than the standard safes but had the same depth. The three box models were similar in height and width to the 11 × 13 but were shallower.

5. Files were single-drawer pull-out units. The files were 14 inches tall, 16 inches wide, and varied in depth from 24 to 30 inches. They were made of

lighter-weight steel similar to the small safes and had a one-hour fire rating. SG sold four different files.

6. Media products were new products introduced to provide protection for personal computer data (floppy disks). There were two models in the media family which were produced by placing an additional insulated box inside the two most popular models of standard safe. The additional insulation kept the internal temperature of these safes sufficiently low so that the media was not damaged. Media products had a two-hour (UL) fire rating.

7. Security safes consisted of two types of products, pipes and S-4s. They were a very old product line and were not insulated for fire protection. They were used solely for security purposes. The pipes were circular, in-floor safes which could be installed in either wood or concrete. The S-4s were a rectangular wall safe. There were seven different models in this product family.

Plastic products

8. Plastic products were introduced in late 1984 and quickly became the firm's highest-volume products. These were injection molded top-opening chests which could hold either legal or letter-size hanging file folders. There were seven models in this line. Plastic products had a half-hour UL fire rating.

COMPETITIVE ENVIRONMENT

SG marketed its products as the highest-quality available, offering a three-year warranty on parts and service and a 10-year replacement warranty if the safe was damaged in a fire. SG competed in two distinct markets with its metal and plastic products: mass merchandisers and office product dealers. Mass merchandisers were the high-volume retail outlets (like K-Mart and Caldor) who sold directly to the public. Because they promoted the products heavily, they were concerned mainly with getting the best price and sufficient quantity to guard against stock-outs. The office products dealers were less concerned about price than they were about having a full high-quality product line. Sales of the metal product lines were split 60% to mass merchandisers and 40% to office products dealers, while 80% of the plastic products were sold to mass merchandisers and 20% to office products dealers.

The cost of doing business in the two markets was very similar. The only real differences were the cost of cooperative advertising (about 6% in the mass merchandising market and 1% in the office

products) and freight charges (the office products distributors paid for all of their own freight charges).

Metal products. The market for the insulated metal home and office safes was approximately $160 million at retail with overall growth expected to be 10% per annum. SG was the leader in this market with an approximate 50% share. There were three major domestic competitors accounting for about 10% each and three foreign competitors that together accounted for 20%. The domestic competitors offered similar products to SG but at slightly higher prices. These companies were larger, full-line safe manufacturers who offered the large, commercial-purpose safes as well as the smaller home and office ones. The foreign competitors offered products of slightly lower quality at a much lower price.

Plastic products. SG's recent victory in a patent infringement lawsuit had forced two foreign competitors to stop producing imitations of Sentry's plastic product line. This victory left SG as the sole producer of this type of product. With over 10 years left on the patent, it did not look like competitors would be able to produce similar products in the near future. The plastic products competed with the traditional residential fire protection storage boxes. These were small metal boxes that were insulated with gypsum, a much less effective insulation material than the vermiculite used in the plastic products. The market for residential fire protection boxes was estimated at $100 million retail, with an overall growth of 15% per annum. This market was highly fragmented with many small competitors selling gypsum products.

PRODUCTION PROCESS

SG's corporate headquarters and production facility were located in a 250,000-square-foot building in Rochester, New York. The production and inventory storage areas occupied about 80% of the total space available.

Metal products. SG manufactured in-house the majority of the steel parts for the metal safes. Production started in the Press Department, where cold-rolled steel was cut to the proper length and width on shear presses. Large press brakes were used to form the inner and outer steel jacket parts, doors, and door jambs. The door jambs and frames were spot welded to add strength and create a smoother appearance, and the door hinges were mig welded to add durability.

When all welding was finished, the safe frame and door were filled separately with vermiculite insulation (a mixture of water, chemicals, and cement) and set aside to cure for approximately 24 hours. When the insulation was dry, the safe pieces were cleaned and painted and hung on a large overhead conveyor, which traveled slowly around the factory, to dry. By the time they reached the final assembly area, the pieces were dry and the safe frame, door, and lock were assembled to form the completed safe. The completed safe was then packed for shipment.

Plastic products. SG subcontracted production of the plastic chests and lids. The two pieces were received, inspected, and moved to the Insulation Department, where they were filled with vermiculite and set aside to cure. Since the plastic products did not need to be painted, they were moved directly from the Insulation Department to the Plastic Assembly Department, where the chest body, lid, and lock were assembled and the completed chest packaged for shipment.

COST ACCOUNTING SYSTEM

SG used a standard product costing system to account for inventory transactions throughout the year. The material and labor standards were reviewed annually and updated as needed. The overhead allocation calculation was made at the end of every fiscal year, and the result was used in the next year's standard costs.

The material portion of the standard costs was calculated by multiplying the material content of the products by the standard price per unit. The labor portion of the standard cost was calculated by summing the standard hours per unit for each direct department and multiplying the result by the company's average labor rate of $18.00 per hour (Exhibit 2 contains the standard hours per unit by direct department for representative products in each product line).

There were seven direct manufacturing depart-ments (Press, Spot Welding, Mig Welding, Insulation, Clean and Paint, Final Assembly, and Plastics Assembly). The labor accounts for these direct manufacturing departments included both direct and indirect labor; for example, materials handling was included in the labor accounts. To determine the direct labor content of the products, the Controller's Department calculated the annual percentage of indirect versus direct hours for the entire plant from the payroll records. It then backed this percentage out of the labor figures to give the direct labor standards. In 1987 the average indirect percentage was 22%; consequently, this rate was used in setting the 1988 standards. The indirect labor costs identified by this procedure were called allocated indirect labor and treated as part of overhead.

Overhead contained five major elements: allocated indirect labor, the overhead associated with the seven direct manufacturing departments, general plant costs, shipping and receiving costs, and maintenance costs. The overhead rate for the year was determined by dividing the total overhead of the previous year by the total direct labor costs (Exhibit 3). The resulting overhead rate was multiplied by the direct labor content of the products to give the overhead cost per product. The cost system did not formally differentiate between variable and fixed costs, but the Controller estimated that 75% of production costs were variable.

All other departments, including Engineering, Quality Control, and Materials Management, were considered period expenses and were included in selling, general, and administrative expenses (Exhibit 4 contains the 1987 direct manufacturing department summary cost report, Exhibit 5 the 1987 indirect manufacturing department summary cost report, and Exhibit 6 the 1987 cost report for the selling, general, and administrative departments).

THE PRODUCT COSTING ANALYSIS

Dick Legge, Manager of Special Projects, had joined the company in 1982 after running his own management consulting firm for about 25 years. Dick had recently attended a seminar on competing through manufacturing at the University of Rochester. One of the speakers had outlined how traditional cost accounting systems that allocate indirect and support costs on the basis of direct labor could significantly misstate product costs. This speaker had increased Dick's misgivings about his firm's cost system. When he heard Jack Brush's concern about the accuracy of the reported product costs, Dick agreed wholeheartedly and was asked to undertake a special study to determine more accurate product costs.

Dick commented,

I am not a specialist in cost system design and did not feel equipped to undertake the study on my own. Consequently, I hired a consulting firm to undertake the analysis. The launch date of the C300 was only three months away, so they were given 10 weeks to make a more accurate determination of product costs.

The consulting firm sent Anne Abbot, a recent MBA graduate and CPA, to design the system. She first studied the validity of the direct material and labor accounting systems. Satisfied that these systems were relatively accurate, her major concern was the accuracy of the allocated indirect labor, but because she could see no way in the short term to improve the situation, she turned her attention to the overhead accounts. Anne started with the direct manufacturing department costs. These costs amounted to just under $3 million.

The general ledger had recently been reorganized to allow the direct manufacturing overhead costs to be traced to the departments. Anne reviewed the tracing procedures and decided that the departmental costs were adequate for her purposes. Discussions with plant personnel indicated that these costs could be allocated to the product lines using direct labor hours and then to the products by the number of units produced.

The technique of tracing costs first to the product line and then to the products using the number of units produced was acceptable because of the similarity in the manufacturing processes for products in the same product lines. From an overhead perspective, the products within each line were essentially identical. Therefore, they should have the same overhead traced to them. Using the number of units produced achieved this objective.

The next set of costs Abbot analyzed were the three indirect manufacturing departments. The cost of these departments amounted to just under $9 million. The General Plant Account was the largest

of the three accounts, about $7.5 million. Anne asked Roger Murphy, the Plant Foreman, about the activities that drove these costs. He said that the expenses in the General Plant category were caused by a number of different factors. The amount of supervisory labor spent on a specific product or product line varied depending on the number of direct labor personnel in the department, the complexity of the products produced, and the skill level of the department's employees. Utilities Expense was most closely related to the amount of time machines were running each day in a given department, while the cost of uniforms was determined by the number of people working in a department. The depreciation on certain machines and equipment could be traced to the departments in which the machines were located. The rest of the costs were small and not driven by any particular activity. Abbot analyzed the general plant costs into the five categories identified by Murphy.

For each of these categories, Abbot identified an allocation base to trace the costs to the cost centers. These bases were as follows:

COST CATEGORY	ALLOCATION BASE
Supervision	Direct tracing
Utilities	Management estimate
Uniforms	Head count
Item depreciation	Direct tracing
Other	Manufacturing square feet

Sue Merz, Supervisor of the Shipping and Receiving Department, said that the title of the department should actually be Materials Handling. She identified her group's activities as being 30% shipping, 25% receiving, and 45% material requisitions. Lynn Barber, Manager of the Maintenance Department, said that it was easy to identify what kept her people busy because normal, preventive, and emergency maintenance were performed on the basis of work orders issued. Abbot identified the cost drivers of these activities as follows:

ACTIVITY	COST DRIVER
Shipping	Bills of lading
Receiving	Invoices
Materials requisition	Requisitions
Maintenance	Work orders

Abbot then turned her attention to the selling, general, and administrative accounts. She was concerned that many of the costs contained in these accounts were actually production costs. She interviewed the supervisors of the quality control, materials management, and engineering departments to see if she was right. Her suspicions were borne out by the interviews. John Martin, the Quality Control Supervisor, confirmed that 100% of his department's efforts were related to production. He said that 40% of the department's time was spent on statistical process control, and 60% related to inspection activities. In general, he felt that the amount of time spent on process control was determined by the number of times the product was manufactured. Inspection activity was also driven by production runs because the Quality Control Department examined the first and last items in each production run.

Wayne Kokinda, the Materials Manager, was responsible for overall management of purchasing and inventory scheduling. Wayne said that 70% of the total cost of the Materials Management Department related to purchasing, while the other 30% was related to inventory scheduling. He suggested that Abbot interview the individuals in charge of those two areas, Terry Marlowe and Paul Bovard. Marlowe, the Purchasing Manager, said that the work performed in the department was driven by the number of purchase orders it issued. Bovard, the inventory and production scheduler, said that his work was divided between preparing the master production schedule, expediting important orders, and updating the master data files. While not able to identify easily measured cost drivers, he was able to estimate the time spent in his department on each product line.

Mark Preston, Engineering Department Manager, stated, "Our time is divided almost evenly between developing new products and modifying existing products and production processes." The work performed on existing designs or processes was initiated by engineering change orders and could therefore be traced to specific products or product lines.

Finally, the General Corporate Department contained costs related to the entire building. These costs included building depreciation, property taxes, and building and grounds.

From these interviews Anne Abbot chose the following cost drivers for the activities performed in these departments:

ACTIVITY	COST DRIVER
Quality control	Producting runs
Purchasing	Purchase orders
Inventory scheduling	Time estimated
Engineering (current portion only)	Engineering change orders
Corporate (building)	Total square feet

Using total square feet as an allocation base caused some of the building costs to be traced to the inventory storage and administrative areas of the facility. Abbot allocated the costs traced to the inventory storage areas using percentage of sales, which she felt was an adequate proxy for the area dedicated to each product line. The costs traced to the administrative areas she redefined as selling, general, and administrative costs. The costs transferred from the sales, general, and administrative category amounted to about $3.5 million (see Exhibit 7). This transfer increased manufacturing overhead to about $17.5 million.

After completing the interviews and identifying the cost drivers, Abbot set about collecting the quantity of each cost driver associated with every product line. This process took about four weeks to complete, and from this data Abbot was able to compute the cost per activity (Exhibit 8).

To demonstrate the impact of the conversion to activity-based costing, Abbot generated a comparison of the old and new costs for the highest sales dollar model in each product line (Exhibit 9). Abbot then turned her attention to the C300, the product that had initiated the study.

The C300 decision

The C300 was a new product that the firm planned to introduce in June. It was a plastic chest that could hold 12 file folders, twice the capacity of the largest existing product, the C200. The C300 represented a minor technical breakthrough because of its size. A special way to fill the insulation cavity had to be developed. This process was currently being patented. This patent would increase the firm's hold on the manufacturing technology of plastic products. SG was excited about their new product, which they felt would rapidly become a best seller.

Abbot, after working with the design and manufacturing engineers, was able to estimate the activity-based parameters for the new product (Exhibit 10). Her major concern, as she sat down to estimate the activity-based cost of the C300, was what price she would recommend for the C300 if she were asked her opinion at the upcoming presentation of her study findings.

EXHIBIT 1

SENTRY GROUP

1987 Income Statement

($000)

Revenues
Gross sales		$98,180
Returns, discounts, and allowances		1,360
Net sales		$96,820

Cost of Goods
Material		$34,400
Direct labor		7,960
Overhead:		
Indirect labor	$2,248	
Direct departments	2,676	
Indirect departments	8,916	
Total overhead	$13,840	
Total cost of goods		$56,200
Gross margin		$40,620

Selling, General, and Administrative
Quality control	380	
Engineering	2,810	
Material management	1,190	
Personnel	400	
Corporate	7,000	
Controllers	2,090	
Profit sharing	3,810	
Marketing	1,600	
Sales	14,870	
West Coast warehouse	900	
Fitness center	200	
Total		$35,250
Net Income		$5,370

EXHIBIT 2

SENTRY GROUP

Direct Labor Hour Standards

for Highest-Volume Products

| PRODUCT FAMILY | MODEL | DEPARTMENT | | | | | | | TOTAL HOURS |
		PRESS	SPOT	MIG	INSULATE	CLEAN/ PAINT	METAL ASSEMBLY	PLASTIC ASSEMBLY	
Standard safe	SS100	0.23	0.41	0.17	0.12	0.32	0.41	0.00	1.67
Design '82 (safe)	D120	0.65	0.01	1.28	0.28	0.79	1.82	0.00	4.82
Large safe	LS300	0.88	0.01	3.95	0.36	2.53	2.72	0.00	10.45
Small safe	B250	0.14	0.37	0.00	0.10	0.25	0.43	0.00	1.29
Files	F100	0.38	0.81	0.00	0.12	0.57	1.08	0.00	2.96
Media products	M100	0.29	0.44	2.77	0.14	0.49	0.70	0.00	4.83
Security safe	S150	0.08	0.00	0.85	0.00	0.13	0.01	0.00	1.06
Plastic products	P200	0.00	0.00	0.00	0.07	0.00	0.00	0.24	0.32

EXHIBIT 3

SENTRY GROUP

1987 Overhead Rate Calculation

($000)

Direct Labor	
Total labor dollars	$10,208
Indirect labor dollars (22%)	2,248
Direct Labor Dollars	$ 7,960
Overhead	
Indirect labor	$2,248
Departmental	2,676
General	7,404
Shipping and receiving	748
Maintenance	764
Total overhead	$13,840
Rate Calculation	
Overhead/direct labor	1.74

EXHIBIT 4

SENTRY GROUP
Manufacturing Department Cost Structures
($000)

ACCOUNT	DEPARTMENT							
	PRESS	SPOT	MIG	INSULATE	CLEAN/ PAINT	METAL ASSEMBLY	PLASTIC ASSEMBLY	TOTAL
Direct labor	$972	$1,288	$672	$888	$1,040	$1,908	$1,192	$7,960
Indirect labor	275	364	190	251	294	539	337	2,248
Payroll taxes	228	284	144	180	212	404	232	1,684
Supplies	36	152	0	40	180	64	76	548
Repairs and maintenance	28	24	0	28	52	24	4	160
Safety service	0	4	0	0	4	4	0	12
Die repair	272	0	0	0	0	0	0	272
Total	$1,811	$2,116	$1,006	$1,387	$1,782	$2,943	$1,841	$12,884

EXHIBIT 5

SENTRY GROUP
Indirect Department Cost Structures
($000)

ACCOUNT	GENERAL PLANT	RECEIVING	MAINTENANCE	TOTAL
Salaries	$2,032	$556	$644	$3,232
Payroll taxes	364	96	112	572
Supplies	560	60	8	628
Repairs and maintenance	252	0	0	252
Safety service	28	0	0	28
Depreciation	2,728	0	0	2,728
Uniform	136	0	0	136
Utilities	924	0	0	924
Other	380	36	0	416
Total	$7,404	$748	$764	$8,916

EXHIBIT 6

SENTRY GROUP
Selling, General, and Administrative Department Cost Structures
($000)

ACCOUNT	QUALITY CONTROL	ENGINEERING	MATERIAL MANAGEMENT	PERSONNEL	GENERAL CORPORATE	CONTROLLER
Salaries	$316	$1,462	$924	$284	$2,044	$1,340
Payroll taxes	52	252	160	52	348	232
Supplies	4	60	56	40	75	232
Repairs and maintenance	0	8	0	0	70	112
Depreciation	0	0	0	0	618	0
Utilities	0	0	0	0	0	0
Other	4	28	26	16	0	0
Fees, dues, and subscriptions	0	324	4	4	1,588	56
Travel and entertainment	4	56	20	4	153	56

(continued)

EXHIBIT 6 (*cont.*)

ACCOUNT	QUALITY CONTROL	ENGINEERING	MATERIAL MANAGEMENT	PERSONNEL	GENERAL CORPORATE	CONTROLLER
Product development	0	620	0	0	0	0
Public relations	0	0	0	0	0	0
Market research	0	0	0	0	0	0
Freight-out	0	0	0	0	0	0
Freight-in	0	0	0	0	0	0
Warehouse	0	0	0	0	0	0
Trade show	0	0	0	0	0	0
Commissions	0	0	0	0	0	0
Telephone and postage	0	0	0	0	386	62
Bad debts	0	0	0	0	54	0
Pension and profit sharing	0	0	0	0	108	0
Insurance	0	0	0	0	477	0
Property taxes	0	0	0	0	775	0
Building and grounds	0	0	0	0	249	0
Rent	0	0	0	0	54	0
Co-op advertising	0	0	0	0	0	0
Advertising	0	0	0	0	0	0
Sales literature and mailings	0	0	0	0	0	0
Customer service	0	0	0	0	0	0
Total	$380	$2,810	$1,190	$400	$7,000	$2,090

ACCOUNT	PROFIT SHARING	MARKETING	SALES	WEST COAST WAREHOUSE	FITNESS CENTER	TOTAL
Salaries	$0	$864	$1,048	$472	$140	$8,894
Payroll taxes	0	148	176	60	24	1,504
Supplies	0	24	8	12	32	543
Repairs and maintenance	0	0	0	0	4	194
Depreciation	0	0	0	0	0	618
Utilities	0	0	0	8	0	8
Other	0	44	16	20	0	154
Fees, dues, and subscriptions	0	4	4	0	0	1,984
Travel and entertainment	0	104	404	56	0	857
Product development	0	0	0	0	0	620
Public relations	0	328	0	0	0	328
Market research	0	84	0	0	0	84
Freight-out	0	0	2,140	0	0	2,140
Freight-in	0	0	0	160	0	160
Warehouse	0	0	256	80	0	336
Trade show	0	0	332	0	0	332
Commissions	0	0	4,712	0	0	4,712
Telephone and postage	0	0	0	32	0	480
Bad debts	0	0	0	0	0	54
Pension and profit sharing	3,810	0	0	0	0	3,918
Insurance	0	0	0	0	0	477
Property taxes	0	0	0	0	0	775
Building and grounds	0	0	0	0	0	249
Rent	0	0	0	0	0	54
Co-op advertising	0	0	4,286	0	0	4,286
Advertising	0	0	1,076	0	0	1,076
Sales literature and mailings	0	0	356	0	0	356
Customer service	0	0	56	0	0	56
Total	$3,810	$1,600	$14,870	$900	$200	$35,250

EXHIBIT 7

SENTRY GROUP
Selling, General, and Administrative Costs Transferred
($000)

Quality control	$380
Engineering	1,400
General corporate	850
Material management	1,180
Fitness center	(270)
	$3,540

EXHIBIT 8

SENTRY GROUP
Cost per Unit of Cost Driver

COST TRACED	COST DRIVER	COST PER COST DRIVER UNIT
Press departmental overhead	Press direct labor hour*	$55
Spot weld departmental overhead	Spot weld direct labor hour*	15
Mig weld departmental overhead	Mig weld direct labor hour*	13
Insulation departmental overhead	Insulation direct labor hour*	34
Clean and paint departmental overhead	Clean and paint direct labor hour*	20
Metal assembly departmental overhead	Metal assembly direct labor hour*	12
Plastic assembly departmental overhead	Plastic assembly direct labor hour*	14
Building costs	Direct labor hour*	7
Supervision	Supervision hour	20
Maintenance	Work order	3216
Shipping	Bills of lading	80
Receiving	Invoice	736
Requisitions	Requisition	56
Purchasing	Purchase order	1216
Inventory	Sales ($)	0.0112
Scheduling and storage	Production run	984
Quality control engineering	Engineering change order	3,425

*Excludes indirect labor

EXHIBIT 9

SENTRY GROUP
Comparison of Reported Product Costs for Highest-Volume Products

PRODUCT FAMILY	MODEL	UNIT VOLUME (000)	SALES PRICE	EXISTING SYSTEM COST	MARGIN	ABC SYSTEM COST	MARGIN
Standard safe	SS100	75	$180	$106	41%	$106	41%
Design '82 (safe)	D120	2	256	204	20	274	−7
Large safe	LS300	1	570	414	27	450	21
Small safe	B250	16	106	70	34	70	34
Files	F100	1	172	148	14	220	−28
Media	M100	1	676	382	43	448	34
Security safe	S150	10	146	72	51	41	72
Plastic products	P200	450	30	22	27	20	33

EXHIBIT 10

SENTRY GROUP

Estimated Activity-Based Parameters C300

PER UNIT	PRODUCTION VOLUME	
	50,000	70,000
	COST DRIVER QUANTITY CONSUMED	
Material	$40	$40
Insulation direct labor hours*	0.2	0.2
Plastic assembly direct labor hours*	0.3	0.3
Supervision hours	0.15	0.15
TOTAL PRODUCED		
Work orders	6	7
Bills of ladings	500	650
Invoices	35	50
Requisitions	2,000	2,500
Purchase orders	70	90
Sales ($ millions)	$4.5	$5.6
Production runs	100	125
Engineering change orders	10	10

*Excludes indirect labor hours

Schrader Bellows (A)

INTRODUCTION

In a diversified company, a few great businesses often sustain a whole kennel of dogs. Within divisions, one or two fabulously profitable product lines frequently support a slew of miserable money-losers. And within product lines, it is common for a small portion of the range to subsidize an astonishing number of unimportant products whose true ROI can easily be worse than −100%. Our traditional cost accounting systems systematically mask the damage caused by the losing divisions, product lines, and products. Sorting out the true profitability of business units, product lines, and of individual products is at the heart of strategic analysis.

This sentiment was expressed by William F. Boone, Vice-President of Planning and Development at Scovill, Inc. In 1983, Boone, a 1977 Harvard MBA, was analyzing the product profitability of the Schrader Bellows Automation Group, one of six Scovill divisions. Prior to accepting his current position at Scovill, Boone had worked for Bain & Company and for The Strategic Planning Institute.

Scovill, a diversified group of manufacturing companies, had 1983 sales of $743 million, operating income of $71 million, and net earnings of $27 million (Exhibit 1). In addition to Schrader Bellows, Scovill owned Schrader Automotive, the world leader in tire valve manufacturing; the Apparel Fasteners Group, producers of fasteners for the clothing industry; Yale Security Group, whose product line included Yale locks; Hamilton Beach, a leading full-time producer of electric housewares; and Nu-Tone, a producer of built-in products for the home such as radio-intercoms, exhaust fans, and door chimes.

Schrader Bellows Automation Group was created in 1979, the year after Scovill purchased Bellows International and amalgamated it with Schrader Fluid Power operations. The new group was viewed by Scovill as a world leader in pneumatic controls. Its strategic advantages were a broad line of quality products, the largest direct salesforce and distributor network in the industry, and a strong market position in emerging industrial countries.

In 1983 Schrader Bellows accounted for 13% of group sales but only 6% of operating income. In 1979, in contrast, it had accounted for 15% of sales and 21% of operating income. In the last five years, Schrader Bellows had lost profitability almost continually (Exhibit 2) and was viewed as a problem division by Scovill senior management. Management of the division attributed the declining profitability to sales decreases caused by a dramatic drop in demand for capital goods.

THE FLUID POWER INDUSTRY

Schrader Bellows competed solely in the pneumatic segment of the fluid power market. This segment contained numerous competitors, each with its own specialized niche, producing a set of nonstandard products that could not be replaced by a competitor's equipment without major circuit redesign. This practice resulted in each firm having a captive customer base.

In recent years, foreign competitors, especially from the United Kingdom and Japan, had introduced many well-received standardized components. Industry experts were predicting that standardized parts would gradually dominate the fluid power market.

Schrader Bellows had analyzed the competitive markets in which it operated and had identified 13 major and numerous minor competitors. While each product line could be analyzed as a separate competitive market, management had found it productive to treat the product groups as the unit of analysis and had estimated the market share of each major competitor in its four product groups (Exhibit 3).

PRODUCTS

Schrader Bellows produced over 2,700 pneumatic control products in its Wake Forest, North Carolina plant. These were grouped into four major product groups and a number of other minor products that were either experimental in nature (e.g., robots) or supplemented the productive output of other Scovill divisions (e.g., automotive tire valves). Total 1983 revenue from Wake Forest was just over $20 million. The plant was expanded in 1978 when the Bellows manufacturing facilities had been integrated into Wake Forest. There were several other Schrader Bellows plants throughout the world, but Boone had identified Wake Forest as the focus for the initial investigation because of the large number of different products manufactured at that plant.

The air preparation and accessories manager since 1966 was Joe Hinton, a 25-year Schrader Bellows veteran. Air preparation and accessories consisted of two main product groups: the filter, regulator and lubrication (FRL) group, and the maintenance, repair, and overhaul parts (MRO) product group.

The FRLs were used to prepare the air passing from a compressor into a compressed air system. Preparation was necessary to lengthen the life of the valves and tools used in the system. Air preparation required three distinct and separate steps: filtration, regulation, and lubrication. Filtration removed the majority of the moisture in the system and particulate matter with a diameter over 5 microns. Regulation maintained a constant downstream pressure even if the compressor was surging. Lubrication prolonged the life of the air valves, cylinders, and rotary tools by reducing friction between moving parts.

While available separately, FRLs were typically sold as a single, integrated unit placed between the compressor and the rest of the air system.

The MRO product group consisted of a hodge-podge of air preparation accessories including blow guns, mufflers, and quick connect couplers. Blow guns are small, hand-held compressed air guns used to direct a blast of compressed air at a recently machined part or at the work area to remove metal and wood chips. Blow guns are relatively simple and inexpensive devices used in almost all metal cutting and woodworking shops. Mufflers, or more properly air exhaust mufflers, are used to silence blasts of compressed air at the exhaust port of valves. They are required by OSHA to reduce air noise below a specified level. Quick connect couplers allow tools to be quickly connected and disconnected from the air line. They are used throughout the typical factory compressed air system.

Hubie Jenks, the product manager for the directional and flow control groups, was a 20-year veteran with Schrader Bellows. Since 1980, he had been the manager of the directional control and flow control valve product groups; previously he had been the assistant product manager. The valve products were used in numerous applications in many industries; a typical use was to control the movement of a part that was being machined.

The directional control valve product line consisted of six major families, all providing the same general service, direction control, but varying in operating conditions permitted, complexity of service provided, and pressure ranges accommodated.

The flow control valve line contained three major product lines all providing the same general service, flow control, but varying in the accuracy of flow control, the ease of adjustment, and the direction of flow control (one or both directions).

The division marketed a complete range of valves, a policy Jenks viewed as fundamental to the firm's marketing strategy. In a recent meeting Jenks remarked, "A full line allows you the opportunity to service the ultimate number of accounts. Many accounts buy a number of products at once and will not multisource; the amount of sales represented by that type of customer is a substantial fraction of the total valve market." Jenks's belief in the value of offering a full product line was strongly shared by the marketing and sales department.

The other product groups included production machine components, pneumatic cylinders, two small robots, and automotive tire valves. The tire valves were being made at Schrader Bellows for the first time; previously, they had been manufactured in the Schrader Automotive plant. Scovill management felt that Schrader Bellows could introduce new production techniques and reduce the cost of manufacture. These tire valves were significantly smaller than the typical Schrader Bellows product and were causing manufacturing a lot of headaches.

The various product groups were sold directly by the firm's salesforce and via distribution houses to the end user. The direct salesforce produced 40% of the domestic revenues through sales to machinery and equipment manufacturers. Schrader Bellows was proud of its direct salesforce and felt it was both the largest and the best in the industry.

Salesforce compensation consisted of two major components, base salary and commissions. In 1985 the salary base averaged $22,000 per year. This varied by $2,000 to $3,000 depending on seniority. Sales representatives on average earned commissions equal to 60% of their base salary. The commission structure was entirely based on planned sales. Up to 75% of planned sales, the salesperson earned a maintenance fee of only ½% of sales. Above that level, the commission rose rapidly to its maximum of 7% for sales above plan.

For FRL and MRO products, OEM sales were not common because Schrader Bellows was generally seen as a high-price producer with little quality advantage (though their FRL line was viewed as the Cadillac of the industry, having several advanced easy-to-maintain features that were only matched by one other competitor). This price disadvantage was less serious in the end-user market because end users typically only buy one or two units and are more interested in delivery and ease of ordering than price.

In comparison to the FRL and MRO products, valves were special-application items that required a salesforce with considerable technical skills. Schrader Bellows valve prices were in the top 25% of the market and typically were about 20% above the market average. In the valve lines, the technical demands of the marketplace, coupled with a perceived quality advantage, allowed the firm to recover its higher than average production costs.

Over the years, the firm's strategy of providing a full product line had resulted in a considerable proliferation of variations for each product. The plant now produced over 2,700 different final products and stocked up to 20,000 parts. Some of these variations were quite simple and required minimal change to the production process. Others, however, required a substantially changed production process. Many of these variations and some of the less popular sized items had relatively small demand and tended to disrupt the smooth flow of production in the plant. For example, it was quite common for a long-run production process to be interrupted because a special variation small-volume product was wanted in a hurry. The existing setup would have to be broken down and set up for the new part. Once the special part had been manufactured, the machine would be broken down and then set up again for the original part. The production personnel at the plant felt that the sales, marketing, and senior management people, who were all located in Akron, Ohio, were not aware of the nuisance these constant interruptions caused.

PRODUCTION PROCESS

There were five manufacturing departments: automatic machining, plating, general machining, assembly, and packing.

Production began in the automatic machining department where bar stock, castings, and forgings were machined. Parts manufactured from bar stock were produced on screw machines, and those from castings and forgings on chucking machines. Both types of machines were automated, designed to produce high-volume parts, and were capable of performing several operations sequentially without human intervention. The two main tasks of the operators were keeping the machines loaded and undertaking in-process inspection.

In the plating department, parts were immersed in large chemical baths and electrochemically plated. Once plated, the completed parts were stored in work in process.

Parts manufactured from purchased parts or subassemblies were produced in the general machining department. This department contained relatively simple machines: drills, lathes, and grinding machines. These machines performed drilling, tapping, shaping, deburring, and finishing operations. Most of the machines were manually loaded and operated, but recently some numerically controlled and automatic loading machines had been purchased.

Finished products and subassemblies were produced in the assembly department. This was a labor-intensive process that used relatively simple machines to assemble the products from the manufactured, purchased, and subassembled parts stored in work in process.

In the packing department, finished products, associated documentation, and spare parts were put in a cardboard box and the box sealed.

PRODUCT COSTING

Product costs were calculated by the firm's computerized standard cost system as the sum of material, direct labor, and overhead costs (Exhibit 4).

The standard material cost of the product was the sum of all the raw material and purchased parts included in the finished product.

The standard direct labor cost of the product was determined by identifying all the direct labor required to produce the manufactured parts and to assemble the product. Direct labor costs were tracked by labor class. In all, there were 15 labor classes with rates varying from $6.50 to $10.00 per hour. The appropriate labor class required by each operation was specified by manufacturing engineering. The wage rate for each class was supplied by the personnel department.

Overhead was allocated based on the number of direct labor hours required to manufacture and assemble the product in each of the five manufacturing departments. Each department had its own overhead allocation rate (Exhibit 5) which represented the total overhead costs associated with the department divided by the expected number of direct labor hours in that department.

The overhead associated with each department consisted of two elements. The first was the overhead directly traceable to that department (e.g., factory space and indirect personnel). The second overhead element was the support department and fixed plant expenses allocated to the manufacturing department (Exhibit 6). This allocation was achieved using a number of different bases.

The total costs of four of the eight support departments (finished goods inventory, purchasing, raw materials inventory, and manufacturing engineering) were allocated to the manufacturing departments on the basis of the number of direct labor hours expected to be charged in each of the manufacturing departments. For example, if the total direct labor hours of the five manufacturing departments was budgeted at 100,000 hours, of which the assembly department accounted for 20,000 hours, assembly would be allocated 20% (20,000/ 100,000) of the total cost of these four support departments.

The total cost of the work-in-process inventory department was allocated to the manufacturing departments on the basis of the percentage of direct labor hours expected to be charged in the automatic manufacturing, plating, packing, and general machining departments (assembly was excluded because it was not responsible for any significant work-in-process costs).

The production and control department cost was allocated to the manufacturing departments on the basis of the ratio of total labor hours (direct and indirect) expected to be charged in each of the five manufacturing departments.

The total costs of the setup and quality control departments were allocated to the manufacturing departments based on the estimates of the workloads associated with each manufacturing department provided by the managers of each department.

The allocated costs from each of the support departments were then added to the overhead costs of the manufacturing departments, creating a separate overhead pool for each manufacturing department. Departmental burden rates were determined by dividing each overhead pool by the direct labor hours worked in that department. To illustrate, assume the assembly department had an overhead cost pool of $480,000 ($120,000 of its own and $360,000 allocated from the support departments) and that 20,000 direct labor hours were expected to be worked in that department. The burden rate for

the assembly department would then be calculated at $24.00 per direct labor hour ($480,000/20,000).

PRODUCT PRICING

Schrader Bellows generally priced its products based on cost, but market considerations came into play at both the beginning and the end of the price-setting process. A target price was set when a new product was first sent to engineering. This target price was based on the anticipated costs and potential market for that particular product. After engineering was complete, the cost to manufacture the product was determined. A standard formula was used to arrive at the selling price. Generally, the objective was to obtain a standard margin of 40% to 45%.[1] This price was evaluated against the target price and any relevant information regarding the market. If the price was too high, either the project would be reengineered in an effort to lower the cost, or the margin would be decreased.

Once a product was in production, its price was reviewed annually when new standard costs were published. If a product's cost was too high, the price was raised, the product was reengineered, or it was dropped (the industry norm was to support a product for five years, after which it was dropped). If none of these options were feasible, the product was left in the line at the old price.

---

[1]For example, if a valve cost $3.52 and a 40% margin was required, the cost was multiplied by 1.67 to give the discounted price of $5.88. If the average discount was expected to be 35%, the discounted price was divided by 0.65 to give the list price of $9.05.

EXHIBIT 1

SCHRADER BELLOWS (A)

Scovill Five-Year Financial Review

SELECTED FINANCIAL DATA (IN MILLIONS OF DOLLARS, EXCEPT PER SHARE DATA)	1983	1982	1981	1980	1979
Net sales	$742.6	$691.4	$817.9	$793.0	$788.1
Cost of sales	513.9	470.2	572.4	561.3	554.2
Interest on borrowed money	19.8	26.3	26.7	27.4	24.9
Pretax earnings from continuing operations	51.6	23.2	59.8	54.0	65.9
Federal, foreign, and state income taxes	23.6	8.3	27.5	24.4	29.5
Minority interest in net earnings (loss) of consolidated subsidiaries	3.1	(.3)	2.3	2.2	1.1
Earnings (loss):					
From continuing operations	24.9	15.2	30.0	27.4	35.3
From discontinued operations		4.7	(34.5)	(3.4)	(3.3)
Extraordinary credit	2.5				
Net earnings (loss)	27.4	19.9	(4.5)	24.0	32.0
Earnings (loss) per share of common stock:					
Primary:					
From continuing operations	2.30	1.60	3.18	2.92	3.81
From discontinued operations		.50	(3.68)	(.36)	(.34)
Extraordinary credit	.23				
Net earnings (loss)	2.53	2.10	(.50)	2.56	3.46
Fully diluted:					
From continuing operations	2.25	1.56	3.13	2.87	3.69
From discontinued operations		.49	—	(.36)	(.35)
Extraordinary credit	.22				
Net earnings (loss)	2.47	2.05	—	2.51	3.35
Total assets	490.4	460.5	557.8	554.1	573.3
Long-term obligations	86.6	110.0	113.2	129.3	163.1
Cash dividends per share of common stock	1.52	1.52	1.52	1.52	1.43

EXHIBIT 2

SCHRADER BELLOWS (A)

Financial Statistics:

Schrader Bellows Automation Group

1979–1983

($ million)

	1983	1982	1981	1980	1979
Sales	$99.7	$102.5	$123.2	$123.1	$120.2
Operating income	6.0	4.7	12.0	16.9	19.5
Identified assets	92.8	87.5	96.1	97.4	97.2
Capital expenditures	4.0	4.7	5.0	5.8	5.0

EXHIBIT 3

SCHRADER BELLOWS (A)

Market Analysis by Product Group

PRODUCT GROUP (1983 MARKET SHARE AND SALES VOLUME)							
MAINTENANCE, REPAIR, OVERHAUL		FILTRATION, REGULATION, LUBRICATION		DIRECTIONAL CONTROL VALVES		FLOW CONTROL VALVES	
Parker Hannifin	(20%)	Norgren	(30%)	Numatics	(20%)	Deltral	(35%)
U.S. Gauge	(15%)	Watts	(20%)	MAC	(15%)	Schrader	(20%)
Dcublin	(10%)	Wilkerson	(15%)	Schrader	(10%)	ARO	(15%)
Hansen	(10%)	Schrader	(10%)	Others	(45%)	REGO	(10%)
Schrader Bellows	(10%)	Others	(25%)			Others	(20%)
Others	(35%)						
Sales Volume (Wake Forest)							
$4.5 million		$5 million		$6 million		$4 million	

EXHIBIT 4

SCHRADER BELLOWS (A)

Standard Cost Report: Valve 60073

	MATERIAL COST	LABOR COST	OVERHEAD COST	TOTAL COST
Purchased part	$1.1980			$1.1980
Operation				
Drill, face, tap (2)		$0.0438	$0.2404	0.2842
Degrease		0.0031	0.0337	0.0368
Remove burrs		0.0577	0.3241	0.3818
Total cost, this item	1.1980	0.1046	0.5982	1.9008
Other subassemblies	0.3253	0.2994	1.8519	2.4766
Total cost, subassemblies	1.5233	0.4040	2.4501	4.3773
Assemble and test		0.1469	0.4987	0.6456
Pack without paper		0.0234	0.1349	0.1583
Total cost, this item	$1.5233	$0.5743	$3.0837	$5.1813
Cost component	29%	11%	60%	100%

EXHIBIT 5

SCHRADER BELLOWS (A)

Overhead Burden Rates per Direct Labor Hour

DEPARTMENT	ACTIVITY	OVERHEAD BURDEN RATE PER DIRECT LABOR HOUR
201	Assembly	$24.21
203	Automatic manufacturing	67.65
205	Plating	84.16
213	Packing	40.51
214	General machining	40.07

EXHIBIT 6

SCHRADER BELLOWS (A)

Overhead Budget by Department

($ thousands)

Manufacturing			
201	Assembly	$ 337	
203	Automatic manufacturing	671	
205	Plating	290	
213	Packing	352	
214	General machining	955	
			2,605
Support			
230	Work-in-process inventory	104	
231	Finished goods inventory	256	
234	Production control	564	
235	Purchasing	357	
239	Raw materials inventory	77	
240	Setup	1,560	
250	Quality control	531	
260	Manufacturing engineering	1,243	
			4,692
Fixed plant expenses*			2,054
Total overhead			$9,351

*Includes property taxes, product liability insurance, general
maintenance labor, and plant management.

Schrader Bellows (B)

Support department activities are expensive; in a plant such as Wake Forest about 50% of all overhead representing 25% of total manufacturing costs occur in support departments. Conventional cost systems do a poor job of allocating these costs to the products. Our major task at Schrader Bellows was to identify appropriate allocation bases for support department costs so that we could calculate accurate product costs.

PIERRE GUILLAUME, MANAGER OF STRATEGIC PLANNING

INTRODUCTION

In early 1983, William F. Boone, Vice-President of Planning and Development at Scovill, Inc., decided to send two of his people, Paul Bauer, Director of Strategic Planning, and Pierre Guillaume, Manager of Strategic Planning, into Schrader Bellows to determine the profitability of the products manufac-

tured at the Wake Forest Plant. This action was triggered by the continued decline in Schrader Bellows's sales and profits. "We are probably the largest producer of pneumatic products in the world," declared Boone. "So why aren't we making an adequate profit?"

The Planning and Development department

This case was prepared by Professor Robin Cooper.

often acted as internal consultant to Scovill's various divisions. The department's assistance could be requested by division management, but, if the department felt a problem was serious enough, it could initiate its own review. In the case of Schrader Bellows, the initiative came from Planning and Development. Boone explained this decision.

> I was convinced that we needed to reexamine the fundamental principles on which Schrader's cost accounting system was based. While at Bain I was involved in a number of studies designed to determine product line profitability, but we never got down to costing individual products. At the Strategic Planning Institute, I developed interviewing techniques for obtaining from line people fairly accurate allocations of assets and expenses to product lines. These techniques were more efficient than those we had used at Bain.
>
> When you are dealing with high-level strategic issues, you are making binary decisions (stay in business or get out of it). At this level of decision making, determining ballpark figures for profitability is quite sufficient; it's not important whether ROI is −30% or −40%: In either case, you are in bad trouble. Spending lots of time and money to be precise does not improve the accuracy of your analysis, nor does it change your recommendations.
>
> For product costing work, however, we could not be quite so cavalier about the accuracy of our estimates. Nevertheless, I was convinced that the same "soft" analytical techniques I had employed when studying product line profitability to circumvent the vices of average costing could be used to improve the accuracy of individual product costing. I needed an approach that was not concerned as much with precision as with overall accuracy. The typical cost accounting system produces product costs that are very precise and totally inaccurate. I wanted relatively accurate product costs and was not overly concerned with precision.
>
> This is why I chose Paul Bauer and Pierre Guillaume for the job. Paul is a PhD aeronautical engineer with an MBA in finance from Chicago. Pierre combined degrees in economics and law with an MIT MBA. He had also taught accounting to students majoring in data processing. Both had a lot of experience in the trenches gathering data for the Scovill strategic data base, which was organized around 200 individual competitive arenas rather than around the existing accounting system. This meant that we almost always ended up developing P&Ls and balance sheets for pieces of the business which had never been reported separately.

In February 1983, Bauer and Guillaume visited the Wake Forest plant. Bauer commented as follows:

> We started by touring the plant, talking to people, and trying to get a feel for the production process. We both agreed that thoroughly understanding the production process was critical to our ability to identify product profitability.
>
> The most striking aspect of the production process was the great discrepancy between lot sizes. For successful products, large lots of several hundred pieces are manufactured. For the less successful products, lots are typically less than 10 pieces.
>
> Once we understood the production process and related economics, we were able to consider what was required to cost the firm's products properly. The costs of the support departments greatly exceeded the overhead costs of the production departments, and yet the procedures used to allocate support department costs to the products were simplistic and, in our opinion, bore little relationship to the underlying economic reality.
>
> As a matter of practicality, we decided to live with the costing system for the five manufacturing departments.[1] It adequately captured the material and direct labor costs and, for the overhead costs that were directly associated with those departments, allocated them to the products reasonably well. The same could not be said of the allocation of the overhead costs for the eight support departments,[2] and we decided to focus on their assignment to the five manufacturing departments.
>
> We interviewed the heads of each support department to learn what events triggered activities in their departments. Our goal was to identify appropriate allocation bases to distribute support department costs on the frequency of activity-triggering events.

SUPPORT DEPARTMENTS

The eight support departments had a total budget of $4.7 million (Exhibit 1). The three inventory departments and the production control department were managed by the same person; each of the other four had its own department head. The Scovill team interviewed all five department heads extensively.

The first person interviewed was Nancy Massey. Massey, a 20-year Schrader Bellows employee, was responsible for four departments: raw materials inventory (number 239), work-in-process inventory

---

[1]Assembly, automatic manufacturing, plating, packing, and general machining.

[2]Raw material inventory, work-in-process inventory, finished goods inventory, production and inventory control, purchasing, setup, quality control, and manufacturing engineering.

(230), finished goods inventory (231), and production control (234).

Guillaume first asked Massey to describe the activities of the Production Control and Inventory Department personnel.[3]

PG How many people do you have in the Production Control and Inventory Department?

NM Well, I've got five people involved with inventory control plus the supervisor, that's six. And there are another eight including a supervisor in the production scheduling function. That's a total of 14. Oh, and I spend most of my time, say 80%, in this department supervising the people here.

PG How are the schedulers assigned to production departments?

NM Out of the seven, three spend all of their time in 203 and 214. A fourth did some 201 scheduling very early this year but now spends most of his time in 203 and 214 as well. The remaining three schedule setups throughout the plant.

PG What determines the amount of work, the number of hours, that your people spend on scheduling?

NM It's essentially a function of the number of production runs.

PG The number, not the size? In other words, if production runs were twice as big but there were the same number, then your work would still be the same?

NM Yes, that's essentially correct.

PG Good. You mentioned a supervisor. Does he do scheduling as well?

NM Occasionally, when the schedulers are overloaded. The rest of the time he supervises the others. He is there when there is a problem, a production crunch, for example; his responsibility is to get the products out when they are required. He tries to make sure that the right products are assembled, even to the extent of modifying the shop orders so that products can be shipped in time.

PG Let's move on. What generates the work for the inventory control people?

NM Out of the six people involved in inventory control, three are directly responsible for inventory control. They decide how much and when we have to order raw materials and purchased parts. The fourth edits the inventory transactions, and the fifth prepares the paperwork for the shop. The sixth is a supervisor who is responsible for the inventory control people. Also, one of the three responsible for inventory control spends some time running the office.

PG What I need to know is what causes the work for those three people so that we can allocate their costs to the products in a sensible manner. In your opinion, what is the best way to allocate these costs, one that really does a reasonably good job of reflecting the work done here?

SB I don't know if you have talked to the accounting people, but they allocate everything based on direct labor hours.

PG Yes, we have talked to them, and we're trying to look at allocating costs in other ways. Do you believe that direct labor hours is the right way to allocate costs? Is the work in this department directly proportional to direct labor hours?

NM No, not really. In fact, if we only had one product in this plant, we wouldn't need any of the people that we have, even for the same volume of output.

PG Even if there were lots of the product being produced?

NM Yes, because if there were only one product, inventory control would be simple and production scheduling would be nonexistent. We only need inventory control people because we have a complicated production process, and the more production runs we make, the more people we require.

Guillaume and Massey next discussed the Finished Goods Inventory Department.

PG How many people do you have working in the Finished Goods Inventory Department?

NM There are eight people working there.

PG Do they all do the same thing?

NM No, come to think of it, there are nine people working there—the ninth is the supervisor. Let me think about what they do. . . . One is in charge of receiving goods from the assembly department.

PG How is the quantity of his work generated? What's it related to?

NM Well, every time a production run is made in the assembly department, the product is moved into the finished goods department, generally in one batch unless it's a very long run. There is some paperwork involved, but essentially the task is material handling, taking the products to the shelves.

PG He doesn't do any inspection or anything like that?

NM No.

PG OK, so that's one of the eight people. What about the others, what do they do?

NM Let's see, three handle customer orders, and the remaining four handle shipments.

PG For the three who are dealing with customer orders, is the work they do generated by each order? For example, if they handled twice as many orders, would they have twice as much work?

---

[3]These interviews have been edited. All unnecessary passages have been removed. The actual interviews were considerably longer.

NM Not necessarily. The work also depends on the size of the orders, the number of different items ordered, and the quantities involved.

PG Could you be more explicit?

NM Every time a customer order comes in, it generates some work, and depending on the number of items that are requested, the amount of work is going to be different. In fact, even though there is a fixed amount of work required every time a customer order is received, what actually generates most of the work is the number of items on each order. Also, the work depends on how large the order is in terms of dollars.

PG Why is that?

NM First of all, when the order is extremely large, it might have to be shipped in more than one shipment, and that creates additional work for the finished goods people. So, for very large dollar orders, the amount of work required for the three people is higher. The amount of work also depends on the size of the product. When we get an order for flow-control valves, the amount of physical work and handling that's required is not as high as when we get an order for a robot.

PG Let me see if I understand. It sounds like there are two things affecting the workload. First, incoming orders generate a certain amount of paperwork. Then there is the work related to the mass of the products that will be shipped.

NM That's right.

PG What do you estimate is the percentage of time that is spent dealing with the paperwork generated by a customer order?

NM Paperwork is generated at two stages, first by the three people who receive the orders, and second by the four people who ship it.

PG Let's just focus on the three in receiving for the time being. What percentage of their work is standing at a desk?

NM Well, let me think about that. It's definitely more than half.

PG Is it more than 70%?

NM No, it's less than 70%.

PG You're confident that it is between 50% and 70%?

NM Yes, that sounds about right.

PG You mentioned four other people, what are they doing?

NM Well, they are handling shipments, and there the bulkiness of the items is a greater factor than for customer orders.

PG Is it the majority of the work?

NM No, it's more like 50% to 60%.

It took all morning to complete two departments. After lunch, Guillaume and Massey started on the raw material inventory control department.

PG How many people do you have working for you in the raw material inventory department?

NM I have four people working in that department.

PG What do they do?

NM Two of them spend most of their time dealing with the shipments of purchased parts. They handle everything; they handle the receiving documents and transfer the incoming purchased parts to the work-in-process stockroom. The third person works in the raw material area. After the material clears inspection, he moves it into inventory and takes care of the paperwork.

PG What causes the amount of time required to process an incoming shipment to be different? Is there a big difference if the shipment is a large one compared to a small one?

NM No, not for the purchased items because they go directly to the work-in-process stockroom, and unless it's a very large shipment, extremely large, it can be dealt with in one trip, so volume is not a real problem. The raw material is a different question because volume can play a major role in the amount of effort required to move it.

PG So, what you're saying is that, for most of the things coming in, whether it's a large quantity or small, it takes the same amount of time to process. But for some of the heavier raw materials, the sheer volume does in fact necessitate taking several trips to move it into the stockroom.

NM That's right, but there are only on a few large raw material shipments. I would say that the amount of time required really depends on the number of times a product is received rather than the size of the shipment.

PG OK, any other factors that impact the amount of work?

NM Well, there is the fourth individual; I haven't had a chance to talk about him yet. He disperses raw material to the shop floor and again the volume required is really not an issue. It's more the number of times raw material has to be dispersed to the shop floor, either to department 203 or 214.

PG Do you usually disperse the total amount of material required for a production run all at once, or does it go out in smaller quantities?

NM It varies with the size of the run. On a very long run we don't disperse it all at once because the amount of raw material on the shop floor would be too large. On smaller runs, and I would say that's 80% of all production runs, we send it there in a single trip once the setup is completed.

While Guillaume was interviewing Massey, Bauer was talking to Larry Leblanc, head of setup. Leblanc had spent 10 years with Bellows International, joining them directly from high school, and continued with the division after its acquisition by Schrader.

PB How many people do you have in your department?

LL I had 14 people in January and then Joe Peak left, so we are now down to 13 people.

PB OK, are all of your people setting up or do they have other tasks as well?

LL That's a good question. Two of my staff have recently been spending most of their time in the automotive, cylinder, and robotic departments.

PB What's being set up there?

LL It's not really a setup; they have been helping out in those departments.

PB Are they setting up new equipment?

LL Not really setting up new equipment, but making sure that the runs are going properly so that things can be completed and so on.

PB How about the people who really are setting up then?

LL Five work exclusively in the 203 and 214 departments where they spend 100% of their time doing setups on non-NC (numerically controlled) machines. Another two spend, well, in the first quarter one of them did spend a little bit of time in 203 on other machines, but now they spend most of their time setting up the NC machines in departments 203 and 214.

PB When you say setting up, is that what they really do all day long? Because it sounds like you've got more people than one would expect given the number of setups to be done and the average setup time.

LL That's an important observation; first of all, we're doing more setups than we're supposed to.

PB Why is that?

LL Because many times we have to stop long production runs to produce 10 or 20 parts for a special product that needs to be shipped out at the end of the month. We then reset the machines, again, for the long running item. Toward the end of the month our people spend a good deal of time on these setups for short jobs. In fact, in the last week of the month, it may be as much as 20% to 30% of their time. Now, another problem is that you probably looked at the standard setup time, and they're not always very reliable. Some machines take a lot more time to set up than standard.

PB What percentage of the standard setup times do you think are off by at least 50%?

LL That's a difficult question. . . . I wouldn't be able to give you an answer.

PB Is it a lot, or just a limited number? Is it more than 50% of them?

LL No, probably not.

PB Is it more than 10% of them?

LL Certainly more than 10%, somewhere in between; it's hard for me to say.

PB Are there any other activities that these people are doing which is really not setup as such, but they end up doing anyway?

LL Well, I didn't mention the remaining four persons working in assembly. They are setting up, but here there are no heavy machines to set up. Setting up means making sure that all the necessary parts are available when the assembly person starts working. This doesn't take a lot of time, 15 to 30 minutes per setup.

PB OK, so other than that, the rest of the time they really have their hands in the grease?

LL Yes, they do, but in many cases, especially when we have a rush order and we need only produce a very small number of parts for a special product, they end up doing the production themselves because it's not worth turning it over to the regular operator.

PB Can you estimate roughly, take a whole month altogether, what percentage of the setup person's time is really used in doing the direct operator's job? Is it greater than 20%?

LL No, it's less than that.

PB Less than 10%?

LL It varies a lot, maybe a little more than 10% for the five people working in 214. This type of situation happens almost exclusively in that department.

After interviewing Leblanc, Bauer talked to Paul Finks, head of quality control. Like his counterparts, Finks was a Schrader Bellows veteran with many years of service with the firm.

PB How many people are in quality control?

PF I have 13 area inspectors who do quality inspection. I have two senior technicians who have a lot more experience and work as the technical experts on the team. Also, there is one statistical clerk and myself.

PB Where are these people working?

PF For the area inspectors, that's fairly simple. Well, not really. Three of them work exclusively in the 203 and 214 departments. You know we just introduced the automotive department last year; one inspector has been working full time on the quality problems of the automotive department.

PB Now, do you expect his services to be required indefinitely there or is that going to . . .

PF Let's hope not. That's not a normal way of operating, to spend that much time on a single product, but maybe automotive products are different. Even the tolerances required of the machines are different, and we did have more than our share of problems when we first started. I hope that next year we'll be able to spend a lot less time doing automotive inspection.

Going back to your original question, there are two more inspectors who do both the receiving inspections and the assembly inspections, and seven others who work in the whole plant. They work in any department that needs them.

PB What creates the work of the inspectors?

PF The inspectors do first-piece inspection, so every time we set up the machines, they are there to check the quality of the first piece produced. Two also check the quality of the parts that we receive. Every time we receive a shipment, we get one of our people there to check the quality.

PB When you check on the incoming purchase orders, does the size of the sample or the effort required vary, or is it always the same?

PF Good point. It does vary slightly, but we tend to do more random checking on large shipments than on small ones, so essentially it takes about the same amount of time.

PB Which is more time consuming, assembly or receiving inspection?

PF Oh, it's clearly receiving inspection. There is very little quality inspection in assembly.

PB 10% or less?

PF Maybe more than that.

PB As much as 50%?

PF No, less than 30%, between 10% and 30%. Let me try to think. . . . Last week we worked about two days in the assembly area.

PB Two out of five?

PF No, out of 10, there are two people involved. Last week was probably representative of what normally occurs.

PB OK, let's talk about the two people, the technicians. On what activities do they spend the most time?

PF This year they spent a good deal of their time on the automotive products.

PB Other than that, what's the most important time consumer?

PF They probably spend a lot more time in the assembly department than any other.

PB What are the other things that they do? You've got automotive products the most important time consumer, then assembly. . . .

PF Yeah, they are about the same; it's hard to tell.

PB Assembly and automotive require about the same amount of time?

PF This year, yes. I don't expect it to be that way next year.

PB Those two combined, how much of the total time of these two individuals is absorbed in automotive and in the assembly department?

PF Maybe two-thirds of their time.

PB What are the other things that they do?

PF They do have to intervene occasionally in the 203 and 214 department when there is a problem. That's the rest of the . . . not really, because they also spend time on new product development and improving the production process. That's not insignificant.

PB If we say 70% of the time goes to the two activities you discussed, then you've got 30% to allocate. You said they work in 203 and in 214, and then there were these new products. Anything else they do, is there any other activity that they do?

PF They do some administrative tasks, but that's about it.

PB Let's just take those three things, the administrative and the 203 and the 214; how would you divide this 30% that I've got? Is it 10, 10, and 10?

PF No, when I think about it, they probably spend about as much time in 203 and 214 combined as they do in 201 assembly.

PB So, maybe we should change it. Maybe it's not 70%; maybe we can go to 60%.

PF Make it something like 30, 30, 30.

PB OK, we're going to put 30% in automotive, 30% in assembly, 30% in 203 and 214 combined, and then there's 10% in process improvement and product development. Now, for the manufacturing departments, what is the split between 203 and 214?

PF I would say half and half.

PB We've allocated the time of the two technicians to the departments; now what we've got to do is trace that back to the individual products. What's the right way to do that?

PF It's really hard to tell because they don't. . . . Well, let's see. They are called on when there is a problem in the inspection area, but they aren't really there every time an inspection is made. They are only there when there is a problem.

PB Are these problems predictable; are they attributable to an individual product line that's problem prone?

PF Well, if that's the case, I'll put them on it until it's straightened out.

PB Other than that, would you say that. . . .

PF No, we know that certain machines give us more problems than others.

PB OK, there are certain machines that give you problems, but you can't put your finger on a particular problem product?

PF Not really. That would be an interesting study.

PB You don't keep any records?

PF No.

PB You don't have a list of troublesome products?

PF No, but we do keep a list by machine.

PB You mentioned that 10% of the technicians' time was spent on process improvements and product development. Can that be attributed to individual products?

PF It varies quite a bit from year to year. We've been working on process improvement in most of our product lines, so it's really hard to trace it back to specific products.

PB If I understand correctly, in addition to the people we have discussed, there's yourself and one statistical clerk. What do you two do?

PF I supervise the department. I tend to spend more time on administrative tasks, people problems, and so on. The statistical clerk keeps records of the data we are collecting, such as problems by machine, the inspection problems on the automotive products, and so on.

It's hard to break his time down into specific product lines or departments.

At the end of the day, Bauer and Guillaume met to discuss their findings. They first reviewed their notes on the interviews they had carried out the previous days and discussed their writeups (Exhibit 2). Once satisfied that they had captured the details for those departments, they focused on today's interviews.

EXHIBIT 1

SCHRADER BELLOWS (B)
Overhead Budget by Department
($ thousands)

Manufacturing			
201	Assembly	$ 337	
203	Automatic manufacturing	671	
205	Plating	290	
213	Packing	352	
214	General machining	955	
			2,605
Support			
230	Work-in-process inventory	104	
231	Finished goods inventory	256	
234	Production and inventory control	564	
235	Purchasing	357	
239	Raw materials inventory	770	
240	Setup	1,560	
250	Quality control	531	
260	Manufacturing engineering	1,243	
			4,692
Fixed plant expenses*			2,054
Total overhead			$9,351

* Includes property taxes, product liability insurance, general maintenance labor, and plant management.

EXHIBIT 2

SCHRADER BELLOWS (B)

Interview Analysis of the Work-in-Process, Purchasing,
and Manufacturing Engineering Departments
at Wake Forest

WORK-IN-PROCESS

The work-in-process inventory area (230) contained six people. One was a group leader who supervised the other five and helped out when bottlenecks occurred. One of the others was responsible for receipts into WIP from the production plant, while the other four split their time between monitoring inventory in WIP and disbursements to assembly (the split was 40% and 60%, respectively).

PURCHASING

Joe Gahagan was responsible for purchasing (235) and was assisted by a secretary. Orders of raw material and parts for production were made in conjunction with the production control department. This occupied approximately 80% of the department's time. Inventory levels were controlled using the OPT system. Supplies, on the other hand, were ordered as people informed Gahagan or his secretary that stock was low.

MANUFACTURING ENGINEERING

The manufacturing engineering department (260) contained 29 individuals who oversaw the development and determination of the processes required to make parts. These included designing necessary tools and having them made, as well as establishing time standards for the required operations. The department was also responsible for evaluating equipment to verify adequate utilization, improving its efficiency and utilization (i.e., cost reductions), procuring and justifying new equipment, and disposing of unnecessary equipment.

The manufacturing services manager, Hank Eide, had a wide range of duties. He not only supervised his department personnel but often was directly involved in the various activities. He was responsible for the departmental budget, labor grievances, hiring and firing (done in conjunction with the personnel department), and reviewing performance of the personnel in his department.

The six industrial engineers solved problems on the production floor and continually reviewed the manufacturing process for improvements. For example, a particular part was being damaged as it fell from a machine into a basket. The solution was to put tennis balls into the basket. This effectively stopped the parts from damaging themselves. These engineers also made suggestions for new machinery and to improve the plant layout. They handled the coordination with quality control and design. They processed new engineering releases to ensure that the product would be properly produced. Finally, they prepared cost estimates for new or changed products.

There were two numeric control programmers who were responsible for the 10 numerical control machines (lathes and screw machines). The programs specified the sequence of milling, drilling, tapping, which tool to use, what speed to operate at, etc.

Three tool engineers designed all the tools necessary to make the products. The range of tools went from cutting tools to jigs and fixtures. Approximately half of the tools were made in the tool room, and half were subcontracted out. The tool room had 13 people making these parts.

Manufacturing developments operated in an advisory capacity, working with other departments to introduce new techniques and processes. In one dramatic case, the setup time on a machine was reduced from three hours and 56 minutes to 19 minutes with the help of this department. There were four people working in the department.

Schrader Bellows (D-1)

In early 1983, William Boone, Vice-President for Planning and Development at Scovill, Inc., initiated a product costing study at Schrader Bellows, a Scovill subsidiary. The Scovill team, consisting of Paul Bauer, director of strategic planning, and Pierre Guillaume, manager of strategic planning, had visited the Wake Forest plant and interviewed the heads of the support departments. The interviews were completed and the Scovill team had identified the appropriate cost allocation bases. Bauer and Guillaume were reviewing their progress on the product costing study.

Guillaume described the product costing procedure:

> Our first step was to explode the sales data. We took the quantity sold of each end product, determined the individual components contained in the end products, and then estimated the quantity of each component required in 1982.
>
> The second step, costing the components according to the selected allocation bases, was the most challenging. A great deal of judgment was required to allocate the support department costs down to individual components. We also spent a considerable amount of time insuring that the factory and sales, general, and administration costs were appropriately allocated. In our opinion, very few of these costs were truly fixed.
>
> After we completed the allocation of costs to the components, we imploded these costs back to the product level by summing the costs of all components in a given product.

Estimating product costs required an enormous number of calculations. Paul Bauer and Pierre Guillaume had to develop a special computer program. While developing the program, they realized that the processing time would exceed the available daytime capacity of the Wake Forest computer. Fortunately, the Wake Forest IBM 4341 was not being used at night, and this time slot was dedicated to the project. Pierre Guillaume described its use.

> We kept the IBM busy all night all by ourselves. We knew we would use a lot of computer time, but

actual use far exceeded our expectations. It was a long, time-consuming process. You take the output of a run, analyze it, make corrections, run the program, and start again. Each run took about 10 hours. Six hours were required to allocate the costs into their components, and it took another four to implode the costs back to the product level. Fortunately, we did not have to run the explosion routine, which takes another three hours, more than once or twice. The number of things that could go wrong was massive. For example, if a product was sold but not manufactured in 1982, there was no 1982 manufacturing data for that product and, consequently, it was not assigned any setup-related costs. The small-lot-size products interrupting the large-lot-size products caused the number of actual setups per large-lot-size product to be much higher than we had expected.

Bauer and Guillaume spent several months debugging the program and resolving problems like the one just described. Eventually a satisfactory run was achieved. The program produced a list containing the product cost data for about 2,000[1] separate products. Initially, Bauer and Guillaume tried to analyze the data for the entire 1982 production. It rapidly became apparent that a structured analytic approach was required. Guillaume elaborated as follows:

> We needed to analyze the data in a way that made sense to the company. We decided to focus our analysis on one product group at a time. We selected valves for initial analysis because valves are the flagship product of Schrader Bellows. To further limit our analysis, we selected flow control valves for particular attention because they are a small but representative product group. There are only a few major types of flow control valves; 76 distinct items were manufactured in 1982 [Exhibit 1].

The product profitability data for the flow control valve line were transferred to a floppy diskette so that they could be analyzed on an IBM PC.

---

[1]Seven hundred products produced at Wake Forest were not included in this analysis.

This case was prepared by Jane Montgomery, research assistant (under the supervision of Professor Robin Cooper). Copyright © 1985 by the President and Fellows of Harvard College. Harvard Business School case 186-053.

EXHIBIT 1

SCHRADER BELLOWS (D-1)

Flow Control Valve Group

The flow control valve group accounted for sales of $4 million in 1982 and contained three major product lines: micrometer flow control valves, flow control valves, and needle valves.

1. Micrometer flow control valves: Used to control the flow of air in a pneumatic circuit. The micrometer line provided full flow in one direction and adjustable flow in the other. They were typically used in applications where flow settings needed to be changed regularly. The micrometer control knob provided accurate, calibrated flow.

2. Flow control valves: Provided the same function as the micrometer valves but were more precise in their operation. They used a fine screw thread adjustment to allow precise settings which could be secured by a sturdy lock nut. Due to their design, they provided the most effective adjustment and highest flow rate of any control valve in their class. They were typically used in applications where exact flow settings were necessary and where changes were rarely required.

3. Needle valves: Similar to the micrometer valves but provided infinite flow adjustment in both directions.

Flow control valves were manufactured in eight different sizes ranging from ⅛″ to 1½″ in diameter. For each of the eight sizes, up to four different variations were manufactured.

- *Standard valve:* These valves contained seals made of polyurethane, were the least expensive of the various seals, and were applicable to a wide range of different conditions.
- *Viton:* These valves contained Viton 0 rings and poppet seals. Viton had a higher life expectancy than polyurethane in high-temperature settings and was impervious to a wider range of chemicals than polyurethane.
- *Nitrile seal:* These valves contained seals that were better suited to low-pressure applications or where a definite positive seal was required.

The eight different sizes, four different variations, and three product lines produced a possible 96 different products, of which 76 were in the 1982 Schrader Bellows catalog.

Schrader Bellows (E)

INTRODUCTION

The Schrader Bellows strategic cost analysis had demonstrated that a large percentage of the products produced at the Wake Forest facility had negative operating profits and residual incomes (see Schrader Bellows (D-1).

The Scovill team was now faced with the problem of developing an action plan that would allow the firm to take advantage of the findings of the study.

ATTACKING THE PROBLEM

Bauer described the approach they adopted.

Our first step was to approach the product managers to obtain their reactions to the cost analysis. We created a list of action codes representing a set of mutually exclusive actions which could be taken with respect to the unprofitable products. This ensured that the product managers would review and select a course of action for every product with

This case was prepared by Jane E. Montgomery, research assistant (under the supervision of Professor Robin Cooper).

Copyright © 1985 by the President and Fellows of Harvard College. Harvard Business School case 186-054.

a negative residual income. The possible actions included the following:

a. Drop the product.

b. Raise the unit price enough to bring the residual income up to zero.

c. Add a setup charge to the price of any order. The setup charge would be the same whether the order was for 10, 50, or 100 units.

d. No change.

e. Take no action because the validity of the data was questionable. The profitability of this product should be analyzed further.

f. Attempt to reduce the cost of the product.

g. Buy the item outside.

We sent a memo to the product managers [Exhibit 1], asking them to recommend a course of action for all products for which they were responsible. The product managers recommended that action be taken with respect to 1,355 items [Exhibit 2]. They proposed dropping 794 products, repricing 471 to bring residual income to zero, adding a setup charge to 51, reengineering three, and buying 36 outside.

With the results of the product manager survey in hand, Bauer and Guillaume initiated a series of meetings with management of the Wake Forest plant. Key players were Thomas White, group vice-president for Schrader Bellows world-wide, Jack Couchois, manager of the Wake Forest plant, and Joe Reardon, production manager at Wake Forest.

These meetings focused on what products should be dropped. While the product managers had lowered the number of products being considered for elimination, everyone agreed that dropping close to 800 products would be a drastic move. Many believed that Schrader Bellows could not afford to do much pruning of its product offerings because the company's major competitive advantage was its broad product line. The management team was also unwilling to drop a large number of products because they were not adequately convinced that the data were accurate enough to feel confident about such a dramatic paring of the product lines. With these concerns in mind, plant management tried to determine what could be done to rationalize the product line while minimizing the associated risk of lost sales.

After much debate, management developed a list of five characteristics required for products to be identified as safe to drop; the safe products could presumably be eliminated without negative consequences.

1. Low sales volume. If a product had more than $100,000 in sales, it would not be eliminated.

2. Easily substituted with another Schrader Bellows product. If there was no functional difference between the product to be dropped and another product which would continue to be offered, the customer could be sold the alternative product.

3. Known to be a "dog" before the study. There were products which were known to be considerably more difficult to make than the standard cost would suggest. Common sense already indicated that these products were losing money, and this intuition was supported by the cost study.

4. Variation on a main product. Schrader Bellows made many products which had various combinations of additional features beyond those offered on the standard products. These were manufactured in response to the preferences of certain customers. However, in most cases a simpler substitute would be adequate to meet customer needs.

5. No major customer involved. No product would be dropped if there were a risk of losing significant sales of other products to the same customer.

Once these criteria were established, further meetings with the product managers were held to determine which products were to be dropped. Eventually 250 such products were identified.

DETERMINING POTENTIAL SAVINGS

Having identified 250 safe products to drop, Bauer and Guillaume estimated the impact on residual income from eliminating these products (Exhibits 3 and 4). The 250 products represented planned 1984 sales of $1,178,000. Bauer described their approach.

Initially, we estimated that if all of the 1984 safe product planned revenue was lost and all of the associated costs were avoided, the improvement in residual income would be $845,000. In actual fact, we expected, based on our knowledge of the affected product lines, that a significant amount of the revenue would be transferred to remaining product lines which would increase profitability beyond that predicted in my analysis. We believed that our analysis provided a good first approximation of the lower bounds of the potential impact on residual income, although we knew that it was not exact.

After management reviewed the estimate of the increase in residual income, they expressed two concerns. First, because the list of safe products had been developed under the assumption that a limited amount of sales would actually be lost by dropping those products, management wanted to see an estimate based on the assumption that sales of other Schrader Bellows products would replace the eliminated products. Second, they wanted to know what the impact would be on the measures of income generated by the existing cost accounting system. They asked the plant controller, Preston Smith, to write a memo documenting the increase in planned 1984 net income if the 250 products were dropped. The controller predicted 1983 savings of $516,000 and ongoing savings of $761,000 (Exhibit 5).

The Scovill team reviewed the controller's estimate with satisfaction, because both their estimate and the controller's showed savings of around three quarters of a million dollars. They both felt that, although the estimates were not exact, it was clear that there was a large benefit to be derived from dropping the safe products.

After listening to the reactions of plant management and reviewing the plant controller's report, Bauer and Guillaume attempted to gain commitment from the support department managers so that the planned cost savings could actually be realized. They took the list of safe products to the managers of the various support departments and asked them to analyze the potential savings in their departments if the 250 products were dropped. The managers were also asked to commit to making these cuts if the products were in fact dropped.

OBTAINING THE SAVINGS

Finally, an implementation strategy had to be determined. As Bauer described it, "You can't just drop products in this business, a few you can, but most you have to phase out." Thus, there were two possible courses of action: phase out a product in the near future or drop it immediately. A detailed strategy for each course of action was outlined.

If plans were made to drop a product sometime in the near future, three initial steps were necessary. First, a plan for scaling down production and reducing inventory levels was necessary. Second, the date of the announcement of discontinuance of the product had to be coordinated with the balancing of production. Third, a deadline for accepting orders had to be announced.

There were seven additional steps to be taken when it came time to actually drop the product. These seven steps were also required for products that were to be dropped immediately. First, the catalog had to be modified. Second, the product had to be eliminated from the price sheet (the price sheet lists the prices of all products within a particular line, by product number). This second step was very important because customers usually order from price sheets (prices were not listed in the catalog). Therefore, customers might continue to order products which had been dropped if the products were still listed on the price sheets. Bauer recognized that the natural reluctance within the organization to turn down orders made it critical to delete dropped products from the price sheets.

The third step was to educate the sales force. Each sales representative and each distributor had to be informed of the products which were eliminated so that they would not take any further orders for those products. They would also encourage customers to substitute other Schrader Bellows products for the dropped products.

The fourth step was to change the computer data base. Two levels of change were required. First, the pricing information had to be eliminated. But this alone did not preclude sales of the product. Production could still continue, and orders could be taken because price information could be entered manually. A greater barrier could be erected by eliminating the bill of materials and routing information from the data base because production would become more difficult without this information.

The fifth step was to determine the level of spare parts necessary to support the products already in the hands of customers. Warranties and service agreements generally dictated that Schrader Bellows be able to support these products for three to five years. This was a sensitive issue, requiring a thorough understanding of customers.

The sixth step was to analyze the inventory requirements and eliminate items which would no longer be necessary. It would, in most cases, be necessary to scrap any finished goods, work in process, or purchased parts (usually castings) which were associated with the dropped products and which were not required to support existing customers. The raw materials for these products could be sold or put to an alternative use and were not seen as a significant problem.

Once management was convinced that a product had been permanently removed from the product line, it was still necessary to take one final step to prevent the product from being made. Guillaume explained why this step was necessary.

When it comes down to it, there is really only one way to get rid of a product, and that is to burn the engineering drawings and destroy any special tooling. Otherwise, the temptation is too great to let products creep back into the line. If the engineering drawings are available and a customer request for the discontinued product comes in, it becomes too easy to pull out the drawings and put the product back into production. The only effective barrier to production is to make it necessary to start all over as though it were a new product.

PRESENTATION TO DIVISION MANAGEMENT

In late 1983, in Akron, Ohio, the team presented their analysis to division management: Bill Cavanaugh, CEO, Brayton Campbell, Director of Marketing, and Chuck Dombrowski, Controller. Bauer described the presentation.

We had kept division management apprised of our progress as we were working on the study through a series of interim presentations and meetings. We saw the final presentation as a way to really impress on division management the magnitude of the problem.

Everyone seemed to agree that some rationalization of the product line was necessary. Someone reminded the group that duplicate products from the merger of Schrader and Bellows still existed. However, management had difficulty embracing the idea of dropping 250 products. Marketing issues seemed to be their main concern. They said that Schrader Bellows's full product line was a strategic advantage and an important factor in the company's ability to charge premium prices. Thus they were reluctant to make any immediate moves to drop products without first studying the problem themselves. When we concluded the presentation, I was not sure what the eventual outcome would be.

EXHIBIT 1
SCHRADER BELLOWS (E)

TO: Hubie Jenks, Joe Hinton
FROM: Paul Bauer and Pierre Guillaume
DATE: August 28, 1983
SUBJECT: Product profitability analysis

As we have discussed, we need your input on the actions to take with respect to the products which my study predicts have negative residual income. Attached is a form which lists all the products with negative residual income in your product lines. Across the top of each form are seven possible actions, coded A through G. In our previous discussions of the possible steps to be taken, you have expressed certain reservations and concerns about particular courses of action. We have summarized these concerns below and identified by code the action to which they relate. Please use your best judgment as to the appropriate course of action taking these concerns into account. We would appreciate your response as soon as possible.

(continued)

EXHIBIT 1 (*cont.*)

A. Drop the product: Self-explanatory.

B. Raise unit price: The unit price should be raised to bring residual income up to zero.

C. Add a setup charge: This action would be appropriate for products which were ordered in small volumes by only one or two customers. The setup charge would be set to cover the additional costs associated with a short production run.

D. No change: This course of action might be chosen when it is feared that dropping the product might cause customers to take all of their business elsewhere because they would no longer be able to obtain all of their requirements through Schrader Bellows.

E. Questionable data: This category should be chosen when you honestly do not believe the data produced by the cost study. However, this is only a temporary category. We will need to meet to discuss how to resolve the questions about these items.

To our knowledge, there are three reasons why you may find the data questionable. First, for some products you have expressed your belief that the estimates used contained errors large enough to cause the resulting measure of residual income to have the wrong sign. Second, we relied on the cost accounting system to allocate the overhead costs of the direct departments, and there is some evidence that these costs are not always sufficiently accurate. Third, there will be cases where you reject the data not on the basis of any specific problems but rather on gut feelings developed over the course of many years spent dealing with the products.

F. Cost reduce: This action may be recommended for some products which are known to be poorly designed. In most cases, reengineering of the product may be called for, but in some cases redesign of the production process may be suggested.

G. Buy from outside vendor: In some cases, Schrader Bellows produces items for which we have only a very small share in a market dominated by two or three major competitors. Usually these items are made on equipment which had overcapacity (screw machines, for example). The reason for keeping the products in the past was to provide for greater absorption of costs, which, as my study points out, is not a valid reason. Therefore, these products would be good candidates for buying outside.

PRODUCT LINE: MICROMETER FLOW CONTROL	DROP A	REPRICE B	SETUP CHARGE C	NO CHANGE D	QUESTIONABLE DATA E	COST REDUCE F	BUY OUT G
10 200							
10 300							
10 400							
10 500							
10 600							
10 700							
10 900							
11 300							
11 400							
11 500							
11 600							
11 700							
11 800							
11 900							
12 000							

EXHIBIT 2

SCHRADER BELLOWS (E)

PRODUCT LINE	NUMBER IN PRODUCT LINE	NUMBER WITH NEGATIVE RESIDUAL INCOME	DROP	REPRICE	SETUP CHARGE	NO CHANGE	QUESTION DATA	COST REDUCE	BUY OUT
Directional control valves	869	704	401	268	28	—	7	—	—
Flow control valves	140	68	18	36	—	—	13	1	—
FRL	470	373	175	—	—	198	—	—	—
MRO									
Solenoids	270	257	123	95	23	—	16	—	—
Couplers	172	118	35	35	—	—	10	2	36
Hydraulic gauges	51	35	—	8	—	21	6	—	—
Blow guns	53	34	12	17	—	1	4	—	—
Fittings	259	144	30	12	—	101	1	—	—
	2,284	1,733	794	471	51	321	57	3	36

EXHIBIT 3

SCHRADER BELLOWS (E)

Direct and Factory Indirect Costs for Products to be Eliminated ($000)

PRODUCT LINE	DIRECT COSTS			FACTORY INDIRECT COSTS				
	MATERIAL	LABOR	TOTAL DIRECT	SETUP	GROUP LEADER	MATERIAL HANDLERS	OTHER INDIRECT LABOR	TOTAL INDIRECT
Directional control valves	$139	$154	$293	$70	$23	$24	$14	$131
Flow control valves	15	4	19	3	1	1	1	6
FRL	239	49	288	10	6	7	3	26
MRO								
Solenoids	12	9	21	10	3	3	1	17
Couplers	5	1	6	2	0	0	0	2
Blow guns	2	10	12	3	1	1	1	6
Fittings	2	4	6	1	0	0	0	1
Total	$414	$231	$645	$99	$34	$36	$20	$189

EXHIBIT 4

SCHRADER BELLOWS (E)

Summary Costs and Profit Losses for Products to Be Eliminated ($000)

| | | | FACTORY | | | | | WORKING CAPITAL | | |
PRODUCT LINE	SALES	DIRECT COSTS	INDIRECT COSTS	FACTORY OVERHEAD	PERIOD EXPENSES	FIXED COST	OPERATING PROFIT	COST OF CAPITAL	FIXED ASSET COST OF CAPITAL	RESIDUAL PROFIT
Directional control valves	$589	$293	$131	$370	$197	$43	$(445)	$54	$45	$(544)
Flow control valves	35	19	6	13	10	2	(15)	2	2	(19)
FRL	480	288	26	95	144	14	(87)	26	10	(123)
MRO										
Solenoids	42	21	17	35	35	2	(68)	3	2	(73)
Couplers	18	6	2	9	10	1	(10)	2	1	(13)
Blow guns	9	12	6	13	16	3	(41)	1	3	(45)
Fittings	5	6	1	11	14	2	(29)	2	1	(32)
Total	$1,178	$645	$189	$546	$426	$67	$(695)	$90	$64	$(849)

EXHIBIT 5
SCHRADER BELLOWS (E)

TO: Wake Forest Management
FROM: Preston Smith
DATE: September 10, 1983
SUBJECT: Impact of dropping safe products on 1986 production

I received from Paul Bauer and Pierre Guillaume a list of 250 products being considered for elimination. These products were identified as being safe to drop because they met certain criteria established by management. Attached is my calculation of the impact which dropping these 250 products will have on planned 1984 net income.

There are three components of my estimate of the change in net income. These are an increase in operating profit, a decrease in carrying charges due to lower inventory levels, and an after-tax charge to income from writing off the inventory.

The change in operating profit is further broken down into two components: changes in product costs (which will result in lowered costs of goods sold and thus higher net gross profit) and changes in period costs.

The changes in product costs reflect the reduction in direct labor and support department costs made possible by eliminating the safe products. For the sake of clarity, I decided to report these changes as variances in exactly the way the cost system would report them if the products were dropped but the standards were not changed. This approach produces what at first appears to be a contradictory result (i.e., there is no change in standard margin). This is a direct result of our standard cost system, which does not accurately account for the higher unit costs of short production runs. Consequently, if the sales of a short production run product (i.e., a safe product) are replaced by those of a similar but long production run product (i.e., the main product), the cost accounting system will show no apparent change in standard margin.

If we use the 1984 plan standard costs and account for the impact of dropping the safe products, four variances will be generated.

1. Labor variance: We can expect to save some labor by dropping the safe products because the number of short production runs will fall. This will reduce the amount of time spent waiting for setups to be completed, checking the early production parts to ensure they are in tolerance, and, finally, getting up to speed on a new production process. The total savings I have estimated at about $40,000.

2. Burden variance: The reduced number of labor hours required to produce the budgeted output will result in a reduction in burden costs. This variance captures this saving. It is calculated by multiplying the burden rate by the number of direct labor hours saved by dropping the 250 products.

3. Lost absorption variance: The burden variance includes some fixed costs that will not be avoided. This variance corrects for the unavoided fixed costs.

4. Spending improvement variance: The net of the burden and cost absorption variances accounts for the decrease in burden costs due to a reduction in direct labor hours. In fact, we expect even greater savings because the short production runs that will be avoided require relatively high levels of support department activities. Dropping the 250 safe products should produce an additional $120,000 reduction in support department costs.

Many of the period costs can also be reduced by simplifying the product offering. The manufacturing costs, division marketing and sales, and general and administrative expenses are all increased by having a large product offering. The small production run products are responsible for more than their fair share of these costs, and these period adjustments reflect my estimates of the potential savings.

Overall inventory levels can be reduced if we drop the safe products which account for almost $500,000 of current inventory. While we can eliminate all of this inventory, we will have to increase the inventory of the substitute products to support their additional sales activity. I estimate the reduction in inventory carrying charges at $31,000.

Dropping products generally results in obsolete inventory which has to be written off. I have reviewed the current inventory levels of the safe products and estimate the after-tax adjustment to be $245,000. This will be a one-time charge to income.

Impact of Writing Off Inventory in 1983
with No Production and Sales in 1984 of
Products to be Eliminated
($ thousands)

CHANGES TO 1984 PLAN	
Standard margin	$0
Less costs:	
Labor variance	(42)
Burden effect	(224)
Lost absorption	40
Spending improvement	(120)
Increase in net gross profit	346
Period expenses	
Manufacturing	(146)
Marketing	(208)
SG&A	(30)
Increase in operating profit	730
Carrying cost avoided	31
After-tax loss due to writeoff	(245)
Increase in profit after tax	$516

READINGS

The Hidden Factory

Jeffrey G. Miller and Thomas E. Vollmann

While the world's attention is focused on the fight to increase productivity and develop new technologies, manufacturing managers—especially those in the electronics and mechanical equipment (machinery) industries—are quietly waging a different battle: the battle to conquer overhead costs. Indeed, our research shows that overhead costs rank behind only quality and getting new products out on schedule as a primary concern of manufacturing executives.

The reason for this concern is obvious: high manufacturing overhead has a dramatic effect on profit and competitiveness, and manufacturing managers believe themselves to be poorly equipped to manage these costs well. As one senior executive told us, "We've been brought up to manage in a world where burden rates [the ratios of overhead costs to direct labor costs] are 100% to 200% or so. But now some of our plants are running with burden rates of over 1,000%. We don't even know what that means!"

We are convinced that this renewed attention to overhead is not a cyclical phenomenon. No doubt, low capacity utilization accounted for some increase in awareness during the last recession; even so, awareness has remained high throughout the recovery. Overhead costs as a percentage of value added in American industry and as a percentage of overall manufacturing costs have been rising steadily for more than 100 years as the ratio of direct labor costs to value added has declined (see *Exhibit I*). Moreover, in today's environment, production managers have more direct leverage on improving productivity through cutting overhead than they do through pruning direct labor.

As America's factories step up the pace of automation, they find that they are being hit twice: first, overhead costs grow in percentage terms as direct labor costs fall (everything has to add up to 100%); and second, overhead costs grow in real terms because of the increased support costs associated with maintaining and running automated equipment.

Exhibit II shows how overhead as a percentage of value added increases as a representative industry—electronics—moves down its product-process life cycle.[1] Highly customized and low-volume specialty businesses, such as those in the government systems segment of the industry, run job-shop-type operations with a relatively low ratio of overhead to direct labor. By contrast, in businesses producing high-volume standardized products in automated environments, as in the microcomputer segment of the industry, the ratio of overhead to direct labor cost is notably greater.

Our data suggest that across the spectrum of U.S. industry, manufacturing overhead averages 35% of production costs; the comparable figure for Japanese products is 26%, despite the fact that the Japanese have been rapidly automating. The differential is particularly large in the electronics and machinery industries, where American overhead accounts for 70% to 75% of value added, and Japan's for 50% to 60%. (See the [Authors' Note on Research Methods] for a description of the methods and data we used.)

---

[1] See Steven C. Wheelwright and Robert H. Hayes, "Link Manufacturing Process and Product Life Cycles," HBR January-February 1979, p. 133, and "The Dynamics of Process-Product Life Cycles," HBR March-April 1979, p. 127.

Exhibit I.   Components of value added

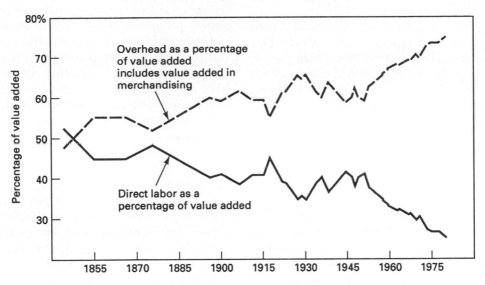

A FOCUS ON TRANSACTIONS

For managers, the critical step in controlling overhead costs lies in developing a model that relates these costs to the forces behind them. Most production managers understand what it is that drives direct labor and materials costs, but they are much less aware of what drives overhead costs. True, we do have models that accountants use—as they do engineering standards and bills of material —to relate overhead costs to products produced. But these models do not so much *explain* overhead costs as *allocate* them.

Exhibit II.   Overhead as a percentage of value added in five segments of the electronics industry

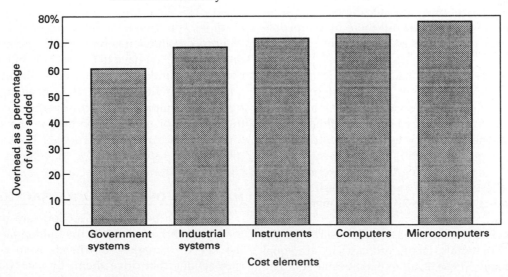

Source: Developed from data in the 1983 report of the American Electronics Association

Most of these efforts use the engineering standards and bills of material models that we do understand as the basis for allocating overhead costs that we do not understand. These efforts base overhead burden rates on direct labor, materials, or machine hours. The problem with this approach is that the driving force behind most overhead costs is not unit output or direct labor. Overhead costs do usually correlate with unit outputs, but that does not mean that unit outputs "cause" overhead costs. In fact, acting as though they were causally related leads managers to concentrate on output measures or on direct labor rather than on the structural activities that determine overhead costs. (See the [section] entitled "Overhead Costs Defined.")

Unit output drives direct labor and materials inputs on the actual shop floor that we all think of when we envision a factory. But in the "hidden factory," where the bulk of manufacturing overhead costs accumulates, the real driving force comes from transactions, not physical products. These transactions involve exchanges of the materials and/or information necessary to move production along but do not directly result in physical products. Rather, these transactions are responsible for aspects of the "augmented product," or "bundle of goods," that customers purchase—such aspects as on-time delivery, quality, variety, and improved design.

To see clearly how the hidden factory creates overhead costs, we must identify the basic types of transaction that are carried out there by the people whose wages and salaries account for the following costs:

Logistical transactions, which order, execute, and confirm the movement of materials from one location to another. These transactions are processed, tracked, and analyzed by many of the indirect workers on the shop floor as well as by people in receiving, expediting, shipping, data entry, data processing, and accounting. For the electronics industry, we estimate that processing such transactions accounts for 10% to 20% of total manufacturing overhead.

Balancing transactions, which ensure that the supplies of materials, labor, and capacity are equal to the demand. These result in the movement orders and authorizations that generate logistical transactions.

The people involved in processing such transactions include purchasing, materials planning, and control personnel (who convert master schedules and customer orders into materials requirements and purchase and shop orders) as well as human resource staff (who convert these demands into labor requirements). Also included are managers who process and authorize forecasts and who turn orders into production plans and master schedules. We estimate that these transactions also account for 10% to 20% of manufacturing overhead in electronics manufacturing.

Quality transactions, which extend far beyond what we usually think of as quality control, indirect engineering, and procurement to include the identification and communication of specifications, the certification that other transactions have taken place as they were supposed to, and the development and recording of relevant data. In the electronics industry, quality transactions add up to some 25% to 40% of manufacturing overhead.

Change transactions, which update basic manufacturing information systems to accommodate changes in engineering designs, schedules, routings, standards, materials specifications, and bills of material. These transactions involve the work of manufacturing, industrial, and quality engineers, along with a portion of the effort expended in purchasing, materials control, data entry, and data processing.

Change transactions can occur over and over again. The first time you design a product, for example, you transact a bill of materials, every time you process an engineering change order (ECO) for that product, you have to transact the bill again. The doing and undoing of logistical, balancing, and quality transactions that result from change transactions lead companies to incur overhead costs twice, three times, or more, depending on the stability of their manufacturing environments. Overall, change transactions represent 20% to 40% of overhead costs in electronics manufacturing.

MANAGING OVERHEAD TRANSACTIONS

If, as we believe, transactions are responsible for most overhead costs in the hidden factory, then the key to managing overheads is to control the transactions that drive them. By *managing transactions,* we mean thinking consciously and carefully about which transactions are appropriate and which

AUTHORS' NOTE ON RESEARCH METHODS

The research on which the data and conclusions in this [reading] rest comes from two different sources. Most of the quantitative data come from the 1984 "North American Manufacturing Futures Survey," which we administer. Insights into overhead cost structures in the electronics industry—and the managerial problems and issues surrounding them —come from structured interviews and data analysis of four electronics factories in the United States and from subsequent follow-up visits to numerous other plants in the electronics and other industries in the United States and the Far East. The Boston University Manufacturing Roundtable sponsored both of these data-gathering efforts.

The Manufacturing Futures Project is an annual survey of the competitive strategies, concerns, recent activities, and plans that North American manufacturers are making to improve their operational effectiveness. In the 1984 survey, respondents included more than 200 senior manufacturing executives in as many different business units (the typical title of the respondents was vice president of manufacturing). Participating business units came from a broad range of industries, which we categorized in five classes: electronics, consumer packaged goods, machinery, basic industries (chemicals, metals, paper), and other industrial goods. In 1984, the third consecutive year we administered the survey in North America, it was also administered to more than 200 business units in both Japan and Europe by our collaborators at Waseda University in Tokyo and at INSEAD in France.

The "Manufacturing Futures Survey" contains more than 50 multiple-part questions. A small number (those relating to managing overheads) formed the basis for the analysis in this [reading]. For example, one survey question required respondents to indicate on a five-point scale the degree of their concern about 32 potential problem areas. The top five concerns were as follows (the number in parentheses indicates the mean scaled score given each potential concern across all respondents to the survey):

1. Producing to high quality standards (3.98).
2. Introducing new products on schedule (3.56).
3. High or rising overhead costs (3.55).
4. Low indirect labor productivity, including white-collar work (3.44).
5. Yield problems and rejects (3.28).

People in the electronics and machinery industries were the most concerned with overhead costs and indirect labor productivity, although concern about these areas was high in all five industry groups analyzed. To narrow the focus of our subsequent investigations, we decided to concentrate on the problems of managing overhead in the electronics industry. Our rationale was that this industry group had proved to be something of a bellwether for other industries during the history of the Manufacturing Futures Project.

Moreover, numerous plant visits convinced us that many of the problems in managing overhead in this fast-changing industry were reflected in other industries, especially in the machinery group. The very high levels of capital investment and energy consumption required in the basic and consumer goods industry groups substantially change the cost structure (and thus the nature of the problems of managing overhead), although we think that much of what we have to say is relevant for those groups.

Our field investigations included extensive tours and interviews at four plants in the electronics industry—two focused on components manufacture and two on the assembly of high-volume equipment. Needless to say, we also spent considerable time discussing overhead costs with both accountants and managers from the plants.

To develop comparable data on overhead costs, we followed several conventions. First, we lumped all overhead costs into one pool. Second, we unbundled all costs so that they fell into mutually exclusive categories. For example, we put all depreciation and space costs in the "facilities" category, even though a particular company might follow the practice of allocating depreciation costs to organizational subunits like purchasing and rolling them up into a total purchasing cost (which we would put in the "materials overhead" category).

are not and about how to do the important transactions most effectively. Manufacturers have rigorously applied this type of analysis to direct labor since the days of Frederick Taylor. Now that overhead costs far exceed direct labor costs, however, managers should redirect their analytical efforts.

Transaction analysis

The design criteria used in developing most products and production processes rarely take overhead costs into account, let alone the transaction costs involved in alternative designs. It is possible, for example, to eliminate numerous transactions by designing short-cycle production processes without any work-in-process (WIP) inventory that would require logistical, balancing, or quality transactions. This is what the Japanese have done with their "just-in-time" philosophy of process design, which "pulls" work through the factory only as needed by operations downstream. This approach eliminates much of the need for elaborate and time-consuming WIP-tracking or shop-floor control systems.

One electronics product that was redesigned to meet competitive pressures provides a vivid example of what a low-transaction production system can do. Prior to the redesign, the product contained more than 700 parts, most of which had to be ordered from a supplier on a weekly basis and then placed in a materials inventory before being withdrawn in batches and taken to the final assembly area. The plant shipped each week's output to a finished goods inventory in the company's distribution system. A count of the number of monthly transactions required by this system is as follows:

Ordering transactions	= 700 parts × 4	= 2,800 transactions
Receiving transactions	= 700 × 4	= 2,800
Materials transactions (in and out of inventory)	= 700 × 4 ×2	= 5,600
Materials authorizations	= 700 × 4	= 2,800
Total transactions		= 14,000 per month

After careful study, management decided that:

1. Changes in product design and vendor specifications could reduce the part count from 700 to 200.

2. The factory could issue blanket orders instead of separate purchase orders for materials and could provide vendors with monthly shipping rates. The need for additional parts would be signaled by the return of an empty container of standard size.

3. A simple receiving and inspection procedure that calls for the packing slip to be sent directly to accounting on receipt of the container could replace the current complicated process. As a result, the company would need to send only one check per month to each vendor for goods actually received.

4. Delivering parts directly to the floor could eliminate the materials inventory, the necessity of putting materials away, the issuing of authorizations to withdraw them, and the work of pulling the materials out again.

5. A smoothed production flow would make quality problems immediately apparent and change management's focus from extensive record keeping to prevention and immediate correction.

This factory is now well on its way to implementing a production system with far fewer monthly transactions (see top of p. 351).

Needless to say, the overhead costs of this factory have plummeted, as have inventory costs. In some areas—receiving, for example—the number of transactions has actually increased, but a painstaking examination of the steps involved in carrying out transactions in the hidden factory has greatly simplified the flow of work and cut total transaction costs. Managers had only to study the transaction process of the hidden factory in the same way they have long examined the production process of the visible factory.

Another way to improve transaction-based overhead is to reduce the "granularity" of the data that are reported. Every manufacturing system embodies decisions about how finely and how frequently transaction data are to be reported. It makes no sense to process more data than needed or more often than needed.

One company, for example, found that its quality transaction system was collecting and keeping quality data on every possible activity —despite the very poor quality of its products. The quality department often complained that

Ordering transactions	=	200 parts × 1	=	200	transactions per month
Receiving transactions	=	200 × 20 days × 2	=	8,000	
Materials authorizations	=	0	=	0	
Materials transactions	=	0	=	0	
Total transactions			=	8,200	

it never had time to analyze the data, which just sat in file cabinets and computer files, because it spent all its time collecting. By focusing on the few key areas where most of the quality problems existed, the department was able to improve quality dramatically while it reduced costs. It processed quality transactions more intensively in the key areas and much less intensively where things were running smoothly.

Stability

Perhaps the simplest way to reduce the number of transactions is to stabilize the manufacturing environment. Many American companies are now aggressively trying to implement Japanese just-in-time approaches, but visitors from Japan are often quite surprised at what they see here. In Japan, the first principle is stability, and great effort goes into engineering the process down to the finest detail and into training workers to follow instructions to the letter. Level loads, balanced work flows, and good housekeeping all help ensure that the unexpected does not destabilize the operations.

Every time an ECO is issued, a schedule breaks down, or a quality problem erupts, a wave of new transactions flows through a plant. The policy of "making it right the first time" applies to the processing of transactions just as it does to the making of products. Not only do these changes increase the number of transactions; they also have an important secondary effect. Instability in plant schedules and performance causes many plant managers to overstaff their work forces so that the plants can react to unexpected peak loads in transaction volume. As one veteran plant manager said, "You've

got to keep shock troops in ready reserve to handle the problems that come up."

One reason for the low percentage of value added attributed to overhead in Japanese factories is that their plants are more stable than ours. Their way of handling ECOs is a case in point. *Exhibit III* shows the frequency with which Japanese and U.S. electronics plants authorize design changes. The Japanese process fewer ECOs than do their American counterparts (about two-thirds fewer) and authorize these changes much further in advance and thus allow for more stable, level transaction loads. With more planning, there are fewer errors.

Automation

One of the most frequently discussed ways to reduce the overhead costs associated with the hidden factory is automation. Robots can have a role in sophisticated materials control systems that automate logistical transactions; lasers can read bar codes and eliminate the need for data entry operators to record movement transactions manually; computer-aided inspection can help reduce the costs of processing quality transactions; a smoothly running materials requirements planning system can make the processing of balancing transactions cheaper.

The cost of processing transactions manually can easily be ten times as great as processing them automatically. The issue is not only the cost of the transaction, however, but also the effectiveness of the transaction process. In addition to the costs of reading, distributing, filing, and retrieving, manual transactions often have a much more serious problem: they take too long. Response time is clearly a major issue in American manufacturing today, yet we know of companies that take 5 to 15 working days to turn a customer order into the proper form for manufacturing. A manual transaction based on retrieving information from a file cabinet, reading the document to understand the conditions, making the transaction, dispatching the results, and refiling can easily take 100 times longer than a comparable

OVERHEAD COSTS DEFINED

In principle, manufacturing overhead is easy to define: it includes all the direct and allocated costs of manufacture other than direct labor and purchased materials. Among these costs are:

- Indirect labor, including the wages of hourly workers who do not directly contribute to the manufacture of a product but consisting mostly of labor dedicated to materials handling, maintenance, quality control, and inspection.
- General and administrative expenses such as personnel administration, cost accounting, security, salaries for plant management, and direct labor supervision as well as corporate allocations for shared services and corporate staff.
- Facilities and equipment costs such as insurance, depreciation of plant equipment, and tooling. These costs also include rents and other facilities-related expenses such as energy and utility costs. (Note that in process-based industries, energy costs may comprise the single largest component of overhead and total costs. Our data suggest that energy accounts for about 4% of the total manufacturing costs for a typical plant in the electronics or machinery industries.)
- Engineering costs such as the salaries of manufacturing, industrial, and other engineers concerned with the design and maintenance of the production process itself.
- Materials overhead costs, including those related to the procurement, movement (with the exception of those shop floor materials-handling costs relegated to the indirect labor category), and coordination of raw materials, components, subassemblies, and finished products. These costs also include the salaries of purchasing, production planning, receiving, stockroom, traffic, and manufacturing systems personnel.

This figure shows the average distribution of these cost categories in the four electronics plants we examined. None of these plants kept its overhead accounts in exactly the fashion we have described. Although their basic categories were the same, each had invented a somewhat different nomenclature and taxonomy for keeping track of these costs. To arrive at a relatively consistent—and comparable—set of numbers, we had to recast the costs at each of these plants.

Table   Manufacturing overhead cost elements in the electronics industry

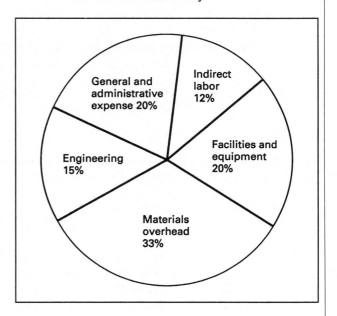

transaction done in a computer-supported environment.

Perhaps the most important means of automating transactions is using computer systems that are so well integrated that data need only be entered once. In virtually every large company, however, there is still a massive redundancy of transactions due to the existence of subsystems that cannot "talk" to one another. These problems exist both within manufacturing and between manufacturing and other functions.

Integrated systems offer more than efficiency; they can also improve accuracy and understanding. When the same data are kept in several places and separate organizational units independently calculate such facts as monthly shipments, the result is redundant records, redundant transaction processing, and general confusion. It is not unusual for managers to ask production, marketing, and finance to provide the unit shipment data for one product and to get three different answers.

Properly designed and integrated computer

Exhibit III. **The frequency of ECO authorizations in the U.S. and the Japanese electronics industries**

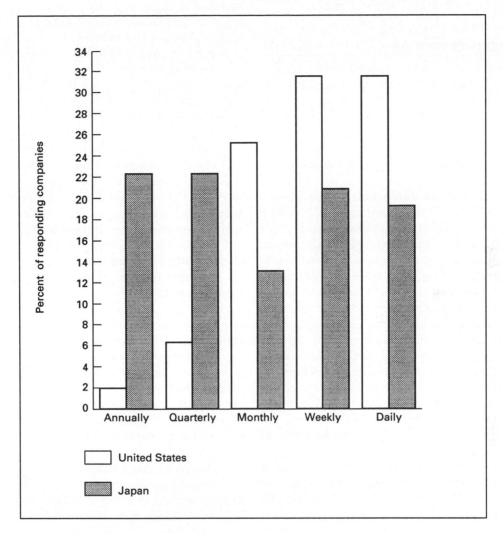

systems should lead to transactions being made only once—and to less confusion. Good systems adhere to the rule of encoding only new data: never design a transaction so that it requires data already in a computer to be reentered by hand. In far too many factories, we see people typing in data like part numbers while they look at computer-generated documents for the numbers.

Another type of data integration unites manufacturing data bases with those of other functional areas. Most familiar is the link between engineering and manufacturing established by CAD/CAM systems, but there are others with equal or greater potential impact. One company, for example, is integrating its complex multiplant network with an equally complex order entry and customer service network so as to reduce overhead costs, increase delivery speed and effectiveness, and improve the accuracy of its order entry—configuration processes (a major source of quality problems). Another company is seeking to improve the efficiency of its large financial staff by linking its financial data base with its manufacturing data base and thereby to eliminate double entries and boost its ability to relate manufacturing plans to financial performance.

A BALANCED APPROACH

There are, then, three general approaches to managing overhead costs more effectively: (1) analyzing which transactions are necessary and improving the methods used to carry them out, (2) increasing the stability of operations, and (3) relying on automation and systems integration. Of the three, U.S. manufacturers seem most enamored of the last.

Selectively applied, transaction automation and integration can be an important tool for reducing overall costs and for raising competitiveness in other dimensions as well. In too many instances, however, this tool has the reverse effect. Managers frequently justify this approach on the basis of substituting capital for labor, but they often forget that they are also replacing direct labor with overhead expense. As one operations manager has complained, "All that we succeeded in doing with our monstrous new computer system was to replace $10-an-hour workers with $30-to-$50-an-hour technicians whom we can't hire anyway because of their scarcity." According to another operations manager, "When we automated, direct labor expense was reduced, but total costs increased because of the increase in overheads."

In many of these instances, no one bothered to do a complete analysis of the impact on transaction volumes and costs as activities moved to middle management levels. Some companies even applied their old burden rates to the direct labor costs projected after automation.

A second and perhaps more serious problem occurs when manufacturers automate transactions that are not really necessary in the first place. One company that had recently built an advanced "factory of the future" later removed the automated guided vehicle system and a major portion of the automatic storage and retrieval systems that it had installed in order to reduce the cost of its internal logistical transactions. After installation the company found that it had simplified the transaction flow so much that no automation was necessary after all.

Another company, while evaluating a bar code system, recently discovered that its justification for the system disappeared when it eliminated the needless paperwork that had flowed among receiving, inspection, accounting, and production. The original projection had been for a two-year payback on the bar code system (based on the elimination of the clerical workers needed to produce the paperwork), but closer examination showed that most of that clerical reduction would come from just eliminating the unnecessary transactions.

The lesson, then, is to seek a balanced approach to managing overhead. Automation does not solve all problems; in fact, it may create some unless handled carefully.

As American managers face up to the task of controlling manufacturing overhead, they will have to go beyond process analysis in its usual sense and learn how to analyze transactional processes. Managers will also have to learn when and where to automate the transaction process, how to integrate it in manufacturing and across functions, and how and where to stabilize that process to its greatest strategic effect.

Finally, manufacturing managers will have to look beyond accounting conventions to analyze and categorize costs in a way that has functional meaning. We believe that the answer does not lie in inventing new accounting systems alone. This is a problem for the accountants to solve if they can; certainly it will help if they do. But no amount of bookkeeping magic will let manufacturing managers avoid one of the strategic necessities of the future: understanding how to manage the hidden factory.

The Rise of Activity-Based Costing—Part One: What Is an Activity-Based Cost System?

Robin Cooper

Volume-based cost systems often distort reported product costs when dealing with product diversity in the form of size or volume. For this reason, activity-based cost systems—those that trace costs to products according to the activities performed on them, independent of volume—are gaining prominence. In this [reading]—the first of a four-part series—the author examines the bias introduced by volume-based cost systems and shows how this distortion can be corrected with activity-based systems.

In recent years, a new development in product costing techniques has quietly gained attention. The new method is known as activity-based costing, and it represents an evolutionary extension of the two-stage procedure that underlies most modern cost systems.[1]

Conventional cost systems focus on the product in the costing process. Costs are traced to the product because each product item is assumed to consume the resources. Conventional allocation bases thus measure only attributes of the individual product item: the number of direct labor or machine hours or material dollars consumed. By contrast, activities are the focus of the costing process in activity-based cost systems. Costs are traced from activities to products based on the product's demand for these activities during the production process. The allocation bases used in activity-based costing are thus measures of the activities performed. These might include hours of setup time or number of times handled.

Not only the nature of allocation base used by activity-based cost systems but the number of allocation bases used to trace costs in the second stage differs. Whereas a conventional system uses, at most, three second-stage allocation bases—direct labor hours, machine hours, and material dollars are the most common bases—an activity-based system makes use of many bases, including setup hours, number of times ordered, and number of times shipped.[2]

In this [reading], I will illustrate a simple activity-based cost system with a series of examples and then demonstrate some of the conditions under which such a system reports more accurate product costs than a conventional direct-labor-hour system. In particular, we will explore the effect of varying product volume and size on reported product costs.

CONVENTIONAL PRODUCT COSTING

The following example illustrates some of the disadvantages associated with conventional forms of product costing.

Example 1.[3]   Company A manufactures four products: P_1, P_2, P_3, and P_4. All are produced on the same equipment and by similar processes. The products differ either by size (small and large) or by volume (low and high) in a single production run. Exhibit 1 summarizes the characteristics of each product. The four products consume material, direct labor, machine hours, setup, material handling, and parts administration costs. Exhibit 2 presents the quantity and dollar value of each input by product.

Company A employs a cost accounting system that consists of one cost center—the entire facility—that traces costs to the product by means of direct labor hours. Overhead costs reported by the system are given in Exhibit 2. The product costs reported by this system would remain the same if machine hours or material dollars were used instead to trace costs to the products. The additional allocation bases would not affect reported costs because all three bases are perfectly correlated.[4]

An analysis of the overhead costs traced to the

Reprinted from *Journal of Cost Management* (Summer 1988), pp. 45-54; with permission.

Exhibit 1. Company A Product Characteristics

PRODUCT	QUANTITY PER YEAR	MATERIAL $ PER UNIT	DIRECT LABOR HOURS PER UNIT	MACHINE HOURS PER UNIT
P_1	10	6	0.5	0.5
P_2	100	6	0.5	0.5
P_3	10	18	1.5	1.5
P_4	100	18	1.5	1.5

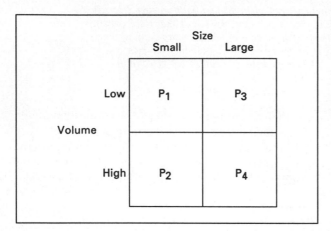

products by the direct labor hour system leads to two conclusions: the high-volume products cost the same to manufacture as the low-volume products and the cost of the large products is three times that of the small ones. The reason for these relationships is clear. The high-volume products, in total, consume 10 times the number of direct labor hours required by their low-volume counterparts. Therefore, the cost system traces 10 times the overhead—as well as 10 times the material dollars and direct labor hours—in total, to them. Because the number of high-volume products manufactured is 10 times

that of the low-volume products, the unit costs are the same.

The large products, for their part, consume three times the number of direct labor hours as their small counterparts. Therefore, the cost system traces three times the overhead —as well as three times the material dollars and direct labor hours—in total, to the large products. Because the products are manufactured in equal numbers, the unit cost of the large products is three times as high.

Intuitively, these reported product costs make only partial sense. Although most managers are likely to be comfortable with the relationship between the reported product costs of the large and small products, many would raise an eyebrow at the high-volume products costing the same as their low-volume counterparts. Economies of scale must come into play.

In fact, all of the reported product costs are highly distorted. The source of this distortion lies in the choice of a single allocation base—direct labor hours—to trace costs to the products. This allocation base cannot accurately trace all input costs consumed in Company A to the products because it assumes that when the number of items of a product manufactured doubles, so does the input cost consumed by that product. Allocation bases that make such an assumption are called volume-related allocation bases. Typical volume-related allocation bases include direct labor hours, machine hours, and material dollars.

Using volume-related allocation bases alone to trace costs to products distorts reported product costs if some of the product-related activities are unrelated to volume. For example, a low-volume

Exhibit 2. Product Costing Data for Company A

ANNUAL INPUT CONSUMPTION PATTERNS AND DOLLAR VALUE BY PRODUCT

PRODUCT NO	MATERIAL ($)	DIRECT LABOR HOURS	MACHINE HOURS	NO OF SETUPS	NO OF ORDERS	NO OF TIMES HANDLED	NO OF PART NUMBERS	TOTAL OVERHEAD COSTS
P_1	60	5	5	1	1	1	1	
P_2	600	50	50	3	3	3	1	
P_3	180	15	15	1	1	1	1	
P_4	1,800	150	150	3	3	3	1	
Units Consumed	2,640	220	220	8	8	8	4	
Dollar Value	$264	$2,200	$3,300	$960	$1,000	$200	$2,000	$9,924

(continued)

Exhibit 2 (*cont.*)

OVERHEAD COSTS REPORTED BY THE COST SYSTEM

OVERHEAD CONSUMPTION INTENSITY			REPORTED OVERHEAD COSTS		
	DIRECT LABOR			OVERHEAD TRACED	REPORTED UNIT COST
Dollar value	$9,924.00	Consumption Intensity	$ 45.11		—
Units Consumed	220	Direct Labor Hours That Product P_1 Consumes	5		
		Costs Traced		$ 225.55	$22.55
Consumption Intensity	$ 45.11	Direct Labor Hours That Product P_2 Consumes	50		
		Costs Traced		$2,255.50	$22.55
		Direct Labor Hours That Product P_3 Consumes	15		
		Costs Traced		$ 676.65	$67.66
		Direct Labor Hours That Product P_4 Consumes	150		
		Costs Traced		$6,766.50	$67.66

OVERHEAD COSTS REPORTED BY AN ACTIVITY-BASED COST SYSTEM

OVERHEAD CONSUMPTION INTENSITIES

	DIRECT LABOR HOURS	NO OF SETUPS	NO OF PART NUMBERS
Total	$5,764.00	$2,160	$2,000
Units Consumed	220	8	4
Consumption Intensity	$ 26.20	$ 270	500

REPORTED OVERHEAD COSTS

	DIRECT LABOR RELATED	NO OF SETUPS RELATED	NO OF PART NUMBERS RELATED	OVERHEAD TRACED	REPORTED UNIT COST	DIFFERENCE FROM EXISTING SYSTEM (%)
Consumption Intensities	$ 26.20	$270	$500	—	—	—
Product P_1 Consumes	5	1	1			
Costs Traced	$ 131.00	$270	$500	$ 901	$ 90.10	299.55
Product P_2 Consumes	50	3	1			
Costs Traced	$1,310.00	$810	$500	$2,620	$ 26.20	16.18
Product P_3 Consumes	15	1	1			
Costs Traced	$ 393.00	$270	$500	$1,163	$116.30	71.88
Product P_4 Consumes	150	3	1			
Costs Traced	$3,930.00	$810	$500	$5,240	$ 52.40	− 22.55

product produced once a year is ordered and handled once and a high-volume product manufactured three times a year is ordered and handled three times. This happens despite the fact that 10 times as many high-volume products are manufactured as low-volume ones. To accurately trace these volume-unrelated costs requires a system that costs activities, not products.

ACTIVITY-BASED PRODUCT COSTING

In an activity-based system, the cost of a product is the sum of the costs of all activities required to manufacture and deliver the product. In Example 1, five activities are required: ordering the parts, transporting the parts to and from the machines, setting up the machines, machining the parts, and administering the part numbers. Many of these activities are unrelated to the volume of a production run. For example, doubling the volume of a product does not require doubling the number of setups or part orders. A simple volume-related allocation base cannot capture the complexity of the relationship between volume and lot or order size.

To trace costs deriving from activities unrelated to volume requires allocation bases that themselves are independent of volume. For example, setups can be costed by dividing all setup-related costs by total setup hours to yield an hourly setup cost. This figure can then be used in conjunction with the allocation base setup hours to trace setup costs to the product.

The allocation bases used by activity-based cost systems are termed *cost drivers.* In our example, a variety of cost drivers can be used to trace volume-unrelated costs, including:

- Setup hours.
- Number of setups.
- Material handling hours.
- Number of times handled.
- Ordering hours.
- Number of times ordered.
- Part number administration hours.
- Number of part numbers maintained.

Three of the cost drivers—the number of setups, orders, and times handled—are perfectly correlated in the example, as noted in Exhibit 2. An analysis of the production process shows why. Products are ordered only as required and handled only when being produced, which requires that the machines be set up. Consequently, the decision to initiate a production run drives the three activities—ordering, material handling, and setup.

When cost drivers are perfectly correlated—because of the interrelationship among the underlying activities—the cost of these activities can be aggregated in a single cost pool. Any one of the correlated cost drivers can then be used to trace costs to the product.

Volume-related costs can still be traced using direct labor hours, because this is an appropriate cost driver. The activities being traced include material-related costs (e.g., incoming freight), direct labor–related costs (e.g., fringe benefits), and machine-related costs (e.g., electrical power). Although in practice three cost drivers—material dollars, direct labor hours, and machine hours—might be required, in our example, the perfect correlation of the three cost drivers allows us to make a second aggregation of costs without distorting the reported product costs.

The overhead costs reported by an activity-based cost system are given in Exhibit 2. Analyzing the differences in the overhead costs reported by the activity-based and volume-based[5] cost systems leads to three important observations:

- The difference in the reported product costs of low-volume products is greater than that of high-volume products.
- The difference in the reported product costs of small products is greater than that of large products.
- These two trends reinforce one another.

To pinpoint the sources of the biases in reported product costs, it is useful to introduce two pairs of examples. In the first, the effect of production volume, or volume diversity,[6] on the product costs reported by volume-related and activity-based systems is explored. In the second, the effect of product size, or size diversity, is examined. When the individual effects of volume and size are understood, their combined effect can be evaluated.

VOLUME DIVERSITY

The following two examples examine the ability of volume-based and activity-based cost systems to accurately trace product costs when products differ by volume.

Example 2A. Company B manufactures two products, P_1 and P_2. P_1 is a small, low-volume product. P_2 is a small, high-volume product. Both are produced on the same equipment and by similar processes. The two products consume six input resources: material, direct labor, machine hours, setup, material handling, and parts administration. Exhibit 3 presents the quantity and dollar value of

Exhibit 3.   Product Costing Data for Company B

ANNUAL INPUT CONSUMPTION PATTERNS AND DOLLAR VALUE BY PRODUCTS

PRODUCT NO	MATERIAL ($)	DIRECT LABOR HOURS	MACHINE HOURS	NO OF SETUPS	NO OF ORDERS	NO OF TIMES HANDLED	NO OF PART NUMBERS	TOTAL OVERHEAD COSTS
P_1	60	5	5	1	1	1	1	
P_2	600	50	50	3	3	3	1	
Units Consumed	660	55	55	4	4	4	2	
Dollar Value	$ 66	$550	$825	$480	$500	$100	$1,000	$3,521

OVERHEAD COSTS REPORTED BY VOLUME-BASED COST SYSTEM

OVERHEAD CONSUMPTION INTENSITY			REPORTED OVERHEAD COSTS		
	DIRECT LABOR			OVERHEAD TRACED	REPORTED UNIT COST
Dollar Value	$3,521.00		Consumption Intensity	$ 64.02	—
Units Consumed		55	Direct Labor Hours That Product P_1 Consumes	5	
Consumption Intensity	$	64.02	Costs Traced	$ 320.10	32.01
			Direct Labor Hours That Product P_2 Consumes	50	
			Costs Traced	$3,201.00	$32.01

OVERHEAD COSTS REPORTED BY AN ACTIVITY-BASED SYSTEM

OVERHEAD CONSUMPTION INTENSITIES

	DIRECT LABOR HOURS	NO OF SETUPS	NO OF PART NUMBERS
Total	$1,441.00	$1,080.00	$1,000.00
Units Consumed	55	4	2
Consumption Intensity	$ 26.20	$ 270.00	$ 500.00

REPORTED OVERHEAD COSTS

	DIRECT LABOR RELATED	NO OF SETUPS RELATED	NO OF PART NUMBERS RELATED	OVERHEAD TRACED	REPORTED UNIT COST	DIFFERENCE FROM VOLUME-BASED SYSTEM (%)
Consumption Intensities	$ 26.20	$270	$500	—	—	—
Product P_1 Consumes	5	1	1			
Costs Traced	$ 131.00	$270	$500	$ 901	$90.10	181.48
Product P_2 Consumes	50	3	1			
Costs Traced	$1,310.00	$810	$500	$2,620	$26.20	−18.15

Exhibit 4. Product Costing Data for Company C

ANNUAL INPUT CONSUMPTION PATTERNS AND DOLLAR VALUE BY PRODUCT

PRODUCT NO	MATERIAL ($)	DIRECT LABOR HOURS	MACHINE HOURS	NO OF SETUPS	NO OF ORDERS	NO OF TIMES HANDLED	NO OF PART NUMBERS	TOTAL OVERHEAD COSTS
P_3	180	15	15	1	1	1	1	
P_4	1,800	150	150	3	3	3	1	
Units Consumed	1,980	165	165	4	4	4	2	
Dollar Value	$198	$1,650	$2,475	$480	$500	$100	$1,000	$6,403

OVERHEAD COSTS REPORTED BY VOLUME-BASED COST SYSTEM

OVERHEAD CONSUMPTION INTENSITY			REPORTED OVERHEAD COSTS		
	DIRECT LABOR			OVERHEAD TRACED	REPORTED UNIT COST
Dollar Value		$6,403.00	Consumption Intensity	$ 38.81	—
Units Consumed		165	Direct Labor Hours That Product P_3 Consumes	15	
Consumption Intensity	$	38.81	Costs Traced	$ 582.15	$58.21
			Direct Labor Hours That Product P_4 Consumes	150	
			Costs Traced	$5,821.15	$58.21

OVERHEAD COSTS REPORTED BY AN ACTIVITY-BASED COST SYSTEM

OVERHEAD CONSUMPTION INTENSITIES

	DIRECT LABOR HOURS	NO OF SETUPS	NO OF PART NUMBERS
Total	$4,323.00	$1,080	$1,000
Units Consumed	165.00	4	2
Consumption Intensity	$ 26.20	$ 270	$ 500

REPORTED OVERHEAD COSTS

	DIRECT LABOR RELATED	NO OF SETUPS RELATED	NO OF PART NUMBERS RELATED	OVERHEAD TRACED	REPORTED UNIT COST	DIFFERENCE FROM VOLUME-BASED SYSTEM (%)
Consumption Intensities	$ 26.20	$270	$500	—	—	—
Product P_3 Consumes Costs Traced	15 $ 393.00	1 $270	1 $500	$1,163	$116.30	99.80
Product P_4 Consumes Costs Traced	150 $3,930.00	3 $810	1 $500	$5,240	52.40	−9.98

the input by product as well as the overhead costs reported by both a volume-based cost system and an activity-based cost system.

Example 2B. The case of Company C is identical to that of Company B except that its two products, P_3 and P_4, are large, low-volume and large, high-volume products, respectively. Exhibit 4 presents the quantity and dollar value of the input by product as well as the overhead costs reported by both a volume-based cost system and an activity-based cost system.

A comparison of the two sets of reported overhead costs clearly demonstrates that the volume-based system overcosts high-volume products in relation to their low-volume counterparts.[7] The reason for this cross-subsidy lies in the relative quantities of input consumed by the products. The high-volume products consume 10 times as many material dollars, direct labor hours, and machine hours as the low-volume products. But the high-volume products are set up, ordered, and handled only three times as often and have the same number of parts numbers to administer. The volume-related cost system ignores these differences in relative input consumption of overhead resources. It assumes that the high-volume products, in total, consume 10 times the amount of all input resources. The result: the high-volume products are overcosted. The activity-based system, on the other hand, recognizes the differences in relative input consumption and traces the appropriate amount of input to each product.

The volume-based systems in Examples 2A and 2B exemplify this bias by reporting product costs of $32.01 for the high-volume and low-volume small products and $58.21 for the high-volume and low-volume large products. By contrast, the activity-based cost system reports product costs of $90.10 for the small, low-volume product, $26.20 for the small, high-volume product, $116.30 for the large, low-volume product, and $52.40 for the large, high-volume product. These costs reflect the complexity of input consumption. The low-volume products incur higher reported product costs because they consume more of the volume-unrelated input per item than their high-volume counterparts. Two additional observations can now be made:

- For the same product, the volume-based system reports different product costs for Company A than for Companies B and C.
- Again, for the same product, the activity-based system reports product costs for Company A that are identical to those reported for Companies B and C.

Because the three firms manufacture the same products using the same manufacturing process, the inability of the volume-based cost system to report consistent costs in the three companies indicates a general failure to accurately report product costs. By contrast, the activity-based cost system passes this test with flying colors.

SIZE DIVERSITY

The following two examples examine the ability of volume-based and activity-based systems to accurately trace product costs when products differ by size.

Example 3A. Company D manufactures two products P_1 and P_3. P_1 is a small, low-volume product, and P_3 a large, low-volume product. Both are produced on the same equipment and by means of similar processes. The two products consume six input resources: material, direct labor, setup, machine hours, material handling, and parts administration. Exhibit 5 presents the quantity and dollar value of the input by product as well as the overhead costs reported by both a volume-based cost system and an activity-based cost system.

Example 3B. The case of Company E is identical to that of Company D except that its two products, P_2 and P_4, are small, high-volume and large, high-volume products, respectively. Exhibit 6 presents the quantity and dollar value of input by product as well as the overhead costs reported by both a volume-based cost system and an activity-based cost system.

These two examples clearly demonstrate that the volume-based system overcosts large products in relation to their small counterparts. The reason for this cross-subsidy again lies in the relative quantities of input resources consumed by the products. The large products consume three times as many material dollars, direct labor hours, and machine hours as the small products. Therefore, a cost system that relies solely on volume-based second-

Exhibit 5.   Product Costing Data for Company D

ANNUAL INPUT CONSUMPTION PATTERNS AND DOLLAR VALUE BY PRODUCT

PRODUCT NO	MATERIAL ($)	DIRECT LABOR HOURS	MACHINE HOURS	NO OF SETUPS	NO OF ORDERS	NO OF TIMES HANDLED	NO OF PART NUMBERS	TOTAL OVERHEAD COSTS
P_1	60	5	5	1	1	1	1	
P_3	180	15	15	1	1	1	1	
Units Consumed	240	20	20	2	2	2	2	
Dollar Value	$24	$200	$300	$240	$250	$50	$1,000	$2,064

OVERHEAD COSTS REPORTED BY VOLUME-BASED COST SYSTEM

OVERHEAD CONSUMPTION INTENSITY		
		DIRECT LABOR
Dollar Value		$2,064.00
Units Consumed		20
Consumption Intensity		$ 103.20

REPORTED OVERHEAD COSTS	OVERHEAD TRACED	REPORTED UNIT COST
Consumption Intensity	$ 103.20	—
Direct Labor Hours That Product P_1 Consumes	5	
Costs Traced	$ 516.00	$ 51.60
Direct Labor Hours That Product P_3 Consumes	15	
Costs Traced	$1,548.00	$154.80

OVERHEAD COSTS REPORTED BY AN ACTIVITY-BASED COST SYSTEM

OVERHEAD CONSUMPTION INTENSITIES			
	DIRECT LABOR HOURS	NO OF SETUPS	NO OF PART NUMBERS
Total	$524.00	$540	$1,000
Units Consumed	20	2	2
Consumption Intensity	$ 26.20	$270	$ 500

REPORTED OVERHEAD COSTS

	DIRECT LABOR RELATED	NO OF SETUPS RELATED	NO OF PART NUMBERS RELATED	OVERHEAD TRACED	REPORTED UNIT COST	DIFFERENCE FROM VOLUME-BASED SYSTEM (%)
Consumption Intensities	$ 26.20	$270	$500	—	—	—
Product P_1 Consumes	5	1	1			
Costs Traced	$131.00	$270	$500	$ 901	$ 90.10	74.61
Product P_3 Consumes	15	1	1			
Costs Traced	$393.00	$270	$500	$1,163	$116.30	− 24.87

Exhibit 6. Product Costing Data for Company E

ANNUAL INPUT CONSUMPTION PATTERNS AND DOLLAR VALUE BY PRODUCT

PRODUCT NO	MATERIAL ($)	DIRECT LABOR HOURS	MACHINE HOURS	NO OF SETUPS	NO OF ORDERS	NO OF TIMES HANDLED	NO OF PART NUMBERS	TOTAL OVERHEAD COSTS
P_2	600	50	50	3	3	3	1	
P_4	1,800	150	150	3	3	3	1	
Units Consumed	2,400	200	200	6	6	6	2	
Dollar Value	$ 240	$2,000	$3,000	$720	$750	$150	$1,000	$7,860

OVERHEAD COSTS REPORTED BY VOLUME-BASED COST SYSTEM

OVERHEAD CONSUMPTION INTENSITY			REPORTED OVERHEAD COSTS		
		DIRECT LABOR		OVERHEAD TRACED	REPORTED UNIT COST
Dollar Value		$7,860.00	Consumption Intensity	39.30	—
Units Consumed		200	Direct Labor Hours That Product P_1 Consumes	50	
Consumption Intensity	$	39.30	Costs Traced	$1,965.00	$19.65
			Direct Labor Hours That Product P_2 Consumes	150	
			Costs Traced	$5,895.00	$58.95

OVERHEAD COSTS REPORTED BY AN ACTIVITY-BASED COST SYSTEM

OVERHEAD CONSUMPTION INTENSITIES		DIRECT LABOR HOURS	NO OF SETUPS	NO. OF PART NUMBERS
Total		$5,240.00	$1,620	$1,000
Units Consumed		200	6	2
Consumption Intensity	$	26.20	$ 270	$ 500

REPORTED OVERHEAD COSTS

	DIRECT LABOR RELATED	NO OF SETUPS RELATED	NO OF PART NUMBERS RELATED	OVERHEAD TRACED	REPORTED UNIT COST	DIFFERENCE FROM VOLUME-BASED SYSTEM (%)
Consumption Intensities	$ 26.20	$270	$500	—	—	—
Product P_2 Consumes	50	3	1			
Costs Traced	$1,310.00	$810	$500	$2,620	$26.20	33.33
Product P_4 Consumes	150	3	1			
Costs Traced	$3,930.00	$810	$500	$5,240	$52.40	−11.11

stage allocation bases will trace three times the cost to the large products.

As in the preceding volume-diversity example, however, an analysis of the actual consumption pattern shows that even though the large products consume three times the volume-related input, they consume the same amount of the volume-unrelated input. Consequently, the large products are over-costed by the volume-based system. The activity-based system, on the other hand, recognizes the differences in relative input consumption and traces the appropriate amount of input to each product.

The volume-based cost systems in Examples 3A and 3B exemplify this bias by reporting product costs of $51.60 and $154.80 for the small and large low-volume products and $19.65 and $58.95 for the small and large high-volume products, respectively. By contrast, the activity-based system reports product costs of $90.10 and $116.30 for the small and large low-volume products and $26.20 and $52.40 for the small and large high-volume products, respectively.

The volume-based cost system reports different product costs for the same products, depending on the company in which they are manufactured. The activity-based cost system reports the same product costs, irrespective of the company in which the products are made.

THE VOLUME-SIZE INTERACTION

The companies cited in Examples 2 and 3 can be considered subsets of Company A and Example 1. Companies B and C demonstrate the bias of volume diversity, Companies D and E the bias of size diversity. Company A demonstrates the interaction of these two biases. The small, low-volume product is doubly undercosted; instead of assessing its true cost of $90.10, the volume-based system reports a product cost of $22.55. The large, high-volume product, on the other hand, is doubly overcosted; instead of being costed at $52.40, its reported cost is $67.66. The two biases reinforce each other, however, they are not simply additive. The errors in the reported product costs in Companies B and C (that result from volume diversity) cannot be added to the errors in Companies D and E (that result from size diversity) to obtain the error in reported product costs traceable to size and volume diversity in Company A.

ESTIMATING THE BIAS

Once the source of the bias in reported products costs is understood, it becomes obvious that small, low-volume products will be undercosted and large, high-volume products will be overcosted. However, it is no easy task to estimate whether products of intermediate size and volume will be over- or undercosted or by how much. In the case of our simple example with only four products, we can make some educated guesses. The large, high-volume product consumes, in total, 30 times as many volume-related input as the small, low-volume product. However, the large, high-volume product is overcosted by only $15.26 and the small, low-volume product is undercosted by $67.55. At least one of the intermediate products, therefore, must be undercosted.

As it turns out, both intermediate products are undercosted. Given the difficulty in estimating the direction of the bias, it is not surprising that the magnitude of the bias proves even harder to pinpoint. In a realistic setting—with hundreds or thousands of products and multiple sources of bias—it is unreasonable to expect managers to make even approximate estimates of the direction and magnitude of biases in reported product costs.

THE GENERAL PRINCIPLE

The distortions to reported product costs caused by volume and size diversity in the case of a volume-based cost system are in fact variants of the same underlying phenomena. This can succinctly be stated as:

> When the quantity of volume-related input that a product consumes does not vary in direct proportion to the quantity of volume-unrelated input consumed, volume-based cost systems will report distorted product costs.

This nonproportionality can arise in several ways, including:

- Production volume diversity—Illustrated in Example 2.
- Size diversity—Demonstrated by Example 3.
- Complexity diversity—Complex products may consume more volume-related input though not necessarily more volume-unrelated resources.
- Material diversity—Materials that take longer to machine may consume more volume-related input relative to volume-unrelated input.
- Setup diversity—The time required to set up a machine varies, depending on the product being manufactured, so that the proportion of volume-unrelated to volume-related input consumed may vary by product.

The types of product diversity that lead to bias in the product costs reported by a volume-based cost system are numerous and common and can be removed only through use of an activity-based cost system. These systems are necessarily more complex than their conventional counterparts. Capturing the economics of the underlying production process and the way in which products demand activities requires using cost drivers that are measures of the activities performed on the product. In general, many such cost drivers are required to report accurate product costs. In our simple example, it was possible to reduce the number of drivers to three because most of the cost drivers were perfectly correlated. Had this correlation not occurred, the activity-based cost system would have had to use all seven cost drivers in order to report accurate product costs.

Activity-based costing systems clearly are more accurate in many settings than their conventional volume-based counterparts. In part 2 of this series, I will discuss the conditions under which managers should consider adopting an activity-based cost system.[8]

NOTES

1 Activity-based costing is also referred to as transaction-based or process costing; for a description of the two-stage cost tracing procedure, see Cooper, "The Two-Stage Procedure in Cost Accounting: Part One," *Journal of Cost Management for the Manufacturing Industry* 1 (Summer 1987), pp. 43–51; and "The Two-Stage Procedure in Cost Accounting—Part Two," *Journal of Cost Management for the Manufacturing Industry* I (Fall 1987), pp. 39–45.

2 In part three of this series, I will discuss how to select allocation bases for activity-based cost systems.

3 This example is based loosely on the John Deere Company. See R.S. Kaplan, "John Deere Component Works," Harvard Business School Cases 9-187-107 and 9-187-108.

4 For a discussion of the significance of the correlation of direct labor hours and machine hours on reported product costs, see Cooper, "When Should You Use Machine-Hour Costing?" *Journal of Cost Management for the Manufacturing Industry* 2 (Spring 1988), pp. 33–39.

5 The firm's cost system is hereafter referred to as a volume-based system, underscoring its reliance on volume-related allocation bases.

6 Product diversity occurs when a product differs systematically according to some parameter such as volume or size.

7 The only distortion in reported product costs results from the procedure used to trace overhead. Consequently, only overhead costs are compared hereafter.

8 For a discussion of the symptoms of a poorly designed cost system, see Cooper, "Does Your Company Need a New Cost System?" *Journal of Cost Management for the Manufacturing Industry* I (Spring 1987), pp. 45–49.

The Rise of Activity-Based Costing—Part Two: When Do I Need an Activity-Based Cost System?

Robin Cooper

Activity-based cost systems (ABCSs) focus on activities rather than products, which helps to prevent the distorted product costs that can arise from the use of traditional cost systems based on volume. Instead of the allocation bases now commonly used—direct labor, machine hours, and material dollars—ABCSs use secondary bases that trace inputs whose consumption varies directly with the number of items produced and also other bases that trace inputs whose consumption does not vary with quantity. The result, ideally, is far more accurate product costs.

Part one of this series of [readings] introduced the concept of activity-based costing (ABC).[1] An activity-based cost system (ABCS), by focusing on activities instead of products, overcomes the distorted product costs inherent to traditional volume-based cost systems. These distortions can arise for a number of reasons, including the following:

1. Production volume diversity;
2. Size diversity;
3. Complexity diversity;
4. Material diversity; and
5. Setup diversity.

In volume-based costing, costs are allocated to products using a small number of second-stage allocation bases, typically one that varies directly with the volume of the product produced.[2] The most commonly used bases are direct labor hour, machine hours, and material dollars.

In contrast, an ABCS uses many second-stage bases to allocate costs to the products. Some of these bases are used to trace inputs whose consumption varies directly with the number of items produced, while others are used to trace inputs whose consumption does not vary with quantity. Examples of the second class of allocation bases include the number of setups and number of feet moved. These additional allocation bases allow the ABCS to better capture the economic nonproportionalities inherent in production and, hence, report more accurate product costs.

Unfortunately, every second-stage allocation base requires measuring some unique attribute of each product. For example, using setup hours as the allocation base requires measuring the number of setup hours consumed by each product. Measuring these attributes can be expensive, and there is no guarantee that the cost of the additional measurements required by an ABCS will be offset by the benefits. This [reading] explores the conditions under which the benefits of an ABCS exceed the costs of implementation and operation. In particular, it demonstrates that three factors—the sophistication of the firm's information systems, the cost of errors, and the diversity of the firms products—all play an important role in the justification of an ABCS.

THE OPTIMAL COST SYSTEM

To understand the role that these three factors play in the justification of an ABCS, it is useful to introduce the concept of the optimal cost system, for example, the system that minimizes the sum of the cost of measurement (those costs associated with the measurements required by the cost system) and the cost of errors (those costs associated with making poor decisions based on inaccurate product costs). When products are diverse, the cost of measurement and the cost of errors are inversely related. Simple cost systems impose low measurement costs, but by reporting heavily distorted product costs, they can cause managers to make poor (i.e., costly) decisions. More complex systems, by distorting product cost

Reprinted from *Journal of Cost Management* (Fall 1988), pp 41–48, with permission.

less, can produce better decisions—but only at a cost.

Improvements to cost systems net diminishing returns as the system becomes more complex. Initial improvements to a simple cost system (for example, implementing a number of cost centers instead of only one) significantly decrease the distortion of reported product costs and, hence, the cost errors; the cost of implementing the more complex system is more than offset by the benefits of more accurate product costs.

Added improvements often require measurements that are inherently more expensive and have less impact on the reported product costs. For example, to trace supervision costs more accurately might require that supervisors fill in time sheets showing, by product, how they spend their time. But completing these sheets might consume 20 percent of the supervisors' time, which is an expensive undertaking.

Adding even more improvements to what is already a complex cost system requires making expensive measurements, yet provides only a minimal increase in the accuracy of reported product costs. For example, attaching electrical meters to each machine to record power consumption by product might minimally improve estimates of power consumption that were formerly done by allocations.

The point at which the marginal cost of an improvement just equals the marginal benefits of the improvement defines the optimal cost system. (See Exhibit 1.) A result of the trade off between the cost of measurement and the cost of errors is that the *optimal* cost system is not the most *accurate* cost system. The degree of approximation (or distortion, depending on your point of view) in product costs depends on where the optimum occurs. If the optimum demands accuracy exceeding that reported by the best traditional cost system, then an activity-based system is required.

The position of the optimal cost system is affected by changes in the three factors: cost measurement, cost of errors, and product diversity. If the cost of measurement can be reduced while the other two factors remain unchanged, the position of the optimal cost system will move to the right and more accurate product costs will be reported. (See Exhibit

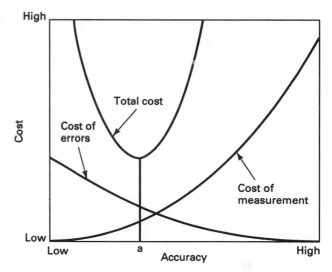

Exhibit 1. Optimal Cost System

2.) Similarly, if the cost of errors increases while the other two factors remain constant, the optimum system will again move to the right. (See Exhibit 3.) Finally, increased diversity of the product offering reduces the accuracy of reported product costs and

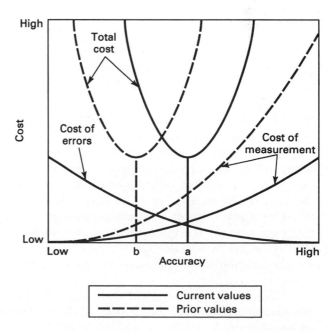

Exhibit 2. Decreasing the Cost of Measurement

Exhibit 3.   Increasing the Cost of Errors

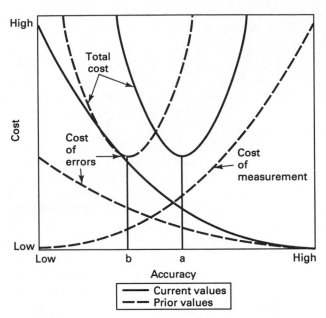

also moves the optimum to the right. The effect of the decreased accuracy is to increase the cost of errors and, hence, justify additional measurements.

HOW THE THREE FACTORS CHANGE

The three factors—the cost of measurement, the cost of errors, and the diversity of products offered—change continuously over time. Understanding how and why these changes occur provides insights into the condition that favors activity-based costing rather than product costing.

DECREASING COST OF MEASUREMENT[3]

The high cost of measurement frequently makes it uneconomical to undertake measurements solely for product costing purposes. Fortunately, experience shows that virtually all of the information required by an ABCS is already available. Given this availability, the cost of measurement consists of two elements: (1) The cost of routing the information to the cost system and (2) the cost of undertaking the calculations required to compute product costs.

The cost of measurement is changed by the introduction of new information technology, such as computerized shop-floor planning systems, nu-

merically controlled machinery, and more powerful, less expensive computers.

With a computerized production floor scheduling system, more information about the products already exists in electronic form. This information can then be supplied to the cost system at virtually no cost. For example, the shop-floor control system captures information about the number of production runs. This information can, in turn, be used to estimate the number of movements of material.

The introduction of numerically controlled equipment, especially when it is under the control of a central computer, increases the quantity of machine-readable information about the production process. For example, numerically controlled equipment can directly measure, set up, and run times even in environments in which the operators simultaneously run multiple machines producing different products.

Finally, cost systems typically perform a large number of calculations to compute product costs. Therefore, the cost per calculation can be a major component of measurement costs. Of course, the cost per calculation has fallen dramatically in recent years with improvements in information-processing technology. This cost reduction has effectively removed any computational barrier to the development of ABCS. For example, a powerful microcomputer can now run the cost system of a sizable facility. Ten years ago, a mainframe would have been required; twenty years ago such a system would have been impossible.[4]

INCREASING COST OF ERRORS[5]

The cost of errors can take several forms; for example:

- Making poor product-related decisions, such as aggressively selling unprofitable products, setting prices inappropriately, or introducing products into unprofitable niches;
- Making poor product-design decisions, such as increasing the number of unique parts in a product to reduce its direct labor content when the cost of maintaining those parts exceeds the labor savings;
- Making poor capital investment decisions based on overhead savings that do not materialize; and
- Making inaccurate budgeting decisions about the level of operating expenses required.

The major cause of changes in the cost of errors across time is related to the degree and nature of competition faced by the firms.

Increased competition. Competition generally increases the cost of errors because there is a greater chance that a competitor will take advantage of any errors made. For example, the profit margin of an overcosted product might look unattractive, but this does not matter unless a competitor decides that the product is worth chasing and the firm mistakenly decides to drop the product.

More focused competition. If the competition remains the same, but one or more competitors decide to adopt a focused production strategy, then full-range producers will require more accurate product costs. Focused production, by reducing the diversity of products offered, causes the competitors' traditional volume-based cost systems to report less distorted product cost. This increased accuracy allows focused competitors to make better pricing decisions and thus develop superior marketing strategies.

More creative competition. When competition becomes creative it can change how the product is sold and render the first costly system obsolete. One recent example was a firm that had bundled two products together: The first product was a machine that customers rented; the other was a fastener that customers purchased in large volumes and attached using the machine. The rental fees for the machines were purposely set low to attract customers. Since the machines and fasteners were customized and had to be used together, the customer became captive. The price of the fasteners was set high enough to cover not only the costs of the fasteners, but also the unrecovered costs of the machines, plus a profit. Reflecting this strategy, the firm's cost system overcosted fasteners by tracing all overhead costs (including those related to the attaching machines) to fasteners and none to the machines. A competitor, in an attempt to increase market share, found a way to unbundle the two products and sell the fasteners at a 20 percent discount, which was approximately the percentage of costs due to the machine. This unbundling forced the first firm to redesign its cost system to report separate product costs for the attaching machines and the fasteners.[6]

Deregulation. Deregulation also forces firms to compete in new ways. When both the products offered and their prices are regulated, the firm survives by controlling its overall efficiency, not by managing its competitive position. The cost systems of many regulated firms reflect this reality by measuring the cost of functional activities, not the cost of products. However, a more accurate knowledge of product costs becomes imperative when unregulated competitors appear on the scene, cut prices, and start "cherry picking" products. Thus, when deregulation looms on the horizon, managers of regulated firms often display a sudden interest in knowing their product costs.[7]

A firm that was once a captive supplier, but is suddenly allowed (or forced) to compete, faces a change virtually identical to deregulation. The existing transfer-pricing system used to "price" products often acts similar to a regulated pricing system. One firm that recently went through this experience discovered that its cost system was causing it to price products inappropriately. The prices attracted business that the firm did not want and caused the firm to refuse business it really wanted. Realizing that the cost system was the culprit, management decided to develop a new product costing system that more accurately reported product costs.[8]

A more subtle way in which the cost of errors has increased across time lies in the change in the overhead structure of most firms. Over the last 150 years, overhead has relentlessly increased as a percent of value added.[9] This increase has caused many cost systems based on direct labor hours to report increasingly distorted product costs over the life of the products. Many firms, realizing this problem, have shifted to systems based machine hours. Although the conversion to machine hours provides more accurate product costs (under certain conditions),[10] it is not the whole story.[11]

As overhead becomes more important, so does the effective management of overhead. Traditional cost systems, with their reliance on a few volume-based allocation bases, make it difficult (if not impossible) to understand the relationship (considering both mix and volume) between the products produced and the appropriate level of overhead. An ABCS, in contrast, provides insights into these relationships and thus leads to better management of overhead.[12]

DECREASING THE ACCURACY OF REPORTED PRODUCT COSTS[13]

Traditional cost systems can report highly distorted product costs when the products consume a diverse mixture of inputs. The following managerial actions increase product diversity and thus reduce the overall accuracy of reported product costs:

- Introducing new products;
- Adopting new marketing strategies; and
- Improving production processes.

The introduction of a new product or product line with a cost structure different from existing products can increase the distortion of reported product costs. The distortion occurs because cost systems report *average* product costs, so the new average is less representative of actual costs of the old and new products being produced than even the old average was of just the old products. A classical example of this problem occurs when a cost center contains both manual and automated machines. As long as the products passing through the center use the different types of machines in about the same proportion, reported product costs will not be significantly distorted. If the new product uses the automated machines more intensely, however, it will be undercosted if direct labor hours are used to allocate costs to products.

New product introductions can cause distortions in product costs to increase in more subtle ways. If the support functions required by a new product (setup and inspection time, for example) are greater than those of existing products, too little overhead will be allocated to the new products unless the system is designed to capture this diversity in products. These distortions can arise slowly as the new products gain in volume relative to existing products. For example, one firm recently introduced a new line of plastic products. Because the firm did not have high enough volume to do its own molding, it purchased molded parts. The firm's older, metal products were purchased as sheet metal and then cut and welded to create the desired shapes. The firm's cost system, which was based on direct labor, spread the support overhead related to metal fabrication over both metal and plastic products, thus undercosting the metal products and overcosting the plastic ones.

Changing the product strategy can also make a cost system obsolete. The decision to market in low-volume niches requires increased production of low-volume products. Conversely, the decision to produce standard parts in a specialty shop requires increased production of high-volume products. These changes result in distorted product costs if the cost system is not designed to trace overhead appropriately.

Volume-based cost systems generally cannot differentiate adequately between overhead consumed by high- and low-production volume products.[14] Fortunately, as long as the range of volumes produced is low (say a ratio of 5:1 for the number of items in the largest to smallest batches), product costs are still reasonably accurate. But if the ratio exceeds 10:1, the risk of highly distorted product costs increases. For example, one company with a large variety of products sold some of the products in high volumes, thus some production lots contained thousands of items. Other products were sold in low volumes and produced in production lots containing only tens of items. As a result, the firm's volume-based cost system produced highly distorted product costs, which led management erroneously to believe that the low-volume products were highly profitable.[15]

Introducing a new production process can also cause a cost system to give distorted product costs. For example, introducing automated production processes such as flexible machining uses *less* direct labor, but it requires *more* support functions such as programming and special engineering support. Products manufactured on the new machine, therefore, get allocated much less cost than is appropriate. Conversely, the cost of those products *not* manufactured on the new machines correspondingly goes up. In one company, for example, the firm had completely revamped its production process. Machines that required continuous direct supervision were replaced with machines that required little attendance. This allowed each operator to watch over several machines at once, perform off-line setups, and also do inspections. Unfortunately, the company's cost system, which was based on direct labor, was *not* completely revamped. As a result, it failed to capture the changed economics of production and reported distorted product costs.

DEFINING COST SYSTEM OBSOLESCENCE

Even though the cost of measurement, the cost of errors, and the diversity of a firm's product offering often change, firms seldom redesign their cost systems. Therefore, as the years go by, the changes in the three factors accumulate. For example, if a firm installs a computerized shop-floor control system, then encounters increased competition a few years later, and also adds a number of products of various kinds over the life of a cost system, the combination of changes could end up making the cost system obsolete. Consequently, deciding if an ABCS is justified requires taking into account all the changes that have occurred since the existing cost system was installed.[16]

COST OF A NEW SYSTEM[17]

The typical cost system appears to last for ten years or more. This longevity is a direct outcome of the perceived magnitude of the costs of redesigning a cost system. These costs create a significant barrier to the introduction of a new cost system and include identifying the individuals (internal or external) to design the system, obtaining acceptance from management of the need for a new system, designing and implementing the new system, tying it into the other information systems of the firm, training management in its use, and creating a team to maintain the new system. (See Exhibit 4.) A cost system is obsolete and should be changed when the net present value of the benefits from improved product costs is greater than the redesign costs. (See Exhibit 5.)

This perspective on the obsolescence of cost systems can be depicted as an archery target. (See Exhibit 6.) At the center of the target is a bull's-eye area: "True" costs[18] fluctuate with the machine used to produce the product, the operators running those machines, and myriad other factors that cause the actual resources consumed to vary. The further the band of the optimum cost is from the bull's eye, the less accurate the product costs produced by the optimum system are. The breadth of the band, for the optimum cost system, results from day-to-day fluctuations in reported product costs and from changes in the three factors that affect the position of the optimum cost system.

The existing cost system is similarly represented by a band once removed from the center of the target than the optimum cost system. The third and widest band represents the range over which rede-

Exhibit 4.   Redesign Costs as a Barrier to Cost Systems Change

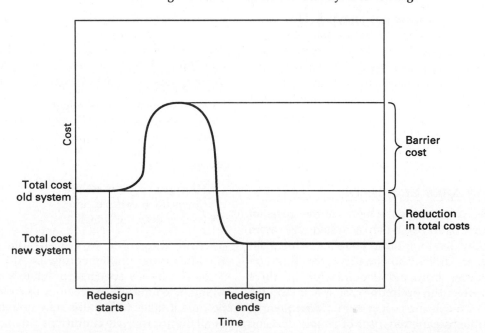

Exhibit 5. When is the Cost System Obsolete?

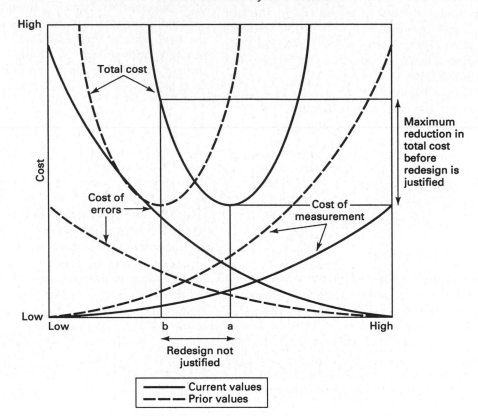

signing the cost system is not justified. This band always contains the band for the existing cost system, but if it does not also contain the band for the optimum system, the cost system is obsolete and replacing the existing cost system is justified (see "a" in Exhibit 6). If the widest band does contain the band for the optimum system, then the existing cost system is not obsolete and replacing it would not be cost-justified (see "b" in Exhibit 6).

WHEN IS AN ABCS REQUIRED?

An ABCS is justified whenever the costs of installing and operating such a system are more than offset by its long-term benefits (which, although real, are difficult to quantify). This trade-off differs for every firm and depends on the three factors that affect the optimum cost system and the adequacy of the existing cost system. Consequently, it is impossible to generate a set of simple decision rules to answer the question, "Do I need an ABCS?" It is possible, however, to define the conditions when an ABCS is most likely to be justified. Specifically, implementing an ABCS is advisable if the existing cost system was designed when:

- Measurement costs were high;
- Competition was weak; and
- Product diversity was low.

But now:

- Measurement costs are low;
- Competition is fierce; and
- Product diversity is high.

Any firm about to redesign its cost system should consider implementing an ABCS even if all of the conditions specified previously are not prevailing. The long-life expectancy of cost systems and the time it takes to install a new one make waiting for all the appropriate conditions a dangerous strate-

Exhibit 6.   The Accuracy Target

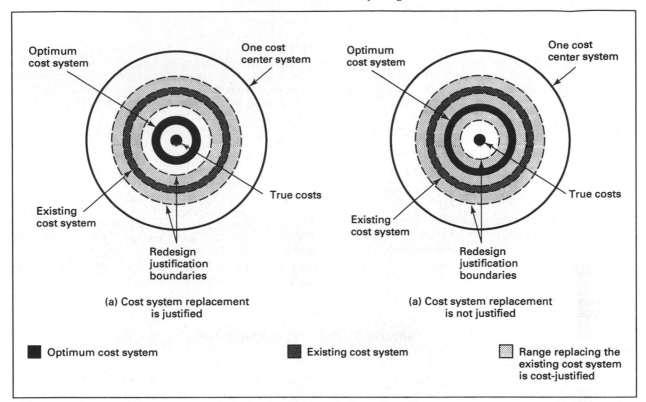

(a) Cost system replacement is justified

(a) Cost system replacement is not justified

■ Optimum cost system   ■ Existing cost system   ▨ Range replacing the existing cost system is cost-justified

gy because of the tendency to keep the "new" cost system even though it too has become obsolete. Instead, firms should monitor how well their cost systems are performing and how much the three factors have changed over time to anticipate obsolescence before it causes major problems. By doing so, a firm has enough time to decide whether an ABCS is required and, if so, to design and implement it before the obsolete existing system can do much damage.

NOTES

1 See *Journal of Cost Management* (Summer 1988).

2 See Cooper, R., "The Two-Stage Procedure in Cost Accounting," Parts One and Two, *Journal of Cost Management* (Summer 1987, Fall 1987).

3 In recent years, most firms have decreased the cost of measurement. However, some firms have managed to increase the cost of measurement by allowing their information infrastructure to decay. One firm I recently visited had just discontinued a direct labor report that

captured the actual time spent on each product. This report was used in a special study as the basis for generating more accurate estimates of the direct labor content of products than the standards. Without this report, the firm will have a harder time determining direct labor costs per product to the same degree of accuracy.

4 It may seem incredible to claim that a cost system for a sizable facility can be run on a personal computer (PC), but I have just completed a project to install such a PC-based ABCS for a $100 million facility producing several hundred products. The millions of calculations required to cost these products are performed in under fifteen minutes.

5 The cost of errors has not increased for all firms. In some environments, the level of competition has decreased. Under these conditions, firms apparently do not simplify their cost systems. Four reasons appear to drive this decision: (1) Most firms have simultaneously decreased their cost of measurement, which tends to offset the decreased cost of errors; (2) management is concerned that competition will return and does not want to risk needing a second new system in the near future; (3) the decrease in competition moves manage-

ment attention away from the issues of product costing; and (4) the redesign is not cost justified.

6 See Cooper, R., and D. Bottenbruch, "Mueller-Lehmkuhl GmbH," Harvard Business School case 9-178-048.

7 For an example of the type of system common to regulated industries and how that system changes under deregulation, see Kaplan, R.S., "Union Pacific" case series, Harvard Business School 9-186-176/7/8.

8 See Kaplan, R.S., "John Deere Component Works (A) and (B)," Harvard Business School cases 9-187-107/8.

9 See Miller, J.G., and T.E. Vollmann, "The Hidden Factory" *Harvard Business Review* (September-October 1985).

10 See Cooper, R., "When is Machine Hour Costing Appropriate." *Journal of Cost Management* (Spring 1988).

11 See part 1 of this series. *Journal of Cost Management* (Summer 1988).

12 See Kaplan, "John Deere Component Works."

13 Not all firms have increased their product diversity. Some have focused their factories, others have introduced new production processes such as just-in-time that reduce the significance of product diversity.

14 See part 1 of this series, *Journal of Cost Management* (Summer 1988).

15 See Cooper, R., "Schrader Bellows" case series, Harvard Business School 9-186-272.

16 A well-managed cost system will be modified from time to time. For example, the introduction of automated machinery in a manual cost center might require that center be split into two. The magnitude of the cumulative change should be viewed in the light of the existing systems (as modified).

17 In some facilities, the savings from redesigning the cost system can be augmented by a major reduction in the cost of measurement. This usually occurs when the existing system measures the consumption of direct labor by the products in excruciating detail. For example, one facility I visited reduced the number of direct labor measures a month from 30,000 to 300. This allowed direct labor to be more productive and reduced the time spent in accounting compiling and correcting the data.

18 True product costs are normally unobtainable because of joint costs and measurement problems.

The Rise of Activity-Based Costing—Part Three: How Many Cost Drivers Do You Need, and How Do You Select Them?

Robin Cooper

The design of an activity-based costing system depends largely on two considerations: How many cost drivers to use and which cost drivers to use. The factors that affect these choices include the desired accuracy of reported product costs, the diversity of products manufactured, the relative costs of the activities traced, and the degree of volume diversity. Three factors that affect the final selection of cost drivers are measurement costs, the correlation of the cost drivers to actual consumption of the activities, and the behavioral effects of various cost drivers.

This article—part three of a series on activity-based costing—discusses the factors that should be considered when designing an activity-based cost system. In particular, it explores *how many* cost drivers should be included and also *what types* of cost drivers should be used.

To set this [reading] in perspective, part one of the series[1] introduced the concept of activity-based costing. It demonstrated that, if the product mix produced in a facility is diverse, an activity-based cost system reports more accurate product costs than a traditional cost system (i.e., one that is based

Reprinted from *Journal of Cost Management* (Winter 1989), pp. 34–46, with permission.

on volume). Part two of the series[2] continued the discussion of activity-based costing. It pointed out that firms facing intense competition and having both high product diversity and low measurement cost are best suited to taking advantage of the increased accuracy offered by an activity-based costing system.

INTRODUCTION

Activity-based costing systems achieve their improved accuracy over traditional volume-based cost systems by using multiple cost drivers (instead of just one or two) to trace the cost of production activities in a process to the products that consume the resources used in those activities.

Unfortunately, the number of activities performed in a typical facility is so great that it is not economically feasible to use a different cost driver for each activity. Instead, many activities have to be aggregated and a single driver used to trace the costs of the activities to products. For example, every time a new batch is run in a metal-cutting operation, new tools have to be drawn from the tool room, inserted, and qualified. The feeds and speeds of the machine must be altered, parts moved from inventory storage to the shop floor, the first part has to be inspected, the batch scheduled, and so on. Despite this complexity, a well-designed activity-based costing system might use only one or two cost drivers to trace the setup costs of associated activities to the products. For example, it might use the cost drivers "number of setups" and "number of feet moved."

Using only two drivers to trace the cost of so many different activities generally introduces distortions into reported product costs. The difficulty of designing good cost systems lies in achieving a system that is economical to maintain yet does not introduce excessive distortions.[3] Using a single driver to trace the cost of multiple activities to products raises the issue of which driver to use. For example, if the cost of the various activities (i.e., setup, scheduling, and material movement) in the foregoing example are aggregated, should the cost driver chosen be *number* of setups, setup *hours*, or *number of times scheduled?*

The art of designing an activity-based costing system can thus be viewed as making two separate but interrelated decisions about the number of cost drivers needed and which cost drivers to use. As will be shown, these decisions are actually interrelated, because the type of cost drivers selected changes the number of drivers required to achieve a desired level of accuracy.

NUMBER OF DRIVERS REQUIRED

The minimum number of cost drivers required by an activity-based costing system depends on the desired accuracy of reported product costs and on the complexity of the product mix being produced. The desired level of accuracy plays an obvious role. As the number of cost drivers used increases, the accuracy of reported costs rises. Consequently, the greater the desired level of accuracy, the larger the number of drivers required to achieve that accuracy.

The complexity of the product mix plays a more subtle and complex role in determining if the costs of two (or more) activities can be aggregated and traced using a single cost driver without introducing unacceptable levels of distortion. In fact, three factors determine if a single driver is acceptable: (1) product diversity, (2) the relative costs of the activities aggregated, and (3) volume diversity. These factors are discussed in the following sections.

Product diversity. Products are said to be diverse when they consume activities in different proportions.[4] According to this definition, therefore, two products are considered diverse if one of the products requires five inspection hours per 100 direct labor hours and the other product consumes only one inspection hour per 100 direct labor hours. The simple example that follows demonstrates the effect of product diversity on reported product costs.

Example 1. A production facility produces equal quantities of two products, A and B. Both products are produced in equal-size batches of fifty units. Two activities are required of products A and B: inspection and machining a surface. These two activities cost the same amount per hour. Both products also consume one hour of machining per unit. However, it takes ten hours to inspect the first unit of A produced and five hours to inspect the first unit of B produced.

The degree of diversity between any two products with respect to two activities can be measured by:

1. Calculating the ratio of the two activities consumed by each product. In Example 1, the ratio for

product A is ten inspection hours per fifty machine hours for each batch. For product B, the ratio is five inspection hours per fifty machine hours for each batch of product B.

2. Dividing the higher ratio by the lower to measure the degree of diversity. In Example 1, this means dividing 10/50 by 5/50, which yields a quotient of 2.

The importance of product diversity can be seen by indirectly tracing the costs of the activity inspection to products A and B assuming that the cost driver used is machine hours.[5] This cost driver simply traces equal amounts of inspection to both products, because one unit of each product consumes one machine hour. If the cost driver chosen is machine hours, therefore, 7.5 hours of inspection is traced to each batch of both product A and product B:

$$\frac{10 \text{ insp. hrs. for A} + 5 \text{ insp. hrs. for B}}{50 \text{ machine hrs. for A} + 50 \text{ machine hrs. for B}}$$
$$= 7.5 \text{ inspection hrs. traced to each batch of both A and B}$$

Since product A actually requires twice as much inspection time as product B, the product costs that result from using machine hours as the cost driver are clearly distorted. Product A, the high consumer of inspection costs, is undercosted; product B, the low consumer of inspection costs, is overcosted.

The ratio of actual to reported inspection cost for a batch of product A is 1.33 (10/7.5) and for product B, it is 0.67 (5/7.5). This simply means that, for the activity inspection, the cost required by product A is actually 1.33 times its reported cost. For product B, the actual cost is only 0.67 of the reported cost for inspection. The greater the diversity between two products, the greater the distortion that will be introduced. For example, if the diversity in the above example had been ten instead of two (that is, if product B required only one hour of inspection for the first product produced instead of five), then the ratio of actual to reported product costs for product A would have been 1.82 (10/5.5) and for product B, 0.18 (1/5.5). This assumes, of course, that the cost driver chosen is again machine hours. Therefore, the inspection hours per batch traced to each product is 5.5. That is,

$$\frac{10 \text{ insp. hrs. for A} + 1 \text{ insp. hrs. for B}}{50 \text{ machine hrs. for A} + 50 \text{ machine hrs. for B}}$$
$$= 5.5 \text{ inspection hrs. traced to each batch of both A and B}$$

The distortion introduced by product diversity is surprisingly large. If the cost system is to report inspection costs to within plus or minus 50 percent of actual (a relatively undemanding objective), then the driver machine hours is acceptable for tracing inspection costs only if the "inspection to machining" diversity of the two products is three or less. In practice, much higher degrees of diversity are common.

Graphing product diversity. The degree of distortion in the reported inspection costs of products A and B that results from higher or lower product diversity can be displayed graphically. (See Exhibit 1.) The distortion curve for A, the product requiring greater inspection time, is convex. At one, there is no product diversity, but as diversity increases (i.e., the ratio deviates from one), the curve rises asymptotically. It approaches 2.00 at high degrees of diversity. (See the upper section of Exhibit 1.) The distortion curve for B, the product requiring less inspection time, is also convex. Again, there is no diversity at one. As diversity increases, the curve falls asymptotically and approaches zero at high degrees of diversity. (See the lower section of Exhibit 1.)

Relative cost of the activities. The relative cost of the various activities is a measure of how much each activity costs as a percentage of the total cost of the production process. The simple example already shown can be modified to demonstrate the effect of the relative cost of various activities on reported product costs for several products.

Example 2. A production facility produces equal quantities of two products, A and B, in equal-size batches containing fifty units. Two activities are required to produce these products: inspection and machining a surface. The activity inspection costs $40 per inspection hour, and the activity machining a surface costs $10 per machine hour. Both products consume one hour of machining per unit, but it takes ten hours to inspect the first unit of A produced and five hours to inspect the first unit of B produced. The relative cost of the activities is 37.5

Exhibit 1. Actual-to-Reported Product Costs—Sensitivity to Product Diversity

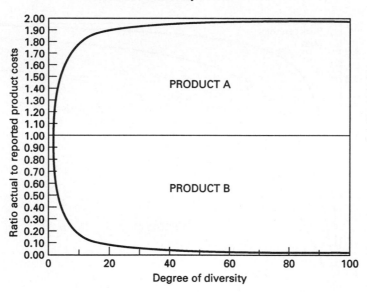

percent of total costs for inspection versus 62.5 percent of the total costs for machining.

The relative cost of the two activities, inspection and machining, is measured by dividing the cost of each activity consumed in the period by the sum of the total cost of the two activities. (See Exhibit 2.)

The relative cost of the activities being aggregated is important because the higher the relative cost of an activity the larger the distortion that will be introduced by inaccurately tracing its consumption to the products. For example, if an activity accounts for 20 percent of the cost of a particular product, then tracing twice as much of that activity to the product will cause reported product costs to be 20 percent too high, but if the activity accounts for only 0.2 percent, then the distortion introduced will be only 0.2 percent.

In Example 2, using machine hours as the cost driver for tracing the costs of both activities, machining a surface and inspection, introduces distortions into reported product costs. The driver machine hours will trace equal amounts of both activities to each product. Thus, products A and B will each report traced costs of $800 (i.e., half of the $1,600 total activity costs shown in Exhibit 2). These reported costs can be compared with the actual costs of $900 for product A and $700 for product B. (See

Exhibit 2. Calculating the Relative Costs of the Activities Inspection and Matching a Surface

ACTIVITY	PRODUCT	HOURS/ BATCH	COST/ HOUR	COST/ BATCH	TOTAL COST	PERCENT
Inspection	A	10	40	$400		
	B	5	30	200		
					$600	37.5%
Machining a surface	A	50	10	$500		
	B	50	10	500	1,000	62.5
Total cost for both activities					$1,600	100.0%

Exhibit 3. **Actual-to-Reported Costs—Sensitivity of Product A to Relative Cost Differences of Activities**

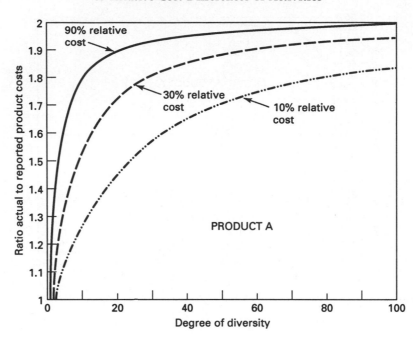

Exhibit 2.) The ratios of actual to reported product costs for the two products are 1.125 (900/800) for product A and 0.875 (700/800) for product B.[6]

The distortion in the reported product costs of products A and B that results from product diversity and from differences in the relative cost of the two production activities can be displayed graphically (see Exhibits 3 and 4.)[7] As Exhibit 3 shows, the distortion curves for product A maintain their convex shape, but as the relative cost of the inspection activity decreases, the resulting distortion in reported product costs rises more slowly. The same pattern occurs in the distortion curves for product B. (See Exhibit 4.) Again, the distortion curves maintain their convex shape, but as the relative cost of the inspection activity decreases, the resulting distortions get relatively smaller as well.

The higher the relative cost of the inspection activity, the greater the distortion introduced. For example, if a 50 percent distortion in reported overhead costs is acceptable and the inspection activity has a relative cost of 10 percent compared with the machining activity, then the products have a diversity ratio of 20 before use of the cost driver

machine hours introduces excessive distortion. But if the relative cost of the inspection activity increases to 30 percent, the maximum diversity allowable is seven. At a relative cost of 50 percent, diversity is five. Thus, as the relative cost of inspection climbs, the maximum acceptable diversity decreases rapidly.

Volume diversity. Volume diversity occurs when products are manufactured in batches of different sizes. If the production volume of two products differs by a factor of 100 (which is not uncommon), the production, order, and shipping batch sizes will differ significantly. Activity-based costing systems use cost drivers that adjust for the effect of different production volumes. Traditional volume-based cost accounting systems do not.[8]

The simple example used so far can be further adapted to demonstrate the effect of volume diversity on reported product costs for products that display product diversity.

Example 3. A production facility produces two products—A and B. Two activities are required to produce these products: inspection and machining a

Exhibit 4. Actual-to-Reported Costs—Sensitivity of Product B to Relative Cost Differences of Activities

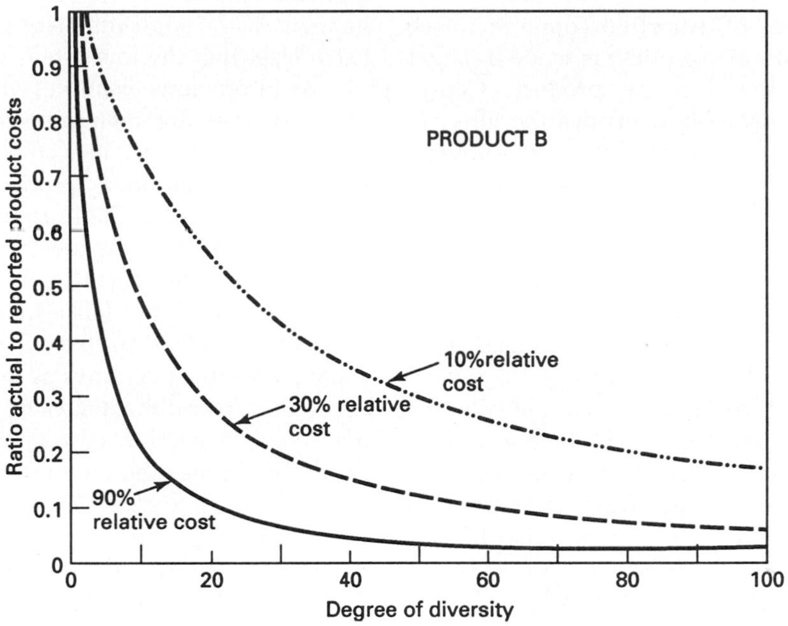

surface. The two activities cost the same per hour. Both products consume one hour of machining per unit, but it takes ten hours to inspect the first unit of A produced and five hours to inspect the first unit of B produced. A production batch of product A contains fifty units, and a production batch of product B contains five units.

The volume diversity of two products is measured by dividing the batch size of the high-intensity product by the batch size of the low-intensity product. In Example 3, therefore, products A and B demonstrate volume diversity of 10 (50/5).

The importance of volume diversity can be seen by tracing the costs in Example 3 of the activity that is *unaffected* by volume—that is, inspection—to products A and B using the *volume-based* cost driver —machine hours. The total number of machine hours consumed for one batch of both product A and B is 55 (50 + 5). The total number of inspection hours for one batch of A and one batch of B is 15 (10 + 5). Since producing one unit of both product A and product B consumes one machine hour, the cost driver machine hours will trace 15/55 hours of inspection to each unit of products A and B. Conse-

quently, a batch of product A will receive 13.64 hours of inspection (50 × 15/55) and a batch of product B 1.36 inspection hours (5 × 15/55). The ratio of actual to reported inspection costs for products A and B will therefore be 0.733 (10/13.64) and 3.67 (5/1.36) respectively. Note that, unlike in previous examples, product A is now overcosted and product B undercosted. However, if batch sizes are reversed and product A is manufactured in batches containing only five units (instead of fifty) and product B in batches of fifty units (instead of five), then the volume diversity becomes 0.1 (5/50). The ratio of actual to reported inspection costs is then 7.35 (10/1.36) and 0.37 (5/13.64) respectively. Note that, as in previous examples, product B is now overcosted and product A undercosted.

Product diversity and volume diversity play virtually identical roles in creating distortion. The distortion introduced by volume diversity reinforces the distortion introduced by product diversity if the high-intensity product (product A in the examples here, since it requires far more inspection time than product B) is made in smaller batches than the low-intensity product. Consequently, a high-intensity, low-volume product will be doubly undercosted, while a low-intensity, high-volume product will be doubly overcosted.

The two sources of distortion counteract each other if the high-intensity product is made in larger batches than the low-intensity product. Consequently, if volume diversity overrides the effect of product diversity, a high-intensity, high-volume product will be overcosted, while a low-intensity, low-volume product will be undercosted. The reverse will hold true if the effect of product diversity dominates. Volume diversity will dominate if the degree of volume diversity is greater than the degree of product diversity. If the degree of volume diversity equals the degree of product diversity, the reported product costs will be accurate. (Graphically, the ratio of actual to reported costs will be one.)

The distortion in the reported inspection costs of products A and B that results from different levels of product and volume diversity can also be displayed graphically. (See Exhibits 5–8.) Due to the magnitude of the potential distortions introduced by volume diversity, two graphs are shown for each product. Exhibits 5 and 7 illustrate what happens if the high-intensity product (product A in the exam-

ples given here) has a smaller batch size than the low-intensity product (product B in these examples). Exhibits 6 and 8, on the other hand, illustrate what happens if the high-intensity product has a larger batch size than the low-intensity product.

As in previous examples, the shapes of the two sets of curves are maintained: The high-intensity product (product A) has convex curves, and the low-intensity product (product B) has concave curves. In Exhibit 5, the reported cost of product A climbs more rapidly the lower the degree of volume diversity. More importantly, the distortion increases as volume diversity falls. In fact, if the volume diversity is only 0.04 (i.e., a batch of product B contains twenty-five times as many units as a batch of product A) and the degree of diversity is ten, then the actual inspection cost of product A is almost twenty-five times the amount reported.

The opposite relationship occurs in the distortion curves of product B, the low-intensity product. As Exhibit 6 shows, the higher the volume diversity, the faster and greater the distortion introduced. If the volume diversity is twenty-five (i.e., a batch of product A contains twenty-five times as many units as a batch of product B), then, at a product diversity

Exhibit 5. Actual-to-Reported Costs—Sensitivity of Product A to Volume Diversity (Batch Size Smaller)

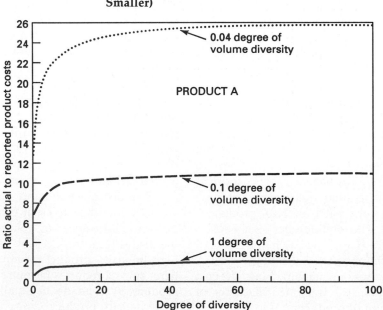

Exhibit 6.   Actual-to-Reported Costs—Sensitivity of Product A to Volume Diversity (Batch Size Larger)

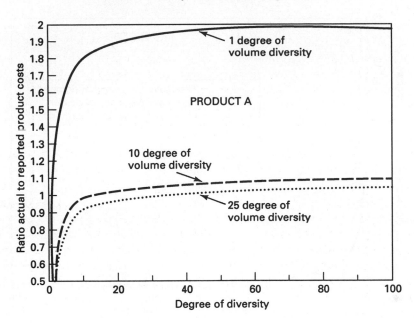

Exhibit 7.   Actual-to-Reported Costs—Sensitivity of Product B to Volume Diversity (Batch Size Smaller)

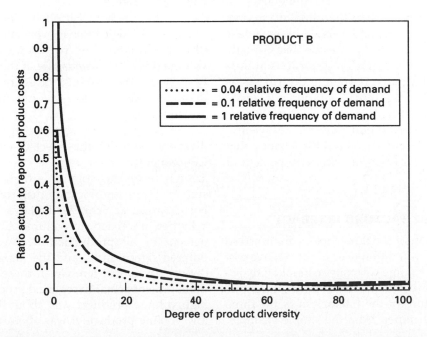

Exhibit 8. **Actual-to-Reported Costs—Sensitivity of Product B to Volume Diversity (Batch Size Larger)**

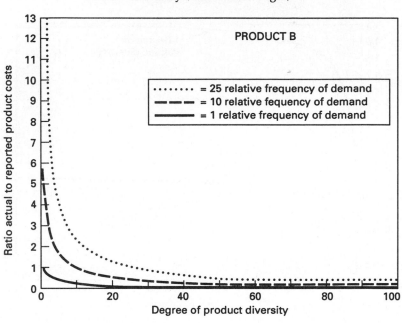

of ten, product B has an actual inspection cost that is more than twice its reported product costs. Similar analyses can be derived for Exhibits 7 and 8.

Note that, if a 50 percent distortion in reported inspection costs is acceptable and the degree of volume diversity is ten, then the range of product diversity in which distortion levels are acceptable is six to twenty. In practice, this means that virtually all products will have significant distortions in their reported inspection costs. If volume diversity is as high as twenty-five, the range of product diversity that results in acceptable levels of distortion is centered on a degree of product diversity of twenty-five (as expected), and there is little chance that actual inspection costs will be within 50 percent of reported.

HOW THE THREE FACTORS INTERACT

The interaction of the three factors discussed so far (product diversity, differences in the relative cost of activities, and volume diversity) cannot be realistically modelled using a two-product example. However, the nature of the interaction of the three terms *can* be determined from the simple example.

Specifically, the higher the relative cost of the activities that are not volume-related, the greater the distortion introduced by using a volume-based driver to trace their costs to products (all else remaining constant). Product and volume diversity either reinforce or counteract each other. They reinforce each other if the high-intensity product has a volume diversity less than one and counteract each other if volume diversity exceeds one. If the volume diversity exceeds the product diversity, its effect will dominate and the low-volume products will be undercosted.

In many practical settings, the effect of volume diversity overrides the effect of product diversity. Consequently, if the relative cost of activities that are not related to volume is high, traditional cost systems report significantly distorted product costs. For example, at Schrader Bellows,[9] the cost of the activities unrelated to volume totaled about 40 percent of all production overhead. Batch sizes differed significantly, and the maximum degree of diversity was over ten. Given these facts, the maximum ratio of actual to reported product costs for the high-volume products was about 0.80 and for the low-volume products it was about ten.

In practice, identifying how many cost drivers are needed calls for a mixture of judgment and analysis. The first step is to identify the inputs having large dollar values. The second step is to consider how diverse the products are and in what volumes they are produced. Isolating the highly diverse products allows the designer to identify which of the major inputs can be aggregated without introducing excessive distortion into reported costs. The designer of the cost system can then analyze the smaller dollar-value inputs to see which of them can be aggregated with major inputs and which need to be aggregated separately.

SELECTING THE APPROPRIATE COST DRIVERS

Once the minimum number of required cost drivers is determined, the appropriate cost drivers can be selected. Three factors should be taken into account when selecting a cost driver:

1. The ease of obtaining the data required by that cost driver (cost of measurement);
2. The correlation of the consumption of the activity implied by the cost driver and the actual consumption (degree of correlation); and
3. The behavior induced by that driver (behavioral effects).

These factors are discussed in the following sections.

Cost of measurement. Activity-based systems achieve their increased accuracy by using more cost drivers than their volume-based counterparts. To reduce the cost of measurement associated with these drivers, activity-based systems try to use drivers whose quantities are relatively easy to obtain. This is accomplished in part by substituting drivers that capture *indirectly* the consumption of activities by products. For example, the driver inspection hours can be replaced by the driver number of inspections. This replacement is usually acceptable if the duration of each inspection is about the same. (See the following section for a more detailed discussion of this point.)

Using cost drivers that capture the *number of transactions generated by an activity* instead of cost drivers that capture *duration of the activity* is an important technique for reducing measurement costs in the design of activity-based costings. The

technique is important because many such transaction-based drivers can be used. Examples include:

- Number of orders processed;
- Number of shipments processed; and
- Number of inspections performed.

The data required for these cost drivers is readily available because a transaction is generated every time the activity is performed. For example, a material requisition is required every time material is moved from inventory to the shop floor.

The measurement cost associated with a cost driver also depends on whether the data required by that driver is already available or has to be specially determined. In recent years, computer technology has dramatically reduced the cost of measurement of many cost drivers. This reduction has occurred in two ways. First, the information required by many cost drivers is already available in the firm's existing information systems.[10] For example, the number of production runs for each product or component is typically available directly from the materials resource planning (MRP) system. Second, the cost of measuring many cost drivers has decreased. For example, throughput time (the time it takes a product to pass through the production process) is often used in just-in-time environments to trace overhead costs (or just some overhead costs) to products.[11] Throughput time can be an expensive cost driver to use in production processes that do not have automatic product-tracking systems (such as bar coding), because it requires manually tracking the throughput time of every product produced. With bar coding, however, tracking costs become negligible. Remote sensing also makes it easier for operators to clock in and out and thus measure setup times.

Degree of correlation. The use of cost drivers that only indirectly capture the consumption of activities by products entails a risk that the cost drivers will introduce distortions into reported product costs because they do not accurately capture the actual consumption of the activities. For example, if inspections take varying amounts of time (inspection-time diversity), using number of inspections as a cost driver will not correlate perfectly with use of inspection hours as a cost driver. Thus, if number of inspections is the cost driver used, a product that requires a longer inspection will be undercosted, while a product that requires only a short inspection will be overcosted.

How well a given cost driver captures the actual consumption by products of an activity is measured by the correlation of the quantities of each activity that the driver traces to the products versus the actual consumption of the activity by the products. The normal statistical definitions of correlation cannot be used to help select cost drivers, however, because the designer is interested in both the overall accuracy (i.e., how accurate are product costs on average) as well as the specific accuracy for individual products (i.e., how accurate is the reported cost of product x). This problem can best be illustrated by example.

Exhibit 9 shows the actual consumption of an activity by four products (P1, P2, P3, and P4) and the quantities associated with four potential cost drivers. Cost driver 1 has a low degree of correlation; it poorly captures the consumption of the activity. Using cost driver 1 to trace costs will cause all reported product costs to be inaccurate. Cost driver 2 captures the consumption of the activity by the first three products perfectly but is hopelessly wrong for product 4. Using it to trace costs will report fairly accurate costs for all products except P4, whose reported costs will be excessively high. Cost driver 3 has a medium degree of correlation; it does not capture the consumption of the activity by all four products perfectly, but is never that far off. If cost driver 3 is used to trace costs, the reported product costs will be fairly accurate. Finally, cost driver 4 is perfectly correlated; it captures the consumption of the activity by all four products exactly. Using it to trace costs will introduce no distortions.

Exhibit 9. Degree of Correlation of Four Cost Drivers

	P1	P2	P3	P4	DEGREE OF CORRELATION
Quantity of Activity Consumed	1	2	2	3	
Cost Driver 1	5	1	5	1	Low
Cost Driver 2	1	2	2	10	Low
Cost Driver 3	1	1	2	2	Medium
Cost Driver 4	1	2	2	3	High

Correlation is important in the selection of cost drivers for both volume-related activities and activities unrelated to volume. For example, if direct labor hours is the cost driver used to trace the cost of the electrical power consumed by the machines, the reported product costs will be distorted if direct labor hours is not perfectly correlated with the consumption of electrical power.[12] The importance of correlation depends in part on the relative cost of the activities being traced. As the relative cost increases, the degree of correlation required to obtain a specified level of accuracy also climbs.

Transaction-based cost drivers are rarely perfectly correlated with the actual consumption of an activity because they assume that, regardless of the product being produced, the same quantity of the activity being traced is consumed. For example, if the cost driver used is number of orders processed, the system assumes that every order is processed identically. The distortion that results from this assumption can be reduced if the orders can be split into categories that consume different quantities of inputs. For example, it may take longer to order an item of raw material than it takes to order a purchased part. The distortion introduced by using number of orders processed can thus be reduced by using two cost drivers: number of raw material orders processed and number of purchased parts orders processed. The selection of imperfectly correlated cost drivers can thus increase the number of cost drivers required to obtain a desired level of accuracy.[13] For example, in one company studied, materials overhead was split into three separate pools—one for steel, one for castings, and one for purchased parts.[14]

Behavioral effects. In selecting cost drivers, the effect that use of a particular cost driver will have on the behavior of individuals in the firm has to be considered. In general, a cost driver affects behavior if individuals feel that their performance will in some way be evaluated based on the cost per unit of that cost driver or the quantity of that driver consumed. The importance of behavioral effects should not be underestimated. For certain companies, the decision to implement an activity-based costing system can be justified on behavioral grounds alone.

Behavioral effects can be beneficial or harmful. Beneficial behavior occurs, of course, when the behavior that results from use of a particular cost driver is desired. For example, if a firm wants to reduce the number of unique parts it processes to simplify activities such as incoming inspection, bill of material maintenance, and vendor qualification, the firm may assign the costs of these activities to products by using number of parts as the cost driver. Similarly, if designers are rewarded based on their ability to design low-cost products, they can be induced to design products that contain fewer parts.

However, care has to be taken if cost drivers are used to modify behavior, because if too many costs are traced via the cost driver, too much "beneficial" behavior may result. For example, if reducing the number of parts causes designers to give up functionality required by the marketplace (just to reduce part numbers), the induced behavior will be harmful.

Harmful behavior occurs if the behavior reinforced by use of a particular cost driver is undesirable. For example, one company ensured the manufacturability of new products by manufacturing prototypes on the same equipment used to produce existing products. Although use of number of setups as the cost driver will appropriately trace many setup-related costs to the prototypes, the designer may choose a different driver (one that distributes the cost of inspections over all products) to avoid potentially harmful behavioral effects. For example, high reported prototype costs may cause the production manager either to reduce the number of prototypes passing through the facility (by charging research and development a high price for the production of prototypes) or to find ways to make the prototypes more efficiently (by developing a special prototype production line). Both these actions compromise the objective of ensuring new product manufacturability.

HOW THE THREE FACTORS INTERACT

Measurement costs, degree of correlation, and behavioral effects interact because each can be associated with a different cost. These costs include:

- Measurement costs;
- Cost of errors (as the correlation falls, the distortion in reported product costs increases and thus, more errors occur in decisions relying upon them[15]; and
- Cost of behavior induced (this is the only cost that can be both positive and negative).

The designer's objective is to design a cost system that provides the most benefit for the lowest overall cost. Thus, a cost driver that induces beneficial behavior but is expensive to use and has a relatively low correlation may still be selected if the behavioral effect dominates. For example, if the behavioral objective is to reduce throughput time, throughput time may be chosen as the cost driver for certain activities even though there is little correlation between the activities and throughput time. In contrast, a driver that is expensive to measure *and* induces harmful behavior but has a high degree of correlation may be selected if the cost of errors dominates. This can occur, for example, if competition is severe and knowing accurate product costs is a strategic necessity.

Two major tasks facing the designer of an activity-based costing system are deciding the number of cost drivers required by the system and then selecting those drivers from the alternatives available. This column explored the factors that require the use of multiple cost drivers, including:

- *Desired accuracy level of reported product costs.* The higher the accuracy desired, the more cost drivers required.
- *Degree of product diversity.* The greater the degree of product diversity, the more cost drivers required.
- *Relative cost of different activities.* The greater the number of activities that represent a significant proportion of the total cost of the products, the more cost drivers required.
- *Degree of volume diversity.* The greater the range of batch sizes, the more cost drivers required.
- *Use of imperfectly correlated cost drivers.* The lower the correlation of the cost driver to actual consumption of the activity, the more cost drivers required.

Factors that affect the selection of cost drivers include:

- *Cost of measuring the cost driver.* The lower the cost, the more likely the cost driver will be selected.
- *Correlation of the selected cost driver to the actual consumption of the activity.* The higher the correlation, the more likely the cost driver should be used.
- *Behavior induced by use of the cost driver.* The more desirable the behavior induced by using the driver, the more likely the driver is to be selected.

NOTES

1 See *Journal of Cost Management* (Summer 1988).
2 See *Journal of Cost Management* (Fall 1988).

3 See part two of this series for a discussion on the concept of the optimal cost system.

4 Part one of this series demonstrated the effect of size diversity on reported product costs.

5 The cost of an activity is said to be directly traced when the cost driver measures the actual consumption of that activity and indirectly when it measures something else. For example, the costs of the activity "inspection" are directly traced by the cost driver "inspection hours" and indirectly traced by the cost drivers "number of inspections" and "machine hours."

6 In Example 1, the distortions in reported *inspection* costs were discussed. In this section it is the *total of inspection and machining costs.*

7 These curves were generated using a different definition of relative cost, namely, "the percentage of total costs of a product that consumes one hour of each activity." Had the original definition been used, as the degree of diversity climbed the cost of the activity "setup" would have had to fall to maintain the same relative cost. In practice, this does not occur because the relative cost is a reflection of the degree of diversity of *all* the products produced.

8 See part one of this series for an example that demonstrates the impact of different production volumes on reported product costs in volume-based and activity-based cost systems. Part one also demonstrated how cost drivers can be selected to reduce the distortion caused by different relative demand frequencies.

9 Harvard Business School case 9-186-272.

10 Part two of this series discussed the impact that computerization has had in general on the cost of measurement.

11 The use of throughput or cycle time costing is explored in the "Tektronix: Portable Instruments Division" case series 9-188-142/3/4.

12 See R. Cooper, "When Should You Use Machine Hour Costing?" *Journal of Cost Management* (Spring 1988), pp. 33–39.

13 This is why the minimum number of drivers required is obtained by determining if the costs of two activities can be traced using a single cost driver without introducing excessive distortion.

14 See "John Deere Component Works," Harvard Business School case 9-187-107/8.

15 See part two of this series for a more detailed discussion on the cost of errors.

Implementing an Activity-Based Cost System

Robin Cooper

This [reading] describes a structured approach to implementing activity-based cost systems that has been used successfully by a number of companies. The first of this structured approach requires making several decisions up front to determine what characteristics the system will have (e.g., will it be a stand-alone system, and how accurate must the new system be?). The second stage consists of a structured implementation methodology consisting of various steps (e.g., designing the system, appointing an implementation team, collecting data, and building support for the new system).

The inadequacies of existing cost accounting systems have recently been the focus of much research,[1] at least four books,[2] and a full-blown project by Computer Aided Manufacturing-International, Inc. (CAM-I). Together, these efforts have identified many failings of traditional cost systems —in particular, their inability to report product costs to a reasonable level of accuracy. Some research has proposed that the distortion in reported product costs could be reduced by the use of an activity-based cost (ABC) system. In ABC systems, the focus of the cost accounting system becomes *activities* instead of *products*.[3]

Apparently, practical applications of activity-based costing have become possible only recently.[4] Only a few ABC systems have ever been document-

Reprinted from *Journal of Cost Management* (Spring 1990), pp. 33-42, with permission.

ed,[5] and the oldest of these is less than ten years old.[6] Even less has been written about how to implement ABC systems.[7]

STRUCTURED APPROACH TO IMPLEMENTATIONS

This [reading] describes a structured approach to implementing ABC systems that several companies have used successfully. The systems were relatively inexpensive to implement: Typically, they cost less than $100,000 and required about three people working full-time for between four and six months.

The structured approach described here can be broken into two major segments. The first segment describes design choices that should be made before starting an implementation. These choices define the characteristics of the system that will emerge. The second major segment describes the steps taken to successfully implement an ABC system. These steps help determine what will be the actual design of the system and how well it will be accepted.

DECISIONS TO MAKE UP FRONT

At least six major decisions need to be made before an ABC system can be implemented. These are as follows:

1. Should the system be integrated with the existing system or should it be a stand-alone system?
2. Should a formal design be approved before implementation?
3. Who should take "ownership" of the final system?
4. How precise should the system be?
5. Should the system report historical or future costs?
6. Should the initial design be complex or simple?

To illustrate the factors that have to be taken into account when making these decisions, the next section discusses the choices that an early adopter of ABC made. The decisions were made by a planning group that included the controller of the facility, the leader of the design team, and the author.

DECISION 1: A STAND-ALONE SYSTEM[8]

Several factors led the planning group to leave the existing cost accounting system in place and to develop a stand-alone, micro-computer-based ABC system for the initial application. First, the existing system was a corporate system. A lengthy approval process would have been required to make any significant changes. Second, it was possible to implement a stand-alone system relatively quickly and inexpensively largely because the company did not have to develop software that would integrate the new ABC system with the company's other information systems (such as the general ledger). Finally, integrating an ABC system with the existing financial system would have required the approval of the external auditors, which would have been another potentially time-consuming and expensive process.

The decision to use a stand-alone system was not without its costs. First, some of the data required by the ABC system were already available on the existing system and, therefore, had to be reentered and stored redundantly. Once reentered, the data had to be maintained to keep them up-to-date, which over time could become a major burden. In addition, no one was certain how to manage the repercussions that were bound to occur when the two systems—the old system and the new, stand-alone ABC system—reported different product costs and thus suggested two different courses of action.

DECISION 2: NO FORMAL DESIGN DOCUMENT

The planning group decided to implement the ABC system immediately and not go through a lengthy design-approval process. Consequently, the team never developed a formal design document. This decision was made because too little was known about the design of ABC systems to be able to design a "good" system on paper without first undertaking most of the data gathering and analysis phase of the project. For example, all the interviews had to be completed before the team could identify the important activities performed by the company.

Another reason for not developing a formal design was to facilitate making changes in the design of the system as more information was received. In particular, the controller worried that presenting a formal design document up front would prematurely restrict the ability of the design team to change the system design as they gained experience. Finally, senior management had given the controller the task of implementing a new system: They were confident of the controller's ability to do so and showed little interest in formal design reviews.

DECISION 3: A MANAGEMENT— NOT A FINANCIAL—SYSTEM

One of the primary objectives the plant controller had in implementing the new system was for it to be viewed as a *management* system instead of a financial system. The controller wanted production and engineering to "take ownership" of the system.

Multidisciplinary team.   To achieve this objective, the implementation team included members from several disciplines other than finance. This was done to foster commitment to the new system throughout the company. The group also believed that having a multidisciplinary team would improve the design of the new system, because nonfinancial members of the team could be counted on to contribute detailed knowledge about production and engineering to the design of the system.

There were several potential drawbacks to having a multidisciplinary team, however. One concern was that functional managers would not assign high-quality personnel to work on the team. Another concern was that nonfinancial members of the team might require intensive training about the design of cost systems. As it turned out, this concern proved to be irrelevant: The functional managers were keen to support the project because they perceived a strong need for a better cost system. The training issue for nonfinancial members of the group was resolved by simply lengthening the design seminar by one day.

Selection criteria.   Several important criteria were identified for selecting team members. The candidates had to be the following:

- Intelligent;
- Flexible in their approach to problem-solving; and
- Knowledgeable about the plant.

Note that knowledge of cost accounting was *not* considered a criterion for selection although it was felt that at least one member of the team had to understand the firm's existing accounting systems.

Using these criteria, four team members were selected:

- The team leader was an engineer who had been working in the strategic planning group (and, incidentally, initiated consideration of an ABC system for the company);
- A factory cost accountant who had production experience and a working knowledge of the firm's accounting system;
- A production supervisor; and
- An industrial engineer with many years' experience.

DECISION 4: REDUCED PRECISION

The planning group decided that the premise for designing the new ABC system should be: "It is better to be approximately right than exactly wrong." Accepting this premise allowed the activity-based system to rely heavily on estimates derived from interview data. These estimates would necessarily be relatively imprecise. For example, a supervisor might say: "I spend about 30 percent of my time in that center" when the actual time spent might be as high as 40 percent or as low as 20 percent. Wherever possible, estimates were cross-checked to minimize errors. The imprecision of the activity-based system, which reported costs to the nearest dollar, can be contrasted to the precision of the existing cost accounting system, which reported costs to four significant figures.

Reduced precision was acceptable because the activity-based product costs were going to be used for strategic decisions, such as which types of business to actively pursue and which to avoid. These decisions are based on a number of factors, including product costs. Therefore, it was considered unlikely that the relative imprecision inherent to the activity-based system would affect the ultimate decisions reached. For example, if the reported activity-based cost of a product was $25 plus or minus $2 and the selling price was exactly $12, it was unlikely that a decision to drop the product would change whether the reported product costs were $23 or $27. In contrast, if the existing accounting system reported a cost of $5.4362, a different decision would have been made.

The decision to accept "soft" interview data in the activity-based system reinforced the decision to build a stand-alone system. If the decision had been to integrate the ABC system with the existing financial systems of the firm, the external auditors would have had to sign off on the change. The planning group was concerned that the interview data would be difficult to verify, which meant that the external auditors might have had trouble accepting the new system. A stand-alone system avoided the need for such a review.

The alternative to using interview data—with its inherently low precision—was to introduce time measurement systems for all salaried employees. The planning group decided that this alternative would be inappropriate because of the costs of a time measurement system, the likely resistance to such a system, and the time it would take to implement a system and collect sufficient data for the new cost system. In any case, the decision to rely on interview data could be revisited once the success of the activity-based system was determined.

DECISION 5: AVERAGE ANNUAL HISTORICAL COSTS

The group also decided to develop a system that reported average annual historical costs instead of estimated future costs. Thus, the system was designed to answer the question: "How much did it cost us to manufacture the products *last* year?" The system was not designed to answer the question: "How much will it cost to manufacture products *next* year?"

Several practical considerations motivated this decision. First, an historical approach guaranteed that the reported product costs would capture all the economics of production and would reflect the actual production processes used to produce the company's products. The planning group was concerned that if they tried to develop an *estimated future cost system,* they might be accused of wishful thinking (e.g., "I am sure that next year we will be 15 percent more efficient in this area.").

Since the activity-based system reported product costs that were to be used for strategic decisions, the group felt that any distortion introduced by using historical data would be acceptable. The production processes and product mix at the facility in which the system was introduced were not changing so rapidly that the historical data would be obsolete. The group also believed that management had developed intuitions about "true" product costs for the previous year and that confirming these intui-

tions would enhance the credibility of the new system. Finally, the traditional costs provided a bench mark against which the activity-based costs could be compared.

An annual period was viewed as the appropriate period over which to average costs for a number of reasons:

1. Year-end closing procedure (such as physical inventories) forced many year-end measurements to be more accurate than their monthly counterparts;

2. A year was long enough for many short-term variations in the consumption of resources to average out;

3. Since the budgeting cycle at the company was annual, the variability in many costs became apparent only as the budget was prepared each year;

4. Most of the records required by the ABC system were available for the prior year but not for earlier years, which meant that it was impossible to develop averages that spanned more than a year;

5. The production processes used to manufacture some of the products were changing sufficiently rapidly that taking an average over more than a year might introduce more distortions than it removed.

The decision to report historical product costs was viewed as a temporary one. Once the ABC system was established, the possibility of developing forward-looking activity-based product costs could be explored. In the meantime, however, historical activity-based product costs could provide the basis for making product-related decisions.

DECISION 6: A COMPLEX SYSTEM THAT COULD LATER BE SIMPLIFIED

The group decided to design a complex system and then to simplify it. This approach was adopted primarily to ensure that the new system did not tell the "wrong story."[9] For example, a simple activity-based system might suggest that a product costs $20, while a complex system might suggest that the product costs $25. Since this system was the first that the group had implemented, it wanted to explore the trade-off between accuracy and the cost of measurement.

There are risks to building complex activity-based systems. Users can be overwhelmed by the details provided by the system. The cost of implementing and maintaining a complex system can also become excessive. The solution selected by the planning group was to build an admittedly complex system and then to simplify it later to an acceptable level of both accuracy and complexity.

These six "predesign" choices reduced the time that it took to implement the new cost system. For example, the decision to develop a stand-alone system rather than an integrated system removed the need to develop interfaces with other systems, avoided having to go through a review by the external auditors, and made it possible to accept a tolerable degree of imprecision. Reducing the time required for implementation was also important, because the planning group wanted to demonstrate that an activity-based system could be implemented in a reasonable time frame at an acceptable cost.

IMPLEMENTATION PLAN

The planning team developed a structured implementation plan to help ensure the success of the pilot study. The three major objectives were:

1. To ensure that the implementation team knew enough about the theory and practice of ABC to allow the team to design an appropriate system;
2. To ensure that management learned enough about the theory of ABC and its potential benefits so that management could accept and use the findings of the project; and
3. To make sure that the design and data gathering phase of the project would be performed efficiently.

The implementation plan that was used has the following seven steps or phases:

1. Seminar on ABC;
2. Design seminar;
3. Design and data gathering;
4. Progress meeting;
5. Executive seminar;
6. Results meeting; and
7. Interpretation meetings.

Each is discussed in the following sections.

SEMINAR ON ABC

The on-site seminar consisted of a short lecture for members of the plant management team about ABC. This lecture was followed by a discussion. The objectives of the seminar were:

- To introduce plant management to the concepts and benefits of ABC;
- To discuss the characteristics of their facility that made it a candidate for an activity-based system; and
- To identify the requirements for the members of the design team.

The seminar lasted about two hours.

DESIGN SEMINAR

The design seminar had two primary objectives[10]:

- To educate the implementation team in the concepts of ABC; and
- To ensure that the implementation team understood the implications of the decisions made by the planning group.

As it happened, the design seminar also served to create a strong team identity, which proved to be a major factor in the successful implementation of the new system.

The design seminar lasted four days. During this period, members of the design team used five computer-based training exercises that provided "hands on" simulated design experience. These exercises covered such issues as the following:

- How to identify activity centers;
- How to identify methods to assign costs in the first and second stages; and
- How to collect data.

DESIGN AND DATA GATHERING

The design and data gathering phase was broken into two parts. First, the direct material and direct labor standards were examined. Then overhead was analyzed to identify the activities that were driving it (i.e., what the cost drivers were).[11]

Overhead was analyzed using the following steps:

- Identify (through interviews) the major activities performed in the facility;
- Determine the cost of those activities;
- Identify (again through interviews) what drove those activities;
- Determine the quantities of each cost driver associated with every product; and
- Compute activity-based product costs.

Overhead was broken into the following major components:

- Salaried wages;
- Indirect hourly wages;
- Maintenance and repair;
- Depreciation and taxes;
- Fringe benefits; and
- Other resources (e.g., supplies, tools, utilities, and project spending).

The first five components represented about 80 percent of the total overhead of the facility.

Salaried wages.   Salaried wages were assigned by estimating the salary cost of each department. This estimating was necessary because, unlike the direct labor force, salary scales varied significantly by department. For example, engineering salaries were systematically higher than personnel salaries. This difference in salary levels meant that tracing salaries using an average salary times number of salaried hours (which is how direct labor was assigned) would have been inappropriate. Doing so would have introduced excessive distortions into the product costs reported by the ABC system.

Departmental salary totals were estimated based on the following:

- Pay scales and the head count;
- Job titles;
- Hours of overtime worked; and
- Years of seniority for each department.

Where necessary, adjustments for interdepartmental movements were made.

Once the departmental totals were determined, each salaried employee was interviewed. The objectives of the interviews were to understand the key responsibilities of each position and the activities performed. If more than one person held the same position, the interview also focused on why more than one person was needed in that position or department. The interviews identified three categories of salaried employees:

- *The product-related category* dealt with specific products. In interviews, these employees could identify the products that caused the activities that kept them busy. This category included such job functions as production supervision and quality control.
- *The equipment-related category* dealt with specific equipment. In interviews, these employees could identify the equipment that caused the activities that

kept them busy. This category included such job titles as manufacturing engineering and maintenance supervision.

- *The administration-related category* dealt with administrative support. In interviews, these employees could not identify products or equipment that caused the activities that kept them busy, but they could identify the people that they managed or supported. This category included such job titles as personnel, plant managers, and secretaries.

The cost of the product-related category of salaried employees was relatively easy to assign to products. In interviews, these employees identified the percentage of time that they spent either on particular products or activities. If the time spent was identified by product, the costs were assigned directly to the appropriate products. If employees broke down their time according to activities (e.g., handling quality complaints) rather than products, the costs were assigned to the products according to the number of transactions that they generated. Thus, for example, the cost of quality complaints was assigned to products according to the number of quality complaints associated with each product. In some cases, transaction measures were not available. When this unavailability was the case, a general measure (e.g., the number of production hours per product) was used.

Employee costs identified with equipment were assigned to the activity center that contained that equipment. These costs were then assigned to products using machine hours or number of setups.

Administration-related salaried wages represented only a small percentage of the total and consisted mainly of wages for the personnel department. Since this department was predominantly occupied with issues related to the salaried and hourly work forces, the costs of this category were assigned to products according to salary head counts and total labor hours respectively.

Indirect hourly wages.   Indirect hourly wages were assigned to products based on information obtained from interviews of the salaried supervisors of the indirect work force. These interviews focused on the following:

- Number of employees supervised;
- Division of labor that existed in the group; and
- Activities that kept the group busy.

This information was then used to identify the cost pools into which the costs would be assigned. For example, the costs of the material-movement department were split among the following:

- Forklift drivers servicing operations;
- Forklift drivers loading rail cars and trucks for shipping; and
- Forklift trucks servicing finished goods inventory.

The wages of indirect hourly labor did not vary systematically by department. These wages were, therefore, estimated using a single wage rate, after adjusting for different levels of overtime. For example, costs associated with material handling were assigned to products on the basis of the number of moves products required, while the costs associated with forklift trucks that serviced operations were based on the number of forklift moves. The number of moves was estimated by dividing the annual volume of production for each product by the average load size of a forklift carrying that product.

Maintenance and repair.   Maintenance and repair costs were assigned to products based on the information obtained by interviewing the maintenance and repair supervisors about the characteristics of the various types of equipment. Since the activities that generated the work were equipment-related, the costs were assigned in the same way as the equipment-related category of salaried wages: first to the activity center that contained the equipment and then by machine hours to products.

Depreciation and taxes.   Depreciation and tax costs included the depreciation and taxes on three different types of fixed assets:

1. Machinery and equipment;
2. Property; and
3. Buildings.

The costs associated with machinery and equipment were assigned directly to the activity centers containing the equipment and then by machine hours to the products. These costs were considered identical to the equipment-related category of salaried wages and to the maintenance and repair component.

Depreciation and tax costs for property and building were more difficult to assign to products. These costs were assigned to the activity centers according to square footage. However, no product-related activities could be identified that caused these costs. Even though no activities could be identified, the team decided to assign these costs to the products using machine hours. This decision was made to keep the costs assigned by the existing cost accounting system and the costs assigned by the ABC system comparable.[12]

Fringe benefits.   Fringe benefits consisted of the benefits for both the salaried and hourly work forces. The benefit packages differed between these two groups and thus had to be assigned separately. The salaried fringe benefits were assigned to activity centers and products using the same bases as those used to assign the salaried and hourly wage costs.

Other resources.   The other, less significant components of overhead were assigned according to the same principles as the major components. Each component was investigated to discover the activities that caused the costs to be incurred. The costs were then assigned to the activity centers and products using some measure of the level of consumption that each activity caused.

Process of assigning overhead.   It took about three months to assign overhead for the first time using an ABC approach. The team conducted about 200 interviews, each lasting approximately an hour. Over 50 potential assignment bases were identified.

The final design of the ABC system was complex: The design identified 630 distinct activities (costs for each of which had to be determined), used over thirty different bases in the first stage to assign costs to cost centers, and then used over forty different bases in the second stage. This complexity can be compared to the simplicity of the company's existing cost accounting system, which contained one cost pool and used only one second-stage basis (direct labor hours).

Product costs reported by the ABC system and the company's existing cost accounting system differed dramatically: The change in overhead assigned to products varied from −50 percent to +200 percent. It should be noted, however, that the cost accounting system used previously—with its one cost pool and one cost driver—was not the best traditional system that could have been designed for the facility. Therefore, comparisons between the costs reported by the company's existing system and the costs reported by the new ABC system are not conclusive in determining the benefits of ABC. The design team therefore decided that the appropriate bench mark against which to compare product costs reported by the ABC system was the best traditional system possible.

To determine the "real" shift in reported product costs resulting from adopting an activity-based approach, the product costs reported by the "best" traditional system were determined.[13] These costs were then compared to those reported by the ABC system. When this comparison was made, the ABC system still reported significantly different product costs from those reported by the more sophisticated traditional cost system. All products were affected. The average product cost changed by 24 percent (which was computed as the average of the absolute difference in product costs divided by the traditional costs).

PROGRESS MEETINGS

The design team kept the plant's management informed about progress made throughout the entire design and data gathering phase. Members of the team attended several monthly plant staff meetings to report their findings and to discuss the problems they had encountered. These progress meetings had two main objectives: to ensure that the design was appropriate and to allow plant management to develop some "ownership" of the system's design.

In these meetings, the plant's managers played an important role by helping to identify several errors that the team had made in its design and data gathering procedures. The plant managers also helped solve some especially difficult design problems. For example, the managers identified one source of material usage that the team had missed.

EXECUTIVE SEMINAR

An executive seminar was held for the plant's management to explain ABC in more detail than had been possible in the first seminar. The seminar helped build commitment to the ABC system, prepared management for the results of the project, and suggested the types of actions they should consider once the results were available.

The seminar gave the design team a chance to describe the final design of the new ABC system and to explain how the results would be disseminated. (The team noted that the first set of activity-based product costs was likely to change—some significantly—as management discovered better ways to assign costs to products. The design team was concerned that these changes would raise doubts about the accuracy and stability of the ABC system. After the design team discussed this concern with management, it was agreed that activity-based product costs would be made available to only a limited number of people until everyone agreed that they were stable and could be "published.")

RESULTS MEETING

When the activity-based costs became available, a select group of managers and engineers was assembled to analyze the results. These managers and engineers were selected because, for at least one major product for which they were responsible, the activity-based costs differed significantly from those reported by the company's existing cost accounting system.

The final design of the ABC system was explained to the managers, who were taken through the conceptual design so that they would understand how the ABC system differed from the existing cost accounting system. (This refresher was considered necessary because of the time that had elapsed since the executive seminar. Also, several of the managers who attended had not been to the executive seminar.)

The overall impact of the changes to product costs was then discussed based on a comparison of the traditional versus the ABC system's reported product costs. After the comparative list of product costs was discussed in depth, the group identified several high-priority products that it thought required extra attention. The managers responsible for those products arranged meetings with the implementation team to investigate in more detail the reasons for the differences in product costs.

INTERPRETATION MEETINGS

Interpretation meetings were held after the results meeting. These meetings focused on how to interpret the activity-based product costs and the actions that should be taken based on them. These meetings had two components.

First, the engineers responsible for the products that had been identified as "high priority" in the results meeting visited the design team and began an exhaustive analysis of the activity-based product costs. In particular, the engineers checked to see that they agreed with the way that costs were assigned to the products and that no major mistakes had been made in determining the proportion of the various activities consumed by the selected products.

Second, the interpretation meetings explored the actions that should be taken in light of the new ABC product costs—including finding ways to change the production process to reduce costs. For example, the ABC system confirmed the intuitions of some engineers that parts requiring a large number of dies were expensive to manufacture. In particular, these parts required higher levels of maintenance, setup, and other die-related activities. The firm therefore began exploring ways to manufacture products using fewer dies.

SUMMARY

ABC systems have attracted attention in recent years because they provide three major benefits:

- More accurate product costs;
- An improved understanding of the economics of production; and
- A picture of the economics of activities performed by a company.

To date, however, the literature on ABC has focused primarily on how the theory was developed instead of how an ABC system would be implemented.

The method for implementing ABC systems explained here makes it possible for a multidisciplinary team of three people to have an ABC system in place at a total cost of about $100,000 per system within a reasonable time—between four and six months. As more ABC systems are implemented and as the concepts become more widely understood, the degree of education required in the implementation methodology will decrease. (This decrease has already been observed at the parent corporation, which has by now used the same approach to implement another ten ABC systems.)

The parent of the corporation considered in this article has reacted favorably to ABC in general and also to the approach for implementing an ABC system. Other firms have also implemented successful ABC systems by following the same approach.

Nonetheless, the structured approach explained here does not guarantee success: It excludes many important factors that must be considered. (For example, it ignores the critical role a "champion" of a new ABC system can play in selling the system.[14]) However, this approach does provide a starting point for managers who are considering implementing an ABC system.

NOTES

1 Robin Cooper, "You Need a New Cost System When. . . .," *Harvard Business Review* (January–February 1989): 77–82; Robin Cooper and Robert S. Kaplan, "How Cost Accounting Distorts Product Costs," *Management Accounting* (April 1988): 20–27; Robert S. Kaplan, "Yesterday's Accounting Undermines Production," *Harvard Business Review* (July–August 1984): 95–101; Robert S. Kaplan, "One Cost System Isn't Enough," *Harvard Business Review* (January–February 1988): 61–66.

2 J.Y. Lee, *Managerial Accounting Changes for the 1990s* (Artesia: McKay Business Systems, 1987); M. Bromwich and A. Bhimani, *Management Accounting: Evolution not Revolution* (London: CIMA, 1989); H. Thomas Johnson and Robert S. Kaplan, *The Rise and Fall of Management Accounting Relevance Lost* (Boston: Harvard Business School Press, 1987); C. Berliner and James A. Brimson, *Cost Management for Today's Advanced Manufacturing: The CAM-I Conceptual Design* (Boston: Harvard Business School Press, 1988).

3 Robin Cooper, "The Rise of Activity-Based Costing—Part One: What Is an Activity-Based Cost System?" *Journal of Cost Management* (Summer 1988): 45–54; Robin Cooper, "The Rise of Activity-Based Costing—Part Two: When Do I Need an Activity-Based Cost System?" *Journal of Cost Management* (Fall 1988): 41–48; Robin Cooper, "The Rise of Activity-Based Costing—Part Three: How Many Cost Drivers Do You Need, and How Should You Select Them?" *Journal of Cost Management* (Winter 1989): 34–46; Robin Cooper, "The Rise of Activity-Based Costing—Part Four: What Do Activity-Based Systems Look Like?" *Journal of Cost Management* (Spring 1989): 34–46; Robin Cooper and Robert S. Kaplan, "Measure Costs Right: Make the Right Decisions," *Harvard Business Review* (May 1988): 96–103; John K. Shank and Vijay Govindarajan, "Unbundling the Full Product Line: The Perils of Volume-Based Costing" (Dartmouth College Tuck School working paper, Dartmouth College, 1987).

4 George J. Staubus, *Activity Costing and Input-Output Accounting* (Homewood, IL: Richard D. Irwin, 1971); Peter F. Drucker, "Managing for Business Effective-

ness," *Harvard Business Review* (May–June 1963): 33–60.

5 Robin Cooper, "Schrader Bellows," *Harvard Business School Case Series 186–272;* Robin Cooper and Peter B.B. Turney, "Hewlett-Packard: Roseville Network Division," *Harvard Business School Case Series, 198–117;* Robin Cooper and Peter B.B. Turney, "Tektronix: Portable Instruments Division," *Harvard Business School Case Series 188–142/143/144;* Robin Cooper and K.H. Wruck, "Siemens Electric Motor Works (A)," *Harvard Business School Case Series 189–089;* Robert S. Kaplan "American Bank," *Harvard Business School Case Series 187–194;* Robert S. Kaplan, "John Deere Component Works," *Harvard Business School Case Series 187–107/108;* Robert S. Kaplan, "Kanthal," *Harvard Business School Case Series 190–002/003.*

6 There is evidence that ABC systems emerged earlier in nonmanufacturing settings. Rail form A, for example, which was developed in 1938; can be represented as an ABC system. See Robert S. Kaplan, "Union Pacific," *Harvard Business School Case Teaching Note 187–058.*

7 There are articles about the implementation of cost systems in general. See, e.g., Carolyn R. Stokes and Kay W. Lawrimore, "Selling a New Cost System," *Journal of Cost Management* (Fall 1989): 29–34; Michael D. Shields and S. Mark Young, "A Behavioral Model for Implementing Cost Management Systems," *Journal of Cost Management* (Winter 1989): 17–27. However, these articles deal with the implementation of any type of cost system rather than the implementation of ABC systems in particular.

8 For a more extensive discussion on the benefits of using stand-alone systems, see Robert S. Kaplan, "The Four Stage Model of Cost Systems Design" (Harvard Business School working paper, 1989).

9 The shift in product costs caused by adopting an ABC system is caused primarily by the interaction of two functions: (1) the cost of the activity being assigned to the products and (2) the degree of diversity of the products in terms of that activity. How those two factors interact is not always obvious. Building a complex system virtually guarantees that all important interactions will be reflected in the activity-based product costs. For a discussion on how these factors interact, see Cooper, "The Rise of Activity-Based Costing—Part Four."

10 Later versions of the design seminar had a third objective: to train the implementation team to use the ABC software developed in this first implementation.

11 A review of material and labor standards is not relevant to this article. However, any firm undertaking an ABC project should ensure the adequacy of its direct material and labor costs.

12 The "value" of tracing these costs to the products was drawn to the engineers' attention when the product costs reported by the ABC system were discussed.

13 This system consisted of multiple cost centers—one for each major class of machine.

14 For example, see, Shields and Young, "A Behavioral Model for Implementing Cost Management Systems."

6

USING ACTIVITY-BASED COST SYSTEMS
TO INFLUENCE BEHAVIOR

Many Western companies, in the post-World-War-II era, gained competitive advantage through superior product design and functionality. The products designed and made by these companies had superior performance to those marketed by competitors. Customers were willing to pay premium prices for the enhanced performance from the products. In these companies, design engineers, who developed products that brought new and expanded functionality to the company's customers, played a dominant role. Manufacturing played a subordinate role. It was given product designs late in the product development cycle and directed to develop the manufacturing processes that enabled the new products to be brought to the marketplace. In one manager's words, "Manufacturing was viewed as the necessary evil to get customers to part with their money." Frequently, the products could not be produced reliably and efficiently and often were delivered late. But customers still purchased the products because they offered performance unavailable from competitors.

During the 1980s, the Western companies received a double shock. First, inflation stopped and, for U.S. companies, the dollar strengthened against the yen. The combination of broken inflation expectations and a strong U.S. dollar meant that companies could no longer simply raise prices to cover the costs of manufacturing inefficiencies. Second, and more important, these same companies found themselves competing against Japanese companies who were now offering virtually the same functionality in their products but with higher reliability and much lower prices.

The Western companies, as they studied the steps required to offer more competitive products, discovered the need to make breakthrough improvements in the quality and reliability of their products and to lower their manufacturing costs even for high-performance products. The search led the companies to adopt total quality management (TQM) and just-in-time (JIT) manufacturing philosophies that emphasized zero defects and continuous flow of materials through the production process, and to motivate their engineers to design products that could be manufactured more efficiently.

As companies promoted TQM, JIT, and design for manufacturability (DFM) activities, they discovered that their efforts were hindered by the signals produced from their traditional cost accounting systems. These systems, designed when manufacturing processes were manual,[1] measured the direct labor content of products with exquisite

---

[1]For electronics companies, the old processes involved hand-wiring and soldering of components to boards.

precision and allocated all indirect and support costs based on products' direct labor content. The companies' contemporary manufacturing processes, however, were now highly automated, with direct labor frequently accounting for less than 5% of total manufacturing expenses. Thus, while efforts were being made to improve materials flow, reduce setup times, and design products with fewer and more common components, the cost system kept stressing reduction of direct labor, direct labor efficiencies, and overhead absorption based on standard direct labor hours earned. These antiquated systems rewarded the performance of managers that were able to keep labor busy even if the labor was frequently building unnecessary inventory and products ultimately discovered to be out of conformance. In addition, the financial systems required tens or even hundreds of thousands of direct labor measurements each month, despite direct labor expenses being a minor portion of total manufacturing expense.

Companies came to realize that they would be unable to achieve their TQM, JIT, and DFM goals while retaining their existing cost systems. New systems emerged that attempted to measure more accurately the costs of product design and process complexity. The companies discovered, however, that attempts to improve the production process for existing products were limited by the constraints of the existing product designs. Once a product has been designed, it becomes very difficult to reduce manufacturing costs significantly. For companies producing products with short life cycles (frequently called high-technology companies), cost reduction projects are more effective if they focus on future products rather than existing products. Some estimates indicate that up to 90% of the cost of a product is determined during the design phase. The potential savings from better design for future products, especially when existing products are near the end of the useful product life cycle, will be much higher than attempting to make major reductions in existing product costs.[2]

Activity-based cost systems play a role in implementing design for manufacturability by helping the product designers understand the economic implications of their design choices.[3] Several companies, however, rather than build complete activity-based systems, chose to build simple systems that would be easy to understand by product designers and process engineers. The companies deliberately chose activities and cost drivers that would immediately start to influence the behavior of product designers. For example, understanding that a manual insertion is three times as expensive as an automatic insertion helps designers choose between two alternatives that have different material costs and different quantities of the two types of insertions. The cost system designers chose cost drivers that penalized the use of low-volume, unique parts. They wanted to get maximum leverage in encouraging the next generation of products to be designed with fewer and more common components.

To focus cost reduction and design for manufacturability, the activity-based system must be well understood by individuals who are expected to use the information it generates. For this reason, activity-based systems deliberately designed to influence behavior tend to be simpler than systems designed to report accurate product costs. The danger of simplicity is that the reported product costs are not as accurate as they could be, thereby contributing to poor decisions. In particular, if too many costs are assigned

---

[2]C. Berliner and J. A. Brimson (eds.), *Cost Management for Today's Advanced Manufacturing: The CAM-I Conceptual Design* (Boston: Harvard Business School Press, 1988), pp. 156–57.
[3]Material in this section is drawn from Robin Cooper and Peter B.B. Turney, "Internally Focused Activity-Based Cost Systems," in R.S. Kaplan (ed.), *Measures for Manufacturing Excellence*, pp. 291–305.

via a given driver, the message being sent, "reduce the number of times this activity is performed," can become too strong and cause harmful behavior to be induced. If the reported cost per unit of a cost driver is biased upward, "improvements" might be made that are not cost-justified. If the designers learn that the messages from the cost system are inaccurate, they will lose faith in the activity-based system and start to ignore it just as many have learned to ignore the signals from traditional cost systems.

OPERATIONAL CONTROL AND STRATEGIC PROFITABILITY ANALYSIS: SEPARATE SYSTEMS?[4]

Some companies have attempted to use their activity-based cost systems not just to inform managers' and engineers' decisions on products and processes but also for monthly control and reporting. These companies may be confounding the two different functions that cost systems perform in organizations. Activity-based systems help managers make better strategic decisions on products and processes and influence engineers' product design activities. Operational control and performance measurement systems provide accurate, short-term feedback to facilitate learning and promote efficiency on operating processes. These two functions are quite different in their information requirements, and it seems unlikely that one system can perform both functions effectively.

Accurate Consumption Measures versus Estimates of Resource Consumption   Recall (from chapter 4) that operational control systems should be based on accurate measures (the Q measure) of resource consumption by operating departments. For the activity-based system, however, the expenses of all the organization's resources should be assigned to the products or services that consume these resources. It may not be cost-effective to measure accurately the quantities of resources consumed by individual products. But the activity-based cost system designer must still estimate the quantity of all resources demanded, product-by-product and customer-by-customer. Thus, the product costing system will have many more subjective estimates than will the information reported to managers by the operational control system.

Timeliness   Second, the reporting period for the activity-based system will be much longer than for the operational control system. Information on the total resources consumed by products and customers is used to direct managers' attention to design, manufacturing technology, and pricing and product-mix decisions. Decisions regarding product design, introduction, abandonment, and pricing are strategic matters that should not be based on short-run fluctuations of manufacturing efficiencies. A system that attributes all organizational resources semiannually or annually is usually sufficient. Even with only annual updates, managers can use the system throughout the year to influence new product design, product introductions, process improvements, and pricing decisions. A good system will calculate unit costs for all key activities (e.g., labor and machine hours, energy usage, materials, and support) so that the projected expenses from introducing a new product or changing the design of an existing product can be estimated based on the product's demands on the organization's resources. Also, the impact of significant process improvements, to lower the cost of performing a key activity, can be reflected in revised product and customer profitabilities.

---

[4]Material in this section is drawn from Robert S. Kaplan, "One Cost System Isn't Enough," *Harvard Business Review* (January-February 1988), pp. 61–66.

Fixed and Variable Cost Assumptions

With the longer time perspective of the strategic profitability measurement system, many expenses are considered variable that, for cost control and responsibility reporting purposes, have been treated as fixed. The activity-based system reflects the consumption of resources by products and customers, and, with this philosophy, almost all organizational resources become variable, not fixed, resources. This distinction between the long-run variability assumption of strategic profitability systems and the short-run fixed nature of many operating expenses leads to the large volume variances reported when activity-based cost systems are used as budgets for monthly reporting.

System Scope

The operational control system collects expenses by each responsibility center. The activity-based cost system, in contrast, collects expenses from across all the organization's operating units. Expenses traced to a product will include not only direct materials, labor, and factory support, but also the expenses of resources required to design, sell, deliver, service, and improve the product. Thus, traceable expenses will include costs incurred in engineering design, process improvement, purchasing, information systems, financial and cost analysis, sales and marketing, and general administration.

Thus, relative to operational control systems, strategic profitability measurement systems involve more subjective estimates, are updated much less frequently, assume that almost none of the organization's resources are unaffected by decisions and actions made about products and customers, and accumulate and report expenses that cut across normal functional and organizational lines.

THE EVOLUTIONARY MODEL OF COST SYSTEMS DESIGN[5]

Some companies are attempting to purchase or develop a single global system to perform both managerial functions (operational control and strategic profitability measurement) and to report data for the external, financial reporting function. Financial executives, in particular, tend to believe that their companies cannot run with multiple financial and cost systems. They feel that their company must march to a single drummer so that it would be infeasible to produce external financial statements with one system, attempt to motivate and evaluate managers with a second system, and make strategic decisions on pricing, distribution channels, product mix, product design, and process technology with yet a third.

We have seen, however, several instances in which companies have implemented major changes in their operational control and strategic profitability systems, without requiring that an entirely new global system be acquired and installed. Attempting to reconcile the diverse assumptions between operational control and strategic profitability measurement systems about expense variability, frequency of reporting and updating, requirements for accuracy, the role for subjective judgments about resource consumption, and unit of analysis seems well beyond the capabilities of existing systems. Rather than make compromises along these important dimensions, companies have retained their official system for financial reporting purposes and supplemented this system, using the power of distributed computing, to develop local, managerially relevant operational control and strategic profitability measurement systems.

Information for these localized systems is down-loaded from existing financial accounting, production, engineering, marketing, logistics, and order-entry sales sys-

[5]Material in this section is drawn from Robert S. Kaplan, "The Four-Stage Model of Cost Systems Design," *Management Accounting* (February 1990), pp. 22–26.

tems. Thus, the company can continue to operate with a single, integrated data base. The intelligence and processing for operational control and profitability measurement, however, resides in local processing units. Companies following this incremental, decentralized approach have been able to develop and install the new systems for operational control and profitability measurement at a local site using only a few people working for several months. This resource commitment, in people, time, and financial expense, is far lower than the multimillion-dollar purchases of new cost systems made by other companies; purchases that mainly installed the traditional thinking of their previous cost system into a modern, 1990-vintage computer. That is, companies attempting to purchase a single global cost system actually may acquire a system that collects all the data in a common format and prepares reports on a consistent basis throughout the company. But the information from the expensive centralized systems will still be too aggregated, delayed, and filled with allocations to be useful for operational control and performance measurement, and the systems will still distort product and customer profitabilities. In effect, they will have automated and integrated the problems and limitations of their existing systems.

The alternative scenario is for companies to develop localized systems for operational control and for product and customer costing while retaining their official system to perform the cost allocations and expense summaries required for financial reporting. As companies experiment with, gain confidence in, and eventually standardize their operational control and strategic profitability systems, they can prepare GAAP financial statements from these managerial systems. The actual expenses needed to prepare periodic financial statements can be captured from the operational control systems that are monitoring daily, weekly, and monthly spending activities. The assignment of these expenses to products for inventory valuation can be done using the more accurate methods developed for the strategic profitability measurement of products and customers. Some expenses assigned to products that cannot, according to GAAP, be allocated to inventory values can be stripped away. Expenses that could not be causally assigned to individual products, but which according to GAAP must be allocated to inventoried products, can be allocated on an arbitrary and simple basis (much as is done today for all indirect expenses).

In this manner, financial statements will be prepared from systems that have been designed explicitly to provide managerially relevant information. This approach is exactly counter to the philosophy of present systems in which companies attempt, unsuccessfully, to develop managerially relevant information from systems that primarily satisfy external requirements. Working from a managerial to a financial system is preferable because the informational needs for operational control and strategic profitability measurement are much finer (i.e., more detailed) than that required for external financial reporting. In summary, companies can start to develop improved decentralized systems for operational control and for product and customer profitability analysis. The advantages of decentralized development include a much lower cost for development and implementation, the flexibility and ease of modifying single-purpose systems, and the considerable opportunities for organizational learning and acceptance. Eventually, these developments will lead to future systems in which the two managerial systems—one for product and customer profitability analysis, and one for on-line feedback and performance measurement—will be integrated with each other. Periodic financial statements will be prepared by excerpting information from the two systems and performing special reconciliation calculations to bring the information into conformance with externally determined reporting standards.

CASES

Tektronix: Portable Instruments Division (A)

The existing cost system did not reflect the realities of our assembly-based production process. We only required about 4% labor to build the product, and yet the cost accounting system was burdening on direct labor. This required an enormous number of transactions to track each stage of production. There was a widespread belief that material usage was a cost driver and that the current system did not reflect that cost driver. Management was quite concerned that we did not have adequate product costs and did not know where to place our strategic emphasis.

BRUCE ANDERSON, DIVISION CONTROLLER

Tektronix (Tek), headquartered in Beaverton, Oregon, produced a wide range of electronic equipment systems and software. The company's sales were divided into three product classes; instrument products, design automation and display products, and communication products. Sales in fiscal year 1987 were about $1.4 billion and net income before taxes was $103 million.

Tek's principal product since its founding in 1946 was the oscilloscope (scope), an instrument for measuring and displaying graphically the timing and magnitude of electrical phenomena. Over the years, Tek had developed a reputation as an engineers' company. Engineers were expected to design instruments from the ground up. Tek products were typically the reference for products in the marketplace (i.e., the products that other companies tried to emulate).

Tek had sold portable oscilloscopes since the 1950s, but a portable version did not exist prior to the introduction of the first battery-powered transistorized oscilloscope in 1961. Portables was created as a separate division in 1983 and split into two divisions in 1984. One of these divisions, Portable Instruments, handled high- and medium-performance oscilloscopes, and the other handled lower-priced models.

THE PORTABLE INSTRUMENTS DIVISION

The Portable Instruments Division (PID) viewed itself as a product differentiator, not a low-cost producer. Its strategy was to set the standards that the rest of the industry would try to emulate. Its competitors would analyze each new generation of Portable's products and then try to produce them less expensively. Competitors often achieved this objective because they could study the Portable's design and simplify it by taking advantage of the introduction of new lower-priced technology in the time lag between when Tek's engineers had designed the product and when the product was introduced in the marketplace. To survive, PID had to keep moving the reference, their products, toward more functionality and performance for the dollar. Reflecting this strategy, only one of the products PID sold in 1987 had been produced in 1983.

In 1983, PID sales were less than $100 million with a return on operating assets of −20%, down from its historical norm of 20% to 25%. The negative return reflected the severe price war that had started when Japanese competitors entered the market in 1981 and set prices 25% below PID's prevailing prices. To protect market share, PID had matched the Japanese prices even though these prices were often below the reported cost of their products. The resulting losses were acceptable to the parent corporation in the short run. But PID's management knew that large losses would not be acceptable in the long run.

To match the Japanese prices and make a profit, PID embarked on an ambitious program of continuous improvement. Many of the existing manage-

This case was prepared by Professor Robin Cooper, Harvard University, and Professor Peter B. B. Turney, Portland State University.

ment teams were replaced with new managers whose sole objective was to turn the business around. The new team began to introduce just-in-time (JIT) production processes, total quality control (TQC), and new management styles, such as people involvement (PI), in which the labor force was allowed to become highly involved in making decisions.

In early 1983, Joe Burger was on assignment, from another Tektronix division, to study how to reduce the cost of the 2400 Series of oscilloscopes. He observed a number of managerial, technical, and process-oriented problems with the product line. For example, inventory levels were high and cycle time was over 30 days.

In late 1983, Joe Conrad, the PID group manufacturing manager, asked Joe Burger to head a special task force charged with solving these problems. Following the successful completion of this project in February 1984, Burger was appointed manufacturing manager of the 2400 Series product line and was promoted to PID manufacturing manager when the division was formed in August 1984.

The 2400 line of analog real-time oscilloscopes (ART) was designed to display the time and magnitude of electrical phenomena in real time (i.e., as they occurred). The 2400 line contained two lines, the 2445 and 2465, which comprised five different models. Each model was available with custom options to tailor the scope for specific applications such as communications, avionics, and the design, manufacture, and service of raster scan devices. The total number of different scopes available was about 15.

Burger described the 2400 line production process and the changes and events that had occurred through early 1987.

> The production process consisted of many functional islands: Etched Circuit Board (ECB) insertion, ECB assembly, kit prepping, ECB testing, ECB repair, final assembly, test, thermal cycle, test/QC, fitting the cabinet, finishing, boxing for shipment, and shipment. In addition, master and final assembly scheduling, modification control, order processing, and manufacturing engineering were service groups, not integrated into the production process.
>
> Due to the structure of the production process, each activity required a sequence number and inventory location, a large number of transactions, supporting paperwork and people to support it. A significant

amount of work-in-process inventory was always on hand. Several large computer-controlled carousels were employed to handle this inventory.

> Realizing the need to change the original 2400 Series manufacturing process, management had implemented a pilot JIT line to begin a learning process that would result in improvements to the production process. This effort had mixed results—the output was low and not predictable—the problem was that management had reduced the work-in-process inventory prior to solving enough of the problems in the process. Consequently, the "excess" inventory was still needed as a buffer between each functional area, and its absence disrupted production.

Burger then described the actions taken.

> My first objective was to consolidate the functionally oriented production activities into an integrated system. Initially, we were able to move just about everything but the wave solder system and ECB testers. We created an open work area, one that allowed eye contact and a visual overview of the entire production area. People, WIP, and problems were all out in the open. By bringing the areas together and eliminating the excessive WIP, we were able to reduce the floor space to 5,500 square feet, down from 10,000. We were now prepared to begin our JIT "journey."
>
> We defined JIT as the continuous elimination of all waste. We did not limit this to activities on the production floor. We included functions such as new product introduction, procurement, stockroom, and the vendors, as well as production. Though we did not initially control many of these service activities, we did treat them as members of the team. This allowed us to create the integrated system we knew would be necessary.
>
> The implementation of JIT in these activities was coordinated but did not occur simultaneously. In particular, JIT was implemented in production on a different schedule from that in the materials function. I controlled all the activities in production, so I could make changes rapidly. It was more difficult to make changes in the materials function, however, because this required working with vendors, changing component specifications, and solving product design problems. Many of the people and organizations involved were outside my span of control, and change took a lot longer to implement.
>
> I gave the materials function one immediate goal: to provide the production group with JIT deliveries of fit-for-use material. Initially, this required additional people to work with vendors, to screen materials for defective units, and to ensure that production's need for materials was covered 100% of the time with nondefective units. Our costs and inventory of

raw material went up, initially, but the goal of JIT delivery of fit-for-use material was met. Once this goal was met and sustained, a lot of effort was put into solving vendor specification and design problems. Eventually, we saw a significant reduction in material-related costs and raw material inventory levels.

The immediate advantage for production was an assured flow of quality components to meet their production needs. Production was able to focus on their own problems, including technical problems, poorly trained people, and inadequate equipment and tools. Production worked rapidly to solve these problems, first on an interim basis, and then on a permanent basis. Cycle time fell as a result, placing pressure on production to increase the first-pass rate. This drive to reduce cycle time and increase first-pass rates became the ongoing focus for all production personnel.

Following the consolidation, it became obvious that a significant amount of time was being wasted doing labor reporting, a carryover from the functionally structured past. When we requested the elimination of this reporting, the Finance Group offered a challenge: "Reduce the cycle time to less than 10 days and you can stop tracking (value added) through labor reporting."

In March, the cycle time was approximately 30 days. At the time of the challenge, the cycle time had already been reduced to approximately 12 days. The 10-day cycle time was achieved in a very short time and many benefits resulted: Labor reporting was simplified, WIP was significantly reduced, and the need to closely track material at each work station was eliminated.

Within the next six months, we had integrated many of the previously functional services. The automatic board test system was removed from its climatized, isolated room and put into the ECB build area. Operators were trained to test their own boards and correct and learn from their mistakes. Incoming inspection provided a person to resolve reject material issues—this person "lived" on the line; vendors were immediately contacted when we encountered problems.

PRODUCTION PROCESS

By 1985, the production process had undergone its first major transition toward a fully integrated JIT process. At this time, production was organized into two areas: machine insertion on the lower floor of the facility, and assembly on the upper floor. Machine insertion had not been moved in line with assembly on the upper floor because it used super machines which serviced multiple products, and

divisions and were not suited to in-line manufacturing.

Machine insertion

The machine insertion area (MI) inserted various components into flats (large boards that contained up to eight separate circuit boards) which were supplied by Tek's Forest Grove plant. The flats were silkscreened and then inserted with integrated circuits (ICs), axial and radial components, and hardware.

Assembly

Flats arrived in assembly from Machine Insertion on kanban carts.[1] The flats were pulled from the carts as required. When all the flats had been removed from a cart, the cart was taken downstairs and exchanged for a full one. The arrival of the empty cart triggered the production of a new batch of flats in MI.

A pull system was used throughout the assembly process. If there were fewer than the specified maximum number of flats in a kanban, this was the signal to the immediately preceding work station to build more flats. The actual number of boards built was determined by the shortfall in the kanban and the daily production goal.

The assembly process could be split into five distinct operations:

- Manual insertion (Prewave soldering)
- Wave solder
- Manual insertion (Postwave soldering)
- Final assembly
- Testing

The oscilloscopes were then moved to the finishing area where the cabinet was put on, a final functional and safety test was completed, and the soft options (e.g., power cords, additional or special probes, service manuals) were packaged with the scope. The scope then moved to a small finished goods area before being shipped to the customer. It took about five days from entry to the assembly area

---

[1]A kanban provided a physical limit on the number of parts, subassemblies, and finished items that could be stored. PID used carts, baskets, and square areas of tables to store work-in-process inventory. These storage points were called kanbans.

to this point. The finished goods inventory area was designed to hold up to 300 units.

COST ACCOUNTING SYSTEM

There were over 100 cost centers in the entire Portable Instruments Plant including about 25 production cost centers. The 2400 line was produced in seven of these production cost centers, although some of these produced products other than the 2400.

The existing system allocated overhead based on direct labor hours, with a separate rate calculated for each manufacturing cost center. Determining the burden rates required calculating frozen standard hours (FSH) and current standard hours (CSH) for each product in each production cost center. Per-unit FSH was the average of the actual number of direct labor hours consumed by a product over a period of a week or more. It was calculated once a year at the end of the fiscal year and was set equal to the most recent CSH at that time. CSH differed from FSH in that it was updated frequently, often weekly, to reflect reported labor efficiencies.

Production cost center overhead consisted of direct and indirect cost. Direct cost was incurred within or directly traceable to the cost center. Total indirect manufacturing costs were allocated among the cost centers based on budgeted FSH.

The system costed products by determining the cost of a single FSH hour in each production cost center. This was calculated by dividing a quarter's actual direct and indirect overhead in the cost center by the total number of FSH earned in that center during the previous quarter. FSH earned was the number of products manufactured, multiplied by the FSH per unit of the product to get the product cost. The rate was updated each quarter.

The CSH system was designed to report on the efficiency of the direct labor force. The labor efficiency reports were very detailed and were prepared on a daily or monthly basis. Efficiency was measured at the cost center level for each major step in the production process and for each individual employee.

Three types of efficiency variance were calculated at the cost center level each month: the method change variance, the volume variance, and the efficiency variance. The method change variance re-

flected the over- or underabsorption of labor and overhead resulting from changes in the production process (standard labor and overhead rate multiplied by the difference between the center's frozen earned standard hours and the current earned standard hours). The volume variance reflected over- or underabsorption of labor and overhead resulting from differences between planned and actual production (standard labor and overhead rate multiplied by the difference between planned and actual FSH). The efficiency variance measured the over- and underabsorbed labor and overhead resulting from differences between current standard hours and the actual hours paid (standard labor and overhead rate multiplied by the difference between CSH and the actual hours paid). These three variances were calculated for each of the seven cost centers, generating 21 different variances per month. Efficiency variances were not broken down by product.

An efficiency rating was calculated for each major step in the production process. Efficiency was calculated for a large number of operations including sequencing, IC insertion, axial component insertion, radial component insertion in the machine insertion department and hand insertion, flow soldering, additional hand insertion, testing (several tests were separately measured), assembly (several steps were separately measured), burn in, and final testing.

In addition to these functional efficiency measures, the cost system also reported on the efficiency of each individual employee daily. In departments where the operations were of short duration, such as hand insertion, it was not unusual for the employee to make over 50 entries a day. In such departments, it often required about 20 minutes a day for the employee to complete the reports. Most employees chose to complete these reports at the end of the day rather than on an ongoing basis.

Each employee was expected to fill in the quantity produced and the amount of time required to produce it. These data were then used to compute an efficiency measure that formed the basis for the employees' performance evaluation. While these production numbers were policed, employees tended to overestimate the number produced. These optimistic estimates could snowball because, to show improved efficiency against a standard that was updated weekly, an employee would have to report even higher output to compensate for the overestimation in the previous reports.

The quantity of data collected and its poor quality produced many problems. Employees complained about the amount of reporting they had to undertake, and the first-line managers grumbled about the amount they had to review. The inventory group was unhappy about the accuracy of the records and the impact the optimistic reporting had on inventory valuation. In particular, they cited the shop floor misreporting output as the major cause of the semiannual writedowns that were required when the physical-to-book comparisons were made. Accountants and line managers had similar complaints because they were expected to reconcile the reported hours to paid hours, and these rarely agreed. The accounting staff was displeased about the burden of correcting the numerous errors as well as having to process over 35,000 labor transactions and 25,000 inventory transactions per month.

There were many symptoms that suggested that this system was already obsolete and would be unable to adapt to the new changes in the production process. In particular, the emergence of a private engineering cost system, distinct from the financial system, indicated that many managers distrusted the product costs reported by the financial system. This engineering cost system used CSH rather than FSH and treated certain manufacturing support costs that were expressed as period costs in the standard cost systems as product costs.

Another reason to replace the existing system was its complexity and unwieldiness. About 18 months were needed to train a new individual to use the system; moreover, it was not clear that anyone fully understood it.

CHANGING THE COST SYSTEM

In 1985, satisfied with their progress on the manufacturing process, management turned its attention to the design of a new cost accounting system. Their first step was to assess the need for cost information. Management identified three distinct uses of cost: special, management, and legal. Special costs were costs derived for special situations, such as make-versus-buy decisions, where the average costs reported by the cost system were inadequate. Management costs were the costs reported by the product costing system. These were used in designing products and guiding cost reduction efforts. Legal costs were the costs used to value inventory for financial accounting purposes.

After these uses for cost information had been identified, the firm embarked on a three-year program to replace the existing accounting systems. The first change was the implementation of an integrated business system that tied together the information used by manufacturing, accounting, and all other areas of the firm.

The second change was to simplify the accounting procedures. Reporting labor performance for each operation was abandoned, reducing the number of monthly labor transactions from 35,000 to less than 100. The number of inventory transactions was reduced by a similar extent, and the number of variances was reduced to three. This simplification freed up the time for a considerable portion of the accounting staff to work on the management cost system and special costing exercises.

The third change was the design of a new cost accounting system for the 2400 Series line of scopes. Management believed that the existing cost system did not reflect the realities of the new production process. Direct labor accounted for only 4% of the manufacturing cost, yet the accounting system used direct labor as the exclusive basis for allocating overhead. The direct labor content of PID's products had been constantly decreasing over recent years, while overhead costs were increasing. The result was that labor-based overhead rates were rising and had become absurdly high.

High overhead rates convinced engineers that the way to reduce overhead costs in products was to reduce labor. As a result, the focus of cost reduction programs had been the elimination of direct labor. Inevitably, since much of overhead was not driven by direct labor, this reduction did not have the desired effect, and overhead rates had continued to spiral upwards.

Given these facts, management was concerned that the product costs reported by the existing system were inaccurate and were not helping them guide the strategic emphasis of the divisions. In 1985, it decided to create a special project team to redesign the cost system. The team initially consisted of Mike Wright, financial systems application manager, and Jeff Taylor, summer student intern. They were later joined by John Jonez, manager of cost accounting.

PHASE 1: MATERIAL BURDENING

Bruce Anderson, division controller, stated the following:

> The problem of the existing system was its inability to recognize the "true" cost of purchased parts. Therefore, it did not allow the engineer to understand the tradeoff between parts proliferation and direct labor content. For example, we had hundreds of different resistors when a dozen would have sufficed. It was costing us money to maintain more and more active parts. Our objective was to reduce the number of vendors so that we could achieve JIT delivery and 100% quality. We believed this would increase our flexibility and reduce our overall costs. We were very worried about part number proliferation and felt that the material burdening system would help reduce it and keep it under control.

Jonez described his assignment to develop a new overhead allocation method.

> As a first step, we established a set of characteristics to guide the new allocation for the new method. We decided that the method must be intuitively logical and easily understandable by management. In addition, it should allow a more accurate correlation of cost to products, thus providing better support for management decisions such as make-versus-buy decisions, product design decisions, product phase-out and start-up decisions, and strategic pricing decisions. Most important, it must support the just-in-time manufacturing strategy of the division. Finally, it needed to provide information that was accessible by decision makers.

The team recognized that the chosen allocation method had to be accepted and supported by management. The time was right for change because almost everybody believed that the current method of burdening was inequitable and because accounting was convinced that the division's burdening method could be improved.

Initially, the team assumed that the new burdening method would be used for inventory valuation as well as for management purposes. This view was abandoned, however, when it was realized that the new burdening method might change the reported valuation of inventory. One concern was that this change might conflict with reporting consistency. PID also wanted to maintain the option of changing the burdening method for management purposes in the future without having to seek corporate accounting, auditing, and IRS approval. Another reason to keep legal costing separate from management costing was the desire to report full product costs. PID therefore adopted the idea of management costs, which would use the new burdening method and would coexist with the financial costs for inventory valuation. One difference between the two systems was that more elements of costs were included in the new system. Purchasing costs, for example, were treated as a period cost in the old system, whereas the team preferred to include them in the product cost.

In its study, the team discovered that about 50% of overhead costs were related to materials (material overhead costs, or MOH). These costs included the costs of planning, procuring, inspecting, storing, and distributing materials. It was felt that an allocation base should be selected that was relevant to these activities. The remaining 50% of overhead would, for the moment, continue to be allocated using direct labor.

After some preliminary analysis, the following alternative allocation bases were identified:

1. Material dollars
2. Number of parts
3. Number of part numbers.

Material dollars burdening calculated an MOH cost per dollar of material cost. For example, if the budgeted annual MOH was $8,200,000 and budgeted total material purchases was $70,000,000, the material dollar overhead rate would be $.0117 of MOH per material dollar.

The second method calculated a single burden rate that was applied to each part specified in the bill of materials. If a bill specified 100 discrete parts and the number used was five times each, the material overhead for the assembled item would be 500 multiplied by the rate per part.

The third method determined a different rate for each part depending on the volume of usage. If there were 6,000 part numbers, there would be 6,000 rates. Each rate was calculated using a two-step procedure. The first step determined the standard burden cost for each part number. The second step divided the standard burden cost by the volume of each part number to obtain the cost per part for that part number. This calculation produced lower rates for high-volume parts and higher rates for low-volume parts (Exhibit 1).

Step 1:

$$\frac{\text{material overhead cost (MOH)}}{\text{number of active part numbers}} = \frac{\text{annual cost to}}{\text{carry a part number}}$$

Step 2:

$$\frac{\text{annual cost to carry a part number}}{\text{annual usage of the part number}} = \frac{\text{MOH rate}}{\text{for each part}}$$

To make a choice from among these three methods, the team had to understand what costs should be included in MOH, to identify the factors that caused those costs, and to determine their relative materiality. After consultation with management, the team broke MOH into the following distinct components:

1. Costs due to the value of parts
2. Costs due to the absolute number of parts
3. Costs due to the maintenance and handling of each different part number
4. Costs due to each use of a different part number.

This breakdown showed that the costs incurred due to the frequency of the use of parts categories (2 and 4) were secondary to the cost of carrying each different part number (3). The costs due to the value of parts were similarly quite small.

The cost of carrying each different part number resulted from a number of activities that had to be carried out for each part number. These activities included planning, scheduling, negotiating with vendors, purchasing, receiving, handling, delivering, storing, and paying for each part number. The more part numbers there were, the more these activities had to be performed.

Given these findings, the team concluded that the total MOH cost of the parts could reasonably be expected to decrease with the use of a smaller number of different part numbers. This cost reduction was the result of two factors. First, higher volume discounts could be achieved by replacing low-volume unique parts with high-volume common parts. As the number of part numbers was reduced, it was also likely that the number of vendors would be reduced. This would, in turn, reduce the demand for vendor-related activities. Second, the total manufacturing overhead needed to support an operation with fewer unique part numbers would be less than the current amount. While overall cost reduction would not be immediate, management believed that the part number allocation method would increase the awareness of the costs associated with part number proliferation. This awareness would influence engineering decisions and result in real cost savings over time.

On reviewing these facts, management decided that the chosen allocation measure for MOH should focus on the second factor—the reduction of overhead through the reduction of part numbers. They felt that the third method, an allocation measure based on part numbers with a specific rate for each part number, best captured the relationship between material overhead and part numbers. Consequently, after the team made a series of presentations to management, the method received general acceptance.

Under this method, the MOH cost for each instrument was computed from the part numbers in the instrument's bill of materials. The rate for each part number was multiplied by the number of times that part was used in the instrument. The resulting cost was aggregated for all part numbers in the bill (Exhibit 2). Instruments with larger numbers of parts and/or a higher percent of unique parts carried a higher MOH cost.

During these presentations, the following advantages were identified for adopting the part number method:

1. The part number method was the most accurate of the three because it reflected the differential consumption of materials-related activities by the products. An instrument designed with many unique components, for example, would be correctly given a cost penalty. The method would also avoid penalizing high-volume products which, while they might contain a number of different parts, consumed relatively few material related activities per material number.

2. The method would provide engineers with a listing of all parts and the material overhead cost associated with each part. This information would be helpful in determining the value of a new part versus an existing common part and encourage reducing the number of part numbers and increasing the proportion of common parts used in the instruments. Such a

listing did not currently exist, and engineers relied on their own judgment in making such evaluations.

The disadvantages of using the part number method were identified as follows:

1. Certain products might be allocated an excessive amount of overhead. The cost allocated to products with infrequent options, for example, might exceed the true cost of adding the options. Products that were being phased out, where little effort was being expended, might also be overcosted.

2. It was the most difficult of the three methods to implement and would require the most computer resources to maintain.

3. It was the most complex method and probably the most difficult for management to understand. For example, management might draw the erroneous conclusion that the material overhead costs of $687.50 were variable with each part number because eliminating one part number in the data base would not reduce total material overhead costs by this amount. Nor would the division save $2.00 in out-of-pocket costs using one fewer low-volume part. Over time, however, and with a sufficient reduction in part numbers, the consumption of materials-related activities and overhead cost would go down.

Given this long-term variability of part-number –related costs, management had difficulty attaching any specific meaning to the $687.50 rate. It was merely an average calculation based on the current overhead cost structure and the current set of part numbers used by the division.

EXHIBIT 1

TEKTRONIX: PORTABLE INSTRUMENTS DIVISION (A)
Number of Part Numbers
Overhead Cost Computation
(Example)

Expenses in the MOH pool =	$5,500,000	
Number of active part numbers =	8,000	
Annual cost to carry each part number =	$\dfrac{\$5,500,000}{8,000}$	= $687.50
− High usage part		
Annual usage of example part number =	35,000 units	
MOH rate for example part number =	$\dfrac{\$687.50}{35,000}$	= $.02
− Low usage part		
Annual usage of example part number =	350 units	
MOH rate for example part number =	$\dfrac{\$687.50}{350}$	= $2.00

EXHIBIT 2

TEKTRONIX: PORTABLE INSTRUMENTS DIVISION (A)

Product Cost Information Using

Material Burdening Approach

Model	A	B	C	D	E	TOTAL
Volume	3,000	3,000	750	400	300	7,450
Selling price	$3,590	$5,550	$7,150	$8,400	$9,200	$38,902,500
Costs:						
Material	$2,000	$2,400	$3,350	$4,100	$4,200	$18,612,500
Labor	250	260	320	380	390	2,039,000
LOH	300	360	250	500	540	2,529,500
MOH	150	160	320	650	700	1,640,000
Other	200	250	350	450	460	1,930,500
Total cost	$2,900	$3,430	$4,590	$6,080	$6,290	$26,751,500
Gross margin	$690	$2,120	$2,560	$2,320	$2,910	$12,151,000
Percent	19.22%	38.20%	35.80%	27.62%	31.63%	31.23%

LOH = Labor Overhead
MOH = Materials Overhead

Tektronix: Portable Instruments Division (B)

Cycle time became an issue as we began to drive inventory down. It became obvious in a return-on-assets environment that reducing cycle time and hence inventory takes the pressure off pricing. So we have a real push on reducing inventories and assets. Cycle time is a limit beyond which you cannot go however efficient you become. If a product is not designed for expeditious cycle time, you cannot get away from processing time that is designed into the product. If you can't reduce processing time, you will always have more inventory in the system than desired.

Cycle time burden, where longer cycle time products have higher reported costs, should cause an organization to focus on reducing the factors that cause cycle time to be long. Very low cycle times are beneficial because, to get them, everything has to be right: the people, the components and the purchased parts. To get to really low cycle time, you have to be a world-class manufacturer.

BRUCE ANDERSON, DIVISION CONTROLLER

PHASE 2 CYCLE TIME BURDENING

After the material burdening system had been running successfully for over a year, management felt it was time to review the design of the product costing system. About half of the manufacturing overhead was still allocated using direct labor, and the principal concern was to find an alternative allocation method for this large pool of cost.

A second special product costing study was

conducted in the summer of 1987 to identify the allocation measure that would replace direct labor. At the time of the study, PID allocated process-related overhead—manufacturing overhead not allocated using material burdening—using frozen standard labor hours (FSH). Historically, it was believed that direct labor had been a critical manufacturing resource, and FSH had thus been a good indicator of effort. In the current manufacturing

This case was prepared by Professor Robin Cooper, Harvard University, and Professor Peter B. B. Turney, Portland State University.

process, however, the direct labor content had shrunk to approximately 3.5% of total product cost. At this low level, it was unlikely that direct labor was still a good indicator of effort.

Due to the introduction of JIT and the simplifications in the accounting measurements, it also became increasingly difficult to use FSH as a basis for allocating overhead. Since labor reporting had been discontinued, FSH were estimated for a product when it was introduced and remained constant over the life of that product; that is, FSH were not updated for changes in the design of the product or the process. FSH represented an ideal quantity of direct labor and did not reflect factors such as quality differences that would affect the amount of direct labor used by each product. Consequently, FSH failed to measure accurately the direct labor consumed by each product, and this inaccuracy increased across the life of the product.

The conclusion of the cycle time study team was that cycle time—the total time required to produce an instrument—was the preferred allocation measure. A report prepared on completion of the product costing study summarized the appeal of cycle time.

> Cycle time costing is based on the theory that the cost of a product is related to the time required to produce it. Thus, attention will be focused on decreasing process time and WIP through increased manufacturing efficiency and quality. Cycle time costing should be implemented in the PID Division as an alternative to direct labor in allocating conversion costs. This measure is more relevant to the current manufacturing environment and is a more accurate reflector of cost.[1]

Cycle time was defined as the total process (manufacturing) time required to produce an instrument. This was the elapsed time from the beginning of main board build to the end of packaging when the instrument was moved into the finished goods inventory (Exhibit 1). This time frame encompassed all the process-related overhead that would be allocated using cycle time.

Process overhead included depreciation on equipment, indirect labor (including manufacturing managers and manufacturing engineering dedicated to process support), direct labor and payroll load,

---

[1]"Management Cost Project, Final Report" (Paul R. Oldhouse).

and property, maintenance, utilities, and floor space associated with manufacturing. Process overhead was divided into several cost pools, one for each distinct manufacturing process or product line.

Cycle times were measured at PID by recording the time and date on a "cal" (calibration) card which accompanied the instrument through the manufacturing process. After the product was packaged, the time and date were again recorded. The cycle time was computed based on manufacturing hours per day (eight hours per shift) in each product line. Nonmanufacturing time, such as weekends, was not included in cycle time. Cycle time was monitored over a number of days, and then an average was computed for each instrument type.

In the future, cycle time could be measured automatically using bar coding. Bar coding enabled cycle time to be recorded and tracked continuously. Product costs calculated using bar codes would be more accurate; they would be based on the most recent cycle time information. In addition, manufacturing would be able to monitor cycle time more closely and appreciate the variability of the production process.

The cost of bar coding was quite low. Terminals and readers (wands) were already in place at the end of the process in finished goods, and additional hardware would only be needed at the beginning of each line. Only one reader would be needed for the 2400 Series line, and the cost of programming to record the time and date automatically was low.

It was hoped that management would accept the cycle time concept. Management interviews revealed a widespread belief that cost was related to the time required to produce an instrument. Management also felt that cycle time was closely related to the level of WIP inventory, quality, flexibility, and customer service. These beliefs were reflected by the use of cycle time as a key measure of manufacturing performance.

The study team identified a number of advantages and disadvantages of using cycle time as an allocation measure.

1. Cycle time was a broader measure of cost consumption than FSH. FSH included only the time of direct labor, whereas cycle time also included machine time and the time required for non-value-added activities such as test time and queuing time. Cycle time was also updated every six months and

thus would reflect changes in the manufacturing process and in the design of the product. FSH were set when a product was introduced and not changed over the life of the product.

2. Cycle time was considered to be a good indicator of cost and effort in PID's continuous process-type manufacturing environment in which relatively homogeneous products underwent similar steps in production. The study team confirmed this by studying the relationship between cycle time and the cost of each of the following constituents of process overhead:

> a. *Indirect labor.* Manufacturing managers and process engineers reported that they spent more time with products that had long cycle times.
> b. *Payroll load and paid-not-worked.* Direct labor time was a component of cycle time, so it made sense to allocate labor-related overhead on the basis of cycle time.
> c. *Depreciation.* The study showed that instruments with longer cycle time spent more time on depreciable equipment such as test equipment.
> d. *Property, maintenance, utilities, supplies.* An instrument with longer cycle time spent more time on the production floor. It was assumed that property, maintenance, utilities, and supplies were consumed proportionately to the time the instrument spent on the floor.
> e. *Direct labor.* Direct labor was a component of cycle time, so cycle time was a good measure of the incurrence of this cost. Also, in JIT production, the line people performed tasks not traditionally included in direct labor, such as the rework of defective products, troubleshooting, and repairing equipment. Cycle time captured this nontraditional component of direct labor time.

The disadvantages of using cycle time were as follows:

1. Cycle time (as defined) failed to capture direct labor time spent on a parallel process. In the presence of a parallel process, the cycle time measurement might fail to reflect all the resources consumed in the manufacturing process. Parallel processes, however, typically used little direct labor, space, or other resources. They also improved the flexibility of production.

2. Cycle time was difficult to measure on low-volume products. There was considerable variability in cycle time from one instrument to another, so it was desirable to have a sufficient number of observations to calculate a reliable average cycle time (Exhibit 2). This issue would be less important, however, when bar coding was introduced.

3. The calculated cycle times (Exhibit 3) did not include time spent in the thermal environmental chamber, which was considered a necessary process to ensure quality. Including this time in cycle time might encourage managers to reduce the time spent in the cycle chamber, which would increase the risk of shipping defective units to the customer. All instruments, however, were required to spend the same amount of time in the thermal chamber, so the omission of chamber cycle time had no impact on the absolute time differences between product types.

COMPUTING PRODUCT COSTS

The process overhead for each instrument was computed using the formula given in Exhibit 4. The calculation resulted in lower costs for instruments that had shorter cycle times (Exhibit 5). An analysis of these cycle times revealed that instruments with additional options, and instruments with quality problems, had higher cycle times.

EXPECTED BENEFITS

Other reasons were given to support the use of cycle time. These included the following:

- *Quality.* Cycle time included test, rework, troubleshooting, and repair time. Instruments with quality problems spent more time in each of these functions, so cycle time would capture quality-related cost differences between products. This was an important benefit because quality played an important role in the success of PID's products.
- *Capacity.* As cycle time was driven down, capacity increased. This reduced capacity cost, or made resources available for use elsewhere.
- *Work in process.* WIP decreased as cycle time was reduced. Reduced WIP increased manufacturing efficiency and flexibility.
- *Manufacturing complexity.* Instruments requiring a more complex manufacturing process had longer cycle times. It was expected that a focus on cycle time would encourage design engineering to improve the manufacturability of products.
- *Mixed model lines.* It was believed that cycle time would encourage mixed model lines for similar products. Such product line flexibility was a lot less expensive than maintaining separate product lines for each product.

In late summer 1987, the team completed its project and presented its findings to management. Senior management now faced the decision of whether to introduce cycle time costing.

EXHIBIT 1

TEKTRONIX: PORTABLE INSTRUMENTS DIVISION (B)
Manufacturing Cycle Time

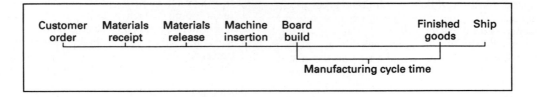

EXHIBIT 2

TEKTRONIX: PORTABLE INSTRUMENTS DIVISION (B)
Measured Cycle Times

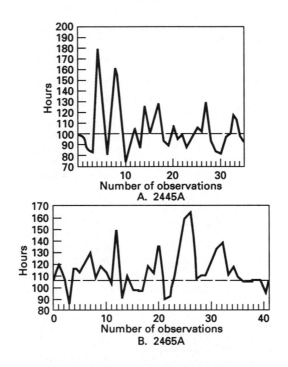

A. 2445A

B. 2465A

EXHIBIT 3

TEKTRONIX: PORTABLE INSTRUMENTS DIVISION (B)
Average Cycle Times (hrs)

Model	A	B	C	D	E	TOTAL
Cycle Time Hours (Average)	100	105	110	125	130	106

EXHIBIT 4

TEKTRONIX: PORTABLE INSTRUMENTS DIVISION (B)
Calculation of Product Cost
Using Cycle Time Allocation

$$CT/unit \times vol = cycle\ units\ (cu)$$

$$\$\ pool/total\ cu = \$/cycle$$

$$\$/cycle \times cu\ per\ instrument\ type = \$/instrument$$

$$\$/instrument/vol = \$/unit$$

EXHIBIT 5

TEKTRONIX: PORTABLE INSTRUMENTS DIVISION (B)
Overhead Cycle Time/Cost Computation
(Example)

---

product line conversion cost
(direct labor plus conversion overhead) $5,000,000

product line cycle units 975,000
$ per cycle unit = $5,000,000/975,000 = $5.13

Short Cycle Time Instrument

average cycle time = 100 hours
volume = 3,000 units
instrument cycle units = 100 × 3,000 = 300,000
total instrument conversion cost = $5.13 × 300,000 = $1,538,461
conversion cost per unit = $1,538,461/3,000 = $513

Long Cycle Time Instrument

average cycle time = 200 hours
volume = 500 units
instrument cycle units = 200 × 500 = 100,000
total instrument conversion cost = $5.13 × 100,000 = $513,070
conversion cost per unit = $513,000/500 = $1,026

Hewlett-Packard: Roseville Networks Division

We want our designers to use as many common parts as possible and we want those parts to come from the minimum number of vendors. In addition, we want the designers to design printed circuit boards so that as many components as possible can be auto-inserted. This means they must not put parts either too close together or too close to the edges of the board.

However, to maintain competitiveness we must allow the designers to take advantage of new technologies. For example, four or five conventional common parts might be replaced by a single integrated circuit (IC) that costs less and is more reliable. Sometimes, we want the designers to use new technologies even when they are unique parts that cannot be autoinserted.

We want our cost system to provide the designer with the appropriate economic information to make the necessary tradeoff between common/autoinsertable parts and new technologies.

TIM HASTRUP, ENGINEERING PROJECT MANAGER

INTRODUCTION

Hewlett-Packard (HP) produced computing and electronic measurement equipment for the electronics, telecommunications, aerospace, aircraft, automotive, and scientific research industries. In 1988 the company had sales of approximately $10 billion and employed 86,000 people worldwide.

The Roseville Networks Division (RND) was one of four Hewlett-Packard divisions that designed and marketed networking products and one of two divisions that also manufactured these products. In 1988, networking products accounted for several hundred million in sales, about two-thirds of which were produced by RND.

PRODUCTS

RND's products were actually a combination of boards and connector cables—circuit boards and connector cables that networked or connected computers to each other and to peripheral devices such as terminals. Boards were used, for example, to connect a terminal to a minicomputer, to connect a personal computer such as Hewlett-Packard's Vectra to a local area network (LAN), or to connect a LAN to a data center or to a global communications network. Networking boards were also used to connect noncomputer devices, such as medical instruments, to a computer. In total, RND produced several hundred boards for different end products. Many of these boards were produced in low volumes. On average, there were two end products for

every board. A typical end product consisted of a board, a cable, and a manual. Networking products had very short lives, and these lives were getting shorter every year. By 1988 the average RND product was under two years old. In addition, the number of different products produced was proliferating as the need for communications increased. Consequently, in 1987, to maintain an up-to-date product offering, RND introduced a new product, on average, every month and implemented a production change to existing products on average every day.

PRODUCTION PROCESS

The production process consisted of attaching electronic components to the circuit boards. The main production steps to produce a board were as follows:

- *Start station.* Boards were loaded manually into titanium fixtures in the starter station according to the production schedule. A bar code identifying each board was attached to the carrier, and the carrier was forwarded to the automatic insertion machines.
- *Automatic insertion.* Automatic insertion required three different types of machines each designed to insert a different class of component. DIP inserters were used for Dual Inline Package integrated circuits, (i.e., the leads were in two parallel lines), axial insertion for axial (i.e., the leads and the component were in a straight line), and radial insertion for radial (i.e., the leads formed a circle below the component) components.

This case was prepared by Professor Robin Cooper and Professor Peter B. B. Turney, Portland State University. Copyright© 1989 by the President and Fellows of Harvard College. Harvard Business School case 189-117.

There were four DIP inserters. These were used in serial fashion, each board moving from one machine to the next. The serial layout had been adopted to eliminate the setup costs associated with changing the components in the DIP magazines. To allow this layout to function given the very high number of automatically insertable components in the products, the engineers had designed special high-volume carousels to increase the number of slots (feeder tubes to hold magazines of distinct components). This in-line layout coupled to the additional slots in the carousel enabled 588 different components to be inserted without a part setup.

There was one axial inserter which was used to insert axial components. These were supplied to the axial inserter in the form of a tape created by a sequencer. Again, due to the high number of automatically insertable axial components, the engineers had extended the sequencer so that it could create tapes containing most of the required axial components. The sequencer tape was fed directly to the axial inserter.

The radial inserter was a recent acquisition. This machine inserted radial components from magazines. Prior to its purchase, few radial components were used in the division's products, and these were manually inserted. Currently, the number of different radial components automatically inserted was sufficiently small that they could all be loaded into the machine at once.

- *Manual insertion.* Components that could not be inserted using insertion machines, or whose volume was too low to justify using automatic insertion, were inserted using semiautomatic Royonics machines. The titanium carrier was placed on the Royonics machine, and the bar code on the carrier was scanned using a wand. Software in the Royonics machine presented and identified the appropriate components for insertion and illuminated the holes where the components were to be inserted. The Royonics machine was connected to an automatic storage unit, called a Paternoster, which contained about 1,000 bins of components. The bins were rotated automatically until the bin containing the required components was accessible.
- *Wave solder.* After manual insertion, the boards were placed in a wave solder machine. The wave solder machine automatically fluxed, heated, soldered, and then cooled the boards. The boards moved directly into a washing machine where they were washed to remove any residual flux and dried. Once soldered and washed, the boards were placed on an automatic conveyer that delivered them to the Final Assembly area.
- *Final assembly.* Parts that would be damaged by the soldering or washing process, were too large for the

automatic insertion equipment, or required field replacement were manually inserted in Final Assembly.
- *Board test.* The boards were functionally tested using a number of standard tests in the Performance Verification and Defect Analysis departments. The amount of time required for testing varied considerably from board to board, with the total testing time varying from one hour to 10 hours. Boards that failed the functional tests were repaired prior to forwarding to the packaging department.
- *Packaging.* In the Kitting and Shipping department, boards were combined with required cables and manuals and packed in boxes for shipment. About 1,000 boxes were shipped each work day.

COST DRIVER ACCOUNTING

In 1984, the cost accounting system at RND was a facility-wide direct-labor-dollar-based system. The move to automation over the years had significantly reduced the direct labor content of the products. For example, in the three-year period from 1978 to 1981, the direct labor content alone had fallen from 6% to 3% of total production costs, and by 1988 the ratio had fallen below 1%. This low labor content created overhead burden rates that were over 400%. As the rate climbed, management began to question the validity of the product costs reported by their cost system and the behavioral effects that the cost system was having on the design process.

As an augmentation to the standard cost system, product engineering had developed the MAKE (manufacturing knowledge expert) model. This model had the ability to identify alternative components and make recommendations about how to reduce the cost of the design. Embedded in the MAKE model was a cost estimation model that differed significantly from the division's traditional cost system. It was this model that triggered the design of the new cost system. As Debbie Berlant, Manager of Cost Accounting, said,

When we discovered that the engineers were using a different definition of product costs to make their design decisions, we knew we were in trouble and had to change our existing cost system. Finance decided that whatever the designers needed we would give them. The MAKE model was actually an off-line cost system. It came in useful in the design process because we could model the effect of the changes we were making without changing the official cost system. Consequently, the MAKE model tended to be one generation ahead of the cost system.

The new cost system that was developed from the MAKE model was known as cost driver accounting (CDA) at RND. John DeLury, Controller, commented on the objective of CDA.

> The purpose of cost driver accounting was not to prevent the engineers from introducing new costly technology. Rather it was to get the engineers to think about cost, and not to go for elegance every time. Cost driver accounting put product costs on the backs of the engineers. It encouraged them to design for manufacturability as well as functionality.

COST SYSTEM REDESIGN

The first modification to the official cost system was implemented in the first half of 1985. The factory was broken into five cost centers—automatic insertion, manual insertion, final assembly, product verification, and defect analysis. In the two insertion and final assembly departments, direct labor costs were traced to the products using the number of insertions. The direct labor cost per insertion was calculated by dividing the budgeted direct labor dollars for the coming six months by the budgeted number of insertions for the period. The number of tests performed was the basis used to trace costs in the other two departments. The direct labor cost per test was calculated for the next six months by dividing the budgeted direct labor dollars by the budgeted number of tests.

The facility-wide overhead was then allocated on the basis of budgeted direct labor dollars to give a full cost of each insertion or test. The overhead rate was about 400%, so the full cost of each insertion and test was about five times the direct labor cost.

The second modification was implemented six months later in the second half of 1985. The overhead was split into two parts, one relating to production and the other to procurement. Procurement costs included the cost of purchasing, storage, product logistics, document specifications, planning, and material engineering. All other costs were viewed as production costs. The procurement overhead costs were traced to the products using the number of parts that the product contained. The production overhead costs were traced as before.

In the first half of 1986, the system was again modified. Production overhead was traced to each major production area. This allowed five production

department overhead rates to be calculated—one for each cost center. In addition, direct labor was now treated as an overhead item. Labor vouchering was discontinued except for nonproductive activities such as building prototypes and performing rework.

Production overhead costs were traced to the product using the number of insertions and the number of test hours. The number of insertions was used in the two insertion and the final assembly departments. The number of test hours was used in the product verification and defect analysis departments.

The move to test hours reflected the design team's discomfort with the original choice of number of tests. This was because some boards required tests that were a lot longer than the tests on other boards and consumed more resources. Consequently, number of test hours was considered to be more accurate.

In the second half of 1986 the automatic insertion department was split into three separate centers—start station (this is where the boards were placed in the titanium carriers and their bar code identification attached), axial insertion (where the axial components were inserted), and DIP insertion (where the dual in-line package integrated circuits were inserted).[1]

These changes were made at the insistence of engineering. One of the engineers had designed a board that contained a lot of axial components but few DIPs. The cost system generated a product cost that the engineer felt was out of line with reality. His analysis of the situation suggested that it was much cheaper to undertake axial insertion than DIP insertion. The accounting department's analysis supported this contention, and the system was correspondingly modified.

The cost of the start station was traced to the products using the number of assemblies (boards), as the activities in this area were driven by the number of boards. Each board had to be inserted in the carrier and bar coded. The costs of the axial and DIP insertion operations were then traced to the products using the number of insertions in each area.

A second modification was also introduced at

---

[1]The radial inserter had not been acquired at this time.

this time. The final assembly department was split into two centers—wave soldering and final assembly. The cost of the wave soldering area was traced using the number of assemblies, since each assembly had to be wave soldered and the number of solder joints required (i.e., number of components) did not change the time or cost of soldering.

Finally, the cost of kitting and shipping (the packaging department) had historically been treated as a period cost. The cost driver approach suggested that these costs could be traced to the products using the number of assemblies. The number of assemblies was chosen because each assembly had to be kitted and packed and the size of the assembly did not have much effect on the resources required to kit and ship the product.

In the first half of 1987, the division changed the way the procurement costs were traced to the products. The procurement costs were split into two pools; one related to the number of assemblies and the other to the number of parts. The costs traced using the number of assemblies included production planning, product logistics, product specification, and marketing services (which was responsible for the scheduling activity). The costs traced using the number of parts included purchasing costs, parts storage costs, parts specification, and material planning.

In the first half of 1988, the costs of the final assembly area were split in two. The first area related to manual insertion. Here the parts that could not be wave soldered were inserted. These parts included large VLSI chips, sockets, edge connectors, and any heat-sensitive or bulky components. These costs were traced to the products using number of insertions.

The second area was manual solder, where hand-inserted components and jumper wires were hand soldered. Not all of the hand-inserted components had to be soldered. EPROMS, for example, were socketed so that they could be replaced in the field. Jumper wires were used to connect printed circuits together. They were viewed by most engineers as necessary evils that should be removed by redesigning the boards as quickly as possible. The costs of this area were traced to the products using the number of solder joints.

The final change made in the first half of 1988 was the introduction of a radial insertion area. This

was required by the purchase of a large radial inserter. The costs of this area were traced to the product using a cost-per-radial insertion.

In mid-1988 some potentially critical limitations in the design of the cost system were becoming apparent. In particular, the current system ignored the volume of usage of each component. Since some costs were incurred because the component was used irrespective of the volume used, the existing cost system overcosted high-volume products and undercosted low-volume ones.

The solution proposed for this problem was a volume-sensitive model. The proposed volume-sensitive model included changes in the costing of each production process. The cost of each process, including labor costs, would now be broken into three pools, each with a different cost driver. The first cost pool contained the costs of getting a board to the process. These costs were divided by the number of assemblies handled in each process to obtain a cost per assembly for each process. The second cost pool included the costs of inserting components into the board in each process. These costs were divided by the number of insertions to obtain a cost per insertion. The third cost pool contained the costs related to setting up the machines. These were the slot costs. This pool was divided by the number of different part numbers inserted to give a per-part-number cost. This part-number cost was divided by the number of components of each part number inserted to give a per-insertion charge. Under this approach, a low-volume component had a higher per-insertion cost than a high-volume one.

In the DIP insertion area, this new three-cost-pool approach significantly changed reported product costs. The part-number cost pool in this area contained the labor, equipment, and support costs associated with the carousels that had been installed on the DIP machines. This pool was divided by the number of slots available on the carousel to obtain a cost per slot. Each slot was dedicated to one part number, so the cost of a slot was assigned to each unique part carried in the carousel. The cost per slot was then divided by the semiannual volume of each part number to obtain the cost per part for that part number.

Fred Huang described why he recommended slot costing.

Slot costing has evolved as a joint project of engineering, manufacturing, and accounting, but I was the one who first suggested charging a rental fee for the use of a slot on the DIP machines. I was concerned that the overhead in the plant might go up because we were setting up new part numbers during the design of the boards. I felt that the slots had a special economic value, and I wanted the cost system to reflect this value.

Debbie Berlant described the likely impact of slot costing.

I believe that slot costing will have a major impact on decision making because it will tell us what it really costs to occupy a slot. In particular, I see slot costs affecting new product decisions such as making or buying a board and phase-out decisions to obsolete or continue making a board.

Tim Hastrup explained the relationship between the number of part numbers and the use of DIP machine capacity.

If we had fewer low-volume parts we would not need so many slots. This is important because our capacity is not limited by insertion capacity but by the number of part numbers we can handle. When we buy a machine today we buy it to increase the number of part numbers we can handle, not to increase the number of insertions we can perform.
Currently we have four DIP machines arranged sequentially. The purpose of this sequential arrangement is to increase the number of part numbers that are available for insertion into a particular board. If each machine has 200 slots, then our total part number capacity per board is 800.
If we halved the number of part numbers, we could convert from a single four-DIP machine line to two parallel two-machine lines. This would significantly increase our insertion capacity. Currently all boards must go through all four machines even if a particular machine contains no components for that board, so converting to two parallel lines would permit us to keep the machines busier. Idle time would also be less because boards would no longer be sitting in queues waiting for machines they do not use. Setup time would also be somewhat reduced.

THE DESIGNERS

The way the designers interacted with the cost accounting and the MAKE model was to develop a series of heuristic design rules that allowed them to make design tradeoffs. The experienced engineer had developed many such rules. Fred Huang, Product Developer, described the type of rules that he used.

1. Manual insertion was three times as expensive as automatic insertion.
2. Introducing a new part into the HP parts list cost the firm $25,000.
3. Introducing a new part to RND that was already on the HP parts list cost the division about $5,000.
4. Connectors that could not go through the wave solder machine and had to be manually inserted, or needed special presolder treatment, added $2 to $3 to the overhead cost of the board.
5. Reliability was critical, and selecting components that had high reliability was better than selecting components that did not. This rule favored using preferred vendors and parts whose breakdown rates and safety margins were known. Each breakdown in the field cost at least $1,000.
6. Time to market was critical, and selecting components that were still under development was risky. If a component was selected that was very new and the production capacity was yet to be established, there was a risk that the component would not be ready when it was required. Using a new component cost between $1,000 and $100,000 per component depending on the risk of nonavailability.
7. Ease of availability was similarly critical. Selecting a component that had excess production capacity in the industry and could be supplied by multiple vendors reduced the risk of component shortages. The rule of thumb used to adjust for availability was that a low-availability component had an additional cost of 10 times its material cost.
8. Using existing designs was sensible. If an existing function or circuit could be used, this was better than starting afresh. Designing a new function or circuit cost from $10,000 (one month of engineering time) for a small project to $30,000 (three months of engineering time) for a large project. In addition, the delay in time to market added 10 times the out-of-pocket cost. The additional cost for a large project was therefore $300,000.

Once designers had developed these heuristics, they did not have to keep going back to the cost system for cost information. However, every time a new cost driver was implemented, the designers would study the effect on the economics of production and adjust their design rules accordingly.

For example, if the cost system said a product cost $100 before the new driver was introduced and $150 afterwards, the designers would ensure that they knew why the change in reported product costs had occurred. The engineers considered understanding the reasons behind the shift in product costs important because the complex mix of products meant that every time a new cost driver was introduced reported product costs of at least some products changed dramatically.

Huang described his use of reported product costs in the design process.

> I do not design to minimize the reported cost of the product, as this will change across time with the introduction of new cost drivers. Instead, I design what I think is the lowest cost product for a given level of reliability and functionality. It is important not to design to minimize the MAKE model cost because the model does not capture all of the relevant costs.
>
> We could improve the model to capture more costs, but we would risk it becoming too complex to understand and hence use. This is especially true for new college hires. They have never been taught to design with cost in mind. If we give them the MAKE model and say, "go for it", they cannot cope. It is better to give them a few rules at a time and slowly bring them up to speed.

The risk of designing to minimize reported product costs surfaced early on in the development of the cost system. An engineer designed a product to minimize reported product costs and was considered by some a hero. That was until the next change in the MAKE model was introduced. That change caused the reported product cost to go through the roof. The old model showed that automatic insertion cost one-tenth of manual insertion, whereas the new model showed it cost one-third.

The engineers saw both benefits and drawbacks to the MAKE model and hence cost driver cost system. In particular, they saw four major benefits and three major drawbacks. The benefits identified were as follows:

> 1. All engineers could use the same numbers to justify their designs. With the MAKE model supplying the cost information, everyone used the same heuristic rules to assess design tradeoffs.
> 2. The MAKE model provided a useful training tool to help establish the economic design heuristics and to sensitize the engineers to the cost of their design choices.
> 3. The MAKE model gave the engineers a good idea of what was really being spent on the products and

helped them understand trends in the economics of design.
> 4. Even though the MAKE model did not capture all of the design costs, it helped identify areas where redesign either of existing products or potential products was called for. For example, one product that contained a very high number of components was redesigned, and the annual savings on the redesign were estimated at $1 million, leading to a payback of under one month.

The drawbacks identified were as follows:

> 1. There was a tendency on the part of some engineers to use MAKE model data in ways that a broader perspective would not support. This tended to occur when some of the issues that needed to be taken into account were outside the MAKE model. For example, recently a new product was introduced based on the product costs reported by the MAKE model. These costs assumed a sales volume that more careful analysis would have suggested was unrealizable.
> 2. The cost system and the MAKE model were heavily reliant on accounting rules. The engineer did not believe that these rules were always appropriate.

Huang commented as follows:

> You need to understand the limitations of the MAKE model before you use it. I have learned to use it properly now, but it took a time. If you do not realize that it is an accounting, not a design, model you can make serious mistakes. It is designed to spread costs the best way possible, but that may not be the best way to report costs for design purposes and other important decisions.

Overall, the engineers were pleased with the cost driver accounting cost system and MAKE model. However, they had mixed feelings about the way the two were implemented. Kyle Black, Engineering Project Manager and Huang's boss, commented as follows:

> My initial reaction to the continuous changes in the cost system was anger. I felt it was unacceptable to have cost changes all the time. I wanted one set of numbers that I could rely on. My next reaction was frustration about how little anyone understood the economics of production. My next reaction was to accept the challenge and put it straight. We created a lot of tighter relationships between accounting, research and development, manufacturing, and marketing. We were all learning about the business. Now we are in the training mode. We have broken the back of the cost system design problem and are now refining it and our intuitions on the economics

of product design. Overall, the whole experience forced us [the engineers] to understand our design process. We lost the "not invented here" syndrome and started understanding the benefits of leverage —using existing designs.

I would have preferred one transition, but I do not believe it could have been done that way. Account-

ing simply did not understand enough about the production and design process. If we had attempted one transition, we would have risked freezing the firm on the first system we designed; we would not have changed it to reflect the new insights we gained from it.

Zytec Corporation (B)

In the U.S. we have not been emphasizing the right things in operations because we have been using the wrong measurements. The key to getting people to move in the direction of just-in-time manufacturing and total quality control is to change the measurement system. If we don't learn how to do this, eventually all of our manufacturing will be done in other countries.

The measurement system is important because people behave according to the way we measure them. Therefore, we must measure them according to the way we want them to behave. We want to increase the linearity of our production, reduce our cycle time, and increase our yields. Therefore, these are the measurements we should take.

GARY FLACK, VICE-PRESIDENT OF MANUFACTURING

INTRODUCTION

Zytec Corporation produced power supplies for a variety of electronic products such as medical equipment, telephone switching equipment, and hard disk drives. A power supply is a device that converts alternating current wall voltage into the low direct current voltage required by components such as the integrated circuits contained in electronics products. Zytec was formed in 1984 when three executives from Control Data Corporation (CDC) purchased the Power Supplies Operation of Magnetic Peripherals, a subsidiary of CDC. They acquired the division via a leveraged buyout.

Zytec was a relatively small player in the highly fragmented U.S. power supply market in which there were over 400 U.S. and offshore companies competing for a $4 billion market for power supplies rated between 250 and 1,500 watts. Zytec had just over 1% of the overall market and was only one-third the size of its largest competitor. Its sales of about $60 million ranked it number 6.

Zytec manufactured primarily high-volume complex power supplies for large electronics compa-

nies. In 1989 Zytec expected to manufacture about 50 different products for 15 different customers. Two of these products were expected to account for about 40% of total sales and two customers for about 60% of sales.

PRODUCTS

Zytec's business consisted of five major business lines.

- *Imprimis:* This was the major business line at the time the firm was purchased. Its sales increased to $66 million in 1984 but, as anticipated, soon began to decrease. In 1989, sales were expected to be about $8 million. This line was still considered to be profitable by management.
- *Black box:* These were power supplies designed by Zytec engineers. Design work was undertaken in Eden Prairie. Sales of black boxes in 1989 were expected to be about $15 million. Management believed that they were still losing money on the black box line.
- *White box:* These were power supplies designed by the customer. They were similar in function and appearance to black boxes. Some white boxes were partially

This case was prepared by Professor Robin Cooper and Professor Peter B. B. Turney, Portland State University. Copyright © 1990 by the President and Fellows of Harvard College. Harvard Business School case 190-066.

designed by Zytec engineers. These were called grey boxes. Sales of white boxes in 1989 were expected to be $24 million. Management felt that this product line was reasonably profitable.

- *Spares:* These were replacement power supplies or circuit boards for products Zytec no longer produced. Sales in 1989 were expected to be $2 million. Management considered this business to be quite profitable.
- *Repair center:* The repair center repaired other manufacturers' products as well as their own. Its 1989 volume was expected to be $3 million. The repair center was considered the most profitable of Zytec business lines.

PRODUCTION PROCESS

Zytec's production process consisted of eight product cells, each designed to manufacture a different type of product. Some product cells were dedicated to a single product, while others were used to manufacture many different types of products. The production process for the typical power supply consisted of the following major steps:

- *Board preparation:* The printed circuit boards were purchased primarily from a Minnesota supplier. When necessary, they were prepared before moving to autoinsertion. Preparation could take many forms, including masking areas of the board so that they would not be soldered by the wave solder machine, and adding hardware such as stakes.
- *Insertion:* Axial components were automatically inserted after they were sequenced. Sequencing consisted of creating a tape of the axial components in the order in which they were to be inserted. Integrated circuits were inserted semiautomatically. Large components that could not be automatically inserted were manually inserted.
- *Wave solder:* Once the boards were inserted, they were wave soldered. Wave soldering consisted of fluxing, soldering, washing, and drying the board.
- *Secondary insertion:* Components that could not be wave soldered were hand soldered. These included magnetic components, such as transformers, and other heat- or water-sensitive devices.
- *In-circuit testing:* The fully inserted boards were in-circuit tested. This testing exercised every component and determined automatically whether they were meeting specifications.
- *Lead attachment:* In this step, the leads were attached. The leads connected different circuit boards together and were prepared in a parallel operation to the main production process.
- *Assembly:* The circuit boards were assembled into the

sheet metal container. These containers were purchased from a local supplier.
- *Vibration test:* The assembled power supply was vibration tested.
- *Burn-in:* The typical power supply was run fully loaded for 20 to 24 hours at relatively high temperatures (40 to 65° C). Some simple power supplies only required 10 to 12 hours of burn-in.
- *Final test:* The power supply was subjected to a full final test. As much of this testing as possible was automated. Once the final test was completed the products were packaged on the line and sent to the shipping department.

CONTINUOUS IMPROVEMENT PROGRAM

In the first year after the acquisition, sales volume increased rapidly. However, in the third quarter of the second year, sales volume fell dramatically. This decrease was due to the entry of the foreign competition into the disk drive market. The competition introduced a higher-quality product at reduced price. As sales of U.S.-manufactured drives fell dramatically, the market for Zytec products also decreased. Third quarter 1985 sales were 40% of the previous quarter. Zytec management reacted quickly to the downturn.

Zytec's initial response to the downturn in sales was to shut the plant down for six weeks, calling people back to work as needed. In addition, everyone in the firm accepted a reduction in pay. Its second response was to begin an ambitious program to improve its overall production efficiency. Zytec introduced just-in-time (JIT) production techniques; their total quality commitment was increased; and people involvement was introduced. Significant implementation of JIT began in March 1985, and by late 1986, the majority of the production process was operating under JIT.

One outcome of this transition was a rapid decrease in work-in-process inventory levels during June, July, and August 1986 as average cycle times fell 78.5%. Overall, inventories fell from about $17 million to about $6 million in 1985 and 1986. This reduction provided the cash flow to fund the losses of the next few years. Without this cash flow, the firm would not have survived.

A total quality commitment program was initiated in 1984. This program also yielded impressive improvements. For example, the "plug and play performance," the percentage of Zytec products that provide trouble-free performance on customer receipt, increased from the low 90s to 99.5%. In 1987, the quality program was extended to include manufacturing process yields, the percentage of product produced that required no manufacturing rework. The 1988 manufacturing process yield target was 90%.

An Implemented Improvement System (IIS) was introduced in 1987. IIS was modeled on an approach developed in Japan. It placed the responsibility of making any improvements on the person making the suggestion. This was consistent with the people involvement portion of Zytec's continuous improvement program. It instilled a belief in the operators on the line that they had the ability to improve the process themselves. It generated far more improvements than the suggestion box approach.

Finally, Zytec introduced Management by Planning (MBP) in 1988. MBP was modeled after a system developed in Japan as a means of encouraging employee involvement under IIS. Management defined the overall mission of the firm, and the employees developed their own improvement targets consistent with that mission.

As part of the MBP system, management identified six objectives that were believed to be critical to the success of the firm.

1. Improve total quality commitment.
2. Reduce total cycle time.
3. Improve Zytec's service to customers.
4. Improve profitability and financial stability.
5. Improve housekeeping and safety.
6. Increase employee involvement.[1]

All departments were expected to identify improvement targets for these six objectives. For example, the automatic insertion area might identify its total quality commitment and cycle time targets as "improve yields 2% and reduce average cycle times 5% in 1989."

The continuous improvement program was extremely successful. Overhead was significantly reduced. For example, in a four-year period one product's reported cost fell from $530 to $325.

However, management still believed that further improvements were possible.

UPDATING THE COST SYSTEM

In late 1986 accounting turned its attention to the cost system. Management already knew that the existing system required excessive direct labor and inventory transaction measurements. Over the last five years, direct labor as a percent of total cost had been falling and was expected in the next three years to fall to 7%. However, the cost system still measured direct labor as if it were a significant cost element. Similarly, the system had not been modified to adapt to the reduction in work-in-process inventory. By 1986, the move to JIT had reduced work-in-process inventory to such an extent that visual control and physical counts were considered more appropriate.

The existing system allocated overhead to products using two allocation bases: direct labor dollars and material dollars. About half of the overhead was traced using each allocation base. The production process was broken down into a number of cost centers, and a separate labor burden rate was calculated for each center. A single material burden rate was calculated by dividing total material-related overhead by total material cost. Management was uncomfortable with direct labor allocation for two reasons. First, they did not feel that direct labor was an appropriate allocation base for manufacturing overhead. In particular, on the multi-product production lines, the labor force could easily work on many different products in the same shift. This made it difficult to measure accurately the direct labor content of the products. Second, the increasing levels of automation made direct labor content a poor predictor of the overhead consumed by the products.

Management was uncomfortable with material dollar allocation because some products had high material content while others had relatively little. The material burdening system allocated more of the cost of warehousing, material handling, and purchasing to the high material content products. However, management did not believe that these products necessarily consumed more of the overhead.

The team assigned to redesign the cost system

---

[1]The employee involvement program was established in 1987 to assist employees in understanding Zytec corporate culture and commitment to continuous improvement.

was told to design a system that reinforced the continuous improvement program. After analyzing the six objectives, the design team identified the following potential cost drivers:

- *Linearity:* Linearity measured the average absolute deviation of actual production to the daily production plan. For example, if the planned output is 10 units and the actual output is either 12 or 8 units, the daily linearity is said to be 80%.[2] Linearity was considered important because management believed that the higher the average linearity the lower overall cost would become.

- *Cycle time:* Cycle time measured the average time taken by a product to go from raw material to finished goods. Cycle time was considered important because reducing cycle time could only be achieved by improving the yield to reduce rework and by improving the just-in-time performance of the plant.

- *Supplier lead-time:* Supplier lead-time measured the average time taken by a supplier to deliver an order. In 1989, the overall average supplier lead-time was 74 days. This lead-time had remained relatively unchanged for several years. Supplier lead-time was considered a cost driver because the longer a supplier took to deliver an order, the more raw material and purchased part inventory had to be held.

- *Yield:* Yield measured the average number of pieces that did not have to be reworked. Yield was considered a cost driver because of the high cost associated with rework and the disturbance it caused on the factory floor.

Lynn Richter, Controller, explained the rationale behind the identification of the four drivers.

We wanted to pick a set of drivers that was meaningful to the people on the floor. We wanted these drivers to capture the essence of our drive for continuous improvement program. In particular, we were convinced that the cost system could become a potent tool for behavior modification. The only real limitation that we placed on ourselves was that the cost system could not require any special measurements. We simply did not have the administrative resources.

Linearity is measured for all products. Driving costs on linearity should help us reduce overall costs. Linearity is a measure of flow, and if the factory is flowing smoothly, cost should come down. You avoid the starting and stopping associated with nonlinear production and the relearning required to cope with nonlinearity.

However, linearity is a long-term cost driver. If you can become more linear, eventually your costs will go down. However, from month to month overall costs will not change simply because linearity has improved.

Cycle time is currently measured for the top 80% of production volume. We start the cycle time counter when the board preparation begins and switch it off after the part is packed on the line. Cycle time is an important driver because the only way to reduce cycle time to really low levels is to improve yields. Cycle time is an indirect measure of quality.

Using cycle time as a cost driver forces us to think why we have inventory sitting around and why we have unnecessary steps in the production process. It requires that we determine how much of cycle time is actually build time. If the cycle time is 100 hours and the product is worked on for three to four hours, then the product is sitting around on the factory floor for 96 to 97 hours. Even if we can't avoid the 24 hours required for burn-in, the product still spends an awful lot of time sitting around for no good reason. This ties up cash and increases overhead. We will get cost down if we move the products through the plant rapidly, and that's why we measure cycle time.

Supplier lead-time is only measured for high-volume components. We currently capture the lead-times for about 95% of material dollar purchases. Using supplier lead-time as a cost driver focuses attention on the financial and operational constraints created by our commitments to our suppliers. We have a legal and financial commitment from the time we order a component from a supplier to the time we receive a check from the customer. The major portion of this time is supplier lead-time. We have programs in place for managing accounts receivables, safety stock, and work in process, but not for supplier lead-time. Using supplier lead-time as a cost driver would fill this void. If we can reduce supplier lead-time, we can cut the cost and speed of responding to changing customer requirements.

Yield is measured by our total quality commitment program. Low yield means that we have to duplicate steps in production. In other words, if it doesn't work, you have to do it over and incur additional cost. In addition, this rework leads to lower linearity and a further increase in cost.

Gary Flack explained why he felt measuring linearity, cycle time, and yields would contribute to cost reduction at Zytec.

Linearity is a measure of the stability of the production process. Linearity—the "drum beat" of the JIT manufacturing—is the single most important measure of the health of the operation. If I had to focus on only one factor in JIT, it would be linearity.

---

[2]The absolute value of $(10 - 12)$ and $(10 - 8)$ is 2. The linearity is therefore 80%—$(10 - 2)/10$ stated as a percentage.

Achieving linearity has a beneficial impact on cost. If you eliminate the "hockey stick"—the tendency for production and shipments to ramp up at the end of the month—you eliminate the need for surge capacity. You also eliminate the quality problems associated with the rush at the end of the month. Linearity allows each person in production to focus on reducing cost on a daily basis. Linearity provides the opportunity to get the time down and to do things right the first time.

Cycle time is important because elapsed time has a major impact on quality and cost. You can't achieve high quality if inventory is sitting around. High quality translates into a reduction in cost associated with rework. Reduced time means less inventory and an improvement in efficiency.

Improving yields reduces the mass of production that has to go through the plant. If there are no failures, and work is done right the first time, there is a significant reduction in the effort required to produce the finished product. Reduced yields, however, create costs associated with the poor quality and increases the time required to get the product out the door.

The design team spent several weeks developing the equations to determine product costs using each of the drivers and preparing a presentation to management. The outcome of these presentations was the decision to introduce a two-driver-cost system that used supplier lead-time and cycle time to allocate costs to products. The costs associated with material burden in the existing system would be allocated using supplier lead-time, and those associated with manufacturing would be allocated using cycle time. In addition, reflecting the decision to cease measuring the labor content of their products, the team decided to allocate labor costs using cycle time.

Lynn Richter explained why the design team did not recommend using linearity and yields as cost drivers.

> We were unable to come up with formulae for linearity and yields that represented saleable correlations with cost. With cycle time and supplier lead-time, we were able to convince management in advance that these two factors correlated with cost. We had no confidence that we could similarly persuade management of a correlation between our measures of linearity and yields and cost.

> However, we didn't work hard on convincing management to accept linearity and yields as cost drivers. The plant manager at the time believed that the key issue was total lead-time and that other factors such as linearity and yields would inevitably show up when total lead-time was reduced. So we built the cost system around time. If Gary Flack had been there, we would probably have focused more heavily on linearity and yields.

> We did not want a cost system that manufacturing had to conform to. We wanted to build a system that fit manufacturing's need. They felt that total lead-time was most important, so we constructed a system based on this factor.

To help sell the new system to management, the team developed a simple example, The Sample Company, to demonstrate the calculations (Exhibit 1). Once management had accepted the proposed new system, it was installed. The existing system and the new system were run in parallel so that management could explore the differences in reported costs. During this test period, the existing system was used for all external purposes such as financial reporting and inventory valuation, but the new system was used for all internal purposes.

EXHIBIT 1

ZYTEC CORP. (B)

The Sample Company

A. CYCLE TIME PERFORMANCE

PRODUCT	CYCLE TIME IN DAYS	UNIT SHIPPED[*]
PS 101	1.0	2,000
PS 102	1.5	1,000
PS 201	6.0	50
PS 202	7.0	50
PS 301	4.0	100
PS 401	3.0	600
PS 402	2.0	400
PS 403	3.5	300
PS 404	4.5	500
PS 501	2.0	100
PS 601	3.5	200
PS 701	2.5	70
PS 801	7.0	50
		11,875

[*]Assume units shipped is equal to units produced.

B. SUPPLIER LEAD-TIME PERFORMANCE[*]

PRODUCT	NUMBER OF PARTS	AVERAGE DAYS LEAD-TIME	TOTAL AVERAGE LEAD-TIME	QUANTITY SHIPPED	LEAD-TIME FACTOR	% FACTOR
PS 101	325	76	24,700	2,000	49,400,000	34.29
PS 102	370	71	26,450	1,000	26,450,000	18.36
PS 201	410	71	29,000	50	1,450,000	1.01
PS 202	405	71	28,700	50	1,435,000	1.00
PS 301	390	66	25,900	100	2,590,000	1.80
PS 401	885	59	52,400	600	31,440,000	21.82
PS 402	545	58	31,800	400	12,720,000	8.83
PS 403	220	54	11,900	300	3,570,000	2.48
PS 404	260	53	13,900	500	6,950,000	4.82
PS 501	370	59	21,800	100	2,180,000	1.51
PS 601	300	56	16,900	200	3,380,000	2.35
PS 701	525	55	28,800	70	2,016,000	1.40
PS 801	185	52	9,700	50	485,000	0.33
					144,066,000	100.00

[*]All figures rounded.

Hewlett-Packard:
Queensferry Telecommunications Division

We implemented cost driver accounting primarily to influence the manufacturability of our products. We wanted our engineers to understand the economic consequences of their design choices. We wanted to ensure that our products were both competitively priced and profitable.

JIM RIGBY, DIVISION CONTROLLER

Queensferry Telecommunications Division (QTD) was established in South Queensferry, Scotland, in 1965. Within the broader Hewlett-Packard organization structure, QTD was a part of the Microwave and Communications Group, which in turn was a part of the Test and Measurement Sector. QTD's main business was the design and manufacture of electronic test and measurement equipment for the international telecommunications industry. In 1990, QTD produced eight different product lines containing over 100 different products. These products were designed to monitor, measure, and find faults in telephone lines. In 1990, QTD employed approximately 640 people and was expected to generate revenues of about $100 million.

From the outset, QTD was committed to high quality and customer satisfaction. The emphasis on high quality encouraged a vertically integrated production structure, with the division doing much of the low-level fabrication activity (e.g., sheet metal work) in-house. The emphasis on customer satisfaction led to relatively long product life cycles and a commitment to support products long after they ceased to be produced.

During the 1980s, the telecommunications industry switched from analog to digital technology. This switch reduced product life cycles and accelerated the ongoing shift toward automated production. The switch also allowed several firms with digital circuit design experience to enter the telecommunications market.

THE COST DRIVER ACCOUNTING SYSTEM

Cost driver accounting (CDA) was initially developed by Hewlett-Packard (HP) at its Roseville Network Division in California. It had spread rapidly and voluntarily throughout the organization, and, by 1990, over half of HP's facilities had adopted CDA. The CDA project at QTD began in 1989, and the system was installed for fiscal year 1990, which ran from November to October.

At QTD, CDA was expected to provide the following benefits:

1. Encourage design for manufacturability.
2. Improve QTD's understanding of its true cost structure, thereby facilitating manufacturing cost reduction.
3. Encourage management to support Total Quality Control methodology and eliminate waste.
4. Provide improved information to monitor production performance.
5. Provide improved product cost information to support pricing and other strategic decisions.

The CDA was well received at QTD. As Harry McCarter, Production Supervisor, commented,

In the old days, the only way to reduce the cost of a product was to reduce its labor content. Material and engineering costs were designed into the products and were effectively fixed. Using CDA we can design products so that their material, engineering, and labor costs are minimized.

System Design

In CDA, allocation bases such as direct labor hours were replaced with cost drivers that both captured the underlying economics of manufacture and made it easier for product designers to understand those economics. The cost driver accounting system at QTD contained eight drivers, one for each of the seven major production processes and one for

This case was prepared by Professor Robin Cooper and Professor Kiran Verma of MIT.

materials procurement. The CDA system recognized three distinct processes in board assembly: automatic insertion, manual insertion prior to wave solder, and manual insertion post wave solder. Automatic insertion was performed for two types of components: integrated circuits, and axial components such as resistors and capacitors. Prior to wave soldering, components that could not be inserted automatically due to size or position on the board were inserted manually. In post wave solder, components that would be destroyed by the wave solder process were manually inserted. For all three board assembly processes, the number of insertions was used to drive costs to the products.

In the fourth production process, the wave soldered boards were tested automatically. The cost driver used to assign test costs to products was number of parts tested. This driver was selected because it captured the complexity of the testing process. An alternative driver, test hours, was not considered appropriate because the length of testing did not vary proportionately with the number of parts tested.

The loaded boards were assembled into completed products in the fifth production process. There were three assembly and test production units in which products were assembled and then tested. Different types of instruments were built in each unit depending on the technology used in the product line. One department assembled products just for British Telecom, while the other two assembled the remaining seven product lines. Because assembly was mostly a manual process, labor hours were used to assign assembly costs to products in these departments.

Instrument testing, the sixth process, was an integral part of assembly. Instruments were tested during assembly and on completion. Test hours were used to drive testing costs to the products. The assembly and test unit managers were dissatisfied with this driver for two reasons. First, some tests were automatic while others were manual. These two types of tests consumed different resources. Second, standard tests were designed to ensure that the instrument was operating properly, while special tests were designed to find the cause for an instrument to fail a standard test. The amount of standard testing was captured well by the number of test hours assigned to each instrument. But testing

was effectively random, and the CDA averaged the cost of special testing across all products. Management was still working on identifying better drivers for special testing.

The sheet metal for the cabinets was cut to size, shaped, and prepared in the fabrication department. This was the seventh production process recognized by the CDA. Fabrication was a process scheduled for outsourcing in the near future, and rather than spend time trying to identify a more appropriate drive, management decided to use direct labor hours to drive metal fabrication costs to products.

Procurement activities included purchasing, material handling, and storage. The costs of these activities were driven to the products using direct material costs. There was general dissatisfaction with this driver because procurement contained a number of distinct processes, each requiring a different driver. In the next six to nine months, management expected to complete a special study to determine additional drivers for the procurement process.

SETTING THE RATES

Cost driver rates were determined twice a year. Each department manager was interviewed to identify how much of the department budget related to each production process and hence driver. For example, as shown in Exhibit 1, out of a total budget of $751,800, the quality assurance manager expected to spend $4,000 on the autoinsert process. The total cost of each driver was determined by summing all department costs. This total cost was then divided by the budgeted total driver quantity to give the driver rate. For example, for the second half of fiscal 1990, the cost driver rate of $0.07 per automatic insertion (as per Exhibit 2) was obtained by dividing the total cost of automatic insertion of $248,100 (as per Exhibit 1) by the budgeted total driver quantity of 3,695,200 automatic insertions.

VARIANCE ANALYSIS

Rigby commented on the objectives of variance analysis at QTD.

> Variance analysis has always formed part of our management control process. Our departmental managers are experienced in determining the reasons behind spending, efficiency, and cost varianc-

es, and then utilizing this knowledge in future planning cycles. The ability to manage and control to planned levels has always been an integral measure of a manager's performance and ability at QTD.

Since installing cost-driver–based rates, all levels of management have a finer appreciation of the impact of operating at different levels of planned capacity. They now recognize the need to modify our cost structure according to activity levels or face the consequences, an erosion of margin.

I view the variance report as the beacon that highlights the issues needing explanation and action. We benefit by our ability to recognize, and react to, changes in cost, volume, and profit plans.

In both the U.S. and the U.K., generally accepted accounting principles required that the cost-of-goods-sold figures for financial accounting purposes reflect both the standard costs of manufacturing and any significant variances. Since the cost driver accounting system reported standard costs, variances were required for inventory valuation purposes. Variances were also used to help evaluate the monthly performance of department managers. For example, how well they managed spending was evaluated via departmental spending variances.

The process of evaluating the managers of the three assembly and test production units highlighted a shortcoming in the existing design of the cost driver accounting system, which treated the three units as if they were a single unit. Consequently, the variances were computed as if there was only one assembly and test area. The unit managers were unhappy with this approach because they felt that the cost structures of the three units were different and therefore each unit should be evaluated individually. This dissatisfaction caused accounting to determine separate rates for each of the three units. As the managers had suspected, the cost driver rates for the second half of 1990 turned out to be quite different (see Exhibit 3).

Unit B's rates were particularly high because it was currently introducing many new products. At present, these new products were being produced in low volumes but were expected to be produced in much higher volumes in the future. The current low production volumes led to high cost driver rates because Unit B was staffed with a full complement

of personnel even though it was producing below capacity.

A full complement of personnel was maintained because of HP's corporate policy against layoffs. As Rigby commented.

One of the challenges of our business is to manage the reduction in the direct labor force without having any forced redundancies. I am pleased to say that HP has never been forced to lay people off. This is an impressive achievement considering that the technology is moving at such a rate that demand for manufacturing people is literally decreasing daily. Our adoption of CDA has increased this tendency by demonstrating the financial advantages of choosing automatic over manual insertion.

Rigby strongly felt that the three assembly units should be treated as a single entity in the CDA.

I'm not at all keen to have three different sets of driver rates for assembly. Basically, because of the scale of the operation, we have split production into three separately managed units. However, it is the same basic process. Unit C benefits greatly from the injection that we get from the British Telecom Contract, so it has the lowest rates. Reporting three different sets of rates will create trouble. I do not want to have engineers telling me that they want their product, when it's launched, to be manufactured in units A, B, or C because the cost structure is inherently different. That's why I want to report only one set of driver rates.

Variance analysis was also performed for each of the eight cost driver processes identified by the cost driver accounting system. The following variances were calculated every month for each driver:

• The *spending variance* captured the difference between actual purchases and budgeted purchases for the month.
• The *volume variance* captured the difference between the actual quantity of cost driver units consumed in the month and the budgeted quantity calculated at the standard rate for that cost drive.

THE BRITISH TELECOM CONTRACT

In 1984, QTD bid aggressively for a major contract with British Telecom. This bid was for a new product that was significantly different from the other products produced at QTD. The British Telecom product consisted of printed circuit boards that were rack mounted and did not require any cabinets or special assembly. The request-for-bid was given to two companies with the expectation that they would share in the business if their quotes were competitive. Despite bidding aggressively by pricing the contract on an incremental basis, the QTD bid was higher than its competitors. Consequently, it was awarded only $3 million of the British Telecom business that year.

The original contract was thought to be a one-time deal. However, in subsequent years, British Telecom placed requests-for-bids every year to the two companies. The amount of work offered to each firm was based on the bid price and the reliability of delivery achieved in the prior year. In the last six years QTD had been awarded business ranging from $3 million to $12 million per year.

The ability to meet British Telecom's delivery requirements was a major consideration in being awarded the contract. Since QTD did not know for sure whether an order would be placed, how big the order was going to be, or when it would be placed, it was forced to budget for an anticipated level of activity that included an estimate of the size of the contract.

At the end of fiscal 1989, British Telecom placed an order with QTD for $13 million production in fiscal 1990. In the first quarter of fiscal 1990, however, Telecom postponed delivery of $8 million of its purchase until the last quarter of 1990. This postponement caused production levels in the first half of fiscal 1990 to drop below budgeted levels (see Exhibit 4). The second quarter was the worst hit, even though actual volume in the second quarter exceeded that of the first quarter. Rigby commented,

> When the production volumes dropped in the first half of the year, we began to encounter volume variances. These variances were not significant in the first quarter, but by the second quarter they were very high. In a perfect world, spending would drop to offset lower production volumes. However, in environments like ours where we retain our employees, it is almost impossible for spending to be cut back when volume drops in a period.

The total volume variance for the first quarter was $43,000 unfavorable. The unfavorable volume variance for the second quarter was nearly $1,000,000 (see Exhibit 5). A variance of this magnitude was thought likely to attract the attention of the auditors and therefore require restatement of year-end inventory values. To avoid reporting large variances in the second half of fiscal 1990, QTD management decided to compute the cost driver rates for the second half of fiscal 1990 using lower production volumes that reflected the postponement of the British Telecom contract.

The postponement of the contract and its impact on the firm caused Rigby to question the cost driver accounting system. He voiced his concerns in a meeting with Finlay McKenzie, General Manager of QTD.

JR The British Telecom contract is different from our core business. We price it incrementally and, therefore should cost it incrementally. Averaging cost driver rates across the two types of business makes our core business look a lot more profitable than it really is. I think we should develop two sets of cost driver rates, one for the core business and the other for the British Telecom contract. I did a quick analysis of the British Telecom Contract, and its driver rates are very different (Exhibit 6).

FM I don't know how you can say that the British Telecom business is different from our core business. The way I look at it, our core business consists of two elements: base business, consisting of small orders from a wide base of customers, and big deals, which are large orders from the national telecommunications firms. Big deals range from $0.5 million to $4.0 million. The British Telecom contract is simply a larger version of a big deal.

JR That's not right, Finlay. We don't discount other big deals to the same extent that we discount the British Telecom contract. Besides, even though we get business from British Telecom every year, its size and uncertainty make it inherently more risky than the core business.

FM Again, I don't agree. The British Telecom contract has been with us for the last five years and will probably be with us for the next 10. There is no difference between our winning four $2 million big deals and getting an $8 million order from British Telecom. The risks are just the same. The British Telecom contract is a cash cow. It funds the development of new products for our core business. The cost system as designed reflects the reality of our business.

EXHIBIT 1

QUEENSFERRY TELECOMMUNICATIONS DIVISION

Department Overhead Analysis by Process: Second Half Fiscal 1990 Budgets Revision
$(000)

	AUTO INSERT	PRELOAD	BACKLOAD	AUTOTEST	INSTRUMENT ASSEMBLY	INSTRUMENT TEST	PANEL FAB	PROCURE	TOTAL $
Quality	4.0	1.2	1.0	4.0	49.5	532.6	13.4	146.1	751.8
Manufacturing management	11.0	56.4	21.3	24.8	49.6	162.7	24.6	38.8	389.2
Materials management	10.9	22.1	13.0	3.8	28.9	61.4	14.2	1,995.9	2,150.2
Fabrication							441.6		441.6
Assembly	146.7	557.3	218.3	8.9	609.7	1,193.7	39.0		2,773.6
Engineering	75.5	97.7	21.8	110.4	74.1	44.4	—	67.0	490.9
Total	248.1	734.7	275.4	151.9	811.8	1,994.8	532.8	2,247.9	6,997.3

EXHIBIT 2

QUEENSFERRY TELECOMMUNICATIONS DIVISION
Manufacturing Cost Driver Rates
Fiscal 1990

| | | RATES | |
PROCESS	DRIVER	FIRST HALF STANDARD	SECOND HALF STANDARD
Autoinsert	Parts Inserted	$ 0.09	$ 0.07
Manual insert Prewave solder	Parts inserted	0.23	0.24
Manual insert Postwave solder	Parts inserted	0.70	0.75
PC autotest	Parts tested	0.04	0.04
Instrument assembly	Labor hours	50.84	58.34
Instrument test	Test hours	63.36	82.60
Fabrication	Labor hours	59.69	40.88
Procurement	% of direct material	26.68%	26.51%

EXHIBIT 3

QUEENSFERRY TELECOMMUNICATIONS DIVISION
Cost Driver Rates for the Instrument Assembly and Instrument Test Departments
for the Second Half of Fiscal 1990

| | INSTRUMENT ASSEMBLY | | | | INSTRUMENT TEST | | | |
	UNIT A	UNIT B	UNIT C	TOTAL	UNIT A	UNIT B	UNIT C	TOTAL
Quality	22.1	14.1	13.3	49.5	272.8	146.2	113.6	532.6
Manufacturing management	27.4	10.1	12.1	49.6	83.4	50.3	29.0	162.7
Materials management	13.9	7.2	7.8	28.9	26.0	19.5	15.9	61.4
Fabrication	—	—	—	—	—	—	—	—
Assembly	321.7	131.4	156.6	609.7	405.5	434.9	353.3	1,193.7
Engineering	24.7	24.7	24.7	74.1	14.8	14.8	14.8	44.4
Total	409.8	187.5	214.5	811.8	802.5	665.7	526.6	1,994.8
Number of operations	7.21	2.32	4.39	13.92	8.82	4.47	10.86	24.15
Cost per operation	$56.84	$80.94	$48.89	$58.34	$91.03	$148.93	$48.51	$82.60

EXHIBIT 4

QUEENSFERRY TELECOMMUNICATIONS DIVISION

Budgeted and Actual Spending and Production Levels

for the First Half of Fiscal Year 1990

| | SPENDING ($ THOUSANDS) | | | | VOLUME (THOUSANDS) | | | |
| | BUDGET | | ACTUAL | | PLAN | | ACTUAL | |
	Q1	Q2	Q1	Q2	Q1	Q2	Q1	Q2
Autoinsert	$214	$225	$207	$203	1,946	2,662	1,566	1,709
Manual insert prewave solder	422	441	396	373	1,672	2,120	1,389	1,325
Manual insert postwave solder	160	167	149	141	210	257	173	168
PC autotest	91	91	91	58	1,866	2,505	1,891	1,936
Instrument assembly	415	433	384	392	8.1	8.6	9.0	6.4
Instrument test	918	966	860	891	13.4	16.5	13.7	12.8
Lower-level fabrication	292	315	264	402	5.1	5.0	6.2	6.0
Procurement	1,191	1,227	1,190	1,288	4,267	4,800	4,150	3,860
Total	$3,703	$3,865	$3,541	$3,748				

EXHIBIT 5

QUEENSFERRY COMMUNICATIONS DIVISION

Manufacturing Overhead Variances

for the First Half of Fiscal Year 1990

$(000)

| | SPEND VARIANCE | | VOLUME VARIANCE | |
	Q1	Q2	Q1	Q2
Autoinsert	7	22	(34)	(86)
Manual insert prewave solder	26	68	(65)	(183)
Manual insert postwave solder	11	26	(26)	(62)
PC autotest	—	33	1	(23)
Instrument assembly	31	41	46	(112)
Instrument test	58	75	19	(234)
Lower-level fabrication	28	(87)	47	54
Procurement	1	(61)	(31)	(251)
	162	117	(43)	(898)

EXHIBIT 6

QUEENSFERRY TELECOMMUNICATIONS DIVISION

Driver Rates for British Telecommunications Contract

for the Second Half of 1990

	BUDGETED ($000)	DRIVER VOLUMES	DRIVER RATES
Autoinsert	85.3	1,797.2	0.05
Manual prewave solder	46.0	1,099.0	0.04
Manual postwave solder	18.5	53.4	0.35
PC auto test	82.8	2,382.8	0.04
Instrument assembly	214.5	4.39	48.89
Instrument test	526.82	10.86	48.51
Lower-level fabrication	54.2	1.9	28.50
Procurement	65.0	2,485.0	2.62%

READINGS

Cost Accounting and Cost Management in a JIT Environment

George Foster and Charles T. Horngren

The just-in-time (JIT) philosophy and methods are being adopted by an increasing number of organizations. What impact will JIT have on cost accounting, cost management, and management accounting? This [reading], based on discussions with managers of domestic and foreign organizations that have adopted JIT and on public accounting and consulting firms engaged by such organizations, examines that impact.

In the broadest sense, JIT is a philosophy that focuses on performing activities as they are needed by other internal segments of an organization. Four fundamental aspects of JIT are:

- All activities that do not add value to a product or service are eliminated—This includes activities or resources that are targets for reduction or elimination (e.g., inventory held in warehouses or storage areas and work in process that must be handled and stacked several times before becoming finished goods).
- There is a commitment to a high level of quality— Doing things right the first time is essential when there is no time allowance for rework.
- Continuous improvements in the efficiency of activities are strived for.
- Simplifying and increasing the visibility of value-adding activities are emphasized—This helps identify activities that do not add value. For example, a walk through a JIT plant will instantly reveal if work-in-process inventory has been eliminated.

JIT also refers to operations management methods in such functional areas as purchasing, production, distribution, retailing, and even in such administrative areas as payroll and accounts payable. For example, JIT purchasing is the purchase of goods so that delivery immediately precedes demand or use. JIT production is a system in which each component on a production line is produced as needed by the next step in the production line. JIT purchasing can be adopted by retailers, wholesalers, distributors, and manufacturing organizations; JIT production can be adopted only by manufacturing organizations. Exhibit 1 presents an overview of the ways in which JIT is used.

PURPOSES AND CHOICES IN COST ACCOUNTING

Cost or management accounting systems have two major purposes: product costing, and planning and control. Cost accounting techniques for fulfilling these purposes include:

- Cost/benefit tests for designing and changing management accounting systems—Elaborate systems are expensive and time-consuming, but managers authorize their installation and adaptation only if doing so will sufficiently improve collective operations.
- Product costing and control systems that are tailored to underlying operations, not vice versa.
- Control devices in all product costing systems— These systems include responsibility accounting, budgeting, and variance analysis.
- Various sources of management information in addition to management accounting systems.

JIT is primarily a change in underlying operations, and, as with any significant change in operations, serious consideration should be given to changing the accompanying accounting system. JIT accounting systems are merely applications of long-standing cost accounting concepts. In addition, JIT operations illustrate that the financial measures provided

Reprinted from *Journal of Cost Management* (Winter 1988), pp. 4–14, with permission. Portions of this paper appeared in the June 1987 issue of *Management Accounting*.

Exhibit 1.   JIT: A Philosophy and a Set of Operating Methods

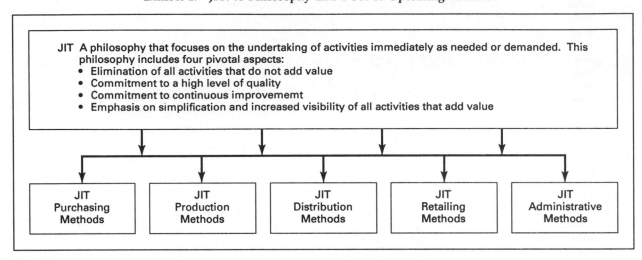

by cost accounting systems are only one means of planning and control.[1]

JUSTIFICATIONS FOR CHANGES IN COST ACCOUNTING SYSTEMS

The changes in cost accounting suggested in this [reading] will yield the following benefits:

- More accurate product cost information—Uses include decisions on pricing, product mix to produce or sell, and cost-based reimbursement contracts. The management accounting system is the primary source of product cost information.
- Better control of cost incurrence—In a JIT environment, the focus is on reducing total costs for the organization as a whole, not individual costs or departmental costs. Changes can take two forms:
  —Fewer or no dysfunctional decisions often associated with the existing cost accounting system.
  —Advantageous comparison of accounting versus nonaccounting variables in cost control.

The internal accounting system is only one of several sources of cost control information. Other sources include personal observation, administrative approval mechanisms, and such nonfinancial measures as setup times and the percentage of defective products.

- Reduced costs of the system—Many existing cost accounting systems are expensive, complex, and time-consuming for both managers and accountants. A key element of JIT is that it simplifies all activities, including cost systems and such operational areas as purchasing and production.

JIT PURCHASING

With JIT purchasing, the acquisition of goods is scheduled in such a way that delivery immediately precedes demand or use. In some industries, JIT purchasing has long been an accepted practice (e.g., industries dealing with such perishables as baked goods, fresh flowers, and fresh fish). Today, JIT purchasing is being adopted by organizations that acquire nonperishables. These organizations previously ordered lots much larger than required by short-run demand or use and often stored inventory in large warehouses for weeks or longer.

Characteristics of operating activities.   Organizations that adopt JIT purchasing report a substantial increase in individual deliveries, each containing fewer units. The costs and time associated with purchasing activities have been reduced by:

- Decreasing the number of suppliers and, consequently, the resources devoted to purchase negotiations—For example, Apple Computer reduced its vendors from 400 to 75, and IBM Corp cut its suppliers from 640 to 32.
- Stipulating price and acceptable quality levels in long-term agreements with suppliers, thus eliminating negotiations for each purchase transaction—When purchasing goods, some JIT adopters use an advanced delivery schedule (ADS) that defines the daily (or even hourly) delivery schedule for a time period (e.g., a month). Clearly, firms using an ADS must have a high degree of certainty regarding de-

mand or production for the time period covered. For example, several Toyota plants freeze the production schedule at least one month in advance.

- Having purchasers establish programs to inform vendors about quality and delivery requirements— These requirements can be stringent, bearing high penalties for nonconformance. For example, Hewlett-Packard has contracts that specify "if [the supplier] misses a four-hour window more than three times in a year, their contract is up for renewal.[2]
- Using shop-ready containers—Activities associated with packing and unpacking are examples of how non-value-added costs are often incurred. Having the correct number of units in individual containers is emphasized, diminishing all facets of material handling (e.g., the use of large material-handling equipment).
- Costs for incoming quality inspection programs are reduced—The number of quality inspectors can be reduced or even eliminated.

The goals set by firms switching to JIT purchasing are ambitious. A consultant gave the following example of how "specific improvement goals are typically very aggressive": supplier productivity and price improvements (30%); total inventory and lead time reduction (90%); quality without inspection (100%); schedule performance (100%).[3]

Implications for cost accounting. JIT purchasing can affect a cost accounting system in one or more of the following ways.

It increases the direct traceability of costs. In a traditional purchasing environment, many material handling and warehouse costs are incurred for multipurpose facilities that service different product lines. Organizations typically classify the costs of operating such facilities as indirect costs. In a JIT purchasing environment, the material handling facilities are often dedicated to a single retail area or a single production line. Such operating costs can be classified as direct costs. Consequently, in a JIT purchasing setting, there can be an increase in the direct traceability of costs to individual retail areas or production lines.

It changes the cost pools that are used to accumulate costs. In traditional purchasing environments, separate cost pools are frequently used for such activities as purchasing, material handling, quality inspection, and warehouse facilities. These costs are allocated to production departments in one of two ways:

- Each cost pool is separately allocated to each production department.
- Purchasing, warehouse, and related costs are collected in one or more aggregate cost pools and are then allocated to each production department.

In an ideal JIT purchasing environment, the warehouse would be eliminated and material handling costs would be reduced. Exhibit 2 summarizes these changes in materials movement. If an organization formerly allocated purchasing, material handling, quality inspection, and warehouse costs separately, the JIT accounting system will reduce the number of such indirect cost pools. At the very least, the warehouse cost pool will vanish. Other cost pools may be combined because of the former pools' diminished materiality.

JIT changes the bases used to allocate indirect costs to production departments. If an organization previously collected purchasing, warehouse, and related costs in a single cost pool, the composition of this pool will change. This has implications for the choice of an allocation base.

Surveys of cost allocation methods report that floor space occupied in a warehouse is a commonly used allocation base for purchasing and material handling costs in traditional purchasing environments. In a pure JIT environment, there is no warehouse; hence, warehouse space is unavailable as an allocation base. Such allocation bases as the dollar value of materials or the number of deliveries may better capture the cause and effect relationship between purchasing and material handling activities and indirect cost incurrence.

It reduces emphasis on individual purchase price variance information. In traditional purchasing environments, many organizations place great emphasis on purchase price variances. Favorable purchasing price variances can sometimes be achieved by buying in larger quantities to take advantage of price discounts or by buying lower quality materials. In JIT environments, the emphasis is on the total cost of operations, not just on purchase price. Such factors as quality and availability are given greater emphasis, even if they are accompanied by higher purchase prices. Firms using JIT purchasing attempt to achieve price reductions by having long-term agreements with suppliers rather than by seeking

Exhibit 2.   Materials Movement in Traditional and JIT
Purchasing Environments

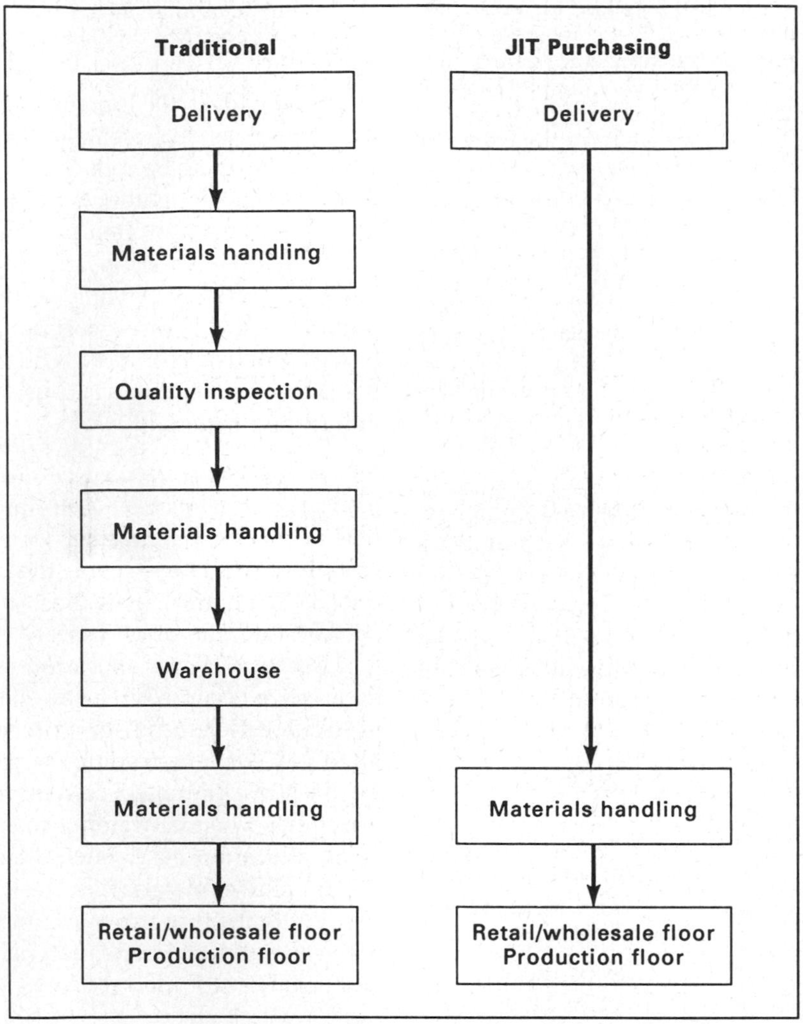

large quantity, one-time purchases that result in sizeable holdings of materials or subcomponents.

As always, the cost accounting system should be adapted to the underlying operating activity. In JIT purchasing, the underlying process focuses on long-term commitments that reduce total operating costs. Purchase price variances for each delivery have much less significance under JIT.

JIT reduces the frequency or detail of reporting of purchase deliveries in the internal accounting system. In a JIT purchasing environment, the number of

deliveries of goods (e.g., raw materials) increases substantially. Organizations have sought to reduce the costs of processing information in the internal accounting system in one or more of the following ways:

• Batching, or summarizing, individual purchase deliveries to avoid a separate transaction for each delivery. When there is an ADS, the transaction may relate to the period of the delivery schedule. When there is no ADS, the individual deliveries may be batched on a weekly basis and only the aggregate of the deliveries recorded as a transaction.

- Using an electronic transfer system in which the initial purchase order (or delivery schedule) automatically sets up electronic data transfers at the delivery date and electronic funds transfers at the payment date.
- Reorganizing the accounts payable department so that it operates as an assembly line. An electronics company initially adopted this approach at one of its plants but subsequently moved to batching purchase deliveries when the reorganized department was "splitting at the seams" and was "archiving mountains of documents."[4]

The appendix to this [reading] describes a backflushing costing system that reduces the information recorded in the internal accounting system. Backflushing can be extended to the purchasing function so that the first recording of materials in the internal accounting system occurs when a finished good using those materials is completed.

Exhibit 3 links the justifications for changes in the cost accounting system with each of the specific changes associated with JIT purchasing described in the preceding sections.

JIT PRODUCTION

Characteristics of operating activities.   In a JIT production environment, each component is produced as needed by the next step in the production line. Key elements of JIT production include:

- The production line is run on a demand-pull basis, so that activity at each workstation is authorized by the demand of downstream workstations. Work in process at each workstation is therefore held to a minimum.

Exhibit 3.   Justifications for Cost Accounting Changes for JIT Purchasing

- More accurate product cost information.
  —Changes in direct traceability of costs.
  —Changes in cost pools.
  —Changes in allocation bases.
- Better control of cost incurrence.
  —Reduced emphasis on individual purchasing price variance information, increased emphasis on total cost of operations. (This minimizes dysfunctional operating decisions often associated with existing cost accounting system.)
- Reduced system costs.
  —A reduction in the frequency or detail of purchase delivery reporting.

- Emphasis is placed on reducing the production lead time (the time from the first stage of production to when the finished product leaves the production line). Reduced lead time enables a firm to better respond to changes in demand; it also reduces changes in supplier orders.
- The production line is stopped if work-in-process is defective. In JIT, there are no buffer inventories at each workstation to keep workers busy. Stoppage is counter to traditional economic-lot-size assumptions concerning the length of the production run. Organizations adopting JIT production continually strive to reduce parameters that are assumed constant in economic lot size formulas (e.g., the setup cost for machinery at a workstation).
- Emphasis is on simplifying activities on the production line so that areas in which non-value-added activities occur are highly visible and can be eliminated. Some firms adopting JIT production methods restructured the layout of their plants. Much emphasis is placed on streamlining material handling between successive workstations. A consultant noted that "one of the many benefits will be the elimination of the dinosaurs—the forklift trucks."[5]

Dramatic improvements have been reported by firms adopting JIT production methods. Exhibit 4 presents examples of efficiency improvements at five companies; the values shown are representative of those reported by a diverse set of organizations.[6] Significant changes in operations underlie these improvements. Accordingly, major changes in the cost accounting area should be expected.

Organizations adopting a JIT production approach are making one or more of the following changes.

Exhibit 4.   Efficiency Improvements with JIT Production Methods

	RANGE OF PERCENTAGE IMPROVEMENT FOR 5 COMPANIES (%)
Manufacturing Lead Time	83–92
Inventory: Raw	35–73
WIP	70–89
Finished Goods	0–100
Changeover Time	75–94
Labor: Direct	0–50
Indirect	21–60
Space	39–80
Cost of Quality	26–63
Purchased Material	6–11

Increasing the direct traceability of some costs.
Direct traceability of cost items has been increased in two ways.

Change in underlying production activities. The costs of many activities previously classified as indirect costs have been transferred to the direct cost category in JIT plants. For example, production line workers in JIT plants perform plant maintenance and plant setups. Previously, such activities were often performed by other workers who were classified as indirect labor.

Equipment suppliers to JIT plants are increasingly asked to supply equipment that facilitates high-speed changeover of tools by production workers, online monitoring of quality, and online packaging and labeling.

For those firms retaining direct labor as a separate cost category, changes in the set of production activities increase the direct traceability of costs to individual product lines. This means that indirect cost pools associated with such activities as plant maintenance and setup are likely to be eliminated (or combined with other cost pools because of the previous pools' diminished materiality).

Change in the ability to trace costs to specific production lines or areas. Even if underlying production activities are unchanged, data may be captured more economically. There is increased use of time clocks, minicomputers, and bar-coded identification codes for production workers (as well as materials, parts, and machines). This has made it more cost-effective to trace costs to specific production lines or areas. Improvements in data bases relating to machine use are also facilitating the development of cost functions that better capture cause and effect relationships at the plant floor level.

IBM is an example of a company that is exploring ways to increase the ratio of directly attributable product costs to total product costs. Controllers at plants where this ratio has been increased said that it improves sourcing decisions and competitive analysis, allows for cost reductions and improves competiveness, and improves expense information to manage product cost (increases visibility and awareness of expense items).[7]

Eliminating (or reducing) cost pools for indirect activities. This change is related to increased traceability of costs and can be achieved in several ways:

- Change underlying production activities as described.
- Eliminate activities that do not add value. Prime targets for elimination in a JIT environment are:
  —Storage areas for work-in-process inventory.
  —Storage areas for spoilage, waste, reworked units, and scrap.
  —Material handling facilities for transportation between the production line and storage areas— Machines or workstations are adjacent to each other so that materials and components can be moved by the workers themselves or on short conveyor belts. Increased emphasis also is given to the design and packaging of materials and components so as to reduce the need for large bulk containers that require forklifts.

Elimination of the items listed may result in the elimination of associated cost pools.

Reducing emphasis on individual labor and overhead variances. In many traditional plants, much of the internal accounting effort is devoted to setting labor and overhead standards and to calculating and reporting variances from these standards. Firms implementing JIT production methods report reduced emphasis on the use of labor and overhead variances.

When defined at the production cell level, labor variances create incentives for workers in each production cell to ignore the effect of their actions on other production cells. In JIT plants, the emphasis is on total plant performance, not on the performance of each cell. At one of its semiconductor plants that is run on a JIT production basis, Motorola has eliminated all labor and overhead standards. The benefits reported include reduced dysfunctional aspects associated with focusing on individual production cells and reduced administrative expenses.

Firms retaining variance analysis stress that a change in focus is appropriate in a JIT plant. The emphasis is on variance analysis at the plant level with the focus on trends that may be occurring in the production process rather than on the absolute magnitude of individual variances. (The notion of continuous improvement that underlies a JIT philosophy means that standards will be revised at shorter intervals than in traditional plants.)

Reducing the level of detailed information recorded on work tickets. A key aspect of a JIT philosophy is the simplification of all activities. There are several ways in which work tickets have become simplified in JIT production.

The production process is changed so that there are fewer materials parts per finished product. This can be achieved by redesigning the product so that fewer parts are used or by increasing the percentage of components assembled elsewhere.[8]

Only direct materials are recorded on work tickets; all other costs are expensed to the period. Several JIT plants that produce products with a low percentage of labor costs have adopted this approach.

A job costing system is changed to a process costing or backflush product costing system. Exhibit 5 compares job, operation, process, and backflush costing systems in terms of the level of detail with which individual product information is recorded. Job costing contains the most detailed level of information about individual product units; the individual job is the focus of product costing. Process costing typically has been viewed as being at the other end of the spectrum; an individual process for a given time period is its focus. Job costing typically is associated with batch manufacturing, and process costing with constant-flow manufacturing (often called continuous-flow manufacturing). Operation costing is a hybrid costing system combining elements of job and process costing.

The appendix to this [reading] describes and illustrates the relatively new backflush costing system used at several JIT plants. Exhibit 5 indicates that extreme backflushing is even less detailed than a process costing system in terms of the recordkeeping for each product unit.

Most firms making changes in their basic costing systems for plants using JIT production have adopted one of three approaches:

- Switch from a job costing to a process costing system. The effect of adopting JIT production methods is that the production line is run on a constant-flow basis; not surprisingly, some of these firms are switching to process costing. Another rationale for adopting process costing is that with the increased emphasis on quality in JIT production plants, there is more homogeneity in the units processed. JIT puts great emphasis on eliminating spoilage and reworked units. Spoilage and reworked units are an important source of heterogeneity in work tickets in non-JIT production plants.

- Switch from a more detailed to a less detailed process costing system. Omark Industries[9] made the following changes in three of its product lines:

Number of Cost Centers

PRODUCT LINE	PRE-JIT	JIT
Chain Saws	18	4
Sprockets	5	3
Bars	4	1

- Switch from a job- or process-costing system to a backflush costing system. Most firms adopting the backflush approach use two triggers to make entries into the internal accounting system. The first trigger is the purchase of materials or components; the second is the completion of production or the sale of a finished good.

These simplifications have led to sizable reductions in individual accounting entries for product costing in JIT prouction plants.

The level of detailed information recorded about labor costs is reduced. In many organizations, labor costs are a declining percentage of total manufacturing costs. Organizations adopting JIT production methods have adapted to the declining materiality of labor costs by:

- Retaining direct labor as a separate direct cost category but reducing individual labor classifications. An industrial machine manufacturer reduced labor classifications at one of its plants from 26 to five over a three-year period in which it adopted JIT production methods. This reduction is consistent with a JIT philosophy that emphasizes teams, not individuals.

Exhibit 5. Reporting Detail in Product Costing Systems

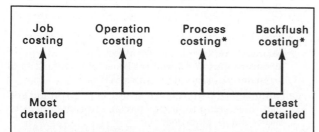

Note: * Depending on the desire for detailed tracking, some observers would switch the positions of process costing and backflush costing on this continuum. In any event, backflush costing has more characteristics of process costing than of job costing.

JIT plants train workers for many activities. Such training increases flexibility regarding the assignment of workers to individual work cells. (Plants with a high level of unionization have reported difficulty in negotiating these reductions in labor classifications with unions.)

- Abandoning labor as a separate direct cost category. The alternative treatments of labor costs are:
  —Classification of labor costs as a part of an indirect manufacturing cost pool that is allocated to units of production.
  —Classification of labor costs as a period cost that is immediately expensed.

Of course, abandoning direct labor as a separate cost category precludes the use of direct labor as an allocation base.

One example of altering labor cost reporting is the Milwaukee plant of Harley-Davidson. Direct labor was less than 10% of the product cost. When direct labor was recorded as a separate cost category, 65% of cost accounting efforts were devoted to administrative work related to these labor costs, including the setting of labor standards, the correction of wrong entries associated with labor, and attempts to reconcile the labor reported on job tickets with the total labor time available. Harley-Davidson concluded that the effort did not meet a cost/benefit test, and the company now combines direct labor and overhead costs into a single conversion cost pool.[10]

Piecework payment plans are being eliminated in JIT plants. Therefore, labor costs can be recorded in far less detail. The elimination of piecework plans drastically reduces the transactions reported per worker. Piecework plans create incentives for workers to produce, even though there is no demand for the finished good. In a JIT plant, management prefers workers to be idle rather than to produce for inventory.

Exhibit 6 links the justifications for changes in the cost accounting system to each of the five specific changes associated with JIT production.

COST MANAGEMENT IN A JIT ENVIRONMENT

Cost management in JIT plants includes several activities, many of which also apply to plants not using JIT.

Cost planning.   This is undertaken before production commences, and in some cases before the

Exhibit 6.   Justifications for Cost Accounting Changes for JIT Production

- More accurate product cost information.
  —An increase in direct traceability of some costs.
  —Elimination (or at least reduction) of several activities classified as indirect.
- Better control of cost incurrence.
  —Reduced emphasis on individual labor and overhead variances, which minimizes dysfunctional operating decisions often associated with existing cost accounting system.
- Reduced system costs.
  —A reduction in the level of detailed information recorded on work tickets.
  —A reduction in the level of detailed information recorded about labor costs.

production line is constructed. Plant engineers and product designers play important roles in cost planning. Their aim is to design the product and the production line with a mix of cost, quality, deliverability, and flexibility that reflects senior management's strategy. In the design of production lines for JIT plants, great emphasis is placed on eliminating all activities that do not add value to the product.

Cost reduction.   This is undertaken in both the preproduction and production stages. At several Japanese plants that use JIT, cost reduction targets are set for each product (e.g., a 25% cost reduction target for a product in its first year). Product line workers are all members of cost reduction circles that seek ways to achieve the cost reduction targets. Each year individual workers are required to submit a specific number of cost reduction ideas to be discussed by the cost reduction circle.

Cost control.   This is undertaken when production starts. The sources of information for cost control activities include:

- Personal observation by production line workers.
- Financial performance measures (e.g., inventory turnover ratios and variances based on standard costs for materials, labor, and overhead).
- Nonfinancial performance measures (e.g., production lead-time, setup time, percentage of product defects, and schedule attainment).

The general trends at both the shop production-cell level and at the plant level that have been observed in JIT plants are a declining role for financial measures, and an increasing role for personal observation and nonfinancial measures in cost control activities. The reasons for these trends include:

- Production workers play a pivotal role in cost control activities. They directly observe nonfinancial variables on the plant floor. Hence, nonfinancial variables are intuitive and easy to comprehend.
- Dramatic reductions in lead times in JIT plants place a premium on the timeliness of data when controlling costs. Measurements taken on the plant floor are inevitably the most up-to-date data available.
- Increased recognition is being given to early pinpointing and controlling of cost drivers (i.e., the underlying causes of costs). The focus is on before-the-fact, rather than after-the-fact, control. For example, workers are encouraged to reduce setup times, minimize scrap, and minimize the number of reworked units.
- The internal accounting system in a JIT plant typically contains little cost control data about actual product costs at individual production cells. For example, under the backflush costing method, no tracking is made of product cost accumulation as products move through successive work cells.

Inventory turnover measures. Inventory turnover is a key performance measure in JIT plants. For example, at one of its plants using JIT production methods, a consumer products company in England now computes separate inventory turnover ratios for each product line and for raw materials and components, work in process, and finished goods. This company still records work in process with a process costing system. (For companies using extreme backflush costing, cost measures of work in process are not recorded in the internal accounting system.)

Cost reduction target measures. Comparisons of actual product costs with target product costs play an important role in organizations that emphasize cost reduction activities. For example, an automotive company in Japan has targets for the materials costs associated with individual product lines. Separate material costs are accumulated for each product variation in its product line in order to gain insight into how cost reduction ideas are leading to lower product costs.

JIT IS SIMPLIFICATION

There is no single blueprint for cost accounting and cost management in a JIT environment. Rather, there is considerable variation in the changes made —for the cost pools used, allocation bases chosen, costing system adopted (job, operation, process, or backflush), and types of performance measures used. However, the changes observed share a underlying commonality—specifically, a movement toward simplification of cost accounting practices. This commonality is part of the JIT theme to simplify all activities. Activities that add value can be further improved, and those that do not can be eliminated.

Many organizations reject JIT as inappropriate for them. Nevertheless, JIT methods have proven that any significant change in underlying operations is likely to justify a corresponding change in the accounting system.

If a company's accounting system is still creaking along on outdated engines, managers are probably not being served optimally in their attempts to cope with today's and tomorrow's challenges and operations. Thus, the flurry of attention to JIT is beneficial even if it only prods managers and accountants to make a zero-base review of their existing cost accounting systems, regardless of whether the underlying operations are using JIT purchasing or production methods.

APPENDIX: BACKFLUSH COSTING

A backflush costing system focuses first on the output of an organization and then works backward when applying costs to units sold and to inventories. The term *backflush* probably arose because the trigger points for product costing entries can be delayed until as late as sales, when costs finally are flushed through the accounting system. In contrast, conventional product costing systems track costs through work in process (WIP) as the focal account, beginning with the introduction of raw materials into production.

The following three examples demonstrate backflushing. Example 1 illustrates the elimination of a separate WIP inventory account. Examples 2 and 3 are more dramatic departures from widely used product costing systems.

EXAMPLE 1

A hypothetical company, Silicon Valley Computers (SVC), has two trigger points for making entries in the internal accounting system:

- Trigger point 1—The purchase of raw materials and components.
- Trigger point 2—The manufacture of a finished good unit.

SVC manufactures keyboards for personal computers. For the month of April, there are no beginning inventories of raw materials, WIP, or finished goods. The standard material cost per keyboard unit in April is $19. For product costing, SVC combines labor costs and indirect manufacturing costs into a single conversion cost category. The standard conversion cost per keyboard unit in April is $12. SVC has two inventory accounts:

TYPE OF ACCOUNT	NAME
Combined raw materials and WIP	Inventory: raw and WIP
Finished goods	Finished goods

Incurrences of conversion costs are charged to responsibility centers under backflush costing just as in other costing systems. Applications of conversion costs are made to products at various trigger points. Any conversion costs not applied to products are written off immediately as expenses incurred in the period. For example, all unfavorable variances are charged as period expenses. (For simplicity, Examples 1 to 3 assume that all actual costs and standard costs are the same.)

SVC uses the following steps when applying costs to units sold and to inventories:

Step one

Record the raw materials purchased in the reporting period. Assume that April materials purchases were $1,950,000.

Inventory: raw and WIP	$1,950,000
Accounts payable	$1,950,000

Step two

Record the incurrence of conversion costs during the reporting period. Assume conversion costs were $1,200,000.

Conversion costs	$1,200,000
Accounts payable accrued payroll	$1,200,000

Step three

Determine the number of finished units manufactured during the reporting period. Assume that 100,000 keyboard units were manufactured in April.

Step four

Compute the standard cost of each finished unit. This step typically uses a bill of materials and an operations list, or equivalent records. For SVC, the standard cost per unit is $31 ($19 standard material cost + $12 standard conversion cost).

Step five

Record the cost of finished goods manufactured in the reporting period:

Inventory: finished goods (100,000 units @ $31)	$3,100,000
Inventory: raw and WIP	$1,900,000
Conversion costs	1,200,000

Step six

Record the cost of goods sold in the reporting period. Assume that 99,000 units were sold during the month.

Cost of goods sold (99,000 units @ $31)	$3,069,000
Inventory: finished goods	$3,069,000

The end of month inventory balance for April is:

Inventory: raw and WIP	$50,000
Inventory: finished goods (1,000 units @ $31)	31,000
	$81,000

The elimination of the WIP account considerably reduces the amount of detail in the internal accounting system. (There still may be tracking of units on

Exhibit 7.   Example 1—An Overview of Backflush Costing

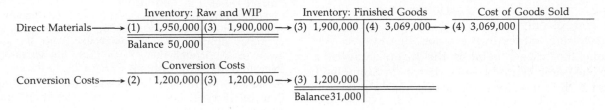

the production line, but there is no "costs attach" tracking through work tickets in the internal accounting system.

Exhibit 7 provides an overview of the accounts affected in Example 1.

EXAMPLE 2

A variant of Example 1 is a backflush costing system whose second trigger point for making entries into the internal accounting system is the sale, rather than the manufacture, of a finished unit. See Exhibit 8.

Two rationales given for this variant system are:

- To remove the incentive for managers to produce for inventory—Under the "costs attach" assumption implicit in job, operation, and process costing, period expenses can be reduced by producing units not sold and by increasing WIP.
- To increase the focus of managers on a plantwide goal (producing saleable units) rather than on an individual subunit goal (e.g., increase labor efficiency at an individual production center).

This variant has the same effect on net income as the immediate expensing of all conversion costs. Under this approach, the inventory account is con-

fined solely to raw materials (whether they are in storage, in process, or in finished goods). No conversion costs are inventoried. The summary accounting entry is:

Cost of goods sold	$3,069,000
(99,000 units @ $31)	
Inventory	$1,881,000
Conversion costs	1,188,000

At the end of each period, an adjusting entry is made that immediately expenses the conversion costs incurred but not attributed to units sold:

Period expenses	$12,000
Conversion costs	$12,000

The end-of-period inventory account is $69,000 ($50,000 in raw materials still on hand and $19,000 in raw materials embodied in the 1,000 units manufactured but not sold during the period).

Under this variant, there is no account for finished goods inventory because the trigger for making the second set of entries is sale rather than manufacture.

Exhibit 8.   Example 2—An Overview of Backflush Costing

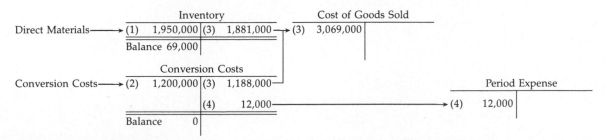

EXAMPLE 3

The simplest version of a backflush product costing system has only one trigger point for making product costing entries in the accounting system. Assume this trigger point is the manufacture of a finished unit. With the same data as in Examples 1 and 2, the summary entry is:

Inventory—finished goods	$3,100,000
Accounts payable	$1,900,000
Conversion costs	1,200,000

At the end of the period, the $50,000 of raw materials purchased but not yet manufactured into finished units will not have been entered into the internal product costing system. This variant of a backflush system is less feasible if there are significant inventories of raw materials and WIP.

NOTES

1 C. Horngren, "Cost and Management Accounting: Yesterday and Today," in E. Bromwich and A. Hopwood (eds.), *Research and Current Issues in Management Accounting* (London: Pitman, 1986), p. 37.

2 V. Wright, "The Effect of Zero Inventories on Cost (Just-in-Time)." *Cost Accounting for the '90s: The Challenge of Technologies Change* (Montvale NJ: National Association of Accountants, 1986), p. 157.

3 T. Arenberg, "Vendor Support Systems—Partners in Profit," *Readings in Zero Inventory* (American Production and Inventory Control Society, 1984), p. 98. Further discussion of JIT purchasing is in C. Horngren and G. Foster, *Cost Accounting: A Managerial Emphasis*, 6th ed. (Englewood Cliffs NJ: Prentice-Hall, 1987), pp 724–726.

4 Wright, "The Effect of Zero Inventories on Cost (Just-in-Time)," p. 158.

5 B. O'Connor, "Just-in-Time Vendors Are Coming," *Reading in Zero Inventory* (American Production and Inventory Control Society, 1984), p. 95.

6 H. Johansson, "The Effect of Zero Inventories on Cost (Just-in-Time)," in *Cost Accounting for the '90s: The Challenge of Technological Change* (Montvale NJ: National Association of Accountants, 1986), p 145. Numerous examples of improvements associated with JIT are given in R. Schonberger, *World Class Manufacturing* (New York: Free Press, 1986).

7 R. Kelder, "CIM and Traditional Cost Accounting Practice" (Presentation at AME Cost Accounting Conference. Chicago: November 1986).

8 An example is the Hewlett-Packard personal computer. The HP150B had 550 part numbers, the next model (HP150C) had only 120 part numbers. See J. Patell, "Adapting a Cost Accounting System to Just-in-Time Manufacturing: The Hewlett-Packard Personal Office Computer Division" (Working Paper, Stanford University, 1986).

9 G. Sanchez, "Manufacturing Accounting Cost System" (Presentation at AME Cost Accounting Conference, Chicago: November 1986).

10 R. D'Amore and W. Turk, "Just-in-Time Accounting at Harley-Davidson" (Presentation at AME Cost Accounting Conference. Chicago: November 1986).

RECOMMENDED READING

HEARD, J. "JIT ACCOUNTING." *Readings in Zero Inventory.* American Production and Inventory Control Society, 1984.

HOLBROOK, W., and EILER, R. "ACCOUNTING CHANGES REQUIRED FOR JUST-IN-TIME PRODUCTION." *American Production and Inventory Control Society Conference Proceedings.* 1985.

HORNGREN, C., and FOSTER G. *Cost Accounting: A Managerial Emphasis,* 6th ed. Englewood Cliffs NJ: Prentice-Hall, 1987.

MASKELL, B. "MANAGEMENT ACCOUNTING AND JUST-IN-TIME." *Management Accounting* (UK) (September 1986), pp 32–34.

NEUMANN, B., AND JAOUEN, P. "KANBAN, ZIPS AND COST ACCOUNTING: A CASE STUDY." *Journal of Accountancy* (August 1986).

The Human Element:
The Real Challenge in Modernizing Cost Systems

Thomas B. Lammert and Robert Ehrsam

Are traditional cost accounting systems holding back the factory of the future? Many contend that they are and often with good reason. It is easy to produce examples of techniques and methods of traditional systems that are at odds with the realities of the new manufacturing environment:

- Direct labor based overhead rates,
- Large plant-wide overhead pools,
- Poor differentiation of fixed and variable costs,
- Lack of focus on material or machine-oriented costs,
- Focus on individual task measurement versus flow and output, and
- Limited focus on the cost of quality.

The prevalence of such examples has led critics like Eli Goldratt, the co-founder of Creative Output, to cite cost accounting as the major obstacle to making U.S. manufacturing competitive. (See the May 1987 issue of *Management Accounting*, and *The Goal: A Process of Ongoing Improvement* published by North River Press.)

But the real problem and challenge lies not in the technical but in the human elements of the cost management system. Modernized cost management systems technically can handle the concepts most often associated with a modern manufacturing facility. New systems can be designed to recognize properly the new realities of cost behavior and the associated cost drivers. But management thinking and reliance on traditional performance measurement factors also must change.

John Phippen, vice president of Mattel Toys, is responsible for the design and installation of the company's new worldwide cost system. According to Mr. Phippen, management involvement and training was a critical element in the design process. He explained that training seminars were held for Mattel management personnel throughout system

conceptual design, detail design, and implementation phases. "We showed them what was coming and obtained their acceptance. Then we showed them the end product and how to use it," Mr. Phippen said.

The movement toward the factory of the future occurs in phases. In the first phase of "Process Simplification," Just-In-Time (JIT) and Total Quality Control (TQC) philosophies are implemented. Manufacturing cells also can be introduced in this phase. Once the process has been simplified, or even while it is still under way, additional automation will logically follow. Initially this occurs in "islands" that are not linked or integrated, but the goal for the factory of the future is achievement of a Computer Integrated Manufacturing (CIM) environment.

As the company moves toward complete and integrated automation, the effectiveness and efficiency of the process as a whole takes increasing precedence over concerns about individual operations. The company learns that efficiencies at individual operations do not necessarily translate into an overall efficient process. As processes are simplified and automation becomes widespread, work in process inventories should diminish. The throughput time for an individual operation can become very short. Combined with the reduced queue time between operations, total throughput time also decreases. As a result of higher fixed equipment costs, capacity utilization gains in importance.

In contrast to this increasing capital intensity, the role of labor—particularly "traditional" direct labor—diminishes. Few individual operations are labor-paced and the process as a whole bears little, if any, relationship to consumption of direct labor resources.

These facts may be lost by the plant manager who continues to focus attention almost exclusively on efficiency at the individual work station level

Reprinted from *Management Accounting* (July 1987), pp. 32-37, with permission.

despite the increase in automation and the fact that the plant clearly is moving toward the continuous processing mode of operation. Nor is the individual to blame when performance measurements and incentive systems oriented nearly exclusively to individual unit efficiencies reinforce his behavior.

As consultants, we have seen how total costs for the plant continued to rise, and customer delivery promise dates often were missed. Yet, the performance measurement systems indicated that operations were good because all work stations were reporting high efficiency rates!

In these cases it is not difficult to determine the reason for the problems and propose a solution. To maintain high individual unit efficiencies, long production runs are the rule, even if overall production is not balanced or matched well with demand. The results are large work-in-process inventories used as "cushions" and a build-up of WIP material from orders that are "poor runners" or require rework (rework time lowers efficiency). Finished good inventories also are large.

However, when management measurements of performance are restructured to focus on throughput, utilization of plant capacity, customer delivery, inventory levels, and total product cost; a significant turnaround occurs. Total plant costs decrease and customer satisfaction improves.

When the JIT philosophy has been adopted, work-in-process inventory is viewed as a liability instead of an asset. Raw materials, components, and subassemblies do not arrive at a work station or point in the manufacturing process until they are needed—"just-in-time." Production is "pulled" through the manufacturing facility in a noninterrupted fashion rather than "pushed." As a result, raw material and especially work-in-process inventories are minimized or nearly eliminated.

Efforts also are made to minimize setup time. At the same time with TQC, quality also receives major emphasis. Ironically, this leads to the elimination of separate inspection departments because everyone, including suppliers, is now responsible for quality. Statistical Process Control (SPC) techniques often are adopted on the shop floor. Also, quality is built into the product at the design engineering level.

The underlying principles in this period of process simplification are high quality levels ("zero defects") and elimination of waste. Some rearrangement of machinery, equipment, and the plant layout almost always accompanies these changes. In this environment, individual work station inventory count points and productivity levels for the individual operations are not relevant. The greater emphasis is on the process as a whole.

As the JIT environment advances, the company often establishes manufacturing cells dedicated to the production of a major component, subassembly, or even an entire high volume product. All the machinery, equipment, and personnel required to perform a series of operations are located within the cell. With high volume product families, the cell concept is expanded to a subplant or "focused factory" level. Often a cell involves diverse combinations of operations that are machine intense, or on occasion, labor intense. Again the emphasis is on the process as a whole—the cell inputs and outputs.

As the movement toward automation continues, machining centers and the use of robotics technology become more common. In this phase, traditional "direct" labor is difficult to differentiate from indirect labor. Usually, the total labor intensity of the operation is far less than the capital or machine intensity. Hence, the traditional focus on direct labor is now nearly meaningless.

When the company achieves a CIM environment, the numerous islands of automation are linked together and integrated via the computer. The need for "real time" information to support the manufacturing process is significantly increased. Many diverse products are produced in small lots or even in lots of "one" so flexibility also is key.

COST ACCOUNTING TECHNIQUES AND METHODS

The system designed to manage costs in this changing environment should not be concerned with calculating and reporting inventory counts nor with the efficiency of production rates at individual operations. Individual direct labor efficiency measurements should be dropped. Rather, measurements should focus on the quality, effectiveness, and efficiency of the total process. Generally, material counts only should be calculated and reported for process inputs (raw material) and process outputs (finished items).

"Specific identification" is the rule for the new cost system. Whenever feasible and practical, costs are directly assigned to a process or a product. Allocations are minimized. They should be limited to costs that are truly general in nature such as building insurance.

Because the role of direct labor has been minimized, direct labor based overhead rates should be discarded. In developing product costs, overhead must be applied on other more appropriate bases. In many cases, particularly in machining centers, machine hours will probably be the basis that best reflects consumption of resources.

Consideration also should be given to applying depreciation on the basis of process outputs using a units-of-production concept rather than on any time factor. This is not a new idea. The mining industry has been charging depreciation as well as depletion in this manner for many years.

As a result of greater product specialization, only one overhead rate is needed for each manufacturing cell. While each cell is different and requires individual analysis, overhead generally will be applied on some measurable unit of output or major unit of consumed resources (input). Except in the very unusual case of high overall labor intensity, all labor costs will be a portion of the overhead cost pool for that cell. The "cell conversion cost" becomes the new key performance measure.

Simplification of the cost accounting system and its support costs also can be a side benefit when modern manufacturing methods are adopted. After implementing manufacturing cells, one company was able to measure productivity and base inventory accounting solely on the cell's units of output. As a result, the clerical support cost for shop floor reporting was cut to a third of its former level.

It is extremely important that the cost of under-utilized capacity be identified and measured. The practical capacity concept should be employed in designing the cost system. Knowledge of all fixed costs associated with any gap (idle capacity) between the practical capacity of the overall process and the amount of production actually planned will highlight the importance of high capacity utilization.

The movement to the highly automated CIM environment requires the cost management system to be responsive to the need for a substantial amount of information, often including performance measures, on a "real time" basis. This should not be difficult because even today the source data is available and can be easily captured and processed by the computer. The same computer controlling the process usually can be programmed to provide the new information.

In the factory of the future, the traditional definition of product cost needs to be expanded. The sum of all costs directly associated with the manufacturing process may well be *less* than the total of engineering and product development costs. The dollar level of investments in manufacturing technology are increasing. Rapidly changing product and process technologies are causing shorter product life cycles.

These factors all increase the risk of product obsolescence. What now, in this scenario, is the economic life of a specific major CIM investment? The cost management system must begin reporting cost information for a product's entire life cycle by associating all development costs directly to specific products and product lines.

Quality represents another major performance measurement area. Most systems are not designed to easily capture, sort, and report this new category of "*cost*" information. The results, however, are well worth the effort.

Consider the case of a major integrated steel manufacturer that measured the cost of quality at one finishing plant. The company had to make some assumptions and accept the fact that costs such as processing scrap would not be included. Yet, the costs that it was able to capture and *directly* associate to quality were over 10% of sales—higher than direct labor!

In his book, *Quality Is Free: The Art of Making Quality Certain*, Phil Crosby correctly claims that "quality is free," but the cost of unacceptable quality—both internal and external—is high. Cost management systems must be designed to readily measure and report these costs.

Actually for many years to come, modern manufacturing facilities will require cost management systems that combine these new techniques and methods for most of their operations with traditional techniques for the portion of their operations that remain labor intense job shops. The cost system must be flexible enough to accommodate a broad variety of manufacturing environments.

MATERIALS MANAGEMENT

Traditionally, materials management costs have been assigned to general plant overhead cost pools and applied to products on the basis of direct labor. The material cost of a product has been viewed as strictly the direct purchase price. As material cost becomes a larger component of total product cost, there will be an increased emphasis on understanding the costs associated with ordering, receiving, storing, moving, and preparing purchased materials for the manufacturing process. The modern cost management system should capture materials-related costs in separate overhead cost pools and assign them to products through a material cost overhead factor.

One of our clients, a large consumer durable goods manufacturer, made some major changes in marketing and manufacturing strategies when the material-based overhead concept was adopted. With the new material overhead rate more properly applying materials-related overhead costs to products, management saw costs go up for material intense products, including those with "outsourced" components. Conversely, costs went down for those products with more "value added" (labor and/or capital intensity). This new information led to the elimination of some product lines, a redirection of sales force efforts, and the reconsideration of earlier decisions to expand outsourcing of components.

THE REAL CHALLENGE

Enough time and talent is now being dedicated to designing new cost management systems to properly support the needs of the modern manufacturing facility. Individually—or as a part of an organized effort—U.S. industry has the tools to overcome most of the *technical* design issues. As these new systems approach the implementation stage, however, more attention must be paid to the *human behavioral element* of cost management. If this dimension is ignored, all previous design efforts have been a tremendous waste of time and effort. The new system is doomed to fail!

We recently designed a new cost management system to better reflect the changed manufacturing

environment of a large multiplant manufacturer of industrial components. We also assisted with education and training for all levels in the organization. Now that implementation is under way, top management's commitment and support for both the new system and more appropriate performance measurements are proving to be key elements in acceptance.

Yet, even this enlightened management team could not accept a system that totally broke with the past. We proposed new costing techniques that required capitalizing some indirect costs that formerly were expensed as incurred. The increased inventory level that resulted would adversely affect a key measure of management performance—return on net assets (RONA). Although performance measurement and compensation factors could have been adjusted easily to account for the changes proposed, management was reluctant to accept the changes. Now, an even greater investment in education would be required.

When top managers discovered that the new costing techniques also would have caused an overall decrease in gross margin as well as shifts in margin levels by product and product line, they elected not to fully implement the proposed changes. Consistency with historical data would now be lost. This "inconsistency" would cause confusion in comparative analysis and with future price quotations. In this case, tradition reigned over improved cost management information and performance measurement!

Like any other major change, making a successful transition to the new cost management system appropriate for the modern manufacturing facility requires top management commitment and support plus an intense program of education and training. Obviously, this training will include a large contingent of cost accountants, cost analysts, and financial or cost managers.

Unfortunately, these individuals may be the least receptive to change! Many of them have built their careers on traditional cost accounting systems. In many cases, they have been so involved in the details of the traditional system that they have not recognized the "big picture" changes that have occurred in cost structure and behavior because of advances in manufacturing technology. They must be made to understand that plantwide, direct labor-based overhead rates, for example, are now inappropriate in the development of product costs. They also must recognize that the traditional benchmarks for measuring cost and operating performance need to be changed.

This "reeducation" effort for cost and financial personnel must be fairly intense, centering on a thorough discussion of the changing manufacturing environment. Real life demonstrations, possibly in a case study format, of the new cost management system's concepts and principles would be most effective. In any such training, the benefits of the new system and the deficiencies of the old must be made readily apparent.

By contrast, the education efforts for manufacturing and engineering personnel will not require discussion of the changes in manufacturing. They have been intimately a part of them! Rather, these individuals must be educated in the meaning and use of the new system's performance measurement factors. These managers probably can suggest other relevant factors specific to their own experience that also should be measured. Finally, the financial and nonfinancial managers need training in how to work as partners in using the benefits of the system. Top management will have to reinforce these efforts by asking only questions based on the new performance measures.

Most enlightened companies, which have spent considerable resources in designing new cost systems, recognize that cost management training is a key component of the management development process. Bob Aspell, vice president, at Wang Laboratories, asked Ernst & Whinney to design a cost management course which became a part of the Wang management training program. Wang believed that the addition of this course would facilitate the successful implementation of cost management system changes at Wang.

The final phase in the successful implementation of the modernized cost management system involves the development of performance measurement and reward systems. From the organization's overall goals through top management's bonus factors and down to the individual line and staff manager's objectives, performance must be measured in terms of the new cost system. In many organizations the existing management by objective (MBO) or similar type of performance review system is the perfect vehicle. Nothing works better in behavior modification than linking the desired response to financial rewards!

BREAKING DOWN THE BARRIERS

Cost managers must look to the future. To ensure the continued responsiveness of the new cost management system, they must pursue their continuing education in modern manufacturing technology. One way to accomplish this would be to assign cost managers to periodically work in manufacturing departments. Likewise, it makes sense to consider assigning industrial or manufacturing engineers and operating personnel to cost accounting departments, either permanently or as a developmental assignment.

Barriers between the disciplines must be broken down in the factory of the future. Down the road we should expect to see less of a differentiation between line and staff positions. The formal cost accounting department should become smaller as more responsibility for cost reporting, analysis, and control is driven down to the shop floor. Cost, like quality, must become everyone's responsibility.

A Behavioral Model for Implementing Cost Management Systems

Michael D. Shields and S. Mark Young

This [reading] presents a general model for developing behavioral and organizational strategies for implementing cost management systems (as opposed to cost accounting systems). Although the focus is on firms with advanced manufacturing technologies (AMT)—including Just-In-Time/Total Quality Control (JIT/TQC), robotics, flexible manufacturing systems (FMS), islands of automation, and computer integrated manufacturing (CIM)—the strategies also apply to other types of firms, even those in service industries.

Current cost accounting systems are often inadequate for planning, controlling, motivating, and evaluating the products, processes, and personnel in modern manufacturing environments.[1] The first comprehensive response to these inadequacies has been made recently by Computer Aided Manufacturing—International, Inc. (CAM-I), which has developed a new conceptual model of a cost management system (CMS) to help firms plan and control the costs of AMT.[2] The next task involves implementing such a model.

Successfully establishing an effective CMS requires a change in corporate philosophy from "managing by the numbers" to "managing by commitment to continuous improvement."[3] The central assumption is that the success a firm will have in changing to this philosophy depends on the extent to which the firm develops an implementation strategy that focuses on behavioral rather than technical issues. Like other organizational innovations, implementing a CMS brings a host of changes. However, since a CMS has a direct impact on the performance evaluation of personnel, products, and processes, its implementation affects the entire organization and not simply one or two subsystems.

COMMITMENT TO CONTINUOUS IMPROVEMENT

Managing by commitment to continuous improvement is an operating philosophy that many successful firms have adopted. Fostering an environment that wins the commitment of employees to continuous improvement also lays the foundation for successful implementation of a CMS. Since accounting numbers help management sustain and increase the rate of continuous improvement, those numbers can be used to set goals and monitor progress toward improvement. In turn, the organization must reward all employees (through the use of performance-based compensation and long-term employment contracts, for example) for their willingness to make this commitment through activities. Examples of a commitment to continuous improvement include eliminating non-value-adding activities (such as moving, storage, and waiting time), reducing cycle time (by increasing production efficiency), and increasing quality (by eliminating problems in the production process that lead to errors and defects). Having this commitment leads to innovation and the creation of high-quality products, which are characteristic of a successful firm.

THE "SEVEN Cs" MODEL

AMT firms should manage their cost-generating activities by using what can be called "The Seven Cs Model" (see Exhibit 1). The goal of a CMS is to identify opportunities for, and monitor progress toward, continuous improvement. But it is not enough for managers alone to be committed to continuous improvement; all employees must adopt this philosophy. This is accomplished by developing a corporate culture that will align the goals of employees with those of the firm. In other words, culture is the means of successfully managing the

Reprinted from *Journal of Cost Management* (Winter 1989), pp. 17-27, with permission.

Exhibit 1.   Seven Cs Model: Implementing the CAM-I Cost Management System

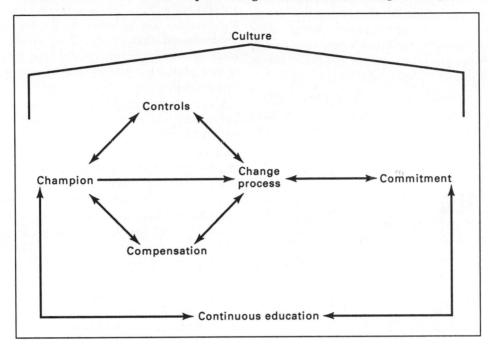

activities and behavior that cause costs. Employees must understand the impact their behavior has on costs, continuous improvement, and the rewards they receive for continuous improvement.

The key person in this process is the CMS champion—the person primarily responsible for implementing the CMS. To be successful, the CMS champion must spearhead the process of change that culminates in a commitment to continuous improvement. This is accomplished by the use of organizational controls, appropriate compensation programs, and continuous education. In the following sections, a detailed analysis of each of the Seven Cs is provided.

Culture.   Focusing initially on corporate culture is important for two reasons. First, research shows that a firm's culture affects its performance. Second, fostering the most appropriate culture accelerates the rate of continuous improvement.[4] Definitions of corporate culture range from the abstract to the commonsensical. For example, Stanley Davis defines culture as "the pattern of shared beliefs and values that give the members of an institution meaning and provides them with the rules of behav-

ior in their organization."[5] Marvin Bower, on the other hand, states that culture is simply "the way we do things around here."[6]

An elaboration of the first of these definitions yields the following definition: "Corporate culture is the mindset of employees, including their shared beliefs, values, and goals." For instance, shared goals include an emphasis on products and processes, high quality, and reliability. Shared values and beliefs include trust, collaboration, and honesty.

Types of cultures.   Research[7] indicates that there are three broad types of corporate cultures: (1) functional, (2) dysfunctional, and (3) ill-defined. While functional and dysfunctional cultures may vary in intensity, this discussion centers on the development of a strong functional culture. A culture is "strong" if it has clearly articulated beliefs, values, and goals that can be expressed either qualitatively or quantitatively. Qualitative expressions, such as company mission statements or slogans (GE's "Progress is our most important product," for example), often are rallying points to sustain and increase the motivation of employees. Quantitative expressions include specific financial

RESISTANCE TO CHANGE AND CHANGES IN THE WORKPLACE

Many factors contribute to the resistance of an organization and its employees to change. The following are the most important factors to consider when a cost management system (CMS) is being planned and implemented.

Effects of implementation on short-term profits. Many senior executives may resist the introduction of a CMS and the philosophy of continuous improvement on the grounds that they reduce short-term profits and earnings per share. This affects the firm's performance in the capital markets and thus affects executive compensation.

The key to overcoming this resistance is for senior executives to realize that a firm's performance in the capital markets depends on expectations about the present value of the firm's expected future cash flows. Public companies should therefore disclose (and indeed publicize) plans for implementing innovations. Particular emphasis should be given to why the innovations are beneficial and how they will ultimately improve financial performance. With this information, investors and their advisors can adequately assess long-term future cash flows. In addition, evaluations of senior executives and executive compensation should not be based solely on short-term measures.

Changes in performance measures. Implementing a CMS will alter the reported performance (and possibly, as a result, performance evaluations) of many employees, products, technologies, and activities. Naturally, the changes pose the greatest threat to those whose reported performance will decrease simply because of the implementation of the CMS. Consider, for example, a worker on a production line whose compensation is threatened by the introduction of a CMS (which provides different measures of his performance) and also, possibly, a new compensation system. Another example is a product manager whose product line becomes unprofitable under a CMS because of new cost allocation procedures.

To reduce resistance to change, firms should use counseling and education programs to describe the changes that will occur in reported performance and performance evaluation systems. These programs should start before changes occur to reduce

problems of resistance. Clear rationales should be given for the changes, including the benefits that employees will realize as a result of them. Among the benefits are a better and more secure work environment that results from employment in a more profitable and successful firm, a fairer performance evaluation system, and increased compensation because of the higher profits.

Changes in the profile of the work force. The introduction of new technology and a CMS results in a general trend to increase the scope of many employees' jobs. The relative sizes of existing employee groups and their required skills also change. These issues are discussed next.

Generalists. An important way to realize continuous improvement (based on integration, innovation, flexibility, and speed) is to have employees who are generalists rather than specialists.[1] This is critical for breaking down functional myopia in employees. An important consequence of having employees who are generalists is that jobs are enriched. Each employee has more job variety, which enables employees to make larger contributions to the success of the firm. The Japanese have used this generalist strategy quite successfully to achieve long-term goals.[2] Of course, one implication of having generalists is a significant reduction in the number of job classifications. Another implication is the increased importance of having effective continuous education programs.

An effective way to create generalist employees is to rotate employees between jobs periodically. This also enriches jobs by increasing variety. The Japanese implement job rotation by having engineers and managers spend their first ten to fifteen years rotating through manufacturing, accounting, engineering and other areas, spending a few years in each. This strategy of creating generalists by the use of teams and job rotation is inextricably linked to the Japanese policy of lifetime employment.

Physical workers. The introduction of robots and other automated technology will eliminate many physical jobs, such as materials handlers and assemblers. Those workers remaining may be retrained as production technologists, who as generalists will know much more about an AMT firm's overall production process than current specialists. Many of these new jobs will require more skills and offer more variety than the jobs that now exist.

Some workers will be retrained to monitor the new technology.[3] An important issue is designing these jobs to make them sufficiently interesting and stimulating to keep employees alert. Research on monitoring and vigilance indicates that people do not always attend conscientiously to their monitoring responsibilities. For example, extensive evidence about pilots who fly the new automated airplanes like the B-757 and the B-767 revealed their frequent lack of attention (some bordering on criminal neglect) to the current status of flights.[4] If even experienced, highly trained pilots—whose very lives are on the line—are poor at continuous monitoring, what monitoring performance can be expected of production employees? Therefore, a policy of job rotation (perhaps even every few hours) may be necessary to keep people alert to continuous and accurate monitoring.

Information workers. Technological advances will also increase the number and kinds of information workers responsible for designing and implementing software and hardware systems.[5] Implementing a CMS and the philosophy of continuous improvement will require a heavy investment in continuing education for information workers. As the source of many innovations (e.g., in software, management systems, R&D, and activity and process improvements), these workers are the key to the long-run success of AMT firms.

Information workers who will be radically affected by the introduction of a CMS are accountants, internal auditors, and bookkeepers. They could prove the most resistant to a CMS, because they have based their careers on developing and operating the existing cost accounting systems.[6] Many of the tasks they perform will either be eliminated or delegated to teams. Tasks that will be eliminated include those that will be automated by computer software and processing (e.g., bar codes to track inventory). Other tasks will be simplified because of reductions in (or elimination of) activities brought about by the use of JIT.[7] A firm that operates with JIT, for example, will also have less inventory and paper trails that require internal auditing, which means a reduced need for internal auditors.[8] Finally, some accounting tasks that involve routine score-keeping can even be delegated to the direct line employees.

Deskilling, alienation, and sabotage. Many of the new jobs, such as the production technology generalist and the information worker, should provide more job variety and satisfaction for workers. However, for many physical workers, there is the potential for deskilling (a reduction in the number and kind of tasks performed) and increased alienation from new work that these employees may find unsuitable.[9]

There are three potentially negative consequences of deskilling and alienation. First, they may cause worker unrest and result in more clashes between unions and management. Second, more errors and accidents may occur, either because employees become bored with performing simple, tedious tasks or because they rebel against a work system they find unfair.

The worst outcome from deskilling and alienation is actual organizational sabotage. Sabotage may occur in many different ways, such as tampering with the CMS to slow its implementation, individuals banding together to oppose the changes, or gaming with the CMS. Saboteurs, or "technology assassins,"[10] are most likely to be workers on the verge of losing their jobs or workers who find their new jobs unsuitable. There are at least three ways to combat such resistance. First, the championship team and its supporters must involve all organizational members to obtain their input and to explain fully why the changes are beneficial and necessary. Starting educational programs as soon as possible will also combat resistance. Second, the firm should retrain those workers whose jobs become obsolete. Third, the changes must be implemented over a reasonable time period.

Union relations. Unions will certainly monitor the implementation of a CMS, which can result in changes in job classifications and responsibilities, new performance standards and measurements, and altered compensation systems. Top management and the CMS champion must therefore work closely with union leaders. The "best managed" U.S. companies have taken great pains to foster strong, congenial relations with their unions.[11]

As new technology is implemented, one potential problem that AMT firms will have to address is the job displacement of union members. A recent study reports that the managements at several firms have agreed to create a higher paying classification for workers performing AMT jobs to increase their seniority in the firm. This decreases their chances of being laid off while they are retrained.[12]

NOTES

1 R. Harvey, "Factory 2000," *Iron Age* (June 4, 1984), pp 27–58; R. Schonberger, *World Class Manufacturing: The Lesson of Simplicity Applied* (New York: The Free Press, 1986).

2 J. Lincoln, M. Hanada, and K. McBride, "Organizational Structures in Japanese and U.S. Manufacturing," *Administrative Science Quarterly* (1986), pp 338–364.

3 K. Ebel, "Social and Labour Implications of Flexible Manufacturing Systems," *International Labour Review* (March-April, 1985), pp. 133–145; S. M. Young and J. Davis, "Factories of the Past and of the Future: The Impact of Robotics on Workers and Management Accounting Systems," in D. Cooper and T. Hopper (eds) *Critical Accounts* (London: McMillan, in press).

4 E. Weiner, "Beyond the Sterile Cockpit," *Human Factors* (Feb. 1985), pp 75–90; E. Weiner, "Fallible Humans and Vulnerable Systems: Lessons Learned From Aviation," in J.A. Wise and A. Debons, *Information Systems: Failure Analysis NATO ASI Series, Volume 32* (Berlin: Springer-Verlag, 1987).

5 R. Kaplan, "Measuring Manufacturing Performance: A New Challenge for Managerial Accounting Research," *The Accounting Review* (Oct. 1983), pp 686–705.

6 T. Lammert and R. Ehrsam, "The Human Element: The Real Challenge in Modernizing Cost Systems," *Management Accounting* (July 1987), pp 32–37.

7 G. Foster and C. Horngren, "Cost Accounting and Cost Management in a JIT Environment," *Journal of Cost Management* (Winter 1988), pp 4–14.

8 R. Barefield and S.M. Young, *Internal Auditing in a Just-in-Time Manufacturing Environment* (Sarasota, Fla.: The Institute of Internal Auditors, 1988).

9 H. Shaiken, *Work Transformed—Automation and Labor in the Computer Age* (New York: Holt, Rinehart and Winston, 1984).

10 D. Leonard-Barton and Kraus, "Implementing New Technology," *Harvard Business Review* (Nov.–Dec. 1985), pp 102–110.

11 J. O'Toole, "Employee Practices at the Best Managed Companies," *California Management Review* (Fall 1985), pp 35–49.

12 R.E. Walton and G.I. Susman, "People Policies for the New Machines," *Harvard Business Review* (March-April 1987).

goals that are clearly defined by budgets or overall profit and cost targets. Other characteristics of strong cultures are specific norms of behavior, members who are considered organizational heroes (an innovative CEO like Lee Iacocca, for example), and effective communication networks.

A strong functional culture is nurtured by high worker involvement and participation, long-term employment (in many instances), goal congruence between employees and management, and a pervasive feeling of teamwork. Overall, employees feel that performing their work well benefits both them and the firm. In contrast, a strong dysfunctional culture is run by management fiat, which causes employees to have poor attitudes and low commitment toward the firm, which ultimately leads to a high turnover of employees. An ill-defined culture is one whose members do not have similar values, beliefs, and goals. Such an organization is simply a collection of individuals who happen to be employed by the same firm.

Both strong functional and strong dysfunctional cultures are often associated with higher performance than ill-defined cultures. Strong functional and strong dysfunctional cultures may lead to better performance than ill-defined cultures, but there are differences between their short- and long-term performance. In the short term, strong dysfunctional cultures may produce better performance (at least on paper) than strong functional ones, because individuals who manage by the numbers attempt to maximize short-term indicators. In the long term, though, a strong functional culture should foster a healthier organization. Its focus on continuous improvement should ultimately result in better performance.

Champion. Almost all successful innovations are initiated and implemented by a zealous, voluntary champion.[8] Champions often have strong entrepreneurial skills and are willing to gamble their jobs on the success of the innovations they sponsor. Due to the significance of the changes brought by a CMS, the champion must usually be someone at a fairly high level in the firm. A CMS champion often collides with supporters of a particular product or technology, because the CMS will change how that product or technology is evaluated. Therefore, top management support for the CMS champion is essential. Other characteristics of champions include the ability to motivate others, the political savvy concerning when to bend organizational rules, and the knowledge of how to acquire all the resources needed for the implementation.

Despite the importance of having a CMS champion, no one person can do it all alone—an implementation team guided by the CMS champion is needed. The team includes:[9]

1. The champion himself;
2. A sponsor (or Godfather)—often someone in top management—who can ensure that the project has the necessary political and financial support;
3. A project manager responsible for administration; and
4. An integrator with strong behavioral skills who can manage conflict and facilitate communication.

Change process. The champion implements the change process (the third C) through three of the remaining Cs: compensation, controls, and continuous education. Each is discussed later in this article. The key elements in the change process are discussed in the following sections.

Top management support. Having the support and commitment of top management is a necessary first step to the successful implementation of a CMS.[10] Without this commitment and support, agents of change like the champion and his team will be blocked by bureaucracy (i.e., being forced to go through the "right" channels) and by employees intent on protecting their own turf. For instance, if a change means usurping a manager's power, top management support may reduce the potential conflict between the champion and the manager.

Financial resources. Changing to a CMS cannot succeed without the necessary financial support. Funding is required for the development and implementation of information processing technology, new software, and continuing education.

Resistance to change. Perhaps the biggest challenge in successfully implementing a CMS is individual and organizational resistance to change.[11] (See [Box] for a discussion of the important issues.)

Time frame. For the implementation of a CMS to be successful, a realistic time frame—five years is a good estimate—has to be allowed.[12] Knowing that major changes are slow to be adopted should help organizational members adjust and also allow the cultural changes to set in slowly.

Each organization must decide how best to evaluate changes in the reported performance of products, technology, managers, and activities that result from the introduction of the CMS. For example, if a manager's product line profitability changes as a result of the CMS, management can do one of two things: Either it can use the new evaluation procedure immediately to drop the product line and fire the manager or it can give the manager sufficient time to change his activities to reduce costs. If management chooses the latter (which is probably the wiser choice), this will also allow them more time to decide what the new cost standards and performance evaluation system should be. Of course, it may be that the product should be dropped and the product manager reassigned. However, this is fundamentally a strategic management issue—top management needs to reevaluate all of its strategies in light of the new costs.

Strategy. The scope of the change is an important decision. Three strategies have been advocated: evolutionary, revolutionary and greenfield/pilot. Another strategic consideration is whether the change should be driven from the top down or from the bottom up. (See [Box] for a discussion of these matters.)

Commitment. Changes in AMT and competition occur at such a rate that the only constant is change. In implementing a CMS, a firm's goal should be to foster a new organizational mindset whose central philosophy is managing by commitment to continuous improvement. Referring back to Exhibit 1, it is clear that commitment is by no means an end in itself. In fact, there is a loop back from commitment via continuous education to the champion. As the loop goes back to the champion, compensation and controls are once again used to develop a higher level of commitment to continuous improvement. The commitment and support of top management and every employee should enable the philosophy of managing by commitment to continuous improvement to become the new mindset of

STRATEGIC CONSIDERATIONS IN IMPLEMENTING A COST MANAGEMENT SYSTEM

In planning and implementing a cost management system (CMS) three possible strategies can be followed.

The *revolutionary strategy* attempts to bring about a change simultaneously in all parts of a firm. The benefit of this strategy is that it may provide a coordinated, centralized, and relatively quick change, which may increase the probability that the desired CMS and philosophy are achieved throughout the firm. The costs of this strategy are the enormous and immediate implementation cost and the disruptions imposed on the entire firm (plus the chance that the firm may not recover if the implementation is not successful).

The *evolutionary strategy* attempts to implement the innovation in a domino pattern, one operating unit changing after the other. A benefit of the evolutionary strategy is that the entire company does not simultaneously experience complete upheaval. Further, if the change fails in one unit, only its progress is impeded and the innovation or the implementation process can be improved before it is tried again. The cost of this strategy is that change occurs at a slower rate; by the time the entire organization switches to the new system, it may be obsolete.

Recent studies[1] suggest that successful innovations are associated with either the evolutionary strategy or a third possible strategy called the *greenfield strategy (or pilot project)*. The greenfield strategy involves setting up a new, model operation to introduce the innovation. This strategy allows the firm to start from scratch and build from the ground up based on an ideal design.

Top-down vs. bottom-up strategy. Another strategic consideration in planning and implementing in CMS is whether the changes should be driven from the top down or from the bottom up. The benefit of the top-down strategy, as with the revolutionary strategy, is the centralized, coordinated nature of the change process. However, top-down strategies usually involve more employee resistance, because in many cases they have had little involvement and participation in changes that greatly affect their jobs. In addition, management often does not take advantage of the employees' local information. Hence, the changes that they suggest may go against what the employees believe to be the best work methods.

A bottom-up strategy employs participative decision making and other employee involvement techniques intended to increase the initiation and acceptance of changes. This strategy allows employees to contribute their local information to help implement the changes. If a bottom-up strategy is used, then it is crucial to involve all employees early and use educational programs to extol the benefits of the new system. Problems with this strategy are that employees may not initiate change unless they believe it is in their own best interest, and the content and process of change may not be what the owners and managers desire.

The best approach is probably a strategy that is simultaneously top-down and bottom-up. This dual strategy provides a higher probability of successful implementation.[2] There should be extensive involvement and participation of all employees, but top management should develop the basic outline and process for the implementation. Then, the employees should deal with the specific aspects of the implementation that affect them. The critical issue is to develop an organizational culture in which all employees voluntarily participate and reach a consensus about the why, what, and how of the CMS and the philosophy of managing by commitment to continuous improvement.

NOTES

1 J. Quinn, "Managing Innovation: Controlled Chaos," *Harvard Business Review* (May-June 1985), pp 73–84; D. Leonard-Barton and Kraus, "Implementing New Technology," *Harvard Business Review* (Nov.-Dec. 1985), pp 102–110.

2 L. Greiner, "Patterns of Organizational Change," *Harvard Business Review* (May-June 1967), pp 119–130; Kanter, *The Change Masters* (New York: Simon and Shuster, 1983).

AMT firms. These changes in mindset can be facilitated by using controls, compensation, and continuous education, which are described next.

Controls. Controls should be designed and implemented to increase both the rate of continuous improvement and the probability that a firm's strategy will be achieved. Generally, the strategy of AMT firms is characterized in behavioral and organizational terms as emphasizing various mixes of integration, innovation, flexibility, diversity, efficiency, speed, and quality. There are three controls that the CMS champion may employ to achieve this strategy: JIT/TQC, organizational structure, and teams.

JIT/TQC. The successful implementation of JIT/TQC, the emphasis of which is on simplification, continuous improvement, standardization, zero defects, and elimination of waste, is necessary for the successful implementation of AMTs. An important benefit derived is that the basis of control shifts from paper reports to visual control. Visual control by both supervisors and peers is more timely and less expensive, which makes it more effective and efficient than control by reference to feedback information in control reports. An important aspect of visual control is to post publicly (e.g., on the shop floor) information about current performance to encourage continuous improvement.

Organizational structure. An organization's structure is the extent to which its activities and job responsibilities are vertically and horizontally differentiated. Most contemporary manufacturing firms are differentiated vertically into many discrete levels (typically with at least ten levels between the workers and the president) and horizontally by products, technology, geography, and functional areas. This multidimensional differentiation creates a series of dissimilar organizational subunits, each of which is focused mainly on its own empire (e.g., the marketing function for a particular product line in the Northeast). To overcome this myopic focus, a firm must use such controls as budgets, formal lines of authority, and standard rules and operating procedures to integrate and coordinate its various subunits.

This vertical and horizontal structuring is not conducive to developing the necessary behavioral and organizational characteristics of a successful AMT firm. Qualities such as innovation, integration, flexibility, and speed, which are required to pursue continuous improvement, are not as likely to develop. To resolve this problem, we believe that firms need to be radically restructured. For example, less differentiation would require a lower investment in controls to integrate and coordinate activities.

For an AMT firm to sustain a high level of continuous improvement, it must be successful at developing and implementing innovation. Research has found that firms with high levels of innovation have what is called an organic structure.[13] Their characteristics include a flat organizational structure with little vertical differentiation, decentralization of power and decision making, low formalization of rules and procedures, low job specialization, high concentrations of professionals with widely shared knowledge, and an emphasis on horizontal rather than vertical communication. This organizational structure results in a higher probability that innovations will be developed and implemented.

Teams. Teams are the critical unit of behavior for control purposes in successful, innovative AMT firms.[14] Teams of workers, managers, marketers, engineers, and information specialists that cut across traditional functional boundaries reduce myopia and turf wars. Some teams should also include suppliers of technology and materials and also transporters and distributors. Teams that cut across the traditional functional areas should be the basic unit of organizational structure and control for continuous improvement in AMT firms. Each vertical level of a firm should comprise teams that coordinate the activities of subordinate teams. An AMT firm will be more effective when there are a small number of team-based vertical levels—only four to six levels from workers to top management, for example, instead of the typical ten to twenty levels. This flatter structure is designed to encourage integration, innovation, flexibility, and speed.

The central idea in designing the horizontal structure is to pull technology and products to the market based on demand rather than push technology and products on the market. Designing the structure of a firm based on pull does not preclude being ready to satisfy demand for new products immediately. The basic idea of the pull philosophy is to have products available upon demand. The implication is that teams should be primarily based on the products of a firm. One benefit of teams structured by products is that manufacturing becomes more focused, which reduces the number of indirect employees and indirect costs, which increases the direct traceability of costs to products.

Compensation.   The CMS champion can use compensation to control behavior and motivate employees to increase the rate of continuous improvement. Compensation systems used in manufacturing firms typically focus on the individual. Employees are paid based on time, skill, and performance, with a heavy emphasis on results of the current period. However, AMT firms must modify these traditional systems to achieve their strategic goals.

Five important changes to compensation systems should be made. First, these systems need to be directly tied to creating and sustaining continuous improvement. Examples include bonus compensation tied to reductions in the number of parts per product, process variability, cycle time, engineering change orders, and increased manufacturing cycle efficiency. Second, compensation should be contingent on both team performance and individual skills. Third, the emphasis on current performance should be replaced by an emphasis on longer-term performance. Fourth, the compensation system must encourage employees to be innovative by allowing them to take some risks. Lastly, companies must increase their use of nonfinancial compensation to create an atmosphere of positive reinforcement. These considerations on compensation are detailed next.

Mix of performance and skill.   JIT requires a compensation system that does not motivate employees to produce more than is currently needed. The approach frequently taken in manufacturing—a piece rate system with a unit bonus for each unit produced in excess of a standard—is not effective for motivating employees to produce a target output level.[15]

An effective compensation system to motivate employees to produce a targeted level provides maximum compensation when actual output equals the targeted quantity (or standard output) of acceptable quality (e.g., zero defects). This maximum compensation is reduced for deviations over and under the target. Such a compensation system[16] (which is consistent with the JIT philosophy) can be expressed algebraically as:

$$C = F - P(T - A)$$

where

C = total compensation
F = fixed compensation
P = penalty (i.e., negative bonus) per unit of output
T = target output
A = actual output

It is not necessary that there be symmetrical penalties for actual output over and under the target output. The values of P should depend on the opportunity cost of overproduction and underproduction relative to current demand.

Teams.   Except for skill-related compensation, compensation should be based on team performance to foster team spirit, cooperation, and continuous improvement. Compensation can further be linked to the performance of combinations of teams that are formed according to the firm's strategy. For example, one team may be responsible for developing, manufacturing, and marketing a product in a particular geographic area, with similar teams having responsibility for the same product elsewhere. To reinforce the importance of having a successful product worldwide, all of these teams can be grouped together. Thus, an employee's compensation would be based on his skills, his team's performance, and the combined performance of all of the teams that manage the product.

Long-term orientation.   A long-term orientation must be taken on compensation. Employees must be motivated to maximize performance (i.e., minimize cost) over the life cycle of a product or AMT. An effective approach taken by many firms for senior management is to base compensation on a three- to five-year performance period. For example, a bonus earned at the end of year three can be based on performance during years one through three.

Innovation.   Compensation systems in AMT firms should be designed to foster innovation, which means that prudent risk taking should be encouraged. The key is to realize that firms with a high rate of innovation have many more failures than successes. Thus, it is critical to motivate employees to initiate enough experiments to generate a sufficient number of successes, while not severely penalizing them for failures. To encourage experimentation, compensation can be tied to the number of experiments attempted and suggestions made. To reduce risk aversion, it may be desirable to make a high percentage of the expected total financial compensation equal to an employee's fixed salary, since this will reduce the financial penalty when there is failure. Another option is to compensate employees for bearing risk by increasing the percentage payout (e.g., percentage of profits earned as pay), which allows successful experiments to offset unsuccessful ones.

Nonfinancial compensation.   Peters and Waterman[17] found that excellent companies used nonfinancial rewards much more than did other firms. These firms found many ways to celebrate success— particularly successful experiments and innovations. Nonfinancial rewards have been important in creating an atmosphere of positive reinforcement and success. For example, giving pins, badges, medals, trophies, dinners, and parties for innovations and other successes creates and sustains an atmosphere of success, innovation, cooperation, and continuous improvement. Another effective and inexpensive nonfinancial reward is the public posting of performance improvements and suggestions.

Continuous education.   The term *continuous* education, rather than *continuing*, is used because it reflects the importance of making education ongoing—from one educational module to another. In contrast, continuing education is more commonly associated with the periodic (and often infrequent) returns to education. Continuous education is the final key to successfully implementing a CMS for two reasons: First, continuous education can be the cornerstone of a program designed to develop a culture of managing by commitment to continuous improvement. Second, continuous improvement requires constant innovation, which is facilitated by exposing employees to new information. All employees should participate in continuous education programs. The spirit of this implementation is captured by changing the name from *training*, the term that is typically used in industry, to *education*.

Who.   A recent survey[18] of manufacturing firms indicates that, during the previous year, only 31 percent of all employees in the companies surveyed received training. For those who received training, the mean number of hours per year was thirty-five. Middle management was the employee group that received the most training, and the average for them

was only forty-four hours per year. To cite another example, in 1981 corporations spent \$3,300 per worker on physical assets, but only \$300 per worker on training.[19] These figures indicate an inadequate commitment to educating employees.

Obviously, the technical aspects of the CMS need to be taught to engineers, managers, and accountants. However, of equal or greater importance is educating all employees, particularly the production workers, in how to perform their tasks more effectively. For example, Hagedorn[20] concluded from discussions with corporate training directors that firms need to provide an average of four to eight hours per week of education to each employee to prepare them to work in an AMT factory. The key is to create a culture in which workers want to find better ways of accomplishing activities.

This approach is founded on the recognition by top management that employees are the most important asset of their firm. Continuous education increases the value of these human assets. To embed this idea further, firms should account for these improvements in human assets as they do with other long-term assets—by capitalizing and amoritizing the cost of education programs (or, more accurately, the increased value of the firm that results from employees' increased skills and innovations).

What.   Continuous education should focus initially on the dysfunctional behavior induced by managing by the numbers. It should then provide examples of managing by commitment to continuous improvement. The implementation of the CMS and its potential impact on performance must also be discussed.

Employees need to be grounded in the technical aspects of the CMS (such as activity and lifecycle accounting) to understand how to make effective decisions regarding pricing, mix and volume, make versus buy, and capital investments. The new compensation systems should be explained to increase the motivation of employees to adopt the philosophy of continuous improvement. This shows employees why it is in their best interest to increase product quality and reduce the cost of non-value-added activities.

How.   The traditional training approach used by most firms (i.e., formal, separate, and short training programs) is inadequate. Instead, these formal programs should be augmented with informal education—making every employee both a teacher and a student. Continuous education is also vital for increasing the effectiveness of creating generalists through job rotation and cross-training.

One implementation strategy is to use indirect employees (staff and support) to teach direct employees how to perform activities previously performed by the indirect employees. For example, line operators can be taught routine preventive maintenance activities (e.g., lubricating machines), which would free scarce maintenance workers to attend to more complex activities such as overhauls and breakdowns. Several benefits arise from this shifting of responsibilities. Line operators have richer, more varied jobs; skilled maintenance workers can apply their skills to more complex activities; fewer maintenance workers are needed; preventive maintenance is done more frequently; and direct traceability of costs is increased.

CONCLUSION

To compete successfully in today's manufacturing environment, the decisions and actions of AMT firms and their employees must be guided by a cost management system. This requires firms to change their philosophy from managing by the numbers to managing by a commitment to continuous improvement. Because human behavior plays such an important role in cost management, the focus of this [reading] has been on developing a behavioral model to detail the many variables that must be considered to implement a CMS successfully.

NOTES

1 H. T. Johnson and R. Kaplan, *Relevance Lost: The Rise and Fall of Management Accounting* (Boston: Harvard Business School Press, 1987).

2 CAM-I, Cost Management System (CMS), Phase I, *Conceptual Design Document* (Arlington, Tex.: CAM-I, 1987).

3 Johnson and Kaplan (1987). op. cit.

4 T. Peters and R. Waterman, *In Search of Excellence—Lessons from America's Best Run Companies* (New York: Harper and Row, 1982).

5 S. Davis, *Managing Corporate Culture* (Cambridge, Mass.: Ballinger, 1984).

6 T. E. Deal and A. A. Kennedy, *Corporate Cultures—The Rites and Rituals of Corporate Life* (Reading, Mass.: Addison-Wesley, 1982).

7 Deal and Kennedy, op. cit.; W. Ouchi, *Theory Z* (New York: Basic Books, 1981); Peters and Waterman (1982)., op. cit.

8 J. Quinn, "Managing Innovation: Controlled Chaos," *Harvard Business Review* (May-June, 1985), pp 73–84; C. M. Crawford *New Products Management* (Homewood, Ill.: Richard D. Irwin, Inc., 1987).

9 D. Leonard-Barton and W. Kraus, "Implementing New Technology," *Harvard Business Review* (Nov.-Dec. 1985), pp 102–110.

10 R. Kanter, *The Change Masters* (New York: Simon and Schuster, 1983).

11 G. Zaltman and R. Duncan, *Strategies for Planned Change* (New York: John Wiley & Sons, 1977); J. Kotter and L. Schlesinger, "Choosing Strategies for Change," *Harvard Business Review* (March-April 1979), pp 106–114.

12 Quinn (1985)., op. cit., and J. Ettlie, "Innovation in Manufacturing," in D. Gray, T. Solomon and W. Hetzner (eds.) *Technological Innovation: Strategies for a New Partnership* (New York: North Holland, 1986).

13 T. Burns and G. Stalker, *The Management of Innovation* (London: Tavistock Publications, 1961); R. Hall, *Organizations: Structure and Process,* Third Edition (Englewood Cliffs, N.J.: Prentice-Hall, 1982).

14 Ettlie (1986)., op. cit.; Hagedorn, H., "The Factory of the Future: What About the People?," *Journal of Business Strategy* (1984), pp 38–45; Harvey (1984)., op. cit.

15 J. Heard, "JIT Accounting," in *Readings in Zero Inventory* APICS, 1984, pp 20–23.

16 S. M. Young, "Participative Budgeting: The Effects of Risk Aversion and Asymmetric Information on Budgetary Slack," *Journal of Accounting Research* (Autumn 1985), pp 829–842; S. M. Young, M. D. Shields, and G. Wolf, "Manufacturing Controls and Performance: An Experiment," *Accounting Organizations and Society* (unpublished article).

17 Peters and Waterman (1982)., op. cit.

18 J. Gordon, "Where the Training Goes," *Training* (Oct. 1986), pp 49–60.

19 "Firing Up Support for CIM," *Industry Week* (Nov. 2, 1987), pp 49–97.

20 Hagedorn, (1984)., op. cit.

Another Hidden Edge—Japanese Management Accounting

Toshiro Hiromoto

Much has been written about why Japanese manufacturers continue to outperform their U.S. competitors in cost, quality, and on-time delivery. Most experts point to practices like just-in-time production, total quality control, and the aggressive use of flexible manufacturing technologies. One area that has received less attention, but that I believe contributes mightily to Japanese competitiveness, is how many companies' management accounting systems reinforce a top-to-bottom commitment to process and product innovation.

I have studied management accounting systems at Japanese companies in several major industries including automobiles, computers, consumer electronics, and semiconductors. Although practices varied greatly, several related patterns did emerge. These patterns differentiate certain aspects of Japanese management accounting from established practices in the United States.

Like their U.S. counterparts, Japanese companies must value inventory for tax purposes and financial statements. But the Japanese don't let these accounting procedures determine how they measure and control organizational activities. Japanese companies tend to use their management control systems to support and reinforce their manufacturing strategies. A more direct link therefore exists between management accounting practices and corporate goals.

Japanese companies seem to use accounting systems more to motivate employees to act in accordance with long-term manufacturing strategies than to provide senior management with precise data on costs, variances, and profits. Accounting plays more of an "influencing" role than an "informing" role. For example, high-level Japanese managers seem to worry less about whether an overhead allocation system reflects the precise demands each product makes on corporate resources than about how the system affects the cost-reduc-

tion priorities of middle managers and shop-floor workers. As a result, they sometimes use allocation techniques that executives in the United States might dismiss as simplistic or even misguided.

Accounting in Japan also reflects and reinforces an overriding commitment to market-driven management. When estimating costs on new products, for example, many companies make it a point not to rely completely on prevailing engineering standards. Instead, they establish target costs derived from estimates of a competitive market price. These target costs are usually well below currently achievable costs, which are based on standard technologies and processes. Managers then set benchmarks to measure incremental progress toward meeting the target cost objectives.

Several companies I studied also de-emphasize standard cost systems for monitoring factory performance. In general, Japanese management accounting does not stress optimizing within existing constraints. Rather, it encourages employees to make continual improvements by tightening those constraints.

The following cases highlight some of the differences between management accounting in Japan and the United States. My intention is to be suggestive, not definitive. Not all Japanese companies use the techniques I describe, and some U.S. companies have adopted approaches similar to what I have seen in Japan.

ALLOCATING OVERHEAD

American executives have been barraged with criticism about how long-accepted techniques for allocating manufacturing overhead can distort product costs and paint a flawed picture of the profitability of manufacturing operations. Accounting experts challenge direct labor hours as an overhead allocation base since direct labor represents only a small percentage of total costs in most manufacturing environments. They argue that a logical and causal relationship should exist between the overhead burden and the assignment of costs to individual products. They believe that an allocation system should capture as precisely as possible the reality of shop-floor costs.

Japanese companies are certainly aware of this perspective, but many of the companies I examined don't seem to share it. Consider the practices of the Hitachi division that operates the world's largest factory devoted exclusively to videocassette recorders. The Hitachi VCR plant is highly automated yet continues to use direct labor as the basis for allocating manufacturing overhead. Overhead allocation doesn't reflect the actual production process in the factory's automated environment. When I asked the accountants whether that policy might lead to bad decisions, they responded with an emphatic no. Hitachi, like many large Japanese manufacturers, is convinced that reducing direct labor is essential for ongoing cost improvement. The company is committed to aggressive automation to promote long-term competitiveness. Allocating overhead based on direct labor creates the desired strong pro-automation incentives throughout the organization.

The perspective offered by Hitachi managers seems to be shared by their counterparts at many other companies. It is more important, they argue, to have an overhead allocation system (and other aspects of management accounting) that motivates employees to work in harmony with the company's long-term goals than to pinpoint production costs. Japanese managers want their accounting systems to help create a competitive future, not quantify the performance of their organizations at this moment.

Another Hitachi factory (this one in the refrigeration and air-conditioning equipment sector) employs an overhead allocation technique, based on the number of parts in product models, to influence its engineers' design decisions. Japanese companies have long known what more and more U.S. companies are now recognizing—that the number of parts in a product, especially custom parts, directly relates to the amount of overhead. Manufacturing costs increase with the complexity of the production process, as measured, for example, by the range of products built in a factory or the number of parts per

product. In plants assembling diverse products, reducing the number of parts and promoting the use of standard parts across product lines can lower costs dramatically.

Using standard parts can also lower materials costs, insofar as it creates possibilities for more aggressive volume buying. Yet on a product-by-product basis, many cost systems fail to recognize these economies.

Consider a factory building several different products. The products all use one or both of two parts, A and B, which the factory buys in roughly equal amounts. Most of the products use both parts. The unit cost of part A is $7, of part B, $10. Part B has more capabilities than part A; in fact, B can replace A. If the factory doubles its purchases of part B, it qualifies for a discounted $8 unit price. For products that incorporate both parts, substituting B for A makes sense to qualify for the discount. (The total parts cost is $17 using A and B, $16 using Bs only.) Part B, in other words, should become a standard part for the factory. But departments building products that use only part A may be reluctant to accept the substitute part B because, even discounted, the cost of B exceeds that of A.

This factory needs an accounting system that motivates departments to look beyond their parochial interests for the sake of enterprise-level cost reduction. Hitachi has adopted such an approach by adding overhead surcharges to products that use nonstandard parts. The more custom parts in a product, the higher the overhead charge.

ACCOUNTING FOR MARKET-DRIVEN DESIGN

By the time a new product enters the manufacturing stage, opportunities to economize significantly are limited. As the Hitachi refrigerator example suggests, Japanese companies have long recognized that the design stage holds the greatest promise for supporting low-cost production. Many U.S. manufacturers, including Texas Instruments, Hewlett-Packard, and Ford, are also making competitive strides in this area. But certain Japanese companies have taken the process even further. They don't simply design products to make better use of technologies and work flows, they design and build products that will meet the price required for market success—whether or not that price is supported by current manufacturing practices. Their management accounting systems incorporate this commitment.

Daihatsu Motor Company, a medium-sized automobile producer that has yet to enter the U.S. market, provides a good example of market-driven accounting practices. It installed the *genka kikaku* product development system in its factories soon after affiliating with Toyota, which pioneered the approach. The *genka kikaku* process at Daihatsu usually lasts three years, at which time the new car goes into production. The process begins when the *shusa* (the product manager responsible for a new car from planning through sales) instructs the functional departments to submit the features and performance specifications that they believe the car should include. The *shusa* then makes recommendations to the senior managers, who issue a development order.

Next comes cost estimation. Management does not simply turn over the development order to the accountants and ask what it would cost to build the car based on existing engineering standards. Rather, Daihatsu establishes a target selling price based on what it believes the market will accept and specifies a target profit margin that reflects the company's strategic plans and financial projections. The difference between these two figures represents the "allowable cost" per car.

In practice, this target cost is far below what realistically can be attained. So each department calculates an "accumulated cost" based on current technologies and practices—that is, the standard cost achievable with no innovation. Finally, management establishes a target cost that represents a middle ground between these two estimates. This adjusted price-profit margin cost becomes the goal toward which everyone works.

At the design stage, engineers working on different parts of the car interact frequently with the various players (purchasing, shop-floor supervisors, parts suppliers) who will implement the final design. As the design process unfolds, the participants compare estimated costs with the target. The variances are fed back to the product developers, and the cycle repeats: design proposals, cost estimates, variance calculations, value engineering analysis to include desired features at the lowest possible cost, and redesign. The cycle ends with the approval of a final design that meets the target cost.

A similar dynamic operates at the production stage, where Daihatsu uses complementary approaches to manage costs: total plant cost management and *dai-atari kanri*, or per-unit cost management.

Reports based on total plant cost management are prepared for senior executives and plant managers. The studies compare budgeted costs with actual costs for an entire factory. Reports generated by the *dai-atari kanri* system are intended for managers at specific workstations. Comparisons between budgeted and actual costs are made only for "variable" charges, which include some costs, like tools, that do not vary strictly with short-term output. Put simply, items subject to *dai-atari kanri* include all costs that can be reduced through workers' continual efforts and process improvement activities—that is, controllable costs.

In production, as in the design stage, Daihatsu does not take a static approach to cost management. During the first year of production for a new car, the budgeted cost reflects targets set during the *genka kikaku* process. This cost is a starting point, however, not an ultimate goal; over the course of the year, it is tightened monthly by a cost-reduction rate based on short-term profit objectives. In subsequent years, the actual cost of the previous period becomes the starting point for further tightening, thereby creating a cost-reduction dynamic for as long as the model remains in production.

GOOD-BYE TO STANDARD COSTS

The market-driven philosophy at Daihatsu and other Japanese companies helps to explain why standard cost systems are not used as widely in Japan as they are in the United States. Standard costs reflect an engineering mind-set and technology-driven management. The goal is to minimize variances between budgeted and actual costs—to perform as closely as possible to best available practice. Market-driven management, on the other hand, emphasizes doing what it takes to achieve a desired performance level under market conditions. How efficiently a company *should* be able to build a product is less important to the Japanese than how efficiently it *must* be able to build it for maximum marketplace success.

Many Japanese companies that have used standard cost systems seem to be moving beyond them. NEC, the diversified electronics giant, designed and installed its standard cost system in the 1950s. The company still uses standard cost reports as a factory management tool and continues to train new employees in the system. But NEC recognizes that it has reached a strategic turning point and it is adjusting its management accounting policies accordingly.

NEC installed its standard cost system when it was supplying a stable product range (mostly telephones and exchangers) at stable prices to a large and stable customer, Nippon Telegraph & Telephone (NTT). Today NEC produces a vast array of products subject to rapid obsolescence and technological change. Its product line poses severe challenges to the standard cost system. The cost standards cannot be revised quickly enough for many products, so variance reports are increasingly open to question. (NEC revises its cost standards every six months, and even then only for a subset of products.) As a result, the company is relying more heavily on departmental budgets than product-by-product variances from standard costs. As with Daihatsu, targets are based on market demands and planned profit levels, and are tightened over time.

The U.S. subsidiary of a major Japanese electronics company takes this budgeting approach even further. Its production and marketing departments operate as separate profit centers. These departments interact to establish internal transfer prices for products. The transfer price is a negotiated percentage of the market price. Under this method, market prices critically influence departmental performance, since market prices are the basis for determining transfer prices. Both the production and marketing functions are encouraged to respond to market demand and competitive trends rather than focus solely on internal indicators.

The company recently extended this approach to its sales department, which is separate from marketing. Selling costs used to be allocated to individual products under a standard cost approach. Now the sales department operates as a profit center and negotiates commission levels with the marketing department. Through the cost system, these commissions are then assigned to products. Thus the marketing department can make product decisions without accepting selling expenses as given, which increases pressure on the sales force to operate as efficiently as possible.

ACCOUNTING AND STRATEGY

The accounting practices I have described do not necessarily represent Japanese practices as a whole. They do, however, point to a central principle that seems to guide management accounting in Japan—that accounting policies should be subservient to corporate strategy, not independent of it. Japanese manufacturing strategy places high premiums on quality and timely delivery in addition to low-cost production. Thus companies make extensive use, certainly more than many of their U.S. competitors, of nonfinancial measures to evaluate factory performance. The reason is straightforward: if a management accounting system measures only costs, employees tend to focus on costs exclusively.

I have encountered many practices designed to capture the nonfinancial dimensions of factory performance. One Japanese automaker wanted to motivate its managers and employees to reduce throughput time in assembly operations. It recognized that direct labor hours measure costs, not the actual time required to build and ship a car. So for time-management purposes, the company has replaced direct labor hours with a variable called managed hours per unit. In addition to direct labor, this new measure incorporates the time required for nonproductive activities like equipment maintenance and product repairs.

In an effort to improve machine and equipment efficiency, many companies are emphasizing preventive and corrective maintenance over breakdown maintenance. (Corrective maintenance means redesigning equipment to reduce failures and facilitate routine maintenance.) This emphasis goes beyond exhorting shop-floor personnel to pay more attention to their machines. Companies regularly measure rates of unexpected equipment failures, ratios of preventive and corrective maintenance to total maintenance, and other variables that track machine performance. These results are widely distributed and evaluated during small group discussions in the factory.

For companies to maintain competitive advantage, employees must be continually innovative. This requires motivation. A product designer must be motivated to play a significant role in cost reduction. Shop-floor workers and supervisors must constantly strive to improve efficiency beyond what "best practice" currently dictates. The Japanese have demonstrated that management accounting can play a significant role in integrating the innovative efforts of employees with the company's long-term strategies and goals.

7

ACTIVITY-BASED SYSTEMS IN SERVICE ORGANIZATIONS AND SERVICE FUNCTIONS

The demand for activity-based analysis for service companies and service functions arises from two sources. First, the past 20 years have seen huge changes in the competitive environment faced by companies in the financial services, transportation, telecommunications, retailing, and health care sectors. Deregulation has spawned new competitors in these sectors and given the companies much greater freedom in setting prices and in determining the mix of products and services offered. This has proved to be a mixed blessing. On the one hand, well-managed organizations with good understanding of their markets, customers, and information technologies can become much more profitable in deregulated, more competitive environments. However, organizations that fail to understand the sources of profitability for their products, customers, and markets can fail more quickly and more decisively once the protective umbrella of regulated prices and restricted entry has been lifted.

Within manufacturing companies, the service functions such as marketing, selling, distribution, service, technology development, and general administration have become much more significant expense categories than in the past. Traditional cost accounting systems, with their emphasis on cost accounting for inventory valuation, have neglected the burgeoning investments and expenses in organizations' service functions.

Sixty years ago, marketing, technology, and corporate administrative expenses were less important than manufacturing expenses. It was only natural that cost systems focused heavily on manufacturing expenses, especially since these systems could build on the information generated by the scientific management and industrial engineers who developed product standards for materials, labor, and overhead. In addition, the nonmanufacturing expenses could not be charged to inventoried products for financial reporting purposes. Cost accountants, wanting to have only a single system and wanting it to be compatible with financial reporting regulations, therefore ignored the attribution of nonmanufacturing expenses to products and customers. Those who did attempt such an attribution found many expenses that appeared common or joint to products and customers, or expenses that seemed mostly fixed in nature and poorly suited for attribution to activities at the product and customer level.

These forces all contributed to measuring the expenses in service organizations by functional category (marketing, research and development, corporate overhead) but not attempting to attribute them to the activities that created the demand for these organizational resources. The financial systems in these organizations emphasized responsibility accounting. Budgets were established for organizational units, actual incurred expenses were measured for the individual organization units, and departmental managers were held responsible for deviations between actual and budgeted expenses. The emphasis was on cost and spending control. For service companies, little or no relevant information was produced to determine the cost and profitability of their individual products, product lines, or customers.

APPLYING ACTIVITY-BASED ANALYSIS TO SERVICE ORGANIZATIONS

Activity-based analysis can be applied in a straightforward fashion to analyze the operating expenses of service organizations. There is no essential difference between the analysis of operating expenses in manufacturing support departments and doing the same tasks for the operating units of service organizations. The analysis starts by examining the expense structure of each operating department and proceeds by determining the factors that create the demands for the functions performed by the department. The cost analyst can apply the Rule of One described in chapter 5. Any department with more than one person cannot be thought of as containing only fixed expenses. Something is creating a demand for the output from that department, and there is too much work for one person to satisfy the demand. The objective, therefore, is to discover the nature of the demand and to quantify it.

When analyzing manufacturing expenses, the demands for support resources arose from product volumes and mix. For financial institutions, such as banks, many of the expenses are driven naturally to products as well—checking accounts, savings accounts, commercial loans, home mortgages, etc. Many expenses for service functions, however, are caused more by demands by individual customers rather than by product demands. Large variations occur in the demands that different customers place on the organization even when they are using the same basic product. One of the qualitative differences between service and manufacturing cost systems, therefore, is the need to model customers' behavior when analyzing the source of demands for service functions. The end result from the analysis must include reports on customer, not just product, profitability.

ANALYZING OPERATING EXPENSES OF SERVICE ORGANIZATIONS

We illustrate the basic principles of activity-based analysis for service organizations with an example drawn from a bank. The principles are general and can be applied to many other types of service organizations. The basic goal of the analysis is to obtain the unit costs for processing transactions from products and customers. The following equation is used:

$$\frac{\text{product unit}}{\text{cost}} = \frac{\text{hourly}}{\text{cost}} \times \frac{\text{product}}{\text{unit time}}$$

The hourly cost is calculated by dividing the operating expense budget for the department by the total number of available hours. For labor-paced operating departments, the available hours are measured by the total people hours available to perform work in the department, reduced by allowable time for vacation days, holidays, and breaks from work during the day. For automated departments, the available hours can be estimated by the number of machines that can perform the function and their available processing times. Both types of departments may require the adjustments for capacity utilization that were discussed in chapter 3. As with manufacturing departments, an operating department may have to be broken into smaller measuring units (cost centers) if too great a variation exists in the hourly cost of performing different types of work within the department.

The estimate of the product unit time is a more complex calculation, involving work measurement processes. Work is measured for each activity in a department that contributes to processing a transaction (such as a check, a deposit, or a cash payment on a loan). For highly repetitive operations, the analyst samples, at periodic intervals, the amount of work performed in a given amount of time. For example, the activity "Encode Items" might have the following history:

SAMPLE	VOLUME	HOURS
1	1,000	0.80
2	1,200	1.00
3	660	0.65
4	800	0.75
5	1,130	1.40
6	1,080	1.35
7	950	0.75
Total	6,820	6.70

From these data, we could estimate the unit time to encode items to be 0.00098 hours per unit (6.7 hours divided by 6,820 units).

For operations that require several minutes or hours to perform, such as those performed by white-collar or managerial employees, the unit times are calculated by first asking the employees to keep track of the time they spend on various activities and then measuring how much output was produced during these time intervals. Typically, the employees are asked to keep a time log for a one- to two-week period. The times for the same task performed by similar employees are averaged to obtain an average unit time for the task. Analysts also use relative value analysis to estimate the times required to perform tasks similar to those actually measured. With relative value analysis, employees are interviewed to gain a consensus about the relative ease or difficulty of performing various tasks.

The activities of professional and managerial employees, who are not performing repetitive activities, are measured by asking these employees to estimate the percentages of their available time they spend on each defined activity. For example, a branch manager may estimate that 40% of her time is spent opening checking accounts, 15% opening savings accounts, 25% processing and approving consumer and mortgage loans, and 20% on general managerial tasks that support all the activities in the bank. The amount of time spent on each of the bank's specific products is then divided by the quantities of each product (number of checking or savings accounts opened, or number of new consumer or mortgage loans) to obtain the unit times to perform that activity for each product.

Once the hourly department costs and the unit times for processing each product type in each department have been calculated, the two quantities can be multiplied together and summed across all the activities to obtain the cost of processing the

transaction for a given product (e.g., the total cost of processing a check or a deposit, of opening a new account, or of granting a loan).[1] With this information, the bank can now calculate the profitability of its various products. For example, the monthly profit of one product—commercial demand deposits—is as follows:

Average monthly balance in customers' accounts (000)				$180,000
Funds credit @ 8%[2]				$ 1,200
Less: product costs				
Deposit tickets	500,000	@	.80	400
Deposit items	1,000,000	@	.06	60
Checks paid	2,200,000	@	.05	110
Cash mgmt. services	80,000	@	.50	40
Return items	25,000	@	.40	10
Overdrafts	28,000	@	5.00	140
New accounts opened	500	@	60.00	30
Product contribution				$ 410

The calculation reveals that the profitability of this product is determined by the average balance in the company's product—commercial demand deposits—and reduced by the expenses associated with handling all the transactions associated with the product—processing deposits, checks, returns, overdrafts, etc.

The analysis is extended by calculating the profitability of individual customer accounts, as in the following example:

		CUSTOMER 1	CUSTOMER 2
Demand deposit balance		$60,000	$60,000
Funds credit @ 8%		400	400
Less:			
Deposit tickets	@ 0.80	32	72
Deposit items	@ 0.06	30	57
Checks paid	@ 0.05	88	72
Cash mgmt. services	@ 0.50	0	22
Return items	@ 0.40	15	40
Overdrafts	@ 5.00	33	11
Contribution		$ 135	$ 59

The two customers hold the same average balance in their demand deposits but make significantly different demands on the bank, through the number of deposits, return items, and use of cash management services. Thus, the profitability of the two customers differs by more than a factor of two. Even larger differences would be revealed for customers holding different average balances in their accounts.

By knowing the profitability of each customer for each type of product (or service),

---

[1]The outcome from these procedures is illustrated in the American Bank case in this chapter.
[2]The internal credit for funds is a transfer price for short-term funds as calculated by the bank's internal treasury department. The department typically engages in continual purchasing and selling of funds in the capital markets.

the organization can perform not only product profitability studies (as shown in the preceding example for commercial demand deposits) but also customer profitability studies. The customer profitability study would aggregate the profitability of each account or product used by the customer across all products offered and used by the customer. This would enable the organization to learn whether losses incurred for a customer in one set of products would be offset by profits earned in other products used by the customer.

Ultimately, service organizations use activity-based analysis to determine profits and losses by product and product line, by customer, and by geographical location. The information helps the organization to retain and defend highly profitable segments and to transform unprofitable segments into profitable ones through actions on pricing, product features, operating improvements, technology introduction, and customer relationships.

MARKETING, SELLING, AND DISTRIBUTION EXPENSES

Companies' spending on marketing, selling, and distribution resources can be analyzed in a similar fashion to the operating expenses we have been discussing for both manufacturing and service companies. Activity-based analysis assigns such expenses to the activities performed for customers, channels, product lines, and regions.[3]

The analysis starts with the basic transaction of a product being sold to a specific customer. The activity-based production expense analysis provides an estimate of the production cost of the product[4] and supplements this with the specific expenses associated with this particular order: the cost of soliciting, processing, and delivering the order, the salesperson's commissions, and any special expediting or design costs.

The production cost and the order-specific costs are subtracted from the selling price to obtain a profit or loss on the individual order. The profit/loss on the individual order can then be aggregated into several branches (see Figure 7.1).

Product-Line Branch The product-line branch captures all expenses associated with sustaining brands, categories, and product lines in the marketplace. Some organizational expenses, such as advertising and technology development, may relate to a specific brand (of detergent, electric motors, workstations). To the extent that such expenses are unrelated to the volume and mix of individual products sold with that brand name, these expenses are best assigned at the brand level. For example, Snappy cereals may include a dozen different package types and variations. The profit/loss for all sales of a Snappy cereal product can be accumulated in the account for the Snappy cereal brand and matched against expenses associated with promoting, advertising, and maintaining the Snappy brand in the marketplace. The profit margin for Snappy cereals can then be determined.

Snappy may be one of six cereal brands that the company promotes and produces. The profit margins for each of these six brands can be aggregated further into a cereal product-line category where expenses are recognized that are attributable to the cereal business but are not specifically assignable to individual cereal brands. Following this procedure reveals a profitability structure for each brand and product line in the company with no allocations of expenses required.

---

[3]See also the readings by Dudick, Johnson and Loewe, and Bellis-Jones that accompany this chapter.
[4]For purposes of assigning product margins to individual customers, channels, regions, and product lines, we must use an estimate of product unit cost. This estimate is typically obtained by dividing total product expenses by number of units produced.

Figure 7.1.   Activity-Based Profitability Branches

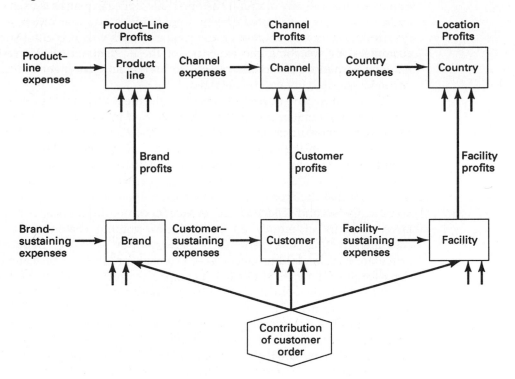

Many research and development expenses can also be attributed to specific brands or product lines but not to individual products. The activity-based approach assigns technology expenses to the specific product lines for which development efforts are performed. This practice ensures that such expenses will not be assigned to product lines for which no development work is done. But the development expenses are assigned at the brand or product-line level because they are incurred to support all the products within the brand or line, and the amount of these expenses is not affected by the number or volume produced of individual products.[5]

After assigning new product development, excess capacity, and other product-line-sustaining expenses, a product-line operating margin can be computed by subtracting these expenses from the sum of the gross margins of all the products sold within the line. This calculation reveals whether the products sold within the line earn enough margin to cover the expenses of activities performed to sustain the product line in the factory and in the marketplace.

Customer Branch   The profit or loss on individual customer transactions can be aggregated into a second branch, measuring the profitability of customers and channels. The first stage of the branch measures total customer profitability by aggregating the profits and losses for all transactions for individual customers and subtracting the *customer-sustaining* expenses traceable to that particular customer. Customer-sustaining activities include maintaining information on the customer and supplying a background level of marketing and

---

[5]Technology expenses to improve individual products would be captured at the product-sustaining level.

sales-call activities. The customer-sustaining expenses, however, must be independent of the volume and mix of actual customer sales since expenses caused by actual volume and mix would be attributed directly to individual customer orders.[6]

Special development and prototyping expenses will also differ substantially across customers. By matching the expenses of these customer-service resources with the margins earned on the products sold to individual customers, a complete picture of customer profitability can be obtained.

Companies have been surprised with their customer profitability results. In addition to the familiar 20-80 rule, where 20% of the customers account for 80% of the sales, some companies have discovered a 20-225 rule, where 20% of the customers generate 225% of the profits. A large number of customers huddle around breakeven profitability, and the least profitable 20% of the customers lose 125% of the profits, leading to the 100% of the profits actually earned by the company. More surprising, initially, is that the most unprofitable customers tend to be among the top 10 in sales volume. On second reflection, the managers come to understand that you cannot lose large amounts of money on isolated, low-volume customers. Only a few large customers, acting in a particularly perverse way—making frequent, unpredictable orders for nonstandard products, with extensive product changes and delivery expediting—can lose as much as 125% of a company's profits. Once the customer profitability structure has been revealed, managers can take a variety of actions, starting with pricing and delivery terms, to transform large, unprofitable customers into profitable ones.

The profits (and losses) of individual customers within a distribution channel can be aggregated into an overall channel profitability figure by subtracting the expenses of opening and sustaining the channel. *Channel-sustaining* expenses could include advertising, promotion, convention, and catalog expenditures that are independent of the quantity and mix of actual customer sales within the channel.

By separating expenses for brand and product-line-sustaining activities from those required to sustain individual customers and channels, a clearer picture of where money is being earned and lost emerges. Each branch and stage of the profit tree sees only expenses (and assets) that can be causally assigned to activities performed for it. The expenses incurred for individual customers or distribution channels would not be allocated to brands or product lines and, conversely, the advertising and technology expenses for brands and product lines would not affect the profitability calculations of customers and channels. The goal is to map the organization's profitability from a variety of viewpoints while eliminating the arbitrary allocations that traditionally have distorted profit and return on capital calculations.

Other Profit Branches In addition to assigning expenses and assets to production facility, product line, and channel profitability branches, companies may find that a profit branch for sales location may explain some portion of organizational expenses. For this branch, products sold from sales offices or to customers in a given geographical region may require a certain level of local sales effort. Such expenses would be directly charged to that region and matched with the contribution margins of products sold within that region. Several regions can be aggregated together to produce a country- or continent-wide profitability

[6]The analysis of customer and brand profitability should not be limited to accurate attribution of revenues and expenses. Company assets, including working capital components like inventory and accounts receivable, can be assigned so that returns on capital employed can be calculated for individual products, brands, product lines, and customers.

figure. Another profit branch could represent expenditures on new products. This branch would receive expenses and assets but no revenues, since, by assumption, the expenditures and assets assigned to this branch represent investments in future products.

Extending the profit tree in this manner enables companies to analyze virtually all corporate overhead expenses and assign them to the activities and objects (facilities, brands, customers, sales locations) that create the demand for the services. Perhaps the only corporate resources not assignable would be the expenses of the senior corporate management group (and their offices and airplane) that would be required independent of the size and scope of the organization. Any resources beyond this core skeletal group (the corporate-sustaining resources) should be assigned to the activities that create the demand for the additional staff and associated resources.

SUMMARY

The activity-based profitability analysis traces the demands for all organizational resources to activities performed for products, product lines, plants, customers, and channels. The profitability map that emerges from the analysis directs the attention of managers to products, facilities, customers, and regions that are unexpectedly profitable or unprofitable. Traditional costing systems, using allocation procedures that spread operating expenses evenly across all products and customers, make the organization's profitability map look much like the plains of Nebraska: flat in every direction. The ABC profitability map looks more like the terrain of California, where high Rocky Mountain peaks of profitability lie juxtaposed near the Death Valley craters of losses.

The profitability map is not used naively to close plants or drop customers or products merely because the activity-based analysis reveals them to be unprofitable. The more accurate map of the terrain points to where careful analysis and specific actions will enable managers to transform craters of losses into peaks of profits and to raise the profit peaks even higher. By capturing in an integrated and comprehensive fashion the interactions among product design, production processes, and marketing and selling efforts, the activity-based analysis focuses managers' attention on the critical territory in which decisions and actions can create the greatest rewards.

CASES

Union Pacific (Introduction)

COMPANY HISTORY

The Union Pacific System was formed in December 1982 upon the consolidation of the Union Pacific, Missouri Pacific, and Western Pacific railroads. As measured by track mileage, with 22,000 route miles in 21 states, the merged system is the third largest railroad in the U.S. The combined system operates a fleet of 108,000 freight cars and 3,200 locomotives. It serves 10 of the country's top 20 ports and links West Coast and Gulf Coast ports with the key midwestern gateways of Chicago, Kansas City, St. Louis, and Memphis (see route maps in Exhibits 1 and 2). Major commodities hauled by the System are grain, food, coal, soda ash, chemicals, construction aggregates, metals and ores, auto parts, autos, forest products, merchandise, and consumer products. Financial statistics of the Union Pacific System are presented in Exhibit 3.

COMPANY ORGANIZATION

Union Pacific has the functional organization that is typical of most major railroads. The operating department is the largest department of the company. Representing more than 80% of the company's employment and budget, it moves and manages trains, operates the locomotive and car fleets, and builds and maintains track, yard, and other facilities. It is divided into groups:

- *Transportation* is responsible for train and yard operations and car management.
- The *engineering* department builds and maintains the right-of-way, signal systems, and all buildings and structures.
- *Mechanical* maintains the fleet of locomotives and railroad cars.

Together, these three groups in the operating department account for 89% of annual railroad operating costs (see Exhibits 4 and 5).

The remaining 11% of operating costs are divided among six general and administrative departments.

The marketing and sales department identifies potential shippers and sells the services of the railroad company. In addition to market development and direct selling activities, the marketing department performs pricing analysis, market and competitive research, contract and tariff administration, economic forecasting, and industrial development. It also maintains records on rates and routes.

The finance department provides cost, profit, and financial planning and analysis for the railroad. It also performs strategic planning as well as the traditional accounting functions of record keeping, customer billing, payments to suppliers, cash management, preparation of accounting and tax statements, and internal audit.

The law department provides a complete range of legal services for the company. It represents the company's interests in commercial, governmental, and regulatory affairs and participates in litigation and other legal matters including real estate, contracts, environmental issues, labor, and personnel.

The labor relations and personnel department is involved with hiring and training of employees, labor relations, benefit and salary administration, management development, staffing, employee assistance, and employee communications.

The purchasing and materials department is responsible for annual spending of $1.5 billion on behalf of the system, purchasing items as diverse as spikes, computers, and locomotives. It manages inventories of $200 million spread among 25 different locations.

The information and communication systems department applies computer technology for routine data processing applications (payroll, billing, inventory control) and for support of operations,

This case was prepared by Professor Robert S. Kaplan.

control, cost analysis, real-time freight car management, locomotive maintenance, and engineering applications. The department's communication responsibility includes both data and voice, including the installation, operation, and maintenance of the largest privately owned and operated microwave system located on railroad property.

RAILROAD OPERATIONS

The goal of a railroad is to provide cost-effective transportation and distribution services to shippers. At the heart of these services is the physical movement of a loaded car from an origin to a destination.

1. The process begins when a shipper contacts a railroad customer service center (CSC) to request a freight car or trailer. The shipper specifies the type of car and the date it is needed. The order is then placed in the computer where the car management system selects a car for the order.

2. The rail carrier supplies the customer with the empty car to be loaded. The computer system provides information on the supply and demand for empty equipment and facilitates decisions on how to deploy the available car supply to meet demand.

3. Once a car has been delivered to the shipper, it becomes subject to demurrage rules. Demurrage is a tariff which encourages shippers to load and unload cars quickly. The customer generally has 24 hours to load a car and 48 hours to unload. After these allotted times have expired, the customer is subject to demurrage charges.

4. When the car is loaded, the shipper provides a bill of lading to the railroad. Two methods are commonly used. The most direct method occurs by a computer-to-computer electronic data interchange from the shipper to the railroad. Alternatively, the shipper calls a customer service center, which enters the bill of lading data through a terminal into the railroad's computer system.
The bill of lading represents the contract between the carrier and shipper. Once the information is entered, a waybill is generated that contains information on the shipper, destination, route, freight charges, and commodity. The waybill can also specify the routing for the shipment, in which case the computer system would assign a trip plan for the car's entire trip over the Union Pacific System.

5. When the CSC is notified that the loaded car is released for movement, the computer generates a work order to begin the car's trip plan. A switch or local crew goes to the customer's location, gets the loaded car, and takes it to the railroad's classification yard where the car will be attached to the proper outbound train.

6. When a train is built and ready to go, a train list and work order document is generated by the computer. All the cars on the train are listed with information on destination, weight, commodity, load or empty status, and hazardous material status, as well as the work that is to be performed enroute. The conductor updates the work order as the train picks up or sets out cars enroute.

7. Unless a shipment is being carried in dedicated train service (for example, unit coal trains or double-stacked container movements for a single customer) or is traveling only a short distance, the car will probably travel on several different trains during its journey. Each time the car enters a yard, it goes through the classification process so that it can be switched onto the proper outgoing train for the next leg of its trip. This classification step is the largest single cause of delays and unreliability in rail transportation. If a car misses its scheduled connection, it must wait in the yard for the next scheduled train that is handling cars for its destination.

8. When the car reaches its destination, the receiver is notified and the car is delivered. After the car is unloaded, it becomes available for another shipment.

INTERMODAL

Railroads have responded to the vigorous competition from trucks by developing intermodal transportation. Intermodal transportation uses two or more forms of transportation to provide better service to a customer. For example, a railroad could contract with a shipper to pick up a container from a ship or provide a truck to the customer's site. These items are then moved to a railroad site (intermodal terminal) where they are loaded on special cars: Container on Flat Car (COFC) or Trailer on Flat Car (TOFC). After traveling a distance over rail lines, the container or trailer is then dropped off at an intermodal terminal near the receiver's site and delivered to the receiver by highway. For intermodal operations, Union Pacific has established 25 to 30 terminals. Both publicly known and confidential contract rates exist for all corridors.

YARD OPERATIONS

The yard switching of cars when originating, interchanging, and terminating shipments represents one of the most expensive parts of railroad operations. Frequently, a railroad's profitability will be determined by the yard manager's ability to provide reliable, fast service with a minimum number of crews and engines.

Yard operations consist primarily of assembling cars from various sources into blocks headed for individual destinations. These blocks can then be combined into trains. Both loaded and empty cars are stored on classification tracks. Computerized yard inventory information provides the location of every car in the yard. Based on this information and the computerized waybill information for each car, a switch list is prepared describing how yard personnel should move cars around to build blocks for outgoing trains.

Two switching procedures, flat and gravity, are employed. Flat switching requires a great deal of back-and-forth movement, especially if the cars have not been blocked very well. To reduce the time expense associated with flat switching, Union Pacific has built strategically located hump yards that provide much faster switching. In gravity switching, a string of cars to be sorted is pushed over an artificial hill or ''hump'' so that gravity can take them down into the classification tracks. Switches, under continuous computer control, channel each car onto the proper classification track. Retarders regulate the speed of each car's descent from the hump.

In the most modern electronically controlled hump yards, the retarder and switch control systems accept switch list data containing the destination track of each car, yard inventory information, physical yard characteristics (length, grade, and curvature of each track), individual data on the speed and rollability of each car on both curved and straight sections of track, and other factors affecting car movement, such as wind velocity and direction. Using this extensive data base, the computer controls the retarders and switches so that each car rolls just far enough up the track to be coupled with cars already in place.

The shipper's decision

Three key factors, in addition to the availability and condition of a particular type of car, affect a shipper's choice among transportation alternatives: the expected length of time necessary to complete the shipment, the reliability of the service, and the rate charged for the shipment.

DELIVERY TIME

Railroad delivery times can be competitive with motor carrier delivery for long-distance hauls of time-sensitive shipments. But trucks will typically have a service advantage over single car shipments, especially when carrying commodities that do not require expedited service. The switching of individual freight cars from one train to another can interject lengthy delays into the elapsed time from shipper pickup to customer delivery. Restrictive work rules and labor agreements and the technology and economics of railroads produce additional idle or nonproductive time during which cars are not moving toward their destination. A railroad has its best delivery performance when the car is part of a dedicated or long-haul train with few or no intermediate switches.

SERVICE RELIABILITY

Numerous studies have shown that shippers place a high premium on service reliability. Frequently, shippers are willing to pay higher rates or accept slower service to obtain more reliable delivery times. Thus, for those markets in which rail service has been less reliable, railroads have tended to lose market share to motor carrier service. In the deregulated environment, however, price has become more important and railroads have begun to win back business by being the low-price bidder.

RATES

Until recently, all railroad rates were regulated by the ICC. The process of changing rates was extremely slow, making it difficult for railroads to respond to market conditions. The rate for carrying a specific commodity was typically based on the value of the commodity itself rather than on the cost of carrying it. Low-priced bulk commodities such as coal and grain had low shipping rates while higher-valued products, such as manufactured goods, were charged much higher rates even though the cost of moving them may have been identical to (or lower than) the low value commodities. The railroads, by the end of 1980, had more than 75,000 rate tariffs on file with the ICC, mostly on a case-by-case basis. Despite a goal to have the overall structure of rates yield a fair return on investment to the railroads, individual rates could range from 95% to more than 200% of long-run variable cost. Railroads were prohibited from working out specialized customer contracts. Also, despite the announced goal of having rates yield a competitive return on railroad investment, the industry average return on investment was under 3% throughout the 1960s and 1970s.

While ICC rate regulation can hardly be blamed for all of the railroads' recent ills, it nevertheless contributed to a severe decline in railroads' market share of intercity freight transportation. In 1929, railroads moved 75% of all intercity service, but their share had declined to less than 40% by the 1970s. (The loss was principally to trucks and pipelines.) But more than losing physical volume, the railroads found that they lost their high-rate, high-margin traffic to trucking and retained mainly their low-margin business.

DEREGULATION

The environment for railroad shipping arrangements was completely changed by the Staggers Rail Act of 1980. The Staggers Act granted the railroads for the first time the right to negotiate individual contract terms and rates with shippers. These rates could either be for one-time shipments or for multiple movements over a period of time. Private contracts have been written for periods up to 20 or more years. Following its initial approval of a private contract between a railroad and a shipper, the ICC has no jurisdiction over the level or enforceability of a contract since voluntary agreements are assumed to be acceptable to both parties.

The ICC's jurisdiction over published rates is limited to those instances in which a railroad has market dominance for the transportation involved. Market dominance is assumed if the price-to-variable-cost ratio is more than 180% and if there is no effective competition for the traffic.

Accordingly, rates which are not controlled by competitive market forces may be submitted to the ICC for a determination of reasonableness. The ICC considers a number of factors, including the variable cost of performing the service, but it has abandoned its earlier standards based on value of service. By mid-1985, approximately 60% of all rail shipments moved under published tariffs that specified a particular commodity, origin, and destination. There is substantially less rate litigation since enactment of the Staggers Act, but the ICC still decides many rate cases, especially those involving heavy traffic flows with substantial revenues at stake.

While railroads were attempting to cope with their deregulated environment, other forces were also at work to challenge the industry. The changed regulatory climate and more relaxed attitude toward large mergers at the ICC were leading to major shifts in the concentration of the railroad industry. In 1978, the five largest railroads—Conrail, Burlington Northern, Southern Pacific, Union Pacific, and the Atchison, Topeka, and Santa Fe—had 43.9% of the total operating revenues of the Class I line-haul railroads. After a series of mega-mergers in the railroad industry during the next five years, the five largest Class I freight railroads in 1984—CSX (Chessie System), Conrail, Norfolk Southern, Union Pacific System, and Burlington Northern—had 67.8% of the operating revenues. With the pending merger of the Southern Pacific with the Atchison, Topeka, and Sante Fe railroad, and the pending purchase by Norfolk Southern of Conrail, the five-firm concentration ratio could rise to 84.7%.

A leading regulatory economist[1] commented on the impact of deregulation and increased competition in the entire transportation industry, encompassing airlines, trucking, and railroads.

> Perhaps the chief benefit of deregulation is that it has increased efficiency substantially. Regulated thinking had the regulators, not the consumers, as the most important customer. There was little incentive to plan or to pinpoint the sources of markets that were successful and those that were failures, nor to keep costs under control and be responsive to consumer desires. In contrast, deregulation is leading to a substantially more efficient industry, one in which cross-subsidy is absent, a diversity of price/ service options are present, and cost-minimizing behavior is prevalent, both in delivery systems and in other operating costs.
>
> These changes are coming about because of fundamental changes in the way firms are conducting business. In every aspect of corporate activity, deeply rooted changes are taking place. Companies are finding that they must be driven by market opportunities and financial needs, not by regulatory considerations. They must calculate their costs on a market-by-market basis and must learn to base price on cost, competitors' prices, and market strategy. Regulatory principles such as value of service, nationwide rate averaging, and so on cannot survive in a competitive environment. Corporations are seeking to develop products and to market them strategically and to find niches which confer some economic benefit. . . . All in all, a more vibrant, competitive, and innovative spirit emerges from deregulation.

---

[1]Elizabeth Bailey, "Price and Productivity Change Following Deregulation: the U.S. Experience," *Economic Journal* (1986).

EXHIBIT 1
UNION PACIFIC (INTRODUCTION)
Union Pacific
Missouri Pacific
Western Pacific

EXHIBIT 2
UNION PACIFIC (INTRODUCTION)
Western U.S. Railroads

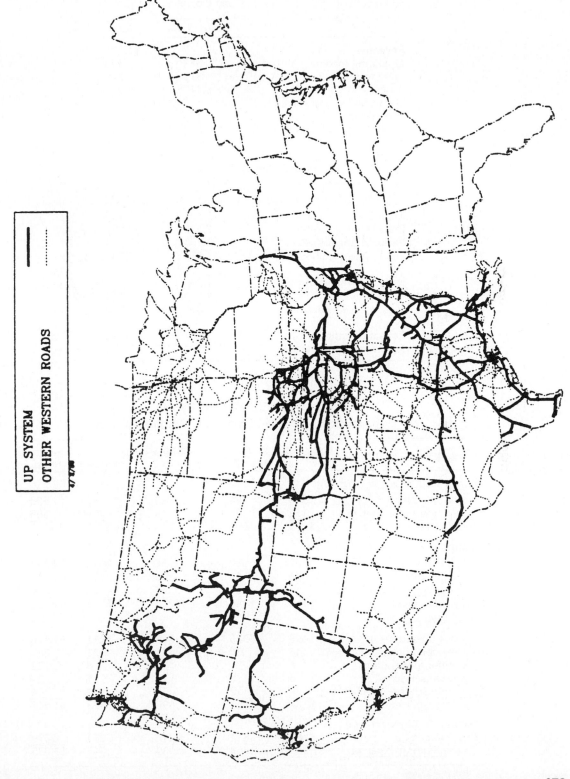

UP SYSTEM
OTHER WESTERN ROADS

EXHIBIT 3

UNION PACIFIC (INTRODUCTION)

Union Pacific System: Financial and Operating Statistics

	1984	1983
Revenues	$3,942	$3,701
Operating income	549	466
Net income	311	240
Assets	6,443	5,952
Depreciation, amortization, retirements	236	233
Capital expenditures	607	341
Maintenance expenditures	824	698

Transportation Statistics

	1984	1983
Main line	13,891	13,850
Branch line	7,683	7,937
Yards, siding, other	13,304	13,064
Total system (miles)	34,878	34,851
Rail track miles replaced	1,060	552
Track miles reballasted	4,806	3,574
Ties replaced (thousands)	2,813	1,758
Operating ratio	86.1	87.4
Revenue tons per train	2,272	2,196

EXHIBIT 4

UNION PACIFIC (INTRODUCTION)

Total Union Pacific System: 1984 Expenses by Categories (000,000)

	SALARIES & WAGES	MATERIALS & SUPPLIES	PURCHASED SERVICES	GENERAL	TOTAL
Way & structures					
Administration	$43	$4	$0	$7	$53
Repair & maintenance	162	91	45	210	509
Total way & structure	$205	$95	$45	$217	$562
Equipment					
Locomotives	$82	$80	$8	$112	$282
Freight cars	76	51	208	120	454
Other equipment	7	10	53	20	90
Total Equipment	$165	$141	$268	$251	$826
Transportation					
Train operations	$498	$388	$19	$211	$1,116
Yard operations	148	30	21	71	269
Common operations	6	1	6	8	22
Special services	3	0	23	1	27
Administrative support	79	2	21	31	134
Total transportation	$734	$421	$90	$323	$1,567
General & administrative					
Total G&A	$183	$12	$(70)	$254	$379
Total operating expenses	$1,288	$668	$333	$1,045	$3,335

EXHIBIT 5

UNION PACIFIC (INTRODUCTION)

Total Union Pacific System: 1984 Percentages of Expenses by Categories (000,000)

	SALARIES & WAGES	MATERIALS & SUPPLIES	PURCHASED SERVICES	GENERAL	TOTAL
Way & structures					
Administration	1.3%	.1%	.0%	.2%	1.6%
Repair & maintenance	4.9	2.7	1.3	6.3	15.3
Total way & structure	6.2%	2.8%	1.3%	6.5%	16.9%
Equipment					
Locomotives	2.5%	2.4%	.2%	3.4%	8.5%
Freight cars	2.3	1.5	6.2	3.6	13.6
Other equipment	.2	.3	1.6	.6	2.7
Total equipment	5.0%	4.2%	8.1%	7.5%	24.8%
Transportation					
Train operations	14.9%	11.6%	.6%	6.3%	33.5%
Yard operations	4.4	.9	.6	2.1	8.1
Common operations	.2	.0	.2	.3	.7
Special services	.1	.0	.7	.0	.8
Administrative support	2.4	.1	.6	.9	4.0
Total transportation	22.0%	12.6%	2.7%	9.7%	47.0%
General & administrative					
Total G&A	5.5%	.4%	−2.1%	7.6%	11.4%
Total operating expenses	38.6%	20.0%	10.0%	31.3%	100.0%

Union Pacific (A)

INTRODUCTION

The cost numbers we get from The Planning and Analysis Group will be the bottom line, and no salesperson will quote a price below estimated cost. We need to have confidence in the numbers provided to us. Cost accounting is too complex a subject for me to be comfortable having marketing managers developing their own formulas or rules of thumb.

George Craig, Senior Vice-President for Marketing and Sales for the Union Pacific System, was commenting on the highly competitive environment for railroads in the deregulation era. Success in this environment mandated much tighter linkages between accounting and marketing than had ever been required during the first 100+ years of railroading.

A railroad sells only three things: equipment, service, and price. Before 1980, price was determined by tariffs filed with the Interstate Commerce Commission (ICC) and therefore was not an issue except when we competed against other forms of transportation. Probably less than 15% of customers' decisions were determined by price. After the Staggers Rail Act, while service and equipment are still factors, 85% of our business is now won by being the low-price bidder. Even in our Intermodal business, in which we believe delivery time and service is critical, we recently lost a contract on only a $25 per trailer differential despite offering delivery 24 hours faster than our competitor. Now that really hurts.

This case was prepared by Professor Robert S. Kaplan.

We also enter into many long-term contracts, and we had better be sure that our prices cover our costs. We have over 5,000 contracts whose duration ranges from six months to 20 years. If we price too low on these contracts, we're going to put ourselves out of business.

On the other hand, if we price too high because our cost estimates are too conservative, we will lose lots of bids and sacrifice future growth. Some opportunities for bidding, especially for large utility companies, may arise only once every 15 years. That's why it is really critical for us to understand and know our true costs.

COST ACCOUNTING

All accounting reports are subject to ICC reporting requirements which were modernized effective January 1, 1978.

Rail Form A, the venerable costing formula developed earlier this century by the ICC, takes the total operating expenses for a railroad and links them to the activities (service units) that are felt to best explain the incurrence of these expenses. Examples of such service units are gross ton miles, locomotive unit miles, train miles, car days, and engine switching minutes. ICC cross-sectional statistical studies of the railroad industry have estimated the average percentage that is variable of any given cost category (see Exhibit 1). The variable cost is then allocated among the various service units. After a long sequence of calculations, the total cost per service unit is obtained; that is, the cost per gross ton mile, cost per engine switching minute, etc. (see Exhibit 2 for a simplified format of Rail Form A). Appendix A contains an excerpt from an ICC publication describing the assignment of railroad operating expenses to service units.

The accounts specified in Rail Form A provided the chart of accounts used by Union Pacific to collect and control its costs into the 1960s. At that time, two major efforts were undertaken to improve its cost measurement system.

COST OUT ALL TRAFFIC (COAT) SYSTEM

In 1965, the company initiated an effort to develop the COAT (Cost Out All Traffic) system. The COAT system worked from the waybill for each carload move.

The waybill provided information on origin, destination commodity, lading tons, car type, and car ownership (whether a system, private, or a foreign[1] car). For any given move, the shortest distance between origin and destination was estimated. The system averages computed in Rail Form A were then used to cost out the move. For example, costs that were assumed variable with gross ton miles were assigned based on the length of the move and the weight of the shipment. Costs based on car miles or carloads could similarly be apportioned. The cost of using a private or foreign car was estimated based on time and mileage charges applicable to that car, whereas depreciation, maintenance, and repair of system-owned cars were calculated based on Rail Form A averages. The Rail Form A averages of frequency of intertrain switches, interchange (between two roads) switches, and pickup and delivery costs were also included and costed to the move.

Union Pacific management recognized that the move-by-move cost and profitability information provided by COAT was not very accurate. Any time system-wide or industry-wide averages were used to cost out individual moves, the data could only provide a very rough estimate of the actual costs. Train size could vary greatly from the assumed average size, road conditions differed over the system and had a major impact on running costs, and switching time could vary by yard and by region. Also, the Rail Form A costs could understate the cost of special features which had been provided to attract certain forms of traffic. For example, along certain lines, extra-strength rail had been installed to carry the anticipated heavy traffic.

Thus, the COAT data could provide only a flag, a signal, for where more detailed analysis should be undertaken. But the more detailed analysis required an enormous work effort to determine whether the Rail Form A assumptions were valid in particular circumstances.

Despite these limitations, cost and profitability information from COAT alerted the company to instances where it could seek rate increases from the ICC on currently unprofitable business. Occasionally, Union Pacific tried to exit markets where it felt it was losing money, out-of-pocket, and where it

---

[1]A system car is one owned by Union Pacific, a foreign car is owned by another railroad, and a private car is owned by a shipper or a private car line.

could not get rate relief. Conversely, the COAT system also signaled which business looked highly profitable. Special attention was then devoted to keep that business and to make sure that rates were not raised which would jeopardize losing that business to other transportation forms.

MANAGEMENT COST CONTROL SYSTEM

In 1968, a project to develop a Management Cost Control System (MCC) was initiated. MCC was a responsibility accounting system designed for the hierarchy of cost centers in the railroad. Approximately 5,000 cost centers were identified throughout the system; the operational definition of a cost center was either who spent money or who authorized an expense. About 1,500 different cost codes were used to accumulate expenses for all the cost centers.

Each cost center manager received a monthly report summarizing actual expenses in the cost center, with a comparison to budget and last year's expenses. (Exhibit 3 shows the first page of a monthly report for a locomotive repair facility.) Summary reports could be prepared by grouping cost codes into more aggregate categories and also by grouping similar cost centers within the same district.

Exhibit 4 shows the summary, by major expense categories, of the costs of the locomotive repair facility detailed in Exhibit 3. Exhibit 5 is the monthly summary of costs for all locomotive repair facilities, by location, and Exhibit 6 summarizes locomotive repair costs by major expense category. Similar cost reports are prepared for subunits in the engineering and transportation departments.

Special reports summarizing monthly and year-to-date operations were prepared for senior managers at the railroad's headquarters in Omaha. Exhibit 7 shows a monthly summary for the mechanical department featuring the cost of administration, diesel fuel, locomotive maintenance, and freight car maintenance. These costs are shown normalized by various activity measures: power unit miles, horsepower miles, serviceable locomotive and cardays, freight car miles, and gross ton miles. Exhibit 8 shows freight crew costs per thousand gross ton miles by geographical district. Exhibit 9 is the first page (of a nine-page report) showing operating statistics by train symbol; a train symbol denotes a particular regularly scheduled train that runs between two hubs. The following monthly train statistics are displayed and compared to the corresponding month in the prior year:

- Average tons/train
- Average horsepower/train
- Average initial terminal delay (ITD) minutes
- Average final terminal delay (FTD) minutes
- Average road speed
- Crews called

These monthly and year-to-date summaries were frequently accompanied by extensive tables and charts to facilitate analysis of unusual conditions and trends.

The MCC system was first installed in the early 1970s. For several years, it was run in parallel with the ICC system (used to generate data for Rail Form A and other ICC reports). Eventually, as the system became accepted and actively used as a management reporting tool, MCC became the sole internal system.

THE FUTURE

As deregulation loomed over the horizon in the late 1970s, Union Pacific management knew that many old ways of doing business would not survive. More aggressive attention to marketing and pricing would clearly be necessary. MCC and COAT were among the most advanced cost systems in the entire industry. But would they be adequate for the turbulent years ahead?

EXHIBIT 1

UNION PACIFIC (A)

Variability Percents Used in Rail Form A Application

(Based on Study by ICC Section of Cost and Valuation)

FREIGHT EXPENSE VARIABLE	RELATED OUTPUT (%)	
Maintenance of way and structures		
Yard and way switching tracks	Yard and train switching hours	55%
Running tracks	Gross ton miles	57
Other	Tons of revenue freight	60
Maintenance of equipment:		
Yard locomotive repairs	Yard switching locomotive unit miles	82
Train locomotive repairs	Freight gross ton miles	68
Freight car repairs	Freight car miles	86
Other	Tons of revenue freight	79
Transportation—rail line:		
Yard expenses	Yard switching hours	96
Train expenses	Freight train miles	97
Station employees—platform	Not applicable	100
Other	Tons of revenue	44
Freight tax accruals	Tons of revenue	72
Traffic, miscellaneous operations, and general	Other operating expenses	70

EXHIBIT 2

UNION PACIFIC (A)

Rail Form A Formula Costs

COST CATEGORY	VARIABLILITY (%)	VARIABLE COST	GROSS TON MILES (GTM)	LOCOMOTIVE UNIT MILES (LUM)	ENGINE MINUTES (EM)
Transportation					
Yard switching fuel	96	xxx			xxx
Train fuel	97	xxx	xxx	xxx	xxx
Yard enginemen	96	xxx			
.		.	.	.	
.		.	.	.	
.					
Maintenance of equipment					
Locomotive repairs—yard	82	xxx			xxx
Locomotive repairs—road	68	xxx	xxx	xxx	xxx
.		.	.	.	.
.		.	.	.	.
.		.	.	.	.
Maintenance of way					
Rail yard switching track	55	xxx			xxx
Rail running track	57	xxx	xxx	—	—
Total expense			xxx	xxx	xxx
Total activity (units)			GTM	LUM	EM
Unit cost:					
Total expense/number of service units			$/GTM	$/LUM	$/EM

EXHIBIT 3

UNION PACIFIC (A)

Form 3860—Final

Management Cost Control Report

Detail of Costs For December 1976

MGE COST AND PROFIT ANAL 50
1427

9:219   NORTH PLATTE DIESEL FACILITY-LOCO DEPT

INDEX NO. 06-035

| CURRENT MONTH | | | COST | DESCRIPTION | YEAR TO DATE | | |
ACTUAL	VARIANCE FROM BUDGET	LAST YEAR	CODE		ACTUAL	VARIANCE FROM BUDGET	LAST YEAR
17,149	2,748•	4,931•	1100	OFFICERS	185,713	12,913•	42,199•
69,945	11,065	9,016•	1111	SUPERVISORY PERSONNEL-AGRMNT	816,906	134,693	115,089•
3,139	1,523-	1,686•	1112	SUPERVISORY PERSONNEL-NON AGRMNT	27,097	6,985-	1,504•
:,382	27-	199•	1114	CHIEF AND ASSISTANT CHIEF CLERK-NON AGRMNT	15,106	1,153	1,484•
2,491	653	1,032•	1122	PROFESSIONAL AND ADMINISTRATIVE-NON AGRMNT	36,948	1,291	6,242•
2,682	1,337-	1,469•	1124	TECHNICAL AND CLERICAL-NON AGRMNT	23,243	7,103-	9,405•
10,396	56	76•	1137	GENERAL CLERICAL PERSONNEL-AGRMNT	136,050	6,205•	27,949•
78,336	11,912	2,434	1201	REP & MNTCE LOCO-PROPULSION ENGINES	986,130	73,427	157,523•
2,242	758-	1,089	1202	REP & MNTCE LOCO-TURBOCHARGERS	28,138	10,719-	5,201-
18,256	3,145	1,019	1203	REP & MNTCE LOCO-TRACTION MTRS-EXCL GEARS	224,852	26,418	31,209•
101,812	22,519	24,839•	1204	REP & MNTCE LOCO-OTHER ELECTRICAL	1,194,245	253,803	310,544•
24,301	5,706	919•	1205	REP & MNTCE LOCO-RUNNING GEAR	288,823	56,970	41,463•
149,938	86,504	13,556•	1206	REP & MNTCE LOCO-OTHER REPAIRS	1,721,891	1,028,900	223,272•
11,865	7,662	517	1208	REP & MNTCE LOCO-PAINTING	168,249	58,408	25,113•
34,194	37,496	1,713•	1211	REP & MNTCE LOCO-FEDERAL INSPECTIONS	411,342	417,067	61,717
16,034	1,065•	1,692•	1212	REP & MNTCE LOCO-LUBRICATION	189,172	15,398•	71,099•
15,051	4,532	480•	1213	REP & MNTCE LOCO-WHEEL TRUING	155,880	78,747	11,796
1,429	1,397•	1,141•	1221	REP & MNTCE CABOOSES-GENERAL	6,246	5,280•	5,424•
79	79•	79•	1231	REP & MNTCE FRT CARS-CAR BODY & UNDERFRAME	90	90•	40
			1233	REP & MNTCE FRT CARS-COUPLERS & CRAFT GEARS			68
		39	1234	REP & MNTCE FRT CARS-BRAKE EQUIPMENT	185	185•	369
35	35•	35•	1236	REP & MNTCE FRT CARS-INTERIOR LOADNG DEVICE	35	35•	35•
			1239	REP & MNTCE FRT CARS-OTHER REPAIRS	57	57•	10
			1241	REP & MNTCE FRT CARS-INSPECTION	21	21•	21•
			1242	REP & MNTCE FRT CARS-LUBRICATION			45
7,508	8,454	319•	1251	SHOP ORDER LABOR	108,890	99,859	13,017
			1252	STORE ORDER LABOR	54	54•	54•
56	38	141	1371	REP & MNTCE AUTOMOTIVE EQUIPMENT	496	616	257
769	646•	387•	1380	REP & MNTCE WORK EQUIPMENT	6,505	5,062•	3,996•
8,181	7,251-	1,830•	1390	REP & MNTCE SHOP & POWER PLANT MACHINERY	89,750	5,138	15,057•
			1403	CLEANING COVERED HOPPERS	623	623•	623•
			1406	CLEANING & SERVICING CABOOSES	81	81•	45•
			1409	FREIGHT CAR SERVICING	-577	577•	532•
			1500	DISMANTLING ROAD AND EQUIPMENT PROPERTY	22	22•	22•
			1510	CLEARING WRECKS	83	83•	83•
104,207	28,989•	11,191•	1530	FUELING & SERVICING LOCOMOTIVES	1,264,974	391,842•	580,647•
			1540	TRANSFER OR ADJUST LOADS	571	571•	412•
8,670	1,631•	3,144•	1630	EQUIPMENT OPERATORS	77,157	4,117	26,001•
			1640	POWER PLANT LABOR	78	78•	36•
26,675	1,796•	3,301•	1691	MISCELLANEOUS LABOR-AGRMNT	299,636	11,136•	94,279•
			1699	UNDISTRIBUTED-PAYROLL ERRORS			25
39,350	2,495	4,883•	1740	HOSTLERS	448,306	47,680	62,555•
			1791	BACK PAY-NON OPERATING	356,294	356,294•	213,857•
			1792	BACK PAY-OPERATING			11,507
		38,382	1793	ACCRUED LIABILITIES-NON OPERATING	313,773-	313,773	627,545

• VARIANCE - UNFAVORABLE

485

EXHIBIT 4

UNION PACIFIC (A)

Mechanical Department—North Platte Diesel Shop

Detail of Expenses

(December 1976)

	CURRENT MONTH					YEAR TO DATE				
	ACTUAL	DEVIATION				ACTUAL	DEVIATION			
		BUDGET		LAST YEAR			BUDGET		LAST YEAR	
	($)	($)	(%)	($)	(%)	($)	($)	(%)	($)	(%)
Payroll & related expenses:										
Straight time	758	153	16.8	82*	12.2*	8,913	1,813	16.9	1,771	24.8*
Overtime	39	15	28.2	3*	10.5*	480	110*	29.7	23	4.6
Accrued liabilities and back pay	40	23	36.4	38	$$$	42	42*	$$$	425	90.9
Health & welfare	47	5*	14.0*	1	4.6	629	121	16.1	184*	41.3
Vacation accruals		66*	$$$	25*	117.5*	577	53*	10.1*	139*	31.8*
Holiday	66	1*	$$$	37*	125.9*	319	319*	$$$	82*	34.8*
Sick leave	1	*	2.2*	*	48.3*	27	27*	$$$	5*	24.6*
Other allowances	4	13*	9.2*	3*	176.4*	72	17*	32.2*	30*	72.8*
Payroll taxes	159	37*	$$$	34*	27.1*	1,763	47*	2.7*	410*	30.3*
Vacation pay—Actual							410*	$$$		
Total	$1,119	66	5.6	146*	15.1*	$12,826	906	6.5	2,175*	20.4*
Less credits:										
Investment accounts		*	$$$*	1*	$$$*	·–	*	30.3*	2*	73.8*
Other credits	9 –	11	54.8*	2	26.7	122 –	125*	50.5*	36*	23.0*
Total credits	9 –	11*	55.1*		3.4	123 –	125*	50.4*	39*	24.1*
Net payroll & related expenses	1,109	55	4.7	146*	15.2*	$12,703	780	5.7	2,214	21.1*
Material & supplies:										
Repair parts & material	392	9	2.3	3	.8	4,924	164*	3.4*	836*	20.4*
Lubricants	217	13*	6.6*	63*	41.2*	2,618	216*	9.0*	335*	14.7*
Gasoline	1	1	56.9	1	16.3	11	17	60.3	7	37.7
Shop supplies	31	4	12.4	28	47.4	380	48	11.2	1*	.3*
Locomotive & train supplies	6	5	46.6	15	70.3	84	61	42.2	39	32.1
Miscellaneous materials & supplies	40	3	7.9	25	38.0	730	208*	39.9*	210*	40.5*
Total material & supplies	689	11	1.5	8	1.2	8,750	462*	5.5*	1,336*	18.0*
Utilities	26	17*	217.7*	5*	24.1*	249	165*	197.3*	126*	103.3*
Repair & maintenance contracts		*	241.3*		50.1	7	4*	195.8*	3*	79.1*
Miscellaneous contracts	3	1*	152.2	2*	226.5*	16	1*	8.4*	2*	21.9*

EXHIBIT 4 (cont.)

	CURRENT MONTH					YEAR TO DATE				
	ACTUAL	DEVIATION				ACTUAL	DEVIATION			
		BUDGET		LAST YEAR			BUDGET		LAST YEAR	
	($)	($)	(%)	($)	(%)	($)	($)	(%)	($)	(%)
Travel & entertainment	20	15*	$$$		$$$	6	1*	33.1*	2	24.3
Miscellaneous expenses			324.7*	12*	146.5*	96	37*	64.5*	160*	250.5*
Less credits to operating expenses:										
Investment accounts		3*	95.6*	*	61.1*	6	50*	114.2*	34*	122.5*
Other credits		2*	$$$*	2*	$$$*	1–	24*	93.6*	20*	92.4*
Car cleaning trans to transportation						.–		$$$		$$$
Cab clean & service TFD to transportation						.–		$$$		128.6
Total credits		5*	97.2*	2*	93.4*	3	74*	105.6*	54*	107.8*
Total mechanical operating expenses	1,850	24	1.3	158*	9.3*	21,833	33	.1	3,896*	21.7*
Total North Platte diesel shop	1,850	24	1.3	158*	9.3*	21,833	33	.1	3,896*	21.7*

EXHIBIT 5

UNION PACIFIC (A)
Mechanical Department—Locomotive Facilities
Summary of Expenses
(December 1976)

Date Prepared 01-12-77
Time Prepared 20.42.03

	CURRENT MONTH					YEAR TO DATE				
	ACTUAL	DEVIATION				ACTUAL	DEVIATION			
		BUDGET		LAST YEAR			BUDGET		LAST YEAR	
	($)	($)	(%)	($)	(%)	($)	($)	(%)	($)	(%)
Locomotive facility—Omaha	13,813	11,980*	653.3	11,880*	614.7*	35,843	14,050*	64.4*	20,302*	130.6*
Locomotive facility—No. Platte	1,850	24	1.3	158*	9.3*	21,833	33	1	3,896*	21.7*
Locomotive facility—Salt Lake	1,006	67	6.3	44*	4.6*	12,272	1		1,731*	16.4*
Locomotive facilities—East Dist.	555	76	12.0	1	.3	7,247	94*	1.3*	725*	11.1*
Locomotive facilities—West Dist.	1,378	134*	10.7*	28	2.0	16,887	2,141*	14.5	2,315*	15.8*
Total locomotive facilities	18,604	11,945*	179.3*	12,053*	183.9*	94,084	16,251*	20.8*	28,972*	44.4*

EXHIBIT 6

UNION PACIFIC (A)

Mechanical Department—Locomotive Facilities

Detail of Expenses

(December 1976)

	CURRENT MONTH					YEAR TO DATE				
	ACTUAL	DEVIATION				ACTUAL	DEVIATION			
		BUDGET		LAST YEAR			BUDGET		LAST YEAR	
	($)	($)	(%)	($)	(%)	($)	($)	(%)	($)	(%)
% Payroll & related expenses:										
Straight time	3,040	480	13.6	325*	11.9*	35,757	5,409	13.1	6,451*	22.0*
Overtime	146	29	16.9	90	38.1	2,109	615*	41.1*	41*	2.0*
Accrued liabilities and back pay			$$$	170	$$$	174	174*	$$$	1,836	91.3
Health & welfare	162	83	34.0	8	5.0	2,522	359	12.4	678*	36.8*
Vacation accruals	229	23*	11.2*	120*	110.2*	2,965	298*	11.1*	516*	21.0*
Holiday	264	264*	$$$*	149*	130.2*	1,280	1,280*	$$$*	313*	32.4*
Sick leave	9	9*	$$$*	1*	20.8*	113	113*	$$$*	7	6.0
Other allowances	24	6*	33.1*	8*	51.0*	350	131*	59.9*	140*	66.6*
Payroll taxes	643	80*	14.2*	133*	26.2*	7,159	573*	8.6*	1,560*	27.8*
Vacation pay—actual		199*	$$$*				2,163*	$$$*		
Total	4,521	11	.2	469*	11.5*	52,435	418	7	7,858*	17.6*
Less credits:										
Investment accounts	32 —	11	57.1	2*	5.8*	335 —	92	38.1	28	9.2
Other credits	78 —	72*	48.1*	23	42.5	989 —	764*	43.5*	213*	17.7*
Total credits	110 —	61*	35.4*	21	23.9	1,324 —	672*	33.6*	185*	12.2*
Net payroll & related expenses	4,410	49*	1.1	448*	11.3*	$51,110	253*	.4*	8,043*	18.6*

Material & supplies:										
Repair parts & material	1,700	663	28.0	661	27.9	31,138	3,081*	10.9*	8,110*	35.2*
Lubricants	385	105	21.5	50	11.6	5,245	252	4.5	181*	3.5*
Fuel	4	4*	$$$*	.	6.6	54	54*	$$$*	24*	85.4*
Gasoline	15	1*	9.2*	1	6.6	143	20	12.2	4	3.2
Shop supplies	97	2	2.6	81	45.6	1,486	243*	19.6*	246*	19.8*
Locomotive & train supplies	21	7	26.2	22	50.9	266	78	22.7	36	12.0
Miscellaneous material & supplies	259	48*	23.1*	25	8.8	3,096	604*	24.2*	612*	24.6*
Total material & supplies	2,483	725	22.6	842	25.3	41,431	3,632*	9.6*	9,134*	28.2*
Utilities	92	22*	31.3*	23*	33.9*	972	150*	18.3*	155*	18.9*
Repair & maintenance contracts	8	1	15.1	6	43.9	104	17	14.1	1	.9*
Miscellaneous contracts	13	,	.3	*	2.9*	197	40*	25.8*	48*	32.1*
Travel & entertainment	3	.	3.4	3	46.4	59	11*	22.8*	5	8.1
Miscellaneous expenses	34	19	122.2*	14*	68.2*	326	138*	73.6*	244*	297.6*
Less credits to operating expenses:										
AAR billing credits	1	*	$$$*	*	$$$*	1 –	4*	67.7*	1*	46.1*
Investment accounts	24	12,562*	$$$*	12,395*	$$$*	24	11,828*	99.7*	11,035*	99.7*
Other credits	2 –	24*	90.4*	23*	89.9*	58 –	285*	83.0*	325*	84.8*
Car cleaning trans to transportation	–	*	40.7*	.	23.9	8 –	3	90.5	2	48.0
Cab clean & service TFD to transportation	2 –	2	252.7	.	9.0	24 –	15	162.2	8	50.0
Total credits	11,557	12,586*	$$$*	12,418*	$$$*	117 –	12,099*	99.0*	11,351*	98.9*
Total mechanical operating expenses	18,604	11,949*	179.5*	12,053*	183.9*	94,084	16,309*	20.9*	28,972*	44.4*
% retirements		4	$$$				57	$$$		
Total locomotive facilities	18,604	11,945*	179.3*	12,053*	183.9*	94,084	16,251*	20.8*	28,972*	44.4*

EXHIBIT 7

Union Pacific (A)
Union Pacific Railroad Company
Mechanical Department Cost Report
October 1983

	October 1980	Net Change From Last Year[1] ( ) = Increase Amount	Percent	Year-To Date 1980	Net Change From Last Year[1] ( ) = Increase Amount	Percent	Twelve Month Average 11/79 - 10/80	Change From Last Year ( ) = Increase Percent
Administrative:								
CMO-Staff & Adm.	$ 1,104,926	$ (47,916)	(5)	$10,329,793	$ (255,692)	(2)	$ 993,778	(4)
C&S Engr.-Staff & General	144,439	(20,600)	(19)	1,290,845	(27,212)	(2)	122,367	3
Total Administrative	$ 1,249,365	$(68,516)	(7)	$11,620,638	$(282,904)	(2)	$1,116,145	(3)
Diesel Fuel								
Cost Per:								
Power Unit Mile	$ 2.29	$ .17	8	$ 2.16	$ .11	5	$ 2.01	13
Million Horsepower Miles	$ 730.81	$ 11.10	2	$ 699.24	$ 14.62	2	$ 648.95	10
Power Unit Hour	$ 61.37	$ 1.20	2	$ 59.47	$ 1.14	2	$ 54.95	9
Service Loco. Day	$ 518.46	$ 40.71	9	$ 490.25	$ 22.15	7	$ 459.99	11
Locomotive Maintenance:								
Cost Per Power Unit Mile								
Direct (Labor & Matl.)	$ .8189	$ .0465	6	$ .7577	$ .0606	8	$ .7330	11
General	.1091	.0697	42	.1516	.0326	20	.1519	18
Lubricants	.0778	$ .0059	9	.0657	$ .0028	5	.0609	9
Total Cost/Power Unit Mile	$ 1.0058	$ .1221	12	$ .9750	$ .0960	10	$ .9458	12
Cost Per Million Horsepower Miles								
Direct (Labor & Matl.)	$ 271.88	$ (3.22)	(1)	$ 246.69	8.64	4	$ 235.91	8
General	36.22	19.15	37	49.14	8.09	16	48.88	15
Lubricants	25.84	.40	2	21.31	.13	1	19.59	6
Total Cost/Mil. Horsepower Miles	$ 333.94	$ 16.33	5	$ 317.14	$ 16.86	6	$ 304.38	9
Cost Per Power Unit Hour								
Direct (Labor & Matl.)	$ 22.81	$ (.16)	(1)	$ 20.90	$ .69	4	$ 19.98	7
General	3.04	1.63	37	4.18	.68	15	4.14	15
Lubricants	2.17	.04	3	1.81	.01	1	1.66	5
Total Cost/Power Unit Hour	$ 28.02	$ 1.51	5	$ 26.89	$ 1.38	5	$ 25.78	9
Cost Per Serviceable Loco. Day								
Direct (Labor & Matl.)	$ 192.88	$ 11.21	7	$ 172.26	11.87	7	$ 167.04	8
General	25.69	16.48	42	34.46	6.98	18	34.61	16
Lubricants	18.33	1.41	9	14.94	.51	4	13.87	7
Total Cost/Serviceable Loco. Day	$ 236.90	$ 29.10	13	$ 221.66	$ 19.36	9	$ 215.51	10
Freight Car Maintenance								
Cost Per Hundred Freight Car Miles								
Direct (Labor & Matl.)	$ 3.9080	$ .1697	4	$ 4.1538	$ .1253	3	$ 3.9282	8
General	1.0314	(.0124)	(1)	.9862	.0638	7	.9538	8
Lubricants	.0107	.0041	34	.0163	.0039	24	.0165	23
Total Cost/Hund. Freight Car Miles	$ 4.9501	$ .1525	3	$ 5.1563	$ .1929	4	$ 4.8985	8
Cost Per Thousand Gross Ton Miles								
Direct (Labor & Matl.)	$ .5764	$ .0289	5	$ .6114	$ .0269	5	$ .5796	10
General	.1521	(.0006)	-	.1452	.0114	8	.1407	10
Lubricants	.0016	.0006	34	.0024	.0006	23	.0025	26
Total Cost/Thous. Gross Ton Miles	$ .7301	$ .0289	4	$ .7589	$ .0389	5	$ .7228	10
Cost Per Serviceable Car Day[2]								
Direct (Labor & Matl.)	$ 4.3282	$ .3032	7	$ 4.5222	$ .0038	-	$ 4.3162	3
General	1.1423	.0168	1	1.0737	.0374	4	1.0481	3
Lubricants	.0119	.0050	36	.0178	.0037	21	.0181	21
Total Cost/Serviceable Car Day	$ 5.4824	$ .3250	6	$ 5.6137	$ .0449	1	$ 5.3824	3

[1] Includes Inflationary Wage, Material Price, and Fringe Benefit Increases Foreign Excluded

Planning and Analysis Department
Omaha - December 1, 1980

EXHIBIT 8

UNION PACIFIC (A)

Through and Local[1]
Comparison of Through and Local Freight Crew Cost
per Thousand Gross Ton Miles after Deflation
for Wage Increases Granted

	JAN. 1978 CREW COSTS PER 000 GTM	JAN. 1978 DEFLATED FOR WAGE INCREASES[2]	JAN. 1977 CREW COSTS PER 000 GTM	VARIANCE AMOUNT	PERCENT
Nebraska	.537	.504	.509	−.005	−1
Wyoming	.628	.589	.566	+.023	+4
Kansas	.602	.565	.662	−.097	−15
Eastern district	.581	.545	.554	−.009	−2
Utah	.776	.728	.680	+.048	+7
California	.896	.841	.773	+.068	+9
South Central district	.816	.765	.711	+.054	+8
Idaho	.816	.765	.838	−.073	−9
Oregon	.934	.876	.911	−.035	−4
Northwestern district	.868	.814	.869	−.055	−6
Total system	.674	.632	.647	−.015	−2

[1] Does not inlcude zone locals.
[2] Compound wage inflation effect of 6.6% removed.
− favorable, + unfavorable.

EXHIBIT 9

UNION PACIFIC (A)

DIR	SYMBOL	AVG. TONS/TRAIN			AVG. HP PER TON			AVG. LID MINUTES			AVG. TID MINUTES			AVG. FID MINUTES			AVG. ROAD SPEED			CREWS CALLED		
		CURR YEAR	PRIOR YEAR	PER CHG	CURR YEAR	PRIOR YEAR	PER CHG	CURR YEAR	PRIOR YEAR	PER CHG	CURR YEAR	PRIOR YEAR	PER CHG	CURR YEAR	PRIOR YEAR	PER CHG	CURR YEAR	PRIOR YEAR	CHG	CURR YEAR	PRIOR YEAR	CHG
E	AENP	6,623	4,844	29	1.7	2.5	32-	40	42	5-	43	36	19				48	46	4	31	30	3
E	ACNP	6,610	7,307	17	1.9	2.0	3-	109	18	508	51	5	920				44	45	2-	28	58	51-
E	ACUE	2,875	2,918	1-	4.7	4.6	4-	24	18	33	13	21	35-				31	27	14	62	60	3
E	AFCCP	7,142	4,935	44	1.3	2.0	35-	12	4	200	8	3	166				37	42	11-	92	90	2
E	AKU	5,227	4,919	6	1.2	1.7	29-	2	36	94-	6	37	83-				24	24		23	59	61-
E	ARIP	7,110	6,641	6	2.0	1.7	17	63	74	14-	96	83	15				40	41	2-	25	31	19-
E	AYT	7,727	7,857	1-	1.8	1.9	5-	19	16	19	21	30	30-				30	30		350	257	36
E	APV	5,536			0.0	2.4		3			11						44			167		
E	ASPK	4,134	4,652	11-	3.4	3.1	9	15	15		28	22	27				39	40	2-	216	245	11-
E	AMFR	5,012	4,949	16	1.9	2.5	24-	41	21	95	28	23	21				31	36	13-	61	172	64-
E	BAX	2,652	2,602	1	3.6	4.5	20-	15	24	37-	20	24	16-				53	36	5-	102	111	8-
E	EAG	7,546	9,006	1-	1.1	1.1		30	28	7	25	30	18-				33	39	15-	98	89	10
E	BKL	7,546	6,297	19	1.1	1.4	21-	28	30	6-	62	36	72				33	34	15-	84	83	7
E	FMFA	3,761			3.2	0.0		49			47						26			24		
E	FMNP	4,159			2.9	0.0		25			27						30			69		
E	FAP	5,675	3,460	66	1.7	3.8	55-	60	43	33	32	26	23				47	42	11	32	32	
E	ONFL	3,527			3.1	0.0		35			48						27			39		
E	YVVO	3,177			3.9	0.0		79			63						21			14		
E	BPUE	13,263			0.6	0.7		11			20						32			20		
E	YUZ	6,454	4,511	7-	3.5	3.0	16	8	6	33	71	51	39				30	27	11	33	41	19-
E	CN	4,534	4,507	7	3.0	3.4	11-	29	25	16	35	28	25				32	37	13-	310	342	9-
E	CNAP	6,636	5,654	12	1.4	1.7	17-	66	25	22-	71	74	4-				43	44	2-	30	31	3-
E	CGALE	8,922	6,175	44	1.1	1.8	39-	11	12	9-	20	26	23-				30	27	11	89	27	229
E	CGSTR	2,961			6.0	4.9		27			36						49			10		
E	CPUE	13,390	13,635	1-	0.7	0.7		30	15	57	23	16	43				37	34	8	13	28	5-
E	CIP	9,746	7,344	15	1.3	1.9	5-	29	42	68-	22	43	48-				48	56	14-	43	29	48

APPENDIX A

RAIL FORM A

ASSIGNMENT OF EXPENSES TO SERVICES AND
ASSOCIATION OF THE EXPENSES WITH SERVICE UNITS

EXPENSE GROUP AND SERVICE TO WHICH ASSIGNED	SERVICE UNIT WITH WHICH ASSOCIATED	EXPENSE GROUP AND SERVICE TO WHICH ASSIGNED	SERVICE UNIT WITH WHICH ASSOCIATED
Maintenance of Ways and Structures		Depreciation, freight-train cars	
		Mileage portion (70%)	
Yard and way switch tracks:		Running	Car miles
Related to distance	Car miles	Switching	
Unrelated to distance	Cars	Related to distance	Car miles
		Unrelated to distance	Cars
Running tracks	Gross ton miles	Time (car-day) portion (30%)	
		Running	Car miles
Station and office buildings		Switching	
Running	Gross ton miles	Related to distance	Car Miles
Station platform	Carload tons	Unrelated to distance	Cars
Other station (clerical)		**Transportation—Rail Line**	
Line-haul traffic	Carload		
Terminal switching	Cars	Dispatching: running	Gross ton miles
Other structures		Station platform labor	Car load tons
Running	Gross ton miles		
Switching		Station labor, nonplatform	
Related to distance	Car miles	Train work, running	Gross ton miles
Unrelated to distance	Cars	Station clerical	
		Carload traffic	Carload shipments
Maintenance of Equipment		Switching	Carload cars
		Special services	Carload shipments
Locomotive repairs			
Running	Gross ton miles	Yard and train expenses	
Switching		Running	Gross ton miles
Related to distance	Car miles	Switching	
Unrelated to distance	Cars	Related to distance	Car miles
		Unrelated to distance	Cars
Freight-train car repairs		**Traffic, General, and Miscellaneous**	
Mileage portion (70%)			
Running	Gross ton miles	General office clerks—waybills	
Switching		Station clerical	
Related to distance	Car miles	Line haul	Carload shipments
Unrelated to distance	Cars	Switching	Carload cars
Time (car-day) portion (30%)			
Running	Car miles	General office clerks—claims	
Switching		Loss and damage	
Related to distance	Car miles	Line haul	Carload tons
Unrelated to distance	Cars	Switching	Carload cars switched
Depreciation, locomotives		Loss and damage	Apportioned over all other expenses
Running	Gross ton miles		
Switching			
Related to distance	Car miles	Traffic, general office	Apportioned over all services
Unrelated to distance	Cars	expenses, taxes, miscellaneous	

Union Pacific (B)

By the late 1970s, Union Pacific executives realized that a new competitive era would soon be unleashed. In addition to its traditional competition from other transportation forms, primarily trucking, and from surviving railroads after a wave of consolidations and mergers, the expected sharp reduction in ICC rate regulation would radically change the nature of competition. In this new environment, effective cost measurement systems would be essential if Union Pacific were to remain a vigorous competitor.

In late 1980, the CEO of Union Pacific asked John Rebensdorf, the head of the planning and analysis department, to develop a new system to measure the railroad's profits by line of business. The goals of the new system were easily explained.

> In a regulated environment, prices are set to cover the costs of the least efficient producers. With deregulation, prices will be established by the most efficient producers. We need to know our costs if we are going to be able to price aggressively, meet our competition, and maximize our profitability.

The recently developed Management Cost Control (MCC) system (see Union Pacific, A) provided valuable information on cost incurrence at detailed cost center levels. These data could be aggregated up to provide overall cost and productivity information on the railroad's transportation, engineering, and mechanical departments. While useful for cost control, MCC was not directly helpful to marketing managers, who wanted cost information on individual carload moves as they attempted to win business away from trucks and other railroads.

The Cost Out All Traffic (COAT) system provided estimates of the cost of each move, but the estimates were based on system- or industry-wide averages, with some of the parameters arising from studies done decades earlier. The estimates, therefore, did not reflect particular traffic patterns, train sizes, and operating procedures of Union Pacific, much less the considerable variation that existed within the Union Pacific system.

Basically, the railroad operated with two completely independent financial systems. The revenue system was driven by the waybills produced for each move. The tariff on a waybill was a function of the origin and destination of the move, the type of commodity being moved, the weight of the shipment, the type of car used, plus any special features associated with the move. The specific costs, however, of a particular move could not be easily computed since the MCC system collected data only by the operating functions of the railroad: transportation, engineering, mechanical, and general and administrative.

Both systems, the revenue and the MCC system, performed effectively the functions for which they were designed. Overall railroad profits could be computed by subtracting all incurred costs from the revenues produced. But computing profits only on a system-wide basis was not very helpful in the emerging competitive environment for railroads. Management knew that certain of its business must be highly profitable whereas other lines of business were close to breakeven or losing money. Some individual moves were costed manually to reflect specific movement parameters, but this approach was cumbersome and time consuming. Without being able to relate specific costs incurred to the revenues produced on an individual move, product-line, or customer basis, it would be difficult for Union Pacific to use its new pricing freedom effectively.

TRAIN AND CAR MOVEMENT COST SYSTEMS

By 1985, the cost and profit planning area of the planning and analysis group had developed an integrated set of systems to cost out prospective and actual car moves. Extensive statistical studies had been performed to understand cost behavior and to choose service units that could be used to compute unit costs. These unit costs, derived from operating expenses and operating statistics, were combined with actual car and train moves to provide cost estimates for individual carload moves. Three sepa-

This case was prepared by Professor Robert S. Kaplan.
Copyright © 1985 by the President and Fellows of Harvard College. Harvard Business School case 186-178.

rate systems had been developed and linked together.

Train unit cost system

The goal of the Train Unit Cost (TUC) System was to develop train-related expenses on a train symbol and location specific basis. For example, costs would be collected for train ABC running from Los Angeles to North Platte, Nebraska. For each such train, the entire run was broken down into crew districts. A crew district is a segment of 100 to 300 miles that represents the basic unit of measurement for transportation, train, and engine crew expenses. The data input to TUC are daily train symbol operating statistics and specific crew wages by location. The train symbol operating service units include number and type of cars, number of locomotives, carload weights, gross ton miles, locomotive horsepower, locomotive miles, and train miles. These data are entered from each crew district via an on-line work order system and run in a batch mode on the system's central computer during the late night/early morning shift to prepare a daily Train Statistical Record.

Depreciation and repair costs for freight cars, locomotives, and cabooses were computed from the UP unit cost systems. Basically, these unit costs provided estimates of locomotive repair and depreciation costs per locomotive unit mile. These locomotive costs could then be allocated to freight carried by each train. Freight car repair and depreciation expenses were computed by another unit cost system and were directly allocated to a particular freight movement.

Fuel consumption was measured for each train and location based on locomotive units, train speed, gross ton miles, track conditions, and geography. The allocation was accomplished by an engineering model that predicted fuel consumption. At present, it was considered too expensive to measure actual fuel consumption by specific train symbol and location.

Finally, each train-related expense was divided by the gross ton miles for each train symbol to calculate train unit costs by symbol and location. The train-related costs per gross ton mile were transmitted to the two-car movement costing systems: Consolidated Profit Measurement System (CPMS) and Network Cost System (NCS). Appendix A provides a sample calculation from the Train Unit Cost System.

CONSOLIDATED PROFIT MEASUREMENT SYSTEM

The Consolidated Profit Measurement System (CPMS) estimated the cost and profit of every railroad shipment. The system started with the estimated revenue of each shipment as collected by the waybills. The shipment was matched against actual car and train movements, as collected in the Train Unit Cost System and another car movement history system, to determine the actual operating parameters and service units for the shipment. That is, the system located the train used to carry the shipment and determined the actual train characteristics: horsepower of locomotives, number of cars, tonnage, car miles, transit time, and routing.

Additional operating features were identified such as whether the car was leased or owned, whether the move resulted in an empty car return trip, the switching locations, and whether location-specific costs such as drayage and ramping were required. The planning and analysis group identified 21 primary cost categories to be measured when computing the total cost of a move. A summary of these 21 cost components is presented in Exhibit 1. An example of a sample CPMS computation appears in Appendix B.

By early 1985, the CPMS was able to match successfully shipment revenues with actual car moves more than 95% of the time. When a match with an actual car movement could not be made, averages for the previous month for that type of car movement were used to cost out the move. By using actual train movements to cost out a move, the CPMS calculation accounted for the variation in actual operating decisions. The estimated cost of a particular move was a function of the number and type of locomotives used, train weight, the speed of the train, the particular routing chosen, the number and location of switching activities, car type and ownership, and lading weight.

CPMS reports indicated where the railroad was and was not profitable and why, down to a detailed car-by-car basis. Profitability could be measured by the following:

- Market manager responsibility
- Shipper
- Commodity
- Traffic corridor
- Ramp
- Location (origin, destination, interchange)
- Equipment type

The CPMS cost calculations were run daily based on the automated revenue reporting system for completed trips and the Train Unit Cost System. By mid-1985, CPMS was costing out 6,000 to 8,000 carload movements each day plus almost that many movements of empty cars. Even though CPMS costed records on a daily basis, a summary profitability report was prepared only on a monthly basis. This monthly report consisted of four large books of printouts plus an executive summary. It was distributed only to the most senior management of the railroad. The estimated costs and profits by commodity, location, and train symbol were considered highly valuable and sensitive information. Hence, access to CPMS was restricted. Marketing people could, by request, get CPMS information move-by-move. An on-line system was being developed to permit access to the CPMS data base.

The CPMS was a retrospective system, providing monthly feedback on the profitability of actual carload moves. While a great advance over the highly aggregate and average cost-based COAT system, additional information was needed to support marketing and sales personnel. Marketing and sales managers needed cost estimates to price bids for prospective movements. In the old (regulated) days, special studies would be performed to cost out a particular move. Five full-time people performed these special studies, but they could not handle very many such requests. With deregulation, the planning and analysis group could envision receiving hundreds of requests each day from marketing and sales for cost estimates or rate changes.

NETWORK COST SYSTEM

The Network Cost System (NCS) was a recently developed on-line model that permitted the cost of prospective moves to be estimated. It was designed to support the marketing department in preparing bids for new business. NCS developed both historical and projected cost estimates for specific moves

based on detailed movement parameters specified by users.

In principle, the NCS would have required estimating costs between every possible origin and every possible destination. But the number of possible origin and destination combinations was so high that a simplified network approach was used for the system. With the network approach, each possible origin and destination was associated with its nearest hub. Any move to an origin or destination was assumed to go through its nearby hub. With this assumption, it was only necessary to calculate costs along the branch from each station to its neighboring hub and then to compute costs between adjacent pairs of hubs. The network approach permitted a considerable savings in computer code and running time.

A request by the marketing department for a cost estimate from the Network Cost System needed to contain at least the following information:

- Movement type (TOFC/COFC, manifest) and service level
- Origin
- Destination
- Routing (branches and main routes: hub to hub)
- Commodity type (STCC code)
- Car type (box, covered hopper, refrigerator [reefer], TOFC, automobile; also owned versus foreign car)
- Empty return assumption
- Commodity (lading) weight
- Time period for costs (today, in six months, one year from now)

For TOFC/COFC:

- Number of trailers/containers on flatcar
- Type of trailer/container

After receiving such a request, the Network Cost System estimated the costs of the proposed move. Exhibit 2 shows the format for output from NCS.

The total cost of a move was broken down into major cost categories: car, locomotive/caboose, overhead, train, terminal, and loss and damage. Each of these major cost categories was further broken down into subcategories (e.g., train cost included the costs of fuel, wages, maintenance of way, roadway depreciation, and line haul). All costs were summed to produce a total cost per car.

Because of the different time periods over which costs were incurred and the inherent jointness of many of a railroad's costs, the costs of prospective moves were prepared under various assumptions. The most-used classification was long-term variable cost. Even within this classification, NCS prepared two estimates. The ledger cost figure estimated depreciation and repair expense based on the book value of long-term assets (e.g., freight cars, locomotives, fixed plant, and track). The replacement cost figure used estimates of the replacement cost of long-term assets when computing depreciation, repair, and maintenance expenses. A fully allocated cost, again both ledger and replacement, was also computed.

The collection and allocation of costs for a particular move followed the same method used to prepare a CPMS estimate (see Exhibit 3).

The NCS cost estimate of a proposed commodity movement could vary significantly based on actual operating decisions such as the number and horsepower of locomotives, assumed train speed, routing used, and number of cars per train. Line-specific historical averages were used to estimate these parameters with the data coming from the actual operating parameters collected and stored in the Train Unit Cost System. Sensitivity analysis on train sizes, routing, car type/ownership, lading weight, and time period could be performed.

Most of the requests to NCS were to cost out the move of a carload shipment which would be part of a larger train. In addition, however, NCS had the capability to estimate the cost for a unit train; that is, a train entirely dedicated to a particular shipment. Unit train requests were most common for coal trains, TOFC, and intermodal operations.

Greg Broderick, director of the cost and profit planning area in the planning and analysis group, commented on the use of the NCS system.

> By the summer of 1985, we were getting about 500 requests per day from the marketing people for cost analyses from NCS. In the current commercial environment, marketing and sales people need the capability to change rates every day. Without NCS, we would have needed 65 people doing nothing but preparing cost studies for bids, and probably doing these with lots of errors.

EXHIBIT 1

UNION PACIFIC (B)
CPMS Cost Components
(Primary Components)

COST COMPONENT	DESCRIPTION
1. Wage	1. Train crew wage costs. Actual wage costs by train symbol, including fringes.
2. Fuel	2. Train fuel consumption cost for train movement between origin/destination terminals. Fuel consumption estimated for each train reflecting actual train operating characteristics
3. Locomotive repairs/ depreciation	3. Repairs reflect cost of maintaining locomotives including both labor, fringes, and material. Depreciation represents the recovery of the purchase cost over the economic life.
4. Maintenance of way	4. Consists of the costs of maintaining track and roadway, including labor, fringes, and material.
5. Roadway depreciation	5. Includes recovery of ownership costs on road property such as roadway buildings, office buildings, and other miscellaneous depreciable structures.
6. Other line haul	6. Major items include costs of dispatching trains, signal operation and maintenance, servicing locomotives, shop machinery, repairs/depreciation, and car inspection.
7. System car—repairs/ depreciation	7. Repair costs of maintaining system cars, including labor fringes and material. Car depreciation reflects the purchase cost of a car and the recovery of the recovery of the cost over its economic life.
8. Foreign/private car— mileage and per diem	8. Cost reflects the per diem and/or per mile charge for foreign or private cars while on company's lines.
9. Car overheads	9. Includes wages of car department supervisory personnel (e.g., shop foreman) and other indirect costs associated with repair of cars.
10. Locomotive overheads	10. Wages of locomotive department supervisory personnel and other indirect costs associated with the repair of locomotives.
11. Transportation overheads	11. Wages and supplies of local transportation supervisory personnel and other transportation department staff.
12. General overheads	12. Costs of mechanical, engineering, and transportation department activities as well as other general and administration, traffic, and support functions.
13. Joint facility cost	13. Charges incurred for movement of car within or over facilities of another or group of railroads.
14. Reciprocal switching	14. Charges incurred when the industry is located on another railroad and the terminal is open to reciprocal switching.
15. Switching	15. Switching costs are incurred when a car is (1) switched from a train to an industry, (2) switched from one railroad to another railroad, or (3) switched from one train to another. Costs include wages and fringes, supplies, fuel, locomotive repairs and depreciation, and maintenance and depreciation on yard tracks.
16. Other terminal	16. Major costs include expenses associated with preparing waybills and paperwork involved with car movement and cleaning cars.

EXHIBIT 1 *(cont.)*

COST COMPONENT	DESCRIPTION
17. Loss & damage costs	17. Loss and damage costs are claims paid out to shippers for commodities lost or damaged during shipment.
18. Drayage	18. Drayage includes the costs of moving a van over the road from the industry location to the ramping point, or vice versa. Costs include driver wages, fuel, and maintenance and depreciation on tractors.
19. Other TOFC/COFC costs	19. Includes ramp/deramp expense (labor and fuel) and depreciation on specialized equipment (cranes) used in the loading/unloading process.
20. Van rental	20. Rental cost for vans while on UP system.
21. Appurtenance rental	21. Rental on multilevel racks on a flatcar.

EXHIBIT 2

UNION PACIFIC (B)

Format for Network Cost System Estimate

	LONG-TERM VARIABLE		FULLY ALLOCATED	
	LEDGER	REPLACEMENT	LEDGER	REPLACEMENT
Car—System				
Repairs				
Depreciation				
Locomotive/caboose				
Repairs				
Depreciation				
Overhead				
Car				
Transportation				
Locomotive				
General				
Train				
Fuel				
Wages				
Maintenance of way				
Roadway depreciation				
Line haul				
Terminal				
Switching				
Other terminal				
Reciprocal switch				
Joint facility				
Loss & damage				
Total/car				

APPENDIX A

Development of train unit costs

I. System developed unit costs
   Locomotive depreciation per locomotive unit mile
   Locomotive repairs per locomotive unit mile
II. Train symbol operating costs by location
   System developed unit cost × train symbol operating statistic
   Crew wage cost from accounting department information
   Train fuel estimate × price per gallon
III. Train symbol unit costs by location
   Train symbol operating costs ÷ train symbol gross ton miles

Train unit cost per gross ton mile locomotive repairs

I. System developed unit cost
   Locomotive repair cost per locomotive unit mile—$.7407
II. Train unit cost system
   A. Train statistics:
      Z200 train of February 3, 1985
      Locomotive unit miles—300
      Gross ton miles—500,000
   B. Locomotive repair cost per gross ton mile

1. SYSTEM DEVELOPED UNIT COST		LOCOMOTIVE UNIT MILES		TOTAL TRAIN LOCOMOTIVE REPAIR COST
$.7407	×	300	=	$222.21

2. TOTAL TRAIN LOCOMOTIVE REPAIR COST		GROSS TON MILES		LOCOMOTIVE REPAIR PER GROSS TON MILE
$222.21	÷	500,000	=	$.000444

Sample train and car movement

TRAIN

Symbol	: Z200, XZ, Z400
Date	: February 1985
Origin city	: City A
Destination city	: City E

CAR

Identification	: ABX 003301
Date	: February 1985
Origin city on Z200 train	: City A
Destination city on Z400 train	: City D

Appendix A (cont.)

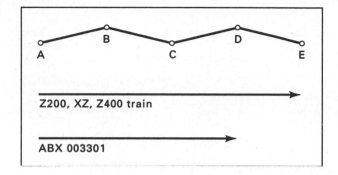

Train symbol operating statistics from train costing system

TRAIN SYMBOL Z200, ZX, Z400

CREW DISTRICT	TRAIN MILES	LOCOMOTIVE UNIT MILES	TRAIN WEIGHT	GROSS TON MILES	NUMBER OF CARS
A-B	100	300	5,000	500,000	90
B-C	50	150	5,500	275,000	100
C-D	150	300	4,500	675,000	80
D-E	200	600	4,000	800,000	70

TRAIN SYMBOL CREW WAGES
FROM ACCOUNTING DEPARTMENT

TRAIN SYMBOL Z200, ZX, Z400

CREW DISTRICT	CREW WAGES
A-B	$1,050
B-C	440
C-D	1,283
D-E	1,500

Car movement operation statistics

Identification	: ABX 003301
Date	: February 1, 1985
Train symbol	: Z200, XZ, Z400
Origin city	: City A
Destination city	: City D
Car gross weight	: 90 tons
Number of terminals	: 2
Terminal switching minutes	: 7 minutes
Miles by crew district	

A-B	100
B-C	50
C-D	150

(continued)

Appendix A (cont.)

Application of unit costs in the car movement costing systems

UNIT COSTS DIRECTLY FROM UNIT COST SYSTEMS

UP SYSTEM DEVELOPED UNIT COST		CAR MOVEMENT OPERATING STATISTICS	TOTAL COST
DESCRIPTION	VALUE		
Station clerical cost per terminal	$ 5.75	× 2 terminal minutes =	$11.50
Terminal switching cost per minute	$ 3.20	× 7 terminal minutes =	$22.40

UNIT COSTS REFINED THROUGH THE TRAIN UNIT COST SYSTEM

TRAIN UNIT COST DESCRIPTION	CREW DISTRICT	UNIT COST VALUE	CAR MOVEMENT OPERATING STATISTICS	TOTAL COST
Fuel cost per gross ton mile	A-B	$.0017	× (90 tons × 100 miles) =	$15.30
	B-C	$.0021	× (90 tons × 50 miles) =	$ 9.45
	C-D	$.0007	× (90 tons × 150 miles) =	$ 9.45
Wage cost per gross ton mile	A-B	$.0021	× (90 tons × 100 miles) =	$18.90
	B-C	$.0016	× (90 tons × 50 miles) =	$ 7.45
	C-D	$.0019	× (90 tons × 150 miles) =	$25.65

Example of CPMS computation of car movement cost and profit

COMPLETED CAR CYCLE

```
Car ID:   ABX 003301      CSN: 0027421902      Own:  P
Type:  B       AAR:  B300     L/E:  L       STCC:  XXXXXXX     Lad:  034
Tare:  056       Start:  850201 13 52       End:  850206 05 20
Consignor:  ABC Company       Consignee:  XYZ Company
Orig:  City A       Dest:  City D       CGTM:  27,000
Per diem:  0.00       Milg-amt:  0.6300       Transit:  46.00       Car mi:  300
Orig-switch:  7.0       Orig-dtn:  128.0 hrs.
Des-switch:  7.0       Des-dtn:  79.6 hrs.
Intermed-switch:  City B 2.2       Dtn:  14.2hrs.
Intermed-switch:  City C 2.2       Dtn:  17.5 hrs.
```

CAR MOVEMENT DATA

EVENT	DATA	TIME	CITY	STATE	TRAIN
Release	02/01/85	1352	A	XX	—
Term. depart	02/03/85	2200	A	XX	Z200
Term. arrive	02/04/85	0430	B	XX	Z200
Term. depart	02/04/85	1845	B	XX	XZ
Term. arrive	02/04/85	2210	C	XX	XZ
Term. depart	02/05/85	1545	C	XX	Z400
Term. arrive	02/05/85	2000	D	XX	Z400
Act placed	02/06/85	0520	D	XX	—

Appendix A (cont.)

Car movement costed history (cost detail)

LOADED MOVEMENT—CITY A TO CITY D

Wage	$52
Fuel	34
Maintenance of Way	48
Locomotive repairs	12
Locomotive depreciation	6
Line haul	21
Car—mileage	189
Car—per diem	0
Term. switch—origin	22
Term. switch—destination	22
Term. switch—intermediate	12
Transportation overhead	10
Locomotive overhead	2
Car overhead	1
General overhead	56
Roadway depreciation	1
Other terminal	49
Total	$537

CPMS: car movement contribution calculation city A to city D

A. Loaded movement revenue		$1,000
B. Loaded movement cost (city A to city B)	$537	
C. Empty movement cost (city B to city A)	150	
Total cost of movement		$ 687
Movement contribution		$ 313
Movement profitability indicator (PI)		1.45

Massachusetts Eye and Ear Infirmary

Mr. Charles Wood, Executive Director of the Massachusetts Eye and Ear Infirmary (MEEI), was reviewing the results of a new cost accounting system which the hospital had installed in 1976. The new system contained several innovative features, and the past year had been a trial period for it. Mr. Wood was now interested in persuading Medicare and Medicaid to accept the system for reimbursement; Blue Cross had adopted it at the outset of the pilot program. Central to his thinking were two issues: (1) whether the system actually represented a more accurate picture of hospital costs, as proponents of the system claimed; and (2) what impact the system was having on cost containment in the hospital. Wood was also concerned about transferring the system to less specialized hospitals, since

This case was prepared by David W. Young, Assistant Professor, and Patricia O'Brien, Research Assistant, based on the document entitled "Massachusetts Eye and Ear Infirmary: Interrelated Programs for Optimum Cost Effectiveness in Hospital Management," by Charles T. Wood, and with the cooperation of the Massachusetts Eye and Ear Infirmary.

his preliminary feedback from the industry indicated that some individuals questioned whether the system was applicable to a general hospital.

HISTORY OF THE MEEI

In 1974, the MEEI celebrated its 150th anniversary. During the century and a half from its inception in 1824 as a free clinic located on the second floor of Scollay's Building in downtown Boston, it had undertaken a wide variety of innovative and farsighted activities.

By 1977, the independent, nonprofit hospital was admitting 11,273 patients and accommodating 80,000 outpatient visits per year. More striking was the increased demand on the hospital's emergency care. In a decade, emergency visits surged from 10,000 per year to nearly 36,000. (Exhibit 1 details patient statistics for 1977). In addition, the hospital coordinated numerous community outreach programs, including screening clinics to detect chronic disorders, civic group lectures, and the preparation of health care education booklets.

In 1977, a total of 1,100 employees staffed the hospital's three daily shifts. There were 136 eye specialists and 67 ear, nose, and throat specialists on the hospital's staff, and 40 residents and 50 clinical and research fellows received specialty training each year. The hospital's income statement is summarized in Exhibit 2.

BACKGROUND

Dissatisfied with the usual per diem cost accounting methods used in hospitals across the country, Charles Wood became convinced of the need for an accounting system that would allow hospitals to measure the cost of health care more accurately. He contended that the historical approach to structuring hospital rates was clumsy and outmoded. Because it failed to identify the components of patient costs, it placed an unfair burden on the patients or payors who could least afford it. According to Mr. Wood, the present method was leading hospitals into ineffective and cumbersome accounting methods, at the expense of the public.

> For years I've been trying to improve the conceptual basis for identifying the cost of hospital care. Back in the 1950s, I noticed that hospitals' costs were defined differently from state to state, depending on

what qualified for reimbursement. Meanwhile, hospitals would try to make up for deficits by tacking on additional patient fees for services like admissions. These experiments were short-lived because the figures were arbitrary and not rooted in fact, but they stimulated me to think about hospital costs as units of service. We developed our present cost accounting system gradually; first we developed a two-part rate composed of a per diem charge, including nursing, and a hospitalization charge. Then, as we improved data systems, we expanded into our present three-part cost accounting method, which takes nursing out of the per diem portion and costs it out for separate charging.

Wood designed the new system to isolate specific elements of hospital costs. By breaking down the lump sum per diem hospital rate into units which reflected the actual services each patient received, Wood hoped to develop a more equitable cost system. In addition, he thought the extensive information produced by such a system could provide management tools for improving the use of hospital facilities.

Although he designed the system for MEEI's specification, Wood believed it had widespread potential for the hospital industry. In the hospital's 1976 Annual Report, he wrote,

> We have just completed the first full year of using our new cost accounting system, and I am happy to report that by any measure it is working successfully. Our program continues to be watched very closely by other hospitals around the country and by various local, state, and federal government agencies. Our first-year pilot program with Blue Cross of Massachusetts, Inc., exceeded even our expectations, and I hope to be able to report a year from now that the seeds planted this year have taken root and grown. It is particularly important that this approach be demonstrated in a general hospital, which will almost certainly erase any doubts about widespread potential. I am quite confident in the outcome of such a test because, despite the fact that we are a specialty hospital, we have worked with such a variety of conditions and amassed such a broad collection of data that we are certain of successful use in general hospitals.

THE SPLIT COST ACCOUNTING SYSTEM

The split cost accounting system in use at MEEI was built around two basic concepts: (1) that not all days' care in a hospital were equivalent, and (2) that for any given patient, the cost of routine services was a function of three distinct categories of costs that related to three essential elements of a hospital stay—hospitalization, routine daily costs, and intensity of service (what MEEI calls "clinical care") costs. The hospitalization cost is the effort of entering and discharging a patient. It includes scheduling for admission, the admission process, and other one-time operations such as maintaining medical records, preparing a bill, and various discharge-related activities. It also includes a per-patient apportionment of plant and administrative overhead—in effect, the cost of the hospital's availability and readiness. Hospitalization is a one-time cost, regardless of a patient's length of stay, and recognizes that one's entry and presence in the hospital engender costs that are measurable.

The cost per patient day category encompasses the costs related to the patient's length of stay (i.e., the daily costs for room, meals, dietary needs, laundry, routine pharmaceuticals, medical and surgical supplies, and incidentals).

The clinical care component is the cost of direct patient care in accordance with diagnosis, surgical procedures, and the patient's point in progress toward recovery. This component relies on the use of clinical care units. A clinical care unit (CCU) is the numerical value given to a direct service or treatment which is provided to a patient. The CCU's are measures of the amount of time necessary to perform various activities in relation to a patient's care while in the hospital.

Wood emphasized that the system focused only on the services which had traditionally been included in a per diem rate.

It's important to recognize that our new cost accounting system is not a medical measurement system. It's a cost measurement system for productivity. By means of the data base which we created, we were able to develop what might best be called a relative-value scale. This tells us how many clinical care units are needed for the entire range of procedures here at the infirmary. The data base is updated periodically by sampling various procedures to see how they correspond to the existing data base and making adjustments accordingly. Services such as the operating rooms, drug units, lab tests, and other ancillaries are billed separately so that the system focuses only on the ongoing care component of a patient's stay.

MEEI had calculated the amount of effort or clinical care units required by each procedure and came up with a method of specifying the amount of care needed by each patient. Time values for clinical care units are shown in Exhibit 3, and the number of clinical care units necessary for various nursing activities is enumerated in Exhibit 4.

USE OF THE SPLIT COST ACCOUNTING SYSTEM

With the split cost accounting system, the traditional per diem cost for a patient's stay was allocated to the three aforementioned categories. Expenses are distributed by categories in Exhibit 5. During fiscal year 1977, the infirmary's hospitalization charge was $202.69. The daily room rate was $41.25, and clinical care was $4.54 per unit. By using the data base which it had developed, MEEI could predict by diagnosis and surgical procedure how many clinical care units a given patient would be likely to require on each hospital day, from the day of admission to the day of discharge. Wood commented on this approach.

We know, for example, that a child with strabismus (squint) will require 15 clinical care units on the day he is admitted. The far more seriously ill laryngectomy patient, who is largely able to care for himself preoperatively, will require only five clinical care units on the day of admission. By means of our data base, we have been able to develop a workload curve by diagnosis and surgical procedure on a day-to-day basis that can be used to predict clinical care requirements of patients in-house and those to be admitted. (See Exhibit 6.)

We recognize, of course, that every service provided as part of general clinical care is not a direct patient care service. We know that a portion of the time of every member of a nursing shift is spent in activities other than direct care, activities such as conferences with other members of the medical team, consoling the patient, and so forth. So, in determining the cost of a clinical care unit, we developed a ratio of direct patient care time to indirect patient care time and then included indirect care and nursing department overhead along with direct patient care costs in the cost per clinical care unit.

As you might expect, we have found that the costs for various procedures under the new system are radically different from those under the traditional system when we simply used a per diem rate. Thus, not only is the new cost accounting system we have put into effect at MEEI a major departure from systems presently being used in hospitals across the country, but it results in significantly different costs for procedures as well. The split cost accounting system we are using closely aligns charges with diagnosis, surgical procedure, and identified required care.

Margarete Arndt, Director of Patient Services at MEEI, highlighted the differences between the split cost accounting system and the traditional per diem system:

I think one can appreciate the advantages of our cost accounting system by looking at some hypothetical hospital activities for one year. For example, suppose a given hospital had 1,000 admissions during a year, 10,000 patient days, and 100,000 CCUs. Suppose now that patient days decreased to, say, 9,000, while admissions remained the same, or admissions decreased to, say, 900, while length of stay remained the same; or suppose there was an increase or decrease in the intensity of care such that more or fewer CCUs were rendered. You could then make comparisons between the hospital using a split cost accounting system and one using a per diem rate to see the differences. What happens, of course, is that hospitals using a per diem system lose revenue as soon as patient days fall, while at the same time they may be delivering more intensive care on the existing patient days.

EVALUATION OF THE SPLIT COST ACCOUNTING SYSTEM

In reviewing the effects of the new accounting system, Wood first mentioned the advantages of the hospitalization charge.

One of the big differences with our new system is the hospitalization charge. Compared with the present per diem system in use in most institutions, it has a greater impact on the short-stay patient. But it is nevertheless more equitable, since under the per diem system the long-stay patient (mostly the older and sicker patient likely to be less economically endowed) is paying a proportionately larger share of the one-time costs and is, in fact, subsidizing the hospitalization of the short-stay patient.

Wood imagined that, used over a wide geographic area, the system would provide a common denominator to compare rates among several hospitals.

The long-argued question of why day rates have varied so markedly from one institution to another over the years is a result of the day rate being a catchall category for many other cost factors. If the true elements of hospitalization are identified, the cost of providing a hospital room should be mark-

edly closer everywhere in that the same elements are assessed.

Wood added a long-range benefit for the health industry.

By costing out the elements of care and charging patients only for the care they receive, it will no longer be necessary to operate separate institutions or facilities for patients who require different levels of care. These facilities were created because traditional cost accounting systems are inadequate to measure and cost out the work output for each level of care. I mean, currently, patients recovering from long or serious illnesses are moved from acute care facilities to skilled nursing care wings or to nursing homes because each facility charges different basic rates depending on the amount of care they offer. It makes sense that as patients need less nursing care, they no longer want to pay the same per diem rate they paid during their critical illness. With the split cost accounting system, a patient would pay different rates within the *same facility* as his or her needs became less. In addition to the obvious advantages of convenience to patients and saving administrative duplications, the system allows hospitals to effectively compete with skilled nursing facilities.

Arndt pointed out that the system also had a major impact on the hospital's nursing department.

One of the real advantages of the split cost accounting system is that it has eliminated some unnecessary conflict in our decision making. Barbara Corey (Director of Nursing) no longer has to defend the amount of care she has to deliver. Once we have projected CCUs for the year, the nursing staff requirements are all but self-determined. The nursing department can be in a precarious position in hospitals that operate under per diem systems. It is probably the largest department and would be an easy target when cutting expenses becomes necessary. The average hours per care for nursing day statistics means nothing retrospectively because it reflects the census more than anything else. Further, as the length of stay gets shorter and shorter, all you leave for the acute care institution is the very sick-stay period for each patient. If nursing has to budget on a per diem basis, they lose, because they have no statistics to show how much care they delivered. But the CCUs deal with that problem by separating intensity of care from number of patient days.

Corey reiterated, pointing out the impact of the system on her staffing decisions.

Before the split cost accounting system, we really never had anything concrete to hang our hat on

when it came to asking for additions to staff. While
the system can, of course, backfire on you, it does
give us a handle on how much time is being spent.
The CCUs are based on an eight-hour shift, and we
estimate that one nurse can handle about 12,900
CCUs a year. Margarete Arndt can predict pretty
closely what our CCU needs are going to be for each
fiscal year, and then it is a relatively simple matter
for me to determine my staffing needs for the
nursing department. Our curve of estimated CCUs
is updated periodically. Once a year we study our
patients for three months, but that's really the only
additional effort involved. We didn't want to get
into a process where we concurrently clock every
service performed on each patient. Rather, while
every patient gets the individual attention he or she
may require, patients are *billed* according to the
curve that goes with their procedure.

RELATIONSHIP
TO THE BUDGETARY PROCESS

According to Wood, the split cost accounting
system at MEEI played an important role in the
budgetary process.

The split cost accounting system is a significant tool
for stabilizing hospital budget forecasts. Presently,
hospital administrators have a single figure with
which to work: the so-called per diem all inclusive
room rate. In this per diem system, unexpected
declines in patient days can lead to serious block
revenue losses. With the split cost accounting system at MEEI, there are three cost categories with a
potential for adjustment: per patient revenue from
the one-time hospitalization charge (related to
number of admissions), revenue from the daily
room rate charge (related to length of stay), and
revenue from the clinical care units charge (related
to the intensity of clinical care given).

With the per diem system, it is extremely difficult to
put one's finger on where problems are, and when
adjustments are indicated there is a danger that they
will be made in the wrong areas. With the split cost
accounting system, however, with its separate areas
clearly identified, we can easily see which areas are
affected by changes in volume, and adjustments can
be made accordingly.

Because each of these categories has a unit measurement which is rather closely aligned to what actually goes on in the hospital, I can more accurately
measure the degree to which we are meeting our
budget, and when we are over or under budget we
can take appropriate action in the area where the
variance occurs. The result is that, despite inflation
and the uncertainties of running a health care
organization, we are able to operate very close to
budget.

Anthony Reis, Manager of Fiscal Affairs at
MEEI, discussed the impact of the system on budgeting and cost containment.

The split cost accounting system has allowed us to
be more accurate in our budgetary process. Nursing
is about 20% of our total payroll dollars, which
makes it very significant and which in turn makes
CCUs very important. Thus, by building CCUs into
the budget process, we are able to have better
control over the nursing portion of our budget.

It is important to emphasize, though, that the use of
CCUs does not automatically trigger decisions;
rather, it helps us ask the right question. If CCUs are
down, we first try to find out why they are down;
then we can make decisions. So we have a better
tool than the old patient day thing to try to make
better management decisions.

When you have a flat room rate that covers all
routine services, such as most hospitals do, if patient days go down you might make a decision that
you need fewer nurses, which might not be the case
at all. Now we can see more clearly how the costs
break down. Let's assume, for example, that patient
days decrease, but we also see that admissions are
the same. This tells us that those services which
relate to admissions can't be cut back, but perhaps
services such as dietary can be. Next we would look
at the CCUs. Just because patient days are going
down doesn't mean that CCUs are decreasing also,
so we see what's happening; then we decide if we
want to cut back on nursing staff. That to me is the
most important part, but for the general public, of
course, the more important part is fairer billing.

As far as the costs and benefits of this system to the
hospital are concerned, they are very difficult to
measure. However, historically our costs have increased at the rate of the rest of the industry, but
now they are increasing by only about 6% to 7% a
year compared to 12% to 15% a year for the rest of
the industry. Even though we are a specialized
hospital, we essentially do everything the same as
every other hospital, except, of course, we now
group our cost centers into three categories.

Thus, because the split cost accounting system
isolates cost centers and presents a more accurate
financial picture of the institution than the accounting system in general use today, it lends itself to
more effective budget forecasting. Cost centers can
be isolated for the predicted number of patient
discharges for the coming year, and the accurate
figures can be extrapolated for budgeting purposes.
Taking this one logical step further, if we can
prepare accurate budget forecasts based on this split
cost accounting system, we then have the credibility
and confidence to enter into prospective reimbursement programs with third-party payors.

BLUE CROSS REIMBURSEMENT

In 1976 and 1977, Blue Cross was the only third-party payor that reimbursed MEEI according to the split cost accounting system. At the end of the year, Paul Bushnell, Manager of the Blue Cross Office of Health Care Planning, reported favorably on the new system and added his intention to renew MEEI's contract using the split cost accounting method. According to Bushnell, Blue Cross was supporting the system for two major reasons.

First, I would agree with Charley Wood that the new system provided him with better management information to run his hospital. I think this has proven out. This year, his costs and efficiency were far better than the national average. His system did help him hold on to costs; I'd say his argument has merit. Secondly, the system will in the long run save money for Blue Cross, Medicare, and Medicaid. Rather than support a health system with 3,000 to 5,000 empty beds and a proliferation of nursing homes, all of us would benefit by using these beds and ending the duplication of facilities. Currently, the empty beds are probably costing us 70% of the full beds. If we can now provide skilled nursing facility care at reasonable rates in unutilized facilities, we will greatly improve hospital efficiency and save ourselves wasted dollars.

Bushnell added one advantage which, he noted, was still highly conjectural. He thought that accommodating patients in one facility for both their acute and skilled-nursing-care needs could possibly hasten some patients' recovery periods. This would represent a savings for the payor, the hospital, and the patient.

Like Wood, Bushnell has tried to interest Medicare and Medicaid in the split cost accounting method of reimbursement.

The state's reluctance may derive from the fact that their payments would increase, at least initially, under the new system. Because the state sets payment rates from historic cost, they are traditionally less than a hospital's current costs. Using the Massachusetts Eye and Ear's cost accounting system, charges are based on current cost figures. This year, Blue Cross paid an additional $100,000 to MEEI because of our patient mix. We consider this an investment in a more equitable health system and long-range savings. On the other hand, Medicare, because of the types of procedures for which Medicare patients are admitted to the Eye and Ear Infirmary, would pay less to the hospital than under a per diem rate.

Average length of stay and volume distributions are classified by payor in Exhibits 7 and 8.

Bushnell had also tried to persuade several community hospitals to develop split cost accounting systems. He believed that medical and diagnostic data can be standardized as surgical data had at MEEI. He commented on transferring the system to other hospitals.

I am talking to several community hospitals because I definitely think they can use an accounting system like MEEI's. It should have been done long ago, but the catch is the work involved in compiling the standard CCU data from historic records. What we really need is someone to put together one cookbook of clinical care units for the various diagnoses done at community hospitals. Besides, if every hospital devises its own clinical care unit structure, there will be no comparability between hospitals.

During the first year, Blue Cross paid MEEI the full amount they were billed. Bushnell explained that because MEEI was unique in their costing method, Blue Cross lacked any comparative information for the hospital's CCU estimates. Blue Cross, added Bushnell, trusted the hospital and thought their utilization and review process kept their costs at a minimum.

EXHIBIT 1

MASSACHUSETTS EYE AND EAR INFIRMARY
Patient Statistics, 1977

Inpatient Hospital (174 beds)
  Admissions

Eye patients	7,266
ENT* patients	4,007
Total admissions	11,273

  Operations

By eye house staff	1,111
By eye attending staff	6,305
Total eye operations	7,416
By ENT house staff	1,123
By ENT attending staff	2,578
Total ENT operations	3,701
Total operations	11,117

Discharges

Death	16
Autopsies	44%
Patient days	55,606
Average patient census	152
Average length of stay	4.92
Bed utilization	88%
Total discharges	11,295

Outpatient Department (OPD)
  Eye clinic

Total eye visits	57,655

  ENT clinic

Total ENT visits	20,455
Total OPD visits	78,110

Emergency Ward

Eye cases	18,868
ENT cases	16,512
Total	35,380

Ambulatory Surgery

Eye cases	2,186
ENT cases	1,508
Total	3,694

Special Services

Audiology	9,430
Electroretinography (tests)	900
Fluorescein (tests)	2,331
Otoneurology (tests)	466
Ultrasonography (tests)	265
Visual function studies	0
Radiology (exams)	30,588

Laboratories

Eye pathology (specimens)	2,184
ENT pathology (specimens)	11,355
Clinical laboratory (procedures)	93,082
Bacteriology (cultures)	16,166

*ENT = ear, nose, and throat.

EXHIBIT 2

MASSACHUSETTS EYE AND EAR INFIRMARY
Condensed Income Account—1977

Patient service revenue	20,901,732
Adjustments to patient revenue for uncollectible accounts, free care, and contractual allowances	1,582,873
Net revenue service to patients	19,318,859
Other operating revenue	5,866,547
Total operating revenue	25,185,406
Operating expenses	
Patient service (including depreciation	20,887,510
Research and other specific purpose direct expenses	4,586,730
Hospital operating income/loss	(288,834)
Income from donations	—
Hospital net loss from operations	288,834*

*It is the express policy of the Massachusetts Eye and Ear Infirmary that charges only recover cost.

EXHIBIT 3

MASSACHUSETTS EYE AND EAR INFIRMARY
Time Values for Clinical Care Units

1 unit	= 7½ minutes	± 2 minutes
2 units	= 15 minutes	± 5 minutes
4 units	= 30 minutes	± 5 minutes
8 units	= 60 minutes	± 5 minutes
12 units	= 90 minutes	± 5 minutes

Source: M. Poland et al., "PETO—A system for assisting and meeting patient care needs." *Amer. J. Nursing,* 70:1479, (July 1970).

EXHIBIT 4

MASSACHUSETTS EYE AND EAR INFIRMARY
Classification of Patient Needs

CATEGORY	DESCRIPTION	CLINICAL CARE UNIT VALUE
Diet	Feeds self without supervision, or family or parent feeds patient	1
	Feeds self with supervision of staff	2
	Tube feeding every three hours by patient	4
	Total feeding by personnel, or instructing the patient or continuous IV, or blood transfusion. Tube feeding by personnel every three hours.	8
	Tube feedings every 1 to 2 hours	12

EXHIBIT 4 *(cont.)*

CATEGORY	DESCRIPTION	CLINICAL CARE UNIT VALUE
Toileting	Toilets independently	0
	Toilets with minimal assistance	1
	Toilets with supervision, or specimen collection, or uses bedpan. Hemovac output.	2
	Up to toilet with standby supervision, or output measurement every hour. Initial hemovac setup.	4
Vital signs	Routine-daily temperature, pulse and respiration	1
	Vital signs every 4 hours	2
	Vital signs monitored, or vital signs every 2 hours	4
	Vital signs and observation every hour, or vital signs monitored, plus neuro check	8
	Blood pressure, pulse, respiration, and neuro check every 30 minutes	12
Respiratory needs	Bedside humidifier, or blow bottle	1
	Mist or humidified air when sleeping, or cough and deep breathe every 2 hours	2
	Continuous oxygen, trach mist, or cough and deep breathe every hour	4
	IPPB with supervision every 4 hours	8
Suction	Routine postoperative standby	1
	Nasopharyngeal or oral suction prn	2
	Tracheostomy suction every 1–2 hours	4
	Tracheostomy suction every half hour	8
Bath	Bathes self, bed straightened	1
	Bathes self with help, or supervision, daily change of bed	2
	Bathed and dressed by personnel or partial bath given, daily change of linen	4
	Bathed and dressed by personnel, special skin care, occupied bed	8
Activity	Up with assistance once in 8 hours (or exercise)	1
	Up in chair with assistance twice in 8 hours or walking with assistance	2
	Bedrest with assistance in turning every 2 hours or up walking with assistance of two persons twice in 8 hours	4
	Bedrest with turning every hour	12
Treatments	Once in 8 hours	1
	Twice in 8 hours	2
	Three times in 8 hours	4
	Four times in 8 hours	8
	More than every two hours	12

Source: M. Poland et al., "PETO—A system for assisting and meeting patient care needs." *Amer. J. Nursing,* 70:1479 (July 1970).

EXHIBIT 5

MASSACHUSETTS EYE AND EAR INFIRMARY
Classification of Expenses
Fiscal Year 1977

COST PER PATIENT	BUDGETED
Admitting & scheduling	36,341
Accounts receivable & cashier	65,023
Patient services	17,532
Property insurance	23,875
Legal expenses	2,193
Social service	163,253
Medical records & library	185,234
Repairs & maintenance	317,080
Operation of plant	251,208
Housekeeping	511,455
Interest & depreciation	677,481
Free care & bad debts	10,977
Total cost	2,261,652
Admissions	11,200
Cost per patient	201.93
Charge per patient	202.69
Cost per Patient Day	
House officers	184,123
Medical and Surgical supplies	407,916
Dietary	837,382
Laundry ⎱ Linen ⎰	257,730
Pharmacy	168,524
Free care & bad debts	9,053
Total cost	1,864,728
Patient days	53,984
Cost per patient day	34.54
Charge per patient day	41.25
Cost per CCU	
Nursing service—direct cost	1,852,073
Nursing ed.—direct cost	215,145
Nursing Admin. and Supervision	1,133,537
Nursing maint. of plant	11,849
Nursing operation of plant	9,386
Nursing housekeeping	9,194
Nursing laundry & linen	1,251
Nursing cafe	91,843
Nursing depreciation & interest	25,698
Free care & bad debts	16,342
Total cost	3,366,318
CCU	753,373
Cost per CCU	4.47
Charge per CCU	4.54

EXHIBIT 6

MASSACHUSETTS EYE AND EAR INFIRMARY

Sample Distribution of Clinical Care Units

PROCEDURE	DAY OF ADMISSIONS	DAY OF SURGERY	POSTOPERATIVE DAYS											DAY OF DISCHARGE	TOTAL
			1ST	2ND	3RD	4TH	5TH	6TH	7TH	8TH	9TH	10TH	ETC.		
Tonsillectomy and Adenoidectomy	3	24												5	32
Cataract extraction	15	18	14	10	6									6	69
Laryngtectomy and radical neck dissection	5	6	50	36	34	28	17	17	14	12	8	6		6	245
Mastoid tympanoplasty	4	17	21	13	7								6*	6	68
Scleral buckle, primary	15	18	13	8	8	8	8	6						6	90
Vitrectomy pars plana	15	17	21	13	13	13	13	11						9	125
Strabismus surgery	15	9												6	30
Sybmucous resection	3	17												5	25
Laryngoscopy and vocal cord strip	8.5	10.4												9.5	28.4
Corneal transplant	15	21	19	16	12	12	12							6	113

*Through day 15.

513

EXHIBIT 7

MASSACHUSETTS EYE AND EAR INFIRMARY
Average Length of Stay by Financial Class
Fiscal Year 1977

	DAYS
Self-pay	6.19
Blue Cross of Massachusetts	4.01
Out-of-state Blue Cross	6.26
Commercial insurance	4.34
Workmen's Compensation	6.25
Welfare (Medicaid)	4.31
Medicare	5.64

EXHIBIT 8

MASSACHUSETTS EYE AND EAR INFIRMARY
Volume Distribution by Financial Class
Fiscal Year 1977

	DISCHARGES	PATIENT DAYS	CLINICAL CARE UNITS
Self-pay	6.24%	7.81%	7.99%
Blue Cross of Massachusetts	28.44	23.09	23.23
Out-of-state Blue Cross	7.36	9.32	9.00
Commercial insurance	18.47	16.23	16.44
Workmen's Compensation	1.12	1.41	1.51
Welfare (Medicaid)	6.25	5.45	5.41
Medicare	32.12	36.68	36.40
Income per category (actual) (all financial classes)	$2,282,899	$2,389,692	$3,565,770

American Bank

I came to American Bank & Trust Co. after working for several years in public accounting. Some of my former clients had installed elaborate standard cost systems to help them understand their product costs. I didn't see any reason why the same basic standard costing principles used by manufacturing companies I had worked with couldn't be applied to the range of products we offered at the bank.

At the time, American Bank had sophisticated financial systems that tracked where transactions were processed and provided good summary reports on costs incurred in branches and operating departments. But the bank had little idea about what any of its products cost. With the much more competitive environment for the banking industry, it seemed to me essential that we understand where money was being made or lost.

Terry Troupe, Senior Vice-President and Controller, described the motivation for developing and installing an entirely new product cost system at American Bank from 1979 to 1981.

COMPANY BACKGROUND

In 1978, American Bank and Trust Co., headquartered in Reading, Pennsylvania, was one of the 100 largest banks in the U.S. It had total assets in excess of $1.5 billion and more than 60 branches. American operated in a seven-county area of southeastern Pennsylvania: Berks, Schuylkill, Lancaster, Lebanon, Lehigh, Chester, and Montgomery and was the dominant bank in several of these counties. The area was stable and prosperous: The seven counties encompassed only 10% of the total land area but contained over 23% of the state's manufacturing plants, 20% of the farms, and 19% of the retail establishments.

American was a consumer-oriented bank with heavy activity in mortgages and car loans. It benefited from the large base of savings accounts maintained by the older population in several of its counties.

By 1978, American had enjoyed 21 consecutive years of increased earnings. The bank was managed conservatively and believed in a policy of cautious expansion. It had never followed financial fads like mass mailing of credit cards to remote markets or granting of foreign loans. The consolidated balance sheet as of the end of 1978 (Exhibit 1) shows a strong base of non-interest-paying demand deposits and low-rate savings accounts. Exhibit 2 presents the 1978 income statement.

REGULATION IN THE BANKING INDUSTRY

Because of its critical position in the economy, the banking industry had been subjected to extensive regulation during the nineteenth and twentieth centuries. Banking regulation imposed restrictions in three broad areas—pricing, geographic location, and product offerings.

ORGANIZATION STRUCTURE

The organization structure of American Bank is shown in Exhibit 3. The distribution and composition of costs incurred in each organizational group are given in Exhibit 4.

The Trust Group, generating about 8% of the bank's total income, was responsible for managing corporate and individual trusts. The Banking Group, encompassing all branch operations and lending activities, provided the interface between the bank and its customers. Branch tellers processed customers' transactions, such as deposits, withdrawals, and payments, opened new accounts, and accepted loan applications. Branch managers and assistant managers were authorized to sanction loans up to specified amounts that depended on their training and lending experience. If the requested loan amount exceeded lending authority, the application would go to the centralized Loan Committee for review. The Banking Group was organized on a regional basis to

This case was prepared by Sanjay Kallapur, doctoral candidate (under the supervision of Professor Robert S. Kaplan).

be responsive to the particular needs of customers in each county.

The Operations Group processed all the paperwork relating to the bank's transactions. Two subsidiaries engaged in title insurance and the real estate business.

PRODUCTS: LIABILITIES

American Bank provided three basic types of accounts to its customers: checking accounts, savings accounts, and term deposits. Five different checking accounts were offered.

Business checking accounts were intended for business organizations. No interest was paid on these accounts. A service charge was assessed based on the average balance and the number of transactions in each account. The transactions were assigned prices based on unit cost figures published by the Bankers Administration Institute to determine the total charge incurred for each account. A notional funds credit was given on the average balance in the account, based on the 91-day Treasury Bill rate. If the charge exceeded the funds credit, the customer paid the difference. If the funds credit exceeded the transactions charges, the excess credit could either be carried forward as a credit against future service charges or used to satisfy compensating balance requirements on outstanding loans.

American checking accounts had no monthly service or per-check charges provided the customer maintained a minimum monthly balance of $200. If the balance fell below $200, a monthly service charge of $2.00 plus a 10-cent per-check charge was levied.

American really free checking for savers accounts required the customer to maintain a savings account in addition to the checking account. The balance in the savings account earned interest at the regular savings account rate while the balance in the checking account paid no interest. There was no minimum balance requirement, no monthly service charge, and no per-check charge. If the checking account was overdrawn, the bank would transfer the amount from the savings account and honor the check. The bank charged 50 cents for each transfer to cover an overdraft.

American interest/checking plan customers had to maintain a minimum balance of $1,500, all of which could be kept in a 5% statement savings account. There was no monthly service charge or per-check charge. Whenever the customer wrote a check, the amount would automatically be transferred to the checking account. Thus, customers could have a zero balance checking account and earn interest of 5% on their entire savings balances. If the savings balance fell below $1,500, a monthly charge of $2.50 was levied.

Free checking for senior citizens, with no restrictions, was available for anybody over the age of 65 years.

Two savings accounts were offered.

A regular passbook account earned interest at a 4.5% annual rate. The customer could make deposits and withdrawals in person. After each transaction the customer's passbook was updated so that it always showed the correct current balance.

For a *statement savings account*, the customer was sent a monthly statement showing the transactions during the month and the balances. This account enabled the customer to deposit and withdraw through the automatic teller machines (ATMs) in addition to executing transactions with bank tellers. It also permitted deposits by mail. Because the bank believed that it was cheaper to send a single computerized statement of transactions than to record the transactions in person, as in a regular passbook account, the bank paid a higher rate of interest, 5%, on statement savings accounts. (Regulation Q restricted interest on commercial bank savings accounts to 5%; this rate was raised to 5.25% in January 1979.)

The bank also accepted time deposits for fixed periods of time ranging from 90 days to seven years. The interest rates were regulated and varied according to maturity—the longer the maturity, the higher the interest rate. Time deposit rates were always higher than the rate on savings accounts.

PRODUCTS: ASSETS

American Bank had three primary types of loans: commercial, consumer, and mortgages. Commercial loans included standard services such as lines of credit and term loans. In addition, commercial loans were made to farmers, real estate developers, and automobile dealers. These loans would be secured by equipment, working capital, and floor plans on inventory. Consumer loans encompassed revolving credit lines, such as from credit cards, and installment loans, either direct (loans for cars, home improvements, boats, and aircraft) or indirect, when the bank bought loans initiated by a third party, such as a car or furniture dealer. Mortgages were initiated directly by the bank through one of its branches. The end-of-year balances and annual income for each of these three loan categories are shown in Exhibits 1 and 2.

The bank also earned income from fee-based services. Lockboxes, a means to collect cash payments for corporate customers and transfer the payments directly to checking accounts, were offered to companies as a cash management service. Safe deposit boxes were rented to individuals and institutions to store their valuables. Trust services earned fee income based on assets given by corporations, foundations, and individuals for the bank to manage. Title insurance fees were earned through a subsidiary, Berks Title Insurance.

BANKING OPERATIONS

In a typical process flow in a bank for a deposit or withdrawal transaction, a customer enters a branch and deposits a check to a checking account. The teller processes the deposit, giving the customer a receipt. During the day, tellers batch all work they processed, and in-bound couriers pick up the batches and transmit them to the centralized operations center of the bank. In operations, the transactions are first recorded in the proof area. The control desk puts batch headers on each batch and assigns batches to proof operators, who encode the dollar amounts on each check and deposit slip. All encoded work is batched, with debits and credits proved (or verified). Batched work is then brought to the reader/sorter area where the items are sorted into pockets by reading the routing numbers on each transaction item: on-us checks, transit checks, and deposit slips. Each item is also microfilmed.

The on-us checks are sorted by account and sent with the deposit slips to bulk file for long-term storage. The statement rendering process accumulates the filed checks and prepares and mails the monthly account statements. The computer operations department receives a computer tape from the reader/sorter so that deposits and checks can be posted to individual accounts.

EXISTING COST SYSTEM

In the stable regulated environment up to the 1970s, the size of deposits and assets was the critical factor for success in the banking industry. The rates paid on deposits were limited by regulation, leading to high lending margins. As long as the bank had its operating costs under control, profits were assured. The existing cost system, therefore, concentrated on measuring the costs of profit centers. Each branch was considered a separate profit center, and units performing central income-earning activities, such as the corporate banking section and trust operations, were also treated as profit centers.

The costs of centers, such as purchasing and operations, were allocated to other cost centers and to profit centers using a sequential procedure. A reserve for delinquent loans expense was allocated to profit centers based on the volume of loans in each center. The cost of the actual delinquent loans, however, was traced individually to the officer who had sanctioned them. This procedure was followed because officers were frequently transferred, and by the time a loan became delinquent, the approving officer may no longer be attached to the same profit center.

After the sequential allocation of costs was accomplished, profitability statements were prepared. This whole process was performed at quarterly intervals. An example of a branch profitability statement is given in Exhibit 5.

Product profitability reports were also prepared at quarterly intervals to get a rough estimate of the profitability of individual products (see Exhibit 6). This was done in a two-stage process. The first step was the sequential allocation of costs to profit centers. The total costs of each branch were then allocated to products based on a weighted average of the activity of each product in that branch. For example, the activity in demand deposit accounts was measured simply by the number of demand deposit accounts in the branch.

NEW COSTING SYSTEM

In 1978, with competitive pressures increasing and deregulation looming, senior bank executives knew that interest margins would be squeezed in the future. With reduced margins between asset and liability rates, the income from service charges and from fee-based services would become more important to the overall profitability of the bank. The pricing of products, such as cash management and personal checking accounts, that formerly had been subsidized by below-market interest rates on liabilities, would need to be reexamined if they were to remain a significant source of profitability for the future. To determine the service charges for liability accounts, in effect the prices for core products, the bank felt it essential to know the costs of those products. In addition, the rapid introduction of new technology, such as automatic teller machines and Pay-by-Phone, was changing operations in fundamental ways.

Terry Troupe's advocacy for improved product cost information (see opening quote of case) was consistent with the bank's strategic objectives. In 1978 the Chief Executive of the bank had established the improvement of financial systems as a key corporate objective. Troupe believed that the old system, which traced expenses to cost and profit centers, gave little guidance on product and customer profitability. Costs were allocated to where the transaction was processed, not who was responsible (and who received the imputed income) for the account. For example, employees of a large local department store may have opened their accounts in one of American's downtown branches, but the costs of servicing these accounts were incurred in and allocated to the branches where deposits were made and checks cashed.

Troupe also wanted to move from full to standard costs. He did not want product costs to be influenced by capacity utilization, especially for emerging growing business. Troupe believed that product costs should be based on potential capacity.

The bank turned to its auditors, Peat Marwick Mitchell & Co. (PMM), who were installing product costing systems in many banking clients. A discussion with the PMM consulting group convinced Terry Troupe to hire PMM to develop a product cost system for American Bank.

Greg Nolan, the Peat Marwick partner in the Philadelphia office, who had developed the PMM Product Costing System, described his approach.

The financial services industry has experienced difficulty in applying standard cost concepts to operations. Analyzing a complex, white-collar, multiproduct processing environment has traditionally proven to be too time consuming and too expensive. As a result, the industry has used arbitrarily, fully allocated actual costs that turned out not to be very useful for managers.

We developed analytical tools that yielded timely and cost-effective estimates of standard product costs. We calculate standard product unit costs within each organizational unit of a financial institution. Calculating product unit costs within an organizational unit allows us to compute bankwide product costs that are derived from the unit cost building blocks. In this way, we create a flexible product cost data base that can support a variety of uses.

The key aspect of the PMM system was to obtain the unit time required to process each product through each of its activities. A variety of industrial engineering techniques, adapted to the particular environment of banking operations, were employed to study the work performed by each stage to process a banking transaction. For each key processing activity, the analysts attempted to obtain the actual volumes processed of each type of transaction and the time spent processing each type. The studies concluded with an estimate of the unit time to process each type of product at each processing center.

The unit processing times were then multiplied by the hourly cost in each processing center. Hourly costs were determined after discussion with processing unit managers, analysis of budgets, and work measurement to determine the distribution of expenses to the various activities performed by personnel. All personnel costs were considered variable. In addition, FDIC insurance and supplies, such as postage and forms, that varied with production volume were also treated as variable costs. Fixed costs included occupancy costs, depreciation, rentals on fixed assets, and communications and telephone expenses. Both variable and fixed costs were allocated to transactions activities. In the final step, the unit costs for each processing stage were summed to obtain the total cost of processing each type of transaction.

Overhead costs were split between local and corporate. Local overhead represented administrative functions that were product specific. These could be easily aligned and traced to products. For example, loan administration for installment lending was distributed to installment loan products as an add-on percentage to the calculated product cost. The overhead was allocated among the various installment products based on their relative percentage shares of total expense dollars.

Corporate overhead represented those centers or functions that served all the products of the organization. For example, the costs of the human resources area could not be allocated to any particular product line or even geographic location. Corporate overhead costs were considered below the line for product and profit center managers and were allocated across all product lines based on total product expenses. Corporate overhead expenses ranged between 20% and 25% of total operating expenses for commercial banks.

DEVELOPING THE AMERICAN BANK PRODUCT COST SYSTEM

By the end of July 1978, a project team had been constituted at American Bank. Three college graduates were hired by the bank and trained by PMM to perform and complete the study. During the two-year development period, the old cost system was discontinued to reduce the demands on the EDP department facilities. Thus, during this period, no internal cost reports were prepared.

In 1980 the data base of standards for each product was completed. PMM involvement ended in the same year. The data base consisted of standard unit times for each activity in a responsibility center and activity counts for each product. The data were updated every three years. Every time a product profitability analysis was made, the analyst took the standard unit time information from the data base and priced them using information about the current annual rate. Unit activity costs were then multiplied by the number of times the activity was performed during the unit period (month or year) for the product under consideration to get product costs for a unit period. This whole operation had to be done manually because the data base was not yet on a computerized system.

THE PRICING COMMITTEE

In conjunction with the Product Cost Study, American Bank established a pricing committee in September 1979. Previously, a committee of senior executives and staff had reviewed pricing issues in reaction to changes in the marketplace. Such changes were typically initiated by other banks or from nonbank institutions. The new pricing committee was to examine systematically the pricing decisions for all noninterest products and services.

The pricing committee consisted of the group heads of marketing and operations, banking, trust, and finance. In addition, a marketing planning and research representative was appointed to develop market research information; a financial planning representative to provide cost, breakeven, and profit analysis; and a trust group representative to provide trust group advice and counsel. The committee reported directly to the President and CEO.

In making the pricing decision, the committee was directed to

- ensure that each product was profitable;
- recognize the value of product quality, especially measured relative to competitors' products; and
- consider the opportunities in special market segments where the bank had a particularly strong presence.

Whenever line managers felt a need for pricing a product or service, they initiated a pricing request. A pricing project would then be opened by the market research and planning division and a task force organized, consisting of the originator, representatives of market research and planning, financial planning, and other departments as needed.

PRICING PASSBOOK VERSUS STATEMENT SAVINGS ACCOUNTS

One of the first issues brought to the pricing committee was the decision on pricing passbook savings accounts. The passbook account required extensive manual processing of transactions. After each transaction, the teller had to walk about 10 feet to the posting machine and key in the old balance and the amount of the transaction. The teller then had to align the customer's passbook to the next blank line for the machine to print out the transaction and the new balance. The bank believed it much cheaper to handle statement savings accounts since only a single computerized statement needed to be prepared each month.

Even though the higher costs of passbook savings accounts were already reflected in the lower interest rate paid on these accounts, the marketing group wanted to phase out the passbook accounts entirely. Marketing believed that statement savings accounts were the wave of the future. The banking group, however, reported strong resistance to the statement savings account from older customers, who were used to the traditional passbook account. Neither the extra conveniences nor the higher interest rate could make them shift to the statement savings account. Many of these people had lived through the Depression, and the passbook represented tangible evidence and proof of their balances. Some even kept their passbooks in safe deposit boxes. The extra conveniences of the statement

savings account did not mean much to them because they did not have many transactions to make. Often, their only visit to the bank would be on Social Security paydays. That visit to the bank constituted a social event where they could meet their friends. Some bank managers would arrange for coffee and doughnuts on those days.

Using the data from the new product cost system, finance staff analyzed the costs of both statement savings and passbook accounts. A summary of their findings is shown in Exhibits 7 and 8. The pricing committee would soon meet to review the analysis and to make recommendations on the continuance of the passbook accounts. If the passbook savings accounts were to be maintained, the committee must then decide whether to lower the interest rate paid on them further to reflect the higher costs for manual processing.

EXHIBIT 1

AMERICAN BANK

Consolidated Balance Sheet

| | DECEMBER 31, | |
	1978	1977
ASSETS		
Cash and due from banks	$ 70,323,000	$ 66,248.000
Investment securities	398,174,000	368,962,000
Loans:		
Commercial	596,832,000	509,063,000
Mortgage	260,464,000	223,667,000
Consumer	185,034,000	142,129,000
Total loans	1,042,330,000	874,859,000
Less: Reserve for possible loan losses	8,009,000	7,595,000
Net loans	1,034,321,000	867,264,000
Federal funds sold	—	4,000,000
Premises and equipment	21,208,000	18,520,000
Other real estate owned	2,313,000	3,745,000
Accrued income receivable	15,275,000	13,280,000
Other assets	4,528,000	1,919,000
Total assets	$1,546,142,000	$1,343,938,000
LIABILITIES		
Demand deposits	$ 299,914,000	$ 288,751,000
Savings deposits	394,516,000	364,747,000
Time deposits	656,614,000	549,362,000
Total deposits	1,351,044,000	1,202,860,000
Securities sold under agreements to repurchase	8,964,000	5,987,000
Federal funds purchased	16,700,000	—
Other borrowed funds	24,231,000	3,522,000
Subordinated notes	14,850,000	21,850,000
Other liabilities	25,962,000	18,819,000
Total liabilities	1,441,751,000	1,253,038,000
SHAREHOLDERS' EQUITY		
Common stock (par value $5.00)	28,482,000	25,139,000
Stock dividend distributable	2,849,000	—
Surplus	39,679,000	30,246,000
Undivided profits	33,381,000	35,515,000
Total shareholders' equity	104,391,000	90,900,000
Total liabilities and shareholders' equity	$1,546,142,000	$1,343,938,000

EXHIBIT 2

AMERICAN BANK
Consolidated Statement of Income

	YEAR ENDED DECEMBER 31,	
	1978	1977
INTEREST INCOME		
Interest and fees on loans:		
Commercial	$ 51,871,000	$38,303,000
Mortgage	20,757,000	18,607,000
Consumer	19,455,000	15,719,000
	92,083,000	72,629,000
Investment securities income	23,733,000	21,053,000
Other interest income	191,000	1,192,000
Total interest income	116,007,000	94,874,000
INTEREST EXPENSE		
Interest on deposits:		
Savings	18,921,000	17,192,000
Time	42,955,000	33,325,000
	61,876,000	50,517,000
Interest on subordinated notes	1,555,000	1,460,000
Interest on other borrowed funds	1,796,000	486,000
Total interest expense	65,227,000	52,463,000
INTEREST MARGIN	50,780,000	42,411,000
Provision for loan losses	6,310,000	5,715,000
Interest margin after provision for loan losses	44,470,000	36,696,000
OTHER INCOME		
Trust department income	2,910,000	2,461,000
Title insurance income	5,103,000	4,193,000
Service charges on deposit accounts	676,000	577,000
Other operating income	2,151,000	1,896,000
Total other income	10,840,000	9,127,000
	55,310,000	45,823,000
OTHER EXPENSES		
Salaries and employee benefits	21,109,000	18,158,000
Occupancy expenses	2,986,000	2,659,000
Equipment expenses	1,958,000	1,522,000
Title insurance agency fees & commissions	1,963,000	1,500,000
Pennsylvania bank shares tax	1,401,000	1,294,000
Other operating expenses	10,222,000	8,179,000
Total other expenses	39,639,000	33,312,000
Income before income taxes & securities gains & losses	15,671,000	12,511,000
Provision for income taxes:		
Current federal	(897,000)	(790,000)
Current state	60,000	43,000
Deferred federal	340,000	382,000
	(497,000)	(365,000)
INCOME BEFORE SECURITIES GAINS & LOSSES	16,168,000	12,876,000
Securities gains & losses, net of related income taxes	(213,000)	34,000
NET INCOME	$ 15,955,000)	$12,910,000
PER SHARE DATA:		
Income before securities gains & losses	$ 2.60	$ 2.12
Net income	$ 2.57	$ 2.13

EXHIBIT 3

AMERICAN BANK

Organization Chart (1979)

TRUST	BANKING	PRESIDENT MARKETING & OPERATIONS	LOAN ADMINISTRATION	FINANCE	CORPORATE STAFF
Employee benefits	Community	Data processing	Credit info.	Financial management services	Credit policy committee
Estate planning	Corporate	Operations	Loan review	Corporate accounting	Bank investment
Tax & corporate trust	Commercial & equipment financing	Market development	Special loans	Purchasing & expenditure control	Personnel
Operations		Market research	Compliance		Audit
Investment		Corporate communications			Corporate secretary
					Corporate planning

EXHIBIT 4

AMERICAN BANK

Distribution of Operating Expenses among Operating Groups (%)

OPERATING EXPENSES	TRUST	BANKING	MARKETING & OPERATIONS	LOAN AD-MINISTRATION	FINANCE	CORPORATE STAFF	TOTAL	PERCENTAGE OF TOTAL OPERATING EXPENSES
Personnel expense	9%	51%	22%	7%	3%	8%	100%	45%
Loan expense	—	15	—	85	—	—	100	18
Occupancy expense	4	78	11	3	2	2	100	10
Furniture & equipment	3	27	65	2	2	1	100	5
Allocated expenses	8	26	53	4	7	3	100	4
Communications	5	41	45	4	2	4	100	4
Professional fees	5	20	8	24	13	31	100	3
Customer development	4	24	1	—	—	71	100	3
Deposit expense	—	93	8	—	—	—	100	2
Other operating expenses	1	54	6	27	—	12	100	2
Stationary & supplies	5	46	42	2	1	6	100	2
Miscellaneous	6	33	33	6	7	15	100	2
Total	6%	44%	20%	20%	3%	8%		100%

EXHIBIT 5

AMERICAN BANK
Lancaster Avenue
Profitability Analysis for the
Year Ended December 31, 1974
Source & Investment of Funds
(Using Average Balances)

Source of Funds				
Demand deposits			8,592,113	
Time deposits			15,254,543	
Total deposits				23,846,656
Cash reserve requirement			1,408,749	
Investment portfolio requirement			6,405,331	7,814,080
Funds available for lending				16,032,576
Investment of Funds	*Yield*			
Consumer loans	12.69		840,707	
Commercial loans	9.73		340,524	
Mortgage loans	7.49		1,155,312	
Revolving credit loans	11.48		101,410	
Total loans	9.76			2,437,953
Excess or (borrowed) funds				13,594,623

Earnings Statement

Income	*Average Yield*			
Interest from loans	9.76		238,053	
Commissions & service charges			30,478	
Other operating income			4,734	
Investment portfolio income[a]			509,474	
Credit for excess funds	11.27		1,531,706	
Total income				2,314,445
Expense	*Average Yield*			
Personnel expense			109,628	
Interest on time deposits	5.95		908,184	
Other operating expense			92,069	
Interest on borrowed funds			-	
Total expense				1,109,881
Direct Income Before Taxes				1,204,564
Applicable income taxes	48%		578,191	
Contribution toward internal operations				626,373
Charge for internal operations			171,614	
Less applicable income taxes			82,375	89,239
Net earnings contribution				537,134

[a]Taxable equivalent after giving effect to income exempted from federal income taxation.

EXHIBIT 6

AMERICAN BANK

Product Profitability Report: Demand Deposits ($000)

Gross funds	$ 296,141	
Less: float	20,010	
Collected balance	$ 276,131	
Less: reserve requirements	11,045	
Other requirements	6,723	
Net available funds	$ 258,363	

Income	Rate	Amount
On invested available funds	9.552	24,680
Loans and investments—other income	0.151	391
Service charges—deposits	0.104	268
Service charges—return	0.256	660
Total	10.063	25,999

Expenses		
Account maintenance and item costs	6.689	17,281
Net earnings contribution	3.374	8,718

EXHIBIT 7

AMERICAN BANK

Development of Activity Costs: Regular Passbook Account

	OPEN ACCOUNT $	MAINTAIN ACCOUNT $	PROCESS DEPOSIT $	PROCESS WITH- DRAWAL $	CLOSE ACCOUNT $
Branch platform	33.6091	0.2782			4.6376
Branch nonplatform		0.6286	0.9204	0.7407	
Savings control	0.0266	0.0205	0.0114	0.0112	
New account reference and control	0.2340	0.0265			
Data entry	1.4735	0.0222			0.1492
Reader sorter operations		0.0063	0.0134	0.0116	
Micromation services		0.0198			
IRA/legal desk		0.0063			
Special handling		0.0196	0.0059		
Customer info. center		0.0928			
Business account services		0.0006	0.0003		
Data control		0.0071			
Data processing		0.0572	0.0085	0.0061	
Item processing			0.0345	0.0197	
Subtotal	35.3432	1.1857	0.9944	0.7893	4.7868
Corporate overhead @ 24.6%	8.6944	0.2917	0.2446	0.1942	1.1776
Total unit activity costs	44.0376	1.4774	1.2390	0.9835	5.9644

EXHIBIT 8

AMERICAN BANK

Profitability Analysis: Regular Passbook versus Statement Savings

UNIT COSTS

REGULAR PASSBOOK ACCOUNT

ACTIVITY	COST PER UNIT ACTIVITY	MONTHLY VOLUME PER ACCOUNT	UNIT COST PER MONTH
Open account	$44.0376	0.01748	$0.7698
Maintain account	1.4774	1.00000	1.4774
Process deposit	1.2390	0.26209	0.3247
Process withdrawal	0.9835	0.20876	0.2053
Close account	5.9644	0.01748	0.1043
Total (per month)			$2.8815
Cost per year			$34.5775

STATEMENT SAVINGS ACCOUNT

ACTIVITY	COST PER UNIT ACTIVITY	MONTHLY VOLUME	UNIT COST PER MONTH
Open account	$33.8419	0.02500	$0.8460
Maintain account	0.7537	1.00000	0.7537
Process branch deposit	0.7160	0.54711	0.3917
Process ATM deposit	0.7546	0.17129	0.1293
Process mail deposit	0.7214	0.01204	0.0087
Process branch withdrawal	0.9780	0.26837	0.2625
Process ATM withdrawal	0.6781	0.71088	0.4820
Process ATM outgoing transfer	0.6781	0.13806	0.0936
Process balance inquiry	0.0224	0.09989	0.0022
Close account	3.9129	0.02500	0.0978
Total (per month)			$3.0676
Cost per year			$36.8113

Addition Information on Value and Cost of Savings Accounts:

1. Funds from Savings Accounts are used:
   40%—for residential mortgages (current yield: 11%)
   60%—for general pool of funds (current yield: 13%)
2. Operating costs for use of savings accounts funds average 1.5%.
3. The bank must maintain a statutory reserve of 12% of the account balance for each account that uses ATM facilities.

Kanthal (A)

Carl-Erik Ridderstrale, President of Kanthal, described his motivation for developing a system to measure customer profitability.

> Before, when we got an order from a big, important customer, we didn't ask questions. We were glad to get the business. But a small company, competing around the world, has to concentrate its sales and marketing resources. We needed an account management system if we were to achieve our strategy for higher growth and profitability. An account management system as part of the Kanthal 90 Strategy will enable us to get sales managers to accept responsibility for promoting high-margin products to high-profit customers.

HISTORY

Kanthal, the largest of six divisions in the Kanthal-Hoganas group of Sweden, was headquartered in Hallstahammar, a town of 17,000 persons about 150 kilometers northwest of Stockholm. The company's history can be traced back to an ironworks founded in the seventeenth century to exploit the water power available from the stream running through the town. Kanthal specialized in the production and sales of electrical resistance heating elements. "We work for a warmer world," was its motto.

Kanthal had about 10,000 customers and 15,000 items that it produced. Sales during 1985 through 1987 had been level at about SEK 850 million.[1] Export sales, outside of Sweden, accounted for 95% of the total. Summary statistics for the past two years appear in Exhibit 1.

Kanthal consisted of three divisions.

- Kanthal Heating Technology supplied manufacturers of electrical appliances and heating systems with wire that generated heat through electrical resistance. Products included heating wire and ribbon, foil elements, machinery, and precision wire. Kanthal's 25% market share made it a world leader in supplying heating alloys. Sales growth was sluggish in Europe and the U.S., but rapid growth was occurring in the Far East and Latin America.

- Kanthal Furnace Products produced a wide range of heating elements for electric industrial furnaces. Its 40% market share gave it a dominant position in the large markets of the U.S., Japan, West Germany, and the U.K. A new product, Kanthal Super, was generating substantial growth because of its substantially improved performance over conventional materials, including longer service life, lower service costs, and higher operating temperatures.

- Kanthal Bimetals was one of the few companies in the world with fully integrated manufacturing of thermobimetals for temperature control devices used in the manufacture of thermostats, circuit breakers, and household appliances.

Kanthal's manufacturing facilities were located in Hallstahammer, Brazil, the U.K., West Germany, the U.S., and Italy.

KANTHAL 90

Ridderstrale, on becoming President in 1985, saw the need for a strategic plan for Kanthal.

> The company had been successful in the past. We needed to use this base of experience to influence the future. We had to have a consolidated view to ensure that we did not suboptimize in narrow markets or with a narrow functional view. Resources were to be allocated so that we could increase profits while maintaining a return on employed capital in excess of 20%.

The Kanthal 90 plan specified overall profit objectives by division, by product line, and by market. Currently, however, salespersons were compensated mostly on gross sales volume. Higher commissions were being paid for selling obviously higher-margin products, such as Super, and higher bonuses were being awarded for achieving sales targets in the high-margin products. But Ridderstrale wanted to achieve the additional growth planned under Kanthal 90 without adding sales and administrative resources to handle the increased volume anticipated.

> We needed to know where in the organization the resources could be taken from and redeployed into more profitable uses. We did not want to eliminate

---

[1]In 1988, the swedish krona (SEK) was worth about US$ 0.16.

This case was prepared by Professor Robert S. Kaplan.

resources in a steady-state environment. We wanted to reallocate people to generate future growth. According to Ridderstrale,

With our historically good profitability, and lacking any current or imminent crisis, we could not realistically consider laying off people at the Hallstahammar plant. But we wanted to be able to redeploy people so that they could earn more profit for us; to move people from corporate staff to divisions, from the parent company to operating subsidiaries, and from staff functions into sales, R&D, and production. Ideally, if we could transform an accounting clerk at Hallstahammar into a salesman of Kanthal-Super in Japan, we could generate a substantial profit increase.

Exhibit 2 shows the distribution of Kanthal's incurred costs. The existing cost system treated most sales, marketing, and administrative costs as a percentage of sales revenue. Therefore, customers whose selling price exceeded the standard full cost of manufacturing plus the percentage markup for general, selling, and administrative expenses appeared to be profitable, while a customer order whose selling price was below standard manufacturing cost plus the percentage markup appeared unprofitable. Ridderstrale knew, however, that individual customers made quite different demands on Kanthal's administrative and sales staff.

Low-profit customers place high demands on technical and commercial service. They buy low-margin products in small orders. Frequently they order nonstandard products that have to be specially produced for them. And we have to supply special selling discounts in order to get the business.

High-profit customers buy high-margin, standard products in large orders. They make no demands for technical or commercial service and accurately forecast for us their annual demands.

Ridderstrale felt that a new system was needed to determine how much profit was earned each time a customer placed a particular order. The system should attempt to measure the costs that individual customer orders placed on the production, sales, and administrative resources of the company. The goal was to find both hidden profit orders, those whose demands on the company were quite low, and the hidden loss orders, those customer orders that under the existing system looked profitable but which in fact demanded a disproportionate share of the company's resources to fulfill.

Ridderstrale identified the problem with the present method of profitability measurement.

We distribute resources equally across all products and customers. We do not measure individual customer's profitability or the real costs of individual orders. In this environment, our sales and marketing efforts emphasize volume more than profits. In the future, we want Kanthal to handle significantly increased sales volume without any corresponding increase in support resources and to gain the share in our most profitable products.

If we could get more accurate information about our own manufacturing cost structure, as well as the costs of supplying individual customers and orders, we could direct our resources to customers with hidden profits and reduce our efforts to customers with the hidden losses. We might end up with the same market share, so that our competitors would not even see this shift in our strategy, but our profitability would be much higher. To execute such a strategy, however, we need better information about the profitability of each customer, product, and order.

The biggest barrier we have to overcome is the notion that production overhead, selling, and administrative costs are fixed. The definition of strategy is to recognize that all costs are variable. Our salespeople must learn how to deploy resources to their most profitable use.

THE NEW ACCOUNT MANAGEMENT SYSTEM

Per O. Ehrling, Financial Manager of Kanthal, worked with SAM, a Swedish management advisory group, to develop a system to analyze production, sales, and administrative costs at the Hallstahammar facility. He described the philosophy of the new approach.

In our previous system, costs were either manufacturing costs that were allocated to products based on direct labor, or they were selling and administrative costs that were treated as period expenses and were unanalyzed. This treatment may have been correct 100 years ago when we had one bookkeeper for every 10 blacksmiths, but today we have eight bookkeepers for every three blacksmiths. This means that most of our costs today are indirect and our previous system didn't know how to allocate them.

We wanted to move away from traditional financial accounting categories by classifying all organizational costs either as order costs or volume costs. Actually, we did investigate three additional cost drivers—product range, technical support, and new products. But the total costs assigned to these three categories ended up being less than 5% of total costs, so we eliminated them.

Each category of costs in the company was analyzed to determine whether it related more to the volume of sales and production or to handling individual production and sales orders (see Exhibit 3). Interviews were conducted in each department to establish the number of hours worked in each order- and volume-related activity. The hours worked for all activities within each cost center were added, and the percentages of total costs related to order- and volume-related activities were determined.

The manufacturing volume costs, in addition to material, direct labor, and variable overhead, included the costs of production orders to replenish inventory stocks. Only 20% of Kanthal's products were stocked in inventory, but these products represented 80% of sales orders. *Manufacturing order* costs equalled the setup and other batch-related costs that were triggered when a customer ordered a product not normally stocked. Manufacturing order costs were calculated separately for each major product group. The *sales order* costs represented the selling and administrative costs that could be traced to processing individual orderlines (the demand for individual products) in a customer's order. The selling and administrative costs that remained after subtracting sales order costs were treated as *sales volume* costs. The sales volume costs were applied to individual products using a volume factor. The *volume factor* equaled the ratio of total volume costs (total costs less manufacturing order and sales order costs) to the manufacturing volume costs of goods sold. Sample calculations are shown in Exhibit 4.

Bo Martin Tell, Controller of the Furnace Products Division, recalled the amount of tedious work required to collect all the numbers.

> It took almost a year to develop a system to collect the data in the proper form. Even in production, we had problems identifying the costs that related to stocked and nonstocked orders.

INITIAL OUTPUT
FROM THE ACCOUNT MANAGEMENT SYSTEM

Exhibit 5 shows a sample report (from 1987) for a group of Swedish customers, with profit margins on individual orders ranging from −179% to +65%. Previously, almost all of these orders would have appeared profitable. Other reports could be prepared for total profitability by customer, by product group, or by country. Exhibit 6 shows, for a given product group, Finished Wire N, the sales volume and profitability of Swedish customers.

Leif Rick, General Manager of Heating Technology, remembered the initial reactions to the account management reports.

> The study was a real eye-opener. We saw how the traditional cost accounting system had been unable to truly report costs and profits by market, product, and customer.
>
> At first, the new approach seemed strange. We had to explain it three or four times before people started to understand and accept it. People did not want to believe that order costs could be so high; that order costs had to be treated as an explicit cost of selling. Most surprising was finding that customers thought to be very profitable were actually breakeven or even loss customers. Salesmen initially thought the approach was part of a master plan to get rid of small customers. But people who have been working with the system now are convinced of its value and are beginning to take sensible actions based on the information.

Exhibit 7 shows cumulative profits in Swedish operations ranked by customer profitability. The results surprised even Ridderstrale. Only 40% of Kanthal's Swedish customers were profitable, and these generated 250% of realized profits. In fact, the most profitable 5% of the customers generated 150% of the company's profits. The least profitable 10% of customers lost 120% of the profits.

Even more surprising, two of the most unprofitable customers turned out to be among the top three in total sales volume. These two customers had gone to JIT delivery for their suppliers. They had pushed inventory back onto Kanthal, which had not recognized the new demands being placed on its production and order-handling processes by the JIT approach. Moreover, further investigation revealed that one of these customers was using Kanthal as a backup supplier, to handle small special orders of a low-priced item when its main supplier could not deliver. Because of the size and prestige of the two customers, Kanthal people had always welcomed and encouraged their orders. Ridderstrale now realized how expensive it had become to satisfy them.

The immediate problem was to devise a strategy for the large number of nonprofitable customers, particularly the very high-volume ones. Corporate management had started a series of meetings with the general and sales managers of the operating divisions in Sweden to discuss how to handle these customers.

Also, while the account management system had been developed for the Swedish operating divisions, some overseas divisions remained skeptical about the value of the exercise. The account management system was seen as yet another intrusion of the headquarters staff into their operations. Ridderstrale knew he faced an uphill battle gaining acceptance for the account management system around the world.

EXHIBIT 1

KANTHAL (A)

Summary of Operations

	1986	1987
Invoiced sales (MSEK)*	839	849
Profit after financial items	87	107
Return on capital	20%	21%
Number of employees	1,606	1,591

*Million Swedish Krona.

EXHIBIT 2

KANTHAL (A)

Cost Structure

COST COMPONENT	PERCENTAGE
Materials	23
Production salaries and wages	19
Variable processing costs	5
Fixed processing costs	16
Subcontracted services	3
Selling & administrative	34
Total costs	100

EXHIBIT 3

KANTHAL (A)

Order and Volume Costs

TYPE OF PERSONNEL	ORDER-RELATED WORK	VOLUME-RELATED WORK
Production		
Stock replenishment	None	All activities
Production planning	Order planning Order followup	Inventory management
Operators	Setup Startup expense	Direct hours
Foremen	Order planning Order support	Machine problems
Stock	Order input Order output	Order handling
Transportation	Order planning Order handling	
Selling and Administrative		
Management	Offer discussion Offer negotiation	General management
Sales	Offer work Order negotiation Delivery followup	Sales unrelated to orders General public relations Sales management
Secretarial	Offer typing	
Administration	Order booking Order adjustment Invoice typing Customer ledger Supervision	Accounting

EXHIBIT 4

KANTHAL (A)

Sample Calculation of Order and Volume Costs:
By Product Group

Step 1. **Calculate S&A order costs per orderline**

Compute selling & administrative order costs:		2,000,000
Compute number of orderlines:		2,000
Stocked articles	1,500	
Nonstocked articles	500	
S&A costs per orderline:		1,000

Step 2. **Calculate manufacturing order cost for nonstocked products**

Compute manufacturing order costs (for nonstocked articles)	1,000,000
Number of orders for nonstocked articles	500
Manufacturing costs per nonstocked order	2,000

Step 3. **Calculate factor relating S&A volume costs to cost of goods sold** (separate factor calculated for each product group)

Compute total manufacturing and S&A costs:		500,000
Subtract order costs:		
Nonstocked articles: 40 × 2,000	80,000	
Number of orders: 140 × 1,000	140,000	220,000
Total volume costs:		280,000
Manufacturing volume costs of goods sold		200,000
Volume factor: total volume costs/mfg. volume cost of goods sold		1.40

Step 4. **Calculate operating profit on individual orderline for nonstocked article**

Sales value		10,000
Less: manufacturing volume cost of goods sold	4,000	
Volume cost: volume factor × mfg. vol. cost of goods sold		5,600
Margin on volume-related costs		4,400
Less: mfg. order cost for nonstocked article		2,000
Order cost		1,000
Operating profit for orderline		1,400

EXHIBIT 5

KANTHAL (A)

Customer Order Analysis

	Order cost per order line:					572	
	Cost for handling nonstocked item:				Foil elements: 1,508		
					Finished wire: 2,340		

COUNTRY CUSTOMER	ORDER LINES	INVOICED VALUE	VOLUME COST	ORDER COST	NONSTOCKED	OPERATING PROFIT	PROFIT MARGIN
Sweden							
S001	1	1,210	543	572	0	95	8%
S002	3	46,184	10,080	1,716	4,524	29,864	65
S003	8	51,102	50,567	4,576	12,064	(16,105)	−32
S004	9	98,880	60,785	5,148	13,572	19,375	20
S005	1	3,150	1,557	572	2,340	(1,319)	−42
S006	5	24,104	14,889	2,860	4,680	1,675	7
S007	2	4,860	2,657	1,144	4,680	(3,621)	−75
S008	1	2,705	1,194	572	0	939	35
S009	1	518	233	572	0	(287)	−55
S010	8	67,958	51,953	4,576	12,064	(635)	−1
S011	2	4,105	1,471	1,144	0	1,490	36
S012	8	87,865	57,581	4,576	12,064	13,644	16
S013	1	1,274	641	572	2,340	(2,279)	−179
S014	2	1,813	784	1,144	0	(115)	−6
S015	2	37,060	15,974	1,144	3,016	16,926	46
S016	2	6,500	6,432	1,144	3,016	(4,092)	−63

Note: All financial data reported in Swedish krona (SEK).

EXHIBIT 6

KANTHAL (A)

Finished Wire N Customer List

CUSTOMER NUMBER	INVOICED SALES	VOLUME COSTS	ORDER COST	NONSTOCKED COST	OPERATING PROFIT	PROFIT MARGIN
33507	3,969	1,440	750	0	1,779	45%
33508	4,165	1,692	750	2,150	(427)	−10
33509	601	139	750	2,150	(2,438)	−406
33510	13,655	6,014	750	2,150	4,741	35
33511	2,088	350	750	2,150	(1,162)	−56
33512	1,742	637	750	0	355	20
33513	4,177	932	750	2,150	345	8
33514	7,361	3,134	750	0	3,477	47
33515	1,045	318	750	0	(23)	−2
33516	429,205	198,277	9,000	0	221,928	52
33517	31,696	13,128	3,750	0	14,818	47
33518	159,612	58,036	2,250	6,450	92,876	58
33519	48,648	17,872	9,750	12,900	8,126	17
33520	5,012	1,119	750	2,150	993	20
33521	4,933	2,170	1,500	4,300	(3,037)	−62
33522	17,277	7,278	1,500	0	8,499	49
33523	134	120	1,500	4,300	(5,786)	−4318
33524	1,825	523	1,500	0	(198)	−11
33525	13,874	4,914	3,750	6,450	(1,240)	−9
33526	3,762	1,452	750	0	1,560	41
33527	64,875	18,559	3,750	8,600	33,966	52
33528	13,052	5,542	3,000	6,450	(1,940)	−15
33529	39,175	12,683	3,750	8,600	14,142	36
33530	383	87	750	0	(454)	−119
33531	6,962	1,865	750	2,150	2,197	32
33532	1,072	314	1,500	0	(742)	−69
33533	14,050	6,333	1,500	2,150	4,067	29
33534	820	244	750	0	(174)	−21
33535	809	181	750	2,150	(2,272)	−281
33536	1,366	316	750	2,150	(1,850)	−135
33537	155,793	65,718	21,750	49,450	18,875	12
33538	7,593	2,772	2,250	2,150	421	6
Total	1,060,731	434,159	84,000	131,150	411,422	39%

Note: All financial data reported in Swedish krona (SEK).

EXHIBIT 7

Cumulative Profitability
by Customers

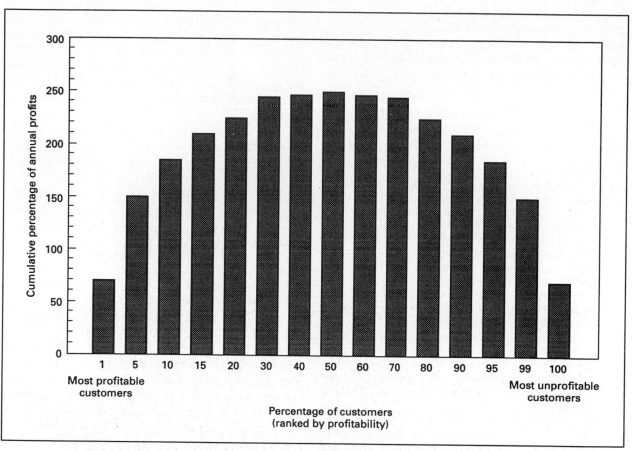

Winchell Lighting, Inc. (A)

INTRODUCTION

In January 1986, Ken Johnson, Vice-President and General Manager of Winchell Lighting, Inc. (WLI), assigned Pamela Wright, Marketing Analyst, and Elizabeth Conrad, Division Controller, to undertake the 1985 WLI Strategic Marketing Analysis. The Strategic Marketing Analysis effort arose from a collaboration, starting in 1982, between WLI management and the members of the planning group of WLI's parent, Hawkes. The goal was to trace marketing costs to individual product lines and channels so that the overall profitability of each line and channel could be determined.

This case was prepared by Professors Robin Cooper and Robert S. Kaplan.

COMPANY BACKGROUND

Winchell Lighting, Inc. manufactured and sold lighting fixtures. Consumer lines were sold through mass merchandisers and wholesale suppliers. Commercial products were sold though contract distributors and industrial suppliers. In 1985, WLI had total revenues of $128 million, generating an operating profit before taxes of $11 million (Exhibit 1).

PRODUCT LINES

The company manufactured thousands of different products, segmented into eight distinct product lines.

1. Consumer Incandescent Fixtures contained a broad range of fixtures designed specifically for easy installation in the residential market. They were all surface mounted, requiring no carpentry work. The products included pendants, close-to-ceiling fixtures, and chandeliers. Residential units were manufactured to less demanding standards than commercial fixtures and were considerably cheaper.

2. Consumer Fluorescent Fixtures contained a small range of surface-mounted fixtures designed specifically for the residential market.

3. Commercial Recessed Fixtures contained fixtures for incandescent bulbs designed to be recessed into the ceiling.

4. Commercial Fluorescent Fixtures contained fixtures for fluorescent lighting designed to be recessed into the ceiling.

5. Commercial Track contained both tracks and the fixtures designed to be attached to the tracks. Tracks were lengths of plastic tubing into which the fixtures could be snapped. Track lighting used conventional incandescent, tungsten-halogen and, recently, compact fluorescent lighting.

6. Commercial Ceiling Fixtures contained high-quality ceiling-mounted fixtures that had a high artistic content.

7. Commercial Wall Fixtures contained a diverse set of fixtures that were wall mounted. Many of these fixtures used the new compact, energy-efficient fluorescent light sources.

8. Commercial External Fixtures contained fixtures specifically designed for external use. These fixtures were of heavy construction to withstand weather conditions that required waterproof electrical connections.

COMPETITIVE ENVIRONMENT

Sales to the consumer markets generated about 15% of Winchell's total dollar volume (see Exhibit 2). WLI was the only company in the two almost independent consumer segments: fluorescent and incandescent. The fluorescent segment was dominated by three U.S.-based competitors—Gold, Conway, and Englehart—who together controlled about 70% of the market. The incandescent segment was more competitive, with three U.S. companies controlling about 70% and imports the other 30% of the market. Most of the U.S. companies used offshore sourcing to match the low cost of imported products.

The commercial market, accounting for the other 85% of Winchell's revenues, had three other full-line producers—Haddon, Conway, and Hobart—plus two companies, Somerset and King, that had gained a respectable percentage of the track and external fixture markets, respectively (see Exhibit 3).

MARKETING CHANNELS

The marketing department was organized along functional lines with separate departments for the three major business segments: Commercial Incandescent, Commercial Fluorescent, and Consumer Products. The Commercial Incandescent department was further split into two administrative areas—contract and industrial sales. The Fluorescent department supported a full line of fluorescent lighting fixtures and sold them to the commercial market through a separate sales force. The Consumer department had its own sales force, which sold consumer products to mass merchandisers and wholesale suppliers.

WLI sold its products through six distinct distribution channels. Two of these channels, mass merchandisers and wholesale suppliers, served the consumer market, and the other four served the commercial market. The channels differed considerably in the amount and method of selling effort required. The six channels were as follows:

1. Mass merchandisers—Mass merchandisers were the large-volume consumer outlets, such as K-Mart, Caldor, and Zayre, that sold directly to the public. They typically carried a small range of lighting fixtures. The mass merchandisers often promoted these products heavily, and WLI provided support for this activity. WLI favored these companies with a liberal returns policy and deep cash discounts. In 1985, mass merchandiser sales amounted to approximately $11 million.

2. Wholesale suppliers—Retail hardware chains (such as True Value and Ace) had formed cooperative associations to obtain bulk discounts based on their combined purchasing power. The associations used central warehouses to store their bulk-purchased merchandise that would be shipped, in small lots, to members on request. In 1985, WLI's sales to wholesale suppliers were $3 million.

3. Contract distributors—WLI provided complete lighting systems for commercial buildings. To compete in this market, WLI employed highly skilled marketing personnel who worked closely with architects. High-quality products and timely delivery were critical for this market segment.

When an architect asked for a bid, the salesperson examined the architect's building plans and generated a complete list of lighting fixtures for the project. This activity required considerable knowledge of WLI's product lines and of local fire, building, and electrical codes. The end document provided a detailed specification for every fixture in a building. Contract sales were nearly $80 million in 1985.

The recessed and fluorescent product lines' sales were not independent in the contract channel. Architects selected the types of fixtures that were to be used, usually a mixture of recessed and fluorescent lights. WLI had little real influence on the type of fixture selected.

4. Industrial suppliers—A large portion of the industrial supplier business was replacement of lighting fixtures. Building owners and operators purchased their lighting fixtures from two types of wholesalers. Master wholesalers, such as Mass Gas and Electric and Standard Electrical Supply, specialized in supplying lighting fixtures to smaller distributors, such as Mass Hardware, who carried a broad range of products for the building trade. Independent stores, such as Commonwealth Light in Boston, carried a large variety of fixtures sold directly to the end users. The independent stores demanded high-quality products and timely delivery but did not require specialized or customized products.

Salespersons to industrial suppliers had to be well informed about the company's products. They regularly called on suppliers to take inventory, assist in the preparation of orders to keep the suppliers adequately stocked, and alert the suppliers about building code changes that would affect WLI products. Intermediary agents and distributors, if applicable, were also involved in this process. In 1985, sales to suppliers totaled $25 million.

5. Government—The United States government occasionally requested a bid for very large volumes of fixtures. Over the years, WLI had not placed much effort into getting listed on the government's acceptable vendor lists. Sales in 1985 amounted to just over $400,000.

6. Original equipment manufacturers (OEMs)—Certain equipment manufacturers required special light fixtures for their products. For example, Sampson Furniture needed recessed fixtures for glass cabinets, and Lamb Cabinets required fluorescent fixtures for its aluminum and glass display cabinets. Since this kind of company was difficult to identify, WLI responded to bid requests but did not actively seek out the business. Once a contract was awarded, the OEMs typically sent in large orders at regular intervals. Sales in 1985 amounted to just over $9 million.

THE STRATEGIC MARKETING ANALYSIS

In 1982, WLI had adopted a product-channel perspective following a cost study performed with the assistance of the Hawkes Strategic Planning Group. Douglas Farish, Vice-President of Strategic Planning at Hawkes, commented on the process of developing the new product-channel perspective at WLI.

In 1981, the Hawkes planning department initiated the development of a strategic data base by business segment. Each Hawkes business was partitioned into much finer segments than were reported by the existing accounting system. Only by disaggregating could we focus on economic units that were reasonably coherent—that is, units within which we had roughly the same share, perceived quality, and profitability.

The existing accounting system, which broke the business into about 150 product groupings, failed to reflect the different costs of doing business in each distribution channel. With marketing expenses exceeding 15% of sales revenue, management wanted to know how each product line was performing in total and by channel. Thus, the product-channel perspective was developed.

As we began the initial marketing cost analysis, we quickly learned that tracing period expenses was more difficult than allocating factory overhead. While in the factory, proxies for cost drivers can often be found where actual data do not exist, the same cannot be said of many selling, general, and administrative activities. To understand the economics of how work was generated in the SG&A departments, we relied heavily on the qualitative information stored in the heads of managers who were most familiar with the activity of each department. The art of this sort of analysis is to be able to quantify the qualitative, that is, to convert the qualitative insights of managers into a quantitative model.

We organized a series of meetings to bring together a number of managers from a given function so that different perspectives on the same issue could be represented. My primary function as moderator of these sessions was to pose the right questions so that we could discover the principal drivers of cost. I also synthesized the estimates given me and fed them back to the managers so that they could judge their reasonableness.

In addition to debriefing knowledgeable managers, we sampled the experience of the sales force to gather qualitative data for the model-building effort. Ultimately, I wanted WLI management to acquire the skill we had developed through experience in reducing soft data to a reasonably reliable model. This was important because the system needs to be revised periodically to reflect changes in the relative importance of the cost drivers and of our expenditure of effort among channels. The system therefore must not be rigid, but rather capable of evolving with the business.

By 1986, the company had developed specific procedures to facilitate the marketing cost study. The analysts started from a channel profitability report in which SG&A expenses were treated as a common or below-the-line cost and not allocated to individual product lines (see Exhibit 4). The difference in gross margins across the six channels reflected the margins earned over manufacturing costs on the products sold through each channel. In the past, if management wanted to know operating profit after fully allocating all costs, the cost analysts had allocated SG&A costs based on sales revenue. Since SG&A expenses were about 25% of sales revenue, the operating profit for each channel equalled the gross margin percentage less 25%.

DESCRIPTION OF MARKETING EXPENSES

The strategic marketing analysis attempted to trace more accurately the selling and marketing expenses to individual channels and product lines. The analysis started from detailed descriptions of each marketing expense category reported in the income statement (see Exhibit 5).

Commissions

WLI products were sold on a commission basis by independent manufacturers' representatives. These representatives often carried a complementary line of products manufactured by other firms, but they were not allowed to carry directly competitive products.

Representatives did not maintain an inventory. They sold to customers, and then WLI shipped the products directly to the customers. The manufacturing representatives received a 5% commission for incandescent products and up to 12½ for fluorescent products. The higher rate for fluorescent sales reflected an historical attempt to increase sales in certain fixture lines.

WLI commercial products were also sold by company personnel who received a flat 5% commission but no base salary. WLI paid benefits such as health, pension, and FICA. Sales personnel absorbed all travel expenses, including any automobile costs. In some instances, a ±½% commission adjustment was made to compensate for the size of the salesperson's territory.

Catalog

The company published three catalogs: fluorescent commercial, incandescent commercial, and consumer. The commercial catalogs were published as three-ring binders to facilitate easy updating and insertion of new product descriptions. Because the product descriptions did not contain price data, the binder arrangement also allowed for price list supplements as required. WLI products were endorsed by *Sweet's Catalog,* the architect's reference manual for all building materials. WLI paid Sweet's to prepare and include separate subsections in the *Sweet's Catalog.*

WLI's contract sales business used the latest lighting technology and, therefore, required up-to-date commercial catalog information. Industrial suppliers also used the catalog, but since they concentrated more on the replacement business and only stocked bestsellers, they could use out-of-date catalogs with little risk. In both instances, products were ordered just as specified in the catalogs; unique designs could not be obtained. All WLI representatives kept copies of the catalogs and passed order requests through to WLI headquarters. Because of the large number of requests for the catalogs, no records were kept at headquarters or by representatives on where the catalogs were sent.

The WLI consumer catalog contained 8 to 10 pages listing all products sold in the mass merchandiser and wholesale supplier channels.

Advertising

Advertising expenditures were primarily the cost of advertisements in trade and industry publications, attendance at trade shows, and the costs of displays and exhibits. The firm placed advertisements in publications such as *Lighting Institute Magazine, Light Fixture Digest* (used by the supplier channel), *Discount News, Do It Yourself,* and the *Hardware Retailer.* Peripheral journals, such as *Architectural Record,* were not generally used.

Two of the most noteworthy trade shows attended were the Lighting Fixture Institute Show and the National Hardware Show. The advertising expenses for these shows included registration fees and the costs of creating and installing the booths, exhibits, and displays.

Cooperative advertising

Cooperative advertising was directed to the consumer market. Mass merchandisers placed color pull-outs in Sunday newspapers. Local hardware stores placed smaller advertisements in local papers. Radio advertisements were used to announce promotions and special prices.

The Advertising Checking Bureau monitored advertising copy for WLI. It received a supply of slicks, a copy of the advertising bill, and a proof of the advertising. WLI then paid the advertisers for their costs up to a cap set at 5% of last year's sales.

Sales promotion

Sales promotions were used to increase sales in both the commercial and consumer markets. Some commercial promotions offered incentives to distributors to purchase WLI products by awarding points based on the number of specified product items ordered. These points were then exchangeable for gift certificates or merchandise at a major department store. Others offered baker's dozen sales, in which the distributor received, say, 12 products for the price of 10. The costs of such promotion schemes included developing, printing, and distributing brochures, mailings, and order forms.

Consumer promotions were product specific. They typically consisted of bakers' dozen or special discount offers to mass merchandisers and wholesale suppliers.

Warranty

Warranty expenses were incurred on major contracts to overcome problems that could only be resolved in the field. Sales returns were not included in warranty expenses but were treated as a direct deduction from sales.

Sales administration

Sales administration expenses included costs that were too small to be treated as separate line items (see Exhibit 6).

Cash discounts

If WLI shipped before the twenty-fifth of the month and payment was received before the tenth of the following month, the customer could take a 2% discount. If WLI shipped after the twenty-fifth of the month, the discount could be taken if payment was received before the tenth of the second month. About 60% of goods were shipped during the first 25 days of each month.

TRACING MARKETING EXPENSES

Wright and Conrad described the procedures they used for assigning marketing costs to the product lines and distribution channels.

PW The distribution of marketing expenses starts with the document describing each component of expense. It formed the basis for our analysis. After we were sure we understood how each expense behaved, we began to develop allocation routines. Obviously, we relied heavily on the procedures used in prior years.

EC Commissions were the simplest to handle. We traced commission payments to the various product lines and then allocated them to channels on the basis of the sales volume of product lines in each channel.

PW Catalog expense was slightly more difficult. We publish three catalogs, one for each of the three business segments. It is easier to talk about the commercial and consumer segments separately.

The WLI commercial catalogs are really a collection of mini product line catalogs that we combine together in a three-ring binder. This approach is economical because it allows us to change one product line catalog without replacing the others. Unfortunately, we do not keep development costs for each product line catalog separately, so we could not break it down any further than the catalog level. This forced us to estimate the relative share of catalog costs by product line and channel.

EC   We used our knowledge of the business to guide us. For example, we knew that the incandescent commercial catalog is used in the contract and industrial supply channels. However, the contract business is always into new products, and it requires the most up-to-date catalogs; we are continuously sending them catalogs. The industrial supply channel is exactly the opposite. In the replacement business, the suppliers usually only stock a limited range of the bestsellers. These tend not to change from year to year, and consequently industrial suppliers are not bothered if their catalogs are not up to date.

PW   In contrast, the *Sweets Catalog* is used only in the contract business. We simply took all of the associated costs for this catalog and assigned them to the contract channel.

     For catalogs that covered several channels, we split catalog costs using the number of different outlets in each channel as the allocation base. We assigned catalog costs to the product lines on the basis of sales dollars in each channel.

     We assigned the cost of consumer catalogs in the same way. The mass merchandisers only stock a limited range of products and do not need a large catalog. But the wholesalers, who stock our entire line, need full-line catalogs. Again, we used our knowledge of the number of outlets and the intensity of use in each channel to estimate their relative share of catalog costs.

EC   Our catalogs do not contain price information because prices change more frequently than the contents of the catalogs. We issue a new price list whenever we want to change prices. The expense of printing and distributing these lists was assigned using the same ratios as we had identified for the catalogs themselves.

PW   Commission and catalog expenses were relatively easy. Advertising, on the other hand, was more difficult because of the range of different activities we undertake. We broke advertising into two sections, trade and cooperative. These two types of advertising are quite different from each other.

EC   Trade advertising in the industry magazines could be easily traced to the three business segments. First, we have project control over all advertising-related costs. Second, we advertise incandescent and fluorescent products separately. Third, the consumer market is reached by different magazines. The real problem was how to allocate the costs among the channels served by each magazine. We felt that some magazines really only served one channel. For example, *The Lighting Ledger* served industrial suppliers and *Discount Store News* reached mass merchandisers. Other magazines, for example, *Electrical Supplies*,

covered several channels, in which case we estimated the relative benefit by channel and allocated the costs accordingly.

PW   Cooperative advertising was completely different. First, it predominantly occurs in the two consumer channels, mass merchandising and wholesale suppliers. Second, the Advertising Checking Bureau invoices could be traced to each channel, which gave us an accurate measure of the advertising expenses in each channel.

     Tracing channel advertising costs to product lines was more difficult. An advertisement often contained pictures of products from several product lines, and there was no easy way to determine how much benefit was attributable to each line. It was simply not practical to count square inches; in any case, in many ads, the largest image was the company name. The local radio spots suffered from the same problem. We were not going to count seconds, and anyway the company name was often the most prominent part of the ad.

EC   In the end, we opted to use sales within the channel to allocate advertising costs to the product lines.

PW   Sales promotions occur at the product and product line level, so we ended up adopting exactly the opposite approach than we had taken for advertising. Instead of tracing costs to the segments or channels, and then to product lines, we traced promotion costs first to products or product lines and then summed up the costs for each product line in a channel. This was relatively straightforward because we record promotion expenses by product code.

EC   We used the same approach with warranty expenses. These occur when we have to go into the field and correct a problem that has developed in a large commercial contract. If the expenditure is above $10,000, then we open a special project. These expenses are easily traced to the channels in which they occurred. However, if the expenditure is below $10,000, then the costs are captured only by product line. These can be allocated to the channels on the basis of the sales of each product line in that channel.

PW   Sales administration is a collection of nine relatively small expense categories. We had to deal with each one separately [Exhibit 7]. We were surprised by how much resources were required by some channels and not by others. The allocations all made sense after we looked at them; it was the magnitude of the effect that was unexpected.

EC   Cash discounts were allocated to channels by selecting large representative accounts within each of the channels and determining their accounts-receivable-to-sales ratio. From these ratios, we computed the day's-sales outstanding (DSO). We used the DSOs to estimate the cash discounts in each channel.

EC   After performing all the analysis, we produced two sets of reports. The first reported the marketing costs as a percentage of sales for each major product line [see Exhibit 8 for an example of the new report for the Commercial Track Lighting product line]. The second added up all the marketing costs in each of our six distribution channels to obtain a new Channel Profitability Report [Exhibit 9]. For the channel report, we also traced the utilization of net invested capital, including working capital items such as inventory and accounts receivable, to individual channels so that we could measure the return on capital for each channel.

PW   The Channel Profitability Report is the most important. It demonstrates how significant the marketing cost analysis really is. The resulting channel profitabilities, returns on investment, and residual incomes are very different from what we used to think they were.

EXHIBIT 1

WINCHELL LIGHTING, INC. (A)

1985 Income Statement ($000)

Sales		$127,960	100%
Cost of sales			
Material	45,529		
Labor	7,082		
Overhead	32,393		
		85,004	67
Gross profit		42,956	33%
Sales and general administrative expenses			
Marketing expenses	20,953		
General/administrative	10,861		
		31,814	25%
Operating income		$11,142	8%

EXHIBIT 2

WINCHELL LIGHTING, INC. (A)

Market Share Analysis—Consumer Products

FLUORESCENT

			SHARE BY CHANNEL OF DISTRIBUTION			
COMPETITORS	MASS MERCHANDISERS	COMMERCIAL SUPPLIERS	CONTRACT	INDUSTRIAL SUPPLIERS	GOVERNMENT	OEM
WLI	15	25	10	10	25	15
Gold	30	25	30	25	20	25
Conway	20	20	10	20	20	30
Englehart	25	10	40	20	30	30
Gellis	10	20	10	25	5	0
% of WLI total product line sales	25	50	5	10	5	5

INCANDESCENT

	SHARE BY CHANNEL OF DISTRIBUTION		
COMPETITORS	MASS MERCHANDISERS	WHOLESALE SUPPLIERS	INDUSTRIAL SUPPLIER
WLI	20	20	20
Commonwealth	25	25	25
Celebrity	25	25	25
Imports	30	30	30
Percent of WLI total product line sales	30	50	20

EXHIBIT 3

WINCHELL LIGHTING, INC. (A)

Market Share Analysis—Commercial Products

RECESSED

	SHARE BY CHANNEL OF DISTRIBUTION		
COMPETITORS	MASS MERCHANDISERS	WHOLESALE SUPPLIERS	INDUSTRIAL SUPPLIER
WLI	15	15	15
Haddon	20	25	25
Hobart	20	10	10
Conway	20	30	30
Others	25	20	20
% of total product line sales	70	20	10

EXHIBIT 3 *(cont.)*

FLUORESCENT

| | SHARE BY CHANNEL OF DISTRIBUTION | | | |
| | | INDUSTRIAL | | |
COMPETITORS	CONTRACT	SUPPLIER	GOVERNMENT	OEM
WLI	10	15	20	10
Haddon	45	45	35	75
Hobart	20	5	5	5
Conway	20	25	25	0
Others	5	10	15	10
% of total product line sales	40	25	15	20

TRACK

| | SHARE BY CHANNEL OF DISTRIBUTION | | |
| | | INDUSTRIAL | |
COMPETITORS	CONTRACT	SUPPLIER	GOVERNMENT	OEM
WLI	20	20	20	
Haddon	20	20	20	
Hobart	20	20	20	
Conway	20	20	20	
Somerset	20	20	20	
% of total product line sales	60	25	15	

CEILING

| | SHARE BY CHANNEL OF DISTRIBUTION | | | |
| | | INDUSTRIAL | | |
COMPETITORS	CONTRACT	SUPPLIER	GOVERNMENT	OEM
WLI	30	30	20	30
Somerset	50	50	50	50
Haddon	15	15	25	10
Other	5	5	5	5
% of total product line sales	30	20	20	30

WALL

| | SHARE BY CHANNEL OF DISTRIBUTION | | |
| | | INDUSTRIAL | |
	CONTRACT	SUPPLIER	OEM
WLI	10	20	10
Conway	50	10	25
Haddon	25	40	50
Hobart	15	20	5
King	0	10	10
% of total product line sales	20	20	60

EXTERNAL

| | SHARE BY CHANNEL OF DISTRIBUTION | | | |
| | | INDUSTRIAL | | |
COMPETITORS	CONTRACT	SUPPLIER	GOVERNMENT	OEM
WLI	50	50	60	50
Conway	30	30	5	30
Haddon	10	10	25	10
Other	10	10	10	10
% of total product line sales	20	20	45	15

EXHIBIT 4

WINCHELL LIGHTING, INC. (A)

Channel Profitability Report

(Existing System)

($000)

	MASS MERCHANDISING	CONSUMER WHOLESALE SUPPLIERS	CONTRACT	INDUSTRIAL SUPPLIERS	COMMERCIAL GOVERN- MENT	OEM	TOTAL
Net sales	10,694	3,120	79,434	25,110	402	9,200	127,960
Material	8,503	2,083	25,089	6,886	99	2,869	45,529
Labor	29	62	4,798	1,437	33	724	7,082
Overhead	150	268	22,172	6,503	154	3,146	32,393
Total	8,681	2,413	52,059	14,826	286	6,739	85,004
Gross profit	2,013	707	27,375	10,284	116	2,461	42,956
Gross margin	19%	23%	34%	41%	29%	27%	34%
SG&A							31,814
Operating profit							11,142
Profit margin							9%
Net invested capital							54,141
Return on investment							21%

EXHIBIT 5

WINCHELL LIGHTING, INC. (A)

Marketing Expenses by Category (000)

CATEGORY	1985 EXPENSES	%
Commission	$7,376	35
Advertising	230	1
Catalog	714	3
Co-op advertising	1,006	5
Sales promotion	1,132	5
Warranty	94	1
Sales administration	8,957	43
Cash discount	1,444	7
Total	$20,953	100

Customer service. Customer service involved order entry and editing using an on-line system. The largest users were the industrial suppliers, who placed many small orders, thereby creating a lot of paperwork, and contractors, who, while only placing a small number of orders, required much telephoning back and forth to establish the correct mixture of products. Other users, such as the OEMs, mass merchandisers, and the government, required little attention.

Customer service expenses were allocated on the basis of management estimates. Contractor and industrial suppliers received the highest amounts because most of the customer service activity was concentrated in those two channels.

Marketing management. Marketing management expenses were the salaries of all of the managers in the marketing department.

Marketing management expenses were allocated proportionally to the time spent by the managers. For functional managers this was relatively easy because they were assigned to particular segments (e.g., a marketing manager and a sales manager). It was more difficult for support function managers because their activities were firm-wide (e.g., research manager and pricing manager). Where possible, the costs of these activities were traced to the channels. Otherwise, they were allocated on the basis of sales dollars.

Sales policy. Sales policy expenses arose from settling disputed claims. Mass merchandisers had the largest numbers of disputed orders, typically complaining about short shipments and other shipment mistakes. They used their large outstanding receivables balances as leverage against the firm and would withhold payment until all issues relating to the shipment were settled. The firm used a commonsense approach on whether to fight. Contractors similarly disputed pricing, shrinkage, and any shortages of the trivial accessories, such as screws, that accompanied their orders. Other channels, such as the industrial suppliers, raised similar issues but to a lesser extent.

Sales policy expenses were first traced to the three business segments and then allocated to the channels using managerial estimates. Within the channels, they were allocated to the product lines using relative sales dollars.

Marketing travel and entertainment. Marketing travel and entertainment expenses consisted of the travel expenditures of the marketing managers. The contract business required extensive travel because there were no regional managers; large individual contracters, the competitiveness of the business, and the technical complexity required a lot of handholding and entertainment by management. The other channels required relatively little travel, typically only for shows and other events.

Marketing travel and entertainment expenses were traced to the person that filed the expense report and hence to the business segment. Certain channels required more traveling than others—for example, the contractor channel, because there are no regional managers. These costs were allocated using a mixture of managerial estimates and sales lars.

Postage. The majority of postage expenditures were related to catalog mailings. They were allocated on the basis of the catalog expenses in each channel.

Administrative travel and entertainment. Administrative travel and entertainment expenses are the costs incurred when the director of marketing, the pricing manager, or marketing analyst traveled to meet contractors, mass merchandisers, and industrial suppliers. The three individuals that charge to this line item were asked to estimate the percentage of their share of these costs by channel.

Warehousing. Warehousing expenses were the costs of keeping finished goods inventory in the warehouse ready for shipment. These costs were allocated to the product lines based on the inventory level of each product line and to the channels by relative sales level.

Meetings. Meeting expenses were incurred for the firm's regular national sales meetings. The costs of national sales meetings were tracked to the three business segments and then allocated to the channels on the basis of managerial estimates.

Fixed expenses. Fixed expenses consisted of a number of different items such as depreciation; heat, light, and power; telephone; building maintenance; supplies and equipment rental charges.

The expenses were allocated to each segment by department using a number of different allocation routines and then to the channels using managerial judgment.

EXHIBIT 7

WINCHELL LIGHTING, INC. (A)

Allocation of Sales Administration Expenses to Channel

| | CONSUMER (%) | | COMMERCIAL (%) | | | |
	MASS MERCHANDISING	WHOLESALE SUPPLIERS	CONTRACT	INDUSTRIAL SUPPLIERS	GOVERNMENT	OEM
Customer service	1	16	38	43	1	1
Marketing management	20	10	60	10	0	0
Sales policy	34	28	30	8	0	3
Marketing travel and entertainment	8	44	43	5	0	5
Postage	8	35	35	23	0	0
Administrative travel and entertainment	21	15	42	21	0	0
Warehousing	5	21	60	14	0	0
Meetings	12	12	42	35	0	0
Fixed expenses	13	18	50	20	0	0

EXHIBIT 8

WINCHELL LIGHTING, INC. (A)

Production and Marketing Costs as a Percent of Sales

Commercial Track Lighting

| | DISTRIBUTION CHANNEL COMMERCIAL | | | |
	CONTRACT (%)	INDUSTRIAL SUPPLIERS (%)	GOVERNMENT (%)	OEM (%)
Sales	100.0	100.0	100.0	100.0
Material	29.5	28.6	34.4	35.3
Labor	15.3	6.5	8.6	8.5
Overhead	25.1	22.0	33.0	28.2
Total	69.9	57.1	76.0	72.0
Gross margin	30.1	42.9	24.0	28.0
Commission	5.9	5.4	2.8	4.0
Advertising	0.2	0.2	0.0	0.0
Catalog	0.6	0.6	0.0	0.0
Co-op advertising	0.5	0.5	0.0	0.0
Sales promotion	0.5	0.5	0.0	0.0
Warranty	0.1	0.1	0.0	0.0
Sales administration	7.2	6.8	4.7	3.8
Cash discount	1.1	1.0	2.8	1.2
Total	16.1	14.7	10.3	9.1
General and administration	8.5	8.5	8.5	8.5
Profit margin	5.5	19.7	5.2	10.4

EXHIBIT 9

WINCHELL LIGHTING, INC. (A)

1985 Channel Profitability Report

(Marketing Cost Analysis)

($000)

	CONSUMER			COMMERCIAL			
	MASS MERCHANDISING	WHOLESALE SUPPLIERS	CONTRACT	INDUSTRIAL SUPPLIERS	GOVERNMENT	OEM	TOTAL
Net sales	10,694	3,120	79,434	25,110	402	9,200	127,960
Material	8,503	2,083	25,089	6,886	99	2,869	45,529
Labor	29	62	4,798	1,437	33	724	7,082
Overhead	150	268	22,172	6,503	154	3,146	32,393
Total	8,681	2,413	52,059	14,826	266	6,739	85,004
Gross profit	2,013	707	27,375	10,284	116	2,461	42,956
Gross margin	19%	23%	34%	41%	29%	27%	34%
Marketing Expenses							
Commission	696	270	4,682	1,344	12	372	7,376
Advertising	46	12	132	38	0	2	230
Catalog	36	14	504	160	0	0	714
Co-op advertising	380	90	416	120	0	0	1,006
Sales promotion	494	128	394	114	0	2	1,132
Warranty	2	2	64	22	0	4	94
Sales administration	908	268	5,696	1,714	20	351	8,957
Cash discount	118	56	892	252	12	114	1,444
Total	2,680	840	12,780	3,764	44	845	20,953
General and administration	907	265	6,740	2,131	36	781	10,860
Operating profit	(1,574)	(398)	7,855	4,389	36	835	11,143
Profit margin	-15%	-13%	10%	17%	9%	9%	9%
Net invested capital[1]	5,447	1,643	33,154	10,974	184	2,748	54,149
Return on investment	-29%	-24%	24%	40%	30%	30%	21%
Residual income	(2,936)	(809)	(433)	1,646	10	149	(2,374)

[1]Allocated on the basis of equipment utilized and working capital levels.

545

Winchell Lighting, Inc. (B)

In spring of 1986, Ken Johnson, Vice-President of Winchell Lighting, Inc., Ted Phillips, Director of Marketing, Pamela Wright, Marketing Analyst, and Elizabeth Conrad, Division Controller, discussed the overall value of the strategic marketing cost analysis.

KJ We sell in several markets, using many distribution channels, each requiring different intensities and methods of selling. Prior to the marketing cost analysis, we virtually ignored the differential costs of marketing our products. We simply added all of the marketing expenses together and treated them as a below-the-line period cost. Our main focus was on gross margin, not on profit margin.

PW The product line distribution channel perspective coupled to the marketing cost analysis provided a better way for us to analyze our business. The study influenced our strategic emphasis. We are now interested in distribution channels, such as government, that we previously ignored and are expending less effort in other channels, such as mass merchandising, that we no longer view as attractive.

TP The study was important in helping us redirect our attention. It is now much easier for management to see things clearly at the divisional level without getting bogged down in the data. The greatest breakthrough is our ability to develop marketing strategies that take advantage of our knowledge of the business. For example, the study helped direct us to a new product, the budget recessed fixture line, and to a new distribution channel, the 100 top builders.

The budget recessed fixture line is aimed at the low-cost end of the market. Our old perspective could have kept us out of the market because the gross margins there are lower than average. The new perspective shows, however, that these fixtures also have low period cost[1] and hence are attractive products.

Similarly, we have aggressively approached the top 100 big residential builders. If we can break into that market by selling to them directly, we will have created a new commercial distribution channel.

The additional insight provided by the study, that the channel costs would be low once the channel was established, enabled us to see this opportunity.

PW We can now identify low-margin niches that we can service economically. We can also identify which product-channel combinations have high or low returns so that we can better manage the competitive environment to increase our long-term profitability. Take our reaction to the external fixture results. We knew we were making good profits but not to the extent we now believe.

KJ Since the study, we have taken several strong actions in the marketplace to protect those products. We have increased the discount structure so that it is more difficult for our competitors to underprice us. We have added technical support so that we are providing a better service than our competitors and, finally, we have increased advertising. By this concerted set of actions, we aim to create entry barriers that keep our competitors out, while still allowing us to earn high profits. If we hadn't undertaken the analysis, we would not have acted so quickly or thoroughly, and we might have lost the advantage.

PW We have also instituted some other pricing and discounting activities aimed at making certain products more attractive to our customers or reducing the loss on others. For example, we increased the discounts on the recessed lighting fixtures for insulated ceilings and reduced discounts on standard recessed. This made insulated ceiling models more competitive while increasing the margin on the standard units.

EC I never really understood that action. I thought the sales of those products were so interconnected that it really doesn't make any difference if we move the discounts around. Each building needs a certain number of insulated and standard recessed fixtures, and the increased discounts on insulated tend to be balanced out by the decreased discounts on the standard line. The new discount structure is not going to change the mix of products sold. So why bother?

TP There is some truth to that. But we want each product to stand on its own, and moving the discount around helps achieve that objective. Also, there are some independent sales of the various product lines, and we definitely do not want to sell those at a loss. It makes good sense to maintain a reasonable profit margin on as many products as possible.

PW We have also increased profits by identifying products that are performing poorly and reviewing what actions we can take regarding them. For example, we discontinued the entire chandelier line and many of the less profitable products we manufacture for original equipment manufacturers (OEM). We also reen-

---

[1]Period costs include marketing, sales, and general administration.

This case was prepared by Professors Robin Cooper and Robert S. Kaplan.

gineered the fluorescent fixture lines, and they are now considerably cheaper to manufacture. They used to be poor performers; now they are very attractive products.

KJ   We should be careful not to overemphasize the effect of the study. We already had the fluorescent project in the pipeline. We knew that fluorescent fixtures were not making adequate profits and had begun to think about reengineering them. The analysis simply confirmed our fears and made us act that much quicker.

TP   Also, while we got rid of the chandeliers, we still sell many other products that are not making an adequate profit. We can't drop them because they are a necessary part of our product offering. Take, for example, standard recessed fixtures. According to the study, we don't make money on them, but, given who we are, we have to continue to sell them. Our entire commercial market strategy is based on being a full-line producer.[2] We sell to customers who are undertaking large construction jobs that require a mixture of fixtures. If we dropped one of these fixture types, we would not be perceived as a full-line producer. If we cherry-pick our lines, we would no longer be competitive with the other full-line vendors.

KJ   That is a more important point than it might at first seem. The strategy we have adopted, of being a full-line producer, is ingrained into the way we do business. It is reflected in our organizational structure, the way the sales force perceives the business, the channels we serve, and the customers we attract. Changing strategy requires that all of these elements be rethought and, if needed, changed. That is not an overnight process.

TP   There are other factors that make it difficult to take advantage of the insights provided by the study. Take government sales, for example. We learned from the analysis that government business was attractive, and we started to promote it a couple of years back. But, if you look at the results, you would never guess we have changed our approach. First, in 1984, the business began to disappear. Then, in 1985, the government substantially decreased the number of bids it requested. This caused a lot of low-ball pricing, and we were not aggressive enough. Consequently, we only gained a small sales increase from the prior year. However, this year we are going to be really aggressive and expect to gain a major share of the market.

PW   The biggest problem was the defense department. We used to have a 50% share in that market, but in 1985 this dropped to 25%. We expect to achieve about a 75% penetration in 1986.

TP   The way the government channel reacted raises an important issue. You simply cannot use the information provided by the analysis without taking into account competitive forces. If our competitors decide to become more active and increase the level of advertising, discounting, or special offers, then we are often forced to do the same even if we have decided on a different strategy. You just cannot turn your back on a product because it is not super-profitable. Most of our products are part of an integrated marketing strategy, and we cannot afford to lose them.

KJ   Remember, our competition is entrenched in the way they do business, and this makes it difficult for us to change our strategy. We keep having to compete with them in ways that are now fundamentally different from where we would want to go. It is just not possible, given our market position, to withdraw from many product markets.

TP   You cannot overemphasize that point. The analysis has shown retail margins to be even worse than we had originally thought. On the surface, our best strategy would be to leave that market. But it is not that easy. A large amount of goodwill for the commercial business is generated by having the WLI name in the consumer market. You cannot put a dollar sign on it, but it's there. You simply cannot turn your back on history.

KJ   When we reentered the consumer market, we effectively committed ourselves to it. You cannot afford to be seen as capricious in the marketplace. Our task is to find ways of making that business profitable.

PW   We are not helpless, though. We have reduced the cooperative advertising cap from 5% to 3%, and this significantly reduces our expenditures on such advertising. We have also decided to put less effort into the wholesale supplier channel. It is by far the least profitable, and we intend to reduce the relative size of that channel.

KJ   The practicalities of business stop us from reacting immediately to the insights provided by the marketing cost analysis. We cannot just drop products, change their prices, or close distribution channels without incurring a substantial penalty in the market as a whole. We are forced to be more subtle: We reduce activity in one market and increase it in another, or we shift discounts to make one product look more attractive and another less so. It would be naive to expect us to drop all poorly performing products. We drop what we can and try to improve the rest. It is a long, slow process, but I am convinced it is the right approach.

KJ   That raises an important point. Demonstrating that the strategic marketing analysis has benefited the group is a difficult proposition. We have never really attempted to prove that the analysis made a difference. We simply reacted to it and, I think, in ways that make sense.

TP   It is probably too soon to tell if it's had a beneficial effect. We have only been using this approach for two

---

[2]In this industry a full-line producer sells recessed, fluorescent, and track ceiling and wall fixtures.

to three years, and we are still learning to take advantage of it. We have only just begun to alter our behavior. Two to three years may seem like a long time to implement a new approach, but it really isn't. First, it took us several years to create a reliable data base; in fact, we are still refining it. It's taken time to modify our data collection procedures to be able to measure accurately, maintain, and store the data required by the new strategic marketing analysis. Second, in the past, we have tended to act too quickly, and, with a project like this, that's dangerous. You rush to use the information provided by the study before you really understand it. This leads to poor decisions and a loss in commitment to the approach. This time, we have been very cautious in the way we have used the data.

PW   It is important to remember that the analysis is only part of what is going on at WLI. We are continuously reacting to changes in the competitive environment and, while the marketing analysis has had an effect, it is difficult to untangle that effect against the background of changing conditions.

KJ   We don't have special strategic marketing analysis meetings where we discuss the findings of the study each year, but that doesn't mean we don't pay attention to the study findings.

EC   One way you might detect the effect of the study across time is to look at the first marketing cost analysis that was completed. It restated the 1982 financials into approximately the same format [Exhibit 1]. Market conditions were different then, and it's not a case of simply comparing results, but it might provide you with some insights if you compare it to the latest analysis [Exhibit 2].

KJ   That might work, but the 1982 market was inherently more profitable. The previous four years had been very busy, and prices had risen correspondingly. The same isn't true of 1985. It is a better year than 1983 or 84 but not as good as 82.

EC   I agree it is difficult to show the effects, but I think it's worth the effort. Another place to look is those new low ROI products quarterly reports. They help us to focus our efforts on the low ROI products. They are designed to highlight the effect of our actions on the low performer product lines such as commercial fluorescent fixtures [Exhibit 3], wall fixtures [Exhibit 4], and residential incandescent [Exhibit 5].

TP   Those reports are a good way to make sure that we do not lose our impetus on the project. I expect to see some real changes in the profitability of the poor performers in the next few years. However, I think it may be too soon to detect anything yet.

PW   If I wanted to demonstrate the effect of the analysis, I would probably look at the sales of recessed fixtures [Exhibit 6]. As we discussed earlier, we have changed the discount structure of the insulated and standard cylindrical products. So there might be something there.

EC   It is possible you might detect something. However, you have to take into account the nonresidential starts for the previous year. We generally use that as a planning guide to sales volume. I have the Dodge's numbers[3] for the same time period, and that should help analyze the sales numbers [Exhibit 7].

TP   The analysis will not be that easy. Architects frequently change the type of fixtures they choose to incorporate in their designs, and that dramatically affects sales. At the moment, recessed fixtures are in, but in the next few years it could easily change back to fluorescent. If you look at the comparison of the two lines, you will see the ratio changes over the years [Exhibit 8].

KJ   Our business is too complex and it changes too rapidly for the effects of any single action to be detectable. The commercial and consumer markets are cyclical, and that dominates anything we have discussed today. We are forced to manage our business on faith. I believe, thanks to the strategic marketing analysis, we are doing the right things and are improving our performance. I cannot prove it, but that doesn't stop me from believing it.

---

[3]Dodge Construction Potentials, Construction Information Group: McGraw-Hill Information System Company.

EXHIBIT 1

WINCHELL LIGHTING, INC. (B)

1982 Channel Profitability Report

(Marketing Cost Analysis)

($000)

	CONSUMER			COMMERCIAL			
	MASS MERCHANDISING	WHOLESALE SUPPLIERS	CONTRACT	INDUSTRIAL SUPPLIERS	GOVERNMENT	OEM	TOTAL
Net sales	9,948	6,982	57,616	19,438	266	9,070	103,340
Material	5,168	2,064	16,683	4,908	74	2,946	31,843
Labor	693	721	3,760	1,276	18	904	7,372
Overhead	2,537	2,750	14,203	4,807	97	3,221	27,615
Total	8,398	5,534	34,646	10,991	189	7,071	66,829
Gross profit	1,550	1,448	22,970	8,447	77	2,019	36,511
Gross margin	16%	21%	40%	43%	39%	22%	35%
Marketing expenses	2,498	1,601	7,470	2,366	22	61	14,018
General and administration	901	689	5,692	1,785	28	808	9,904
Operating profit	(1,849)	(843)	9,808	4,296	27	1,150	12,589
Profit margin (%)	−19%	−12%	17%	22%	10%	13%	12%

EXHIBIT 2

WINCHELL LIGHTING, INC. (B)

1985 Channel Profitability Report

(Marketing Cost Analysis)

($000)

	CONSUMER			COMMERCIAL			
	MASS MERCHANDISING	WHOLESALE SUPPLIERS	CONTRACT	INDUSTRIAL SUPPLIERS	GOVERNMENT	OEM	TOTAL
Net sales	10,694	3,120	79,434	25,110	402	9,200	127,960
Material	8,503	2,083	25,089	6,886	99	2,869	45,529
Labor	29	62	4,798	1,437	33	724	7,082
Overhead	150	268	22,172	6,503	154	3,146	32,393
Total	8,681	2,413	52,059	14,826	266	6,739	85,004
Gross profit	2,013	707	27,375	10,284	116	2,461	42,956
Gross margin	19%	23%	34%	41%	29%	27%	34%
Marketing Expenses							
Commission	696	270	4,682	1,344	12	372	7,376
Advertising	46	12	132	38	0	2	230
Catalog	36	14	504	160	0	0	714
Co-op advertising	380	90	416	120	0	0	1,006
Sales promotion	494	128	394	114	0	2	1,132
Warranty	2	2	64	22	0	4	94
Sales administration	908	268	5,696	1,714	20	351	8,957
Cash discount	118	56	892	252	12	114	1,444
Total	2,680	840	12,780	3,764	44	845	20,953
General and administration	907	265	6,740	2,131	36	781	10,860
Operating profit	(1,574)	(398)	7,855	4,389	36	835	11,143
Profit margin	−15%	−13%	10%	17%	9%	9%	9%
Net invested capital	5,447	1,643	33,154	10,974	184	2,748	54,149
Return on investment	−29%	−24%	24%	40%	20%	30%	21%
Residual income	(2,936)	(809)	(433)	1,646	(10)	149	(2,394)

EXHIBIT 3

WINCHELL LIGHTING, INC. (B)
Low ROI Products Quarterly Reports
Commercial Fluorescent Fixtures
($ million)

| | 1984 | | 1985 | | | |
| | STRATEGIC ACCOUNTING | TRADITIONAL ACCOUNTING | TRADITIONAL ACCOUNTING | | | FULL YEAR |
			Q1–Q2	Q3	Q4	
Sales	$13.2	$13.2	$13.4	$13.4	$13.4	$13.4
Gross profit	5.0	5.0	5.2	5.6	7.8	6.2
Period expenses	3.6	4.4	4.2	4.0	5.0	4.4
Operating profit	1.4	0.6	1.0	1.6	2.8	1.8
Accounts receivable	2.6	3.0	2.8	3.0	2.8	2.8
Inventory	9.6	8.6	6.4	5.2	5.6	6.0
Property, plant, and equipment (PPE)	2.4	2.4	2.6	2.4	2.6	2.4
Current liabilities	1.8	2.0	1.8	1.8	2.2	2.0
Net invested capital	12.8	12.0	10.0	8.8	8.8	9.2
Gross margin (%)	26.3%	26.3%	31.2%	31.7%	44.7%	36.5%
Return on sales (%)	7.4	3.2	5.3	9.1	15.6	10.6
Return on investment (%)	10.9	5.0	8.7	18.2	30.6	19.2

Notes:

1. All quarterly sales profit period expense and operating profit has been annualized for comparison purposes.
2. All accounts receivable, inventory, PPE, current liability, and net invested capital are at period end levels.

EXHIBIT 4

WINCHELL LIGHTING, INC. (B)
Low ROI Products Quarterly Reports
Commercial Wall Fixtures
($ million)

| | 1984 | | 1985 | | | |
| | STRATEGIC ACCOUNTING | TRADITIONAL ACCOUNTING | TRADITIONAL ACCOUNTING | | | FULL YEAR |
			Q1–Q2	Q3	Q4	
Sales	$ 8.1	$ 8.1	$ 8.7	$ 9.9	$10.5	$ 9.3
Gross profit	2.7	2.7	2.7	2.7	3.6	3.0
Period expenses	2.1	1.8	2.1	2.1	3.0	2.4
Operating profit	0.6	0.9	0.6	0.6	0.6	0.6
Accounts receivable	1.2	1.2	1.5	1.5	1.8	1.5
Inventory	4.5	3.9	3.0	2.7	3.3	3.0
Property, plant, and equipment (PPE)	0.6	1.2	1.2	1.5	1.5	1.5
Current liabilities	0.9	0.9	0.9	1.2	1.8	1.2
Net invested capital	5.4	5.4	4.8	4.5	4.8	4.8
Gross margin (%)	33.3%	33.3%	32.2%	28.3%	35.9%	32.2
Return on sales	7.4	11.1	6.3	5.7	6.8	6.4
Return on investment	11.1	16.7	11.4	12.0	14.5	12.7

Notes:

1. All quarterly sales profit period expense and operating profit has been annualized for comparison purposes.
2. All accounts receivable, inventory, PPE, current liability, and net invested capital are at period end levels.

EXHIBIT 5

WINCHELL LIGHTING, INC. (B)
Low ROI Products Quarterly Reports
Residential Incandescent
($ million)

| | 1984 | | 1985 | | | |
| | STRATEGIC ACCOUNTING | TRADITIONAL ACCOUNTING | TRADITIONAL ACCOUNTING | | | FULL YEAR |
			Q1–Q2	Q3	Q4	
Sales	$13.8	$13.8	$ 9.8*	$13.8*	$ 8.2	$10.4
Gross profit	3.4	3.4	2.6	3.4	2.4	2.8
Period expenses	3.0	4.8	2.6	3.2	2.4	2.8
Operating profit	0.4	0.3	—	—	—	—
Accounts payable	2.2	2.2	1.6	2.2	1.2	1.6
Inventory	6.6	7.0	6.2	4.6	3.6	5.2
Property, plant, and equipment (PPE)	1.4	1.4	1.2	1.0	0.8	1.0
Current liabilities	1.4	1.6	1.2	1.6	1.4	1.4
Net invested capital	8.8	9.0	7.8	6.2	4.2	6.4
Gross margin (%)	24.6%	24.6%	26.0%	24.7%	28.8%	26.1%
Return on sales	2.9	1.4	—	2.1	—	—
Return on investment	4.5	2.2	—	4.8	—	—

Notes:
1. All quarterly sales profit period expense and operating profit has been annualized for comparison purposes.
2. All accounts receivable, inventory, PPE, current liability, and net invested capital are at period end levels.

EXHIBIT 6

WINCHELL LIGHTING, INC. (B)
Sales of Commercial Recessed Fixtures 1977–1985
(million)

PRODUCT LINE	1977	1978	1979	1980	1981	1982	1983	1984	1985
Standard	3.6	4.4	5.5	5.4	7.2	7.2	6.8	9.4	9.6
Insulated	4.2	6.2	6.6	6.6	9.0	8.4	8.8	9.4	10.2
Total	7.8	10.6	12.1	12.0	16.2	15.6	15.6	18.8	19.8

EXHIBIT 7

WINCHELL LIGHTING, INC. (B)
Nonresidential Construction Starts 1977–1985
(million square feet)

1977	1978	1979	1980	1981	1982	1983	1984	1985
1,050	1,150	1,369	1,195	1,166	915	989	1,210	1,195

Source: Dodge Construction Potential, Construction Information Group: McGraw-Hill Information System Company.

EXHIBIT 8

WINCHELL LIGHTING, INC. (B)

Sales of Commercial Recessed and Fluorescent Fixtures 1977–1985

(million)

PRODUCT LINE	1977	1978	1979	1980	1981	1982	1983	1984	1985
Recessed	7.8	10.6	12.1	12.0	16.2	15.6	15.6	18.8	19.8
Fluorescent	6.1	7.2	6.8	9.4	11.3	11.8	12.9	13.2	13.4

Manufacturers Hanover Corporation: Customer Profitability Report

MANUFACTURERS HANOVER ANNOUNCES NEW STRUCTURE TO SHARPEN ITS APPROACH TO CUSTOMERS AND MARKETS:
Streamlined, Flatter Organization Redeploys Executives Closer to Customers and Provides Greater Flexibility
(News Release, May 15, 1990)

COMPANY

Manufacturers Hanover Corporation (MHC), after several difficult years of credit loss recognition, primarily from Latin American lending, had emerged with a strengthened financial position. The company now was attempting to profit from its strong North American multinational customer base. With total assets in excess of $60 billion (down from a high of more than $75 billion in 1985), MHC was the eighth largest commercial bank in the U.S. Tangible equity as a percentage of assets had rebounded from a low of 2.9% at year end 1987 to 5.2% by the end of 1989. Exhibit 1 summarizes recent financial performance and ratios.

Thomas S. Johnson, formerly President of the Chemical Banking Corporation, was hired in December 1989 as President of MHC and heir-apparent to John F. McGillicuddy, Chairman and Chief Executive Officer. The reorganization announced in May 1990 gave Johnson major responsibility for the global banking group of MHC, which encompassed six major market and product segments. The six group executives reporting to Johnson headed the North America markets, Europe, Asia, merchant banking, trading and treasury, and Financial Institutions and Distribution groups. The remainder of the bank's operations were organized into three other major market groups: Developing Markets (including Third World countries), Regional Banking, and Operating Services (also called GEOSERVE), a unit formed in 1989 to handle all the bank's information and transactional services such as cash management, funds transfer, corporate trust, securities processing, and trade services.

THE FOCUS ON CUSTOMERS

The deregulated banking environment of the 1980s led to greatly expanded products offered by commercial banks for customers. These products generated fee-based income, an attractive alternative to the shrinking interest-rate margins earned on traditional lending activities. MHC's Trading and Treasury group engaged in interest rate swaps, foreign exchange transactions, private placements, underwriting, and securitization. Merchant Banking

This case was prepared by Professor Robert S. Kaplan.

provided financing for leveraged buyouts (LBOs), mergers and acquisitions, venture capital, and equity investment. MHC found that its credit customers provided an excellent base for marketing these fee-based products.

Herb Aspbury, Group Executive for the North American Markets Group, described the changing banking environment.

> In the past, corporate lending was the primary driver of bank profitability. The margins we earned on commitments and actual lending were so attractive that any credit-worthy loan we could make was bound to be profitable. The 1980s turned our world upside down. Relationships that had been highly profitable in the 1960s and 1970s became unattractive as profits margins from commercial lending contracted. In addition, commercial lending was consuming our scarcest resource: equity. The new fee-based services, offered by our product groups, provided profitable new opportunities for the bank without requiring heavy equity commitments.
>
> Most of our multinational companies, however, do not want to shop each of their individual financing transactions. These companies had become "overbanked," and they wanted to reduce the number of financial institutions that called on them. By dealing with only a limited number of banks, companies recognized that some business they give to a bank is a reward for providing other key products and services. The commercial lending units, therefore, had to become responsible for marketing the entire bank.
>
> Customers were also becoming more sophisticated about our own performance with them. Many of them surveyed their treasury managers worldwide and gave us an annual report card on how well MHC served their company. We were in a position where our customers were grading us but we couldn't grade our customers.

MHC's financial system was focused on profit center reporting, treating its geographical and product groups as separate reporting entities. Each department manager attempted to meet budgeted profitability goals. Up through the 1970s, this system reflected well the underlying economics of the bank. Commercial lending enjoyed high interest-rate margins that encouraged strong growth in lending activities. The auxiliary merchant and investment banking services were limited in scope and did not contribute greatly to overall bank profitability.

The banking world of the 1980s, however, required interdependencies among the different banking groups, and traditional profit center reporting no longer captured well the underlying economics of the bank. Commercial lending to a large multinational company might be unprofitable because of razor-thin margins and a heavy commitment of equity capital to support the lending relationship. But the lending activity became the entry point for a wide range of profitable merchant banking, treasury, trading, and corporate trust activities that the bank could perform for the client company.

Aspbury recalled the changes in thinking required by the new circumstances.

> We had too many people chasing too many accounts: 1,200 separate corporate relationships. We took a hard look at whether each of these relationships led to other services for the bank. Many didn't. We terminated relationships with several hundred companies, either by raising our lending margins or, more decisively, by curtailing lending activities altogether. We forced our lending officers to be realistic about their customers. For some companies, we were second or third-tier lenders, and we got none of their fee-based product business. With a scarcity of equity capital, there was no way these customers could be profitable lending at 10 basis points over LIBOR.[1] The reduction in number of clients served enabled us to cut the number of people in the lending group from 600 to 300.
>
> But this was only the start of what needed to be done. The various groups of the bank had now become completely interdependent. The North American Markets Group, with profitable relationships with U.S.-based companies, needed the European Group to support our U.S. companies' overseas activities, making calls and perhaps accepting low-margin business there. And we, in the U.S., had to service the European Group's clients that were expanding into North America.
>
> I felt the need for a system that could regularly tell me the total profitability of individual customers to MHC, accumulating the profits earned in all the MHC groups. That way, each group would be more willing to support and promote the work that earned profits in the operating statements of other groups.

PROFIT CENTER REPORTING

Business units were evaluated by a business Profit Center Report (see Exhibit 2). *Interest income,*

[1]LIBOR was the acronym for London Interbank Offered Rate, the interest rate in London at which banks loaned to each other (comparable to the Federal Funds rate in the U.S.).

the main revenue source, represented the interest received from commercial loans. Loan fees were interest-based fees earned by granting various forms of credit to customers. *Interest expense* was calculated either using an internal transfer pool rate or a market rate; the particular rate chosen was determined by the terms of the loan.

Operating income, representing noninterest-based fees, was added to the net interest margin, and *operating expenses* (salary and benefits of departmental personnel, occupancy charges, equipment, and other departmental expenses such as telephone, travel, etc.) were subtracted to obtain the *net contribution before interoffice*. This net contribution figure was the key performance measure for lending groups.

Cynthia Warrick, Senior Vice-President of the North American Markets Group and one of eight officers reporting directly to Herb Aspbury, commented on the value of the Profit Center Report.

> This report is all right for an officer working with credit-intensive companies in which all the action takes place within the lending activity. For example, last year we arranged the financing for a major acquisition by one of my customers. We earned a $7,000,000 agent's fee and everything was booked within my profit center.
>
> But an officer like Maryann Sudo handles 12 large multinational relationships, and many of their banking activities are in corporate trust, cash management, and international financing. Maryann's customers frequently show low profitability for lending activities, but the business she generates in other banking products with these companies could be highly profitable to the bank as a whole. Another one of my officers, Gerry Hannon, showed a moderate contribution margin for a large company last year, but his work with this customer led to our European Group's booking and syndicating a major financing transaction with the company's Turkish subsidiary. Herb and I believe that Gerry should get some recognition and reward for the fee the bank earned from this transaction.

In 1986, Herb Aspbury attempted to overcome the limitations of the traditional profit center report by developing a Customer Profitability Report (CPR). The first step was to recognize differences in effort required by officers to handle individual customers. Warrick commented on the difficulties this created.

> Officers were asked to fill out time sheets to record how much of their time was spent on each customer. It was a time-consuming job and very tedious. And the people didn't really believe the numbers at the end.

But even the crude results from this early model contained some surprises. Warrick recalled a large midwestern food processor with whom MHC had a long, close relationship.

> We knew that the company didn't pay us well for their credit facilities and other services, but the CPR made it clear that the profits we were earning were far too low for the effort we were expending with them. We took a much harder stance on receiving compensation from them for certain services and were able to bring that company to a satisfactory level of profitability.
>
> With other companies, we had a medium-level credit but no other business. We told our officers that if they could not develop additional MHC business with these companies, we would exit the relationship.
>
> Some company relationships showed up as highly profitable. The report confirmed that we wanted to continue to work closely with these companies. But this profitability would never have been revealed if we looked only at the lending relationship. One company's risk-adjusted ROE for commercial lending was only in the 8% to 10% range, but MHC served as the company's stock transfer agent, and did LBO work, private placements, and interest-rate swaps for their affiliates. Overall, the relationship with the company was among the most profitable the bank had.

John Poplawski was the Senior Vice-President of the Management Reporting Group of the Controllers department. Poplawski had supervised the development of the CPR system as well as the standard unit cost system for all of the bank's transactional products. He had encouraged the commercial lending divisions to participate in the development of CPR but initially found that only Herb Aspbury's North American Markets Group (NAM) actively supported the concept. He recalled that the early CPR reports had large gaps.

> The International people initially performed customer profitability studies only on an as-needed or special study basis. They felt this was adequate for their needs, so they stayed out of the CPR system. Unfortunately, the NAM people thought the report would be perfect the first time it appeared and

didn't recognize all the difficulties of linking a diverse, worldwide bank's operations into a single report. The officers themselves were not always aware of all of the transactions that a given company had with the bank. The officers also griped a lot about the time survey they had to complete. They thought it tedious and a complete waste of time.

THE LOAN PRICING MODEL

Bill Maass, Vice-President and Planning Officer of the Global Bank, had joined NAM in mid-1988 as Planning Officer. He inherited responsibility for refining the Customer Profitability Report. He saw an opportunity to integrate the CPR with a Loan Pricing Model that an outside consulting company had recently introduced into the bank. The Loan Pricing Model (LPM) was designed to determine the profitability of proposed loan transactions. Maass decided to update the model so that a risk-adjusted return on equity (ROE) figure could be produced flexibly and comprehensively.

> Suppose we have an existing line of credit with a major corporation. The company comes to us asking for a large increase in the line, say from its present level of $20 million up to $100 or $125 million, and they want to do this with a 25 basis point spread. We would like to know what the impact will be on our profitability and return on equity. Equity is our scarcest resource, and the amount of equity required for a loan depends on its riskiness. The Loan Pricing Model enables us to evaluate various alternatives for supplying the credit. It's also good for incremental decision analysis, including whether we should retain the loan, syndicate it, or sell it off.

Maass adapted the consultant's simple spread-sheet program into an interactive model that ran on a desk-top computer. Exhibit 3 presents a description of the data inputs required for the LPM.

The model calculated the *risk-adjusted assets (RAA)* of the facility as the sum of the following:

100% × Loans outstanding
 90% × Acceptances
 40% × Unused commitments (original tenor > 1 year)
 20% × Unused commitments (original tenor ≤ 1 year)
 10% × Unused lines of credit
 80% × Standby letters of credit (financial)
 50% × Standby letters of credit (performance)
 30% × Commercial letters of credit

The RAA figure was used for several calculations. MHC had developed a risk-adjusted loan loss provision by specifying a percentage, varying by facility grade, to be applied against the RAA of the facility. This loan loss provision was an expense to be deducted from the proposed revenue from the facility.

Maass also decided to use the RAA to allocate departmental expenses to the facility. In response to the opposition from lending officers to filling out customer-specific time reports, he eliminated the effort reporting system. In its place, Maass used a loan's RAA as a surrogate measure of the effort required to develop and monitor loans. He divided budgeted departmental direct expenses by the planned RAA for the period to obtain a ratio of expense dollars per RAA $. This ratio was used in the LPM to assign departmental expenses to loans. The expense ratio was increased for loans rated as requiring a high level of effort and decreased for loans that required a low level of effort.

The RAA was also used to estimate the amount of bank equity required for proposed facilities. Banks need to have a certain amount of equity to support the risk-adjusted assets of loans and commitments. In the original LPM, the consultant had assumed that risk-adjusted equity was a fixed percentage of risk-adjusted assets. Maass developed a finer partition based on the riskiness of the credit.

FACILITY GRADE	RISK-ADJUSTED EQUITY (RAE)%
1–3	2.0%
4–5	3.4
6–7	5.0
8–10	7.0

The risk-adjusted equity recognized that more capital is required for riskier loans.

The LPM then calculated the income, the risk-adjusted ROE, and the value added or destroyed by the proposed facility (see Exhibit 4). Officers were encouraged to run the model at both 0% utilization and 100% utilization so that they could price the loan to have approximately the same profitability, independent of utilization. If the ROE was below 16%, the officer could contemplate selling off part of the facility. This would reduce income and possibly even ROE, but since the smaller facility would require less bank equity, the total amount of value destroyed would decrease. Maass explained how the current pricing structure for lending led to more loan syndication and sales.

> Ten years ago, facilities were richly priced so that more retention was always more profitable. Now, pricing is so thin that more of a loan could be worse, as revealed by the value added/destroyed calculation. The interactive LPM encourages officers to do more sensitivity analysis on the terms of the deal and on the degree and terms of syndication so that they can determine the optimal amount of the loan for MHC to retain.

The revised Loan Pricing Model led naturally to a more accurate Customer Profitability Report. Maass stated,

> For the LPM, the officer estimates the size and utilization of the facility as well as projected expenses. For the CPR, we use the actual utilization of the facility and the actual departmental expenses. The CPR also evaluates the total relationship we have with the customer, including non-credit revenue streams, not just the incremental lending alternatives that get considered in the LPM. But technically, the profitability and ROE calculations are the same in the two models.

THE CPR INFORMATION SYSTEM

Hilary Gammage, Vice-President, was the Product Manager for CPR. She was responsible for accessing all the bank's data bases, providing the information processing for the report, and developing its form and distribution.

> Conceptually, the CPR seems like a simple concept, but to get this report to work requires an enormous amount of effort. A customer may have a dozen legal entities reflecting domestic subsidiaries, plus all of its international operations. Each entity has its own distinct ID code and each ID code could include dozens of transaction accounts, representing Demand Deposit Accounts (DDA), Loan Accounts, etc. One of the biggest jobs I have is just getting the data to *connect*, to recognize all the accounts the bank has with a given customer. We're still dependent on the knowledge of the account manager and department head for many of these relationships. And in linking with the bank's systems domestically and around the world, we discovered that different units had different cut-off dates for operations, and different ID numbers for the same customers.
>
> For some transactions, the loan may have originated in one location, be funded out of a second location,

and sent to the customer in yet a third location. We have to be able to pull together the threads from all these transactions. Our proof that we have all transactions is to tie to the bank's legal books, but that still doesn't tell us things are linked correctly. Another "linking" problem is attaching the appropriate expenses to each transaction. Loan provisions can be calculated from customer data using Bill Maass's model, but direct and operating expenses don't come with customer tags attached to them. Correct alignment of costs to revenues is a big analysis job and initially needed a lot of local involvement. We also have to link with the Commercial Loan and Exposure databases to get detailed information on opening and closing loans and facility grades and amounts. We access the GEOSERVE database for the profitability of the customer's products supplied by GEOSERVE. And we need to hook up with the Merchant Banking and Treasury and Trading information systems to be able to track the fees they are earning from individual customers. Even today, the CPR reports are far from complete, but we're getting better at including more of a customer's transactions with us in a single report.

Poplawski reinforced the difficulty of linking all the bank's information systems.

> Initially, we couldn't get the cooperation of the International Groups for CPR. But now, with the emphasis on cost control and centralized reporting, they want to participate in the system, and that has made it a lot easier to link overseas operations to NAM's customers.

CURRENT STATUS

The CPR system had been operating in Aspbury's North American Markets group for two years and was generally well accepted despite several remaining limitations. Exhibit 5 shows a sample CPR report for a large customer. Aspbury was looking ahead to getting wider bank acceptance for the concept.

> I sense some resistance to applying the CPR report more widely in the bank because it can expose unprofitable operations, especially in other groups. It will force the bank to confront why it is operating in certain geographical areas and in certain product lines.
>
> We also need to get a longer time-line for evaluating our profitability with customers. Right now, we're running the model quarterly to stay current on our activities, but even a calendar year may be too short for evaluating customer relationships. In any given

year, a company may not use any of its commercial banking relationships. If the company represents a key relationship for us, we need to be patient.

Maryann Sudo, a Vice-President and Relationship Manager in NAM, noted problems she still had with the report.

After each report is issued, we must spend time supplementing and correcting the numbers. Sometimes we can't reconcile to the RAA reported for the customer. We also have to call up the Trust Department to get the profitability of their activities with our customers, and the overseas operations are just beginning to come on to the system. But the systems people seem committed to correcting the errors and making the report work.

At the end of the day, however, the way we use the report is pretty simple. We either increase or decrease our business with the customer, change prices, or even drop companies. We detected two customers in the Midwest who just used us for our credit facilities, which were priced at low margins. Both companies, it turned out, had spread their banking business too thin, across too many banks. We told these customers that we couldn't continue in this way, calling on them several times a year and tying up equity in thinly priced loan commitments.

Interestingly, neither company wanted to terminate their relationship with us. The companies agreed to have us work with them by phone, or when they made trips to New York, helping us to reduce our expenses. We pulled out of both credit facilities. The companies started to use our fee-based services, such as cash management and foreign exchange, much more actively and we see some potential for attractively priced financing. These changes have transformed companies with a 2% ROE into profitable relationships.

We are beginning to use the CPR concept to price out prospective business. For example, we might agree to lend to a Mexican subsidiary of a U.S. company at a competitive price when we have the expectation that the business will lead to some debt/equity swaps. Another customer has asked for a lower price for cash management services. Our enthusiasm in responding to such a request would be determined by the existing ROE of the customer relationship.

Cynthia Warrick, Sudo's manager, also strongly supported the CPR report.

Herb Aspbury keeps pushing us on knowing the profitability of our customer relationships. Some of my officers never turn in a proposal now without a customer profitability report accompanying the analysis. But we're still not picking up enough of the

data. One of our largest customers shows only a 3% ROE and an equity value destroyed of almost $6 million. But the company has all its corporate trust work done by the bank, and the profitability from that isn't yet in the report.

We probably should revisit the expense distribution method. Officers now annotate their CPR reports to note major discrepancies between actual effort and the amount allocated based on RAA. I think we need more accuracy here, but I don't want to return to filling out time sheets. Account managers know in general where they spend most of their time and effort. Perhaps they can just estimate the percentage of effort spent with each of their customers to give us a better picture of the different relationships.

I'm sure we'll solve these data problems in the near future. The big issue that the bank needs to resolve is whether we should double-count the revenues from transactions in each group or whether we should negotiate some fee-splitting arrangement. We're currently advising a major U.S. client on financing for a new venture in Hungary. The bank will earn a large advisory fee for this service, plus a syndication fee when the credit is booked out of the London office, and the normal interest-rate spread on the credit itself. The fees could total $1 million this year. Gerry Hannon, in my region, sourced the transaction with his client and did much of the upfront work, but the transaction will take place in Europe. Who should get credit for the fees?

Herb Aspbury wants to measure success through the profitability of the global relationship. Fee splitting can be too arbitrary. But other group executives want a formal fee-splitting arrangement, perhaps formula-based by type of product, feeling that people will be more motivated if their recorded income is "real" rather than a shadow amount. The bank's bonus compensation is based on recorded profitability, and many top bank executives feel that pay-for-performance could become compromised if too much attention is paid to "shadow profits."

Richard Copeland, Vice-President and Planning Officer of the Developing Markets group, described the problems of attempting to assign profits to the various banking groups.

You might have a Brazilian loan that is funded out of London but managed out of New York. You can transfer the loan revenue from London to New York, but then you should pass back, as well, the expenses from London to New York for operating the loan. And the adjustments should be made on the balance sheet too, to recognize equity commitments.

The choice of how to recognize profits really comes down to two alternatives. Number 1, we can attempt to match expenses against revenues and charge out for services provided to other MHC units; or, Number 2, each unit keeps its own expenses and we fee-split the revenues on deals involving multiple departments. I think we're likely to choose Number 2. Expenses are too difficult to apportion, and charging for services based on costs puts operating units into a cost center mentality that provides the wrong kind of motivation.

The current thinking in the bank was to customize the fee-splitting arrangement by type of product. A marketing officer might make the initial contact for a private placement and then bring in the product specialist, who would place the security with investors. The marketing officer might get 30% of the total fee reflected in his P&L for this work. For a more specialized product, where greater expertise was required by the product specialist, the marketing percentage would be lower, closer to 20%.

Large deals of a special nature, such as receiving advisory fees in excess of $500,000, would be shared on a case-by-case basis. All participants would provide their own judgments about their individual contributions to the deal with the percentages reviewed and finalized at the senior executive level.

Copeland summarized the issues involved.

Tom Johnson keeps emphasizing the importance of teamwork and increasing the ROE of the entire global bank, regardless of where the revenue is earned. But integrating this goal into the messy details of profit and revenue measurement and incentive compensation still needs to be worked out.

We now understand that we must have a Global Customer-Product Profitability Report, similar to what the North American Markets Group initiated. But we will need different reports for the bank's individual profit centers. The bank executives seem chastened by the experience of a large Wall Street investment firm that had allowed double-counting of revenues for all its units. Each SBU thought it was very profitable, but overall expenses continued to grow, and the company as a whole became highly unprofitable and almost failed. If the bank is to focus on ROE, it must know which businesses are pulling their weight and which are not, and which products are the most profitable for the bank given its scarce resources of people and capital.

Product people and marketing people are now having intense discussions about fee-splitting. This dialogue, however, may be what Tom Johnson intends to happen. Our companies want a single relationship with MHC, not to have 20 different people calling on them. In the fee-splitting arrangements currently being discussed, the sharing percentages for the marketing units for most corporate finance products vary between 20% and 30%, so it may not be a big deal which number gets selected for each product.

A marketing officer, however, remained skeptical about the equity of any formula-based fee-splitting arrangement.

I prefer the shadow profitability approach rather than any formula-based scheme. I may work four months on a deal with one of my customers, pulling my product colleagues along, but end up getting credit for only 20% of the fees. This doesn't begin to reflect the contribution I feel I made to the success of the transaction.

EXHIBIT 1

MANUFACTURERS HANOVER CORPORATION:
CUSTOMER PROFITABILITY REPORT

Selected Financial Data

	1989	1988	1987	1986	1985
Income Statement Summary					
Total interest revenue	$6,888	$6,637	$6,324	$6,538	$7,322
Total interest expense	5,254	4,645	4,413	4,506	5,210
Net interest revenue	1,634	1,992	1,911	2,032	2,112
Credit loss provision	1,404	502	2,236	859	623
Noninterest revenue	1,532	1,908	1,433	1,428	1,063
Noninterest expense	2,124	2,120	2,346	2,157	1,955
Income (loss) before extraordinary items	($588)	$ 752	($1,140)	$ 411	$ 407
Balance Sheet Summary					
Total loans	$39,145	$49,024	$55,617	$56,273	$58,466
Credit loss reserve	2,677	2,346	2,652	1,008	814
Total assets	60,479	66,710	73,348	74,397	76,526
Total deposits	41,994	41,714	45,176	45,544	46,261
Long-term debt	3,400	8,136	8,473	7,357	7,867
Shareholders' equity	3,381	3,251	2,704	3,766	3,547
Selected Ratios					
Total equity/total assets	5.59	4.87	3.69	5.06	4.64
Tangible equity/total assets	5.17	4.16	2.90	4.26	3.69
Loss reserve/total loans	6.84	4.78	4.77	1.79	1.39
Number employees (full-time equivalent)	20,034	23,094	28,669	29,912	31,814

EXHIBIT 2

MANUFACTURERS HANOVER CORPORATION: CUSTOMER PROFITABILITY REPORT
North American Division
Monthly & Year-To-Date Comparison
Financial Summary
(units are thousands $)

RUN DATE : 19-JAN-90
FUN TIME : 20:38
CENTER   : 68339   MIDWEST/GREAT LAKES / WARRICK   FOR THE PERIOD ENDING : DECEMBER 31, 1989

	MONTH-TO-DATE 12/31/89						YEAR-TO-DATE 12/31/89					
RETURN ON EARN ASSETS				VARIANCE					VARIANCE		RETURN ON EARN ASSETS	
ACTUAL %	PLAN %	12/31/89 ACTUAL	12/31/89 PLAN	FAVORABLE/(UNFAV) $	%		12/31/89 ACTUAL	12/31/89 PLAN	FAVORABLE/(UNFAV) $	%	ACTUAL %	PLAN %
10.20	9.78	3,141	4,653	(1,511)	(32)	Interest income on loans	45,567	56,921	(11,354)	(20)	10.72	10.10
.01	.03	5	12	(7)	(62)	Tax-free interest adjustment	65	181	(116)	(64)	.02	.03
.35	.58	109	275	(166)	(60)	Total domestic loan fees	2,690	3,297	(607)	(18)	.63	.59
10.56	10.38	3,255	4,940	(1,685)	(34)	Total interest income & fees	48,322	60,399	(12,077)	(20)	11.37	10.72
1.81	.91	558	434	(124)	(29)	Transfer pool expense (net)	10,512	6,260	(4,251)	(68)	2.47	1.11
.45	.43	139	204	65	32	Other interest expense	1,501	2,494	993	40	.35	.44
5.29	6.37	1,629	3,032	1,404	46	LIBOR interest expense	23,010	36,371	13,361	37	5.41	6.45
5.74	6.80	1.768	3,236	1,468	45	Total interest expense	24,511	38,865	14,354	37	5.77	6.90
7.55	7.71	2,326	3,671	1,345	37	Total funding cost	35,023	45,125	10,102	22	8.24	8.01
3.01	2.67	928	1,269	(340)	(27)	Net interest margin	13,299	15,274	(1,975)	(13)	3.13	2.71
3.01	2.67	928	1,269	(340)	(27)	Funds profit	13,299	15,274	(1,975)	(13)	3.13	2.71
2.61	2.77	803	1,321	(518)	(39)	Total operating income	19,321	15,847	3,475	22	4.55	2.81
.77	.59	236	279	43	15	Salary & benefits	2,734	3,175	441	14	.64	.56
.17	.10	51	50	(2)	(3)	Occupancy	596	599	2	0	.14	.11
.03	.06	10	26	16	60	Equipment	201	314	113	36	.05	.06
.22	.20	69	97	28	29	Other operating expenses	394	1,158	764	66	.09	.21
1.19	.95	367	452	85	19	Total operating expense	3,925	5,246	1,321	25	.92	.93
4.43	4.49	1,364	2,137	(773)	(36)	Net cont. before interoffice	28,695	25,875	2,821	11	6.75	4.59
.26	.00	81	0	(81)	0	Total interoffice expense	1,042	0	(1,042)	0	.25	.00
4.17	4.49	1,284	2,137	(854)	(40)	Net income before taxes	27,653	25,875	1,779	7	6.51	4.59
4.17	4.49	1,284	2,137	(854)	(40)	Net income after taxes	27,653	25,875	1,779	7	6.51	4.59
		100,800	85,826	14,974	17	Reference rate loans	125,871	92,285	33,587	36		
		207,031	397,147	(190,116)	(48)	LIBOR loans	242,793	390,773	(147,981)	(38)		
		20,266	45,650	(25,384)	(56)	Money market loans	16,957	46,642	(29,685)	(64)		
		8,817	0	8,817	0	CD-based loans	11,655	0	11,655	0		
		1,525	4,639	(3,114)	(67)	Tax-exempt loans	2,083	5,741	(3,658)	(64)		
		21,436	21,621	(185)	(1)	Fixed rate loans	22,757	22,512	245	1		
		2,656	5,539	(2,883)	(52)	G/L overdraft balances	4,078	5,539	(1,461)	(26)		
		240	0	240	0	Principle adjustments	(1,109)	0	(1,109)	0		
		0	0	0	0	Deferred income FASB 91	0	0	0	0		
		362,771	560,422	(197,651)	(35)	Total loans	425,085	583,492	(138,407)	(25)		
		60,405	70,671	(10,266)	(15)	Total demand deposits	58,301	69,559	(11,258)	(16)		

EXHIBIT 3

MANUFACTURERS HANOVER CORPORATION:
CUSTOMER PROFITABILITY REPORT
Data Input for Loan Pricing Model

To use the Loan Pricing Model, the lending officer entered a number of parameters describing the proposed financing transaction.

1. *Facility Type*[1]
   Line of credit
   Revolving credit
   Term loan
   Standby letter of credit
   Commercial letter of credit
   Banker's acceptance

2. *Facility Grade*
   A numeric grade (from 1 to 10) reflecting the company's risk classification. Similar in concept to a bond rating, most of North American Markets group's customers were in the 4 or 5 category.

3. *Facility Amount and Usage Percentage*
   The size of the facility requested and the officer's estimate of the amount that would actually be used. As more of a facility was used by a company, MHC had to supply more capital to support the loan. Typical pricing for a facility to a highly rated customer could be 10 basis points on the commitment amount and Libor plus 1/4 on the amount actually used.

4. *Tenor*
   Length of commitment; facilities for less than one year were considered less risky than facilities in excess of a year. This split reflected guidelines established by the Federal Reserve Board.

5. *Pricing Index and Spread (in Basis Points)*
   Reference rate
   Libor
   Certificate of deposit
   Money market

6. *Fees (in $ or Basis Points)*
   Amount earned (or paid) as agent, arranger, underwriter, syndicator, or originator; fees could be earned based on commitment, actual usage, and on loan prepayment.

7. *Effort Required (Low, Medium, or High)*
   Officer entered relative amount of effort required for the proposed transaction.

---

[1]A *facility* is the general term used by bankers to describe an agreement or commitment from the bank to lend money when a company needs it. A loan would be the amount actually borrowed by the company under the facility arrangement.

EXHIBIT 4

MANUFACTURERS HANOVER CORPORATION: CUSTOMER PROFITABILITY REPORT

LMP Calculation of ROE and Value Added/Destroyed

Revenues:	Loan spread	[Interest rate spread $\times$ outstanding balance]
	Value of balances	
	Loan fees	[fees in lieu of compensating balances, facility fees, interest-related commitment fees, loan orgination fees, agent and syndication fees]
	Equity credit[1]	[Risk-adjusted equity $\times$ equity credit rate]
Expenses:	Risk-adjusted loan loss provision	
	Departmental expense allocation (based on RAA and estimated effort required)	
	Expenses of loan syndication and sales	
	Income taxes	

Income = revenues − expenses

ROE = income/risk-adjusted equity.

Value Added/(Destroyed)

MHC estimated that it needed a 16% ROE for its common stock to trade at book value. Loans with an ROE in excess of this 16% rate were considered to add value to stockholders, and loans that yielded less than 16% were destroying stockholder value. A final calculation revealed the amount of stockholder value that was added or destroyed by the proposed transaction.

$$\text{Market-to-book ratio} = \frac{\text{ROE} - \text{corporate growth rate [8.4\%]}}{16\% \text{ [hurdle rate]} - 8.4\% \text{ [growth rate]}}$$

Market value = (market-to-book ratio) $\times$ book value

Book value = Risk-adjusted equity

Value added/ (destroyed) = market value − book value

[1]The equity credit reflects a credit for that portion of the facility funded with interest-free equity.

EXHIBIT 5

MANUFACTURERS HANOVER CORPORATION
Customer/Product Profitability Reporting

FAMILY	FAMILY CREDIT GRADE 5			FAMILY DEPT. 425	12-MONTH PERIOD ENDING 06/30/90	RUN DATE 09/20/90	($000)
	NAD1	MHBD	Subtotal	ITA	BIS	OTHER	
On & off balance sheet							
Loans outstanding	$20,918	$1	$20,919		$8,195		
Acceptances							
Standby L/C S							
Commercial L/C S	2,111		2,111				
Unused commitments	65,838		65,838				
Unused lines	27,548		27,548				
Risk-adjusted assets	50,642	1	50,642				
Risk-adjusted common equity	1,801	4	1,805				
Income statement							
Net interest income	$203	−$0	$203		$647		
Domestic loan fees	76		76				
Commitment fees	24		24				
L/C fees	3		3				
Agent fees							
Syndication fees							
Other fees (credit only)	−3		−3				
Noncredit fees	258	33	291		17		
Value of balances required for credit: excess/(deficient)	21	0	21		89		
Required for noncredit	339		339				
(Deficient)	−329	−0	−329				
Additional value	49		49				
Equity credit	174	0	174				
Total revenue	815	33	848				
Expenses							
Risk-adjusted loan loss provision	$152	$0	$152				
Direct	152		152				
Net interoffice (credit & general)	64		64				
Net interoffice (noncredit)	220		220				
Corporate overhead	66		66				
Other balance sheet charges	41	0	41				
Pre-tax income	120	33	154				
Net income	70	21	91				
Return on equity	4	521	5				
Value added/(destroyed)	−$2,872	268	−2,604				

(continued)

EXHIBIT 5 *(cont.)*

FAMILY	FAMILY CREDIT GRADE 5	FAMILY DEPT. 425	12-MONTH PERIOD ENDING 06/30/90	RUN DATE 09/20/90	($000)
Investment banking					
Acquisition finance					
Risk exposure					
Foreign exchange					
Structured finance					
Private placement					
ESOPS					
Mergers & acquisitions					
Corporate advisory					
Capital markets					
L S & S (bid notes)	−7				
Agent bank services					
Other					
Total	−7				
BIS					
AIM					
Sovereign risk group					
Total					
ITA					
Bond trustee					
Comm. paper issuance					
Escrow					
Other corporate trust					
Dividend reinvestment					
Reorganization					
Other stock transfer					
Coupon paying					
Institutional custody					
Master trust					
Other instit. asset					
Total					
Cash management					
Collection services	15				
Disbursement services	71				
Interplex					
Total	86				
Total MHC revenue	1,593				

READINGS

Why SG&A Doesn't Always Work

Thomas S. Dudick

With global competition increasing, U.S. manufacturing companies are giving their nonmanufacturing costs much closer scrutiny than they've traditionally done and with good reason. Over the past ten years, selling, general, and administrative (SG&A) expenses have been rising as a percentage of the total cost of doing business. Today, because of higher selling, advertising, warehousing, and other costs, it's not unusual for SG&A to approach 50% or more of a company's manufacturing costs. In the high-technology sector, SG&A can easily approach 100% of manufacturing expenses.

To achieve better control over nonmanufacturing costs, manufacturing executives are developing more precise measures of their SG&A expenses. Many manufacturing companies, however, continue to make the mistake of relying on "one size fits all" methods of allocating SG&A costs. I have observed this process many times in the course of my work as a manufacturing cost consultant. It can be found in every industry and in companies that are well managed in other respects.

In organizations that take a production-line approach to SG&A, the controller typically uses the percent-of-sales, cost-of-sales, or some other arbitrary method of allocation. When percent of sales, one of the most common methods, is used, the corporate controller simply divides the total corporate sales revenue by the total companywide SG&A expense and applies the resulting percentage to all product lines. If, for example, the company's SG&A cost is 10% of its sales revenue, then that's the percentage the company controller will charge to each product line based on its sales. Under the cost-of-sales method, the controller charges each product line an SG&A amount based on its share of

manufacturing cost (materials, direct labor, and factory overhead).

Although the use of such standardized, across-the-board methods simplifies SG&A cost accounting for company accountants working under the pressure of having to meet financial reporting deadlines, these arbitrary measures can distort the profitability of a company's different product lines and market segments. Profits can be inflated and losses understated using broadbrush SG&A accounting methods. While a variety of distortions are possible, there are, as we shall see, several ways of correcting for them.

MATERIALS COST DISTORTIONS

When a company's raw materials costs vary greatly among its product lines, severe distortions in SG&A costs can result if accountants use conventional percent-of-sales or cost-of-sales methods of allocation.

The president of a sewing notions company I know of had been puzzled by the profit performance of his woolen goods line. Although his woolen goods sales had been steadily increasing, the line showed a loss. Because wool had a higher materials cost than the company's other products, it had a low gross margin. The president discovered that the profit for the woolen goods line was being penalized because the company's use of the percent-of-sales expensing formula meant that wool's high materials cost resulted in an overstatement of its SG&A costs.

The company controller suggested that they use a conversion cost ratio, which would eliminate profit distortions caused by differences in raw materials costs. To construct the conversion ratio, the controller added up the company's direct factory labor and overhead and divided it into the total SG&A expense. He used the resulting conversion ratio to allocate SG&A costs to each product line based on each line's direct factory labor and overhead. Now the woolen goods line showed a profit, while the other lines showed reduced net income.

Although a conversion cost ratio is usually an improvement over the percent-of-sales method, it too has built-in distortions and therefore should be used with caution. If a company has certain product lines with a high percentage of finished components bought from vendors, those lines will incur much lower conversion costs. Their SG&A charges would be understated and their profitability inflated.

FINE-TUNING SG&A COSTS

Is there a better method? Since any across-the-board measure—including a conversion ratio—can lead to distorted perceptions of profitability, the best solution is to develop a finely tuned allocation method that will give more precise measures of the SG&A costs incurred by each of a company's product lines. Each of the following cases illustrates how a specific type of distortion can be avoided using more accurate SG&A cost information.

Product-line distortions

Confronted with intensifying foreign and domestic competition, the senior management of an electronics company decided to review its manufacturing and nonmanufacturing costs. As part of that review, it looked at how the company's accountants were calculating SG&A expenses for each of the corporation's major product lines.

Up to that time, the company's accounting staff had been using the percent-of-sales method for allocating SG&A expenses to each of the manufacturing divisions. Some division managers were dissatisfied with the result, among them the vice president of the television division. He complained that his division's SG&A charge was inflated because his product line used high-cost finished components—picture tubes and cabinets.

The problem arose because these components had a high percentage of materials content in the selling price. This inflated his division's SG&A

allocation in comparison with other divisions whose materials content was much lower as a percentage of sales. As Part A of *Exhibit I* shows, the television line had a pretax loss of 3.9% using the percent-of-sales method. Its share of the corporate SG&A was 24% during that period. To get a more accurate measure of each line's profit-and-loss performance, a specialist from marketing and another from manufacturing services developed a more precise SG&A allocation formula.

The marketing specialist pointed out that reliable information was readily available to break down the selling expenses for each product line. Fully 90% of the selling cost consisted of payroll expenses. After the specialist identified which product lines were handled by the different salespeople, the annual payroll costs for each product line could be calculated. The remaining nonpayroll component, 10% of the cost, was allocated on the same basis as the other 90%. Warehousing costs could be allocated to each product line by counting the number of bays used to store each product. Percentage rates of space utilization could then be calculated by product line.

Advertising expenses would continue to be allocated on the traditional percent-of-sales basis because the company's advertising campaigns usually promoted the corporation and its entire product line as a whole. Allocating promotional costs posed no problem either because promotions were always carried out on an individual product-line basis.

The manufacturing services specialist recommended that the corporate purchasing department charge each product line according to the amount of material it actually used. Formerly, corporate purchasing had consolidated the purchase of high-volume materials used in all product lines. He recommended that the industrial relations department charge each product line according to its percentage share of the total number of employees. Finally, he suggested that corporate accounting and data processing costs be parceled out to the various product lines on the following basis:

- Payroll costs would be charged based on the number of employees in each division.
- Customer billing costs would be allocated according to the number of invoices or invoice lines for each division.

Exhibit I.   How SG&A Cost-allocation Methods Affect Pretax Profits

PRODUCT LINE	PART A CONVENTIONAL PERCENT-OF-SALES METHOD		PART B NEW PRODUCT-SPECIFIC METHOD	
	SG&A CHARGE AS A PERCENTAGE OF TOTAL CORPORATE SG&A	PRETAX PROFIT	SG&A CHARGE AS A PERCENTAGE OF TOTAL CORPORATE SG&A	PRETAX PROFIT
Television	24.0%	(3.9)%	17.2%	(1.4)%
Cathode-ray tubes	17.7	5.4	10.2	9.1
Phosphors	2.0	16.5	1.2	20.0
Television components	27.9	15.4	28.4	15.3
Electronics	2.4	7.4	3.3	4.5
Fabricated parts	6.0	13.1	2.6	17.9
Lighting products	20.0	22.0	37.1	14.5
Total	100.0%		100.0%	

- Sales reports prepared by corporate staff would be allocated on the basis of the same ratio used to charge sales office overhead to each product line.
- Internal auditing expenses would be charged to each product line by multiplying the number of auditor days spent in each division by the auditor's per diem fee.

The manufacturing services specialist also suggested that corporate quality control costs be divided according to the number of QC employees assigned to each division. Other corporate services that couldn't easily be charged to each product line could be allocated by simply dividing those costs by the number of product lines. Each line would absorb an equal amount of the costs on the assumption that these services were equally available to all divisions at any time.

Top management implemented the specialists' recommendations. The impact of the new method on the profit performance of each of the company's product lines can be seen in Part B of *Exhibit I*.

The results confirmed what the vice president in charge of the television division had long suspected: his division's financial performance had been depressed under the old SG&A allocation measure. The product-specific SG&A method reduced his division's share of corporate SG&A from 24% to 17.2% and his division's pretax loss from 3.9% to 1.4%. The new method also led to a near doubling of the cathode-ray tube division's profit—from 5.4% to 9.1%.

Market segment distortions

A company's cost accounting system may also fail to capture accurately the SG&A costs of selling to different market segments. A manufacturer of power cords, switches, sockets, and other electrical fixtures sold to three different market segments: original equipment manufacturers, retail outlets (replacement market), and building contractors (distributor market). In the past, the company had made no effort to analyze its SG&A costs by market segment; it simply assessed a flat SG&A percentage against all sales. The company's controller finally recognized the need to allocate SG&A costs based on the real costs of selling to each market. More finely tuned SG&A cost information would give top management a better picture of the true profitability of the different market segments.

The controller requested managers in the different departments to calculate advertising, warehousing, selling, and other nonmanufacturing costs for the three market segments. Warehousing costs, for example, could be parceled out according to the space used in serving the different market groups. The hours spent by the sales force in the field were also logged and allocated to the different market segments.

As *Exhibit II* shows, the new method for allocating SG&A revealed substantial disparities in costs among the three segments in most expense categories—disparities not caused by differences in the kinds of electrical products sold in each market.

Freight, packing, and warehousing costs, for example, were much lower for the OEM market than for the other two markets. The reason, the controller learned, was that OEMs typically order in bulk. Packing and freight costs for the replacement market were much higher because orders placed by hardware stores and other retailers are usually smaller and more varied. The cost of selling to the OEM market was also lower because the company's salespeople didn't have to call on OEM accounts as

frequently as on accounts in the other two markets. What top management learned was that the OEM market was more profitable than had been assumed.

Distortions caused by low volume

The percent-of-sales method for allocating SG&A costs can be especially troublesome when sales of one product line constitute a very small percentage of total sales. The CEO of a sunglasses manufacturing company decided to add a line of hair combs. Because demand for sunglasses is seasonal, he had excess capacity on his plastic-molding machines. He would incur no additional selling costs because his salespeople could easily sell the comb line when calling on their sunglasses accounts.

The CEO told the controller to charge the comb line for its fair share of SG&A costs, and the controller did so using the percent-of-sales method. The marketing group had projected that combs would account for 15% of the company's $21.5 million in total revenue, and the controller used that percentage to calculate the comb line's share of SG&A. (The comb line's share of revenue was small because its unit cost was much lower than that of the sunglasses line.)

Exhibit II.   Itemized SG&A Costs by Market Segment

ITEMIZED EXPENSES	OEM MARKET	REPLACEMENT MARKET	DISTRIBUTOR MARKET
Selling	3.1%	4.3%	4.4%
Warehousing	1.4	2.7	2.4
Packing	1.7	3.5	2.5
Advertising and promotion	1.8	3.5	3.2
Bad debts	0.1	0.9	0.3
Freight	0.9	2.0	1.3
Administration*	2.6	2.3	2.6
Total SG&A as a percentage of sales	11.6%	19.2%	16.7%

*Administration includes any remaining costs after direct charges have been made to the various manufacturing units. The direct charges include such services as payroll, billing, accounts payable, and any other corporate charges that can be specifically identified by location. These represent costs that would have been incurred by the individual plants as manufacturing overhead if they were completely decentralized.

The company's SG&A expense (excluding sales commissions) was assessed as a fixed monthly cost. Based on sales projections, total SG&A would amount to approximately $3.8 million a year (or 18% of total sales). The controller apportioned 15% of the monthly SG&A charge ($48,462) to combs and 85% ($274,620) to sunglasses.

The comb line's low share of total revenues led to erratic fluctuations in its profit performance. When sunglasses sales dipped during the off-season, the effect on the comb line's share of sales was magnified—because of the comb line's smaller percentage of revenue. The SG&A cost for sunglasses varied no more than three percentage points, from 11% in April to 14% in June. In sharp contrast, the SG&A cost for combs swung from 21% in April to 13% in June.

As the controller explained to the CEO, the erratic profit performance of the comb line resulted from the magnified impact of the sharp change in sunglasses sales on the comb line's percentage of revenue. This caused combs to be overcharged for SG&A. More sales effort was required to sell sunglasses; advertising, promotion, and packaging costs were also much higher for sunglasses.

The controller solved the problem by charging the comb line a flat 5% of total corporate SG&A. This reduced the variability in the comb line's SG&A from 7% of sales in April to 4% of sales in June. He explained that although month-to-month variation in profitability would still occur, the profit figures for combs would be more accurate and stable using the new, more realistic SG&A percentage figure.

When companies rely on undifferentiated, "one size fits all" cost accounting methods without regard to important differences among product lines and markets, measures of profitability can become distorted. Since SG&A costs can vary widely among a company's products or markets, more precise methods for allocating SG&A will give management a more accurate reading of each product line's profit.

There is, however, an important caveat to be made. Corporate controllers must decide how far to go in breaking down SG&A expenses. It may not pay, for example, to count the number of phone calls made or salesperson hours spent in the field per account in allocating selling costs to a product line. Too much refinement may impose unjustifiable record-keeping costs.

A good case can be made, however, that reasonably detailed breakdowns should be carried out since in most cases SG&A percentage breakdowns will need to be made only once during the year, when the annual financial plan is developed. With more accurate cost and profit measures, management can know which product lines and markets most deserve corporate resources and attention.

Customer Profitability Analysis

Robin Bellis-Jones

Fuelled by pressure from the City, the post-war retail sector has merged, acquired and rationalised to the point where a limited number of major retailers can wield great purchasing power at the expense of their suppliers. The latter, in terms of their commercial clout, remain relatively fragmented and powerless except where a particularly strong brand name exists. In this increasingly competitive environment, customer service has become a key element in the battle for both volume and margin.

Suppliers have often responded by either increasing discounts or increasing the level of service available to their retailers, hoping that the additional volume generated will protect *their* profits. Howev-

Reprinted from *Management Accounting* [UK] (February 1989), pp 26-28, with permission.

er, the additional volumes or services often create extra activity—and cost—which more than offsets the additional margins generated.

Confusion in this key area has led to a certain amount of conflict between accounting and marketing staff and has led to a proliferation of courses such as 'Marketing for Accountants' and 'Finance for Non-Financial Managers'. But although such courses increase understanding, they do not address the fundamental commercial issues.

In fact many companies have resigned themselves to low, decreasing profitability on the grounds that the trading environment is 'becoming more difficult'. But the reality is that they squander otherwise profitable parts of their business by supplying service at *below* true cost.

Sophisticated analysis of all costs and revenues generated by outlet, rather than simply the gross margin less trade discount, is the solution.

Companies need to be able to quantify and present the implications of the trading relationship so that it can add *real* value to commercial decisions. Such an approach should answer key questions which conventional accounting fails to address—questions such as:

• Does market sector X meet our profitability criteria? Has it ever? Can it ever? If so, how?
• Which account generates the greatest profit contribution and how best can we protect it?
• What are the maximum discount/service packages we can afford in the next round of negotiations with our largest customers while still meeting our profit objectives?
• What type of account should we focus our new business effort on for maximum profitability?
• Do our large accounts really make money? Under what conditions are we prepared to walk away from that volume and what will we have to do as a consequence?
• Does this product contribute sufficiently to profitability to justify retaining it in the range?
• Should we stay in this market?

If these questions cannot be answered accurately then the success of related decisions will be minimal.

Crucially, competitors who do understand how their costs are driven can significantly enhance their profitability against the sector trend.

THE BARRIERS TO MEASURING ACCOUNT PROFITABILITY

Although most companies recognise the need to answer such questions most are constrained by the following factors:

• Conventional accounting philosophy is inappropriate to this type of analysis.
• Most companies are organised along functional lines, where the operations being quantified cross several functional boundaries. Often, some functions won't support such analysis, thereby devaluing the effort of others—a kind of 'functional myopia'.
• Some companies feel it's inappropriate to allocate the cost of providing a service to those who receive it.
• Many companies place strong emphasis on the measurement of profit centre performance. Although this orientation is valuable in measuring overall performances, it is also introverted in that it does not focus on customer performance at the individual level—the level at which many commercial decisions are made.

As a result of these constraints few companies get beyond measuring account profitability at the level of gross margin net of trade discount; they prefer to focus on easy rather than valuable measurements. In other words most companies understand the issues but do not know how to resolve them.

This [reading] describes a solution which provides an immensely powerful and flexible means of quantifying and understanding the trading relationship, as well as a means of supporting key commercial decisions.

We describe the technique as customer profitability analysis (CPA).

CUSTOMER PROFITABILITY ANALYSIS

CPA demands that *all* costs relevant to the trading relationship with any particular customer outlet are taken into account. This is necessary because gross margin net of trade discount is *not* an accurate measure of profitability. This approach is illustrated in Figure 1.

The CTN (confectioner/tobacconist/newsagent) outlet shown in the diagram provides a graphic example. At face value it generates a high level of contribution but, once all of the variable costs of each service aspect are taken into account, it is in fact marginally *unprofitable*.

Some outlets suffer a much more severe reduc-

Figure 1.

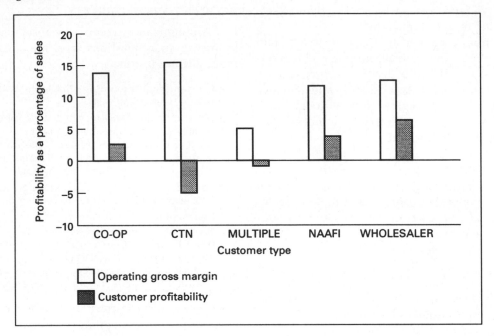

tion in profitability than others. Whatever the effect, however, reduced profit is caused by those overhead costs which vary with both activity, timescale and customer type and which could and should touch on most functions within the business. The following list is a sample cross-section of such overheads:

- Quality control
- Merchandising
- Salesforce
- Retrospective discounts
- Distribution
- Purchasing
- Promotions
- Financing costs
- Enquiries

The fundamental question which needs to be asked of each overhead element is, 'What aspect of the relationship with the customer does this support, and how does it vary with activity levels and customer?'. For example, the cost of full-pallet transactions is quite different to that of break bulk; telesales is more time-efficient than a field salesforce; merchandising is required by some outlets but

not others; some customers demand pre-priced goods whereas others do not.

These questions become particularly important when it is recognised that:

- activity-related costs which support the relationship with the customer independently of product costs can account for up to 60 per cent of sales value;
- when expressed as a percentage of sales value these costs can vary widely depending on both the type of customer and the level of activity.

As no two customers are the same, profitability can vary enormously from one customer to another. None of these variations is revealed by conventional accounting technique and their extent is illustrated in Figure 2.

IMPORTANCE OF THE TRANSACTION

Relating these variations to the customers responsible is the problem. Conventional accounting has failed to recognise that the *transaction* is the common denominator between product and customer outlet and is therefore the *ultimate profit centre*. Exchange of goods as recorded against a single

Figure 2.   Variability of Costs

Total sales	*Customer-driven variations in cost as a percentage of sales*
Discounts and Adjustments	0 - 25
Selling and Order-taking	2 - 20
Storage and Distribution	2 - 35
Production and Purchasing	20 - 70
Marketing and Advertising	1 - 20
Gen Admin and Fixed Costs	10 - 30
Profit	◀ SCOPE FOR MASSIVE PROFIT VARIATIONS

product line item on a sales invoice is the most refined level of identifiable transaction.

Undertaking analysis at this level of detail means that the undesirable necessity to use 'averages' is removed, so the results are far more credible. This change in accounting philosophy means the overall profit and loss account can be re-analysed to produce an individual profit statement for each customer outlet. Subsequently these may be re-analysed to examine entire multiples as single entities or, further still, to look at an entire market sector, such as all multiples, as a whole.

CPA integrates the cost effect of *all* functions into the customer base and highlights the relationship between individual actions and policies—and their impact on each customer account.

CPA can require a significant mainframe 'number crushing' resource—PCs are still too small. However, once this stage is complete customers have a flexible profitability database capable of analysis in a wide range of ways, each dependent on the nature of the question being asked.

ANALYSIS OF THE CUSTOMER PROFITABILITY DATABASE

A full CPA will cover *all* products sold to *all* outlets over a defined period of time. The profitability database therefore tends to be large and require

analytical techniques to help focus management attention on the most urgent issues.

A particularly powerful technique is decision grid analysis (DGA). This plots each account on a graph of profitability against volume of business (see Figure 3). It highlights all outlets against four key categories, each of which will require a different managerial response. It is also the first step in defining what characterises a profitable or unprofitable customer, so providing the sales and marketing effort with a stronger focus on attractive accounts. Other techniques, such as cumulative outlet contribution analysis (COCA), also highlight how major resources (and assets) frequently stand behind those accounts that only generate marginal or negative contributions. They also illustrate graphically the extent of total profit erosion by accounts with servicing costs above the margins which they generate. Figure 4 is typical of the result of such analysis. These frequently identify examples of profit erosion to the extent of 10 to 20 per cent of that profit which has already been generated.

However, although such analyses make interesting reading, they are of no value unless they lead to action. The four main ways of achieving this are:

• productivity improvements;
• account engineering;

Figure 3.   Decision Grid Analysis

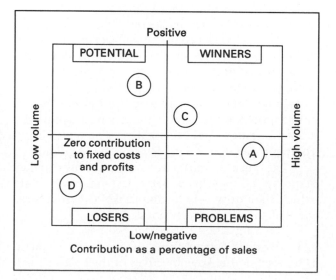

Figure 4. Cumulative Outlet Contribution Analysis

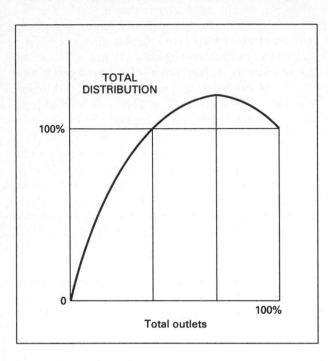

- commercial strategy;
- competitor modeling.

Productivity improvements

Before embarking on a CPA exercise it is essential to make sure that the company's overall operations are as cost effective as possible.

Many achieve a competitive level of productivity by undertaking reviews of technology, utilisation, performance and planning in each function. But, although yielding some benefits, such reviews are generally limited because they are function-based; they cannot take account of inefficiencies within the web of interfunctional relationships on which every company depends for its day-to-day operations.

The quickest, most effective way of fully understanding all overhead activities—and the costs which they drive—is to undertake a thorough review of overhead effectiveness.

The total quality approach we have developed at Develin and Partners aims to ensure that resource is focused on the key objectives of the business and the needs of the customer and not on discretionary, unnecessary activities.

As a methodology it has proved outstandingly successful; it can typically save between 10 and 20 per cent of all overhead costs *and* enhance customer service.

Account engineering

Account engineering asks critical questions and compares and evaluates answers. Its purpose is to enhance the profitability of the supplier to an acceptable level for each outlet. For example:

- What will be the impact of distributing to major customers via their national distribution centres rather than through our own network?
- How will EDI affect my cost structure?
- What is the implication of serving small accounts through third-party wholesalers?
- Which are the least profitable accounts and how can their profitability be most easily improved?

Four factors key to successful account engineering are understanding that:

1. Customer expectations of service, in all its forms, *can* be managed.
2. Internal cost structure *must* be modified to reflect any changes resulting from account engineering.
3. The implementation of account engineering decisions must be carefully planned and the results clearly monitored.
4. Top management commitment is essential, especially in view of the cross-functional nature of the effect of some decisions.

The adoption of account engineering is the equivalent to exchanging a shotgun for a sniper's rifle. It is the suppliers' equivalent of the retailers' use of direct product profitability in supporting commercial decisions.

Commercial strategy

A clear view of customer profitability is essential for evaluating and developing a sound commercial strategy; it is the only way of linking the company's external trading relationship at customer level to its internal cost structure. This is not an end in itself but merely a base for developing a more credible and focused strategy. It complements the supplier's understanding of the market, the players within it and the company's competitive positioning.

Competitor modelling

Competitor modelling is a natural extension of CPA. The supplier achieves this by establishing an understanding of the customer profitability profile of his own company and the differences between himself and a target competitor. By evaluating these differences it is possible to assess which customers, segments and activities of the target competitor are most vulnerable to competitive action. Such evaluation is a valuable supplement to both market intelligence and intuitive feel for the right decision.

Currently CPA is an exception in a few of the more advanced companies. Five years from now CPA will be a routine part of the planning and control process for many companies in the retail sector. In ten years its extension into competitor modelling will be a frequent occurrence.

SUMMARY

Customer profitability analysis fills a crucial gap in the range of analytical and management accounting tools available to management:

- It puts the customer first—at the centre of the analysis.
- It quantifies the trading relationship and measures account profitability.
- It is a powerful analytical tool.
- It emphasises the concepts of 'right first time' and 'total quality'.
- It replaces the shotgun with the sniper's rifle and allows the supplier to identify precisely which accounts are eroding overall profitability—and those which are contributing to it.
- It enables senior management to make major decisions relating to the shape of the customer base with a much greater degree of confidence than has been possible so far.
- It integrates the effort of the company across functional boundaries in pursuit of customer satisfaction.
- It can provide a basis for constructive dialogue between buyer and seller to improve margins.

Finally, suppliers have a responsibility to understand the customer-profitability implications of their trading relationships. This is not simply because of their responsibility to their employees and shareholders but also so that they are in a position to develop a sensible, *mutually advantageous*, dialogue with their present and future customer base—the most valuable asset they have.

How Weyerhaeuser Manages Corporate Overhead Costs

H. Thomas Johnson and Dennis A. Loewe

Having discovered from experience in the early 1980s that drastic budget cuts are not an effective procedure for controlling corporate overhead costs, the Weyerhaeuser Company in 1985 developed a procedure for identifying and managing activities that cause indirect corporate costs.[1]

Referred to by company personnel as a "charge-back" system, this procedure resembles allocation procedures for managing overhead that became popular in the 1970s. But the resemblance between Weyerhaeuser's charge-back procedure and allocation procedures is deceptive. Accountants regard allocations as an effective indirect means of controlling overhead costs by influencing managers' cost consciousness.[2]

Weyerhaeuser's charge-back procedure attacks overhead directly by giving managers decision rights over activities that consume resources. The Weyerhaeuser procedure is akin to state-of-the-art methods of strategic cost management that have been applied in factory settings.[3] Weyerhaeuser Company extends the concept of strategic cost man-

Reprinted from *Management Accounting* (August 1987), pp. 20-26, with permission.

agement to overhead costs incurred outside the factory, specifically to corporate headquarters overhead costs.

COMPANY BACKGROUND

Weyerhaeuser Company is principally engaged in the growing and harvesting of timber and the manufacture, distribution, and sale of forest, pulp, and paper products. Consolidated 1986 sales totalled $5.7 billion and total assets amounted to $6.6 billion. The company owns approximately six million acres of commercial forest land in the United States and, additionally, has long-term license arrangements in Canada covering approximately 12 million acres. In 1986, the company employed approximately 37,500 employees and was ranked in Fortune's top 100 companies.

The company is organized into three principal business groupings: Weyerhaeuser Forest Products Co., Weyerhaeuser Paper Co., and Diversified and Specialty Businesses. Through unconsolidated subsidiaries, the company also is engaged in real estate development and construction and in financial services. Supporting these major businesses is a holding company comprising 14 corporate service departments. Total overhead costs for these groups and the administrative and selling functions within the operating companies totalled $477.3 million in 1986. By comparison, the company's 1986 earnings totalled $276.7 million. Management of corporate overhead obviously is not a trivial exercise for this company.

Since 1985, corporate service departments must "charge back" all costs to users. These charge-backs are no mere allocations. They attribute costs to the service departments' use of resources by carefully analyzing the activities that drive the consumption of corporate resources. And they prompt profit-oriented responses because users and suppliers are now free to acquire or sell these corporate services outside the company in the market.

An example of the charge-back system at work is provided by Financial Services Department (FSD), a staff unit in the corporate controller's department that is responsible for all central accounting activities, including consolidations, general accounting, salaried payroll, accounts payable, accounts receivable, and invoicing. At the start of a fiscal year, FSD supplies a complete statement of charges for its services to 42 user units in the company. The charges are based on specific activities that give rise to consumption of resources in FSD. Table 1 lists activities occurring in FSD and describes very broadly the bases for charging the cost of these activities to the business units of the Weyerhaeuser Company. Here is a description of the bases used to charge-out each activity in FSD:

- *Consolidations and Database Administration.* Consolidation charges are based on hours spent on activities. All consolidation activities support a specific unit, division or business and therefore are charged-out directly. These activities include report preparation, reconciliations, special projects or analyses, and report changes required by reorganizations or systems modifications. Database administration charges generally are based on the actual costs of developing new reports plus ongoing costs to produce the reports. Costs for new reports are based on estimates supplied by the Information Services (I/S) staff and approved by the sponsor. Ongoing costs include an average computer-and-print charge per report for the estimated number of times the report will be produced.

- *General Accounting.* Separate charge-out rates are determined for analytical, clerical, and systems employees in general accounting. Rates determined for analytical and clerical support staff include each employee's fully loaded salary, training costs, corporate service charges, supplies, telephones, travel, and an amount for management support. Systems staff and computer costs are specifically identified where possible and the remainder is allocated based on an estimate of usage. Each employee in general accounting determines the percentage of his or her time spent supporting operations or staff groups. These percentages are charged-out at the specific rates determined for clerical and analytical support staff.

- *Salaried Payroll.* Users are charged per capita for each person whose salary is processed through the salaried payroll unit of FSD. This charge includes costs of providing a bi-weekly check/earnings statement and annual W-2; special pays including bonus payments, commissions, and recognition awards; deferred compensation payments and tracking; reporting and paying taxes to appropriate taxing authorities; and processing relocation expenses.

- *Accounts Payable.* The accounts payable unit of FSD conducts four distinct sets of activities: micrographics, control and support, packaging accounts payable, and corporate accounts payable. Different charge-outs are developed for each activity. Charge-outs are based on the following percentages:

    Micrographics: percentage of time spent filming documents and percentage of the prime computer's time used for document storage and retrieval.

Table 1. Weyerhaeuser Company
Financial Services Department (FSD), 1986
($000's)

FSD ACTIVITY CENTERS AND THEIR MAJOR ACTIVITIES	TOTAL	BASES FOR CHARGING COSTS OF ACTIVITY	CHARGES TO WEYERHAEUSER DIVISIONS FOR FSD ACTIVITIES				
			PAPER COMPANY	FOREST PRODUCTS CO.	WRECO ET AL.	STAFF GROUPS	HOLDING COMPANY
Consolidation and Data Base Admin.	$1,147		$14	$122	$4	$28	$979
—Report preparation		$/hour					
—Database administration		$/report					
General Accounting	2,437		625	875	66	270	601
—Analytic and clerical support		$/hour					
—Systems		$/report					
Salaried Payroll	1,071		269	321	280	145	56
—Issue checks; maintain files		$/paycheck					
Accounts Payable	1,411		306	607	42	315	141
—Micrographics		$/hour					
—Control and support		$/document					
—Packaging accounts payable		$/invoice					
—Corporate accounts payable		$/invoice					
Accounts Receivable	2,787		903	1,663	221	0	0
—Cash application		$/invoice					
—Customer file		$/customer					
Invoicing	1,203		152	967	77	7	0
—Mill sales coding		$/transaction					
—Domestic invoicing		$/invoice					
—Export documentation		$/document					
Total	$10,056		$2,269	$4,555	$690	$765	$1,777

Control and Support: percentage of documents handled for each unit. This typically includes stuffing and mailing of paychecks, invoices, and vendor payments.

Packaging Accounts Payable: percentage of machine paid invoices is the basis for charging to the paper company units.

Corporate Accounts Payable: percentage of all invoices processed.

- *Accounts Receivable.* This unit incurs two types of costs, systems costs and people costs, in each of two activities—cash application and customer file. Charge-outs for cash application are based on invoice volume through the system and charge-outs for customer file are based on number of customers on the file. The invoice counts sometimes are weighted for businesses with special complexities in customers' invoices that require manual cash application.

- *Invoicing.* An average rate for salaries, overtime, and fringe costs is multiplied by the percentage of the invoicing unit's time spent on various services such as mill sales coding, domestic invoicing (both internal and third-party sales), and export documentation. The unit's time allocation is based on each employ-

ee's estimate of his time spent supporting various activities and businesses. Telephones, floor space, and management costs are also charged-out on the same percentage basis. Costs specifically identified as supporting a particular business (e.g., costs of print shop, message center, document delivery fees, bank fees, and outside employees dedicated to specific tasks) are charged to that business.

This information gives managers of units that use FSD's service a good understanding of their expected charges for corporate overhead services during the coming year. Each user of a corporate service has a clear idea of the charge per unit of services he or she demands (e.g., reports prepared, hours of clerical accounting staff, employees paid, invoices processed, customers billed, etc.). Managers of user units, if dissatisfied, are free to challenge (and have challenged) FSD's charges by securing bids for comparable services from outside the company. Likewise, the manager of FSD is free to sell services outside the company. To date, no user unit in Weyerhaeuser Company, after raising a challenge, has elected to take over any of the services that FSD provides.

One staff service unit that has suffered successful challenges to its charges is the Information Services (I/S) Department. Built around a large mainframe computer system about 10 years ago, I/S provides central computing, programming, and systems design services. Low-cost alternatives to its service, especially distributed microcomputer equipment, have appeared just in the last few years. Challenges from users who can employ newer computing and telecommunications technology have forced I/S to cut charges, to lay off a large number of its employees, and to embark on a major campaign to sell services to users outside the firm.

Other corporate staff groups employ similar techniques to identify the activities that drive their costs and to charge users of their services accordingly. For example, General Counsel maintains time and materials logs just as any law firm must do to bill its clients. Corporate Services charges for telephones, floor space, and all general office supplies and services. Corporate Communications charges for developing promotional campaigns, artwork, video and television services, and printed materials. The Treasurer's Department charges for credit management, and so on.

A few corporate staff activities cannot be charged directly to an originating business or product line. Examples include activities of the Tax Department, which prepares the federal income tax return, and activities of Corporate Consolidations and DBA that involve preparation of the annual report and SEC 10K. These activities support the holding company itself and, as such, are charged back to the holding company as a separate "business unit." Isolated into a small and discrete set, these activities can be managed by the president and executive vice president of administration.

This charge-back system provides for rational management of activities that consume corporate overhead resources. The activities do not occur at the discretion of the supplying service unit, without regard either to user demand or to alternatives available in the market. Charges to users are not the traditional cross-subsidized allocations, based on company-wide denominators, that reward intensive users of overhead resources and penalize light users.

Compare the charge for accounts receivable maintenance that a user division pays, for instance, with an allocation that is pro-rated over divisional revenues. In the latter case, divisions with thousands of small-volume retail customers—the divisions that likely cause the consumption of most of the accounts receivable resources in FSD—are charged relatively much less for the service they receive than are divisions with small numbers of high-volume industrial customers. The Weyerhaeuser charge-back system mitigates against the misuse of resources that usually is associated with such cross-subsidized allocations.

BENEFITS AND RESULTS

Managers of corporate staff functions typically fight a defensive battle to obtain and maintain their funding levels. Unlike the manufacturing and selling segment of a company, who can demonstrate a bottom-line contribution to profitability, staff groups often are viewed as a necessary evil that is carried on the shoulders of revenue producers. As such, they are constantly challenged to control costs and to be more effective.

A major benefit of identifying and charging users for overhead activities is the clear identification of users with the demand for services. No longer can operating units disassociate themselves from the costs of "overhead" activities they require to serve their customers.

A related benefit of this charge-back system is that line and staff groups understand better the nature of the services being provided and their associated costs. In fact, this benefit comes in three parts. The first is the understanding among line groups of the role they play in creating staff services and the responsibility they have for funding the level of services they request. Second, direct funding of service activities makes suppliers of staff services more responsive to real business needs, rather than being immersed in their own self aggrandizement. Unfunded activities simply do not survive.

The third benefit is the team building that occurs between staff groups and the business units they support. Of necessity, the staff groups must meet with their line counterparts to agree on services, service levels, and costs. In the service process there is a natural exchange of strategic and tactical business direction that is absorbed in the staff group. Because both groups have put some "skin in the game," a dynamic team relationship is created that draws them toward shared vision and goals. While this team relationship does not eliminate all incentives to pursue sub-optimal gaming strategies, it undoubtedly contributes to a sense of shared purpose now pervading Weyerhaeuser Company that resembles the spirit of a small business more than the stereotypical spirit of a large multinational firm.

These benefits arising from Weyerhaeuser's charge-back procedure are analogous to benefits attributed to just-in-time (JIT) procedures for managing factory operations. In both charge-back and JIT systems, demand for customer output (not plans for using resource inputs) triggers the decision to engage people in work. Activities are "pulled," not "pushed," into action. Consequently, charge-back procedures, like JIT procedures, link processes closely and expose outcomes promptly and clearly. Personnel who charge directly for service activities develop, therefore, a keen sense of ownership for the *quality* of outcomes.

In time the charge-back system should enhance the profitability of the company. In the case of Weyerhaeuser's Financial Services Department, an $11-million budget was reduced $250,000 in the first year of the charge-back system. In itself, this reduction is not remarkable—a cost-cutting program in a department of almost any business can register a savings of this relative size in one year. The reduction in Weyerhaeuser's FSD is unusual as it was achieved by FSD personnel and their "customers" controlling activities that generate costs, not by FSD personnel merely embarking on a program to cut costs. Moreover, these savings were passed back to the line business. Consequently, these savings are likely to be permanent, not eroded in coming years by waves of incremental budget increases.

WHAT IS REQUIRED

To manage corporate overhead successfully in this fashion requires two essential conditions. First, senior management must possess vision and staying power if demand for overhead activities is to determine the levels of service to be provided. This staying power requires a policy of demanding charge-outs for services of all staff groups without

exception. The natural tendency is for empowered staff groups to resist charging for their services, of course. Charging invites detailed scrutiny of their services and costs.

The second condition required to manage corporate overhead is a spirit of flexibility among staff personnel. This spirit must start with the department head of a staff unit and must permeate the entire staff group. Absent a strong conviction from the top to charge for service activities, and an understanding of how to react to service demands throughout the rest of the organization, a fortress mentality can emerge that ultimately may require personnel changes and/or the elimination of some or all of the services they provide.

A POWERFUL TOOL

Existing management accounting procedures fail to control overhead creep in part because they address symptoms, not causes, of costs. Among the procedures that management accountants recommend for controlling indirect costs are allocations aimed at stimulating cost-conscious behavior, corporate reorganizations aimed at stimulating cost-conscious behavior, corporate reorganizations aimed at eliminating redundant personnel, across-the-board budget cuts, and exhortation. Because they direct managers' attention toward cost numbers rather than toward the resource-consuming activities that eventually cause costs, these procedures do not help managers control activities that consume resources.

Existing cost management procedures fail to control overhead creep because they assign responsibility for indirect costs to people whose activities consume overhead resources—the suppliers of services—not to people who demand overhead services in order to serve the final customer. For example, an accounting department manager is held responsible for the cost of preparing customer invoices. The marketing department manager who decides the number and volume of customer sales seldom is held responsible for the cost of invoicing. In this situation, the management accounting system cannot inform managers if the supply of services effectively meets the demand for services.

The charge-back system, while not without

flaws, elevates the management of corporate overhead to a much higher level of sophistication than usually found in most management accounting textbooks. Although interdependencies and inseparable joint costs sometimes limit its use, it is a powerful tool for managing most overhead costs. It prompts managers to trace corporate service costs directly to the consumption of resources, rather than allocate them, mysteriously, as indirect costs. When company units have the power to buy and sell services on the outside, the system helps eliminate the concept of "fixed" overhead costs. Service units that cannot profitably sell services either in the company or on the outside are forced to liquidate company-owned resources that provide unwanted services.

1 The background leading up to Weyerhaeuser Company's development of a new overhead cost control system in 1985 is described in H. Thomas Johnson, "Organizational Design versus Strategic Information Procedures for Managing Corporate Overhead Cost: Weyerhaeuser Co., 1972-1986," in William J. Bruns and Robert S. Kaplan, eds., *Accounting and Management: Field Study Perspectives.* Harvard Business School Press, Boston, 1987.

2 Garth A. Blanchard and Chee W. Chow, "Allocating Indirect Costs for Improved Management Performance." *Management Accounting.* March 1983, pp. 38–41.

3 For more on strategic cost management in manufacturing, see H. Thomas Johnson and Robert S. Kaplan, *Relevance Lost: The Rise and Fall of Management Accounting.* Harvard Business School Press, Boston, 1987.